THE SUBTLE ANATOMY OF CAPITALISM

Edited by

JESSE SCHWARTZ
San Diego State University

GOODYEAR PUBLISHING COMPANY, INC.
Santa Monica, California

Library of Congress Cataloging in Publication Data

Main entry under title:

The Subtle anatomy of capitalism.

   Bibliography: p. 501
     1. Economics—Addresses, essays, lectures.
  2. Marxian economics—Addresses, essays, lectures.
  3. Neoclassical school of economics—Addresses,
essays, lectures.   4. Capitalism—Addresses,
essays, lectures.   I. Schwartz, Jesse G.
HB34.S83   330.12'2   76-26192
ISBN 0-87620-871-5

In the crises of the world market, the contradictions and antagonisms of bourgeois production are strikingly revealed. Instead of investigating the nature of the conflicting elements which erupt in the catastrophe, the apologists content themselves with denying the catastrophe itself and insisting, in the face of their regular and periodic recurrence, that if production were carried on according to the textbooks, crises would never occur. Thus the apologetics consist in the falsification of the simplest economic relations, and particularly in clinging to the concept of unity in the face of contradiction.

—KARL MARX

Library of Congress Catalog Card Number: 76-26192

ISBN: 0-87620-871-5

Y-8715-8

Current Printing (last number)
10 9 8 7 6 5 4 3 2 1

Printed in the United States of America

Production Editor: Pam Tully
Designer: Leon Bolognese
Compositor: Sandy Bennett

CONTENTS

Introduction

Some years ago I published a collection of readings bringing together criticism of academic economics.[1] I had imagined that an upsurge was sweeping the social sciences for it was clear that literature, political science, sociology and economics were in a state of crisis. I thought they would emerge reborn. I thought that the social sciences would soon shed their antiquated premises of social harmony, "individualethik," unthinking acceptance of socioeconomic institutions, and obliviousness to the rhythms and cunning of history.

I was mistaken.

Today, one can still walk into classrooms and find the professors endlessly elaborating "utility," "consumer sovereignty," and the "marginal productivity" of land, labor, and capital.

Walk downstairs and one will come upon astute discussions of whether political science can be "value-free" and of the wonders achieved by American "pluralism."

Across the campus in the psychology building, professors with sophisticated techniques will be measuring "social deviancy" and the "modification of behavior" with the very delicate application of electric shocks.

No, not much has changed. The textbooks have discovered an "energy crisis," a "recycling problem," and have added whole sections on "worsening Phillips curve problems." One recent text boasts that "isoquant-indifference curve analysis has been deleted in favor of numerical tables."

I. AN AUSTERE SCIENCE

Hardly a month passes without the appearance of another textbook on macroeconomics. How similar they are! All are expressions of the same narrow underconsumptionist view, called Keynesian. The problem, we are told, is that of a deficiency of aggregate demand; there is an insufficiency of purchasing power to command the mass of commodities thrown on to the market. A "finely tuned" manipulation of federal spending and taxation, we are told, will insure "steady growth."

One would imagine that a learned endeavor to encompass the workings of the economy as a whole would devote much attention to the alternating periods of expansion and decline of output and employment that have occurred regularly in the United States for over 150 years. During each of the precipitous crises of 1873, 1884, 1890, 1893, 1907, 1920, and 1929, the illogical character of the system was plain. That capitalism should be called into question during each regularly recurring crisis is evidently too unsettling to the finely tuned sensibilities of the academic economists. Alas, courses on the "business cycle" are no longer taught. Instead the textbooks speak of "macroeconomic shocks"

or "fluctuations in income and output." These, we are told, are mere accidental deviations from a golden path of never-ending accumulation, the *ultima Thule* of economic policy.

Soon after Ricardo's death, arguments for socialism based upon scientific insights began to appear.[2] Honest inquiry gave way to the need to reply to the Ricardian socialists and, later on, Karl Marx. The academics devoted themselves to composing pastoral idylls. For example, Alfred Marshall, doyen of nineteenth-century academics, could not bring himself to speak of the business cycle or crises in the many editions of his *Principles*; instead he has bequeathed to untold generations graphic illustrations of "supply and demand." This, in spite of the prolonged and severe depression of the 1890s just before his eyes! From this same milieu of evasiveness arose the delicate doctrines of "utility" and "general equilibrium" which are inflicted upon students to this very day.

We devote Part I of this book to discussing the true nature of this rich legacy. The articles by Joan Robinson (Reading 1), E. K. Hunt (Reading 2), and Michael Carter (Reading 3) deal with the logical inconsistencies of modern economics; that by Douglas Kellner (Reading 5) traces the faulty philosophical foundations of modern economics back to Adam Smith's conception of the bourgeois "individual."

In a recent article, "The Idea Shortage: Perplexed Economists Hunt for Ways to Cure U.S. Economy's Woes,"[3] the *Wall Street Journal* noted that despite the worst recession since the 1930s, the economists could only offer "ideas long employed in other nations, or merely old ideas that may be worth a second look." These were: a more active government role taking the form of tax incentives or penalties to reach "goals"; indexation, "learning to live with inflation" by inserting clauses into all contracts to adjust payments to price rises; or more investment—"What this country needs is an investment boom!"

These trite conceptions arise from the intellectual impoverishment of American economics. Only when forced by necessity have the academics been willing to forget their "general equilibrium"; this occurred for example in the 1930s when, with all things proclaiming the absurdity of Say's Law, the academics had no alternative, and reluctantly gave it up. (The meaninglessness of Say's Law had been amply demonstrated 100 years before by Karl Marx[4] and several others.)

This overturning of orthodoxy is called the Keynesian revolution. After the war it became the official wisdom of governments. The main point, the breaking out of the "cocoon of equilibrium," as Joan Robinson[5] knowingly tells us, was lost. Indeed, neoclassicalism was largely reconstituted even going so far as to bring back Say's Law, perfect competition, marginal utility, and optimum firms.

> By one simple device, the whole of Keynes' argument is put to sleep. Work out what savings *would be* at full employment in the present short-period situation, with the present distribution of wealth and the present hierarchy of rates of earnings for different occupations, and arrange to have enough investment to absorb the level of savings that this distribution of income has created. Then hey presto! We are back to the world of equilibrium, where savings governs investment and micro theory can slip into the old grooves again. . . .[6]

In Reading 16, John Hotson tells how American academics succeeded in creating a diluted, "bastardized" version of Keynes' teaching.

To understand its conservatism, one must become aware that studying economics in the United States is a process of social conditioning that often systematically weeds out the more inquiring, curious, or radical student. Success goes to those who can intone, with charm and finesse, the harmonies of the "neoclassical synthesis." Aside from such fruitful excursions into the realm of abstract thinking, students are harnessed to the minutiae of the common sense, practical details and statistical manipulation essential to corporate banking, and governmental bureaucracies. This occurs often enough to deter those who, in seeking some understanding of the heavily armored and deeply alienated character of relations between people under late capitalism, turn to economics. To this day, "neoclassicism" dominates the curriculum at nearly every university, college, and high school, even though many of the professors themselves are cynical.

We suggest the Readings in Part III for those wishing to chuck "general equilibrium" into the middle of next week. Peter Bell (Reading 10) and Erik Wright (Reading 11) discuss the many currents in Marx's view of the nature of periodic crises. Shinzaburo Koshimura (Reading 13) presents a theory of how crises propagate from particular industrial sectors to the economy as a whole. These views are remote from Keynesianism, either in its bastardized or legitimate versions. Peter Erdos (Reading 12) tells how "Keynes's scientific achievements marked a point of culmination in the history of non-Marxist economic thought," at the same time contending "that Keynes, when he turned against some neoclassical theses characteristic of the Marshallian-Pigouvian school, remained very much a captive of this school."

II. THE DIALECTICS OF LIVING LABOR

I think it clear that, despite the many obstacles in its path, and its own short-comings, there is at hand a rebirth of political economy. For decades, aside from a few singular contributions, little was accomplished besides more or less recapitulating Marx's arguments. But a new generation is learning for itself.

One discouragement that threatens to encumber many at the onset is the theory of value. It is not hard to see how one can become stuck in the voluminous literature or carried out to sea by the eddies and riptides of the many disputations and arguments. It is no help that academic economists either dismiss it outright or give the most remarkable interpretations. Professor Paul Samuelson of MIT deals with it by saying:

> Marx sought to find in labor a common denominator in which to express values. The modern view is that it is enough, in explaining relative values or relative prices of two goods—say, deer and beavers, . . . —to assert, "Supply (as determined by the difficulties of production) interacts with demand (as determined by tastes and wealth) to determine the exchange or price ratios that we observe in the market."

> But remember that Marx was a nineteenth-century German philosopher: he thought there was a need for an absolute measure of value by which to make commensurable the incommensurables of deer and beaver.[7]

Marx takes value as crystallizing the essence of commodity production. No modern economist dares to follow him here. To do so would be to undermine belief in the naturalness and reasonableness of capitalism, for the theory of value makes the historical specificity of capitalism very clear. Instead the academics invariably appeal to the certainty of perception—the palpable nature of prices. Not surprisingly, Professor Samuelson ignores Marx's argument and speaks rather of laws of *supply and demand.* But before one can speak of supply and demand, there must be at hand masses of material products which have taken on the character of commodities. This presupposes a social division of labor with isolated producers exchanging their products; it implies a mass of humanity, on the one hand, with nothing to sell but their labor power, and on the other, a concentration of machines, buildings, and instruments of production confronting them as *capital.* Small wonder, then, that Professor Samuelson ignores this and confines himself to the "here and now" of supply and demand. As far back as 1821 David Ricardo exclaimed, "The opinion that the price of commodities depends solely on the proportion of supply to demand, or demand to supply, has become almost an axiom in political economy, and has been the source of much error in that science."[8]

Marx's theory of value, as we have said, is an abstraction belonging to the essence of capitalism. Its roots wander back to antiquity. It was nurtured by the thinkers Aristotle, Thomas Aquinas, and the medieval Schoolmen. Later on one finds further reflection in the writings of Nicholas Bardon, William Petty, and Benjamin Franklin. Finally, with Adam Smith, it assumes its classical expression, though not without conflicting and contradictory notions side by side. Ricardo made it the cornerstone of his system, but fell into difficulties by not consistently following through with its implications.

With Marx we find its development in full generality. Using it as an X-ray he could view the physiology of the economy and discern the forces behind the cycles of accumulation and secular trends in prices, wages, rent, and profit all in relation to the changing structure of the mass of social capital. Such things ordinarily are well hidden.

Furthermore, from this way of seeing emerges one of the deepest truths of Marxian political economy; namely, that capital is accumulated through the pumping out of the life energy of working men and women. This occurs through the coercive bond between living and dead labor crystallized into capital. The flow of life energy within a person has much to do with ability to love, to be in harmony with others, to engage in creative work, and his or her general health and well-being. In the present social order, a considerable portion of the life energy of millions of people is displaced and enchained by the recessions, depressions, booms, and inflations of capital. This is veiled by the "civilized" and "democratic" buying and selling of wage labor. The living labor thereby expropriated by capital takes on the seemingly incomprehensible forms of profit, interest, and rent. Most textbooks are a celebration of this world where things, imbued with life, govern men. Marx calls this the fetish that attaches itself to commodities.

The rigor of modern economics consists in designating as "real" that which can only be counted on the ten fingers of ordinary understanding, thereby reducing reality to its external, naturalistic aspects which were already well catalogued in the nineteenth century. The economy is conceived merely in terms of

the factual immediacy—the "here and now" of "supply and demand." Thus academic thinking remains imprisoned in the realm of social appearance without penetrating to the essence of things and their inner laws of motion.

The repressive structure is quite content to see the academics immersed in a fetish-laden world where prices, money, and "supply and demand" are deemed both natural and eternal. Occasionally, however, there is some puzzlement as to why the "analysts" cannot reach agreement among themselves in trying to explain even the most abstruse phenomena such as persistent unemployment and a high rate of inflation.[9]

One last point about Marx's theory is that there appears to some to be a stumbling block in its formal consistency. This is the so-called "transformation of values into prices of production." I feel that its importance has been exaggerated. Let us listen to Marx describe it:

> Capitals of equal size produce commodities of unequal *values* and therefore yield unequal *surplus-values* or *profits,* because value is determined by labour time, and the amount of labour time realized by a capital does not depend on its absolute size but on the size of the variable capital, the capital laid out in wages....
>
> Hence, if *profits* as a percentage of capital, are to be equal over a period, say of a year, so that capitals of equal size yield equal profits in the same period of time, then the *prices* of the commodities must be different from their *values.* The sum total of these *cost-prices* of all the commodities taken together will *be equal to their values.* Similarly the total profit will be equal to the total surplus-value which all these capitals yield, for instance, during one year.... The equalisation of the surplus-values in different spheres of production does not affect the absolute size of this total surplus-value; but merely alters its *distribution* among the different spheres of production. *The determination of this surplus-value* itself, however, only arises out of the determination of value by labour-time. Without this, the average profit is the average of *nothing,* pure fancy. And it could then equally well be 1,000 percent or 10 percent.[10]

That is, the equalization of surplus-values or the establishment of a uniform rate of profit presupposes a whole series of mediations starting from value to surplus value, money, capital, and then accumulation and competition of capitals. (See page 11.) This is a higher level problem that can only be discussed after the elaboration of a theoretical substructure. It is not by chance that it appears in the third volume of Marx's great work. The apparent contradiction between prices of production and values reflects the reality of the competition of capitals, and is fully encompassed by Marx's system. What then are we to make of Bohm-Bawerk and others, who, to this very day, claim this to be an inconsistency in Marx's logic, and use it to "disprove" his whole system.

In my view the solution given by Marx in Part II, Volume III of *Capital,* contains the essentials of establishing prices of production on the basis of values. However, his solution is not complete and some readers remain puzzled. Progress in its unravelling is described by Mario Nuti (Reading 6), and Anwar Shaikh gives a significant and innovative development in Reading 7.

There are only a few studies in which trends in the economy have been measured using the Marxian categories. There are several difficulties in con-

ducting these studies, not the least of which is the ideological basis on which national accounting statistics have been compiled. The paper by Edward Wolff (Reading 8) demonstrates how such obstacles can be overcome. Its conclusions as to changes in the rate of surplus value and the organic composition of capital over a twenty year period of rapid industrialization in Puerto Rico are intriguing and we hope will inspire further inquiries.

Rosa Luxemburg unerringly sought the central contradictions of capitalism in the process of accumulation. There has been much discussion of her attempt to use Marx's reproduction schemas to demonstrate that imperialistic expansion arose from an inner law of capitalist development. Less familiar is her work dealing with armaments; this is outlined by Ken Tarbuck in Reading 9.

III. COST-BENEFITS ANALYSIS IN THE AGE OF PRECISION

The New World of Economics,[11] by Professors McKenzie and Tullock, bravely promises to disclose applications of academic economic concepts to realms hitherto unsuspected. No one can deny, the authors claim, that "the book attempts to break out of the narrow confines of economic subject matter as traditionally defined . . ."[12]

Picking it up, with much anticipation, I turned straightaway to the chapter entitled "Sexual Behaviour." Here was something that threatened to overturn the staid level of conventional discourse and it was coming from the academics themselves. The authors open, courageously enough, by saying, ". . . given the dominance of sex in human experience, one must wonder how economists have been able to avoid the topic in their classes and books for so long."[13]

Such an investigation may seem very remote from the *gravitas* of Marshall's *Principles*, but it is not really, for we are told, "Given that sexual experiences can yield utility like other goods, it follows that the quantity of sex demanded is an inverse function of the price . . ."[14] Further along we find a brilliant usage of general equilibrium: "If the price of sex rises relative to other goods, the consumer will 'rationally' choose to consume more of other goods and less sex. (Ice cream, as well as many other goods, can substitute for sex if the relative prices require it.)"[15] "The value of one's time, as approximated by his wage rate, will determine the cost of the sexual experience."[16]

I thumbed through the pages of Samuelson's "official" textbook and was disturbed to find no mention of this weighty question. It seems that some discombobulation in the price mechanism has not permitted sex to be reflected in market prices. Undeterred, I next looked at the section, "Child Production," where I discovered a rigorous explication of the demand for children, or as the authors call it, "child services."

Obviously the authors have performed a notable service to the profession. We can hardly do it justice here. In fact I know of no praise too high to bestow on this book than to say that it marks the triumph of neoclassical economics.

At the same time, this triumph bespeaks its exhaustion. With what pomp, supply and demand are trotted on stage again and again. The diction of "utility" and "opportunity costs" grows more mannered and the constructions begin to writhe. This reflects accurately enough the paralysis of the late bour-

geois world no longer able to generate new life from within but trying desperately to infer some sort of ethic from the calculus of the auction market.

We have talked of *The New World of Economics* only because, in our opinion, it is representative of scores of books which mirror the senility of a doctrine. The reader seeking to refute the academics on their own grounds should look at the critiques by Kay Hunt (Reading 2), Mike Carter (Reading 3), and Douglas Kellner (Reading 5). Those wishing to consider a view of the world utterly opposed to the textbooks should see Reading 4 by Fredy Perlman.

IV. LOS CHICAGO BOYS

I remember, not so long ago, I looked in at a cocktail party at an annual American Economics Association meeting. It was in a hotel suite in Dallas. There were the usual grim visages, as well as the nervous, put-on smiles. There were hellos. (The same hellos, by the way, ring down the corridors of economics departments each morning. They are the Morse signals exchanged in the fog by seagoing destroyers declaring for the moment a cessation of hostilities.) There was friendly chat. "Your marginal preferences for vodka or whisky?," "Yes, faculty can use the xerox machine for free at my school," "Just read *Neo-Classical Growth with Fixed Factor Proportions*, how titillating!" "I've got a grant to forecast demand for consumer durables through 1984."[17]

It was a conventional gathering of clenched-jawed econometricians and shallow-chested deaf adders. Our host was the economics department of the University of Chicago. What I found disturbing were the large numbers of earnest young people each with a nameplate affixed to a double-breasted tweed. I stared, reflecting upon the awesome forces that had molded them, with apparent success, into the image of *Los Chicago Boys*.

That is the name given by Latins to the illustrious members of the Chicago school of economics. Let us pause for a moment and consider:

Chile: The report of the U.S. senate's select committee on intelligence activities, published on 20 November, has revealed that the CIA station in Santiago and U.S. military personnel helped plan and provide weapons for the kidnapping of General Rene Schneider on 22 October 1970. . . . The CIA found President Eduardo Frei and General Schneider unwilling to participate in a coup to prevent Salvador Allende's election as President by [the Chilean] Congress. U.S. ambassador Edward Korry wrote to Frei saying: "Not a nut or bolt will be allowed to reach Chile under Allende. Once Allende comes to power, we shall do all within our power to condemn Chile and the Chileans to utmost deprivation and poverty, a policy designed for a long time to come to accelerate the hard features of a Communist society in Chile." CIA director Richard Helms was given instructions by President Nixon on 15 September 1970 to "make the economy scream."[18]

The "neoclassical synthesis" strikes quickly! After the coup, the cool reasonableness of international finance capital promptly gave Chile some $2 billion in credits from international organizations and banks, despite the fact that the right-wing military government is virtually bankrupt and cannot meet the payments on its foreign debts. "The banks have been falling all over each

other to make loans."[19] During Allende's regime, loans from abroad virtually ceased.

Two University of Chicago professors, Milton Friedman and Arnold Harberger, have served as unofficial economic advisors to the Chilean junta. Economic policy in Chile is dominated by some of their former students. Upon the advice of these worthies, the junta has administered "shock treatment" to Chile —"huge slashes in government expenditures, drastically tightened credit and the elimination of subsidies on a wide range of necessities. These include bread, dairy products, meats, fruits and vegetables."[20] This at a time when ". . . the number of unemployed is estimated roughly at a third of the labour force: The one modest hot meal a day provided by the Church or other relief group, stands between most of the idle and starvation."[21] Thousands have been killed, concentration camps have been established all over the country, over 100,000 persons have been jailed in three years, trade unions and neighborhood organizations have been closed and all political activity and all forms of free expression prohibited.

The junta's economic measures stem in part from the advice of *Los Chicago Boys*. The stock in trade of these monetary theorists is that governments cause inflation by an irresponsible increase in the money supply and bring about depression by an abrupt contradiction. We can judge the absurdity of this when we consider that from 1854 to 1961 there have been twenty-six business cycles averaging fifty months in length, and we are asked to believe that these regularly recurring phenomena are due to arbitrary and capricious tampering with the money supply. As Marx said long ago, "The superficiality of Political Economy shows itself in the fact that it looks upon the expansion and contraction of credit, which is a mere symptom of the periodic changes of the industrial cycle, as their cause."

These apostles of free trade also advocate the dismantling of the welfare state and habitually tirade against minimum wage legislation. Their ideal is a return to a Golden Age of nineteenth century capitalism.

But, rather than merely administer bromides to students, *Los Chicago Boys* have turned Chile into a laboratory to demonstrate to the world the folly of their doctrine. For the sake of reducing inflation to "the magic level of 5%," a generation is being crushed. Certainly at some level of misery the inflation will abate, as it does in every depression, amidst starving workers and bankrupt capitalists.

May I refer readers to the article "Economic 'Freedoms' Awful Toll" by Orlando Letelier. It appeared in *The Nation,* August 28, 1976. Shortly after, the author, a leading spokesman of the Popular Unity Government (in exile), was assassinated in the streets of Washington.

V. MECHANICAL MARX

Something called "Marxian economics" is becoming quite respectable. In some curricula this subject has been considerably expurgated and cleansed so that it can be easily digested by middle-class students. This "purification" of Marx has only just begun in this country. We can perhaps learn much from Japan, where this has been going on for quite some time. There, one dominating school of

thought occupies itself exclusively with nineteenth century English capitalism. Never a word is ventured about the ghastly contradictions of postwar Japan. Instead, there is endless twaddle about rewriting Marx's *Capital* to present a "pure" theory of value.

A young person turns to political economy as a seeker because he has a yearning for a more vibrant quality of life. But instead of guidance toward a deeper understanding of society, the young student often finds an immensely boring and tendentious rumination over scholastic questions. It is not hard to understand how it is that Marxian economics has been taught at most Japanese universities and colleges for decades. Except for a small number of courageous scholars dedicated to dispelling the illusion of capitalism's integration by exposing its workings as a changeable construction, the majority immerse themselves in a mystical fog. Through a cunning policy of repressive toleration, the academic establishment has evaded serious inquiries into the nature of modern Japanese capitalism. Such subtlety is yet to be achieved in Anglo-Saxon universities, where dissent is dealt with in a more rough and ready fashion.

Another unfortunate trend often found in Marxism is the reduction of reality to a crude economism or mechanistic determinism. The lights and wonders within each are given a mere economic dimension. This brand of Marxism fails to comprehend class consciousness; it can offer no clue as to the barriers and inhibitions embedded within each individual which may prevent his becoming conscious of his objective interests.

The reductionists claim that economic factors are decisive. Surely they run a danger of succumbing to fetishism and treating people as abstractions. One can see in any leftist journal or newspaper the same sonorous, metallic language that comes from the world of alienated labor. Should not the mechanical separation of man on the one hand, and the economy on the other, be left to the textbooks with their momentous gibberish on "the clash between growth and the quality of the environment"?

VI. PRODUCTION OF COMMODITIES BY MEANS OF COMMODITIES VS. PRODUCTION OF COMMODITIES BY MEANS OF CAPITAL AND WAGE LABOR

One of Ricardo's striking demonstrations was that with a rise in the money wage rate the prices of some commodities would rise, but others, strangely enough, would fall. This is called the "Ricardo effect." It was in contradiction to Smith's doctrine that an increase in money wages would lead to an all-around rise in prices.[22] To say just how the prices of various commodities would change is rather involved, for it depends not only on the proportion of capital to labor, in any particular industry, but on the proportions in all the industries that have provided raw materials and semifinished goods and machines.

Back in the 1890s J.B. Clark had proclaimed, ". . . what a social class gets is, under natural law, what it contributes to the general output of industry."[23] For decades after, the neoclassicals devoted themselves to exemplifying this potent stupefier with precision and rigor. They sought to discover the "contribution" of capital to the national product by measuring its marginal product. For this they required a measure of capital in price terms (since they eschewed

Marx's theory, measurement in terms of labor values was out of the question). But the prices of machinery, equipment and so forth change with alterations in the wage rate and hence cannot be defined independently, as required by this theory, to "explain" the wage rate or profit rate.

In 1960, Piero Sraffa published *Production of Commodities by Means of Commodities*. This was a telling critique, dealing in part with the difficulties created by the "Ricardo effect" for any notion of the "marginal productivity" of capital. Joan Robinson had come to a similar conclusion some years before.

The "neoclassicals" responded superciliously at first. "Everybody except Joan Robinson agrees about capital theory," said Professor Solow.[24] But, noticing that their critics could not be silenced with a sneer, the neoclassicals came on with an academic fog. Samuelson,[25] Solow,[26] Levhari,[27] and others tried to conjure artifices that would answer the objections. But they too suffered shipwreck on the rocks of the "Ricardo effect."

"To save the appearances, Ptolemaic astronomy could always add a new epicycle to allow for newly observed aberrations,"[28] declares Professor Samuelson in describing what he sees as heavy-handed attempts to explain recent history in Marxian terms. Surely this is a better description of the forced and rather clumsy attempts of the neoclassicals to salvage their own top-heavy doctrine. It is remarkable that in the latest edition of the "official textbook," the Nobel laureate still presents J.B. Clark's theory of the distribution of income—of the wages going to working people, and the mass of profits accruing to capitalists—as determined by "marginal productivity."[29] Later, in Chapter 30, something called "capital theory" is discussed. He tells us that it "is one of the most difficult parts of economic theory."[30] (What sort of economics is it that relegates the study of capital to a single chapter interleaved between paeans to "supply and demand" and "marginalism," seeing the main problem of the capitalist economy as that of a deficiency of aggregate demand? The classicals, alas, lacking in MIT mathematics, were so crude as to take the accumulation of capital as their fulcrum. The great difficulties that Professor Samuelson sees in "capital theory" arise from the twistings and turnings of the neoclassicals stuck in a mire of logical inconsistencies.) Throughout this chapter we have a wondrous confusion of the rate of interest with the rate of profit; we are treated for example to a diagram showing the profit rate as determined by the intersection of a demand curve for capital and a supply curve.[31]

Only in the Appendix are we offered some mention of *reswitching*, the term used to denote what is essentially the "Ricardo effect." He does say how Joan Robinson has demonstrated the untenability of the concept of marginal productivity, but instead of seeing this as an unanswerable refutation of his 900-page tome, he quickly reduces the argument to a question of whether capital is more like the ethereal, homogeneous, puttylike substance required by the "neoclassical parable," or more like milling machines, forging presses, railroads, refineries, bales of cotton, and horse manure. The problem, you see, is really one of measurement and, having said this, the "wunderkind of American economics" quickly moves on to consideration of profits.

Sad to say, neoclassical economics lacks a theory of profits, so all the Professor can do is to merely catalogue the way profit appears: "as an implicit factor return"; as "a reward to enterprise"; as "a premium for risk bearing"; and as a "monopoly return."

The "capital controversy" of the mid-sixties marks the end of a factitious and worn-out doctrine. The rise and fall of neoclassicism is in a sense tragic when one considers the generations who have been forced to see where the marginal cost cuts the marginal revenue curve; this includes the learned papers, treatises, and theses on Cobb-Douglas production functions and discourses on "neoclassical growth with fixed factor proportions." There is a bit of poetic justice here, because the essence of the matter had been put forth by Ricardo in 1823.[32] But the neoclassicals, when they deigned to consider the classicals and Marx, did so with ill-concealed contempt, apart, of course, from seeing in them the precursors of their own truth. Thus they fell into a trap of their own making.

The ebb and flow of doctrines will of course continue; each one rising and eventually confounded by its partiality and one-sidedness. We must surely agree that as a "prelude to a critique," which was his high object, Mr. Sraffa's book serves its purpose well. It should come as no surprise however, to anyone familiar with the history of ideas, that some have seen in it no less than a new system of political economy, as suggested by the recent titles *The Sraffian Revolution*, or *Post-Marxian Economic Theory*. Some try to show that Sraffa gives precision or clarity to Marx, while others maintain that Sraffa transcends Marx.

Now, if I may state my own view, it is that we are dealing here with vastly different views of the nature and workings of capitalism. Marx starts with the essence of capitalist production, using a historically specific social artifact—the commodity. From its properties he derives a theory of value that is neither an emotive nor artificial construct, but rather an abstraction belonging to the essence of the capitalist economy. Proceeding step by step, he examines the links or mediations:

COMMODITY—VALUE—EXCHANGE—MONEY—CAPITAL—WAGE LABOUR—SURPLUS VALUE—REPRODUCTION—ACCUMULATION—COMPETITION OF CAPITALS—RATE OF PROFIT—MARKET PRICES—CREDIT—BANKING, etc;

whereas with Sraffa, just as with Ricardo,[33] we have:

EXCHANGE—COMPETITION OF CAPITALS

This leap from exchange to the competition of capitals omits a world of understanding. Not surprisingly, such categories as constant and variable capital and surplus value are foreign to Sraffa. This is why I feel it reasonable to say that we are dealing here with different views of the nature and workings of capitalism. This should not be ignored or confounded with light talk of "Ricardo-Marx-Sraffa systems," but should rather be the starting point for further study.

Part IV is devoted to the Cambridge School. In Reading 14, Geoffrey Harcourt discusses the social significance of the work of Piero Sraffa and Joan Robinson, and in Reading 15, Bob Needham tells how the publication of *An Introduction to Modern Economics*,[34] by Joan Robinson and John Eatwell, is a significant step in modernizing the teaching of economics. In Reading 17, Peter Newman formally sets out Sraffa's system to illuminate aspects of its inner structure.

In Part V there is some exploration of the contentions of the Cambridge

and Marxian schools. We are privileged to have a recent paper by Joan Robinson (Reading 18), in which she discusses the contributions of Sraffa and Kalecki. In Reading 19, Alessandro Roncaglia answers attacks upon Sraffa from both the Marxians and marginalists. Alfredo Medio, in Reading 20, expresses the view that Sraffa's work has "rebuilt the cost of production theory of prices on a sounder basis. In so doing, it has also contributed to overcoming certain logical difficulties existing in Marx's theory of prices of production." Then there is the paper by Frank Roosevelt (Reading 21), who sees in the work of Sraffa and the Cambridge school some aspects of the same fetishism of commodities that overwhelm neoclassical thinking. Although the excerpt from Lucio Colletti's *From Rousseau to Lenin* (Reading 22) does not touch upon these issues directly, it has been included to give the reader some idea of the four-mile-deep ocean of understanding within Marx's theory of value.

Finally, in Reading 23, I discuss Marx's critique of Ricardo. I believe that the elements of the debate can be found therein. In my opinion, many of the same shortcomings in Ricardo's work threaten to encumber those who see a new political economy in Mr. Sraffa's contribution.

These papers encompass some central contentions in political economy and the reader is invited to reflect upon them and judge for himself.

VII. POLITICAL ECONOMY

The industrialized, late bourgeois world has become so alien to its inhabitants, its premises so questionable, its triviality of such gigantic proportions, that George Frankl sees in it:

> The extraordinary situation . . . that the work activity as well as its products which have been lost to man now confront him as capital. Capital is externalized and alienated work-energy and the worker is completely dependent upon it. Thus it comes about that the whole edifice of industrial civilization is alien to the worker. As he is merely a means for its operation so it is no more than a means for his livelihood. The alienated industrial civilization consolidates its rule over men by making them dependent upon it and men who have created it are its slaves.[35]

Those able to see the tragedy that American economics is entrapped in the mechanical rigidity of a basic evasion, are often answered with the indisputable argument of being thrown into the street. Frequently this takes the guise of "budget problems." A mysterious evaporation of funds often occurs when the institutionally defined limits of inquiry are trespassed. All the while, the professors unperturbedly keep chewing the cud of bankrupt doctrines of the dullest and most worn-out kind. This, with every sophisticated flourish as the wretched of the earth are starved, clubbed, gassed, and bombed into submission.

Imagine, if you will, a Shaman among an ancient Siberian tribe. By certain rituals, we are told, it is possible for the Shaman to fall into a state of ecstasy, a temporary liberation from time and the space restrictions of the body, wherein he can heal the sick and divine the future. But such illuminations are momentary and soon he sinks back into the bleak asperity of cold and wintry desolation.

A political economist should be like a Shaman. There should be a sense in his or her life of the discrepancy between the society we have and the society it is possible to have. The present is a world in which Monsieur Le Capital and Madame La Terre gyrate frenziedly in their ghostly cakewalk, followed by a torrent of men and women, aged and youthful, in manhood and infancy, all in grim submission. The future is a vision of immense energy—energy that freely associated people can devote to overcoming centuries of armoring, negativity, and distrust in their relations with fellow beings. In this future society, people will create garden cities—temples fit for the human spirit—and they will experience holistic healing in place of the medicine of commerce, so that they can dance, moving their arms and bodies freely, in clear air and sunlight, becoming one with the river.

Such are the waking dreams that give strength and courage to the political economist as he tries to demystify the dialectics of Monsieur Le Capital and humanity.

These visions should suffice to dispel the illusion of elitism among some who think political economy is a special knowledge comprehensible only to a learned few. I think it is closer to truth to say that political economy is rather the study of the simplest "moments" of the complex content of life and consciousness.

> People are the determining factor in any happening in social processes. There is nothing whatsoever that can or will ever happen without basic rooting in people's ways. . . .
> The ocean of human living had but begun to stir before some one hundred years ago. The stillness of the ocean of human living was mistaken by the ripples for the non-existence of an ocean at all. . . . The social upheavals of the first half of the twentieth century are only the first stirrings. . . .[36]

It is not political economists who make the stir, rather it is the stir that makes the political economists.

Jesse G. Schwartz
San Diego
July 4, 1976

NOTES

1. See E. K. Hunt and J. G. Schwartz, *A Critique of Economic Theory*, Harmondsworth: Penguin Books, 1972.

I should like to mention that the opinions expressed in the Introduction are those of the Editor. They do *not* necessarily reflect, even in part, the views of the contributors.

2. See Meek's fine discussion, "The Decline of Ricardian Economics in England," in *Economics and Ideology and Other Essays* (London: Chapman and Hall Ltd.), 1967.

3. *Wall Street Journal*, New York, May 9, 1975.

4. See his discussion in *Theories of Surplus Value*, Part II, Chapter XVII (Moscow: Progress Publishers), 1968.

5. Joan Robinson, "The Second Crisis of Economic Theory," in *Collected Papers*, Volume IV (Oxford: Basil Blackwell), 1973, pp. 92-105.

6. Joan Robinson, ibid. pp. 76-77.

7. Paul Samuelson, *Economics,* Tenth Edition, (New York: McGraw-Hill), 1976, p. 858.

8. David Ricardo, "On the Influence of Demand and Supply on Prices," Chapter XXX of *On the Principles of Political Economy and Taxation,* Vol. I, *Works and Correspondence,* edited by P. Sraffa, Cambridge: Cambridge University Press, 1970, p. 382.

9. See for example *Wall Street Journal,* Sept. 2, 1976.

10. Karl Marx, *Theories of Surplus Value,* Part II (Moscow: Progress Publishers), 1968, p. 190.

11. Richard B. McKenzie and Gordon Tullock, *The New World of Economics: Explorations into the Human Experience* (Homewood, Ill.: Irwin), 1975.

12. Ibid. p. ix.

13. Ibid. p. 49.

14. Ibid. p. 51.

15. Ibid. p. 52.

16. Ibid. p. 53.

17. It is not easy to convey to the reader the vibrations of most economics departments. Much can be inferred from Marlene Dixon's chastened and knowing, "Letter of Resignation," *Insurgent Sociologist,* Vol. V No. 11 Winter, 1975.

18. *Latin America,* Nov. 28, 1975.

19. Quoted in *New York Times,* Feb. 20, 1976, p. 47.

20. *New York Times,* January 25, 1976, p. 49.

21. Ibid. p. 49.

22. "Adam Smith, and all the writers that I know of, maintained that a rise in the price of labor would be uniformly followed by a rise in the price of all commodities. I hope I have succeeded in showing that there are no grounds for such an opinion . . ." David Ricardo, op. cit. p. 46.

23. J. B. Clark, "Distribution as Determined by Rent," *Quarterly Journal,* Vol. 5, 1891, pp. 289-318.

24. Robert M. Solow, *Capital Theory and the Rate of Return,* Amsterdam: North-Holland Publishing Co., 1963.

25. Paul Samuelson, "Parable and Realism in Capital Theory: the Surrogate Production Function," *Review of Economic Studies,* Vol. 29, pp. 193-206.

26. Robert Solow, "The Interest Rate and Transition Between Techniques," in *Socialism, Capitalism and Economic Growth; Essays Presented to Maurice Dobb,* edited by C. H. Feinstein, Cambridge: Cambridge University Press, 1967.

27. D. Levhari, "A non-substitution theorem and the switching of techniques," *Quarterly Journal of Economics,* Vol. 79. pp. 98-105.

28. Paul Samuelson, *Economics,* op. cit. p. 865.

29. Ibid. see Chapter 25.

30. Ibid. p. 598.

31. Ibid. p. 603.

32. See David Ricardo, op. cit. p. xlix.

33. See the section *He Bypasses Mediations to Confound Value and Price* in Reading 23.

34. Joan Robinson and John Eatwell, *An Introduction to Modern Economics,* (New York: McGraw-Hill), 1973.

35. George Frankl, *The Failure of the Sexual Revolution,* (London: Kahn and Averill), 1974, p. 24.

36. Wilhelm Reich, *The Murder of Christ,* (New York: Noonday Press), 1974, pp. 82-83.

PART I
Goodbye to Marginalism

1

The Relevance of Economic Theory

JOAN ROBINSON

Professor of Economics at Cambridge University

The controversy which has been going on for many years amongst theoretical economists about the meaning and measurement of capital must appear to outsiders (including the bulk of the profession itself) as mere scholasticism, yet it has important implications both for the formation of ideology and for understanding the world that we are living in.

Academic teaching for the last hundred years has been concerned much more with the first task than the second. It has been concerned with propagating the ideology of laissez faire and of the beneficial effects of the free play of market forces; it has done more to distract attention from the actual operations of the capitalist economy than to illuminate them. Yet it does not consist merely of slogans; it has an intellectual structure which has fascinated generations of students and provided generations of professors with position and with reputation for the brilliance with which they expound and elaborate it.

Marxists generally dismiss the whole thing as a deception without bothering to understand it; their own categories such as surplus value, variable capital, and organic composition are not defined in a way that brings them to bear on the questions that the academics discuss. Thus the two systems of ideas are not confronted with each other in logical argument, and the choice between them is left to ideological prejudice. Prejudice, of course, as well as academic funds, is heavily on the side of orthodoxy, which thus grows and flourishes undisturbed.

The new criticism, inspired by Piero Sraffa, does not merely mock at orthodoxy. It penetrates into its theoretical system and exposes its weakness from within. The debate is carried out on the plane of logical analysis; when the logical argument has been refuted, the orthodox ideology is left floating in the air, deprived of what it used to claim was its scientific basis.

1

To understand the criticism, we must first survey the scheme of ideas that it is replacing. Modern doctrines are derived from the neoclassical school which established itself as orthodox in the latter part of the nineteenth century and continued in vogue right up until the great slump of the 1930s. One of its main elements was the principle of optimum allocation of scarce means between alternative uses. Consider a situation in which there are given productive

resources, fully specified in physical, engineering terms, a given body of technical knowledge, and a specific list of commodities to be produced. Resources can be used in various combinations to produce any one commodity. This is most easily seen in the case of agriculture, from which the idea was originally derived. An annual output of so many tons of corn can be produced (in the same weather conditions) by a larger labor force working more intensively on a smaller area of land or by a smaller labor force working a larger area. Again, the same labor force and the same area of land can produce a variety of crops—say, more corn and less turnips or vice versa.

This construction illustrates the concepts of *efficiency* and of *opportunity cost.* For any particular combination of commodities, there is a maximum quantity that the given resources could produce when they are fully utilized. It would be inefficient to use them in such a way that more resources produce less output. When production is efficient, in this sense, it would be impossible to produce more of any one commodity without reducing the production of something else. Thus at every point in the range of possible efficient patterns of production each commodity has a marginal opportunity cost in terms of the sacrifice of other commodities which would be required in order to produce a little more of this one. There is a pattern of relative prices, for any given combination of commodities reflecting marginal opportunity costs of each in terms of the rest.

Now, within its proper sphere of operation, this principle is of great importance. Its sphere is the use of limited specific resources for specified ends, in conditions of full employment and full utilization of capacity. This is the reason why the mathematical school in the USSR has been attracted to neoclassical economics, which offers them something they could not find in Marx. In Western orthodoxy, the argument was puffed up to cover the whole of economics. The linchpin of the orthodox defense of laissez faire was the doctrine that, under conditions of perfect competition, a free market will always allocate resources efficiently in the above sense. This part of the argument has never been convincing. The textbooks dwell upon the characteristics of an equilibrium situation while being excessively vague about how a competitive market would actually reach it. But even if it were perfectly correct, this analysis leaves out the most important part of the problem. The market demand for commodities, which allocates resources between uses, is discussed in terms of the tastes of consumers, not of the distribution of purchasing power amongst them. The prices of the "factors of production" are derived from the prices of commodities. All factors are on the same footing—the muscle of a laborer, the knowledge of an engineer, the capacity of a blast furnace to produce iron, of a loom to produce cloth, or of a field to produce corn is each "rewarded" according to the relation of supply to demand for the type of factor to which it belongs. . . . It is usually admitted in the orthodox textbooks that inequalities ought to be corrected, but the main emphasis is upon the proviso that interference must not impair the delicate mechanism of the market.

A different application of the principle of efficiency is the notion of a competitive firm producing a given output at minimum cost; here we are concerned not with physical resources but with expenses. Wage rates, the rate of interest on borrowed finance, and the prices of equipment, materials, power,

etc., are all given by the market; competition compels the individual seller to adopt the method of production with the least expenses per unit of output and keeps the price of the commodity from rising above its cost. Here again the argument has a certain sphere of application, but it is hardly adequate as the "theory of the firm" for latter-day capitalism.

There was another layer in orthodox theory which came from a different source. It was a garbled version of Ricardo. Ricardo set out to find the principles which govern the distribution of the produce of the earth between the classes of society, "the proprietor of the land, the owner of the stock or capital necessary for its cultivation and the laborers by whose industry it is cultivated." This was turned into a theory of distribution between the factors of production, land, labor and capital. These are factors in quite a different sense from those in the "scarce resources" argument. The capital which receives a "reward" is not a blast furnace or a stock of copper already in existence. It is a fund of finance which can be invested in the physical equipment and work in progress appropriate to some line of production. When the investment is successful, the business gradually recovers the original finance from gross profits and reembodies it in whatever form, within its horizon of competence, appears to promise the greatest profitability. The service for which the capitalist receives a "reward" more or less proportional to the amount of finance that he controls (that is, a rate of profit on capital) is described as "waiting" because investment precedes receipts. The factors of production, then, are land, labor, and waiting, receiving rent, wages, and profits. This construction was used as an answer to the labor theory of value—not only labor produces value, capital produces some too. The laborer is worthy of his wage and the capitalist is worthy of his profit.

All this was under the rule of Say's Law—supply creates demand. Equilibrium with full employment of the labor force will always be established except when the monopolistic combinations of workers in trade unions are so foolish as to demand wages in excess of their marginal product.

The whole structure of ideas came to a crash along with the world market in the great slump. Keynes attacked Say's Law and supplied a theory of effective demand but he did not penetrate into the confusions and sophistries of the underlying doctrines.

After 1945 it was taken for granted that near-full employment was henceforth to be maintained by government policy, and the ideology of "growth" displaced laissez faire as the main defense for private enterprise. The economists, therefore, had to bring the accumulation of capital into the center of the picture. They plunged in without a moment's thought, failing to notice the ambiguity in the conception of capital and profit in the neoclassical system. The doctrine that the rate of profit corresponds to the "marginal product of capital" was propagated without inquiring what it was supposed to mean. A whole prosperous profession has been busy for more than twenty years, deriving mathematical propositions, interpreting statistical evidence, and putting out textbooks on this basis, while smothering criticism by a conspiracy of silence.

2

For anyone who has not been mesmerized by neo-neoclassical teaching, the fallacy is easy to see. It consists in confusing the two meanings of capital:

finance controlled by capitalists which earns profits is identified with the physical equipment and stocks which assist labor to produce output. A fund of finance is a sum of money to be invested by buying equipment at current prices or paying for it to be built at current costs. The rate of profit enters into the determination of prices. When the level of money-wage rates is given, the prices at which goods are sold has to be higher if they are to yield a higher rate of profit. The value of a stock of equipment, whether reckoned in terms of money, of labor time, or of a representative "basket" of commodities, is not independent of the rate of profit. The concept of the "marginal productivity of capital" was an illegitimate extension of the "scarce commodities" concept to the sphere of accumulation. The argument is kept going, pupils bewildered, and critics exasperated by constantly jumping from one concept of capital to the other without distinguishing between them.

The formal argument can be stated in a rough and ready way. (Those who want it rigorously must go to Piero Sraffa's *Production of Commodities by Means of Commodities.*) Suppose that, with x-ray eyes, we can see the actual flow of production that is going on over a period of time in an industrial economy, set out in physical terms—tons, pints, and yards, and man-hours of labor. From the goods in being at the end of the period, subtract the physical equivalent of those in being at the beginning. We then have net output in physical terms. In the Marxian scheme, $c + v + s$ are quantities of labor-value. Here c on one side and $(v + s)$ on the other consist of lists of physical items. These physical specifications cannot tell us the prices or rates of exchange between commodities. (There are n equations for n products and $n - 1$ prices.) Nor can they tell us how net output is shared between wages and profits.

Now let us suppose that "prices of production" obtain in this economy, with a uniform rate of profit. Conceptually (not, of course, in real life) the rate of profit may be anything between zero (when wages absorb the whole net product) and the maximum that would obtain if wages were zero. Consider how prices and the value of the stock of capital behave as the rate of profit is notionally varied. If the special conditions required for labor-value prices obtain—the capital/labor ratio is identical for all products—then there is one pattern of prices that is independent of the rate of profit. (At every rate of profit, "prices of production" are proportional to labor-values.) The relative prices of commodities are proportional to the labor-time required to produce them, and the value of capital is governed by the "labor embodied" in physical equipment and stocks. In the general case, relative prices vary with the rate of profit. Products for which the ratio of the value of capital to the wage bill is higher than the average at one rate of profit will show a rise in price relative to the average when the rate of profit is higher and contrariwise. (The "transformation of values into prices" was nothing to make such a fuss about.)

This is a sketch (not an exact statement) of the formal demonstration that a "quantity of capital" has no meaning apart from the rate of profit.

The marginal productivity argument, however, does not rely upon a single set of technical relations. The essential point for the neo-neoclassics was substitution between labor and capital. In the "scarce resources" case, if more land becomes available to a given labor force, output per head goes up. Similarly, they maintained, with more "capital" (without any change in technical knowledge) output per head would rise, while the "marginal product of capital" and

the rate of profit would fall. Sraffa's argument goes on to show that, when a edge) output per head would rise, while the "marginal product of capital" and the rate of profit would fall. Sraffa's argument goes on to show that, when a variety of techniques are compared, a lower rate of profit may be associated with a lower level of output per head just as well as with a higher level.

This was rather shocking. At first the neo-neoclassicals sought refuge in a parable. If "capital" were made of some homogeneous and malleable substance, such as putty, physical equipment would be just like finance. A business is continually recovering finance invested in one physical form from amortization allowances, and may reinvest it in other forms. Similarly putty-capital can be remolded at will. Indeed putty is more convenient than finance, for finance has to submit to risk and is recovered only over a period of time, while putty-capital in the parable can be instantaneously adjusted whenever there is a change in the state of demand. The problems concerned with getting into equilibrium and, indeed, the whole problem of historical time, moving from an irrevocable past into an uncertain future, is left out of the story.

A more subtle line of defense was to confine the argument to the case of labor-value prices (though of course a neo-neoclassical would not put it like that) so that a higher value of capital is necessarily associated with a higher output per head. Next, a sally was made to try to prove Sraffa wrong in the general case. At last the conspiracy of silence was broken. In 1966 (in the so-called reswitching debate) a flood of mathematical argument came in from England, Italy, Japan, India, and Israel. The neo-neoclassics had to admit that Sraffa was right. But:

> He who is convinced against his will
> Is of the same opinion still.

3

The formal argument is just a formal argument, but it opens up questions of the greatest importance.

It destroys the presumption that the rate of profit measures the contribution of investment to national income (let alone to human welfare).

It exposes the fact that the orthodox school has failed to answer Ricardo's question. Indeed, it does not have a theory of distribution at all.

It calls in question the benefit to society of "economic growth" which consists mainly of the accumulation of capital by the great corporations under their own control and for their own purposes ("what is good for General Motors is good for the United States").

It throws a new light on the meaning of the "export of capital" which is supposed to be a benefit to so-called developing countries.

Indeed, it requires a radical reconsideration of all the slogans of orthodoxy.

The transformation of *values* into prices is also a purely formal argument. The question which lies behind it concerns the manner in which a capitalist economy operates. Does the rate of exploitation dominate the rate of profit? That is, does the balance of power in bargaining between employers and workers determine the share of wages in net proceeds, or is it rather the requirements of profits that determine what is left over for wages from a given level of physical output?

The wage bargain is made in terms of money. Marx once argued (in *Value, Price, and Profit*) that strong trade unions can raise real wages and squeeze profits to any extent. We know now that they can sometimes squeeze profits a little bit for a little time, but, in the main, rises in money-wage rates are offset by rising prices (percentage gross profit margins vary very much less than the level of money-wage rates). In a general historical sense, obviously, the social, political, and economic forces that determine the workers' bargaining power are of dominant importance, but from day to day in the private-enterprise system profits have the upper hand.

The theory of profits which is called Keynesian really derives from Kalecki (Keynes did not interest himself very much in the problem of distribution). It belongs to that part of Marx's scheme which is concerned with the "realization of surplus value." The capitalists clearly could not get any profit out of selling commodities on which no more was being spent than the wages earned in producing them. The receipts to cover overheads and profit must come from other sources. The wage bill for investment and rentier expenditure (out of interest, distributed profits, and realized capital gains) comes back through the shops to cover the element of gross profits in sales. "The workers spend what they get and the capitalists get what they spend." An important corollary of this way of working at things is that the proper function of profits in a capitalist economy is to be saved and invested. Expenditure out of "unearned income" (as the tax collectors neatly describe it) merely raises profits at the expense of real wages without contributing to production.

Another corollary is of the utmost importance in understanding the "fiscal crises" of the modern state; government outlay (which has the same effect as capitalist investment) reduces real wages even if the whole increment of expenditure is covered by taxes on profits.

The radical economists who have established a new movement in American universities are generally inclined to say that they always knew that economic theory was a lot of rubbish; it is irrelevant and not worth answering. By this policy they allow themselves to be encapsulated. They are given a course to teach or a paper to examine as a side line, while, in the mainstream, students continue to be demoralized by having to repeat arguments which they vaguely feel to be unsatisfactory without knowing quite why. The radicals ought to be helping them to find the clue. But the neo-neoclassical professors are very agile debaters. The radical has to be well versed in Sraffa and Kalecki if he is going to take them on.

2

The Ideal Foundations of Welfare Economics

E. K. HUNT

Associate Professor of Economics at University of California, Riverside

The extreme individualism that stands as the intellectual foundation of classical liberalism is the ideal reflection of the fact that in capitalism, while production becomes progressively more social in nature, exchange of privately owned commodities makes each individual appear to be subordinated to material processes that are beyond human influence. Each individual appears as an isolated combatant, concerned only with his own being and activities, and struggling to adapt to the forces of market exchange over which neither he nor any other individual can exert any direct control.

> The mutual and universal dependence of individuals who remain indifferent to one another constitutes the social network that binds them together. This social coherence is expressed in *exchange value,* in which alone each individual's activity or his product becomes an activity or product for him. . . .
>
> The social character of activity, and the social form of the product, as well as the share of the individual in production, are here opposed to individuals as something alien and material; this does not consist in the behaviour of some to others, but in their subordination to relations that exist independently of them and arise from the collision of indifferent individuals with one another. The general exchange of activities and products, which has become a condition of living for each individual and the link between them, seems to them to be something alien and independent, like a thing.[1]

The seemingly immutable and impersonal forces of the market have always seemed beneficent, however, to bourgeois economists. From Adam Smith's invisible hand to the welfare economics of contemporary neoclassical economists, the market is seen not as the source of human estrangement and alienation nor as the medium through which bourgeois class rule is effected, but as an institutional framework within which the behavior of isolated, self-seeking, rational individuals will automatically and most efficaciously promote the general welfare.

Modern welfare economics is the most elaborate and refined statement of the ideological implications of the individualism of classical liberalism. All human behavior is reduced to maximizing behavior. Whether the thing being

This article was previously unpublished but contains material which will appear in Hunt, E. K., "A Radical Critique of Welfare Economics" in Growth, Profits and Property, *E. J. Nell, ed. Copyright © 1977 by Cambridge University Press. Reprinted by permission.*

maximized is utility or position on one's preference scale, the fundamental relationships considered are those between people and things rather than those among people. The ends of human behavior (the relative degrees of satisfaction to be gained from consuming various commodities) are taken as metaphysically given and fixed, and all human beings are imagined to be rational, calculating maximizers who pursue these ends solely through the activities of exchanging the commodities and productive resources with which they have been "endowed" (the source and propriety of the endowment is beyond the purview of the analysis).

Individual desires, weighted by market purchasing power, are the ultimate criteria of social values in this theory. Externalities caused by interdependencies of preference orderings (that is, consumption considered as a social activity) can only be handled by treating them as isolated exceptions (of which more will be discussed below). Welfare economics ignores the fact that individual desires are themselves the products of a particular social process and the individual's place within that process. If they did not ignore this, they would have to acknowledge the fact that normative evaluations can be made of totally different social and economic systems and their resultant patterns of individual desires.

This omission is, perhaps, one of the clearest instances of false consciousness caused by the ideological blinders inherent in bourgeois economics' consistent expression of capitalists' class interests. Marx saw this clearly when discussing the antecedents of modern welfare economics:

> The economists express it like this: each person has his private interest in mind, and nothing else; as a consequence he serves everyone's private interests, i.e. the general interest, without wishing to or knowing that he is. The irony of this is not that the totality of private interest—which is the same thing as the general interest—can be attained by the individual's following his own interest. Rather it could be inferred from this abstract phrase that everyone hinders the satisfaction of everyone else's interest, that instead of a general affirmation, the result of this war of all against all is rather a general negation. The point is rather that private interest is itself already a socially determined interest, which can only be achieved within the conditions established by society and through the means that society affords, and that it is thus linked to the reproduction of these conditions and means. It is certainly the interest of private individuals that is at stake; but its content, as well as the form and the means of its realization, is only given by social conditions independent of all these individuals.[2]

This being the case, it is clear that in some deeper or more ultimate sense one can find whose interests are served by each person pursuing their private interests only by understanding the systematic class privileges created and maintained by the social institutions and conditions of capitalist society.

When one examines class privileges and the institutions and the ideologies through which they are maintained, one must conclude that welfare economics is the direct lineal descendent of the doctrines Marx labeled as "vulgar economy." A point of view that "confines itself to systematizing in a pedantic way, and proclaiming for ever-lasting truths, the trite ideas held by the self-complacent

bourgeoisie with regard to their own world, to them the best of all possible worlds."[3] This paper is an attempt to substantiate such a conclusion.

At the heart of welfare economics is the norm of Pareto optimality. This norm grows out of the standard textbook treatments of microeconomic theory (from Samuelson through advanced graduate texts). Standard neoclassical statements of consumption and production theory all lead ultimately to the concept of Pareto optimality. In consumption theory each isolated, maximizing consumer is constrained by a fixed budget. Constrained utility maximization results in commodities being chosen in such proportions that the individual's marginal rate of psychological substitution between any pair will be equal to the ratio of their prices. This means that relative prices accurately reflect the psychic or utility evaluations (at the margin) for every commodity for every consumer—because in a competitive economy every consumer is faced with the same prices. And because prices reflect the relative evaluations of every consumer considered individually, they must, in a capitalist economy where the consumer is "sovereign," perfectly reflect the relative *social values* of commodities.

In production theory each individual business firm with a "continuous twice differentiable" production function is confronted by given prices in a competitive market. A mathematical or geometrical analysis of constrained profit maximization shows each firm choosing a point on its production function where (1) the price of any factor (including labor) is equal to the value of its marginal product; (2) the marginal rate of substitution between any pair of factors is equal to the ratio of their prices; and (3) the marginal rate of transformation between any two outputs is equal to the ratio of their respective prices.

The first of these conditions of profit maximization is equivalent to the neoclassical marginal productivity theory of distribution. It assures us that each factor of production (and, by implication, each human being) receives as income exactly that which it contributes, an ideal which has long served as a bourgeois ideal of distributive justice. The third of these conditions of profit maximization assures us that the prices of commodities accurately reflect the marginal opportunity costs of society forgoing some of any commodity in order to get more of another commodity.

In the competitive world of the neoclassical apologist, every consumer and every firm faces the same set of prizes as every other. This means that in equilibrium the mental evaluation of any pair of commodities by any consumer is a perfect reflection of the technologically determined opportunity cost of producing those commodities. No reallocation of resources through changes in consumption, exchange, or production could *unambiguously* augment the value of the commodities being produced and exchanged. This is Pareto optimality—the fundamental norm of bourgeois economics.

The fundamental rule of Pareto optimality states that the economic situation is "optimal" when no change can improve the position of one individual (as judged by himself) without harming or worsening the position of another individual (again, as judged by himself). A Pareto improvement is a change that moves society from a nonoptimal position closer to an optimal position: "Any change which harms no one and which makes some people better off (in their own estimation) must be considered to be an improvement."[4]

Two points are significant in the Pareto rule: First, in the hands of many nineteenth century reformers the notion of diminishing marginal utility had radical equalitarian implications. If all individuals have similar capacities for enjoyment, and if the marginal utility of income declines as one's income increases, then it follows that an equal distribution of income maximizes the total utility for all of society. Contemporary ideologists avoid this conclusion by insisting that interpersonal utility comparisons are impossible and that statements about the effects on the total social welfare of redistributions of wealth and income are thereby impossible. The insistence that an individual's welfare can only be judged by himself is the means by which these interpersonal utility comparisons are avoided.

The second significant point to note in the Pareto rule is its conservative consensual character. Defined away are all situations of conflict. In a world of class conflicts, imperialism, exploitation, alienation, racism, sexism, and scores of other human conflicts, where are the changes that might make some better off without making others worse off? *Improve the plight of the oppressed, and you worsen the situation of the oppressor* (as perceived by himself, of course)! If there are any important social, political, and economic situations where improving the lot of one person, group, or class is not opposed by persons, groups, or classes, who, by virtue of their roles in the economic, political, and social spheres are their natural antagonists, then such situations are indeed rare. The domain of this theory would, indeed, seem to be so restrictive that it would hardly warrant a serious social scientist's time to investigate it were it not for the fact that the theory is thought to be important not only by the overwhelming majority of bourgeois economists, but by many unwary Marxist economists as well.[5] The theory's ideological content, as we shall see below, is revealed equally in its positive conclusions and in the issues it systematically excludes from investigation.

The neoclassical notion of "market efficiency" encountered in every branch of applied economics, as well as the bourgeois notion of "rational prices" encountered in so many discussions of the role of the market in a socialist society, have absolutely no meaning whatsoever other than the belief that a "free" competitive market will tend toward a Pareto optimal situation in which, *by definition*, resources are said to be "efficiently allocated" and prices are said to be "rational." There is no further criterion or justification for using the words "efficient" and "rational" than the assertion that the particular resource allocation and price structure obtaining in a free competitive market will have some connection with that envisioned in the analysis of Pareto optimality.

Acceptance of the "efficiency" or "rationality" of the free-market solution to the problem of the allocation of resources demands that one accept the social values underlying the analysis. Moreover, one must accept the general framework of empirical and behavioral assumptions as being tolerably good reflections of reality. The only values that count in Pareto analysis are the preferences of each isolated individual weighted by the purchasing power of that individual. Both the individualism and the distributional assumption must be separately considered.

The axiom of individual preferences is extraordinarily constraining. Because in the neoclassical analysis we have no way of evaluating the relative merits of different persons' preferences, we likewise have no criterion for evaluating changes in a given individual's preferences. To be able to do the latter would be

to be able ipso facto to do the former. At the level of abstraction on which this theory is constructed, the only differences among individuals are different preference orderings. There is absolutely no difference in the theory between the change in a given individual's preference ordering and the complete withdrawal from society of one individual and his replacement by a new individual. For this reason the theory can consider neither the historical evolution of social and individual values nor their day-to-day fluctuations. To do so would be to admit the normative incomparability of any two events or situations that are temporally separated; that is, to exclude all real-life phenomena from the domain to which the theory is applicable. On the other hand, to permit such normative comparisons would be to return to the egalitarian conclusions of the "philosophical radicalism" of the early utilitarians and seriously weaken neoclassical economics as an intellectual support of the status quo.

It is therefore obvious that this theory is applicable only where individual preferences or tastes do not change over time. It is equally obvious that every person, including fanatics, lunatics, sadists, masochists, mentally incompetent persons, children, and even newborn babies must always be the best judge of their own welfare. (It might also be added that all decisions must be made individually and never simply by heads of families or other social groupings.) They must have perfect knowledge of all presently available alternatives, and there must be no uncertainty about the future. Unless these conditions are realized, people will find that the utility they expect before an act will have no necessary relation to the utility realized after the act, and individual choices or preferences will have no demonstrable connection to an individual's welfare. This extreme individualism also breaks down when we admit the presence of envy and sympathy, which make one individual's perception of his own welfare depend upon his perception of the welfare of others (that is, of course, a special case of the general problem of externalities, of which more will be discussed below).

The fact that any Pareto optimum can be defended as optimal only in relation to a specific distribution of wealth and income is, perhaps, the most decisive normative weakness of the theory. Although orthodox economists usually admit the incredibly restrictive relativity of any Pareto optimum, they tend to slur over it in passing and hurry on to safer topics before facing the embarrassing consequences of this condition. On the normative assumptions of Paretian analysis itself it can be shown that unless the existing distributions of wealth and income are socially optimal, then a situation that is Pareto optimal may be socially inferior to a large number of situations that are *not* Pareto optimal but that have distributions of wealth and income that are preferable to the one in question. Orthodox economists skirt this issue by inserting one standard sentence: "assume that the existing distributions of wealth and income are ideal *or that the government uses a system of taxes and subsidies to make them so.*"

After stating this standard caveat the bourgeois economist proceeds to his policy analysis using cost-benefit techniques that are based upon the assumption of the normative and empirical adequacy of standard Paretian analysis. Never is there hint of the fact that the government has *never* used its taxing and spending powers to attempt to obtain a just distribution of wealth and power.

The lack of such an admission is not surprising because it would force

orthodox economists to come to grips with the nature of social, economic, and political power—an analysis of vested economic interests and their relation to political power has always been taboo for orthodox economists (and political scientists as well). The reason that no serious effort has ever been made to achieve a more just distribution of wealth and income—and the reason seems painfully obvious—is that the ordinary social, legal, and political means of making such a redistribution are themselves an integral part of the initial distribution of wealth. To possess wealth is to possess political power in a capitalist system. The orthodox economist's hope that political power will be used to redress economic inequities is perhaps his most glaring blind spot.[6] This point will be discussed more fully below.

In practice, economists merely accept the existing distribution of wealth without question. But only rarely do they have the candor to admit that accepting the existing distribution of wealth implies accepting the existing system of law and moral rules (including the laws of private property). More generally, it implies the acceptance of the entire system of social power, all roles of superordination and subordination, as well as the institutions and instruments of coercion through which power is assured and perpetuated. Thus, most of the important issues with which radical economists are concerned are eliminated from the orthodox economists' analyses with the initial assumption of the Paretian approach.

In addition to the above assumptions of individualism and distributional justice, the theory requires many further empirical and analytical assumptions. These make up the familiar textbook recitation of the conditions necessary for equilibrium under pure competition (and no orthodox economist has ever argued for any alternative means of achieving Pareto optimality in a capitalist economy). In another article this writer has discussed these conditions and the utterly ahistorical and grotesquely unreal foundation that they provide for the ideological conclusions of welfare economics.[7]

Few neoclassical economists would argue that the assumptions underlying the theory of competitive equilibrium are realistic, but nearly all accept the social, moral, and philosophical foundations of the Paretian welfare criterion. The lack of realism of the assumptions, however, does not prevent them from advocating the theoretical model as a basis upon which policy making by government officials should be based. The analysis should not, they argue, be considered as descriptive of reality, but as a normative model that can be used to guide government interventions into the marketplace whenever various assumptions necessary for competitive equilibrium are not met.[8] Two comments should be made regarding this view of government interventionism in a capitalist economy.

First, this bourgeois view gives government a shadowy existence. As long as Pareto optimality exists it is nowhere. When an imperfection occurs (it is generally regarded as an isolated occurrence in an otherwise perfect world) the government becomes a *deus ex machina* that restores the system to a state of bliss. It is an aloof, neutral, impartial arbitrator that descends on the scene and enacts an excise tax or gives a subsidy, the only purpose of which is to restore Pareto optimality. If the neoclassical economist is asked about vested interest, about corruption (which is, after all, simply another aspect of the functioning

of the market), about economic and political power, or about class control of government processes, he replies with disdain that these are the concerns of sociologists and political scientists (although one searches in vain for such concerns in orthodox social science).

The second criticism of Pareto optimality as a norm for government policy is even more damaging. Perusing the several necessary assumptions and contemplating the hundreds of thousands of interdependent markets in the contemporary capitalist economy, one is impressed by the certainty that at any moment there are, in fact, innumerable departures from any potential state of Paretian optimality. But according to "the theory of the second best," policies designed to remedy only some and not all of the defects (because simultaneously remedying all would obviously be impossible) will often result in effects diametrically opposed to those envisioned by the authors of these policies. In the words of William J. Baumol:

> In brief, this theory [of the second best] states, on the basis of a mathematical argument, that in a concrete situation characterized by *any* deviation from "perfect" optimality, partial policy measures which eliminate only some of the departures from the optimal arrangement may well result in a net decrease in social welfare.[9]

Where then does this leave the normative theory of Pareto optimality upon which the neoclassical notions of market efficiency and rational prices (not to mention the whole classical liberal argument for laissez-faire capitalism) are based? The answer is obvious. It is riddled by even more acute contradictions than the economic reality from which it springs and for which it attempts to provide an ideological defense.

It is in the treatment of externalities, however, that neoclassical economics becomes involved in the most glaring contradictions. This is not surprising because even though the alienation experienced in capitalist society causes economic activity to be seen as merely so many individual struggles against the laws of the market, which appear as immutable, natural forces, nevertheless the real-life processes of production and consumption are universally social rather than private experiences.

In the usual neoclassical approach, the processes of production and consumption are assumed to have "direct" effects on only one or a few persons who are doing the producing or consuming.[10] Externalities occur when the utility function of one consumer is affected by the consumption of another consumer, or the production function of one firm is affected by the production of another firm, or, most importantly, the utility of an individual is affected by a production process with which he has no direct connection. The traditional neoclassical approach is to assume that, except for a single externality, Pareto optimality exists everywhere. With all prices other than those in the market in question reflecting "perfect market rationality," then through a supposed process of extrapolation and/or interpolation (commonly referred to as "cost-benefit" analysis) the welfare economists claim to be able to simulate what would be the "correct," "rational" market price in the absence of this lone externality.

The cost-benefit analysis by means of which externalities are to be corrected is itself a mere extension of the Paretian theory of allocative efficiency. As E. J. Mishan has stated:

> A person who agrees to apply the principles of allocative efficiency needs no new assumption to extend his agreement to the application of existing cost-benefit analysis. In sum, both the principles of economic efficiency and those of cost-benefit analysis derive their inspiration from the . . . Pareto criterion, and a person cannot with consistency accept the one and deny the other.[11]

The externality being analyzed is not really imagined to be the only actual deviation from Pareto optimality. Rather, it is asserted that this is only a tolerably close approximation to reality. Mishan, for example, asserts that:

> . . . although it is not expected that the economy at any moment in time attains an optimum position, in its continuous adjustments to changes in the conditions of demand and supply, it may not be too far from an overall optimal position for any prolonged period.[12]

So, when in this set of circumstances, we find an externality, the beneficent, impartial *deus ex machina* is again called upon, this time to tax or subsidize in such quantities as to exactly nullify or neutralize the lone externality. Pareto optimality is restored. But the cost-benefit analysis that forms the foundation of the tax-subsidy approach to externalities is an unrealistic as a simple statement that there are no externalities at all, because it rests on the assumption of Pareto optimum prices in all markets except the one in question.[13]

Even more devastating criticism (if such is, indeed, needed) results when we realize that externalities are totally pervasive.[14] When reference is made to externalities, one usually takes as a typical example an upwind factory that emits large quantities of sulfur oxides and particulate matter inducing rising probabilities of emphysema, lung cancer, and other respiratory diseases to residents downwind, or a strip-mining operation that leaves an irreparable aesthetic scar on the countryside. The fact is, however, that most of the millions of acts of production and consumption in which we daily engage involve externalities. In a market economy any action of one individual or enterprise which induces pleasure or pain to any other individual or enterprise and is unpriced by a market constitutes an externality. Because the vast majority of productive and consumptive acts are social, that is, to some degree they involve more than one person, it follows that they will involve externalities. Our table manners in a restaurant, the general appearance of our house, our yard or our person, our personal hygiene, the route we pick for a joy ride, the time of day we mow our lawn, or nearly any one of the thousands of ordinary daily acts, all affect, to some degree, the pleasures or happiness of others. Only the most extreme bourgeois individualism could have resulted in an economic theory that proceeded on the assumption of the existence of only a single externality.

With the recognition of the fact of pervasive externalities the tax-subsidy solution is seen clearly as the fantasy it is. This solution would require literally hundreds of millions of taxes and subsidies (in the United States alone!). More-

over, the imposition of any single tax or subsidy would undoubtedly create totally new externalities because a system of taxes and subsidies, as personalized as this system would have to be, would certainly create new patterns of envy and sympathy with each new tax or subsidy. This envy and sympathy would constitute new externalities for which there would have to be new taxes and subsidies. So the process would go on forever, with an infinitude of taxes and subsidies never getting us any closer to that most elusive of all bourgeois chimeras—Paretó optimality.[15]

The neoclassical view of government implicit in the above discussion is at the heart of bourgeois liberal ideology. It is inseparable from the view of human beings underlying welfare economics. If one studies the leading academic textbooks in microeconomic theory (where neoclassical theory receives the purest statement) one is struck by the implicit assumption of economic and political equality that pervades all the analyses. Individuals are differentiated only by slightly different endowments of commodities and factors of production. They are usually represented by symbols that have utterly no significance beyond the indication that they are different individuals. Each is usually assumed to have some amounts of each commodity and factor of production. When one inspects the total endowments of the individuals, they are relatively equal, though differing in the proportions that each commodity constitutes of the total endowment. Each individual engages in identical forms of maximizing behavior, and each individual benefits by the exchange.

The institutional prerequisites of commodity exchange are provided by the government. They include the protection of property rights, the enforcement of contracts, the issuing, maintaining and regulating of a money supply, and the provision of any other institutions necessary for effective exchange. Because every individual is assumed to benefit by exchange, it follows that every individual benefits from these activities of government. Because in the abstract every individual can own private property and have the contracts into which he enters enforced by the government, there appears an illusion of equality. It is from this illusion of equality that the government appears to be the neutral *deus ex machina* that exists merely to enforce the universally beneficial prerequisites of commodity exchange.

One would search in vain in these microeconomic theory textbooks for any mention of class relations. Indeed one would find no mention of capitalists, of workers, of financiers, or of any other differentiating economic roles into which the maximizing individuals can be placed.

In the best-selling intermediate microeconomic theory textbook of the last twenty years, the theme of the book is stated on page 2:

> We are the participating members of a substantially free-enterprise economy. We consume its milk and honey, its automobiles and entertainment. We own and operate its farms, its filling stations, its factories and its gold mines. We own and command its capital and labor.[16]

The "we" in this passage is never differentiated in any way throughout the book.

This view of human nature and the appropriate role of government originated in a period of transition between feudalism and capitalism. It was based on the notion of the universal "Rights of Man." Feudal landed property was individualized with its lord. It had his rank, privileges and political position. Such landed property was estranged from people generally, and it confronted them as an alien power. The concept of the universal Rights of Man was an attack on the claim of the feudal ruling class that their position was foreordained by divine fiat. The liberals argued that all men should be equal in the abstract sense that any person ought to have the legal right to acquire property and to have that property right defended by government.

When this political and economic philosophy is juxtaposed to the medieval notion that possession of land was divinely decreed and therefore one could not advocate its alienability, we can see that there is an important, but purely formal notion of equality contained in it. All persons can legally alienate land because all belong to the general class of "man." Therefore there are no innate or *a priori* inequalities.

But the actual result of this formal equality must always be inequality. Alienation for one means coercive exclusion for all others. The ways in which land ownership were acquired inevitably meant that ownership would be in the hands of a few and the majority would be forcefully excluded from any rights in regard to the land. Thus, there was a contradiction between the form of the principle of the "Rights of Man" and the inevitable, practical, real content of the principle. Istvan Meszaros has concluded that

> The abstractness and formal-legalistic character of the Rights of Man is determined by the irreconcilable contradiction between content and form: the new *partiality* of motivating content and the formal *universality* of ideological appeal. This is not a conceptual abstractness that could be removed or improved upon. It is an objectively necessary abstractness, determined by the internal contradictions of a concrete historical situation. It is quite impossible to 'demystify' this abstract structure without exposing the contradiction between actual partial content and formally universal ideological appeal.[17]

Neoclassical economists are the contemporary advocates of the Rights of Man. The function of welfare economics is to obscure the "actual partial content" of legal rights by creating the illusion that the "formally universal ideological appeal" is, in fact, descriptive of the concrete reality of each individual living in contemporary capitalist society.

Marxism demystifies this contradiction. Its historical analysis of the class basis of contemporary capitalism reveals that the law of contract enforces the present rules of the capitalist game. Its basic rule is that when two parties have made a bargain, in which one side agrees to transfer to the other certain goods or services in return for some valuable consideration from the other, either can be held to that bargain. This seems "obvious" in our present private-enterprise society, and indeed is a pillar of that society—because workers can thus expect only a set wage for their services and financiers can collect their principal and

interest and landlords their rent and manufacturers the agreed price for their products. It is undoubtedly true that this would be considered an odd and "bad" rule in many other societies, but in capitalist society the law of contract is the socio-legal institution through which power is yielded and coercion is visited upon the weak. The terms of a contract depend upon the initial endowment of salable things (that is, the system of property rights), and the extent and acuteness of the needs of the parties to the contract (that is, the economic inequalities created by the system of property rights). As a former federal judge states: "The main reason that freedom of contract has never been as free as advertised—and it is a painfully obvious reason—is that sellers and buyers are not equal in bargaining power. So the terms of sale will simply reflect the power, or lack of it, that each party brings to the market place. So a market is also a financial slaughter house, where the strong can chop up the weak."[18]

The laws governing property ownership are undoubtedly the most basic laws of capitalism. The most general definition of property ownership laws is that they are codified systems of privileges for some and sanctions or prohibitions for others that relate directly or indirectly to "things" (which may or may not be tangible). Such privileges and sanctions are coercively established and coercively maintained. They form the basis for the hierarchical or class differentiation in society. In capitalism private ownership of the means of production gives less than 1 percent of the population control of all of the more important production processes. With this control goes a legal claim on the surplus of the output that the working class produces above and beyond (1) its own subsistence and (2) the replacement of the means of production used up in the production process.

One lawyer has argued that "while idealism determines the form of law, material interests, specifically the interests of private property, determine its content. The basis of all law is the real, tangible interest in rights of ownership of property...."[19] It is not surprising that this lawyer concludes that "private property cannot, under the present order, be abolished by law," because private property is the basis of the present order.

Based on the laws of contract and property are the criminal laws that enforce repression by the state against those who would violate private property or contract rights. If a man steals a loaf of bread under capitalism, he is guilty regardless of his need or that of his family. One can certainly imagine a better society in which anyone would be thought criminal who would prevent a starving man from taking whatever he needs to stay alive, or in which all necessities were free. If bread is too farfetched an example in the United States (but not in India), then we may point to the laws that would make it a crime to force a hospital to care for someone at gunpoint, but do not make it a crime to turn away a sick man with no money from the hospital door. Such are the inevitable legal consequences of a system built upon the foundations of private property.

The laws necessary to protect each and every privilege of private property are so pervasive that the President's Crime Commission estimated that 91 percent of the American people have committed crimes for which they could have received prison sentences.[20] This raises the important question of which laws are enforced and against whom are they enforced. The commission report concluded that "the poor are arrested more often, convicted more frequently, sentenced more harshly, rehabilitated less successfully than the rest of society."[21]

The commission reported that "white-collar" or upper-class "criminals are only rarely dealt with through the full force of criminal sanctions."[22] On the other hand, a study of law enforcement in a major American city showed that 90 percent of the people arrested had incomes under $5,000 per year. Furthermore, nearly 45 percent of the crimes for which they were arrested were "crimes without victims."[23] The vast majority of these lower-class victims of the legal system lack the financial resources to hold out for a trial and most are forced to plead guilty in order to avoid lengthy detention before their case comes to trial:

> A poor or non-white defendant languishes in jail weeks, months and even years before trial. Nor does this preventive detention count toward whatever sentence may be imposed if the defendant is convicted; thus more pressure is placed on the accused to plead guilty quickly.

> It may surprise most people that there are almost no criminal trials in the United States; but since seventy percent (over ninety percent in some states) of all defendants plead guilty, the need for most trials is eliminated. In 1966 there were 9,895 felonies recorded in New York City; 9,501 of these ended in convictions by a plea of guilty. The pressures on the lower class, poor, or non-white defendants to plead guilty have received little attention; perhaps those who are arrested and detained illegally are generally thought to be guilty anyway.[24]

Such is the actual historical content of the laws that the neoclassical economists consider universally beneficent because they permit the advantages of exchange; and such is the actual content of the actions of the neoclassical economists' beneficent *deus ex machina* that impartially acts to maintain or restore Pareto optimality.

So orthodox welfare economics accepts as the ultimate ethical criteria of social value the *existing* desires, generated by the institutions, values, and social processes of *existing* society, and weighted by the *existing* distributions of income, wealth, and power. Accepting them as such the theory becomes by its very nature incapable of asking questions about the nature of an ethically good society and ethically good men that would be the product of such a society. The desires of the isolated, egoistic, alienated, manipulated "economic man" created by the capitalist social system form the moral foundation upon which neoclassical welfare economics is constructed. The bourgeois economists rest their theory on the assumed impartiality of laws and governments whose basis is clearly the maintenance of the existing structure of privilege and power. The Vietnam war, Watergate, the recent revelations of the systematic, illegal surveillance and disruption of radical groups by the FBI and CIA show that the government will go to incredible lengths to protect these interests.

Nor is welfare economics merely a disconnected branch of bourgeois economics that can be discarded while leaving other areas of applied economics unscathed.

Concepts that are only defensible on the assumption that the Paretian analysis is accepted underlie nearly all policy conclusions of applied economics. Paretian efficiency notions form the basis of the theory of comparative advantage in international trade theory; they underlie most normative conclusions in the neoclassical theory of public finance, most cost-benefit analyses, and nearly every other area in which neoclassical economics culminates in policy

recommendations. Even worse are the rarely defended, sanctimoniously stated cliches and shibboleths about "rational prices" and "market efficiency" in that most ideologically tainted of all neoclassical academic specializations, comparative economic systems, or the analysis of socialist economies.

The pervasive use of subtle variations of the elements of Paretian analysis in most areas of applied economics is inherently conservative. Even when the economist using this analysis has the most progressive and humane intentions, the very foundational presuppositions of welfare economics have a significant tendency to eliminate fundamental social conflicts from the purview of the investigations and to channel his thinking into safe, sterile areas of analysis and to limit him to the use of safe, sterile "tools of analysis." Welfare economics is indeed the contemporary, lineal descendent of the doctrines that Marx labeled as "vulgar economy." But on examination it is evident that this is the very heart and the unifying principle of nearly all applied bourgeois economics. It is for these reasons that I believe the greatest barrier to constructive radical economic analysis for an individual trained in a bourgeois economics department to be the necessity of intellectually transcending the habits of thought inculcated through years of intensive study of neoclassical welfare economics in both its pure and applied forms.

NOTES

1. Karl Marx, *Grundrisse,* ed. David McLellan (London: Macmillan, 1971), p. 66.

2. Ibid., pp. 65-66.

3. Karl Marx, *Capital,* vol. I (Moscow: Foreign Language Publishing House, 1961), pt. I, chap. 1, note p. 81.

4. W. J. Baumol, *Economic Theory and Operations Analysis,* 2nd ed. (Englewood Cliffs, N.J.: Prentice-Hall, Inc., 1965), p. 376.

5. See E. K. Hunt, "Orthodox and Marxist Economics in a Theory of Socialism," *Monthly Review* 24, no. 8 (January 1973), pp. 50-56.

6. This point is developed more amply in W. J. Samuels, "Welfare Economics, Power and Property," in Gene Wunderlich, ed., *Perspectives on Property* (Philadelphia: The Pennsylvania State University Press, 1972).

7. E. K. Hunt, "A Radical Critique of Welfare Economics," in Edward Nell, ed., *Value, Distribution and Growth: Essays in the Revival of Political Economy* (Cambridge: Cambridge University Press, 197-).

8. For a discussion of this view see E. K. Hunt, "Orthodox Economic Theory and Capitalist Ideology," *Monthly Review* 19 (1968), pp. 40-55.

9. William J. Baumol, "Informed Judgment, Rigourous Theory and Public Policy," *Southern Economic Journal* 32 (October 1965), p. 138. For the definitive formulation of the theory of the second best see R. G. Lipsey and Kelvin Lancaster, "The General Theory of the Second Best," *The Review of Economic Studies* 24, nos. 63, 64, 65 (1956-57).

10. By using the adjustive *direct* I am following E. J. Mishan, "The Postwar Literature on Externalities: An Interpretative Essay," *Journal of Economic Literature,* March 1971, p. 2. Excluded are *indirect effects,* which are obtained through changes in relative prices in a Walrasian general equilibrium system.

11. E. J. Mishan, *Economics for Social Decisions: Elements of Cost-Benefit Analysis* (New York: Praeger Publishers, 1973), p. 17.

12. Ibid., p. 80.

13. Ibid., pp. 29-83.

14. For an analysis of the implications of pervasive externalities see R. C. d'Arge and E. K. Hunt, "Environmental Pollution, Externalities, and Conventional Economic Wisdom: A Critique," *Environmental Affairs,* June 1971, pp. 266-86.

15. The most reactionary segment of neoclassical economists, the so-called Chicago School, has a different approach to the treatment of externalities. They advocate the

creation of property rights to pollute. Such rights, they argue, should be freely exchanged in the market with no government intervention. This writer has criticised this approach in "A Radical Critique of Welfare Economics."

16. Richard H. Leftwich, *The Price System and Resource Allocation* (Hinsdale, Ill.: The Dryden Press, 1970, first published 1955), p. 2.

17. Istvan Meszaros, "Conceptual Structure of Marx's Theory of Alienation," in E. K. Hunt and Jesse G. Schwartz, eds., *A Critique of Economic Theory* (Baltimore: Penguin Books, Inc., 1972), pp. 153-54.

18. D. T. Baxelon, *The Paper Economy* (New York: Vintage Books, 1963), p. 52.

19. Kenneth Cloke, "The Economic Basis of Law and State," in R. Lefcourt, ed., *Law Against the People* (New York: Vintage Books, 1971), p. 72.

20. The President's Commission on Law Enforcement and the Administration of Justice, *The Challenge of Crime in a Free Society* (New York: Avon Books, 1968), p. 87.

21. Ibid., p. 151.

22. Ibid., p. 156.

23. Ibid., pp. 149-50, 195.

24. Robert Lefcourt, "Law Against the People," in *Law Against the People,* p. 27.

To Abstain or Not to Abstain (Is That the Question?)

A Critique of the Human Capital Concept

MICHAEL J. CARTER

Assistant Professor of Economics at Notre Dame University

INTRODUCTION

The introduction of the concept "human capital" into economic analysis is generally considered to be one of the most fertile theoretical developments within the discipline since the Keynesian "revolution." In order to avoid confusion, we acknowledge at the outset that not all orthodox economists share this high opinion of human capital theory. Melvin Reder, for instance, notes that there is a problem of allocation of nonhomogeneous labor that the theory merely assumes away rather than solves.[1] Kenneth Arrow seems bothered by the inability of the theory to account for the persistent empirical evidence of discrimination against blacks and by the fact that the valued job skills imparted by liberal arts curricula are unobvious at best.[2] However, the objections of Arrow and Reder are not to the concepts and structure of human capital theory per se. They merely question from different viewpoints the empirical relevance of the perfect information assumption embedded in the theory and assert/ demonstrate that the absence of such information can substantively alter the character of equilibria in labor markets. Although these objections are intriguing in their own right, neither they nor any observed lack of correlation between measured amounts of "human capital" and wage incomes are fatal to the theory. These empiricist critiques merely demonstrate the need for further work on the theory—better model specification, more refined measurements of relevant variables—possibly leading to the conclusion that once again there has been a breakdown in the conditions of perfect competition and, hence, a justification for government intervention to restore that felicitious arrangement wherein private cupidity promotes the "general interest."

In this paper we are concerned solely with the logical or, rather, the ideological structures that underlie the concept of human capital. We will demonstrate through dialectical materialist analysis that the concept of "human capital" has coherence only within a framework that abstracts from essential

This reading was written especially for this book.

differences in real relations. In particular the failure to distinguish value from price and labor from labor power lies at the root of the contradictions embodied in human capital theory. Marx noted long ago that ". . . the transformation of value and price of labor power into the form of wages, or into the value and price of labor itself . . . makes the actual relation invisible, and, indeed, shows the direct opposite of that relation, [and] forms the basis of all the juridicial notions of both laborer and capitalist, of all the mystifications of the capitalistic mode of production, of all its illusions as to liberty, of all the apologetic shifts of the vulgar economists."[3] From this standpoint, human capital theory is merely the most recent and the most vulgar[4] of these apologetic shifts.

THE CONCEPTUAL STRUCTURE OF HUMAN CAPITAL THEORY

The proudest claim that the architects of human capital theory advance for it is that it provides a secure foundation for distribution theory. For instance Jacob Mincer authoritatively intones, "the analysis of causes of income variations in the aggregate and among individuals is returning to the mainstream of theoretical and empirical research. One impressive outgrowth of this shift is the rapidly developing literature on human capital. The human capital approach is intimately related to the study of income distribution: costs and returns to investment are measured in the first instance by earnings differentials."[5] Similarly, Gary Becker announces excitedly, ". . . this approach should demonstrate that such a theory need not be a patchwork of Pareto distributions, ability vectors and ad hoc probability mechanisms, but can rely on the *basic economic principles that have proven their worth elsewhere.*"[6] What are these "basic economic principles," these theoretical beams that prop up the human capital edifice, whose "proven worth" induces Becker to invest his scarce intellectual resources here? They are abstinence theory and marginal productivity theory, or more generally consumer choice theory and production function theory.

The central concept on which human capital theory rests and that permits the application of choice theory calculus to questions of income distribution is the concept of wage income as a return to an investment. Individuals (or their parents) spend time and money in acquisition of "productive" characteristics. The earliest human capital models concentrated on schools as the locus of "human capital" acquisition but quickly expanded to encompass "on-the-job training," and "parental investment in nutrition and time spent with child," as additional sources of human capital accumulation. These expenditures of time and money by parents and later by the child himself are considered to be investments rather than mere consumption because they increase the child's future productivity—that is, they increase his or her ability to produce highly priced commodities in the future. Moreover, these expenditures on human productive skills earn a return in the future in the form of higher wages than would have been earned in the absence of such expenditures. These higher wages accrue to the individual, however, directly because of his higher productivity, not because of his investment. If some individuals were highly productive even without any "investment" in human capital, they would still earn high wages. That is, human capital theory rests on the assumption that economic rewards to individuals

equal their individual (marginal) contribution to production. The theory attempts to add substance to this assumption by explaining the distribution of individual productive abilities (distribution of marginal productivities) among the population on the basis of individual choice theory. Phrased differently, we could say that the specific content of the human capital concept is that the substance of wage income (except for that portion which is a rent on nonreproducible skills) is interest on previous investments. This interest is, however, realized in the form of payments for current productivity.

Having specified the relation of the human capital concept to the production function/marginal product theory of wage determination, let us determine its relation to abstinence (individual choice) theory. The basic assumption on this side is that at any time the individual (or his parents) is faced with a choice between activities that earn income in the present and activities that "sacrifice" present income but increase the individual's productive ability and, hence, future income. Thus during pre-school years a child's parents can opt either to spend time working and earning income or to spend that time talking to the child, playing with him, and so on. Such time spent with the child leads to greater attainment in education and training and, hence, higher future earnings. The value of a unit of human capital "investment" in such cases is equal to the opportunity cost of the parents' time. Thus highly educated, highly paid parents invest more in their child per unit of time spent in the home with the child than do poor working-class parents. Once in school the amount of human capital investment equals the institutional costs undertaken by the parents plus the earnings that the student forgoes in order to stay in school and accumulate more skills. Finally, once in the labor market the young worker with a given amount of already embodied capital faces a choice between jobs with relatively lower salaries that afford him the opportunity to acquire even more skills and those with relatively higher salaries that offer no such opportunities. In each of these situations the individual faces a choice between an income now and a larger income in the future. Those who throughout their lives have invested the most, that is, abstained from the most income, will (assuming equal endowments of initial ability, and equal levels of current investment) in a cross-sectional view of any age cohort have the largest wage incomes and will have contributed the most to production. Thus Jacob Mincer, speaking of the abstract human capital equation relating present wage income to human capital in its expanded expression as accumulated abstinence and compounded interest, glibly notes that, "these formulations incidentally highlight the principle that it is . . . the postponement of earnings that is the basic cause of differentials in earnings."[7]

But more must be said. Why is there a positive rate of return on human capital? On the one side the returns to human capital investment are realized through wages which depend on "marginal productivity," which in turn (for a given level of embodied human capital) depends on the amount of physical capital and the specific technology in which physical capital is embodied. Thus, ultimately, the "demand" for human capital depends on the amount and particular technological configuration of physical capital. On the other side, the "supply" of human capital depends on people's willingness to "abstain" from present income in expectation of higher future income. Why does the "supply" of human capital determined by these individual time preferences remain

sufficiently low that when combined with physical capital "it" has a marginal product sufficiently high to regularly insure a positive rate of return on human capital investment?

This question has never been explicitly posed, much less resolved, by human capital theory, which has remained snugly (and smugly) moored in its partial equilibrium harbor imagining itself safe from the storms raging in capital and value theory. Yet, if we are to understand the structure of human capital theory, we must understand the logic that connects it to the basic economic principles of marginal productivity and abstinence. Therefore let us pursue the question further and attempt to specify the theoretical relations of physical to human capital.

We notice first that in a world of perfect capital markets an individual may borrow to maintain present income and consumption while investing in himself. Of course, he faces a positive rate of interest, which is determined ultimately by individuals' rates of time preference. In this sense the "rate of return" to human capital realized in the form of wage differentials is a recoupment of interest costs. The real "return" accrues to the lender of the funds and is a return to his abstinence—specifically his abstinence from frittering away those funds in present consumption. In the case of the human capital investor who finances his own investment through reduced consumption, the "return" on his investment realized in the form of higher wages is a return to his abstinence and simultaneously a replacement of his implicit interest costs. Similarly, the return to the investor in physical capital can be analyzed as a recoupment of interest costs and simultaneously as a return to abstinence from consumption. From this perspective, then, both types of investment appear formally identical. The ultimate source of the positive rate of return on both is the scarcity of (excess demand for) savings at zero interest rate. The personal distributions of both physical and human capital are determined by individual differences in willingness to forgo present consumption. Thus, if perfect capital markets are assumed, the abstinence on which wage differentials are based is ultimately not abstinence from earnings but abstinence from consumption.

In this general equilibrium sense the ultimate rationale for a positive rate of return on human capital is identical to the rationale for a positive interest rate on physical capital. Indeed the choice between accumulation of physical and human capital appears here as a mere portfolio choice where risks and expected returns on the different types of assets determine in conjunction with individual preferences over these characteristics the optimal mix of such assets. However even at this level with perfect capital markets and absence of exogenous inequalities (such as unequal "ability" endowments) the formal identity of the two types of "investment" is disturbed by two substantive, qualitative differences.

First, the inalienability of embodied human capital precludes the possibility of its being pledged as collateral on loans. Hence, such loans are more risky than loans of physical capital. This drives up borrowing rates in the human capital loan market for those who have no physical assets to pledge as collateral. In particular, individuals from families with low-wage histories and no physical assets may find it impossible to secure the funds to live on in organized markets, and will—regardless of their preferences—be forced to "forgo" investment and work for current income. This outcome obtains even though capital markets

function "perfectly" in a technical sense; indeed, it results precisely through the risk sensitivity of such markets. This inherent institutional restriction on the accumulation of human capital tends to raise the rate of return of human capital investment above that of physical capital and converts the possession of physical capital into a precondition of human capital accumulation.

Second, the "abstinence" from wage income that forms the active substance of human capital investment is just as directly abstinence from work. This is true at least for parental investment of time with the child and for the schooling component of human capital investment. That is, the concrete actions that constitute "human capital investment" elsewhere in neoclassical theory constitute "consumption of leisure." To the linear additive mind of the neoclassical theorist this poses no problem in *principle*. Admittedly education and child care have a "consumption component." But this will be reflected in an increased demand for human capital investment funds, an increase in human capital investment, and a decrease in the equilibrium rate of return on that investment.[8] This same agile mind then notes that the tendency to decrease measured rates of return from this source counteracts to a greater or lesser extent the tendency of rates of return to increase due to human capital's inalienability. Thus measured rates of return on physical and human capital may turn out to be about equal after all. What is forgotten is that this quantitative equalization masks a qualitative divergence. Those with high physical asset levels who can afford to invest reap the consumption benefits of not working but at the same time can earn a rate of return roughly commensurate with that on physical capital. They thus are enabled to have their cake and eat it, too. Those with no or low physical assets on the other side are forced to forgo investment and remain trapped in low-paying, dangerous, and unpleasant jobs.

Thus, even in the fetish world of neoclassical theory where all human relations are resolvable into commodity relations, there is a substantive difference between the commodity human capital and the commodity physical capital. Human capital cannot be alienated from its proprietor. Hence, even with perfect capital markets, the savings/consumption "choice" involved in human capital accumulation is not independent of current productive activity (the work/leisure "choice"). This interdependence manifests itself concretely in two ways. On the one side, prior accumulation of physical wealth appears as the condition of human capital accumulation; on the other, part of the action of human capital acquisition appears as a shift in the form of consumption rather than pure abstinence from consumption. By contrast physical capital is alienable and its accumulation appears as a result of pure savings/consumption choices made independently of current productive activity.

CRITIQUE OF HUMAN CAPITAL THEORY

The analysis of the human capital concept and its relation to distribution theory has remained on the surface of the reified forms of economic appearances systematized in neoclassical theory. Admittedly, we have shown that part of the return to human capital is a monopoly return to possessors of physical wealth, and that the unfettered operation of the market tends to reproduce unequal opportunities for human capital accumulation independent of individual pref-

erences. However, the possession of physical wealth itself insofar as it results from accumulation of physical capital still appears as the result of pure abstinence from consumption either by the individual or by his extension through time, his parents. Thus, the advantage that owners of physical wealth have in human capital accumulation still resides ultimately in individual choices that are prior to and outside the economic relationships as such in which individuals find themselves. Moreover, the analysis suggests that if we wish to remove any restrictions on individuals of the present generation resulting from the profligacy of their forebears all that is necessary is a state-guaranteed loan program for human capital investment.

The point is: Distribution still appears as a relation between amounts of (relatively scarce) "things"; that is, commodities. Individuals are all posited as qualitatively equal in their economic relations with each other. All are owners of commodities, either physical capital or human capital, and relate to each other in exchange on this basis of qualitative equality (and exchange is the only economic relationship in which they confront each other). The only differences between individuals are quantitative—that is, the amounts of scarce commodities they possess. Even these differences are rooted ultimately in the individual's own choices and lie as such outside and prior to the exchange relation itself. If one individual grows wealthier while another remains impoverished, it has nothing to do with the nature of their economic relationship.

In this section we tear aside this veil of appearances and demonstrate through dialectical analysis of the total capital-labor exchange process that the basic source of income differentials resides in the different and qualitatively unequal structural position of labor and capital within that process. That is, the capital relation itself, not individual choice, is the source of wealth on the one side and poverty on the other (poverty here in the sense of exclusion from objective wealth, not necessarily in the sense of absolute want or shortage). The use of the dialectic exposes as the fundamental flaw of neoclassical distribution theory, and human capital theory in particular, the assertion that labor is a commodity with properties identical to any other commodity. We have already seen that even within the neoclassical framework the inalienability of the concrete productive skills that form the substance of the commodity human capital upsets the analogy with physical capital. But within that framework all that is affected by the inalienability of these skills are the relative terms of exchange and accumulation between human and physical capital. Here we show that the consequences of this inalienability cannot be so facilely trammeled up but ultimately undermine the basis not only of human capital theory but of the entire neoclassical capital theory.

To grasp the specific difference between the capital-labor "exchange" and simple commodity exchange let us first specify the elements of the latter.[9] In simple exchange each of the parties to the exchange brings to market a value that is embodied either in a specific physical object or in the general object money. Each is therefore an independent proprietor of physical property. The manner in which each initially obtained his property, whether by force, theft, inheritance, thrift, industry, and so forth, is immaterial to their mutual relationship as exchangers. Their relationship is shaped solely by the exchange values of their respective commodities that determine the proportions at which their goods

exchange. The concrete act of exchange establishes that the goods exchanged are equal as exchange values. Yet each individual exchanges his property for that of the other only if the use value to him of the goods received exceeds the use value (to him) of the goods with which he parts. On the other side each is indifferent to the use values that the commodities have for the other and cares not how the other uses the commodity after the exchange. Thus, while each subject recognizes that they have a common interest in exchange, each serves the needs of the other only to serve himself. Each, therefore, feels himself the dominant subject of the exchange.

Hence in this simple exchange of commodities freedom and equality are displayed—freedom because each gives up his property voluntarily and is "forced" or determined only by his own natural needs; equality because each has the same social relation towards the other (independent proprietor-exchanger) and because equivalent exchange values are exchanged. Moreover if one individual grows richer while the other remains impoverished, then this is of their own free will and is in no way connected with their economic relation to each other. Indeed, the function of the exchange relation in accumulation is here limited to the conversion of value embodied in particular objects and accumulated by some means outside of exchange into money, the general objective form of value. This possibility of conversion of value from one form into another, of course, frees the individual qua commodity producer to specialize, increase the mass thereby of specific objective values brought to market, and exchange these there either for the instruments necessary to further expand his production or for increased money. But the point here is that his wealth grows through his own productive activity, not at the expense of the other and not through his exchange relation with the other. The exchange process merely allows his natural industriousness to assume the specific form in which it can produce the most value.

All of these harmonies, these reciprocities of the commodity exchange process have been derived from the supposition that each party to the process brings to market an objectified value, a commodity separable from himself, and that this commodity is what he exchanges for the particular commodities necessary to sustain his individual production and consumption (and production and consumption are here an individual's own business, have nothing to do with the *form* of the exchange relation as such; although of course they have some bearing on the amounts of particular commodities brought to market and, hence, on the quantitative outcomes of exchange). Now it is the chief business of bourgeois distribution theory and of its most adequate expression, human capital theory, to represent the exchange between the laborer and the capitalist as just such a simple commodity exchange. The capitalist brings to market the commodity physical capital; the worker, the *commodity human capital.* These two are therefore equal independent proprietors each with a mutual and reciprocal need for the other's commodity. The difference between the two commodities (and therefore between their proprietors) is a purely formal one. Both have been accumulated by essentially similar means—abstinence—and for essentially similar purposes—preference for future over present income. In fact, so qualitatively similar are these two commodities H. Capital and P. Capital that we give them the same last name. Small wonder then that these two brothers should find it to their mutual interest to become partners in production and divide the

value of the output between them on the basis of the quantitative contribution of each. The fact that one receives his return in the form of wages, the other in the form of profits is an illusion. At bottom the return to both is interest income (although the profit form is tainted with greater or lesser amounts of risk, which must also be compensated). This then is the wit and wisdom of human capital theory—to reduce all economic relations between individuals to the relation simple commodity exchange, all income categories to the single category interest. These reductions are then represented as the stuff of pure common sense. It never occurs to the human capital theorist that these reductions are made possible only by initially abstracting from the precise differences in real economic relations between the simple form of exchange and its developed capitalist form. That is, everything that distinguished the capital-labor "exchange" from simple commodity exchange is abstracted from at the outset. On this basis the essential identity (mere formal, quantifiable differences) of labor and capital is demonstrated. That is, in human capital theory nothing comes out of the hat that was not first put into the hat. The formal elaboration of the theory is seen from this perspective to be so much magician's hand-waving to distract our attention from the crucial nature of the assumption that labor is a commodity qualitatively identical in exchange to any other commodity.

Let us now drop this assumption and, instead, attempt to grasp the specific differences between labor and other commodities. (Only from this basis can the differences between the labor-capital exchange and simple commodity exchange be grasped.) First, we notice that the worker does not bring any object distinct from himself into the market. He brings only his ability to work embodied in his physical person. Different workers have different specific skills and abilities, but this does not yet concern us. The commonality that they all possess as workers, that which distinguishes them specifically from capitalists or simple commodity producers or other "sellers," is that they have nothing to sell. They have only their ability to work, their capacity to labor. It is this that they sell to the capitalist, or rather they sell the power to dispose of their labor for a certain number of hours; that is, to direct its activities for that time and appropriate its products. Thus, they sell the power to dispose over their labor, not their labor itself. The concrete labor itself must be extracted in the production process. This may seem a fine distinction, but it opens up the possibility that the price (and value) of this right to disposal over labor power need not equal the price and value of labor itself.[10]

So the commodity that the worker brings to market is his capacity to labor, embodied in his physical person. Like all other commodities it has a value determined by its cost of production. This is a fixed sum of money determined by social processes over which the individual worker has no control. The worker has some control over the amount of labor capacity (specific skills, and so forth) that he brings to market, but no control over the value of a particular labor capacity. The forces of competition among workers drive this value always back to its cost of production. (We are here abstracting from the labor market and educational institutions that interfere with this competition and permit the accrual of monopoly rents to some groups of workers. This abstraction is necessary if we are to focus clearly on the pure relation of labor to capital. Only when this relationship is clearly understood can the particular institutions that partially

negate its functioning be grasped in their historic specificity.) Thus, the worker receives the cost of production (reproduction) of his labor capacity. But because this is inseparable from his physical body, this cost of reproduction is nothing other than the cost of reproducing the worker himself in his concrete totality (that is, not mere individual, biological reproduction but reproduction of himself as an average member of a *class* with the average historically and socially determined reproduction needs of that class). Now the worker receives this reproduction value not in the direct form of the goods and services that are the material stuff of his reproduction, but in the form of a money wage that he must subsequently exchange for the material necessaries of reproduction.

Looked at from this side the money wage is just a mediating factor, and at that a vanishing mediation between the worker and the objective conditions of his reproduction. Thus, the object of his exchange with capital is subsistence. This would be obvious if he received his wages in the form of direct goods and services, but because they are received in the form of money, the general form of wealth, it appears that the product of his labor for him is wealth, not subsistence. This illusion is reinforced by the circumstance that the wage is not paid until after the period of labor is completed, and is even further heightened by certain wage forms such as piece-rate wages. Thus to the individual worker it appears that his wages are the result of his individual labor and that by increasing industriousness he can increase his wage. Moreover, the individual worker can occasionally increase his wages in this way, but only as an individual, only as an exception to his class. If this behavior were followed by all workers, all that would result is a minimum of wages for a maximum of work. Similarly, the individual worker by dint of extreme sacrifice and self-denial can occasionally save, and perhaps enough to become a petty capitalist or a minor *rentier*. But again this behavior is possible only as an exception. If wages were to rise generally above historically necessary reproduction costs, so that general savings became possible, it would be a signal to capitalists to increase prices. (Or in some cases such a rise in workers' savings leads to an overproduction crisis, unemployment, consequent wiping out of savings, and so on. Although it is outside the scope of this paper to discuss crises, the present crisis preceded by a period of wage controls, preceded by several years of a steadily rising wage share, is the most immediate concrete instance of the mechanisms sketched here.) The point both with respect to individual savings and individual industriousness is this: The individual as an individual can at times accumulate wealth by these means, but these are the exceptions, not the rule. As average representatives of a class, workers receive the value of their commodity, their labor power. The value of this commodity is determined—as are the values of all commodities—by the cost of its reproduction. This is a value determined prior to the particular worker-capitalist exchange and outside the individual control of either. Thus for the worker as worker the only outcome of his repeated exchanges with the capitalist is reproduction of his capacity to labor; and, moreover, reproduction of this capacity isolated from the objective means of its realization, from objective wealth. Hence, reproduction of himself as worker.

We have examined the capital-labor exchange from the side of the worker. To complete the analysis we turn to the side of the capitalist. Whereas the worker brings to market only his capacity to labor embodied in his physical

self and isolated both from his means of subsistence and from the objective means of realizing his labor in material objects, the capitalist comes to market as the possessor of objective value. That is, the capitalist possesses value in the form of particular raw materials and instruments of production. Everything that the worker is not, the capitalist is. The capitalist is the possessor of objective wealth; the worker, its absence. Although the worker must sell his capacity to labor in order to obtain the material stuff of subsistence, the capitalist is under no such compunction. Therefore the object of the exchange for the capitalist is not subsistence, but an increase in his wealth. Of course if the capitalist were never to throw his exchange value into the circulation and production process but merely contented himself with exchanging it for objects of consumption, he would sooner or later eat all his wealth and cease to be a capitalist. Thus, in this sense the reproduction of his capital and of himself as capitalist requires that he enter into exchange with the worker. Nonetheless, the reproduction of his capital as value and the production of the value necessary to support his consumption needs requires that the immediate object of the capitalist in his exchange with labor be an *increase* in the objective exchange value he possesses. Moreover, the competition of capitals enforces even more strongly on the individual capitalist the need to increase the value of his capital in order to maintain himself as capitalist, but detailed discussion at this point of the interaction of different capitals within the accumulation process would distract attention from our primary theoretical object, the capital-labor relation.

From the standpoint of the capitalist, therefore, the worker's capacity to labor is of interest only insofar as it is a capacity to create value and increase the sum of values possessed by the capitalist. Recall that in our discussion of simple commodity exchange we noted that each party to the exchange would part with a given sum of exchange value only if the anticipated use value to him of the commodities received exceeds the use value of the exchange value with which he parts. Here also the capitalist will part with his exchange value only if the expected use value to him of the commodity purchased *exceeds* the amount of exchange value of which he divests himself. Note that if the capitalist wanted to satisfy some particular, concrete need of his, then he would exchange his money for the particular material objects or personal services that satisfy these needs. (But in these simple exchanges he does not act as a capitalist.) But in his exchange with the worker the capitalist is not purchasing any material object; he is purchasing the right to direct and dispose of the worker's productive activity for a given number of hours. This abstract labor power that the capitalist purchases has as such no concrete, personal use to the capitalist; that is, no use to him as a "consumer." It can only be of use to him as a capitalist, by creating for him a greater sum of exchange value than he had *before* his exchange with the laborer, and this increase in the capitalist's exchange value can come about only if the abstract labor power that the capitalist has purchased materializes itself during the hours it is at his disposal in a quantity of goods whose exchange value exceeds the replacement costs of the physical goods consumed plus the quantity of goods necessary to reproduce the laborer's labor power. That is, the worker's actual physical labor is the use value of his commodity, his capacity to labor. After his exchange with the capitalist, however, this use value exists not for him, but for the capitalist.

Moreover, in simple exchange, consumption of the use values of the goods received by each of the exchangers is a purely personal, individual matter that occurs outside and after the exchange process and consequently has nothing to do with the economic relations of the exchangers. But in the capital-labor exchange process, consumption of the worker's labor power forms an integral part of their economic relation. For in this instance the worker has nothing outside of himself as an abstract capacity to labor to offer the capitalist; his use value to the capitalist is not materialized in an object outside of himself. Consumption of the worker's commodity then is nothing other than the extraction of labor and the appropriation of its product by the capitalist. Marx aptly remarks that in this labor process the worker—who brings only his hide to market—"has nothing to expect but a hiding."[11] Only when the labor process is over and the worker's labor has been materialized in commodities belonging to the capitalist does their economic relation end. Only then is their exchange completed.

Thus, the capital-labor relation is a complex exchange characterized by two distinct economic relations. The first is the exchange of the worker's capacity to labor and create value for a fixed sum of value (the wage). The second relation is the extraction and appropriation of the worker's actual labor in the production process. This second relation is, of course, not an exchange relation at all. Indeed, in this second relation the equality, freedom, and reciprocity that we observed in simple commodity exchange relations are completely *negated*. The capitalist is master, the worker his servant; the worker's activities are determined and directed by the capitalist; the capitalist grows richer at the worker's expense. The worker's own activity and the products of that activity are the property of the capitalist because the worker, forced by his situation as pure subjective labor capacity isolated from property, from the objective means of its own reproduction, has already alienated his labor power and the rights to its fruits in the initial exchange (wage contract). Thus, in production the worker grows poorer by the life force expended while the capitalist grows wealthier by the products in which that creative force is materialized.[12]

Looking at the capital-labor exchange as the unity of these two relations we see that one side, labor, emerges only with the reproduction value of labor capacity, while the other side, capital, emerges with a value larger than that with which it began the process. This surplus value, which accrues to capital through the extraction of more labor in the production process than that necessary to produce the commodities needed to reproduce the laborer's labor power, is the inner fountainhead of capital accumulation. Once capitalist production is fully developed—that is, the mass of past surplus value appropriated by capital has grown to the point where profits derived therefrom are large enough to absorb necessary labor plus some surplus labor into production—then no longer must the invested capital come from any source other than the capital relation itself.[13] That is, past labor alienated by labor power in its exchange with capital and appropriated in production by capital provides itself the funds to purchase present labor power. That which began as a presupposition of the capital relation—that is, separation of labor into individual, isolated, subjective labor power and the social, concentrated, objective mass of exchange value that confronts it in the form of capital—is posited in the fully developed relation as a result of the relation itself.[14]

SUMMARY

We are now finally in position to see the confusions embodied in the human capital concept and in its theoretical foundations (abstinence and marginal productivity theory). First, saving is and always has been the sine qua non condition of all accumulation. But the specific condition of capitalist accumulation, of the increase in the objective exchange value possessed by the capitalist, is not saving but extraction and appropriation of surplus value. That the capitalist cannot eat all this booty pumped out of the worker, but must save some of it if he is to increase his wealth or even to survive as a capitalist, is an unfortunate (from his point of view) fact of life. However, this circumstance should not blind us to the fact that in a *causa per quam* sense the condition or source of capitalist accumulation is surplus value. Surplus value, not savings, provides the fund for capital accumulation. Indeed, savings in this sense is specifically a condition of noncapitalist accumulation. In particular the only fund available to the worker for accumulation is the amount of exchange value he has received for his labor power. Because this sum is equal to the reproduction cost of his labor power, it follows that the historically determined consumption requirements of his class will normally eat up this entire sum. But because these requirements are historically, not biologically, determined, there is the possibility that individual workers may by dint of unusual sacrifice of normal consumption for their class or by unusual industriousness accumulate a small stock of exchange value and become petty capitalists or *rentiers*. Thus for the individual worker thrift is the only available means of accumulation of exchange value, but for the capitalist appropriation of surplus value is the means of accumulation. Abstinence theory in representing savings as the condition of capital accumulation has thus failed to grasp the specific distinction between capitalist and noncapitalist accumulation and postulated the condition of the latter as the condition of the former. Although nothing is more true, nor more trite, than that one cannot simultaneously "have one's cake and eat it, too"; as long as labor creates more value than the value of labor power's own reproduction the capitalist is able to invest his exchange value and at the end of production have enough value both to eat and to reinvest. Thus, through repeated exchanges with labor the capitalist is able not merely to have but to accumulate his cake and eat it, too.

Human capital theory reproduces this fundamental error of abstinence theory—that is, it represents savings, abstinence, as the condition of capital accumulation. However, it compounds this error by identifying human productive skills as capital. We have shown that this notion misses completely the specific relation of labor to capital. Rather, labor as activity is the creator of the objectified value that—appropriated by the capitalist—comes to stand opposite labor, to direct and determine the activity of labor in order to increase the value in the hands of the capitalist. Human productive skills as they appear in action within capitalist production are not commodities, not values, not capital. They create values, but are not themselves values. However, these productive skills as they appear embodied in the physical person of the laborer are a commodity with an exchange value determined, as are the exchange values of all commodities, by their reproduction cost. Thus in this respect these skills do not differ from machines or from any piece of capital equipment. And it is of course this

analogy that human capital theory seizes hold of to represent capital and labor power as equals. Unfortunately for human capital theorists the construction of analogies, no matter how elegant, is not science. What is forgotten in the leap from this analogy to the identity of capital and labor power is that neither capital nor labor power is a "thing." Capital is objectified value, objective wealth, created by labor and alienated from labor power in its exchange with capital. The commodity labor power on its side is directly not an object, it is mere subjective capacity to create value. Hence labor power is the complete exclusion of objective wealth; it is absolute poverty. Thus it is forced to alienate its capacity to create value, to alienate its own labor to capital for a fixed sum of value to sustain itself. Therefore, human productive skills viewed as the commodity labor power are in every way the direct opposite of capital (the objectified values possessed by the capitalist), notwithstanding the fact that the specific values of particular skills and machines are determined by a common process.

The logical errors in marginal productivity theory, the other pillar on which the human capital concept rests, are structurally similar to the errors in the abstinence concept. It is of course perfectly true and completely obvious that machines, human labor, and raw materials are all mutually necessary elements of production. But this has been so for thousands of years under many different organizations of the production process and tells us nothing about the creation of value within capitalist relations of production. Indeed, the inability of either men or machines to produce without the other or without raw materials should warn us against the resolution of the output into marginal *products*. That is, a production process is a totality, a specific combination of particular machines, raw materials, and human labor at the end of which a quantity of some particular product is produced. The entire quantity of product is produced in the process by the entire ensemble of factors. In general, there simply is no basis for imputing any part of the product to any one factor. Thus even as a technical relation the concept of marginal product is a mere mathematical artifact rather than a fact. But in any case, we are interested in values, not products, in social, not technical, relations. The worker exchanges with the capitalist. His labor does not exchange with a machine. We have dissected this exchange between worker and capitalist to demonstrate that it is a specific unity of two separate relations—the exchange relation in which the worker receives the reproduction cost of his labor power, and the production relation in which the capitalist extracts labor from the worker. In collapsing labor and labor power into the single commodity human capital, into a single exchange value, these two relations are collapsed into a single, undifferentiated, simple exchange relation. If the worker receives the value of his labor, his "thing," and this is less than the value of the total output, then the remainder must obviously be the value of the capitalist's "thing," his capital. Of course such reasoning is possible only by abstraction away from the specific differences between labor power and capital, only by ignoring the conduct of capital as capital within the production relation, and so forth.

To summarize: The basic error that vitiates the human capital concept and the theoretical structure on which it is based is the conflation into a single value, a single "thing," of two separate aspects of labor—labor as the commodity, labor power, and actual value-creating labor. Having conflated together these two, and

thereby abstracted away from the specific nature of labor as the use value to the capitalist of labor power, human capital theory announces the qualitative identity of the "thing" labor to the "thing" capital. Thus human capital theory abstracts away from the specific nature of labor as the creator of capital. On the basis of these elegant abstractions, which reduce everything always back to the same thing, production can appear as nothing other than a voluntary combination of qualitatively equal things that mutually exchange their services in return for a share in output quantitatively equal to their individual (marginal) contributions. Thus the specific nature of the capitalist production relation as a conflict in which labor is extracted from the laborer and appropriated by the capitalist is represented as its opposite, a harmonious exchange relation. Finally, because production is represented as mere exchange of values, accumulation must occur outside of the production-exchange relation of labor to capital, each of which can grow wealthier only by means of saving the fruits earned by "its" marginal contribution. Thus saving, the condition specifically of noncapitalist accumulation, is represented as the condition of capital accumulation, and the condition of capitalist accumulation, the appropriation of surplus value through the capital relation, never appears in the theory at all.

POSTFACE

In this paper we have confined ourselves to a systematic exposition of the fundamental misrepresentations of capitalist production that are embodied in the human capital concept and in its associated theoretical framework. We must emphasize again that this critique concerns the inner structure of capitalist relations of exchange and production and is thus prior to particular empirical hypotheses about the actual distribution of wage incomes. We have, however, laid the methodological basis for more concrete investigations of wage determination. The central insights that we have derived and that must inform more concrete studies are: (1) wages are determined by the reproduction cost of labor power, not by the productivity of labor; (2) the capital-labor relation is at its core (the extraction and appropriation of surplus value) a conflict relation; (3) the reproduction cost of labor power is determined historically by the struggle between capital and labor; and (4) the structure of wages as well as the general level of wages is also a historical outcome of this struggle and thus reflects not merely different costs of production of different skills but also attempts by capital to objectively divide the labor force and weaken its class opposition to capital, attempts by fractions of the labor force to limit entry into their particular skill area, increasing hierarchization and bureaucratization of the production process caused by concentration and centralization of capital, and so on.[15]

NOTES

1. Melvin Reder, "A Partial Survey of the Theory of Income Size Distribution," in Lee Soltow, ed., *Six Papers on the Size Distribution of Wealth and Income* (New York: Columbia University Press, 1969), p. 228.

2. Kenneth Arrow, "Higher Education as a Filter," Technical Report 71, Institute for Mathematical Studies in the Social Sciences (Stanford University, September 1972).

3. Karl Marx, *Capital*, vol. I (New York: International Publishers, 1967), p. 54.

4. A *vulgar economist* is one who worships appearances on principle and substitutes pedantic formalization of the world view of the bourgeoisie for analysis of the real relations on which the capitalist mode of production is based.

5. Jacob Mincer, "The Distribution of Labor Incomes: A Survey," *Journal of Economic Literature* 7, no. 1 (March 1970), p. 1.

6. Gary Becker, *Human Capital and the Personal Distribution of Income* (Ann Arbor: University of Michigan Press, 1967), p. 39, emphasis added.

7. Mincer, "Distribution of Labor Incomes," p. 7.

8. *In practice*, neoclassical theorists have an even neater solution to this dual nature of schooling/child care. When middle- and upper-class white women stay home, it is "investment in human capital" and a source of their children's future wealth. When poor, black women do the same thing, their action is "consumption of leisure" and the cause of their present poverty. Thus the same action is in one case a source of wealth and in the other a source of poverty.

9. The discussion of the following two paragraphs is inspired by Karl Marx, *Grundrisse* (Middlesex, England: Penguin Books, 1973), pp. 243-47.

10. The distinction between the legal right to direct the activity of labor for a specific time and the extraction of labor itself has been noted also by H. Gintis in "The Nature of the Labor Exchange: Toward a Radical Theory of the Firm," Discussion Paper 328, Harvard Institute of Economic Research (October 1973). However he emphasizes a different set of contradictions arising from this distinction than those that I develop because his theoretical object is the capitalist firm, while mine is the capital relation itself.

11. *Capital,* p. 176.

12. Obviously, this production relation is a conflict relation. The worker wishes to minimize effort per dollar of wage earned; the capitalist to maximize extraction of labor. The ramifications of this conflict situation for the development of the capitalist firm and for its internal wage structure are analyzed in detail in Gintis, "Nature of the Labor Exchange."

13. Of course historically capital will continue to be formed in part through means not internal to the capital relation itself—most notably through the interaction of capital with noncapitalist modes of production. The explicit introduction of such noncapitalist modes, however, must await a more concrete specification of the capitalist mode than is possible within the scope of this paper.

14. We do not imply here that the actual accumulation of capital is a smooth process merely because the capital relation posits its own preconditions; indeed, precisely because the results/preconditions of capital are the antithetical moments of objectless labor power and objective exchange value existing for itself, the reproduction of the capital relation involves conflicts and reproduction of the objective basis of conflict.

15. For a review of the emergent literature on the historical processes of labor market segmentation and stratification, see M. Carter and M. Carnoy, "Labor Markets and Worker Productivity,"

4

The Reproduction of Daily Life

FREDY PERLMAN
Essayist, journalist, and publisher

The everyday practical activity of tribesmen reproduces, or perpetuates, a tribe. This reproduction is not merely physical, but social as well. Through their daily activities the tribesmen do not merely reproduce a group of human beings; they reproduce a tribe, namely a particular *social form* within which this group of human beings performs *specific* activities in a *specific* manner. The specific activities of the tribesmen are not the outcome of "natural" characteristics of the men who perform them, the way the production of honey is an outcome of the "nature" of a bee. The daily life enacted and perpetuated by the tribesman is a specific *social* response to particular material and historical conditions.

The everyday activity of slaves reproduces slavery. Through their daily activities, slaves do not merely reproduce themselves and their masters physically; they also reproduce the instruments with which the master represses them, and their own habits of submission to the master's authority. To men who live in a slave society, the master-slave relation seems like a natural and eternal relation. However, men are not born masters or slaves. Slavery is a specific social form, and men submit to it only in very particular material and historical conditions.

The practical everyday activity of wage-workers reproduces wage labor and capital. Through their daily activities, "modern" men, like tribesmen and slaves, reproduce the inhabitants, the social relations and the ideas of their society; they reproduce the *social form* of daily life. Like the tribe and the slave system, the capitalist system is neither the natural nor the final form of human society; like the earlier social forms, capitalism is a specific response to material and historical conditions.

Unlike earlier forms of social activity, everyday life in capitalist society *systematically* transforms the material conditions to which capitalism originally responded. Some of the material limits to human activity come gradually under human control. At a high level of industrialization, practical activity creates its own material conditions as well as its social form. Thus the subject of analysis is not only how practical activity in capitalist society reproduces capitalist society, but also how this activity itself eliminates the material conditions to which capitalism is a response.

First published as a pamphlet, Black and Red Press, 1969.

DAILY LIFE IN CAPITALIST SOCIETY

The social form of people's regular activities under capitalism is a response to a certain material and historical situation. The material and historical conditions explain the origin of the capitalist form, but do not explain why this form continues after the initial situation disappears. A concept of "cultural lag" is not an explanation of the continuity of a social form after the disappearance of the initial conditions to which it responded. This concept is merely a name for the continuity of the social form. When the concept of "cultural lag" parades as a name for a "social force" which determines human activity, it is an obfuscation which presents the outcome of people's activities as an external force beyond their control. This is not only true of a concept like "cultural lag." Many of the terms used by Marx to describe people's activities have been raised to the status of external and even "natural" forces which determine people's activity; thus concepts like "class struggle," "production relations" and particularly "The Dialectic," play the same role in the theories of some "Marxists" that "Original Sin," "Fate" and "The Hand of Destiny" played in the theories of medieval mystifiers.

In the performance of their daily activities, the members of capitalist society simultaneously carry out two processes: they reproduce the form of their activities, and they eliminate the material conditions to which this form of activity initially responded. But they do not know they carry out these processes; their own activities are not transparent to them. They are under the illusion that their activities are responses to natural conditions beyond their control, and do not see that they are themselves authors of those conditions. The task of capitalist ideology is to maintain the veil which keeps people from seeing that their own activities reproduce the form of their daily life; the task of critical theory is to unveil the activities of daily life, to render them transparent, to make the reproduction of the social form of capitalist activity visible within people's daily activities.

Under capitalism, daily life consists of related activities which reproduce and expand the capitalist form of social activity. The sale of labor-time for a price (a wage), the embodiment of labor-time in commodities (salable goods, both tangible and intangible), the consumption of tangible and intangible commodities (such as consumer goods and spectacles)—these activities which characterize daily life under capitalism are not manifestations of "human nature," nor are they imposed on men by forces beyond their control.

If it is held that man is "by nature" an uninventive tribesman and an inventive businessman, a submissive slave and a proud craftsman, an independent hunter and a dependent wage-worker, then either man's "nature" is an empty concept, or man's "nature" depends on material and historical conditions, and is in fact a response to those conditions.

ALIENATION OF LIVING ACTIVITY

In capitalist society, creative activity takes the form of commodity production, namely production of marketable goods, and the results of human activity take the form of commodities. Marketability or salability is the universal characteristic of all practical activity and all products.

The products of human activity which are necessary for survival have the form of salable goods: they are only available in exchange for money. And money is only available in exchange for commodities. If a large number of men accept the legitimacy of these conventions, if they accept the convention that commodities are a prerequisite for money, and that money is a prerequisite for survival, then they find themselves locked into a vicious circle. Since they have no commodities, their only exit from this circle is to regard themselves, or parts of themselves, as commodities. And this is, in fact, the peculiar "solution" which men impose on themselves in the face of specific material and historical conditions. They do not exchange their bodies or parts of their bodies for money. They exchange the creative content of their lives, their practical daily activities, for money.

As soon as men accept money as an equivalent for life, the sale of living activity becomes a condition for their physical and social survival. Life is exchanged for survival. Creation and production come to mean sold activity. A man's activity is "productive," useful to society, only when it is sold activity. And the man himself is a productive member of society only if the activities of his daily life are sold activities. As soon as people accept the terms of this exchange, daily activity takes the form of universal prostitution.

The sold creative power, or sold daily activity, takes the form of *labor*. Labor is a historically specific form of human activity. Labor is abstract activity which has only one property: it is marketable, it can be sold for a given quantity of money. Labor is *indifferent* activity: indifferent to the particular task performed and indifferent to the particular subject to which the task is directed. Digging, printing, and carving are different activities, but all three are *labor* in capitalist society. Labor is simply "earning money." Living activity which takes the form of labor is a means to earn money. Life becomes a *means of survival*.

This ironic reversal is not the dramatic climax of an imaginative novel; it is a fact of daily life in capitalist society. Survival, namely self-preservation and reproduction, is not the means to creative practical activity, but precisely the other way around. Creative activity in the form of *labor*, namely *sold activity*, is a *painful necessity* for survival; labor is the means to self-preservation and reproduction.

The sale of living activity brings about another reversal. Through sale, the labor of an individual becomes the "property" of another, it is appropriated by another, it comes under the control of another. In other words, a person's activity becomes the activity of another, the activity of its owner; it becomes *alien* to the person who performs it. Thus one's *life*, the accomplishments of an individual in the world, the difference which his life makes in the life of humanity, are not only transformed into *labor*, a painful condition for survival; they are transformed into *alien* activity, activity performed by the buyer of that labor. In capitalist society, the architects, the engineers, the laborers, are not builders; the man who buys their labor is the builder; their projects, calculations, and motions are alien to them; their living activity, their accomplishments, are his.

Academic sociologists, who take the sale of labor for granted, understand this alienation of labor as a feeling; the worker's activity "appears" alien to the worker, it "seems" to be controlled by another. However, any worker can explain to the academic sociologists that the alienation is neither a feeling nor

an idea in the worker's head, but a real fact about the worker's daily life. The sold activity is *in fact* alien to the worker; his labor is *in fact* controlled by its buyer.

In exchange for his sold activity, the worker gets money, the conventionally accepted means of survival in capitalist society. With this money he can buy commodities, things, but he cannot buy back his activity. This reveals a peculiar "gap" in money as the "universal equivalent." A person can sell commodities for money, and he can buy the same commodities with money. He can sell his living activity for money, but he cannot buy his living activity for money.

The things the worker buys with his wages are first of all consumer goods which enable him to survive, to reproduce his labor-power so as to be able to continue selling it; and they are spectacles, objects for passive admiration. He consumes and admires the products of human activity passively. He does not exist in the world as an active agent who transforms it, but as a helpless, impotent spectator; he may call this state of powerless admiration "happiness," and since labor is *painful*, he may desire to be "happy," namely inactive, all his life (a condition similar to being born dead). The commodities, the spectacles, *consume him*; he uses up living energy in passive admiration; he is consumed by things. In this sense, the more he has, the less he is. (An individual can surmount this death-in-life through marginal creative activity; but the population cannot, except by abolishing the capitalist form of practical activity, by abolishing wage-labor and thus de-alienating creative activity.)

THE FETISHISM OF COMMODITIES

By alienating their activity and embodying it in commodities, in material receptacles of human labor, people reproduce themselves and create Capital.

From the standpoint of capitalist ideology, and particularly of academic Economics, this statement is untrue: commodities are "not the product of labor alone"; they are produced by the primordial "factors of production," Land, Labor and Capital, the capitalist Holy Trinity, and the main "factor" is obviously the hero of the piece, Capital.

The purpose of this superficial Trinity is not analysis, since analysis is not what these Experts are paid for. They are paid to obfuscate, to mask the social form of practical activity under capitalism, to veil the fact that producers reproduce themselves, their exploiters, as well as the instruments with which they're exploited. The Trinity formula does not succeed in convincing. It is obvious that *land* is no more of a commodity producer than water, air, or the sun. Furthermore *Capital,* which is at once a name for a social relation between workers and capitalists, for the instruments of production owned by a capitalist, and for the money-equivalent of his instruments and "intangibles," does not produce anything more than the ejaculations shaped into publishable form by the academic Economists. Even the instruments of production which are the capital of one capitalist are primordial "factors of production" only if one's blinders limit his view to an isolated capitalist firm, since a view of the entire economy reveals that the capital of one capitalist is the material receptacle of the labor alienated to another capitalist. However, though the Trinity formula does not convince, it does accomplish the task of obfuscation by shifting the subject of the question: instead of asking why the activity of people under capitalism

takes the form of wage-labor, potential analysts of capitalist daily life are transformed into academic house-Marxists who ask whether or not labor is the only "factor of production."

Thus Economics (and capitalist ideology in general) treats land, money, and the products of labor, as things which have the power to produce, to create value, to work for their owners, to transform the world. This is what Marx called the *fetishism* which characterizes people's everyday conceptions, and which is raised to the level of dogma by Economics. For the economist, living people are *things* ("factors of production"), and things *live* (money "works," Capital "produces").

The fetish worshipper attributes the product of his own activity to his fetish. As a result, he ceases to exert his own power (the power to transform nature, the power to determine the form and content of his daily life); he exerts only those "powers" which he attributes to his fetish (the "power" to buy commodities). In other words, the fetish worshipper emasculates himself and attributes virility to his fetish.

But the fetish is a dead thing, not a living being; it has no virility. The fetish is no more than a thing for which, and through which, capitalist relations are maintained. The mysterious power of Capital, its "power" to produce, its virility, does not reside in itself, but in the fact that people alienate their creative activity, that they sell their labor to capitalists, that they materialize or reify their alienated labor in commodities. In other words, people are bought with the products of their own activity, yet they see their own activity as the activity of Capital, and their own products as the products of Capital. By attributing creative power to Capital and not to their own activity, they renounce their living activity, their everyday life, to Capital, which means that people *give themselves*, daily, to the personification of Capital, the capitalist.

By selling their labor, by alienating their activity, people daily reproduce the personifications of the dominant forms of activity under capitalism, they reproduce the wage-laborer and the capitalist. They do not merely reproduce the individuals physically, but socially as well; they reproduce individuals who are sellers of labor-power, and individuals who are owners of means of production; they reproduce the individuals as well as the specific activities, the sale as well as the ownership.

Every time people perform an activity they have not themselves defined and do not control, every time they pay for goods they produced with money they received in exchange for their alienated activity, every time they passively admire the products of their own activity as alien objects procured by their money, they give new life to Capital and annihilate their own lives.

The aim of the process is the reproduction of the relation between the worker and the capitalist. However, this is not the aim of the individual agents engaged in it. Their activities are not transparent to them; their eyes are fixed on the *fetish* that stands between the act and its result. The individual agents keep their eyes fixed on *things*, precisely those things for which capitalist relations are established. The worker as producer aims to exchange his daily labor for money-wages, he aims precisely for the thing through which his relation to the capitalist is re-established, the thing through which he reproduces himself as a wage-worker and the other as a capitalist. The worker as consumer exchanges his

money for products of labor, precisely the things which the capitalist has to sell in order to realize his Capital.

The daily transformation of living activity into Capital is *mediated* by things, it is not *carried out by* the things. The fetish worshipper does not know this; for him labor and land, instruments and money, entrepreneurs and bankers, are all "factors" and "agents." When a hunter wearing an amulet downs a deer with a stone, he may consider the amulet an essential "factor" in downing the deer and even in providing the deer as an object to be downed. If he is a responsible and well-educated fetish worshipper, he will devote his attention to his amulet, nourishing it with care and admiration; in order to improve the material conditions of his life, he will improve the way he wears his fetish, not the way he throws the stone; in a bind, he may even send his amulet to "hunt" for him. His own daily activities are not transparent to him: when he eats well, he fails to see that it is his own action of throwing the stone, and not the action of the amulet, that provided his food; when he starves, he fails to see that it is his own action of worshipping the amulet instead of hunting, and not the wrath of his fetish, that causes his starvation.

The fetishism of commodities and money, the mystification of one's own daily activities, the religion of everyday life which attributes living activity to inanimate things, is not a mental caprice born in men's imaginations; it has its origin in the character of social relations under capitalism. Men do in fact relate to each other through things; the fetish is in fact the occasion for which they act collectively, and through which they reproduce their activity. But it is not the fetish that performs the activity. It is not Capital that transforms raw materials, nor Capital that produces goods. If living activity did not transform the materials, these would remain untransformed, inert, dead matter. If men were not disposed to continue selling their living activity, the impotence of Capital would be revealed; Capital would cease to exist; its last remaining potency would be the power to remind people of a bypassed form of everyday life characterized by daily universal prostitution.

The worker alienates his life in order to preserve his life. If he did not sell his living activity, he would not get a wage and could not survive. However, it is not the wage that makes alienation the condition for survival. If men were collectively not disposed to sell their lives, if they were disposed to take control over their own activities, universal prostitution would not be a condition for survival. It is people's disposition to continue selling their labor, and not the *things* for which they sell it, that makes the alienation of living activity necessary for the preservation of life.

The living activity sold by the worker is bought by the capitalist. And it is only this living activity that breathes life into Capital and makes it "productive." The capitalist, an "owner" of raw materials and instruments of production, presents natural objects and products of other people's labor as his own "private property." But it is not the mysterious power of Capital that creates the capitalist's private property"; living activity is what creates the "property," and the form of that activity is what keeps it "private."

TRANSFORMATION OF LIVING ACTIVITY INTO CAPITAL

The transformation of living activity into Capital takes place *through* things, daily, but is not carried out *by* things. Things which are products of human

activity *seem* to be active agents because activities and contacts are established for and through things, and because people's activities are not transparent to them; they confuse the mediating object with the cause.

In the capitalist process of production, the worker embodies or materializes his alienated living energy in an inert object by using instruments which are embodiments of other people's activity. (Sophisticated industrial instruments embody the intellectual and manual activity of countless generations of inventors, improvers, and producers from all corners of the globe and from varied forms of society.) The instruments in themselves are inert objects; they are material embodiments of living activity, but are not themselves alive. The only active agent in the production process is the living laborer. He uses the products of other people's labor and infuses them with life, so to speak, but the life is his own; he is not able to resurrect the individuals who stored their living activity in his instrument. The instrument may enable him to do more during a given time period, and in this sense it may raise his productivity. But only the living labor which is able to produce can be productive.

For example, when an industrial worker runs an electric lathe, he uses products of the labor of generations of physicists, inventors, electrical engineers, lathe makers. He is obviously more productive than a craftsman who carves the same object by hand. But it is in no sense the "Capital" at the disposal of the industrial worker which is more "productive" than the "Capital" of the craftsman. If generations of intellectual and manual activity had not been embodied in the electric lathe, if the industrial worker had to invent the lathe, electricity, and the electric lathe, then it would take him numerous lifetimes to turn a single object on an electric lathe, and no amount of Capital could raise his productivity above that of the craftsman who carves the object by hand.

The notion of the "productivity of capital," and particularly the detailed measurement of that "productivity," are inventions of the "science" of Economics, that religion of capitalist daily life which uses up people's energy in the worship, admiration, and flattery of the central fetish of capitalist society. Medieval colleagues of these "scientists" performed detailed measurements of the height and width of angels in Heaven, without ever asking what angels or Heaven were, and taking for granted the existence of both.

The result of the worker's sold activity is a product which does not belong to him. This product is an embodiment of his labor, a materialization of a part of his life, a receptacle which contains his living activity, but it is not his; it is as alien to him as his labor. He did not decide to make it, and when it is made he does not dispose of it. If he wants it, he has to buy it. What he has made is not simply a product with certain useful properties; for that he did not need to sell his labor to a capitalist in exchange for a wage; he need only have picked the necessary materials and the available tools, he need only have shaped the materials guided by his goals and limited by his knowledge and ability. (It is obvious that an individual can only do this marginally; men's appropriation and use of the materials and tools available to them can only take place after the overthrow of the capitalist form of activity.)

What the worker produces under capitalist conditions is a product with a very specific property, the property of salability. What his alienated activity produces is a *commodity*.

Because capitalist production is commodity production, the statement

that the goal of the process is the satisfaction of human needs is false; it is a rationalization and an apology. The "satisfaction of human needs" is not the goal of the capitalist or of the worker engaged in production, nor is it a result of the process. The worker sells his labor in order to get a wage; the specific content of the labor is indifferent to him; he does not alienate his labor to a capitalist who does not give him a wage in exchange for it, no matter how many human needs this capitalist's products may satisfy. The capitalist buys labor and engages it in production in order to emerge with commodities which can be sold. He is indifferent to the specific properties of the product, just as he is indifferent to people's needs; all that interests him about the product is how much it will sell for, and all that interests him about people's needs is how much they "need" to buy and how they can be coerced, through propaganda and psychological conditioning, to "need" more. The capitalist's goal is to satisfy *his* need to reproduce and enlarge Capital, and the result of the process is the expanded reproduction of wage labor and Capital (which are not "human needs").

The commodity produced by the worker is exchanged by the capitalist for a specific quantity of money; the commodity is a *value* which is exchanged for an equivalent *value*. In other words, the living and past labor materialized in the product can exist in two distinct yet equivalent forms, in commodities and in money, or in what is common to both, *value*. This does not mean that value is labor. Value is the social *form* of reified (materialized) labor in capitalist society.

Under capitalism, social relations are not established directly; they are established through value. Everyday activity is not exchanged directly; it is exchanged *in the form of value*. Consequently, what happens to living activity under capitalism cannot be traced by observing the activity itself, but only by following the metamorphoses of value.

When the living activity of people takes the form of *labor* (alienated activity), it acquires the property of exchangeability; it acquires the form of value. In other words, the labor can be exchanged for an "equivalent" quantity of money (wages). The deliberate alienation of living activity, which is perceived as necessary for survival by the members of capitalist society, itself reproduces the capitalist form within which alienation is necessary for survival. Because of the fact that living activity has the form of value, the products of that activity must also have the form of value: they must be exchangeable for money. This is obvious since, if the products of labor did not take the form of value, but for example the form of useful objects at the disposal of society, then they would either remain in the factory or they would be taken freely by the members of society whenever a need for them arose; in either case, the money-wages received by the workers would have no *value*, and living activity could not be *sold* for an "equivalent" quantity of money; living activity could not be alienated. Consequently, as soon as living activity takes the form of value, the products of that activity take the form of value, and the reproduction of everyday life takes place through changes or metamorphoses of value.

The capitalist sells the products of labor on a market; he exchanges them for an equivalent sum of money; he realizes a determined value. The specific magnitude of this value on a particular market is the *price* of the commodities. For the academic Economist, Price is St. Peter's key to the gates of Heaven.

Like Capital itself, Price moves within a wonderful world which consists entirely of objects; the objects have human relations with each other, and are alive; they transform each other, communicate with each other; they marry and have children. And of course it is only through the grace of these intelligent, powerful, and creative objects that people can be so happy in capitalist society.

In the Economist's pictorial representations of the workings of Heaven, the angels do everything and men do nothing at all; men simply enjoy what these superior beings do for them. Not only does Capital produce and money work; other mysterious beings have similar virtues. Thus Supply, a quantity of things which are sold, and Demand, a quantity of things which are bought, together determine Price, a quantity of money; when Supply and Demand marry on a particular point of the diagram, they give birth to Equilibrium Price, which corresponds to a universal state of bliss. The activities of everyday life are played out by things, and people are reduced to things ("factors of production") during their "productive" hours, and to passive spectators of things during their "leisure time." The virtue of the Economic Scientist consists of his ability to attribute the outcome of people's everyday activities to things, and of his inability to see the living activity of people underneath the antics of the things. For the Economist, the things *through* which the activity of people is regulated under capitalism are themselves the mothers and sons, the causes and consequences of their own activity.

The magnitude of value, namely the price of a commodity, the quantity of money for which it exchanges, is not determined by things, but by the daily activities of people. Supply and demand, perfect and imperfect competition, are nothing more than social forms of products and activities in capitalist society; they have no life of their own. The fact that activity is alienated, namely that labor-time is sold for a specific sum of money, that it has a certain value, has several consequences for the magnitude of the value of the products of that labor. The value of the sold commodities must *at least* be equal to the value of the labor-time. This is obvious both from the standpoint of the individual capitalist firm, and from the standpoint of society as a whole. If the value of the commodities sold by the individual capitalist were smaller than the value of the labor he hired, then his labor expenditures alone would be larger than his earnings, and he would quickly go bankrupt. Socially, if the value of the laborers' production were smaller than the value of their consumption, then the labor force could not even reproduce itself, not to speak of a class of capitalists. However, if the value of the commodities were merely equal to the value of the labor-time expended on them, the commodity producers would merely reproduce themselves, and their society would not be a capitalist society; their activity might still consist of commodity production, but it would not be capitalist commodity production.

For labor to create Capital, the value of the products of labor must be larger than the value of the labor. In other words, the labor force must produce a *surplus product*, a quantity of goods which it does not consume, and this surplus product must be transformed into *surplus value*, a form of value which is not appropriated by workers as wages, but by capitalists as profit. Furthermore, the value of the products of labor must be larger still, since living labor is not the only kind of labor materialized in them. In the production process,

workers expend their own energy, but they also use up the stored labor of others as instruments, and they shape materials on which labor was previously expended.

This leads to the strange result that the value of the laborer's products and the value of his wage are different magnitudes, namely that the sum of money received by the capitalist when he sells the commodities produced by his hired laborers is different from the sum he pays the laborers. This difference is not explained by the fact that the used-up materials and tools must be paid for. If the value of the sold commodities were equal to the value of the living labor and the instruments, there would still be no room for capitalists. The fact is that the difference between the two magnitudes must be large enough to support a class of capitalists—not only the individuals, but also the specific activity that these individuals engage in, namely the purchase of labor. The difference between the total value of the products and the value of the labor spent on their production is surplus value, the seed of Capital.

In order to locate the origin of surplus value, it is necessary to examine why the value of the labor is smaller than the value of the commodities produced by it. The alienated activity of the worker transforms materials with the aid of instruments, and produces a certain quantity of commodities. However, when these commodities are sold and the used-up materials and instruments are paid for, the workers are not given the remaining value of their products as their wages; they are given less. In other words, during every working day, the workers perform a certain quantity of unpaid labor, *forced labor,* for which they receive no equivalent.

The performance of this unpaid labor, this forced labor, is another "condition for survival" in capitalist society. However, like alienation, this condition is not imposed by nature, but by the collective practice of people, by their everyday activities. Before the existence of unions, an individual worker accepted whatever forced labor was available, since rejection of the labor would have meant that other workers would accept the available terms of exchange, and the individual worker would receive no wage. Workers competed with each other for the wages offered by capitalists; if a worker quit because the wage was unacceptably low, an unemployed worker was willing to replace him, since for the unemployed a small wage is higher than no wage at all. This competition among workers was called "free labor" by capitalists, who made great sacrifices to maintain the freedom of workers, since it was precisely this freedom that preserved the surplus value of the capitalist and made it possible for him to accumulate Capital. It was not any worker's aim to produce more goods than he was paid for. His aim was to get a wage which was as large as possible. However, the existence of workers who got no wage at all, and whose conception of a large wage was consequently more modest than that of an employed worker, made it possible for the capitalist to hire labor at a lower wage. In fact, the existence of unemployed workers made it possible for the capitalist to pay the lowest wage that workers were willing to work for. Thus the result of the collective daily activity of the workers, each striving individually for the largest possible wage, was to lower the wages of all; the effect of the competition of each against all was that all got the smallest possible wage, and the capitalist got the largest possible surplus.

The daily practice of all annuls the goals of each. But the workers did not

know that their situation was a product of their own daily behavior; their own activities were not transparent to them. To the workers it seemed that low wages were simply a natural part of life, like illness and death, and that falling wages were a natural catastrophe, like a flood or a hard winter. The critiques of socialists and the analyses of Marx, as well as an increase in industrial development which afforded more time for reflection, stripped away some of the veils and made it possible for workers to see through their activities to some extent. However, in Western Europe and the United States, workers did not get rid of the capitalist form of daily life; they formed unions. And in the different material conditions of the Soviet Union and Eastern Europe, workers (and peasants) replaced the capitalist class with a state bureaucracy that purchases alienated labor and accumulates Capital in the name of Marx.

With unions, daily life is similar to what it was before unions. In fact, it is almost the same. Daily life continues to consist of labor, of alienated activity, and of unpaid labor, or forced labor. The unionized worker no longer settles the terms of his alienation; union functionaries do this for him. The terms on which the worker's activity is alienated are no longer guided by the individual worker's need to accept what is available; they are now guided by the union bureaucrat's need to maintain his position as pimp between the sellers of labor and the buyers.

With or without unions, surplus value is neither a product of nature nor of Capital: it is created by the daily activities of people. In the performance of their daily activities, people are not only disposed to alienate these activities, they are also disposed to reproduce the conditions which force them to alienate their activities, to reproduce Capital and thus the power of Capital to purchase labor. This is not because they do not know "what the alternative is." A person who is incapacitated by chronic indigestion because he eats too much grease does not continue eating grease because he does not know what the alternative is. Either he prefers being incapacitated to giving up grease, or else it is not clear to him that his daily consumption of grease causes his incapacity. And if his doctor, preacher, teacher, and politician tell him, first, that the grease is what keeps him alive, and secondly that they already do for him everything he would do if he were well, then it is not surprising that his activity is not transparent to him and that he makes no great effort to render it transparent.

The production of surplus value is a condition of survival, not for the population, but for the capitalist system. Surplus value is the portion of the value of commodities produced by labor which is not returned to the laborers. It can be expressed either in commodities or in money (just as Capital can be expressed either as a quantity of things or of money), but this does not alter the fact that it is an expression for the materialized labor which is stored in a given quantity of products. Since the products can be exchanged for an "equivalent" quantity of money, the money "stands for," or represents, the same value as the products. The money can, in turn, be exchanged for another quantity of products of "equivalent" value. The ensemble of these exchanges, which take place simultaneously during the performance of capitalist daily life, constitutes the capitalist process of circulation. It is through this process that the metamorphosis of surplus value into Capital takes place.

The portion of value which does not return to labor, namely surplus

value, allows the capitalist to exist, and it also allows him to do much more than simply exist. The capitalist invests a portion of this surplus value; he hires new workers and buys new means of production; he expands his dominion. What this means is that the capitalist *accumulates new labor,* both in the form of the living labor he hires and of the past labor (paid and unpaid) which is stored in the materials and machines he buys.

The capitalist class as a whole accumulates the surplus labor of society, but this process takes place on a social scale and consequently cannot be seen if one observes only the activities of an individual capitalist. It must be remembered that the products bought by a given capitalist as instruments have the same characteristics as the products he sells. A first capitalist sells instruments to a second capitalist for a given sum of value, and only a part of this value is returned to workers as wages; the remaining part is surplus value, with which the first capitalist buys new instruments and labor. The second capitalist buys the instruments for the given value, which means that he pays for the total quantity of labor rendered to the first capitalist, the quantity of labor which was remunerated as well as the quantity performed free of charge. This means that the instruments accumulated by the second capitalist contain the unpaid labor performed for the first. The second capitalist, in turn, sells his products for a given value, and returns only a portion of this value to his laborers; he uses the remainder for new instruments and labor.

If the whole process were squeezed into a single time period, and if all the capitalists were aggregated into one, it would be seen that the value with which the capitalist acquires new instruments and labor is equal to the value of the products which he did not return to the producers. This accumulated surplus labor is *Capital.*

In terms of capitalist society as a whole, the total Capital is equal to the sum of unpaid labor performed by generations of human beings whose lives consisted of the daily alienation of their living activity. In other words Capital, in the face of which men sell their living days, is the product of the sold activity of men, and is reproduced and expanded every day a man sells another working day, every moment he decides to continue living the capitalist form of daily life.

STORAGE AND ACCUMULATION OF HUMAN ACTIVITY

The transformation of surplus labor into Capital is a specific historical form of a more general process, the process of industrialization, the permanent transformation of man's material environment.

Certain essential characteristics of this consequence of human activity under capitalism can be grasped by means of a simplified illustration. In an imaginary society, people spend most of their active time producing food and other necessities; only part of their time is "surplus time" in the sense that it is exempted from the production of necessities. This surplus activity may be devoted to the production of food for priests and warriors who do not themselves produce; it may be used to produce goods which are burned for sacred occasions; it may be used up in the performance of ceremonies or gymnastic exercises. In any of these cases, the material conditions of these people are not

likely to change, from one generation to another, as a result of their daily activities. However, one generation of people of this imaginary society may store their surplus time instead of using it up. For example, they may spend this surplus time winding up springs. The next generation may unwind the energy stored in the springs to perform necessary tasks, or may simply use the energy of the springs to wind new springs. In either case, the stored surplus labor of the earlier generation will provide the new generation with a larger quantity of surplus working time. The new generation may also store this surplus in springs and in other receptacles. In a relatively short period, the labor stored in the springs will exceed the labor time available to any living generation; with the expenditure of relatively little energy, the people of this imaginary society will be able to harness the springs to most of their necessary tasks, and also to the task of winding new springs for coming generations. Most of the living hours which they previously spent producing necessities will now be available for activities which are not dictated by necessity but projected by the imagination.

At first glance it seems unlikely that people would devote living hours to the bizarre task of winding springs. It seems just as unlikely, even if they wound the springs, that they would store them for future generations, since the unwinding of the springs might provide, for example, a marvelous spectacle on festive days.

However, if people did not dispose of their own lives, if their working activity were not their own, if their practical activity consisted of *forced labor,* then human activity might well be harnessed to the task of winding springs, the task of storing surplus working time in material receptacles. The historical role of Capitalism, a role which was performed by people who accepted the legitimacy of others to dispose of their lives, consisted precisely of storing human activity in material receptacles by means of forced labor.

As soon as people submit to the "power" of money to buy stored labor as well as living activity, as soon as they accept the fictional "right" of money-holders to control and dispose of the stored as well as the living activity of society, they transform money into Capital and the owners of money into Capitalists.

This double alienation, the alienation of living activity in the form of wage labor, and the alienation of the activity of past generations in the form of stored labor (means of production), is not a single act which took place sometime in history. The relation between workers and capitalists is not a thing which imposed itself on society at some point in the past, once and for all. At no time did men sign a contract, or even make a verbal agreement, in which they gave up the power over their living activity, and in which they gave up the power over the living activity of all future generations on all parts of the globe.

Capital wears the mask of a natural force; it seems as solid as the earth itself; its movements appear as irreversible as tides; its crises seem as unavoidable as earthquakes and floods. Even when it is admitted that the power of Capital is created by men, this admission may merely be the occasion for the invention of an even more imposing mask, the mask of a man-made force, a Frankenstein monster, whose power inspires more awe than that of any natural force.

However, Capital is neither a natural force nor a man-made monster which was created sometime in the past and which dominated human life ever since.

The power of Capital does not reside in money, since money is a social convention which has no more "power" than men are willing to grant it; when men refuse to sell their labor, money cannot perform even the simplest tasks, because money does not "work."

Nor does the power of Capital reside in the material receptacles in which the labor of past generations is stored, since the potential energy stored in these receptacles can be liberated by the activity of living people whether or not the receptacles are Capital, namely alien "property." Without living activity, the collection of objects which constitute society's Capital would merely be a scattered heap of assorted artifacts with no life of their own, and the "owners" of Capital would merely be a scattered assortment of uncommonly uncreative people (by training) who surround themselves with bits of paper in a vain attempt to resuscitate memories of past grandeur. The only "power" of Capital resides in the daily activities of living people; this "power" consists of the disposition of people to sell their daily activities in exchange for money, and to give up control over the products of their own activity and of the activity of earlier generations.

As soon as a person sells his labor to a capitalist and accepts only a part of his product as payment for that labor, he creates conditions for the purchase and exploitation of other people. No man would willingly give his arm or his child in exchange for money; yet when a man deliberately and consciously sells his working life in order to acquire the necessities for life, he not only reproduces the conditions which continue to make the sale of his life a necessity for its preservation; he also creates conditions which make the sale of life a necessity for other people. Later generations may of course refuse to sell their working lives for the same reason that he refused to sell his arm; however each failure to refuse alienated and forced labor enlarges the stock of stored labor with which Capital can buy working lives.

In order to transform surplus labor into Capital, the capitalist has to find a way to store it in material receptacles, in new means of production, and he must hire new laborers to activate the new means of production. In other words, he must enlarge his enterprise, or start a new enterprise in a different branch of production. This presupposes or requires the existence of materials that can be shaped into new salable commodities, the existence of buyers of the new products, and the existence of people who are poor enough to be willing to sell their labor. These requirements are themselves created by capitalist activity, and capitalists recognize no limits or obstacles to their activity; the democracy of Capital demands absolute freedom.

Imperialism is not merely the "last stage" of Capitalism; it is also the first.

Anything which can be transformed into a marketable good is grist for Capital's mill, whether it lies on the capitalist's land or on the neighbor's, whether it lies above ground or under, floats on the sea or crawls on its floor; whether it is confined to other continents or other planets. All of humanity's explorations of nature, from Alchemy to Physics, are mobilized to search for new materials in which to store labor, to find new objects that someone can be taught to buy.

Buyers for old and new products are created by any and all available means, and new means are constantly discovered. "Open markets" and "open doors" are established by force and fraud. If people lack the means to buy the capitalists' products, they are hired by capitalists and are paid for producing the goods they wish to buy; if local craftsmen already produce what the capitalists have to sell, the craftsmen are ruined or bought out; if laws or traditions ban the use of certain products, the laws and the traditions are destroyed; if people lack the objects on which to use the capitalists' products, they are taught to buy these objects; if people run out of physical or biological wants, then capitalists "satisfy" their "spiritual wants" and hire psychologists to create them; if people are so satiated with the products of capitalists that they can no longer use new objects, they are taught to buy objects and spectacles which have no use but can simply be observed and admired.

Poor people are found in pre-agrarian and agrarian societies on every continent; if they are not poor enough to be willing to sell their labor when the capitalists arrive, they are impoverished by the activities of the capitalists themselves. The lands of hunters gradually become the "private property" of "owners" who use state violence to restrict the hunters to "reservations" which do not contain enough food to keep them alive. The tools of peasants gradually become available only from the same merchant who generously lends them the money with which to buy the tools, until the peasants' "debts" are so large that they are forced to sell land which neither they nor any of their ancestors had ever bought. The buyers of craftsmen's products gradually become reduced to the merchants who market the products, until the day comes when a merchant decides to house "his craftsmen" under the same roof, and provides them with the instruments which will enable all of them to concentrate their activity on the production of the most profitable items. Independent as well as dependent hunters, peasants and craftsmen, free men as well as slaves, are transformed into hired laborers. Those who previously disposed of their own lives in the face of harsh material conditions cease to dispose of their own lives precisely when they take up the task of modifying their material conditions; those who were previously conscious creators of their own meager existence become unconscious victims of their own activity even while abolishing the meagerness of their existence. Men who were much but had little now have much but are little.

The production of new commodities, the "opening" of new markets, the creation of new workers, are not three separate activities; they are three aspects of the same activity. A new labor force is created precisely in order to produce the new commodities; the wages received by these laborers are themselves the new market; their unpaid labor is the source of new expansion. Neither natural nor cultural barriers halt the spread of Capital, the transformation of people's daily activity into alienated labor, the transformation of their surplus labor into the "private property" of capitalists. However, Capital is not a natural force; it is a set of activities performed by people every day; it is a form of daily life; its continued existence and expansion presuppose only one essential condition: the disposition of people to continue to alienate their working lives and thus reproduce the capitalist form of daily life.

5

Human Nature and Capitalism in Adam Smith and Karl Marx

DOUGLAS KELLNER
Assistant Professor of Philosophy at The University of Texas, Austin

I. KARL MARX'S APPRAISAL OF ADAM SMITH

Karl Marx's appraisal of Adam Smith contains a dialectical approach that assimilates into his own theory the enduring insights of Smith into the nature of capitalism and economics, while criticizing those aspects of Smith's work that are, in Marx's view, mere ideology: ideas that reflect the institutional arrangements, behavior, and ideas of the status quo, or that construct an illusory and fanciful model of the real world that legitimates the interests of the ruling class. The ideas of the dominant class become the dominant ideas of the age, Marx believed, and in his view Adam Smith expressed and systematized the ideas on economics and capitalism, science and human nature of the rising and eventually triumphant bourgeoisie. Smith was not, however, for Marx a crass apologist whose ideas were constructed explicitly to defend the interests of the industrialist class. Rather, he saw Smith as a conscientious theorist who expressed the leading ideas of his age, saw deeply into its fundamental tendencies, and fell prey to its illusions. No one can transcend the limits of his age, and Adam Smith could not foresee the problems that the developing capitalist system would produce that began to surface during Marx's life. Marx's complex critique/appreciation of Smith is cogently summarized in a passage in the second volume of *Theories of Surplus Value*:

> Political economy had achieved a certain comprehensiveness with Adam Smith; to a certain extent he had covered the whole of its territory, so that Say was able to summarize it all in one textbook, superficially but quite systematically. The only investigations that were made in the period between Smith and Ricardo were ones of detail, on productive and unproductive labor, finance, theory of population, landed property and taxes. Smith himself moves with great naiveté in a perpetual contradiction. On the one hand he traces the intrinsic connection existing between economic categories or the obscure structure of the bourgeois economic system. On the other, he simultaneously sets forth the connection as it appears in the phenomena of competition and thus as it presents itself to the unscientific observer just as to him who is actually involved and interested in the process of bourgeois production. One of these conceptions fathoms the inner connection, the physiology, so to speak, of the bourgeois system,

> whereas the other takes the external phenomena of life, as they seem and appear and merely describes, catalogues, recounts and arranges them under formal definitions. With Smith both these methods of approach not only merrily run alongside one another, but also intermingle and constantly contradict one another. With him this is justifiable (with the exception of a few special investigations, such as that into money) since his task was indeed a twofold one. On the one hand he attempted to penetrate the inner physiology of bourgeois society but on the other, he partly tried to describe its externally apparent forms of life for the first time; to show its relations as they appear outwardly and partly he had even to find a nomenclature and corresponding mental concepts for these phenomena, i.e. to reproduce them for the first time in the language and in the thought process. The one task interests him as much as the other and since both proceed independently of one another, this results in completely contradictory ways of presentation: the one expresses the intrinsic connections more or less correctly, the other, with the same justification—and without any connection to the first method of approach—expresses the *apparent* connections without any internal relation. Adam Smith's successors, in so far as they do not represent the reaction against him of older and obsolete methods of approach, can pursue their particular investigations and observations undisturbedly and can always regard Adam Smith as their base, whether they follow the esoteric or the exoteric part of his work or whether, as is almost always the case, they jumble up the two.[1]

In this passage Marx appraises Smith as the great explorer who charted for the first time the unexplored terrain of political economy and who formulated much of the language in which later discussions would take place (and ideological battles would be fought!). Smith is lauded for his comprehensiveness, his penetration of the "inner physiology of bourgeois society," and his grasp of important connections between economic categories (and the structures of the capitalist system). But Smith is criticized for a certain naiveté in which he accepts some of the appearances of bourgeois society at face value ("as they seem and appear") and merely "describes, catalogues, recounts, and arranges ... under formal definitions ... the external phenomena of life." Hence Marx believes that Smith's work contains an "esoteric" and "exoteric" method of approach that at once superficially mirrors some aspects of the bourgeois society while it profoundly and correctly conceptualizes other aspects of the society. Much of the development of Marx's own economic theory would consist of a critique of Smith's work and a correction of its inadequacies through constructing an alternative theory.

Marx must have also appreciated the practical-political thrust of Smith's work, which like the Marxian project wanted not only to interpret but to change the world. For Smith believed that an answer to the question of the source of the wealth of nations was of crucial importance for political practice; indeed the very well-being of the nation depended on devising an economic policy based on a correct solution to the problem of maximizing wealth and productivity. Smith, of course, believed that industrial labor and industry were the source of the wealth of nations and that the free functioning of the market without state intervention would provide maximum opulence and human well-being. Although Marx would totally oppose this political position, he could appreciate Smith's

This article was previously unpublished.

attempt to use theory to influence practice and could thus approve the attempt to unite theory with practice in Smith's work.

Marx continually applauded the comprehensiveness of Smith's stupendous work. Both Marx and Smith were engaged in a Faustian attempt to gain an overview of the development and mechanisms of the modern world, to lay bare the structure of the present society, and to chart its future course. Although Smith lacked the Hegelian categories of totality and mediation, he at least attempted to picture the main features of historical development and to uncover the mainsprings of the economic process that was revolutionizing the world. Both Marx and Smith were iconoclasts who were attacking the received wisdom and dominant theories of the time. Marx, following Engels, labeled Smith the Luther of political economy.[2] For Smith believed exchange was the fundamental human activity and argued that labor—human productive activity—was the source of wealth, rejecting the views of his "Catholic" "fetishist" predecessors that the source of wealth lay outside of human activity (in gold, land, bullion, and so on). Hence Smith brought the essence of economics (exchange, labor, commodity, property) into human activity, just as Luther brought the essence of religion into individual religious activity (faith, praying, and so forth). But if Smith was the Luther of political economy, Marx was its Kierkegaard, exploring the manifold alienations that ruptured and fragmented the human being caught in the thralls of the capitalist system.

An examination of Marx's "Economic and Philosophic Manuscripts of 1844" discloses the crucial importance of Adam Smith's work for his own project. After being convinced by Engels' ground-breaking essay, "Outlines of a Critique of Political Economy," that the development of capitalism and industry was the key to the physiognomy of modern society, and that the nature of the rising society was most clearly revealed in the economic theory of Adam Smith, Marx began his own critique of political economy.[3] The first important formulation of Marx's theory is found in his Paris Notebooks of 1844, in which he divides his manuscript into three columns—"The Wages of Labor," "The Profit of Capital," and "The Rent of Land"—thus reproducing Smith's tripartite division of political economy. Marx cites Smith's views on these topics and develops his own theory by critiquing the dominant views of Smith and other writers on economics.[4] Hence Smith was a decisive influence on the development of Marx's theory and from the beginning to the end of his intellectual labors, Marx's vocabulary, problems, and systematic intentions were highly influenced by Smith's work.[5] But Marx's *Auseinandersetzung* with Smith was always *critical* and took the form of a *critique of political economy*. In the rest of this paper we shall examine that critique.

II. MARX'S CRITIQUE OF SMITH

Marx continually developed a methodological/metatheoretical critique of Smith's work. Smith's error, in Marx's view, was assuming that a given social system— capitalism—was a natural, rational, and universal system that would eternally endure as it corresponded to the being of human nature and had constructed a market system that was self-regulating, self-correcting, and thus crisis-resistant. In assuming that capitalism could endure indefinitely, Smith fell prey to the

illusion that Marx felt was the cardinal sin of bourgeois thought: the tendency to universalize the status quo and thus to suppress history and contradiction. That is, Smith, Locke, Kant and the other architects of the dominant philosophy and science of the eighteenth century failed to see that the present system and ideology was a product of a historical matrix and that history consisted of conflict, change, and development. In the Marxist theory of history, every system, institution, and idea is transitory; a product of its age that must eventually give way to a new socioeconomic system, set of institutions and social relations, and ideas and ideologies as the totality of social and economic conditions mature and develop. Change takes place, in the Marxist view, through contradiction, conflict, and struggle. Each historical system generates contradictions embodied in conflicting classes, political parties and ideologies, and this struggle produces historical change, eliminating institutions, ideas, and relations that are no longer adequate to the needs and potentialities of the age. From this standpoint, Smith failed to see that capitalism was a transitory system that was full of contradictions that would result in conflict, crisis, and its eventual demise. Marx's project was to ferret out these contradictions and to chart the course of historical development and the passing away of capitalism overlooked by Smith. Smith's work helped Marx see into the nature of capitalism and Marx saw his work as a corrective that surpassed the deficiencies and limitations of Smith's work.

Underlying the differences between Marx and Smith were conflicting theories of history and methodology. Marxian dialectics is both a theory of history and society and a philosophic-scientific methodology. Marxian dialectics sets out the fundamental categories that describe the totality of social relations in a given society and describes the dynamics of historical movement. Because the central dialectical categories of contradiction and negation are missing in Smith's theoretical apparatus, he was able to assume that capitalism was a smoothly functioning, contradiction-free system, devoid of explosive structural contradictions or agents of revolution. Although Smith's *The Wealth of Nations* contains numerous historical interludes tracing out stages of historical development from the society of hunters and shepherds to the industrialist pinmakers and candlemakers of his day, Smith lacks insight into the logic of historical change (explained by Marx in his theory of contradiction and class struggle) and is instead guided by the Enlightenment philosophy of history, which viewed historical development as a process of evolutionary perfectionism leading to the heavenly city and self-regulating market of eighteenth century capitalist-bourgeois society. History thus revealed in Smith's telling phrase, "the natural progress of opulence." Although Smith's "invisible hand" that guides this process anticipated Hegel's "cunning of reason," it lacked the turbulent dialectic of negation and contradiction found in Hegel and Marx, and instead posited a magical coincidence between private vice and public benefit as the motor of historical change.[6] In the famous passage in Book III of *The Wealth of Nations*, Smith describes the transition from feudalism to capitalism as follows:

> A revolution of the greatest importance to the public happiness was in this manner brought about by two different orders of people who had not the least intention to serve the public. To gratify the most childish vanity was the sole motive of the great proprietors. The merchants and artificers,

much less ridiculous, acted merely from a view to their own interest, and in pursuit of their own peddler principle of turning a penny wherever a penny was to be got. Neither of them had either knowledge or foresight of that great revolution which the folly of the one, and the industry of the other, was gradually bringing about.[7]

In Smith's fanciful theory of the transition from feudalism to capitalism, blind self-interest is the (unconscious) agent of revolution! One might compare Marx's account of this process, which stresses class conflict and the brutal exploitation of the working class upon whose suffering the capitalist system was brought into the world.[8] Indeed, in the passage we have just cited, Smith does not even mention the working class as a participant in the modern age's monumental economic revolution. Critiquing Adam Smith's concept of primitive accumulation, Marx writes in *Capital:*

> Within the capitalist system all methods for raising the social productiveness of labor are brought about at the cost of the individual laborer; all means for the development of production transform themselves into means of domination over, and exploitation of, the producers; they mutilate the laborer into a fragment of a man, degrade him to the level of an appendage of a machine, destroy every remnant of charm in his work and turn it into a hated toil; they estrange from him the intellectual potentialities of the labor-process in the same proportion as science is incorporated in it as an independent power; they distort the conditions under which he works, subject him during the labor-process to a despotism the more hateful for its meanness; they transform his life-time into working-time, and drag his wife and child beneath the wheels of the Juggernaut of capital. But all the methods for the production of surplus-value are at the same time methods of accumulation; and every extension of accumulation becomes again a means for the development of these methods. It follows therefore that in proportion as capital accumulates, the lot of the laborer, be his payment high or low, must grow worse. The law, finally, that always equilibrates the relative surplus-population, or industrial reserve army, to the extent and energy of accumulation, this law rivets the laborer to capital more firmly than the wedges of Vulcan did Prometheus to the rock. It establishes an accumulation of misery, corresponding to the accumulation of capital . . . capital comes dripping from head to foot, from every pore, with blood and dirt.[9]

Marx stresses class conflict as the key to the transition to capitalism and stresses the terrible costs to the working class involved in this historical process. Adam Smith, on the other hand, smoothes over class opposition and assumes a harmonious balance and coincidence of interests among all classes. This is not to say that Adam Smith was totally oblivious to the fact of class conflict or conflicting class interests,[10] but he believed that class conflicts could be resolved and class interests harmonized within the confines of the existing capitalist system. Indeed, "conflicts," or Smith's favored term *competition,* would in the long run strengthen rather than weaken the system. Hence we see that Smith lacks the crucial categories of historical change found in Marx's theory of contradiction, negation, and class struggle.

Underlying differences in their theories of history and methodology are different views of human nature. The motor of Smith's self-regulating market that harmonizes class interests is the dual propensity of human nature to barter and exchange and the relentless drive to pursue one's self-interest. I shall now attempt to show the role of Smith's theory of human nature in his theory of political economy. Very often a thinker's concept of human nature is a key element and constitutive of his or her political, economic, or social theory, and this is dramatically the case with Adam Smith. Let us recall that before Smith became the founder of political economy he was a philosopher whose theory of human nature in *Theory of Moral Sentiments* provided the foundation for an ethical theory.[11] Smith was continually concerned with human motivation and the "well-springs of human action." While working on his economic theory, Smith was constantly dealing with human nature and often explained human behavior in its intercourse with its social-economic environment in terms of his theory of human nature. After all, economics is concerned with some very basic and fundamental human activities—producing, buying, selling, consuming—and it is natural that the theory of a philosopher vitally concerned with the nature of the human species would be informed and shaped by his theory of the economic animal, *homo faber,* who both Smith and Marx distinguished from other species by the human's productive activity.

It is arguable that Smith's economic studies led him to modify his theory of human nature set forth in *Theory of Moral Sentiments* in the direction of postulating a more relentless and consistent theory of egotism, self-interest, and bartering as the primary wellspring of human action, which involved an increasing de-emphasis on benevolence, sympathy, and the social sentiments that he stressed in his earlier work. Possessive individualism triumphed in political economy, just as it did in political theory.[12] The point I wish to stress is that Adam Smith's theory of human nature was the basic prop/support for his theory of the self-regulating market ("the invisible hand"), for his theory of competition and laissez faire, and indeed crucially influenced the construction of his entire theoretical edifice. Smith's theory of human nature is, I shall attempt to show, totally at odds with the theory of Karl Marx, and perhaps Marx's most powerful critique of Smith lies in the implicit/explicit assault on the concept of human nature that played such a fundamental role in Smith's theory and subsequent political theory. I shall now offer a reading of *The Wealth of Nations* to support the claim that Smith's theory of human nature plays a major role at key intervals in the development of his political economy, and shall then outline Marx's critique.

A. The Theory of Human Nature in *The Wealth of Nations*

First, let us note that Smith makes human nature the driving force of historical and economic development. The division of labor, which is the source of society's opulence, is for Smith the "gradual consequence of a certain propensity in human nature . . . the propensity to truck, barter, and exchange one thing for another."[13] The human being is uniquely dependent on other humans for its well-being and is forced to appeal to the self-interest of other humans

to ensure its survival and improve its well-being. The underlying assumption of this position—and of Smith's whole theory—is that the human being is uniquely, deeply, and fundamentally motivated by self-love/egotism. This is expressed in unparalleled candor and even charm in a passage in *The Wealth of Nations* that exposes a clear turn to the primacy of self-interest in Smith's theory of human nature, and devaluation of the role of benevolence, fellow-feeling, and sympathy from Smith's earlier theory in *The Theory of Moral Sentiments*. Note the appeal to *self-love* at two crucial junctures in this passage:

> Man has almost constant occasion for the help of his brethren, and it is in vain for him to expect it from their benevolence only. He will be more likely to prevail if he can interest their self-love in his favor, and show them that it is for their own advantage to do for him what he requires of them. Whoever offers to another a bargain of any kind proposes to do this. Give me that which I want, and you shall have this which you want, is the meaning of every such offer; and it is in this manner that we obtain from one another the far greater part of those good offices which we stand in need of. It is not from the benevolence of the butcher, the brewer, or the baker that we expect our dinner, but from their regard to their own interest. We address ourselves not to their humanity, but to their self-love, and never talk to them of our own necessities, but of their advantages. (*WN*, p. 14)

Smith then argues, "As it is by treaty, by barter, and by purchase that we obtain from one another the greater part of those mutual good offices which we stand in need of, so it is this same trucking disposition which originally gives occasion to the division of labor" (*WN*, p. 15). In Smith's nursery rhyme of the tribe of hunters and shepherds, John L makes bows and arrows and exchanges them for cattle or venison with Jean-Jacques R. John L finds that it is in his own self-interest to solely make bows and arrows because he can get much more meat, clothes, and beer by exchanging his produce with others than if he tended the cattle, raised crops, and brewed beer himself. Moreover, the hunters benefit from John L's production of bows and arrows in that it saves them the trouble of having to make their own tools and implements; hence they can devote their energies to their speciality, producing game for a hungry public. Hence everybody comes out ahead! In Smith's idyllic fable, which has lulled to sleep the critical faculties of countless generations and still provides the self-satisfied punch line for countless economics lectures and chamber of commerce meetings, there is a remarkable coincidence between self-interest and public interest in an exchange society. By following one's own interest one contributes to public well-being. Moreover, it induces one to develop one's own talents and abilities: "The certainty of being able to exchange all that surplus part of the produce of his own labor, which is over and above his own consumption, for such parts of the produce of other men's labor as he may have occasion for, encourages every man to apply himself to a particular occupation, and to cultivate and bring to perfection whatever talent or genius he may possess for that particular species of business" (*WN*, p. 15).

The process of exchange and the emerging market that develops from this "original state of things" (*WN*, p. 64) produces an increasing division of labor and

simultaneously an increased variety of "natural talents" and "dissimilar geniuses." These differences are harmonized in the market where "the most dissimilar geniuses are of use to one another; the different produces of their respective talents, by the general disposition to truck, barter, and exchange, being brought as it were into a common stock, where every man may purchase whatever part of the produce of other men's talents he has occasion for" (*WN*, p. 16). In the exchange society, "Every man thus lives by exchanging or becomes in some measure a merchant and the society itself grows to be what is properly called a commercial society" (*WN*, p. 22). The introduction of money facilitates exchange and becomes the measure of value in the commercial society and the social bond that ties the society of egotists together (*WN*, pp. 25ff.). In Smith's magical and imaginary world, self-interest, money, and the "higgling and bargaining of the market" creates that "sort of rough equality which though not exact is sufficient for carrying on the business of common life" (*WN*, p. 31). Hence the exchange society is supposed to maximize the individual's freedom and equality. Marx brilliantly summarizes Smith's theory in the *Grundrisse* before demolishing it (see p. 82):

> Out of the act of exchange itself, the individual, each one of them, is reflected in himself as its exclusive and dominant (determinant) subject. With that, then, the complete freedom of the individual is posited: voluntary transaction; no force on either side; positing of the self as means, or as serving, only as means, in order to posit the self as end in itself as dominant and primary (*übergreifend*); finally, the self-seeking interest which brings nothing of a higher order to realization; the other is also recognized and acknowledged as one who likewise realizes his self-seeking interest, so that both know that the common interest exists only in the duality, many-sidedness, and autonomous development of the exchanges between self-seeking interests. The general interest is precisely the generality of self-seeking interests. Therefore, when the economic form, exchange, posits the all-sided equality of its subjects, then the content, the individual as well as the objective material which drives towards the exchange, is *freedom*. Equality and freedom are thus not only respected in exchange based on exchange values but, also, the exchange of exchange values is the productive, real basis of all *equality* and *freedom*.[14]

Further, Smith claims that each individual solely following his own self-interest will not only improve his own condition but that of the public and nation as a whole—despite clumsy and harmful state intervention: "The uniform, constant, and uninterrupted effort of every man to better his condition, the principle from which public and national as well as private opulence is originally derived, is frequently powerful enough to maintain the natural progress of things toward improvement, in spite of both the extravagance of government, and of the greatest errors of administration. Like the unknown principle of animal life, it frequently restores health and vigor to the constitution, in spite, not only of the disease, but of the absurd prescriptions of the doctor" (*WN*, p. 326). That the root of opulence is found in an innate tendency of human nature is starkly expressed in the following passage: "But the principle which prompts to save is the desire of bettering our condition, a desire which, though

generally calm and dispassionate, comes with us from the womb, and never leaves us till we go into the grave" (*WN*, p. 324).

After tracing in broad historical panorama "the natural progress of opulence" and championing the commercial society, Smith then comes to his famous passage where he explains how each individual following his self-interest "is in this, as in many other cases, led by an invisible hand to promote an end which was no part of his intention. Nor is it always the worse for the society that it was no part of it. By pursuing his own interest he frequently promotes that of the society more effectually than when he really intends to promote it" (*WN*, p. 423). Commentators have noted that Smith's "invisible hand" metaphor was influenced by mechanistic concepts of society, a deistic idea of Divine Providence, and natural law thought.[15] These metaphysical theories might well have influenced Smith but his arguments for the self-regulating market governed by the "invisible hand" more obviously reveal the visible hand of Mandeville's private vices/public benefit argument. In all the passages we have cited there is no metaphysical natural law talk, let alone whispers of Divine Providence, but rather the position that following one's self-interest (that is, obeying the basic law of human nature) would harmonize public and private interests and make possible a self-regulating market system. Thus underlying Smith's theory of the self-regulating market is his theory of human nature. As we have seen, the market arises out of individual drives and inclinations that are deeply engraved upon the human heart from cradle to grave; Smith's Enlightenment belief in "the natural progress of things toward improvement" is rooted in his postulate of a "uniform, constant, and uninterrupted effort of every man to better his condition"; the wealth of a nation grows from the division of labor that grows out of an innate disposition to barter grounded in the propensity to pursue one's self-interest; "the system of perfect liberty" and free competition requires that each individual relentlessly follow his own self-interest and presupposes that it is a law of human nature that he will; and Smith's laissez-faire politics rests on the assumption that the society of egotists can best maximize their well-being by pursuing their own interests without state interference. In other words, social stability for Smith derives from the rational pursuit of one's self-interest (and not from the State, the system of laws, or constitution as previous political theorists would have it). This summary of Smith's theory should show that his elaborate edifice rests on his theory of human nature.

Hence there has been a tremendous exaggeration of the market mechanism in Smith's theory and an underestimation of the importance of human nature in making it all work. In the passages we have examined where Smith discusses the mechanisms of the capitalist market, what plays the key role is his concept of human nature and not the law of supply and demand, competition, free enterprise, or the like, as our capitalist ideologues would have it. The reason that for centuries there has been a primary stress on the market mechanism in Smith is that capitalist apologists want to posit the existence of a self-regulating crisis-free market as the producer of the wealth of nations, and then want to posit a harmony between human nature and capitalism. In our reading of Smith, one can find the second position in Smith but will find upon closer examination of *The Wealth of Nations* that the success of the market is a product of the working

out of human nature (and not of its own inner, self-regulating, self-contained mechanisms). Moreover, when Smith does construct a model of the capitalist market it is based on the idyllic society of hunters and fishermen, thus grounding his theory of capitalism in a fanciful myth of simple accumulation—as Marx clearly saw. In fact, I believe that Smith's theory of the market is based on a replay of Mandeville's private vice/public benefit argument, which he strips of its moralistic overtones and from which he traces out the "unintended social consequences" that follow from a sustained pursuit of self-interest that is the source of the wealth of nations.[16] Mandeville's discussion of industry, free trade, opulence, and "private vice" (self-interest) had, I believe, a major and generally unappreciated impact on Smith. Although Smith viciously denounced Mandeville's views in *TMS* as "licentious" and termed him a "pot-house philosopher," I believe that Mandeville's ideas haunted Smith and finally won him over in *WN*—as they reflected the reality of the emerging bourgeois society whose outlines were becoming increasingly clear to Smith as capitalism dramatically developed.

There are some unarticulated premises of Smith's theory of human nature and model of how a society of egotists will act and much subsequent social theory consisted of a series of attempts to bring the underlying premises to light and to then draw the appropriate political consequences. The different evaluations of Smith's egotistic man and society of egotists resulted in the conflicting liberal and conservative traditions that accepted many of the premises of Smith's theory of human nature and the market society, but differed as to their evaluation of what the egotist would do in a free market society, unfettered from previous feudal-absolutist shackles, and differed over what role the state should consequently play to protect the market society (that is, private property) and to ensure social harmony. In this context, I might suggest that the main difference between conservatives and liberals is derived from their theories of human nature and consequent theories of the state. Both assume the existence of an atomized individual with an innate, fixed, unchanging human nature that is primarily egotistic, driven by self-interest and competitive instincts. The conservative is frightened and pessimistic about this state of affairs, believing that the aggressive and destructive aspects of human nature must be kept in check by a strong state and authoritarian system of law and order (this is the common thread running through the conservative theories of Plato, Hobbes, de Tocqueville, Freud, Hitler, *Dragnet,* and *SWAT*). The liberal, on the other hand, has a more beneficent and optimistic view of human nature and believes a society that gives free reign to human nature will best develop human potentialities and well-being. Hence the liberal is not afraid, as is the conservative, that human beings will run amok, wreak havoc on one another, and produce chaos and disorder. Rather, the liberal believes—and here Adam Smith is a classic liberal—that all the egotists will smoothly mesh into a market society that at once enables them to give full play to their self-interest and harmoniously resolves all conflicts. This analysis suggests that *The Wealth of Nations*—and subsequent liberalism—presupposes the theory of human nature in Smith's *The Theory of Moral Sentiments,* which stresses the more social, benevolent, and fellow-feeling sides of human nature, for the smoothly running market presupposes that the egotists will play by the rules, respect the law and the other's rights to pursue their self-

interest, and will not utilize crime or violence to pursue their ends. Occasionally the view of human nature in *The Theory of Moral Sentiments* surfaces in *The Wealth of Nations*, as in the passage where Smith discusses justice: "Envy, malice, or resentment are the only passions which can prompt one man to injure another in his person or reputation. But the greater part of men are not very frequently under the influence of those passions; and the very worst men are so only occasionally. As their gratification, too, howsoever agreeable it may be to certain characters, is not attended with any real or permanent advantage, it is in the greater part of men commonly restrained by prudential considerations. Men may live together in society with some tolerable degree of security, though there is no civil magistrate to protect them from the injustice of those passions" (*WN*, p. 670).

This issue raises the old Adam Smith Problem concerning the relationship between Smith's earlier *TMS* and *WN*. It has been hotly debated for two centuries whether the views of human nature in Smith's two major works are completely contradictory, or are compatible and even harmonious. In my view there are both continuities and discontinuities in the relations between Smith's works, but the inconsistencies and contradictions are dominant.[17] It has been argued that there is a harmony between *TMS* and *WN* in that self-interest is operative in *TMS* and that sympathy is operative in *WN*—hence the principles of self-interest and sympathy are said to be operative in both works and to provide complementary and reciprocal aspects of human nature.[18] Let us examine this position a minute. One argument is that exchange in *WN* requires sympathy: putting oneself in the other's place, identifying with his self-interest, discerning as an impartial spectator what are the other's needs and fancies. It is also suggested that exchange elicits a process of mutual approbation in which both participants attempt to win each other's approval by presenting themselves to each other in a sympathetic manner that takes account of the other's self-interest. Hence it is claimed that exchange in *WN* requires sympathy, mutuality, fellow-feeling, reciprocity—central themes in *TMS*—ergo the continuity in Smith's works. *But,* is not the "sympathy" operative in exchange-relations much different from the *moral sympathy* operative in social-moral relations in *TMS*? Is not the "sympathy" in *WN* completely subordinate to economic self-interest? I put myself into another's place in the exchange-relation precisely so that I can best profit from the deal, get the highest price and the lowest cost, or perhaps even mislead, deceive, or exploit the other person. The approbation I seek to win from sympathetic behavior is often a mask for crude self-interest: the hypocritical smile, calculated handshake, and pseudo-friendliness of the salesman. Is not the motor of exchange thus self-interest in its most asocial, egotistic guise? Smith in fact was not so naive as to believe that the sort of sympathy, fellow-feeling, or the like that he portrayed in *TMS* played a major role in exchange. In a passage in *WN* he cynically—and accurately—notes the primacy of a self-interest that has no regard for the public good—and by implication for the other person: "By pursuing his own interest he frequently promotes that of the society more effectually than when he really intends to promote it. I have never known much good done by those who affected to trade for the public good. It is an affectation, indeed, not very common among merchants, and very few words need be employed in dissuading them from it" (*WN*, p. 423). Economics triumphed in

Smith over morality, reducing it to a pale specter of idealism weakly confronting the triumphant materialism of capitalism. Smith thus profoundly shifts the operation of sympathy, making it a means to the end of profit and self-interest, rather than a self-subsistent end in itself. Capital, Marx tells us, transforms everything it touches, and in Smith's theory we see sympathy metamorphosed from a profoundly social-moral virtue in *TMS* to an aspect of capitalist business practice in *WN*. Morality and moral sympathy were a weak counterforce to the juggernaut of capital and gave way time and again to the primacy of material self-interest. This fact of capitalist society is perhaps reflected in the change in emphasis from *TMS* to *WN*.

Unfortunately, Smith, unlike most writers, refused to comment on the relation between *TMS* and *WN*, burned his papers before his death, and left no (known) evidence as to whether he perceived or constructed a change in his theories; nor, as far as I know, have any of his intimate contemporaries thrown any light on the topic. To clarify the issue, I would suggest that there is not only a metamorphosis of sympathy in the shift from *TMS* to *WN* but that there is a changed emphasis from social-moral sympathy to self-love as the motor of human behavior in Smith's writings. It seems reasonable to interpret this shift as a response to the developing capitalist economy that was conceivably changing human behavior before Smith's very eyes, as industry grew, wealth accumulated, cutthroat competition intensified, and economics played a dramatically increasing role in all areas of public and private life, becoming, in Marx's words, the religion of everyday life. A sensitive observer of human behavior with strong empiricist leanings who was writing the first great treatise on capitalism could hardly fail to notice the "great transformation" taking place, and would no doubt take account of this thoroughgoing revolution in his theory.[19] In any case, Capital triumphed in eighteenth century social theory and both the classical liberal and conservative agreed—and this is the basis of their consensus—that a capitalist market economy would maximize opulence, human freedom, and individual well-being and that capitalism—and this is the point I am going to attack—was in tune with the stuff of human nature. Marx of course saw through this ideological fraud and it was his critique of political economy and theory of the alienation of labor that undermined the foundation of the liberal-conservative consensus, first, by uncovering the failings of the capitalist market from a purely technical or economic point of view, and, second, by showing that capitalism was totally at odds with and hostile to human nature and was thus at its core an alienating and inhuman system. It is this latter claim that I shall develop in the remainder of this paper.

B. Marx's Critique of Smith's Theory of Human Nature

Marx points out that the view of human nature in Smith (and other bourgeois producers of ideas) is at best an ideological reflection of the personality type that was coming to be dominant in the rising capitalist society. Smith's bartering animal reflected the nature of the rising merchant-industrialist class for whom business was the center of life. The calculating man of self-interest reflected, Marx said of Bentham, the eighteenth century English storekeeper. The illusion

of Smith and his ilk was their belief that the sort of personality gaining ascendency in their society was identical with human nature at large. This incredible egotism and naive projection of their own personality traits onto a human essence was for Marx evidence of how ideology covered over the facts of the human condition and provided a mystified consciousness that served the interests of the ruling class. For if the human being is primarily egotistical, motivated by self-interest, enamoured by self-love, driven to bartering and higgling as one's fundamental propensity, then capitalist society—a market society—is most in tune with human nature and can best satisfy the human demands and fulfill human strivings. Adam Smith's concept of human nature thus provides an ideological defense of the capitalist economy and legitimation of capitalist practice as being in fundamental harmony with human nature.

Marx's attack on this point of view is devastating. Human beings are not by nature like the egotistical creatures freely consenting to capitalist acts in the texts of political economy and the marketplace of bourgeois society. Rather, we became this way through the development of capitalism, which rewarded and reinforced the relentless pursuit of self-interest; which forced the pursuit of profit and wealth on those who would rule, dominate, and prosper; which created new needs for wealth and luxury that required capital accumulation, bartering, and self-motivated higgling: "Consciousness is from the very beginning a social product," Marx writes, "and remains so as long as human beings exist at all."[20] In Marx's view, one's language, values, ideas, and consciousness develop in an intimate interaction with one's social environment. As he puts it in *The German Ideology*:

> The production of ideas, of conceptions, of consciousness, is at first directly interwoven with the material activity and the material intercourse of men, the language of real life. Conceiving, thinking, the mental intercourse of men, appear at this stage as the direct efflux of their material behavior. The same applies to mental production as expressed in the language of politics, laws, morality, religion, metaphysics, etc. of a people. Men are the producers of their conceptions, ideas, etc.—active men, as they are conditioned by a definite development of their productive forces and of the intercourse corresponding to these, up to its furthest forms. Consciousness can never be anything else than conscious existence, and the existence of men is their actual life-process. . . . Life is not determined by consciousness but consciousness by life.[21]

Marx denies that there is a human essence inhering in all human beings at all times throughout history; rather, each single individual is the "ensemble of social relations."[22] Marx argues that the social relations of production of a given society produce a certain dominant personality type. In his view human behavior does not spring from an innate human essence but is shaped and molded by a given society. Smith naively assumed that the bartering, acquisitive, competitive animal of his emerging market society was identical with the human essence as such, whereas actually Smith was merely describing an emerging personality type that would become dominant in bourgeois society. Hence the harmony between capitalist society and human nature was an ideological fiction.

Moreover, Marx did not think too much of the bourgeoisie's image of human nature, which for Marx reflected their own enslavement to money, commodities, and business and provided but a stunted, fragmented, and alienated view of human nature. Indeed Marx's crucial criticism is that Adam Smith and the political economists had an incredibly one-sided, reductionistic, and impoverished concept of human nature that did violence to the full wealth of human potentialities. The human being, Marx tells us, is a many-sided being with a wealth of needs, potentialities, desires, and possibilities for individual and social development: "Man, much as he may therefore be a *particular* individual (and it is precisely his particularity which makes him an individual, and a real *individual* social being) is just as much the *totality*—the ideal totality—the subjective existence of thought and experienced society present for itself; just as he exists also in the real world as the awareness and the real enjoyment of social existence and as a totality of human life-activity."[23] Adam Smith's egotistical barterer, primarily motivated by self-interest directed at the market, possession, consumption, or the accumulation of capital, falls prey to a "one-sided *gratification*—merely in the sense of *possessing,* of having."[24] Marx contrasts the total, whole, well-rounded human being who cultivates a wealth of human potentialities and relations to the world—"seeing, hearing, smelling, tasting, feeling, thinking, being aware, sensing, wanting, acting, loving"—to the one-sided acquisitive activity of capitalist man who is characterized by "an estrangement of all human senses and attributes," a reduction of human wealth to mere financial gain. In short, Marx believes that "private property" has made Adam Smith's egotistic higgler "stupid and one-sided," a partial, impoverished human being. Marx wants to put "in place of the *wealth* and *poverty* of political economy the *rich human being* and rich human need. The *rich* human being is simultaneously the human being *in need of* a totality of human life-activities—the man in whom his own realization exists as an inner necessity, as *need.*"[25] "Political Economy," Marx ironically writes—and he is referring to Smith and his definition of self-interest in terms of frugality, accumulation, and so on—"this science of *wealth* is therefore simultaneously the science of renunciation, of want, of *saving.* . . . This science of marvelous industry is simultaneously the science of *asceticism,* and its true ideal is the *ascetic* but *extortionate* miser and the *ascetic* but *productive* slave. . . . Self-renunciation, the renunciation of life and of all human needs, is its principal thesis. The less you eat, drink, and buy books; the less you go to the theater, the dance hall, the public house; the less you think, love, theorize, sing, paint, fence, etc., the more you *save*—the *greater* becomes your treasure which neither moths nor dust will devour—your *capital.* The less you *are,* the less you express your own life, the greater is your *alienated* life, the more you *have,* the greater is the store of your estranged being."[26]

Smith's view of human nature was also deficient in that he failed to perceive the crucial role of *labor* in producing a humanized world, in fulfilling human needs, and in developing human potentialities. Labor for Marx was human productive, creative activity *par excellence,* and the human species was distinguished by its capacities for producing out of its imagination, out of its aesthetic sense, out of its freedom and creativity. Smith had an impoverished concept of the human significance of labor, and thus of the very central core of human being. As Marx puts it in the *Grundrisse:*

In the sweat of thy brow shalt thou labor! was Jehovah's curse on Adam. And this is labor for Smith, a curse. "Tranquility" appears as the adequate state, as identical with "freedom" and "happiness." It seems quite far from Smith's mind that the individual "in his normal state of health, strength, activity, skill, facility," also needs a normal portion of work, and of the suspension of tranquility. Certainly, labor obtains its measure from the outside, through the aim to be attained and the obstacles to be overcome in attaining it. But Smith has no inkling whatever that this over-coming of obstacles is in itself a liberating activity—and that, further, the external aims become stripped of the semblance of merely external natural urgencies, and become posited as aims which the individual himself posits—hence as self-realization, objectification of the subject, hence real freedom, whose action is precisely labor.[27]

The radical differences in Marx's and Smith's views of human nature are dramatically revealed in their different evaluations of the capitalist division of labor. Smith champions the division of labor as producing tremendous benefits in increased productivity and efficiency that will spill over and produce increased opulence and well-being for all classes of society. At one point, Smith concedes that the worker becomes a commodity and that the increased division of labor may fragment the human being,[28] but on the whole he is a resolute champion of the capitalist division of labor. Smith's primary focus in fact is on exchange and circulation, and the act of production receives little attention from him. Hence he misses the alienation of labor under capitalism that Marx was to make a primary focus of his theory from beginning to end.[29]

For Marx, the division of labor constitutes an alienation of the human being in several senses. Marx challenges Smith's uncritical praise of the capitalist division of labor in the very beginning of his critique of political economy in the "Economic and Philosophic Manuscripts of 1844":

The accumulation of capital increases the division of labor, and the division of labor increases the number of the workers. Conversely, the number of workers increases the division of labor, just as the division of labor increases the accumulation of capital. With this division of labor on the one hand and the accumulation of capital on the other, the worker becomes ever more exclusively dependent on labor, and on a particular, very one-sided machine-like labor at that. Just as he is thus depressed spiritually and physically to the condition of a machine and from being a man becomes an abstract activity and a belly, so he also becomes ever more dependent on every fluctuation in market price, on the application of capital, and on the whim of the rich. Equally, the increase in the class of people wholly dependent on work intensifies competition among the workers, thus lowering their price. In the factory system this situation of the worker reaches its climax. . . . The division of labor renders him ever more one-sided and dependent, bringing with it the competition not only of men but also of machines. Since the worker has sunk to the level of a machine, he can be confronted by the machine as a competitor. . . . Whilst the division of labor raises the productive power of labor and increases the wealth and refinement of society, it impoverishes the worker and reduces him to a machine. . . .[30]

Marx continues his critique of the alienation of labor under capitalism in the famous passage on alienated labor, which can be read as a direct critique of Smith's views on human nature, labor, and capitalism:

The estrangement is manifested not only in the result but in the *act of production*, within the *producing activity*, itself. How could the worker come to face the product of his activity as a stranger, were it not that in the very act of production he was estranging himself from himself? The product is after all but the summary of the activity, of production. If then the product of labor is alienation, production itself must be active alienation, the alienation of activity the activity of alienation. In the estrangement of the object of labor is merely summarized the estrangement, the alienation, in the activity of labor itself.

What, then, constitutes the alienation of labor?

First, the fact that labor is *external* to the worker, i.e. it does not belong to his essential being; that in his work, therefore, he does not affirm himself but denies himself, does not feel content but unhappy, does not develop freely his physical and mental energy but mortifies his body and ruins his mind. The worker therefore only feels himself outside his work, and in his work feels outside himself. He is at home when he is not working, and when he is working he is not at home. His labor is there-fore not voluntary, but coerced; it is *forced labor*. It is therefore not the satisfaction of a need; it is merely a *means* to satisfy needs external to it. Its alien character emerges clearly in the fact that as soon as no physical or other compulsion exists, labor is shunned like the plague. External labor, labor in which man alienates himself, is a labor of self-sacrifice, of mortification. Lastly, the external character of labor for the worker appears in the fact that it is not his own, but someone else's, that it does not belong to him, that in it he belongs not to himself, but to another. Just as in religion the spontaneous activity of the human imagination, of the human brain and the human heart, operates independently of the individual—that is, operates on him as an alien, divine or diabolical activity—so is the worker's activity not his spontaneous activity. It belongs to another; it is the loss of his self.[31]

Adam Smith ignores these alienating conditions of labor under capitalism and derives his much-acclaimed concepts of freedom and equality from an analysis of the exchange relation. All men are in a sense free in a capitalist market society to exchange whatever they can on the market; they are equal before the laws of supply and demand; they are free to pursue gain and their self-interest as they see fit. Moreover, one can theoretically sell his labor power to whomever one chooses and one is free to seek any occupation for which one is qualified. What Smith fails to note, however, is that one class of individuals is much more free and equal than the other class and that the system of labor and exchange produces gross inequality, lack of freedom, and the destruction of individuality. Crucially, in a class society where one class owns the means of production and the other class must submit to domination and exploitation by the possessing class, the deck is stacked from the beginning in a rigged game. Once again, Marx's critique of Smith is devastating. In a section of the *Grundrisse*, Marx first summarizes Smith's position (see the passage I have already cited) and then demolishes it:

If this way of conceiving the matter is not advanced in its historical context, but is instead raised as a refutation of the more developed economic relations in which individuals relate to one another no longer merely as exchangers or as buyers and sellers, but in specific relations, no longer all of the same character; then it is the same as if it were asserted that there is no difference, to say nothing of antithesis and contradiction, between natural bodies, because all of them, when looked at from e.g. the point of view of their weight, have weight, and are therefore equal; or are equal because all of them occupy three dimensions. Exchange value itself is here similarly seized upon in its simple character, as the antithesis to its more developed, contradictory forms. In the course of science, it is just these abstract attributes which appear as the earliest and sparsest; they appear in part historically in this fashion too; the more developed as the more recent. In present bourgeois society as a whole, this positing of prices and their circulations etc. appears as the surface process, beneath which, however, in the depths, entirely different processes go on, in which this apparent individual equality and liberty disappear. It is forgotten, on one side, that the *presupposition* of exchange value, as the objective basis of the whole of the system of production, already in itself implies compulsion over the individual, since his immediate product is not a product for him, but only *becomes* such in the social process, and since it *must* take on this general but nevertheless external form; and that the individual has an existence only as a producer of exchange value, hence that the whole negation of his natural existence is already implied; that he is therefore entirely determined by society; that this further presupposes a division of labor etc., in which the individual is already posited in relations other than that of mere *exchanger,* etc. That therefore this presupposition by no means arises either out of the individual's will or out of the immediate nature of the individual, but that it is, rather, *historical,* and posits the individual as already *determined* by society. It is forgotten, on the other side, that these higher forms, in which exchange, or the relations of production which realize themselves in it, are now posited, do not by any means stand still in this simple form where the highest distinction which occurs is a formal and hence irrelevant one. What is overlooked, finally, is that already the simple forms of exchange value and of money latently contain the opposition between labor and capital, etc. Thus, what all this wisdom comes down to is the attempt to stick fast at the simplest economic relations, which, conceived by themselves, are pure abstractions; but these relations are, in reality, mediated by the deepest antithesis, and represent only one side, in which the full expression of the antithesis [that is, between capital and labor] is obscured.[32]

This passage encapsulates much of Marx's critique of Smith and returns to my first criticism that Smith often merely describes surface appearances and fails to see the reality of capitalist society; in this case, the extent to which all individuals are dominated by society and that the bourgeoisie's much-touted equality, individuality, and freedom are surface appearances that hide slavery, conformity, and a manifold of societal and class domination. As we have seen, Smith's view of human nature is a superficial reflection of the predominant personality type of the time that hides the full wealth of human nature. In the same vein, his theory of equality and freedom reflects surface appearances that cover over

existing inequality, dependence, exploitation, and wage slavery. Marx's theory of surplus value is intended to call attention to the reality of capitalist exploitation that previous political economists had failed to grasp; Marx conceives his theory of surplus value as one of his major scientific contributions to understanding the workings of the hidden, inner mechanisms of capitalist society, and believes that the major failure of Smith's purely economic theory is a failure to provide an adequate theory of surplus value. Marx's brilliant critique of previous theories of surplus value devotes much interesting material to critiquing Smith's economic theory.[33] These studies show that from the beginning of Marx's development of a critique of political economy to the end, Marx continuously studied and critiqued the works of Adam Smith.

III. CONCLUSION

I should stress in conclusion that Marx's critique of Adam Smith is not limited to demolishing Smith's theory of human nature. In Marx's view, Smith fails to accurately describe many of the realities of capitalist society. Smith's model of the origin of the market society in the society of hunters and shepherds is for Marx an ahistorical myth, an idyll of simple accumulation that covers over the bloody history of capitalism.[34] Smith fails to appraise the fundamental role that monopoly will play in the capitalist economy and fails to see that the state will actively intervene on the side of the monopolists and capitalist ruling class again and again, making a sham out of laissez faire. Smith failed to properly grasp the phenomenon of exploitation and lacked a cogent theory of surplus value. Finally, Smith's mode of the self-regulating market, harmony of class/individual interests, and the invisible hand are in Marx's view but mere myths, ideology concocted to cover over the reality of class conflict, the anarchy of an unregulated market, and a capitalist system full of explosive contradictions that would create periodic crises and bring about eventual collapse.

In the final section of this paper I have stressed Marx's claim that capitalist society is really dreadfully harmful to the human being, that the division of labor, competition, unbridled self-interest, the ubiquity of the market, lust for money and possessions as the end of life, and so forth, are really restrictive of human potentialities and create humanly impoverished, one-sided, alienated human beings. Thus, in Marx's view, rather than being in harmony with human nature, capitalism is profoundly opposed to it. Smith's view of human nature, upon which his theory of political economy rests, was shown to be a mere myth that legitimates powerful and destructive economic interests and that provides ideological support for an alienating and dehumanizing economy. Marx's critique of Adam Smith's concept of human nature, which continues to express the dominant view of capitalist man to this day, is one of his enduring contributions to modern thought and indicates that radical socioeconomic and individual change is necessary to create more human beings and a more humane society.

NOTES

1. Karl Marx, *Theories of Surplus-Value*, pt. II (Moscow: Progress Publishers, 1968), pp. 165-66.

2. The label originates in Engels' "Outline of a Critique of Political Economy," in

Karl Marx and Friedrich Engels, *Collected Work*, vol. III (New York: International Publishers, 1975), p. 422. Marx elaborates on the metaphor in "The Economic and Philosophic Manuscripts of 1844," in *Collected Work*, p. 290.

3. Engels' early article reveals less respect for Smith than Marx was to show and exhibits excessive moralism that was never present in Marx's work. Engels writes: "Modern economics—the system of free trade based on Adam Smith's *Wealth of Nations*—reveals itself to be that same hypocrisy, inconsistency and immorality which now confront free humanity in every sphere." "Outlines of a Critique of Political Economy," p. 420.

4. "Economic and Philosophic Manuscripts of 1844," pp. 235-70.

5. It is interesting to note that Hegel—often touted as Marx's chief intellectual influence and source—was himself deeply immersed in Smith's ideas, which he reproduced in his early writings and in *The Philosophy of Right*. Hence Smith's ideas had a twofold impact on Marx: through his direct study of Smith and through his work on Hegel, who had earlier appropriated many ideas and insights from Smith. For a further discussion of this issue, see Herbert Marcuse's *Reason and Revolution* (New York: Beacon Press, 1960), and George Lukács' *The Young Hegel* (Cambridge: MIT Press, 1976), which has been recently translated and explores the theme in detail.

6. Mazlish suggests in the Library of Liberal Arts edition of *The Wealth of Nations* that "Smith reached, although only gropingly and without using the technical term, the notion of the 'dialectic,' and what is more, the dialectic working itself out in economic terms" (New York: Harper and Row, 1961), p. xix. This is absurd because the central dialectical notions of negation and contradiction are missing in Smith's theoretical apparatus.

7. Adam Smith, *An Inquiry into the Nature and Causes of the Wealth of Nations* (New York: Modern Library, 1937), pp. 391-92.

8. Marx and Engels, "The Communist Manifesto," pt. I; Marx, *Grundrisse* (London: Macmillan, 1973), pp. 459-515; and Marx, *Capital* (New York: International Publishers, 1947), chaps. 25-32.

9. *Capital*, pp. 708-9.

10. See especially *The Wealth of Nations*, bk. I, chap. 8, "On the Wages of Labor," resolved in optimistic faith in progress in a growing cornucopia of opulence that will spill over its bounties to the entire population.

11. Adam Smith, *The Theory of Moral Sentiments*, 1st ed. (London, 1759), hereafter *TMS*.

12. C. M. Macpherson's *The Political Theory of Possessive Individualism* (Oxford: Oxford University Press, 1962) discusses the role of egotism and self-interest in the political theories of Hobbes and Locke. Hartmut Neuendorff discusses the concept of self-interest in Hobbes, Smith, and Marx in *Der Begriff des Interesses* (Frankfurt: 1973).

13. *The Wealth of Nations*, p. 13, hereafter *WN*.

14. *Grundrisse*, pp. 244-45.

15. J. Bronowski and B. Mazlish, *The Western Intellectual Tradition* (New York: Harper and Row, 1960), interpret the "invisible hand" doctrine in terms of "God's providential benevolence" and "man's earthly self-interest"! (*WN*, p. 352). I don't see what God has to do with this and find no appeal to Him as the backbone of the capitalist market in *The Wealth of Nations*.

16. See Bernard Mandeville, *The Fable of the Bees*, ed. F. B. Kaye (London: Penguin, 1924).

17. I might note that, although there is the same continuity/discontinuity evident in the relation between the early and late works of Marx, Marx's work presents more consistency and unity in its totality than does Smith's work, where, in my view, the discontinuities are predominant. To fully demonstrate this would require another paper that would flesh out Smith's theories of self-interest and sympathy in *TMS* and *WN*.

18. The influential work by Glenn Morrow, *The Ethical and Economic Theories of Adam Smith* (New York: 1969, reprint of 1923 ed.) attempted to integrate Smith's *TMS* and *WN* on these grounds. Other attempts include Joseph Cropsey, *Polity and Economy: An Interpretation of the Principles of Adam Smith* (The Hague: Martinus Nijhoff, 1957); and J. Ralph Lindgren, *The Social Philosophy of Adam Smith* (The Hague: Martinus Nijhoff, 1973). Countless articles have dealt with this problem.

19. For an account of the rapid economic development and industrialization and the changes that it wrought on human life from the mid-1700s when *TMS* was conceived to 1776 when *WN* appeared, see Karl Polanyi, *The Great Transformation* (Boston: Beacon Press, 1968); Paul Mantoux, *The Industrial Revolution in the Eighteenth Century* (New York: Harper and Row, 1961); and Fernand Braudel, *Capitalism and Material Life* (New York: Harper and Row, 1973).

20. Karl Marx and Friedrich Engels, *The German Ideology* (Moscow: Progress Publishers, 1968), p. 42.

21. *German Ideology*, pp. 37-38.

22. Karl Marx, "Theses on Feuerbach," *German Ideology*.

23. Marx, "Economic and Philosophic Manuscripts of 1844," p. 299.

24. Ibid., p. 299.

25. Ibid., p. 304.

26. Ibid., p. 309.

27. *Grundrisse*, p. 610.

28. Marx himself cites this passage in *Capital*, chap. 14, sec. 5.

29. Against the view that the notion of alienated labor was a temporary fancy of the young Marx, one can easily show that this theme is always of central importance to Marx and is a thread running through his work from the "Economic and Philosophic Manuscripts of 1844" to *Capital*. Hence although I shall only cite passages from the early Marx here, there are many passages in the later Marx that also speak of alienated labor. See, for example, the first passage from *Capital* quoted in this chapter.

30. Marx, pp. 237-38.

31. "Economic and Philosophic Manuscripts of 1844," p. 274.

32. *Grundrisse* (London: Penguin), pp. 248-49.

33. Karl Marx, *Theories of Surplus-Value* (New York: Progress Publishers, 1969). See especially pt. I, pp. 69-182, and pt. II, pp. 216-36, 342-73, *passim*.

34. See the introduction to the *Grundrisse* where Marx attacks "Robinson Crusoe" approaches to political economy model-building, and the chapters on "Primitive Accumulation" in *Capital*.

PART II

The Hidden Meaning of Things: Profit, Rent, Interest, and Wages

6

The Transformation of Labour Values into Production Prices and the Marxian Theory of Exploitation

DOMENICO MARIO NUTI

Fellow of Kings College, Cambridge

1. CURRENT CRITICISMS

One of the central concepts in the economics of Marx is that of *value* of commodities, defined as the labour socially necessary for their production, or labour directly and indirectly embodied in commodities. Marx's use of this concept has been subjected to very heavy criticism by economists over the last hundred years. Modern economists have argued that value is a metaphysical notion (Robinson, 1962); that Marxian values are a defective price theory (Samuelson, 1957; Arrow and Hahn, 1971); that the problem of the transformation of labour values into production prices is a pseudo-problem because values and prices are mutually exclusive alternatives (Samuelson, 1970, 1971); that nothing can be said by means of Marxian values that could not be said equally well by means of more conventional economics (Samuelson, 1971); that a viable reinterpretation of Marxian values should compute values—in a steady state—to include a profit rate equal to the growth rate of the economy; and that exploitation occurs only when the profit rate is greater than the growth rate, that is, consists only of capitalists' consumption (Weiszäcker, 1971). This approach is regarded as "a generalisation of Marx's exploitation theory" (Weiszäcker and Samuelson, 1971, p. 1194).

In this paper the main features of Marxian value theory are considered within a simple model of production in a capitalist economy in order to discuss these lines of criticism and relate the economics of Marx to some modern economic models, such as those of von Neumann and Sraffa. It is hoped that a better insight is gained in this way into the significance of the Marxian value system, the transformation of labour values into production prices, and the

I wish to thank A. Bhaduri, M. H. Dobb, R. M. Goodwin, A. Roncaglia, R. E. Rowthorn, I. Steedman, and E. Wolfstetter for commenting on an earlier draft. I have also benefited from talking to P. Sraffa and M. Morishima on the topic of this paper. Their assistance does not necessarily imply agreement with the views expressed here. Responsibility for any error is the writer's. This article was published in Polish in Ekonomista, n. 1, 1974, Warsaw.

Marxian theory of exploitation. Throughout the paper the requirements of logic have sometimes overruled the letter of the Marxian text, and it is not claimed that this presentation embodies "what Marx really said."

2. QUANTITIES, VALUES, AND PRICES

Consider a capitalist economy where commodities are produced under constant returns to scale and no joint production, with a single technology using labour and circulating capital. The turnover period of circulating capital is the same in all sectors and is taken as the time unit (Marx, 1885, chap. 15, sec. I). Wages for that time unit are paid in advance, so that the wage bill is equal to the wage fund, and the turnover period of the wage fund is the same as that of circulating capital.[1] The notation is as follows (vectors are *columns*):

$\underline{x}$ is the vector of total gross output produced per unit time;

$\underline{y}$ is the vector of final net output;

$\underline{c}$ is the vector of final output for consumption use in the next period;

$\underline{w}$ is the vector of consumption output consumed by workers; workers are paid a money wage rate w_m at the beginning of the period, and do not save;

$\underline{p}$ is the vector of prices, expressed in terms of the money wage rate w_m per unit of labour time; their dimension is therefore *labor commanded* by commodities. Money prices are given by $w_m p$.

$\underline{\ell}$ is the vector of labour values;

$\underline{a}$ is the vector of direct labour inputs a_{oj} for each commodity j; no commodity can be produced without direct labour or $\underline{a} > \underline{0}$. The working time L of the whole labour force during the period considered is the unit of measurement of labour inputs, i.e., $L = 1$.

$\underline{A}$ is the matrix of input-output coefficients a_{ij}, defined as the amount of the i-th input required per unit of j-th output. Inputs are needed at the beginning of the period and must therefore be produced in the previous period; $a_{ij} \geqslant 0$, but $a_{ij} > 0$ for some i, j, i.e., $\underline{A} \geqslant 0$. Assume also that $\underline{A}$ is irreducible (each commodity enters directly or indirectly into the production of all other commodities). A semipositive irreducible matrix has a strictly positive eigenvector $\hat{x}$, unique to within a multiplicative constant, and a positive eigenvalue λ (the dominant of $\underline{A}$), i.e., $\underline{A}\hat{x} = \lambda\hat{x}$. We define $R = (1 - \lambda)/\lambda$. If workers consumed nothing at all, an economy producing an output $\hat{x}$ would require capital inputs $\lambda\hat{x}$ and produce a physical surplus $(1 - \lambda)\hat{x}$; R therefore is the maximum growth rate or the maximum profit rate of an economic system with technology $\underline{A}$, obtained when $\underline{w} = 0$. The composite commodity of composition $\hat{x}$ is Sraffa's "standard commodity"; while his "standard product" is the net output of a "standard system," i.e., an imaginary system where the labour force is the same as that in the system actually considered and output has composition $\hat{x}$ (Sraffa, 1960, Ch. IV). We assume that the economic system is *productive*, i.e., any vector of gross output $\underline{x}$ requires a vector of material inputs $A\underline{x}$ such that $A\underline{x} < \underline{x}$. Hence $\lambda < 1$, and $R > 0$.

Under these assumptions the economy will be able to reproduce the circulating capital $A\underline{x}$ and still obtain a semipositive vector of net output $\underline{y} \geqslant 0$. Define

the matrix $\underline{B} = \underline{A} + \underline{w}\underline{a}'$. Economic viability at the given wage vector $\underline{w}$ requires also that the strictly positive eigenvector $\underline{x}^*$ of $\underline{B}$ is associated with a positive eigenvalue σ smaller than unity, i.e., $0 < \sigma < 1$. Define $r = (1 - \sigma)/\sigma$; this is the maximum rate at which an economic system with access to that technology and real wage may expand if there is an unlimited labour supply, and is therefore the competitive profit rate corresponding to $\underline{A}$, $\underline{a}$ and $\underline{w}$. The composite commodity of composition $\underline{x}^*$ is von Neumann's commodity (1937); this is how Marx approached the determination of the profit rate in his system (see below, section 7; on the profit rate as "the degree of [capital's] self-expansion," see Marx, 1894, p. 47). We consider an economy with access only to technology $\underline{A}$, $\underline{a}$, and growing at a constant rate g which in a closed economy must satisfy $R \geqslant r \geqslant g \geqslant 0$.

The quantity equations of the system are

(1) $\underline{y} = (I - \underline{A})\underline{x}$

(2) $\underline{c} = [I - (1 + g)\underline{A}]\underline{x}$

The labour value of a commodity is equal to its direct labour input plus the labour value of its inputs other than labour,

(3) $\underline{\ell} = \underline{a} + \underline{A}'\underline{\ell}$, hence

(4) $\underline{\ell} = (I - \underline{A}')^{-1}\underline{a}$

The dominant of $\underline{A}'$ is the same as that of $\underline{A}$, λ, and since $0 < \lambda < 1$ the inverse $(I - \underline{A}')^{-1}$ exists, and since $\underline{A}$ is semipositive and $\underline{a}$ is strictly positive the vector $\underline{\ell}$ is strictly positive and unique. If $g = 0$, $\underline{\ell}'\underline{c} = 1$; values can be interpreted therefore as the employment requirements per unit of output in each sector of a stationary economy. If labour is not homogeneous, as long as differences between types of labour are due to education, "complex" labour can be reduced to "simple" labour by a similar mathematical procedure (Rowthorn, 1973). Therefore values are not metaphysical.

In the customary Marxian notation, the value X of gross output is equal to the sum of the value V of the real wage bill, the value C of circulating capital, and the remaining surplus value S:

(5) $X = \underline{\ell}'\underline{x}$

(6) $S + V = \underline{a}'\underline{x} = \underline{\ell}'\underline{y} = L \equiv 1$

(7) $C = \underline{\ell}'(\underline{A}\underline{x})$

(8) $V = \underline{\ell}'\underline{w}$

(9) $S = \underline{\ell}'[(I - \underline{A})\underline{x} - \underline{w}] = \underline{\ell}'(g\underline{A}\underline{x}) + \underline{\ell}'(\underline{c} - \underline{w})$

The rate of surplus value S/V measures labour performed in excess of labour embodied in wage goods, expressed as a fraction of labour embodied in wage goods, and therefore measures the degree of exploitation. As long as the real wage per unit of labour time is the same in all production sectors, the degree of exploitation is the same throughout the economy by definition.

Prices of production are competitive prices in a situation where the composition of output has been correctly anticipated, for a given profit rate r and in terms of the money wage rate w_m. They are given by

(10) $\underline{p} = (1 + r)\underline{a} + (1 + r)\underline{A}'\underline{p}$, hence

(11) $\underline{p} = [I - (1 + r)\underline{A}']^{-1}\underline{a}(1 + r)$

Since $r \leqslant R$, the inverse $[I - (1 + r)\underline{A}']^{-1}$ exists, the vector $\underline{p}$ is strictly positive and unique; while *money* prices depend on the money wage w_m. For $r = 0$, $\underline{p} = \underline{\ell}$, i.e., values can be interpreted as the prices *in terms of labour commanded* which would prevail if profits were zero and the whole net product were distributed to workers by the price system. For $r > 0$, $\underline{p} > \underline{\ell}$.

Calling Y net national income, P profits, W the wage bill, K the magnitude of circulating capital (excluding the wage fund), all production prices,

(12) $\text{GNP} = \underline{p}'\underline{x}$

(13) $Y = \underline{p}'\underline{y}$

(14) $K = \underline{p}'(\underline{A}\underline{x})$

(15) $W = \underline{p}'\underline{w} = 1$

(16) $P = \underline{p}'[(I - \underline{A})\underline{x} - \underline{w}] = \underline{p}'(g\underline{A}\underline{x}) + \underline{p}'(\underline{c} - \underline{w})$

In general, the price ratios P/W and $P/(K + W)$ obtainable from conventional social accounting differ from the respective labour value ratios S/V and $S/(C + V)$. There are, however, special cases where some or all the ratios measured in value or price terms coincide, namely: when prices are proportional to values, whatever the relative composition of the aggregates; and when the relevant aggregates are homogeneous quantities, whatever the differences between relative prices and values (we neglect other cases where differences in relative prices and values happen to be exactly compensated by differences in relative quantities by pure chance).

(i) Prices Proportional to Values

Outside the trivial case of $r = 0$ when prices *in terms of labour commanded* are actually equal to labour values, the necessary and sufficient condition for prices to be proportional to labour values is that $\underline{a}$ is an eigenvector of $\underline{A}'$ (in which case the associated eigenvalue is the dominant of $\underline{A}$, λ). From

(17) $\underline{A}'\underline{a} = \lambda\underline{a}$, we obtain

(18) $\underline{\ell} = \underline{a} + \underline{A}'\underline{\ell} = \underline{a} + \lambda\underline{a} + \lambda^2\underline{a} + \ldots + \lambda^k\underline{a} + \underline{A}'^{k+1}\underline{\ell} = \dfrac{1}{1 - \lambda}\underline{a} = \dfrac{1 + R}{R}\underline{a}$, and

(19) $(1 + r)^{-1}\underline{p} = \underline{a} + (1 + r)\lambda\underline{a} + (1 + r)^2\lambda^2\underline{a} + \ldots + (1 + r)^k\lambda^k\underline{a} + \underline{A}'^{k+1}\underline{p}(1 + r)$

i.e., $\underline{p} = \dfrac{1 + r}{1 - \lambda(1 + r)}\underline{a} = \dfrac{(1 + R)(1 + r)}{R - r}\underline{a}$

Whenever (17) is satisfied, therefore, prices *in terms of labour commanded* are proportional to labour values,

$$(20) \qquad \underline{p} = \frac{R(1 + r)}{R - r} \underline{\varrho}$$

In Marx's terminology, the organic composition of capital is the same in all sectors; in fact the labour value of circulating capital $\underline{A}'\underline{\varrho}$ is proportional to direct labour $\underline{a}$ in this case, because $\underline{A}'\underline{\varrho} = \underline{A}'\underline{a}\,\frac{1}{1 - \lambda} = \frac{\lambda}{1 - \lambda}\underline{a}$. In this case,

$$\frac{S}{V} = \frac{P}{W} = \frac{\underline{p}'\underline{y} - \underline{p}'\underline{w}}{\underline{p}'\underline{w}} = \frac{R(1 + r)}{R - r}\underline{\varrho}'\underline{y} - 1, \quad \text{that is,}$$

$$(21) \qquad \frac{S}{V} = \frac{P}{W} = \frac{r(1 + R)}{R - r}, \quad \text{and}$$

$$(22) \qquad \underline{p} = \left(1 + \frac{S}{V}\right)\underline{\varrho}$$

(ii) Homogeneous Aggregates

$S/(C + V) = P/(K + W)$. Whether or not prices are proportional to values, if the growth rate is equal to the profit rate the composition of output and circulating capital (including the wage fund) is physically identical and the profit rate is therefore the same whether in price or value terms (or indeed at any other arbitrary system of aggregation weights). If we indicate with an asterisk the magnitude of the different variables when $g = r$,

$$(23) \qquad \underline{w} = \underline{c}^*(1 + g)^{-1} \quad \text{and therefore}$$

$$(24) \qquad \frac{S}{C^* + V} = \frac{\underline{\varrho}'(g\underline{A}\underline{x}^* + g\underline{w})}{\underline{\varrho}'(\underline{A}\underline{x}^* + \underline{w})} = g = r = \frac{P^*}{K^* + W}$$

Golden rule growth, however, is not sufficient nor necessary for the *shares* of profits and wages to be the same in terms of values and prices, and in general $S/V \gtrless P^*/W$. (In the golden rule economy V and S are the same as in any economy with the same wage vector and technology; given the profit rate, W is also the same regardless of the growth rate.)

(iii) Homogeneous Aggregates

$S/V = P/W$. This is the case in an economy producing a net output of composition equal to that of the wage vector w. Sraffa calls this a "subsystem" producing wage goods in the proportions of the wage vector (Sraffa, 1960).

(iv) Homogeneous Aggregates

$S/V = P/W$ *and* $S/(C + V) = P/(K + W)$! This is the very special case where wages, profits and circulating capital have the same physical composition. In this case—whether or not there is golden rule growth—the value and price ratios of profits

to wages coincide, and so do the value and price ratios of profits to capital (including wages). Call b the share of profits in income and s the share of profits reinvested; we then have

$$(25) \qquad sb\underline{y} = g\underline{A}\underline{x} + g\underline{w}, \quad \text{which can be rewritten as}$$

$$(25') \qquad sb\underline{y} = g\underline{A}\underline{x} + g(1 - b)\underline{y}$$

which after elementary manipulation gives from (1)

$$(26) \qquad \underline{A}\underline{x} = \frac{sb - g + gb}{sb + gb}\underline{x}$$

Therefore in this special case $\underline{x}$ is a semipositive eigenvector of $\underline{A}$, and its composition is that of Sraffa's "standard commodity," $\hat{\underline{x}}$. By putting

$$(27) \qquad \frac{1}{1 + R} = \frac{sb - g + gb}{sb + gb} \quad \text{we obtain}$$

$$(28) \qquad b = \frac{g(1 + R)}{R(s + g)}$$

which since $g = sr$ can be written as

$$(28') \qquad b = \frac{r}{R}\frac{(1 + R)}{(1 + r)}$$

If wages were paid at the end of the period we would obtain Sraffa's result: $b = r/R$ (Sraffa, 1960, p. 30).

Here we obtain the same result as in the case of uniform organic composition of capital:

$$(21) \qquad \frac{S}{V} = \frac{P}{W} = \frac{r(1 + R)}{R - r}$$

Whatever the *actual* composition of the wage vector in an economy with technology $\underline{A}$, $\underline{a}$, and profit rate r, the wage level can be expressed as a fraction $(R - r)/R(1 + r)$ of the standard product. But unless workers actually happen to *consume* the standard commodity, in general $S/V \gtrless r(1 + R)/(R - r)$; and unless, in addition, profits also have standard composition, in general $P/W \gtrless r(1 + R)/(R - r)$.

Marx's use of *value* ratios allows for the possibility of consistency, when technology changes, between otherwise irreconcilable propositions of progressive relative immiserisation of the proletariat (the progressive increase of S/V), the tendency of the "value" rate of profit $S/(C + V)$ to fall over time (Marx, 1894, Part III) while the real wage $\underline{w}$ per unit of labour increases, and the profit rate r and the ratio of profits to wages in price terms may move in any direction. The prediction of the fall of *both* V/S and $S/(C + V)$ may have been wrong, but

this needs proving and is not disproved by the observed facts of rising living standards of workers and the existence of an inverse relation between real wage and profit rates (see Steedman, 1971). We cannot speak, *a priori*, of "inconsistencies of [Marx's] inevitable laws" (Samuelson, 1957, p. 893).

3. VALUE AND PRICE

The Marxian proposition that prices equal values requires two important qualifications. First, the proposition does not mean that prices *in terms of labour commanded* by commodities are equal to values. Marx criticises both Smith and Proudhon for confusing labour *commanded by* and labour *embodied in* commodities (Marx, 1956, p. 70; 1847, pp. 54-55). Marx's "prices equal to values" are prices expressed in terms of the labour embodied in the money-price of commodities. In fact for Marx money is commodity-money, and stands for labour embodied in it ("Only in so far as paper money represents gold, which like all other commodities has value, is it a symbol of value," Marx, 1867, p. 128; see also 1939, Vol. I, Ch. "On Money"). If commodities exchange at the same rate as the labour they embody, the labour embodied in the commodity-money wage will be the same as the labour V embodied in the commodity labour power. Calling ℓ_m the value of the commodity money, w_m the commodity-money wage rate, and $\underline{p}_m$ the vector of commodity-money prices,

$$(29) \qquad \underline{p}_m = w_m \underline{p}$$

$$(30) \qquad \ell_m w_m = \underline{\ell}'\underline{w} = V, \quad \text{from which}$$

$$(31) \qquad \ell_m \underline{p}_m = \ell_m w_m \underline{p} = V\underline{p}$$

where $\ell_m \underline{p}_m$ is "labour embodied in commodity-money prices." As long as prices equal values in this sense, this relation holds whatever the commodity serving as money. Hence the proposition "prices equal values" means

$$(32) \qquad V\underline{p} = \underline{\ell}, \quad \text{or} \quad \underline{p} = \underline{\ell}\left(1 + \frac{S}{V}\right)$$

and not $\underline{p} = \underline{\ell}$ as often thought (e.g., by Weiszäcker, 1971, p. 8; Arrow and Hahn, 1971, pp. 45-47).

Second, the proposition "prices equal values" is not, in Marx, an assertion about what actually happens in a capitalist economy, but a provisional *assumption*: "I assume that commodities are sold at their value" (Marx, 1867, p. 519; also, 1885, p. 393; 1894, p. 151 and p. 175; etc.). This contradicts the proposition that the labour theory of value "says that the exchange rate of goods is given by the ratio of their specific labour content" (Weiszäcker, 1971, p. 8; see also Samuelson, 1957, and Arrow and Hahn, 1971, pp. 45-47 for the same interpretation of the labour theory of value as an assertion of how prices are determined). This may be the case for Smith, but does not apply to Marx, for whom this is only a working hypothesis.

The purpose of this hypothesis is to show that profit is not generated in the sphere of exchange by the divergence of prices from values (i.e., of $V\underline{p}$ from $\underline{\ell}$), and that profit arises in the sphere of production *even if* commodities are sold at their relative values: "To explain . . . *the general nature of profits*, you must start from the theorem that, on an average, commodities are *sold at their real values*, that is, in proportion to the quantity of labour realized in them. If you cannot explain profit upon this supposition, you cannot explain it at all" (Marx, 1898, p. 42).

4. PRODUCTION AND EXCHANGE

For Marx, profit arises from the process of production because labour power as a commodity produces more value than is required in its production. This is why exploitation is consistent with contracts between free agents, and is not immediately visible as under other exploitative economic systems (See Marx, 1898).

In the economic systems that have preceded capitalism, the exploitation of workers appears as the direct performance of unpaid labour for masters. "In the corvée, the labour of the worker for himself, and his compulsory labour for his lord, differ in space and time in the clearest possible way. In slave labour, even that part of the working day in which the slave is only replacing the value of his own means of existence, in which, therefore, in fact he works for himself alone, appears as labour for his master. All the slave's labour appears as unpaid labour." "In wage labour, on the contrary, even surplus labour, or unpaid labour, appears as paid" (Marx, 1867, pp. 539-40). "The wage-form thus extinguishes every trace of the division of the working day into necessary labour and surplus labour, into paid and unpaid labour" (*Ibidem*, p. 539).

Whatever appearances, surplus value does not arise from monopolistic conditions in exchange, but from class monopoly of the means of productions. Workers do not sell the commodities embodying their labour; they sell their own labour power (Marx, 1867, p. 167) as a commodity that happens to create more value than is spent in its own production. Marx's reasoning is sometimes based on a subsistence theory of wages; competition among workers in the production of labour power as a commodity, and the existence of a reserve army of labour (Marx, 1867, Ch. XXV) cause workers to get only what is strictly necessary to produce labour power (Marx, 1891a, p. 26). "Subsistence" however should not be taken literally; "In contradistinction . . . to the case of other commodities, there enters into the determination of the value of labour-power a historical and moral element. Nevertheless, in a given country, at a given period, the average quantity of the means of subsistence necessary for the labourer is practically known" (Marx, 1867, p. 171). Wages therefore do not have to be at "subsistence"; they are simply *given* in the Marxian analysis; what matters is that "the value of labour must always be less than the value it produces" (Marx, 1867, p. 538). The fact that other commodities beside labour power produce more of themselves than is needed as their own input—a fact implicit in $R > 0$—is immaterial for this argument; commodities, unlike workers, cannot be exploited, and when commodities are used as inputs they transfer to their product no more labour value than they contain themselves.

This distinctive property of labour power is the real source of profit, and the reason why profit is consistent with "equivalent exchange" (Marx, 1867, p. 194). Suppose prices equal values (in the sense specified in the previous section); "If, . . . the magnitude of value advanced in wages is not merely found

again in the product, but is found there augmented by a surplus value, this is not because the seller has been defrauded, for he has really received the value of his commodity; it is due solely to the fact that this commodity has been used up by the buyer" (Marx, 1867, p. 585). From this angle, profit is simply *unpaid labour*: "The capitalist's profit is derived from the fact that he has something to sell for which he has paid nothing" (Marx, 1894, p. 42).

5. CAPITAL AND EXPLOITATION

Workers' unpaid labour is obscured by all labour appearing to be paid labour, and profit appearing to originate in the "productiveness" of capital. In non-Marxian economics, capital goods are primarily the embodiment of future commodities; their ownership gives title to future commodities, and additional future commodities are forthcoming in the economy because of the existence of capital goods. In the Marxian view, capital is primarily the embodiment of past labour. "The *productivity* of capital consists in the first instance . . . in the *compulsion to perform surplus labour*, labour beyond the immediate need; a compulsion which the capitalist mode of production shares with earlier modes of production . . ." (Marx, 1956, vol. I, pp. 389-90). Profit may appear as reward for the waiting of the thrifty, but if capitalists sacrifice themselves and wait for a while for capital to produce its fruits, workers wait forever and in vain since they never touch the fruits of their unpaid labour embodied in capital goods. Workers have to acquire every year a fresh right to their share by fresh work, while capitalists have already acquired a permanent right to their share; the capitalist's entitlement was not acquired "By his own labour and that of his forefathers," but from "primitive accumulation" (Marx, 1867, p. 582; pp. 713-14).

In Marx's view *all* profit is unpaid labour, whether capital has been acquired by thrift or by force. The central point of the labour theory as a theory of exploitation is that *labour is the only human contribution to economic activity, and the exercise of labour power should be the only way in which a claim to the net product of a nonexploitative economic system is acquired.* Exploitation is the appropriation of surplus value by agents other than the workers as a class; but there is no natural law prescribing class exploitation (Marx, 1867, p. 169).

Marx was aware that even in an economic system where capital goods are socially owned, workers would not be receiving the full value created by their labour, because some labour would have to be performed to produce collective consumption and capital accumulation; the equality of prices in terms of labour commanded and values is not a feature of Marx's socialist economy (Marx, 1891a, pp. 9-10). *If* workers have control over the amounts of collective consumption and capital accumulation, it can be said, as Engels does, that "the workers as a whole, i.e., *all*, would remain in possession and enjoyment of their total product" (Engels's Introduction to the second edition of Marx, 1847, p. 21). Most socialist economies as we know them do not seem to have this kind of control to a sufficient extent, but socialist writers recognise that the *nationalization* of the means of production is only the first step in the process of their *socialization*, i.e., of the establishment of full social control (as opposed to élitist or bureaucratic control) over resource allocation (Brus, 1967, p. 15; Nuti, 1973).

6. TRANSFORMATION

If the organic composition of capital is the same in all productive sectors, the equality of prices and values

$$(22) \qquad \underline{p} = \left(1 + \frac{S}{V}\right)\underline{\ell}$$

becomes a statement of equilibrium production prices. Outside this case, if prices (in terms of labour embodied) were equal to $\underline{\ell}$ profits would be proportional to the variable capital employed in each sector and the ratio between profits and the sum of variable and constant capital—or the profit rate at those prices—would differ in different sectors. This is why prices of production $V\underline{p}$ have to diverge from $\underline{\ell}$, or $\underline{p}$ from $\underline{\ell}\left(1 + \frac{S}{V}\right)$; this divergence being obtained by transforming labour values $\underline{\ell}$ into prices of production $V\underline{p}$.

The contention that "Marx . . . confuses everything by his attempt to maintain simultaneously a pure labour theory of value and an equilization of rates of return on capital" (Arrow and Hahn, 1971, p. 2) cannot be supported by the reading of Marx. "If the commodities were sold at their values . . . the rate of profit in the various spheres would have to vary a great deal" (Marx, 1956, vol. II, p. 28; also, 1894, *passim*).

In his treatment of the transformation of values into prices (in terms of labour embodied), Marx made two mistakes (on a third point Marx was only partially mistaken; see the next section).

(i)   he considered the profit rate to be a simple average of the profit rates prevailing in the economy when $V\underline{p} = \underline{\ell}$ (Marx, 1894, p. 156);

(ii) he determined the "transformed" prices of production on the assumption that inputs were acquired at prices equal to values instead of at the "transformed" prices (Marx, 1894, p. 155; see also the tables on pp. 153-55).

These mistakes, however, can be easily rectified without altering Marx's line of reasoning: (i) the profit rate *is* an average, where however the weights are given by the relative outputs produced not in the actual economic system considered but in a golden rule economy (where $r = S/(C^* + V)$, see section 2 above); (ii) the transformation problem can be formulated by taking inputs at their transformed prices rather than at their values. This is susceptible of rigorous formal treatment and computation.

Define the *Transformation Matrix* $\underline{T}$ as

$$(33) \qquad \underline{T} = V\left[\underline{I} - \left(1 + \frac{S}{C^* + V}\right)\underline{A}'\right]^{-1}(\underline{I} - \underline{A}')\left(1 + \frac{S}{C^* + V}\right)$$

The *Transformation Process* can be both described and computed as

$$(34) \qquad \underline{p} = \underline{T}\underline{\ell}\left(1 + \frac{S}{V}\right), \quad \text{or} \quad V\underline{p} = \underline{T}\underline{\ell}$$

In fact, from (6), (4) and (24) we can rewrite (34) as

$$\underline{p} = V\left(1 + \frac{S}{V}\right)\left[\underline{I} - \left(1 + \frac{S}{C^* + V}\right)\underline{A}'\right]^{-1}(\underline{I} - \underline{A}')(\underline{I} - \underline{A}')^{-1}\underline{a}\left(1 + \frac{S}{C^* + V}\right)$$

$$= [\underline{I} - (1 + r)\underline{A}']^{-1}\underline{a}(1 + r)$$

which we know from (11) to be the correct expression for the prices of production. This transformation is not a metaphysical operation, let alone a question of "erasing" a set of values and "replacing" them with a set of prices (Samuelson, 1971); the transformation is simply a reflection of the operation of competitive markets equalizing the profit rate throughout the economy.

Of course, prices of production could be obtained *directly* from $\underline{A}$, $\underline{a}$ and $\underline{w}$, for instance following the procedure adopted by Sraffa and summarized in equation (11), rather than following the more roundabout Marxian procedure. The point is that Marx's purpose is *not* the determination of relative prices; *on the contrary*, his problem is how to look *beyond* the impact of a positive profit rate on relative prices, in order to find the origin of profit and present the true nature of profit as unpaid labour. The fact that the transformation process also yields a set of relative prices is only a by-product of the analysis. The Marxian insight is that capitalist exploitation is not in the transformation process, in the sphere of competitive exchange of commodities, but in the sphere of production, or rather in the production of labour power as a commodity and its use in the production of commodities.

The statement that profit is the appearance and surplus value is the reality cannot be reversed, as in Samuelson's parody of Marx's own words (1971, p. 417); prices, and not values, are the parameters observed in the market, and if there is a disguise at all it must be prices phenomena disguising value phenomena; labour being the only human contribution to production makes transformation a one-way process.

7. TOTAL PROFIT—TOTAL SURPLUS VALUE

From the view of prices as a transformed form of value, Marx inferred that total profit must be equal to total surplus value: ". . . surplus value and profit are actually the same thing and numerically equal" (Marx, 1894, p. 47). This is correct in the self-evident sense that surplus *product* is not increased by the process of circulation (Marx, 1894, p. 141), but if the proposition is taken literally to mean

$$(35) \qquad \underline{p}'(\underline{y} - \underline{w}) = \left(1 + \frac{S}{V}\right)\underline{\ell}'(\underline{y} - \underline{w})$$

it has no general validity and is only true in special cases.

One of the special cases is that of an economy where net output is a multiple of the wage vector, or $\underline{w} = V\underline{y}$. There

$$(35') \quad \begin{cases} \underline{p}'(\underline{y} - \underline{w}) = \underline{p}'\left(\dfrac{1}{V}\underline{w} - \underline{w}\right) = \left(\dfrac{1}{V} - 1\right)\underline{p}'\underline{w} = \dfrac{S}{V} = S\left(1 + \dfrac{S}{V}\right) \\[2mm] \left(1 + \dfrac{S}{V}\right)\underline{\ell}'(\underline{y} - \underline{w}) = \left(1 + \dfrac{S}{V}\right)\underline{\ell}'(\underline{y} - V\underline{y}) = \underline{\ell}'\underline{y}(1 - V)\left(1 + \dfrac{S}{V}\right) = S\left(1 + \dfrac{S}{V}\right) \end{cases}$$

Samuelson adds the special case where there is equal *internal* composition of capital, i.e., where "*every one of the departments* [including the 'department' producing labour power] *happens to use the various raw materials and machine services in the same proportions that society produces them in toto*," in which case Marx's own transformation procedure would be correct (Samuelson, 1970, p. 415). In general, however, there is no reason for expecting equation (35) to hold. It is not simply a problem of normalization; transformation may alter the evaluation of surplus product generated by exploitation.

The statement that "total profit equals total surplus value" was put by Marx also as a statement that there exists an ideal average commodity whose price (say, Vp_a, an element of $V\underline{p}$) was also equal to its value (say ℓ_a), and where a profit rate would be obtained equal to the average profit rate in the economy; indeed this is how the profit rate in the economy was to be determined: "The average rate of profit . . . is the percentage of profit in that sphere of average composition in which profit, therefore, coincides with surplus-value. Hence, the rate of profit is the same in all spheres of production, for it is equalized on the basis of those average spheres of production which have the average composition of capital. . . . Between the spheres more or less approximating the average there is again a tendency towards equalization, seeking the ideal average, i.e., an average that does not really exist" (Marx, 1894, pp. 170-71).

Here Marx was partly right, partly mistaken. He was right in his idea of an average commodity where the profit rate would be the same whether expressed at prices of production or at values; this is the net output $\underline{x}^*$ of a golden rule economy with the same wage vector and technology.[2] Marx was mistaken, however, in believing that the price of that commodity would be equal to the value of that commodity. There is no reason to expect $Vp_a = \ell_a$, and Medio's claim that for that composite commodity "price equals value" (Medio, 1972, pp. 330-37) is unfounded. However, the important feature of the composite commodity produced in the golden rule economy—which, as Morishima points out, is nothing but von Neumann's ray—is that in the industry producing it surplus value is equal to the profit earned on variable and constant capital at the profit rate r $\left(\text{because } S = r(C^* + V), \text{ or } \dfrac{S}{V} = r\left(\dfrac{C^*}{V} + 1\right)\right)$, and therefore *in that industry values would not have to be transformed for the capitalists operating in it to earn the average profit rate.* As Medio puts it, that industry "normally will have to 'transform' the *value* of its product as a consequence of the 'transformation' carried on in other industries" (Medio, 1972, p. 336).

An average commodity fulfilling *both* basic criteria laid out by Marx (price-value; profit rate the same whether at prices or at values) does not in general exist. A sufficient condition for it to exist is that the composition of the wage vector is the same as that of Sraffa's standard commodity. In that case the von Neumann commodity and the Sraffa commodity coincide; if such imaginary industry was set up in an economy where workers consume the standard commodity (see section 2(iv)), whether or not the economy actually grows under golden rule conditions, the price of that commodity would be equal to its value *and* the profit rate in that industry would be the same whether at prices or values (*Ibidem*).

Needless to say, this is a most special case (though it is far more general than Samuelson's case of uniform *internal* composition of capital, where not only are workers implicitly assumed to consume the standard commodity, but

additional and restrictive assumptions about technology are also made). How-ever, it has been suggested by Eatwell that *if* the rate of surplus value is rede-fined by taking the value of labour power as the value of the commodity-money in which wages are paid ($\ell_m w_m$ instead of the value V of the wage vector), *and if* the standard commodity is used as money, *then* the standard commodity is the average commodity sought by Marx. This approach has two additional advan-tages: (i) this redefined rate of surplus value can be inferred immediately from the properties of Sraffa's standard system, and expressed as a function of the profit rate (see section 2(iv), equation (21); Eatwell does not modify the Sraffian formulation to allow for advanced wages); (ii) this redefined rate of surplus value is the same for a given profit rate, whatever the actual composition of the wage vector; no special assumptions about workers' consumption or the growth of the economy actually considered are required (Eatwell, 1972). The redefinition of the rate of surplus value in this fashion is undoubtedly conven-ient; there are however a series of objections if the purpose of this approach is that of clarifying and tidying up Marxian economics.

Marx only used the notion of value of labour power as the value of the commodity-money wage within the framework of equality of prices and values (for instance, Marx, 1967, Ch. VII, sec. 2), in which case there is no difference between the value of labour power as the value of the wage vector or as the value of the commodity-money wage (see above, section 3). Outside this case the two measurements of the value of labour power would diverge, and the redefined rate of surplus value would not be any better than the actual profits/wages ratio as a measure of the degree of exploitation. For a commodity-money other than the standard commodity, the redefined rate of surplus value would require knowledge of the money wage rate, and hence could not be found prior to the transformation of values into prices; therefore this definition is in general useless from the viewpoint of the transformation process. If the standard com-modity were used as money this problem would not arise because the relative shares in the standard system can be known *prior* to the knowledge of relative prices (see above, section 2(iv)), but for Marx the emergence of a particular commodity as money *is a social process,* (Marx, 1867, p. 86; p. 142) and the commodity-money cannot be arbitrarily chosen. If, as one would reasonably expect, the standard commodity is not the money decreed to be money by a social process, the redefinition of the value of labour power as the value of the money wage is useless from the viewpoint of the transformation problem. Besides, Marx was rather scornful of Ricardo's search for "an invariable measure of value" (Marx, 1939, vol. II, p. 201), which Sraffa's standard commodity purports to be; any commodity-money, Marx argues, is "invariable" with respect to itself (*Ibidem*). In addition, even if one neglected all these objections to the notion of the degree of exploitation as the profits/wages ratio in the standard system, one would still not obtain necessarily the Marxian propositions that "total value equals total price" and that "total profit equals total surplus value."

The *evaluation* of the surplus product at prices (in terms of labour em-bodied) equal to values and at transformed prices is not necessarily the same, except for a few special cases; the transformation process affects the evaluation of the surplus product, and not merely its distribution among capitalists. This, however, does not alter the findings of Marx's analysis on the origin of profit,

his view of profits as exploitation, and his measurement of the degree of exploitation.

8. EXPLOITATION AND NON-MARXIAN ECONOMICS

It is true that there are many statements which could be obtained from bour-geois economics as well as from Marxian economic theory. Instead of saying $V < 1$, we could simply say $W < Y$; instead of $S > 0$, we could say $P > 0$; instead of saying that there is a positive rate of exploitation, we could simply say $r > 0$. But if we do take the view that profits are exploitation, we need an accurate measure of exploitation, and conventional social accounting does not provide an exact measure. The ratio of profits to wages expressed at current prices depends on what commodities capitalists spend their profits on; economies with the same wage vector per unit labour and the same technology might appear to have different degrees of exploitation. The profit rate is not a good measure of exploitation because profit is related not to variable capital but to the whole of the capital stock, i.e., it is always an underestimate of the degree of exploitation (Marx, 1867, Ch. IX). The ratio of profits to wages at labour values indicates how much percent more work than is necessary is performed by labourers to produce their wages, and it is therefore "an exact expression for the degree of exploitation of labour power by capital" (Marx, 1867, p. 218). This is a unit of measurement in which exploitation can be immediately perceived by workers.

Of course a radical economist could go a long way simply by using the current instruments of bourgeois economics. By listing all the conditions that must be satisfied for Paretian efficiency to prevail, one can point out how unlikely it is that any economy could satisfy these conditions unassisted, and ask for radical intervention by the state. If production and distribution are deter-mined by the initial endowment of productive resources, traditional general equilibrium theory points out that any permanent redistribution of income requires a redistribution of the resource endowments, or possibly the expropria-tion of the endowment of productive resources other than labour from those who, somehow, have acquired exclusive control over these resources. Given the appropriate political premises, it is conceivable that the conclusion that pro-letarians of all countries should unite could be drawn from Samuelson's own textbook.

If bourgeois economics has a great untapped revolutionary potential, there remains the fact that the conventional tools of economic analysis have been used to build a powerful apologia for capitalism, not a theory of capitalist exploitation.

The neoclassical tradition in the theory of profit and distribution is char-acterized by the search for natural laws of distribution and a harmonic vision of society. In 1860 Jevons spoke of "the natural laws which govern the relations between capital and labour and define inexorably the rates of profits and wages"; he quite consistently denounced all trade union activity intended to affect wages, as a futile and wasteful activity, since "The competition to obtain proper work-men will strongly tend to secure to the latter their "legitimate share" (sic) of the ultimate produce" (quoted by Steedman, 1971). For J. B. Clark, "What a social class gets is, under natural law, what it contributes to the general output

of industry." Modern versions of neoclassical theory emphasize not so much the natural fairness of the *status quo,* but its basic efficiency (Samuelson, 1948, p. 56 on "consumer sovereignty"; p. 621 on efficiency). Hence although conventional economic theory *could,* and perhaps will, be used to obtain radical statements and from a purely *methodological* viewpoint does not lend itself necessarily to political labels, from a *historical* viewpoint it deserves the label of "bourgeois" that Samuelson obligingly has attached to it (Samuelson, 1971, p. 422).

9. A FALSIFICATION OF MARX

It is a well known proposition that when there are alternative techniques of production, the maximum maintainable rate of consumption per man is obtained— whether technology is unchanged or improves over time in a "neutral" fashion— when the technique is used which would be chosen for a profit rate equal to the growth rate. A simple corollary of this "golden rule of accumulation" is that a central planner in a socialist economy would only be in the path affording the highest maintainable steady rate of consumption if he has been using a price system implying a profit rate equal to the growth rate.

Samuelson and Weiszäcker give a formulation of this corollary and call it "a fundamental theorem that in a sense brings into discount the worthwhileness for planning of Marx's innovations in volume I of *Capital*" (Weiszäcker and Samuelson, 1971, p. 1193). They call their theorem "a generalisation of Marx's exploitation theory" (*Ibidem,* p. 1194). Accordingly, "the rate of exploitation is the difference between the value of consumption and the value of wages, divided by the value of wages" (Weiszäcker, 1971, p. 28).

First, Marx never suggested that labour values should be used for planning purposes; indeed he most explicitly denied that exchange prices in a socialist economy would be equal to labour values (see section 5 above). When Soviet and East European economists refer to the applicability of the law of value to socialist planning, they talk about something else, namely the relative role of markets and plans (see Nove and Nuti, 1972, p. 17; Stalin, 1952). The "law of value" here implies that prices should be geared to the cost of production and demand conditions, and the allocation of resources should be guided by the relation between relative prices and relative costs (see Nuti, 1973, section 5). This kind of discussion should be left to the initiated, and left aside when talking about Marx. Secondly, this so-called "fundamental theorem" has been derived by socialist writers everywhere. It can be found in M. H. Dobb's writings (1969, ch. 8) and in Soviet literature (out of many instances, see Kantorovich and Makarov, 1965, and Terekov, 1967, ch. IV).

Anybody of course is free to define exploitation as he likes. For Pigou, exploitation consisted in the divergence of the wage/price ratios from what would be the case under perfect competition; i.e.: exploitation is caused by monopoly. It may be useful, for some purpose or other, to define "exploitation" in other ways as well: for instance as exploitation between different generations, or races, or regions, or nations, and not just classes. This is legitimate as long as definitions are not unduly attributed to others, and they are consistent with the approach to economic science of whoever provides the

definition. Samuelson and Weiszäcker's definition of exploitation as capitalists' consumption scores badly on both counts.

Imagine a capitalist who optimizes his intertemporal consumption following the standard procedures of the neoclassical theory which Samuelson and Weiszäcker represent, i.e., maximizing his utility via activities of production and exchange. Undoubtedly he will not be indifferent between a given stream of consumption and the same stream of consumption out of profits *plus* entitlement to the capital cumulated by means of the unconsumed part of profits; and rightly so, since cumulated capital is a source of potential consumption, additional to the consumption stream which is being offered to the capitalist. Samuelson and Weiszäcker neglect the capitalists' claim on cumulated unconsumed profits. At least according to Weiszäcker, "interest and growth rates do not diverge much in reality" (Weiszäcker, 1970), i.e., capitalists' consumption must be negligible; in his world of benevolent capitalism, without exploitation as he defines it, transition to socialism would be an instantaneous and painless step.

To say that exploitation is only capitalists' consumption and claim that this has anything to do with Marx does violence to both the letter and spirit of Marxian texts. There is no doubt that any notion of exploitation along the most remotely Marxian lines should regard profits, whether squandered or dutifully accumulated, as an integral aspect of the process of capitalist exploitation. For Marx, *all* profits are unpaid labour (see section 5 of this reading). The only conceivable purpose of this so-called "generalisation" of Marx's value and exploitation theory is that of diluting the politics of the Marxian results.

10. CONCLUSION

Labour values are tangible economic categories, not metaphysical notions. The equality between the labour embodied in the money price of commodities and the labour values of commodities is not, for Marx, a price theory, but a working hypothesis made in order to show that profits originate in the production of labour power as a commodity and in its use in the production of other commodities, and not in the process of exchange. Ratios between economic magnitudes aggregated at prices and at values differ except for a number of special cases: Marx's equal organic composition of capital, Sraffa's subsystem producing wage goods, von Neumann's economy growing in golden rule conditions, Sraffa's standard system if workers happen to consume the standard commodity. Marx's version of the transformation process was defective, but can be formulated and computed rigorously; the transformation of labour values into prices of production is not a "pointless exercise," nor just a matter of replacing one set of values with another, it is the mode of the distribution among capitalists of the profits generated by capitalists' exploitation. The notion of exploitation could be derived from more conventional economic theory, but it is perhaps no accident that it was not derived from it; besides, if the notion of exploitation is accepted Marxian theory provides an accurate measurement of exploitation. A redefinition of Marxian values to include a profit rate equal to the growth rate may have some, though limited, use for socialist planning, but does not extend the notion of "labour value" or make it more viable, it simply destroys the specific feature of this notion. Finally, exploitation may be defined as capitalists' consumption, but this cannot be considered a neo- or new- or after-Marxian definition.

REFERENCES

Arrow, K. J., and F. H. Hahn, *General Competitive Analysis*, 1971.

Brus, W. (Ed.), *Ekonomia Polityczna Socjalizmu*, Warsaw 1967.

Dobb, M. H., *Welfare Economics and the Economics of Socialism*, 1969.

Eatwell, J., "Value, price and the rate of exploitation," (seminar paper), 1972.

Kantorovich, L. V., and V. L. Makarov, "Optimal'ne modeli perspectivnego planirovania," in V. S. Nemchinov (Ed.), *Primenenie matematiki v ekonomicheskikh issledovaniyakh*, Moscow 1965.

Marx, K., *The Poverty of Philosophy* (1847), Foreign Languages Publishing House, Moscow.

——, *Contribution to the Critique of Political Economy*, Berlin 1859.

——, *Capital*, Vol. I (1867), English translation, Moscow 1961.

——, *Capital*, Vol. II (1885), English translation, Moscow 1962.

——, *Critique of the Gotha Programme* (1891a), English translation, London 1933.

——, *Capital*, Vol. III (1894), Foreign Languages Publishing House, Moscow.

——, *Wages, Price and Profit* (in English, 1898), Peking 1965.

——, *Economic and Philosophic Manuscripts of 1844* (1932), English translation, Moscow 1959.

——, *Grundrisse der Kritik der Politischen Ökonomie*, Moscow 1939, French translation Vol. I, 1967; Vol. II, 1968.

——, *Theories of Surplus-Value* (1956), English translation, Moscow 1963.

Medio, A., "Profits and surplus-value," in E. K. Hunt and J. G. Schwartz (Eds.), *A Critique of Economic Theory* (London: Penguin), 1972.

Morishima, M., *Marx's Economics*, 1973.

von Neumann, J., "A model of general economic equilibrium" (1937), *Review of Economic Studies*, 1945.

Nove, A., and D. M. Nuti (Eds.), *Socialist Economics*, 1972.

Nuti, D. M., "The political economy of socialism—orthodoxy and change in Polish texts," *Soviet Studies*, 1973.

Robinson, J., *Economic Philosophy*, 1962.

Rowthorn, R. E., "The reduction of 'complex' to simple labour," (mimeo.) 1973.

Samuelson, P. A., *Economics*, 1948, 6th edition, 1964.

——, "Wages and interest: a modern dissection of Marxian economic models," *American Economic Review*, May 1957.

——, "The 'transformation' from Marxian 'values' to competitive 'prices': a process of rejection and replacement," *Proceedings of the National Academy of Sciences*, September 1970.

——, "Understanding the Marxian notion of exploitation: A summary of the so-called transformation problem between Marxian values and competitive prices," *Journal of Economic Literature*, June 1971.

Sraffa, P., *Production of Commodities by Means of Commodities*, 1960.

Stalin, J., *Economic Problems of the USSR*, 1952.

Steedman, I., "Jevon's theory of capital and interest," *Manchester School*, 1971a.

——, "Marx on the falling rate of profit," *Australian Economic Papers*, June 1971b.

Terekov, L. L., *Otsenki v optimal'nom plane*, Moscow 1967.

von Weiszäcker, C. C., "Ende einer Wachstumstheorie?" *Kyklos*, 1970.

——, *Steady State Capital Theory*, Berlin 1971.

—— and P. A. Samuelson, "A new labour theory of value for rational planning through use of the bourgeois profit rate," *Proceedings of the National Academy of Sciences*, June 1971.

NOTES

1. Marx assumes that workers advance their labour power to capitalists (1867, p. 174; 1956, p. 314), but the production cycle is longer than the interval over which wages are paid, so that wages are paid in advance of the realization of the product (Marx, 1956, p. 314). At any rate profits are made also on the wage fund (1932, p. 38); hence the assumption here of wages paid in advance.

2. The idea that, when the growth rate equals the profit rate, profits and capital are homogeneous magnitudes, is of course as old as the golden rule of accumulation, and was first stated by von Neumann. Within the Marxian context, the proposition that $S/(C + V)$—or indeed the ratio between profits and capital measured at *any* arbitrary set of weights—is equal to the profit rate r under golden rule growth is a simple corollary; it was stated by Morishima in a seminar at Cambridge in 1968. The connection between Marx's "average commodity" and the composition of output under golden rule growth has been made by Medio (1972) and Morishima (1973). This commodity however does not fulfil Marx's condition that its price should be equal to its value.

Marx's Theory of Value and the "Transformation Problem"

ANWAR SHAIKH

Associate Professor of Economics at the
New School for Social Research

I. INTRODUCTION

It is curious that in the almost eighty years since the publication of Volume III of Marx's *Capital*, a major theoretical problem, the infamous "transformation problem," has never been satisfactorily resolved. Throughout Volume I, written by Marx *after* he had already completed the first draft of Volume III, the analysis is based on the assumption that exchanges of commodities take place at prices proportional to their labor values. I will call these prices the "direct prices" of commodities. In Volume III, which was compiled by Engels from the incomplete first draft, after Marx's death, Marx extends his analysis to take into account "prices of production," demonstrating how one can derive these prices from the "direct prices" of Volume I. This derivation, from then on the center of an intense controversy, was the original "transformation procedure."

Opponents of the labor theory of value immediately seized on the apparent incompleteness of Marx's procedure. Bohm-Bawerk, for instance, questioned the tenability of Marx's statement that the sum of prices after the transformation would remain equal to the sum of values; others have pointed out that Marx's procedure contains an "error," because while he transforms the prices of outputs from "direct prices" to "prices of production," he leaves the inputs untransformed. Since commodities appearing as outputs of a productive system are often also inputs into the system, it is argued that Marx's procedure is logically flawed; "direct prices" and "prices of production" are two separate and unrelated phenomena, leading to a "great contradiction" between Volume I and Volume III of *Capital*. More recently, essentially the same point has been made by Samuelson [17], in which he attacks the very idea of a transformation procedure: "Contemplate two alternative and discordant systems. Write down one. Now transform by taking an eraser and rubbing it out. Then fill in the other one. Voila! You have completed your transformation algorithm."[1] As we shall see, this criticism is completely incorrect. It is also somewhat misplaced; if anything, it applies most properly to the neoclassical "transformation procedure" which was the center of the so-called Cambridge Capital Controversies, a procedure in which Samuelson himself was quite prominent.*

On the Marxian side, there have been, of course, many "solutions" to the

transformation problem, from Bortkiewicz's original transformation procedure and its subsequent variants to Francis Seton's important paper [18]. Unfortunately, as even supporters and sympathetic critics of the labor theory of value admit, these "solutions" all suffer from the same basic defects; they show "the formal possibility of a consistent derivation of prices from values"[2] while apparently severing the crucial links between price and value magnitudes which Marx seemed to emphasize in his own procedure. In most discussions of the issue, these links have appeared in the form of the following equalities: of the "sum of prices" and the "sum of values"; of the magnitude of profits and the magnitude of surplus-value; of the profit-wage ratio and the rate of surplus-value; and of the general rate of profit in price terms and the same rate in value terms. As is well-known by now, in any "correct solution" either the first or the second, but not both, can be always made to hold, while in general the other two cannot. What then are we to make of Marx's procedure?

It has been suggested that Marx, having published Volume I in full confidence that the labor theory of value was the correct basis, discovered too late, in writing Volume III, that it was not. But that doesn't work, because we know that Volume I was published well after Volume III had been drafted. Others, perhaps more charitably, have suggested that because the labor theory of value as a theory of relative prices was so much a part of the tradition of classical economics, it was taken over by Marx almost unexamined. A variant of this line of reasoning, which is popular among some Marxists, is that if nowadays we view Marx-as-an-economist as a member of the classical school, it is we who import into Marx's theory of value, which is only nominally similar to that of Smith and Ricardo, the pre-Marxian question of the quantitative relationship between prices and values. In the variant, therefore, the lack of examination is on our part, not that of Marx. Marx was simply not terribly concerned with the quantitative relationship.[3]

To anyone who has read Marx's voluminous comments and critiques of the classical economists, notably in *Theory of Surplus-Value* and in *Capital*, it becomes impossible to ascribe to Marx an unthinking take-over of a labor theory of value from anyone at all. Marx spends literally hundreds of pages discussing values and their relationship, both qualitative and quantitative, to wages, profits and prices; no aspect, no issue, is ignored in these incredibly detailed discussions. So the main line of that argument does not hold up. As for the variant, insofar as it argues that there is a vast difference between the "value" of Smith and Ricardo and the "value" of Marx, it is undeniably correct; where it goes wrong is in jumping from this important fact to the conclusion that Marx either does, or even could ignore the quantitative aspects which dominated the pre-Marxian "value theory."

Consider for a moment the fact that there is a vast difference between Einstein and Newton too, one which stems from different methodologies, different objects of analysis, etc., and extends all the way to differences in concepts and calculations. There is, in other words, what Thomas Kuhn calls a "paradigm break" between the two modes of analysis.[4]

The notion that Einstein and Newton, for instance, treat what appears to be some autonomously defined subject—"Physics"—is an illusion which is fostered by textbook propagandists whose very aim is to treat science as the glorious

---

*For a discussion of this debate as a neoclassical "transformation problem," see Shaikh [19].
*This article, a solution to a problem that has plagued a century of Marxian scholarship,
was previously unpublished.*

and lofty march towards "truth." In reality, however, almost every conception and calculation in Relativity Theory contradicts those of classical physics.

To reduce Einstein to a "tidied up" Newton would therefore be impossible. What is worse, this impossibility would show up in the form of "logical contradictions," "redundancies," and "irrationalities" in Einstein, not in Newton, for the propositions derived from the Theory of Relativity cannot be derived within a Newtonian basis. What can we say, for example, in a Newtonian framework about the fundamental Einsteinian notion that there exists a finite limit, the speed of light, for the velocity of any object? Only that it is clearly wrong, or at best, a notion we (as Newtonians) have no use for in our framework—one which therefore appears "mythical," "metaphysical," "irrelevant."

Insofar as some Marxists have pursued a similar line of argument as to the "reduction" of Marx to Ricardo, they have been making an absolutely crucial point: namely, that by attempting to "reduce" Marx to Ricardo, or to neoclassical economics, the impossibility of this reduction will manifest itself as a series of "contradictions" and "irrationalities" in Marx! What we think we find, on a Ricardian or neoclassical basis, is that Marx is simply incorrect, or at best gets involved in an "unnecessary muddle."[5] What we have in fact demonstrated is that you cannot derive Marx from Ricardo or Samuelson.

Obviously, none of this implies that Marx is above criticism. The point here is that in order to be able to evaluate Marx's solution to some problem, we must first of all define the problem. We must, in other words, *locate* the problem in terms of some general analysis, so that we may see which solutions are adequate and which are not. It has often been said that the hardest part of solving a problem is figuring out the question!

Some Marxists, however, jump from the implications of the difference between Marx and Ricardo to the false conclusion that Marx was, or at least that Marxists could be, unconcerned with the quantitative relationships between prices and values (whether he was and whether Marxist analysis could be are in fact two separate issues, but one leads to the other).

To begin with, the statement that Marx did not in fact consider these matters to be important runs headlong into the contrary evidence of the vast amount of attention Marx's writings give to them; the only way to get around this evidence in turn, is to try and show that the issue itself is irrelevant. In this way the real basis of this line of reasoning turns out to be the argument that Marxist analysis can, and should ignore the quantitative relationship. On the one hand, this argument gets much of its impetus from the persistent, and to some extent, damaging attacks on the "transformation from values to prices"; and on the other, it derives much of its appeal from a reaction against the obvious banality of neoclassical economics, in which relative prices figure so prominently. Nonetheless, the argument is simply untenable, for it is based on an *unspoken* conception about scientific analysis which when made explicit is quite unsupportable: namely, that as a science, the Marxist analysis of capitalism can simply choose to ignore the quantitative aspects of any phenomena, once it has understood the qualitative aspects. Marx himself had a higher opinion of his work:

> Considering what this third book treats, it cannot confine itself to general reflection relative to this synthesis. On the contrary, it must locate and describe the concrete forms . . . The various forms of capital, as evolved in this book, thus approach step by step the form which they assume on the surface of society, in the action of different capitals upon one another, in competition, and in the ordinary consciousness of the agents of production themselves. (*Capital*,* Volume III, Part I, Ch. I, p. 25)

Unfortunately not many Marxists today seem willing to accompany Marx all the way in his arduous journey; and of those that do, even fewer appear to be interested in pulling together and extending, where necessary, the sometimes incomplete analysis of Volume III. The labyrinths of the turnover of capital in Volume II, the "petty detail" of the endless tables of differential rent in Volume III, and certainly the unending controversy about the "transformation problem" must all seem so very tedious, perhaps even dangerously confusing, to those who remain content to bask in the brilliance of Volume I.[6] But Marx at least did not find in the difficulty of a subject a sufficient reason for avoiding it:

> That is a disadvantage I am powerless to overcome, unless it be by forewarning and forearming those readers who zealously seek the truth. There is no royal road to science, and only those who do not dread the fatiguing climb of its steep paths have a chance of gaining its luminous summits. (*Capital*, Volume I, "Preface to the French Edition," p. 21)

II. VALUE AND PRICE

1. Calculation versus Conception

I have, up to now, confined myself to a discussion of the so-called "transformation problem" and of various attitudes toward it. It is, however, a major purpose of this paper to demonstrate that one can, *precisely in the manner set out by Marx*, calculate the "correct prices of production" from values. The link between the two, one so obvious that until recently it seems to have been completely overlooked,** is simply that while Marx's procedure is a perfectly general one, it is only the first step in an iterative transformation from "direct-prices" to "prices of production." But while this extension of Marx's procedure does falsify the so-called "impossibility theorems" on it (most recently voiced by Paul Samuelson), it by no means establishes the need for such a transformation in the first place. As has often been pointed out, "prices of production" can instead be calculated directly from the same "economic data" as "direct-prices." The difference between the two methods of calculation therefore lies not in the end point but in the beginning; that is, it lies not in the magnitude of "prices of production" but in their meaning, in their conception. To reduce the issue of the transformation to one of merely calculation, is simply to reduce Marx to neoclassical economics. And, as I pointed out earlier, the impossibility of such a

---

*All quotes from *Capital* refer to the International Publishers edition, New York, 1967.
**The transformation procedure contained in this paper was first presented in a paper delivered to the Graduate Economics Department of Yale University, February 1973. A similar result was presented by Michio Morishima in "Marx in the Light of Modern Economic Theory: An Inaugural Lecture," London School of Economics, November 1973.

reduction can only "show up" as a "redundancy" in *Marx:* after all, if both methods arrive at the same end point, why bother with Marx's needless "detour" through values?

The question may be put more precisely: in what way is Marx's analysis of value different from that of orthodox economics? What sorts of issues, conceptions, and calculations are specific to it alone? What laws does Marx derive from it which cannot be derived from conventional economic analysis? Unless we make an attempt to answer these questions, any discussion of the "transformation" issue is quite irrelevant: without a proper understanding of the concept of value as it appears in Marx, it is pointless to try and analyze the so-called "transformation from values to prices of production." The discussion of the actual transformation algorithm is therefore postponed until Section III. In this section we must establish its raison d'etre.

2. Basic Method

> Whatever the social form of production, labourers and means of production always remain elements of it. But in a state of separation from each other either of these factors can be such only potentially. For production to go on they must unite. The specific manner in which this union is accomplished distinguishes the different economic epochs of the structure of society from one another. (*Capital,* Vol. II, Ch. I, Section I, p. 34.)

> The specific economic form, in which unpaid surplus-labour is pumped out of direct producers, determines the relationship of rulers and ruled, as it grows out of production itself and, in turn, reacts upon it as a determining element. Upon this, however, is founded the entire formation of the economic community which grows up out of the production relations themselves, thereby simultaneously its specific political form. It is always the direct relationship of the owners of the conditions of production to the direct producers . . . which reveals the innermost secret, the hidden basis of the entire social structure and with it the political form of the relation of sovereignty and dependence, in short, the corresponding specific form of the state. (*Capital,* Vol. III, Ch. XLVII, Section II, p. 791.)

The preceding quotes present a crucial element of the Marxist approach to history: namely, that the specific manner in which production is organized, and surplus-labor extracted from the direct producers, forms the "hidden basis of the entire social structure." For Marx, it follows from this that the concepts adequate to the analysis of any specific historical epoch, including that of capitalism, must necessarily be based on these aspects of its social practice. The struggle for production is the fundamental social practice in all human society; hence the analysis of production is the beginning point of Marxist analysis. The extraction of surplus-labor is the basis of all class societies; hence its study is the source of the concepts adequate to an analysis of all class societies. *Capital* is Marx's application of this approach to the analysis of capitalism.

3. The Production of Commodities

One very important aspect of the social process in which laborers and means of production are united in the *capitalist* mode of production, as opposed to all others, is that under the capitalist mode the overriding aim of production is not production-for-direct-social-use but production-for-exchange. In the caste system of India, for example, the social regulation of productive activity is made starkly visible by the existence of hereditary castes whose members can, and in fact must, perform only those concrete types of labor which are required of their caste. Production is, in this society, production-for-direct-social-use (whatever we may think of that use); distribution of the products of labor is similarly directly regulated.

But in capitalism, we have commodity production. What turns a product (something which is produced) into a commodity (something which is bought and sold) is a specific set of social structures which organize the productive activities (the labor) of society around production-for-exchange. In commodity production, production necessarily implies exchange; exchange is a necessary step in the process of *re*production. Society is organized in such a way that there is no *direct* social regulation of productivity activity: during production people act as individuals, relating only to their products; it is in exchange, therefore, that the true social nature of their existence is forcibly demonstrated to them through the relation of their commodities to those of others. Exchange, so to speak, is a "symptom" of commodity production, and its real limits can only be understood by relating exchange to its "hidden basis"—i.e., to production. It follows, therefore, that in a Marxist analysis the derivation of the categories of exchange, such as money and price, as well as their movements, must necessarily be based on the categories of production. Taken by itself, as an eternal category divorced from any particular type of production, exchange appears to be a smooth, static, inherently equilibrating process: witness the parables of neoclassical economics. Circulation is, to all appearances and purposes, the sphere of freedom, equality and equilibrium. But for Marx, circulation is precisely the sphere in which the contradictions inherent in the production of commodities are "both exposed and resolved";[7] the manner in which these contradictions in production dominate exchange, both qualitatively and quantitatively, is what Marx means by the law of value: "in the midst of all the accidental and ever fluctuating exchange-relations between the products, the labour-time necessary for their production forcibly asserts itself like an overriding law of Nature."[8]

4. Exchange-Value and Value

In all production, concrete (i.e., specific) types of labor and concrete inputs result in a concrete product. Moreover, since the produced inputs themselves must be the products of past labor, we may say that in all production, including commodity production, concrete products are the results of concrete labors, in a given natural context.[9] But commodity production (the production of goods-for-exchange) necessarily implies exchange; and in exchange the distinct qualities which give various commodities their "concreteness" are abstracted from. In exchange, what matters is not the physical properties of iron but how much wheat, or cloth, or coffee, etc., we can get for the iron; hence in exchange we treat every commodity not as a concrete bundle of distinctive qualities, but as the equivalent of specific *quantities* of all other commodities.

Precisely because exchange is a social process which quantitatively compares and equates different products, it is only in those societies which produce for exchange that the product of human labor acquires the property of "quantitative worth." In addition to being useful, they are now also "valuable": they are commodities.

We have to get a little more exact in our terminology at this point. In conventional usage (and with some classical economists), the term "value" sometimes refers to the notion of a useful object, and at other times to the notion of the "quantitative worth" of an object. In order to avoid confusion, therefore, Marx uses the term *use-value* to mean useful object, and the term *exchange-value* to mean the quantitative "worth" of an object. In Marx's terminology, therefore, a commodity is both a use-value and an exchange-value.

It is usually not difficult to explain what is meant by a useful object.* But when we say that a commodity is "worth" something just what is implied? Suppose I say that in barter a bushel of corn is "worth" a ton of iron, and also a yard of silk, and an ounce of gold, and so on. At first glance, what I appear to be saying is that there are many different quantitative expressions for the "worth" of a bushel of corn, depending on which other commodity (iron, silk or gold) I choose to *measure* it by.

But there is a deeper problem here. In order for me to measure the "worth" of corn in terms of gold, for instance, gold must also be "worth" something itself. Otherwise I cannot say how much gold is equivalent to a bushel of corn. It is just like my saying that a stone "weighs" ten grams; what I mean is that on a scale it takes ten pieces of iron called gram-weights to equal the weight of the stone. But clearly, in order for me to carry out this operation, both stone and iron must already possess the property of being "heavy," of having "weight"; the gram-weights don't make stones "heavy," they only measure the already existing heaviness of stones.

Exactly the same conclusion applies to "quantitative worth." The factors which cause commodities to have "quantitative worth" in the first place must be carefully distinguished from the measurement of this "worth." Measuring the "worth" of corn in iron will give a different result from measuring it in gold; but neither measure causes corn to have "quantitative worth." Rather, each merely expresses the preexisting "worth" of corn in terms of some particular commodity.

The question of exchange-value ("quantitative worth") is therefore really a twofold one: first, what is the cause of "quantitative worth"; and second, how is this "worth" actually expressed, measured, in exchange?

If we look at society as a regularly reproduced set of social relations, it becomes very clear that the production and reproduction of the masses of useful objects which correspond to various social needs requires a definite, quantitative distribution of social labor. Each different useful product requires a concretely different type of labor; reproduction of the material basis of the society consequently requires the existence and reproduction of appropriate amounts

*The apparent simplicity of the term useful object or use-value is misleading. Many Marxists, for instance, confuse it with physical object, i.e., a good as opposed to a service. This is definitely *not* the sense in which Marx uses the term use-value.

of different concrete labors. That is to say, social labor from the point of view of its capacity to produce different use-values is what Marx calls social labor in its role as *concrete* labor.[10]

A commodity, however, is more than a mere use-value; it is at the same time an exchange-value, an object possessing "quantitative worth." It follows from this that the very same social relations which endow use-values with the property of "quantitative worth," endow the labor which produces these use-values with the capacity to create "quantitative worth." From this point of view, all commodity producing labor is qualitatively alike and quantitatively comparable: it is what Marx calls "(commodity producing) social labor in its capacity as *abstract* labor."[11]

Therefore, to the question on the cause of exchange-value, Marx's answer is: abstract labor, i.e., labor actually engaged in commodity production, is the cause of exchange-value.[12] Moreover, if we consider the production of a commodity from the point of view of the whole society, it becomes apparent that the commodity's exchange-value represents the total amount of abstract labor-time socially necessary[13] for its production, both directly (in the process of producing the commodity from its material inputs) and indirectly (in the process of producing the material inputs themselves, and the inputs of the inputs, and so on). Marx consequently refers to this total sum of abstract labor-time as the *immanent measure* of a commodity's exchange-value, what he calls its "Value."[14]

The discerning reader will have noticed that I have capitalized the term Value. This is done in order to emphasize the distinctiveness of Marx's use of the term, and especially to avoid confusing it with the term "value" in orthodox economics (where it generally refers to a price of some sort).

It should also be noted here that the Value of a commodity is the *average* amount of abstract labor-time required for its production. The total output of a particular commodity represents* the expenditure of a certain amount of abstract labor-time which under existing conditions is required for its production. In exchange, however, all commodities of a given type are treated alike; each commodity is merely "an average sample of its class,"[15] and as such represents the average expenditure of abstract labor-time.[16]

In order to avoid confusion later on, I will distinguish between the *sum of Values* (the abstract labor-time required to produce the total social product**), the *total Value* of a given branch of production (the Value of its total output),[17] and the *unit Value* of a single commodity (the average Value in the sense defined above). All terms are defined over a given period of time.

*The term "represents" is used here rather than the more common term "embodied." It is clear in Marx, for instance, that it is not the historical cost of a commodity in labor-time, but rather its current cost of reproduction, which determines the magnitude of a commodity's Value. (*Capital*, Vol. I, Ch. 1, p. 39). As such, it is not a question of the labor-time "embodied" in a commodity but of the social cost which the current production of the commodity entails.

**I refer here only to the total *commodity* product. Use-values produced for direct use are not treated here, in spite of their great importance in concrete analyses of actual capitalist societies. Marx himself distinguishes between social *capital* and social *wealth* "of which capital is only a part." (Marx, *Capital*, Vol. II, Ch. x, p. 200).

5. Money and Price

We turn now to the second aspect of exchange-value: how is "quantitative worth" actually expressed in exchange? To this Marx answers: in exchange, the "quantitative worth" of a commodity *must* take the form of money-price. Since exchange is the interchange of two commodities, at first glance it seems obvious that there are as many measures of a commodity's worth as there are other commodities to measure it by. And historically, where exchange is sporadic or irregular, this is in fact true. But as exchange spreads and develops, this variety of different possible measures increasingly becomes a barrier to the smooth functioning of the process; without a point of reference, the direct comparison of every commodity with every other becomes impossibly complex. Consequently it becomes increasingly necessary to socially recognize a given commodity out of those available as the one commodity in which all others are to express their "worth"; this special commodity therefore becomes the universal equivalent, the money-commodity. We will henceforth assume it is gold.*

Notice that money does not by itself cause commodities to have "worth," any more than gram-weights cause stones to have weight. On the contrary, it is only because both gold and the other commodities have "quantitative worth" (exchange-value) in the first place that we can express their worth of commodities in terms of gold. The money-price of a commodity is the "golden" reflection, the external measure, of its exchange-value. It is what Marx calls the *form* taken by Value during exchange.[18]

6. Production and Circulation

The foregoing analysis has focussed on the difference between Value and money-price. Implicit in this distinction, however, is another equally important one: the Marxian distinction between the production of commodities and their circulation.

Production, Marx notes, is the creation or transformation of a use-value.[19] Insofar as the product is a commodity, it belongs to some individual; it enters circulation, therefore, as private property.

Consider the case of two commodity producers, a fisherman and a hunter. They bring definite quantities of fish and game, respectively, to the market for the purpose of exchange; commodities with definite Values representing definite quantities of abstract labor-time thus enter the market-place.

Now what happens in exchange? In the exchange process the two commodity producers negotiate terms under which they will *transfer the titles* to their respective commodity property.[20] But note: the time they spend bargaining over these terms of trade will in no way increase the total amount of fish or game to be had; it will determine only the final pattern of distribution.[21] In fact, insofar as they need to subsist during the actual process of exchange itself, their

---

*It is beyond the scope of this paper to discuss the different forms of money such as token money (metallic and paper tokens of gold and silver) and credit money. In any case, this extension of the analysis cannot be attempted without first resolving it satisfactorily in the simplest case—that of pure gold-money.

costs of circulation, costs of exchange, could appear only as a deduction from the total production and value-creation of both of them. If they commissioned a third [person to perform] these exchanges, and thus lost no labour time directly, then each of them would have to cede a proportional share of his product to [that third person]. . . .

Circulation costs as such, i.e. consumption of labour time or of objectified labour time, of values, in connection with the operation of exchange . . ., are therefore a deduction either from the time employed on production, or from the values posited by production. *They can never increase the value.* They belong among . . . the inherent costs of production resting on capital. (Marx, *Grundrisse*, Notebook VI, pp. 632–633. Emphasis added)

This is a very important point in Marx's analysis. The circulation process is the process whereby commodities change hands, where their titles of ownership are transferred. As such, no commodities and hence *no Value is created in the circulation process.*[22] If anything, part of the previously produced mass of commodities (and hence the Value previously created in production) may be used up just in the struggle over its distribution.

One immediate implication of this is that the categories of circulation are thereby limited by those of production.* Value is created in production, materialized in commodities; *regardless of the actual money prices at which these commodities are sold,* only the same mass of commodities (and hence the same amount of Value) exists after the sales as before. Different price relations will therefore give rise to different distributions of the total commodity-product, and of the total sum of Values, but they cannot by themselves change these totals. It is on this basis that Marx argues:

If commodities are sold at their values, then the magnitude of value in the hands of the buyer and seller remains unchanged. Only the form of existence of value is changed. If the commodities are not sold at their values, then the sum of converted values remains unchanged; the plus on one side is a minus on the other. (Marx, *Capital,* Volume II, Ch. VI, Section 1.1, p. 129)

7. The Importance of Prices

In commodity producing societies the object of production is not direct use, but personal gain through exchange. Individuals produce without any apparent social regulation. Nonetheless, they too exist within a social structure. For each individual to be able to specialize in producing for exchange, others must do so too; for exchange to proceed without rupture, the various products must correspond to the various social needs. Since under this form of social organization the correspondence between the various social needs and the distribution of social

---

*Another implication is that not all labor-time, even if it stems from wage labor employed by capitalists, leads to the creation of Value. This has been a perennial topic of discussion in Marxist literature under the heading of productive and unproductive labor. Though we cannot treat it here, it is important to note that it arises from the distinctive character of the Marxian concept of Value.

labor required to satisfy these needs cannot be brought about directly, it must be done indirectly. What in other societies is a direct evaluation of the importance of a particular type of labor in terms of its concrete product, becomes in commodity producing societies the indirect evaluation of this labor—through the "quantitative worth" of its product. It is only in exchange that the true social nature of commodity production is made apparent; and precisely because commodity production is undertaken for personal gain, for the money which is to be made, *it is the money-prices of commodities that serve as the immediate regulating mechanism of the system.* Far from being a "veil," money constitutes a very important feedback mechanism.

It follows from the above that the laws which determine money magnitudes such as prices, profits, and wages, are of the utmost importance in understanding the laws of motion in capitalism.*

Now of course it was known well before Marx's time that supply and demand were the immediate determinants of actual market phenomena. But even classical political economy was aware that over the course of time the ceaselessly fluctuating interplay of supply and demand was itself regulated by a much more fundamental principle: the Law of Equal Profitability.

For instance, if as a result of market conditions a particular sector's rate of profit rose above the average rate, then the flow of capital would tend to be biased towards that sector, causing it to grow more rapidly than demand, and driving down its market price to a level consistent with average profitability. Conversely, the sectors with low profitability would tend to grow less rapidly than demand, causing their prices and profitability to rise.

The classical economists were thus able to demonstrate that behind the continuously varying constellation of market prices there lay another set of prices, acting as "centers of gravity" of market prices and embodying more or less equal rates of profit. The name given to these regulating prices in classical political economy was natural prices; Marx calls them prices of production. Their discovery was the first great law of prices.

By David Ricardo's time, the problem had moved on to a higher level. What Ricardo sought to do, for instance, was to go one step further and look behind prices of production themselves, to discover *their* "centers of gravity." That is, just as the market price of a commodity was shown to be regulated by its price of production, Ricardo sought to show that this regulating price was itself subject to a hidden regulator—the total quantity of labor time required to produce the commodity, both in its direct production and in the production of its means of production.

> In speaking . . . of the exchangeable value of commodities, or the power of purchasing possessed by any one commodity, I mean always that power which . . . is natural price. (D. Ricardo, 1962, p. 92)

---

*The problem that Marx set himself in *Capital* was to "lay bare the economic law of motion of modern society."[23] But why this task? Because he knew only too well that in *order to change the world it is necessary to first understand it.* In particular, he knew that without an adequate understanding of how the capitalist system operates, of the manner in which its underlying contradictions give rise to the phenomena of regular and violent crises, of increasing wealth alongside increasing misery, of rising productivity which leads to falling profitability, and many others—without an adequate understanding of these *laws* of capitalism, attempts to change it would be doomed to failure.

> The great cause of the variation in the relative value of commodities is the increase or diminution in the quantity of labour required to produce them. (*Ibid.*, p. 36)

There we have it: the *great* cause of the variations in the (relative) price of production of a commodity is the variations in the total labor time that goes, directly or indirectly, into its production. The total quantity of labor time was the center of gravity of the commodity's price of production, just as this price of production was itself the center of gravity of its market price. This was Ricardo's attempt to formulate a second great law of prices.

What Ricardo perceived was that there was an intrinsic connection between the "quantitative worth," the exchange-value, of commodities, and the total labor-time required for their production.[24] This, according to Marx, was Ricardo's great scientific merit.[25] But at the same time Ricardo was trapped by the conceptual framework of bourgeois political economy, which saw all production as being alike. He was consequently unable to distinguish concrete labor, an aspect of all social production, from abstract labor, an aspect which only commodity producing labor takes on. Ricardo therefore misses the difference between Value and the form of Value. Instead of recognizing price as the manner in which the exchange process reflects Value, and developing the various intermediary links between the two, he attempts instead to fuse them together through his law of prices. His failure to adequately distinguish between Value and price is, according to Marx, the first great source of error in his analysis.[26]

In addition to that, however, there is another problem. How can Ricardo attempt to analyze the effects of a uniform rate of profit on prices, asks Marx, when he nowhere discusses what determines the *level* of this rate of profit? And this in turn leads to an even more basic question. A uniform rate of profit is simply a way of saying that profits on different capitals are proportional to the size of these capitals: that is, each capital gets a share of total profit in proportion to its own size. But Ricardo nowhere discusses what determines aggregate profit in the first place. How then can he attempt to isolate the factors which regulate the movements of prices of production when he is missing a crucial ingredient—profit?

It is therefore apparent to Marx that even given the relation between Value and money price which he himself derives,[27] the specific manner in which Value regulates price cannot be developed without first showing how profit arises. And this, as we shall see next, leads Marx to the concept of surplus-Value.

III. SURPLUS-VALUE AND PROFIT

1. The Circulation of Money and the Circulation of Capital

We have up to now focused on the relationship of the circulation of commodities to their production; on the basis of this we were able to derive the categories of Value, money, and price, and discuss their mutual interrelationship. But the very existence of the circulation of commodities within a capitalist mode of production immediately implies that, for those who function as capitalists, the process of circulation is itself a means to realizing a profit: where then does the profit of the capitalist class as a *whole* come from?

Marx begins by noting that once we consider commodity production within the context of capitalist production, the overall process of circulation is in reality two different processes with different functions and hence different laws. In the first process, the owners of commodities (CC) exchange them for money (M) in order to be able to use this money to buy other commodities (CC) for the purpose of consumption.* This circuit in the overall circulation process therefore has the form $CC \rightarrow M \rightarrow CC$, and is the aggregate of the exchanges of one set of commodities for what is, under the existing conditions of exchange, an equivalent set. In this process money is an intermediary between two sets of commodities; once acquired it is spent, and for the individuals involved in it, the process terminates in consumption. Marx calls this "selling in order to buy";[28] in it, money functions as money only.

In the second circuit, however, the owners of money (M) exchange it for commodities (CC) in order to get more money ($M = M + \Delta M$), i.e., in order to make a profit ΔM. Money here is not spent, it is merely *advanced* in order to make more money, through the intervention of commodities. The process of $M \rightarrow CC \rightarrow M'$ tends to be self-perpetuating, since it can always lead into $M' \rightarrow CC \rightarrow M''$, etc. The initiators of this process function as capitalists: $M \rightarrow CC \rightarrow M'$ "is therefore in reality the general formula of capital as it appears prima facie within the sphere of circulation."[29] Marx calls this second process "buying in order to sell";[30] in it, money functions as *capital*. It makes a profit. But how is it possible to make money by merely advancing money?

2. Surplus-Value

The first step in the solution to the problem of profit is to recognize that it is not simply a question of money. Money, after all, represents a command over actual commodities, and hence over the actual labor-time materialized in them. If therefore in the circuit $M \rightarrow CC \rightarrow M + \Delta M$, the profit of the capitalist class (ΔM) is to be something more than a monetary illusion, if it is to represent a potential increment in their real wealth, then *their money profit ΔM must itself be matched by an actual increment in the commodities available, and hence in materialized labor-time.* That is, ΔM must be matched by an increment in the total Value of the commodities represented by CC. This increment in Value necessary for any real profit, Marx calls surplus-Value.

3. Constant Capital

Ostensibly, the process of the formation of capital, as represented by $M \rightarrow CC \rightarrow M'$, is a process occurring wholly within circulation. But Value is itself a result of production; it cannot be created in circulation, and hence neither can the necessary increment in Value, surplus-Value. Surplus-Value, if it is possible at all, can only arise from production. And indeed, if we examine $M \rightarrow CC \rightarrow M'$ more carefully, we find that the first stage involves the purchase of human and nonhuman inputs required for production, whereas the final stage involves the sale of the outputs of production. The commodities purchased as inputs and the commodities sold as outputs are in fact not the same, and it is the intervention of *production* which distinguishes them. The formation of capital, which appears to exist solely within circulation, in reality encompasses a process of production; properly speaking, it should be represented by $M \rightarrow CC \ldots P \ldots CC' \rightarrow M'$, with the stage $CC \ldots P \ldots CC'$ representing the effect of production. Not just production or even just commodity production but, as we shall see, capitalist commodity production.

Means of production and laborers combine in all production. But in commodity production, the means of production are themselves commodities, and as such represent, in their total Value, the quantity of abstract labor-time that was socially necessary for their own production. If we examine the process of production over a period of time sufficiently long so that even the most durable means of production are entirely used up, then it becomes clear that the Value of the means of production must become incorporated into the commodities produced over this period. The bodily forms of the means of production either wear out (as with machines) or are physically incorporated into the product (as with raw materials); but precisely because these means of production are socially necessary under existing conditions, the abstract labor-time represented by them is also (indirectly) socially necessary for the production of the commodities. It is a necessary component of the total Value of the product. From the point of view of Value, therefore, the means of production only contribute as much Value as they actually contain. As such they cannot be the source of the increment in Value upon which any nonillusory aggregate profit must be based; Marx therefore calls the capital advanced in the form of the means of production "constant capital."

4. The Value of Labor-Power

The formation of capital, the process represented by $M \rightarrow CC \ldots P \ldots CC' \rightarrow M'$, presupposes not just commodity production but capitalist commodity production. And under capitalist commodity production, not only are the products of labor bought and sold as commodities, but so too is the very capacity-to-labor itself.

This capacity-to-labor, which Marx calls labor-power, is "the aggregate of those mental and physical capabilities existing in a human being, which he exercises whenever he produces a use-value of any description."[31] In all societies, it is the basis of the productive activities of human beings; but for this fundamental human property to become a thing to be bought and sold, a commodity, it must exist within a specific social context. Not only must the laborer have the legal title to his labor-power, he must also be obliged to sell it and not other commodities. He must be free not only to dispose of his own labor-power as a commodity, but also "free" of the means of production which might enable him to be a producer of other commodities. He must be a wage-laborer.

The Value of the commodity labor-power, like that of every other commodity, is determined by the abstract labor-time socially necessary for its production under existing conditions. Since labor-power is a capacity of living beings, its production implies their continued maintenance and reproduction; hence it implies a given quantity of commodities as means of subsistence,

---

*Marx uses the symbol C to represent commodities (as in $M \rightarrow C \rightarrow M'$) and also to represent constant capital (as in $C + V$). In order to avoid any possible misunderstanding, I will use "CC" for the former and "C" for the latter.

sufficient not only to maintain laborers in their normal state as laborers but also sufficient to support their families so that they may as a class continue to perpetuate themselves.* The Value of the means of subsistence of the total work-force is therefore the abstract labor-time socially necessary for their maintenance and reproduction, and hence is the measure of the Value of their labor-power (V).

When a capitalist purchases the commodity labor-power, he purchases the capacity-to-labor of workers, and in order to utilize this commodity he must extract as much labor-time from these workers as he can. The concrete functions that workers perform in their productive activities involves the transformation of the means of production into specific commodities; as such, the time spent by workers in these activities is itself a quantity of socially necessary abstract labor-time (L), which is in effect incorporated into the commodities. From the social perspective of Value, therefore, workers add a quantity of Value (L) to the Value (C) contained in the means of production they use up.

5. Surplus Labor-Time

Capitalist production begins with the commodities CC, means of production and labor-power; as commodities they represent a definite quantity of Value, $C + V$. In a period of time sufficiently long, the entire Value C of the means of production will be *transferred* to the product. On the other hand, the Value V of labor-power employed in this period is *replaced* with the Value added to L by workers in the form of the amount of labor-time they actually spend in production. Thus while the Value of the initial commodities is $C + V$, the Value of the final product is $C + L$. The formation of capital, which we have represented as $M \rightarrow CC \ldots P \ldots CC' \rightarrow M + \Delta M$, can therefore also be represented by $M \rightarrow (C + V) \ldots P \ldots (C + L) \rightarrow M + \Delta M$. Clearly, *surplus-Value, the Value increment $S = (C + L) - (C + V) = L - V$ which is necessary to match the money increment ΔM can arise if and only if the labor-time (L) put in by workers is greater than the labor-time (V) socially necessary for their reproduction.*

The same result can be derived differently. Imagine for a moment that at any given level of technology, workers in all branches of production work just long enough to produce the commodities necessary for the needs of the working class as a whole and to replace the means of production they use up in this process. Under these circumstances, no matter how "advanced" the technology, there can exist no social surplus, and hence no basis for capitalist profit. If, and only if, workers can and actually do work longer than the time necessary to maintain themselves and the means of production, will there arise a continuing social surplus; the time spent by workers in producing this surplus, their surplus labor-time, is therefore the real basis of capitalist profit. And of course since the

*As in the case of every other commodity, the value of labor-power is given by the average labor-time required to produce the average quantity of means of subsistence of the average labor-power, under existing conditions. But for simple, *unskilled* labor-power, these existing conditions are themselves "the product of historical development, and depend therefore to a great extent on the degree of civilization of a country. . . . In contradistinction therefore to the case of other commodities, there enters into the determination of the value of labour power a historical and moral element. Nevertheless, in a given country, at a given period, the average quantity of the means of subsistence necessary for the labourer is practically known." (Marx, *Capital*, Vol. I, Ch. VI, p. 171).

The issue of skills requires further treatment which cannot be undertaken here. See instead Shaikh [19], Rowthorn [16].

necessary labor-time described above is none other than the aggregate value of labor-power V, the surplus labor-time is none other than aggregate surplus-Value S.[32] Once again we see that surplus-Value is the "hidden basis" of any real capitalist profit.

None of this, by the way, implies that Marx intended the labor theory of value as a theory of property rights, à la Locke or even Proudhon. Marx's goal was a scientific analysis of capitalism, not a mere moral critique.[33]

IV. THE TRANSFORMATION FROM DIRECT PRICES TO PRICES OF PRODUCTION

1. Exchange at Values: Direct Prices

In the Marxist conception of exchange-as-the-circulation-of-commodities, the total labor-time materialized in commodities during their production is the basis for their exchange-value and money-price, while the surplus labor-time materialized in them is the basis of the capitalist profit to be realized from their sale. Without a proper understanding of the quantitative and qualitative relationships between the sphere of production and the sphere of circulation, of the *limits* imposed on circulation by production, the laws of circulation must remain a mystery. Neoclassical economics is a testament to this.

For Marx, it was absolutely critical that the dominance of production over circulation be properly understood. It is in production that capitalist wealth is created and expanded, and Value and surplus-Value are materialized in commodities. Circulation, as we have seen, is the process whereby the previously created use-values are transferred from one hand to another, by means of money-prices.

Two things follow from this. First of all, it is in circulation that the Value magnitudes take their money-forms: Value takes the form of money-price, surplus-Value the form of money-profit; and secondly, neither Value nor surplus-Value are created in circulation, precisely because in this process commodities are merely exchanged, not created. This means that regardless of the actual money-prices involved, there can be no *real* increase in capitalist wealth through circulation.

It is obvious that the most direct way to explore the production and expansion of capitalist wealth is to assume that exchange takes place in proportion to the Values of commodities, so that the money-price of every commodity is equal to its Value relative to the Value of the unit of money (say one ounce of gold). I will henceforth call prices so determined *"direct prices."*

When indeed the analysis is begun this way, as Marx does in Volumes I and II of *Capital*, it becomes clear that none of the basic categories of capitalist circulation, the categories of capital and labor, money and price, and wages and profits, owe their existence to any *deviations* of relative prices from relative Values.

> The conversion of money into capital has to be explained on the basis of the laws that regulate the exchange of commodities, in such a way that the starting-point is the exchange of equivalents . . . the formation of capital must be possible even though the price and value of a commodity

be the same; for its formation cannot be attributed to any deviation of the one from the other. If prices actually differ from values, we must, first of all, reduce the former to the latter, in other words, treat the difference as accidental in order that the phenomena may be observed in their purity, and our observations not be interfered with by disturbing circumstances that have nothing to do with the process in question. (*Capital*, Vol. I, Ch. V, p. 166, text and footnote 1.)

2. The Conceptual Basis for Prices of Production

There is yet another reason for beginning with direct prices (exchange at values): the major *systematic* deviation of relative prices from relative Values arises when commodities exchange at "prices of production." But prices of production are prices which reflect a general rate of profit; and a general rate of profit in turn presupposes the existence of profits. Prior to any question about the formation of a general rate, therefore, is the question about the source of profit.[34] This question leads Marx to surplus labor-time and hence to surplus-Value, and once again the analysis comes to Value.

The path from Value back to price of production involves two major steps. First, one must examine and understand prices and profits in general; this was done through the analysis of the relationship of production to circulation, and of the relationship of Value to money. Second, since prices of production must reflect a general rate of profit, one is led to an analysis of the formation of this general rate out of the individual rates of profit in each sector of production. We turn to this now.

Let us recall that the general process for the formation of capital could be written as $M \rightarrow C + V \ldots P \ldots C + L \rightarrow M'$, where M is the money price of commodity inputs into production: the means of production having the Value C and labor-power having the Value V. M', on the other hand, is the money price of the commodity outputs of production; their total Value is $C + L$. By definition, $S = L - V$.

In money terms, the general money rate of profit is $r = (M' - M)/M$, the aggregate profit $M' - M$ divided by the capital advanced M. In terms of Value, the general *Value* rate of profit is $\rho = S/(C + V)$, the aggregate surplus-Value S divided by $C + V$, the Value of the inputs. Obviously, if prices are proportional to Values, then the general money rate of profit must equal the general Value rate of profit: $r = \rho$.

We now consider two individual circuits of capital involving sectors of production I and J, as represented by $M_i \rightarrow (C_i + V_i) \ldots P \ldots (C_i + L_i) \rightarrow M_i'$ and $M_j \rightarrow (C_j + V_j) \ldots P \ldots (C_j + L_j) \rightarrow M_j'$, respectively. If prices are proportional to Values, then in each sector the sectoral Value and money rates of profit are the same. We need therefore deal only with the Value rates $\rho_i = S_i/(C_i + V_i)$ and $\rho_j = S_j/(C_j + V_j)$.

The first question we must then ask is: are these two Value rates ρ_i and ρ_j generally equal? For *if* they were, then at prices proportional to Values each sector would have the same money and value rates of profit, and no movement of prices would be necessary to equalize the individual rates of profit. To facilitate the answer, Marx rewrites each expression for the value rate of profit by

dividing both the numerator and denominator of each fraction by the Value of labor-power V:

$$\rho_i = \frac{S_i}{V_i} \left| \frac{C_i + V_i}{V_i} \right. \quad \text{and} \quad \rho_j = \frac{S_j}{V_j} \left| \frac{C_j + V_j}{V_j} \right.$$

Each Value rate of profit is therefore itself the ratio of two component ratios: S/V, which Marx calls the rate of surplus-Value, and $(C + V)/V$, which he calls the organic composition of capital. We will deal with each in turn.

A. The Equality of Rates of Surplus-Value

For society as a whole in any given period, the productive activities of workers may be viewed as a certain aggregate quantity of labor-time L. But the very fact that the concrete labor-times of different workers can be added together requires that they have already in some way been made qualitatively equal, that they have been reduced to quantities of some *general* social labor-time, what Marx calls "abstract" labor-time. This reduction of concrete labor-times to abstract labor-time is of course a consequence of generalized commodity production, as discussed in the section on Value (II.4); for our purposes, what is important in this is that it implies that the labor-time of each worker represents a definite quantity of abstract labor-time.[35]

Of the aggregate labor-time L, a certain portion V represents the time socially necessary for the production of the means of subsistence of the working class, and the remainder S, the aggregate surplus labor-time, constitutes the surplus-Value materialized in commodities during their production. If the working day is the same in all branches of production, then each worker adds the same amount of Value to the product, in a given time period (like a day). If the wage rate for a given type of work is the same in all branches, then each worker can purchase the same share of the aggregate means of subsistence; a uniform wage thus represents a given quantity of (abstract) labor-time (say 4 hours a day) which each worker must put in to reproduce the Value of his or her labor-power. Clearly, if the length of the working day (say 10 hours) is indeed the same in all branches, each worker will work the same amount of surplus labor-time (6 hours a day). That is, in each sector, the rates of surplus-Value will necessarily be equal. These rates, therefore, cannot be the source of any differences between the Value rates of profit ρ_i and ρ_j.

B. The Inequality of Organic Compositions of Capital

The above results imply that in any one sector, say sector J, V is an index of the total quantity of labor-time L worked in that sector, since any one hour of abstract labor-time requires the fraction v for its reproduction: $V = vL$. The quantity C, the value of the means of production in this sector, is, on the other hand, an index of the specific types and quantities of commodities which enter into this process of production as means of production. In general, therefore, unless each sector employs the same types of commodities and labor-powers in the same proportions as every other sector, the ratios C_i/L_i and C_j/L_j will differ.

Since V_i and V_j are indexes of L_i and L_j, in general the organic compositions $(C_i + V_i)/V_i$ and $(C_j + V_j)/V_j$ will differ.

To reiterate Marx's conclusion: in general, the sectoral rates of surplus-value will be equal, but the organic compositions of capital will not. Hence in general the value rates of profit will differ from sector to sector.

C. The Deviations of Prices of Production from Direct Prices

Let us now return to the two circuits of capital $M_i \rightarrow (C_i + V_i) \ldots P_i \ldots (C_i + L_i) \rightarrow M_i'$ and $M_j \rightarrow (C_j + V_j) \ldots P_j \ldots (C_j + L_j) \rightarrow M_j'$. We began earlier by noting that if prices were proportional to Values, the money rates of profit $r_i = (M_i' - M_i)/M_i$ and $r_j = (M_j' - M_j)/M_j$ would be equal to the corresponding Value rates of profit $\rho_i = S_i/(C_i + V_i)$ and $\rho_j = S_j/(C_j + V_j)$. If in addition the Value rates of profit were themselves equal to each other, then at direct prices, capital in each circuit would realize the same *money* rate of profit and no movement of prices would be necessary to bring these money rates into line with the general rate.

We have just seen, however, that in general the sectoral rates will differ; if for instance ρ_i was greater than ρ_j, the capital invested in sector I would, with prices proportional to Values, earn a higher money rate of profit than would capital invested in industry J ($r_i = \rho_i > r_j = \rho_j$). *To equalize these money rates, therefore, relative prices would have to deviate from relative values* in such a way as to lower M_i' relative to M_i and to raise M_j' relative to M_j, for only in this way would the higher money rate of profit V_i be reduced and the lower money rate V_j be raised.

In any sector K, M_k' represents the money price of the commodities produced, what I called earlier the sector's total price; M_k, on the other hand, is the money price of the sector's commodity inputs (means of production and labor-power), what Marx calls its (money) cost-price. Since both the total price M_k' and the cost-price M_k are in essence determined by the prices of commodities, any movements of relative prices, including the ones under consideration here, will in general change both M_k' and M_k: the overall price movements necessary for the formation of a general rate can therefore be quite complicated, as Sraffa has so elegantly demonstrated.[36]

Nonetheless, beginning from prices proportional to Values, for any sector I whose Value rate of profit ρ_i is higher than the average Value rate ρ, its total price M_i' must fall relative to its cost-price M_i, in order to bring its money rate of profit r_i into line with the general money rate r. The opposite movement must take place for a Sector J whose Value rate of profit ρ_j is lower than the average Value rate ρ.

Since the differences in the value rates ρ_i and ρ_j upon which these price movements are predicated are themselves a consequence of the differences between sectoral organic compositions of capital, one may equally well say that, beginning from prices proportional to Values, a sector's total price must fall (or rise) relative to its money cost-price according to whether its organic composition of capital is lower (or higher) than the social average, if its particular money rate of profit is to conform to the general rate.

It does not follow from the above, however, that the general *money* rate

of profit will continue to equal the general *Value* rate of profit, once prices deviate from a strict proportionality with Values. To see why, let us recall that M', the aggregate price of commodities, is the total price of the commodities which form the social product. On the other hand, the aggregate cost-price M is the total price of the commodities, the means of production and the labor-power, which form the inputs into the aggregate process of production. Since the price of labor-power is determined by the price of its means of production, the aggregate cost-price M is in effect the total price of the means of production and the means of subsistence.

Suppose the social product was 100 bushels corn and 100 tons iron. M' would be its total price. In general, the aggregate means of production and means of subsistence will also consist of quantities of one or both of these commodities, say 80 bushels corn and 60 tons iron. M would then be their total price. Because these two aggregate "bundles" of commodities will generally differ in their proportions of corn to iron, as is true of the case illustrated above, any movement in the price of corn relative to iron will affect them unequally. Hence *any* movement of relative prices will in general change the ratio M'/M or equivalently, the general rate of profit $r = [(M' - M)/M] = [(M'/M) - 1]$.

The quantity M' is of course the sum of prices, while the quantity $M = M' - M$ is aggregate money profit. The above result may therefore be stated in an equivalent form: in general, *any deviations of relative prices from relative Values, including but not only those which arise from the formation of a general money rate of profit, will make it impossible for both the sum of money prices M' and the sum of money profits M to remain strictly proportional to the sum of Values $C + L$ and the sum of surplus-Values S, respectively.* This result is well known in the debate about the so-called transformation problem; but as it is stated above, it arises in a broader context. In any case, in order to discern its real content, we must examine matters a bit more carefully.

3. Some General Effects of Price-Value Disproportionality

In much of the literature on the "transformation problem," there is a great confusion between Values, prices proportional to Values (what I call direct prices), and prices of production. In particular, since direct prices are so simply related to Values, the general issue of the differences between price and Value, and profit and surplus-Value, tends to be taken up only when we turn to prices of production. All of a sudden, we are confronted with the impossibility of a simple proportionality between Value magnitudes and their money-forms, and it begins to seem as if the analysis of Value is something quite separate from the analysis of price.[37]

For this reason, I have attempted throughout this paper to carefully distinguish between Value, which stems from production, and money-price, which is the form taken by Value in circulation. With this distinction in hand, it is possible to see that money-magnitudes are *always* different, both qualitatively and quantitatively, from Value magnitudes. Marx notes, for instance, that precisely because the form of Value is not the same thing as Value, the determination of money-price is a *complex combination* of its Value elements.

Consider the simplest case, that of direct prices. Suppose the Value of a

gold coin weighing ¼ ounce (which we call a "£")* is ½ worker-hour, while that of a bushel of wheat is 100 worker-hours. The direct price of wheat will then be £200. Even right here, Value (100 hours) and price (£200) are both qualitatively and quantitatively different (though related) magnitudes, with different units.

Now suppose the Value of wheat falls by half, to 50 worker-hours. How will this be reflected in its direct price? Well, says Marx, that depends; if the Value of gold also fell by a half, the money-price of wheat would remain constant at £100; if the Value of gold fell by more than a half, the money-price of wheat would rise even though its Value fell![38] Even in this simple case, therefore, the laws which determine the money-form of Value are more complex than those which determine Value itself. But this is hardly an analytical defect; on the contrary, it is the whole point of theoretical analysis to be able to derive more complex categories from basic ones.

If indeed price and Value are always distinct, what exactly is the "transformation" issue about? Clearly, it is about a *transformation in the form-of-Value*; it is a transformation from the direct expression of Value (direct prices) to a more complex expression (prices of production). What we have to do, therefore, is to see what is altered by this change in form, and what is not.

We begin by noting that what we are considering here is a *pure* change of form. For instance, in the traditional formulation of the transformation we analyze a capitalist society in a simple or extended reproduction, first when exchange is ruled by direct prices, and then when it is ruled by prices of production.** In both cases, the composition and distribution of the use-values is the same: the same mass of commodities is circulated in either case, with the same physical composition of means of subsistence and surplus-product. Thus the same total commodity Value, the same aggregate Value of labor-power, and the same aggregate surplus-Value, is circulated by the two different price-forms. From the point of view of the system as a whole, the transformation leads to no *real* change; all that changes is the manner in which given production relations are manifested in circulation.

From the point of view of individual capitals, however, the situation is indeed different. With direct prices, each capitalist realizes an amount of money equivalent to the surplus-Value contained in the commodities he sells. With prices of production, each sector's money profit is no longer proportional to its surplus-Value; since the sum of Values (and hence the total surplus-Value) circulated is still the same as before, the above change of form has the effect of redistributing surplus-Value from one sphere of production to another.

> The fact that prices diverge from [proportionality with] values cannot, however, exert any influence on the movements of social capital. On the whole, there is the same exchange of products, although the individual

*Originally a "£" represented a pound of silver. Hence the name. Over time, however, while the money-name "£" was retained, the silver or gold content decreased steadily. By Marx's time, a "£" represented roughly 1/3 of a pound of silver, or about ¼ of an ounce of gold (Marx, *Contribution to a Critique . . .* , Ch. II, Sec. 1, p. 72).
**See section IV.4 of this paper, which discusses the calculation of prices of production.

capitalists are involved in value-relations no longer proportional to their respective advances and to the quantities of surplus-value produced singly by everyone of them. (Marx, *Capital*, Volume II, Ch. XX, Section 1, p. 393)

> There is no need to waste words at this point about the fact that if a commodity is sold above or below its value, there is merely another kind of division of surplus-value, and that this different division, this changed proportion in which various persons share in the surplus-value, does not in any way alter either the magnitude or the nature of that surplus-value. (Marx, *Capital*, Volume III, Ch. II, p. 43)

What has been said above in fact applies to any set of prices which differ from direct prices, not just to prices of production. What it shows is that there are *limits* to the effects of different forms of Value, and that these limits arise precisely in the Value magnitudes whose distribution is brought about through these money-forms.

It does not follow from this, however, that the determination of money-prices is of no consequence. Different forms of Value have different *real* effects on individual capitals, and these in turn have different implications for the dynamic process of accumulation and reproduction. It is through the actual movements of money-prices that the system is regulated; as such, the analysis of prices of production (which act as centers of gravity of market prices), and of their relation to Values, is of the utmost importance to concrete analysis. The first step (which in most discussions of the "transformation problem" is the *only* step) along this path is the derivation of prices of production from direct prices.

4. The Calculation of Prices of Production

In general, we may characterize any two circuits of capital as $M_i \to (C_i + V_i) \ldots P_i \ldots (C_i + L_i) \to M_i'$ and $M_j \to (C_j + V_j) \ldots P_j \ldots (C_j + L_j) \to M_j'$.

When exchange is at Values, the money rate of profit in each circuit will equal the Value rate of profit in that circuit. Since Value rates will in general differ from sector to sector, owing to differences in their organic compositions of capital, exchange at Values will imply unequal rates of profit in different sectors, and hence in different circuits of capital.

It follows from the above that the formation of a general rate of profit out of the various individual rates of profit will require that for a sector with a Value rate of profit higher than the social average, the money price of its product M_i' must fall *relative* to its money cost-price M_i, since only this movement will lower its money rate of profit r_i. As we saw earlier in section III.2.C, this *must* hold regardless of how complicated the effects of the formation of a general rate of profit on the overall pattern of prices. And as we shall see immediately, *it is precisely this movement which is captured by Marx's own transformation procedure.*

A. Marx's Transformation Procedure

The example below illustrates the three basic circuits of capital in Marx's analysis: Circuit I represents the production of the means of production themselves,

Circuit II the production of the means of subsistence of the working class, and Circuit III the production of the means of consumption of the capitalist class. The example itself, though from Bortkiewicz, not Marx, is used because it is the standard illustration of the so-called transformation "problem" and appears in most discussions of the issue.

Because we have throughout distinguished between Value and money-price and because the issue at hand centers on differences in their magnitudes, we must be careful with notation. As defined earlier, C_i will represent the value of the means of production of the ith department, V_i the value of the labor-power employed there, and $S_i = L_i - V_i$ the surplus-value produced there; the total value $C_i + L_i$ produced will be designated by W_i. In contrast, MC_i will represent constant capital, the money price of the means of production used in the department, and MV_i variable capital, the money price of the labor-power used there; as before, M_i will be the total cost-price and M_i' the total price of the product. All Value quantities will be in units of (abstract) labor-time, worker-hours, and all money quantities in £'s (¼ ounce gold coins). It is also assumed that each £-coin has a Value of ½ worker-hour.

When exchange is *at* Values, we get the results shown in Table 1. It should be noted that the table has been designed to correspond to the whole circuit of capital, $M \rightarrow (C + V) \ldots P \ldots (C + L) \rightarrow M'$, so that the phases of circulation are clearly distinguished from those of production.

Marx's transformation procedure is simple: noting that in Table 1 the total cost-price $M = £1350$ (column 3) and the total money profit $\Delta M = £400$ (column 10), we get an average rate of profit on social capital of $r = 400/1350 = 29.63\%$.

At existing prices, however, the capital in circuit I, invested in department I, would realize only a 19.05% rate of profit. Thus, in order to raise its money rate of profit to the average level, it must raise its money price. Since its money cost-price is £630, the "normal" profit that it would earn at the average rate of profit is 29.63% of £630, which is £186.67: the level to which it must raise its price therefore is given by $M = £630 + £186.67 = £816.67$. Similarly, department II must lower its money-price to $M = £570.37$, and department III must lower its to $M = £362.96$ (see Table 2).

Table 2 illustrates Marx's transformation procedure. In it, the transformation per se refers to the movements of money-prices, *not* to changes in the Value flows. *Moreover, the direction of movement of money prices M_i' to their corresponding cost-prices M_i is the correct one: M_1' rises relative to its cost-price, and M_2' and M_3' fall relative to theirs.*

B. The "Correct" Prices of Production

From Bohm-Bawerk onwards, critics have argued that Marx's procedure was simply incorrect. They pointed out, for instance, that his transformation leaves the money prices of inputs (MC_i, MV_i) unchanged, whereas a thoroughgoing transformation would change these too. Marxists have countered these charges by claiming that, in any case, one can show the formal possibility of deriving prices of production from direct prices; in the Bortkiewicz method, for example, one can solve for a series of price multipliers which would enable one to trans-

Table 1 / Exchange at Values

$$M \rightarrow (C + V) \ldots P \ldots (C + L) \rightarrow M'$$

	Constant Capital (MC_i)	Variable Capital (MV_i)	Cost-Price (M_i)	Value of Means of Prod. (C_i)	Value of Labor-Power (V_i)	Surplus Value (S_i)	Total Value (W_i)	Value Rate of Profit % (P_i)	Total Price (M_i')	Total Profit (ΔM_i)
(Means of Production)	450	180	630	225	90	60	375	19.05	750	120
(Means of Subsistence)	200	240	440	100	120	80	300	36.36	600	160
(Capitalist Consumption)	100	180	280	50	90	60	200	42.85	400	120
	£750	£600	£1350	375	300	200	875		£1750	£400

Table 2 / Marx's Transformation

$$M \rightarrow (C + V) \ldots P \ldots (C + L) \rightarrow M'$$

Dept.	MC_i	MV_i	M_i	C_i	V_i	(Surplus-Value) S_i	W_i	M_i'	(Money Profit) ΔM_i	(Money Rates of Profit) % r_i
I	450	180	630	225	90	60	375	816.67	186.67	29.63
II	200	240	440	100	120	80	300	570.37	130.37	29.63
III	100	180	280	50	90	60	200	362.96	82.96	29.63
	£750	£600	£1350	375	300	200	875	£1750	£400	

form the exchange-at-Values scheme of Table 1 to the "correct" exchange-at-prices-of-production scheme.[39] Then, depending on whether one prefers the sum of prices or the sum of profits as constant, one can always "normalize" the multipliers derived from the Bortkiewicz method to make one or the other hold, for in general both cannot.

Even if the controversy about the appropriate "normalization," much of which arises from a confusion between Value and money-price, is satisfactorily resolved, the real problem with all of these foregoing transformation procedures remains: they effectively sever the link between Values and money-prices, or at least bury it in algebra, and are forced to reject Marx's own procedure as completely erroneous. Thus for instance in this example, the appropriate algebraic procedure would "jump" us from Table 1, representing exchange at Values, to Table 3 below, which portrays the "correct" price of production scheme under an (algebraically) arbitrary "normalization" which keeps the sum of money-prices (£1750) invariant to the transformation. In all of this, Marx's own transformation, as represented in Table 2, plays no role at all.

Table 3 / The "Correct" Prices of Production

| Dept. | MC_i | MV_i | M_i | $M \rightarrow (C+V) \dots P \dots (C+L) \rightarrow M'$ | | | | | Money Profits | | |
				C_i	V_i	S_i	W_i	M_i	$\triangle M_i$	r_i
I	504	168	672	225	90	60	375	840	168	25%
II	224	224	448	100	120	80	300	560	112	25%
III	112	168	280	50	90	60	200	350	70	25%
	£840	£560	£1400	375	300	200	875	£1750	£350	

C. Marx's Transformation Procedure Extended

Marx himself never goes beyond the transformation procedure he illustrates in Volume III of *Capital*. And yet in several instances, he indicates clearly his awareness of the issue:[40]

> Aside from the fact that the price of a particular product . . . differs from its value . . . the same circumstance applies also to those commodities which form the constant part of (its) capital, and indirectly also its variable part, as the labourer's necessities of life. . . . Under capitalist production, the general law acts as the prevailing tendency only in a very complicated and approximate manner, as a never ascertainable average of ceaseless fluctuations. (*Capital*, Vol. III, Ch. IX, p. 161.)

> The foregoing statements have at any rate modified the original assumptions concerning the determination of the cost-price of commodities . . . Since the price of production may differ from the value of a commodity, it follows that the cost-price of a commodity containing this price of production of another commodity may also stand above or below that portion of its total value derived from the value of the means of production consumed by it. It is necessary to remember this modified significance of the cost-price, and to bear in mind that there is always the possibility of error if the cost-price of a commodity in any particular

sphere is identified with the value of the means of production consumed by it. Our present analysis does not necessitate a closer examination of this point. (*Ibid.*, pp. 164-65.)

To his critics, especially to those for whom only the *calculation* of prices of production has any significance, Marx's postponement of the "feedback" effects of the price-Value disproportionalities is an admission of failure—hence the so-called "great contradiction" between Volumes I and III.

But there is in fact a simple alternative: Let us extend Marx's procedure by progressively "feeding back" the effects of the initial price-Value disproportionalities and see what happens. Table 4 illustrates this extended procedure. In order to emphasize the fact that the transformation and its extension affect only money flows M and M', and not the Value flows $(C+V) \dots P \dots (C+L)$, I have included both. This is somewhat tedious but it does make it clear that Value and surplus-Value are distinct from price and profit, a distinction which arises precisely from the difference between the spheres of production and circulation. But before we turn to this, we must first understand the logic involved.

We begin with exchange at Values (as was previously illustrated in Table 1). Let us now consider for a moment the real content of Marx's transformation procedure. If prices were actually proportional to Values, then rates of profit in each sector would differ from the social average. All other things being equal, either the competition of capitals or the threat of this competition would force the various sectors to adjust the prices of their products in such a way as to realize only the average rate of profit. In Department's II and III, for instance, which would have higher than average profit rates, either the threat of competition or else the actual inflow of capital would lower prices till only the average profit was obtained; in Department I, the reverse would take place.

In any real situation similar to the above, the actual adjustment process would involve changes in both the unit prices and the quantities sold; any actual inflow of capital would lower price through an expansion of supply; conversely, any lowering of price in response to the threat of competition would increase the amount sold.

But what we are interested in here is the pure change of form involved in the equalization of profit rates. And this, for a *given* mass of commodities, is an adjustment process *which leaves the total sum of money prices unchanged*: since the cost-prices have already been incurred by the individual capitalist, the immediate burden of adjustment must fall upon current product prices, and their response in the face of capitalist competition is precisely to rise or fall till the individual rates of profit all equal the existing average rate. This simply means that the unit price of *average* commodity output is under no immediate compulsion to change, because in this case the rate of profit *is* the average rate. The average commodity, however, is only a microcosm of the total mass of commodities: the constancy of its price is therefore equivalent to the constancy of the total sum of prices.

Marx's transformation procedure is merely an application of the logic of this adjustment process. In Table 4, the initial situation under consideration in Step 1A is exchange at Values: the sum of prices is £1750, and the sum of profits is £400. Step 1B then illustrates Marx's own transformation, in which

Table 4 / The Transformation from Direct Prices to Prices of Production*

Dept.	MC_i	MV_i	M_i	$M \to (C+V) \ldots P \ldots W \to M'$					ΔM_i	% r_i	ψ_i (Multiplier**)
				C_i	V_i	S_i	W_i	M'_i			
Step 1A Exchange at values											
I	450	180	630	225	90	60	375	750	120	19.05	—
II	200	240	440	100	120	80	300	600	160	36.36	—
III	100	180	280	50	90	60	200	400	120	42.85	—
	£750	£600	£1350	375	300	200	675	£1750	£400		
Step 1B Marx's transformation											
I	450	180	630	225	90	60	375	816.67	186.66	29.63	1.089
II	200	240	440	100	120	80	300	570.38	130.38	"	0.951
III	100	180	280	50	90	90	200	362.96	82.96	"	0.907
	£750	£600	£1350	375	300	200	675	£1750	£400		
Step 2A Cost-prices adjusted to reflect prices of production of Step 1B											
I	490.00	171.12	661.12	:	:	:	:	816.67	155.54		:
II	217.78	228.14	445.92	:	:	:	:	570.38	124.45		:
III	108.88	171.12	280.00	:	:	:	:	362.96	82.96		:
	£816.66	£570.38	£1387.04					£1750	£362.96		
Step 2B Prices of production adjusted to equalize rates of profit in Step 2A											
I	490.00	171.12	661.12	:	:	:	:	834.12	173.00	26.17	1.021
II	217.78	228.14	445.92	:	:	:	:	562.62	116.70	"	0.986
III	108.88	171.12	280.00	:	:	:	:	353.26	73.26	"	0.973
	£816.66	£570.38	£1387.04					£1750	£362.96		
Final Step "Correct" prices of production											
I	504	168	672	:	:	:	:	840	168	25	1.
II	224	224	448	:	:	:	:	560	112	"	1.
III	112	168	280	:	:	:	:	350	70	"	1.
	£840	£560	£1400					£1750	£350		

*ψ_i = ith price multiplier ≡ (ith price in current step) ÷ (ith price in previous step)
**The actual calculation was done to three significant digits after the decimal point. The numbers shown here are rounded off to two places.

(handwritten margin note: where q.d ↑ 1.50 value disappear)

the immediate process of adjustment redistributes the given mass of surplus-Value (whose magnitude cannot of course be changed in circulation) by raising prices in Department I and lowering them in II and III. The sum of money prices remains unchanged at £1750, and in this instance the sum of money profits also remains at its previous level of £400.

Expressed in proportion to its previous price, which was its direct price, the change in the money-price of Department I is $\psi_1 = 816.67/750 = 1.089$. Similarly, $\psi_2 = 0.951$ and $\psi_3 = 0.907$.

It is only in the next step, Step 2A, that we see the effect of the above deviations from direct prices on the cost-prices in each amount of capital. Since Department I produces the means of production for all departments, its price multiplier $\psi_1 = 1.089$ will imply higher money prices (MC_i) for all means of production. Similarly, since Department II produces the means of subsistence, its price multiplier $\psi_2 = 0.951$ implies a lowering of the money costs of labor-power (MV_i) in each amount. ψ_3, on the other hand, will not affect either component of cost-prices, since Department III produces only commodities for the consumption of capitalists.

Capitalists in each department will now have incurred new cost-prices differing from those in Step 1B. If they were to continue to sell their products at the prices of Step 1, their rates of profit would no longer be equal. This is the case illustrated in Step 2A. The overall effect of the preceding "feedbacks" is to raise the aggregate cost-price from £1350 to £1387.04. Since the sum of prices is unchanged, this results in a decrease of total money profit from £400 to £362.96.

Once again, therefore, capitalists in each sector would be compelled to adjust their individual money rates of profit to conform with the average rate, through the movements of their respective commodity-prices; once again, the average commodity, and hence the total mass of commodities, would be under no such compulsion, so that the total sum of prices would remain constant at £1750.

The resulting situation is depicted in Step 2B. Department I's price, compared to its previous level in Step 1B (and 2A), has risen again, this time by $\psi_1 = 834.12/816.67 = 1.021$, while those of II and III have fallen from their previous levels by $\psi_2 = 0.986$ and $\psi_3 = 0.973$. The pattern of transfer of surplus-Value has therefore been altered once again; moreover, in this case the money form of the mass of surplus-Value (i.e., total money profit) has been altered in magnitude. In the same way, the money rate of profit (26.17%) is no longer simply equal in magnitude to the value rate of profit (29.63%).

In each succeeding step, the procedure may be repeated until the changes from one step to another are negligibly small—and we find ourselves with the "correct" prices of production first illustrated in Table 3! This is not, as is usually the case, on the basis of an alternative to Marx's procedure of transformation, but rather on the basis of its successive application.

The procedure illustrated in Table 4 is quite general. The proof is left to Section VI of the mathematical appendix to this paper.

V. SOME FURTHER CONSIDERATIONS

In the preceding discussion, four important points have emerged in connection with the so-called "transformation problem."

First of all, it is not a case of transforming "Values into prices." Rather, it is a case of transforming one form-of-Value, direct prices, into another form, prices of production.

Secondly, the issue under consideration involves a pure change of form. As such, the transformation from direct prices to prices of production does not involve any *real* change for the system as a whole. The total mass of commodities, and the various portions of it going to each class, remain the same as before. By the same token, so do the sum of Values and sum of surplus-Values. What the transformation brings about is a different division of the total pool of surplus-Value among individual capitalists.

Third, the transformation procedure set out by Marx reflects the inherent nature of the process of the equalization of profit rates. This is a continuously occurring process, and in its pure form it acts by changing prices of individual commodities while leaving the sum of prices of a given mass of commodities intact. In addition, Marx's procedure can be extended in a simple way to derive the "correct" prices of production.

Lastly, in the case of the "correct" prices of production, the money rate of profit will deviate from the Value rate of profit. Like the deviations of prices of production from direct prices, however, the money and Value profit rate deviation is systematic and determinate. Though we do not prove it here, it can be shown that (under any given conditions of production), the money rate of profit will vary with the Value rate.[41]

These connections by no means exhaust the possibilities. The relation between the mass of surplus-Value and its transformed money-form (total money profits under prices of production) still needs to be better specified. So too does the relationship between individual prices of production and the corresponding Values.

Perhaps the most important point to keep in mind is that the laws that Marx derives on the basis of this theory of Value cannot be derived from a theory which *begins* with prices of production. For instance, Marx's distinction between Value and money-price goes hand in hand with a corresponding differentiation between production and circulation. It consequently becomes necessary to distinguish between activities which produce commodities and those which circulate them, and eventually this difference develops in the more complex and powerful distinction between surplus-Value *producing* labor (what Marx calls "productive" labor) and all other types (which Marx relegates to the category of "unproductive" labor). Among other things, an increase in the proportion of unproductive labor (say advertising) to productive labor, for a given level of total employment, would imply a smaller mass of surplus-Value to be shared out, and hence a smaller rate of profit. Such a conclusion has no parallel in orthodox theories of price.

Marx's analysis abounds with similar examples. His theory of money, for instance, is the direct opposite of the Quantity Theory.[42] Similarly, his theory of the falling tendency of the rate of profit, and the theory of accumulation and

crises which stems from it, receive their characteristic form from the distinction between constant and variable capital—precisely a distinction which makes no sense without the notion of Value.

All of this means that if Marx's economic analysis is to be developed, it must first be understood. Or else it must be abandoned altogether. The latter path is no doubt simpler, and certainly more consistent with orthodox economics. If the task is to understand the world in order to change it, then the *adequacy* of analysis, not its "acceptability," is all that matters. And on that basis, it seems to me that Marx's analysis is the most appropriate starting point.

VI. CONCLUSION

It is the function of all scientific analysis to get beneath the surface of phenomena, to reduce their apparent movement to the real: ". . . all science would be superfluous if the outward appearance and the essence of things directly coincided."[43]

The outward appearance of the sphere of circulation is one of freedom, equality, and choice: it is a world whose real inhabitants are inherently-equal-things, commodities, a world into which human beings enter only as representatives of these "natural" democrats: "It is an enchanted, perverted, topsy-turvy world, in which Monsieur le Capital and Madame la Terre do their ghost-walking as social characters and at the same time directly as mere things."[44]

To Marx, the great merit of classical economy was that it saw through, albeit incompletely, this "false appearance and illusion, this mutual independence and ossification of the various *social* elements of wealth, this personification of things and the conversion of production relations into entities, this religion of everyday life. It did so by reducing interest to a portion of profit and rent to the surplus above average profit, so that both of them converge in surplus-value; and by representing the process of circulation as a mere metamorphosis of forms, and finally reducing value and surplus-value of commodities to labour in the direct production process."[45] In this way the classical economists were able to get beyond the simple conceptions generated by the outward appearance of capitalism, penetrating the disguise of circulation and seeing behind it the process of production. But they themselves were trapped by their inability to properly distinguish capitalist production from other historically determinate forms; by taking as given and eternal the concepts generated by the outward appearance of capitalist production, they remained "more or less in the grip of the world of illusion which their criticism had dissolved."[46]

The "world of illusion" Marx refers to represents the conceptions common to bourgeois thinkers; it covers not only the actual analysis of classical economists and of their targets, the vulgar economists, but also the conceptual framework within which they clash. Contained in their agreements and disagreements is an implicit philosophy, an implicit theory of history, an implicit anthropology, and so on.[47] Thus for Marx the critique of classical economy is at the same time a critique of its philosophy, its history, its anthropology. His analysis in *Capital* is necessarily predicated on all of these critiques; the vast distance between Marx and the classical economists, and hence between "value" in Marx and "value" in classical economy, can only be understood if one recognizes

that in solving the problems of the classical economists Marx also breaks with the (often implicit) bases on which they had formulated their questions.

Insofar as the problems to be dealt with center largely on the magnitude of Value, as is often the case in this paper, the real difference between Marx and Ricardo, the difference in their methods, tends to be hidden. Marx's superior ability to solve Ricardo's problems, is, as he himself insists, due to his ability to transcend "the world of illusion" in whose grip Ricardo remains. This superior ability is therefore only a symptom of the real difference between Marx and the classicals. But to those who either explicitly or implicitly reduce Marx to Ricardo, this symptom becomes the real difference itself. Marx becomes a clever, if somewhat mystical, post-Ricardian.

The very same process of reduction often operates even further in the comparison of Marx to neoclassical analysis. Not only are Marx and Ricardo lumped together, but both are reduced to the one-dimensional world of neo-classical analysis. Here, the very conception of the problem to be analyzed is usually neoclassical; even those who reject the flatness of its theory are very often forced to fight their battles on its terms, and hence *within* its general framework.

The so-called transformation problem is a classic example of all this. As it is usually presented, the central issue is one of the *calculation* of static prices of production, and the major point of contention is the presence or absence of a relationship between Marx's transformation procedure and the "correct" one.

I have, as much as possible, attempted to avoid this trap. Certainly the issue of calculation is relevant; but the *conception* of that-which-is-to-be-calculated comes first, for in that conception lies the superiority of Marx's method. The early part of this paper therefore attempts to provide the basis of Marx's conception of prices in general, and prices of production in particular. In this way we are able to resolve many of the confusions surrounding the so-called "transformation problem," as well as being able to demonstrate that the "correct" prices of production can be calculated from values *in the manner suggested by Marx's own transformation procedure.*

Mathematical Appendix

Lack of space makes it impossible to include the mathematical appendix to this reading. However, a copy of the appendix is available on request from the author of this reading.

REFERENCES

[1]   L. Althusser and E. Balibar, *Reading Capital,* translated from the French by Ben Brewster, Pantheon Books, (New York: Random House), 1970.

[2]   W. Baumol, "The Transformation of Values: What Marx 'Really' Meant (An Interpretation), *Journal of Economic Literature,* March 1974, Vol. XII, No. 1.

[3]   A. Emmanuel, *Unequal Exchange: A Study of the Imperialism of Trade* (New York: Monthly Review Press), 1972.

[4]   T. Kuhn, *The Structure of Scientific Revolutions* (Chicago: University of Chicago Press), 1970.

[5]   E. Mandel, "Value, Surplus Value, Profit, Prices of Production and Surplus Capital— A Reply to Geoff Hodgson," *International Socialist Review,* Vol. 2, No. 1, Spring 1973.

[6]   K. Lancaster, *Mathematical Economics* (New York: The Macmillan Company), 1968.

[7]   Karl Marx, *A Contribution to the Critique of Political Economy,* with an Introduction by Maurice Dobb (New York: International Publishers), 1970.

[8]   ——, *Theory of Surplus Value: Volume IV of Capital* (Moscow: Progress Publishers), Part I, 1969; Part II, 1968; Part III, 1971.

[9]   ——, *Capital,* Volumes I–III (New York: International Publishers), 1967.

[10] ——, "Comments on Adolph Wagner's 'Lehrbuch der politischen Okonomie', 1879/80," published as *Karl Marx on Value,* British and Irish Communist Organization, Belfast, 1971.

[11] A. Medio, "Profits and Surplus-Value: Appearance and Reality in Capitalist Production," published in *A Critique of Economic Theory,* edited by E. K. Hunt and Jesse G. Schwartz (London: Penguin Books), 1972.

[12] R. Meek, *Economics and Ideology and Other Essays* (London: Chapman and Hall), 1967.

[13] M. Morishima and F. Seton, "Aggregation in Leontief Matrices and the Labour Theory of Value," *Econometrica,* Vol. 29, 2 (April 1961), pp. 203–220.

[14] M. Morishima, *Marx's Economics* (Cambridge: Cambridge University Press), 1973.

[15] J. Robinson, *An Essay on Marxian Economics,* Second Edition (London: Macmillan; New York: St. Martin's Press), 1969.

[16] B. Rowthorn, "Skilled Labour in the Marxist System," *Bulletin of the Conference of Socialist Economists,* Spring 1974, pp. 25–45.

[17] P. A. Samuelson, "Understanding the Marxian Notion of Exploitation: A Summary of the so-called Transformation Problem between Marxian Values and Competitive Prices," *Journal of Economic Literature,* June 1971, Vol. IX, No. 2, pp. 399–431.

[18] F. Seton, "The 'Transformation Problem'," *Review of Economic Studies,* June 1957, 25, pp. 149–160.

[19] A. Shaikh, *Theories of Value and Theories of Distribution,* Columbia University Ph.D., 1973 (unpublished).

[20] P. Sraffa, *Production of Commodities by Means of Commodities* (Cambridge: Cambridge University Press), 1960.

[21] P. M. Sweezy, *The Theory of Capitalist Development* (New York: Monthly Review Press), 1964.

NOTES

1. P. A. Samuelson [Bibliography Reference 17], p. 400.

2. R. Meek, "Some Notes on the 'Transformation problem'," in Meek [12], p. 150.

3. See, for instance, Mandel [5], pp. 64-65. For a non-Marxist with a similar position, see Baumol [2].

4. Kuhn [4]. The term "paradigm break" is used figuratively here. The notion of a break between the problematic of classical economy and that of Marx, which Althusser [1] discusses, is considerably more precise.

5. J. Robinson [15], p. xi, and Ch. III, especially pp. 20-22.

6. Marxists who attempt to directly apply the abstract categories of Volume I of *Capital* are in a sense reverting to a Ricardian methodology. Marx is careful to point out that a basic flaw in Ricardo's method is that he "jumps" directly from the abstract (value) to the concrete (prices of production, rent, taxes) without tracing the intermediate connections. (Marx, *Theories of Surplus Value,* Part II, Ch. x, Sect. 4.6., p. 191.) It takes Marx three volumes to make that connection!

7. K. Marx, *A Contribution to the Critique of Political Economy,* p. 86.

8. Marx, *Capital,* Vol. I, Ch. 1, p. 75.

9. *Ibid.,* p. 43.

10. *Ibid.,* p. 46.

11. The distinction between concrete labor and abstract labor is similar to (though distinct from) the distinction between productive and unproductive labor. In both cases, the properties of Value and surplus-Value lie at the heart of the matter.

12. Marx [10].

13. Marx uses the term "socially necessary labor-time" in two senses. First, the average quantity of abstract labor-time required to produce a single commodity; this determines the magnitude of its Value (*Capital*, Vol. I, Ch. I, p. 39). Second, the total quantity of labor-time which would be required to produce a given type of commodity in the amount consistent with effective demand; if the actual quantity of labor-time, and hence the actual amount of the product, deviates from the above necessary amount, the market-price of the commodity would deviate from its regulating price. (*Capital*, Vol. III, Ch. xxxvii, p. 635). The first sense of socially necessary relates the commodity to its conditions of production. The second sense relates the mass of commodities to the expressed social need for them.

14. "...he [Adam Smith] confuses—as Ricardo also often does—labour, the *intrinsic* measure of value, with *money*, the *external measure* ..." (Marx, *Theories of Surplus-Value*, Part II, Ch. xv, Section 2, p. 403).

15. Marx, *Capital*, Vol. I, p. 39.

16. The amount of labor-time socially necessary for the production of a commodity is determined by the average conditions of production of the average commodity. If the *average* conditions are altered, as in Marx's example of the introduction of power looms in weaving, then though existing cloth may have required more time than this new average, the magnitude of its value is still determined by the current average, precisely because all cloth of a given quality is treated alike in exchange. Similarly, if hand-loom weavers continue to hang on, then even though it may take them twice as long as the average to produce a bolt of cloth, the *value* of the cloth is nonetheless determined by the average. See Footnote 13 above, also.

17. The total social product is usually defined to include only the commodities newly produced in the given period of time. However, the existence of durable commodities implies that in any given period, "used" commodities and inventories of unsold products may enter exchange as commodities even though they have not been *produced* in that period. In the treatment of fixed constant capital, for instance, this issue becomes important. Marx himself suggests in the treatment of fixed constant capital that the portion which is not used up in the process of production should be counted as part of the annual product (*Capital*, Vol. I, Ch. IX, p. 213). Properly speaking this treatment of fixed constant capital requires Marx's theory of *rent*, and for that reason is not developed in this particular paper. It should be noted, however, that a Marxian treatment of this issue will not be identical with the von Neumann-Sraffa "joint product" approach.

18. Marx, *Capital*, Vol. I, pp. 47-48.

19. Marx, *Capital*, Vol. I, Ch. VII, Section 1.

20. Marx, *Capital*, Vol. II, Ch. VI, Sect. I and Sect. III, p. 149.

21. *Ibid.*, pp. 129-130.

22. *Ibid.*, Ch. V, p. 127. Of course, the circulation process adds to the *money price* of a commodity. As long as Value and price are kept conceptually separate, this presents no problems at all.

23. Marx, *Capital*, Vol. I, "Preface to the First German Edition," p. 10.

24. Marx, *Theories of Surplus-Value*, Part I, pp. 164-167.

25. *Ibid.*, p. 166.

26. *Ibid.*, Ch. X, Section A. See also pp. 106, 164, 174-176.

27. In *A Contribution to the Critique of Political Economy* [7], Marx begins by assuming that commodities exchange at Values, and then poses a series of objections to this assumption as a challenge to his own beginning. Of these, the "last and apparently the decisive objection" has to do with the fact that commodities with no Value can possess exchange-value. This problem, he says, "is solved in the theory of rent." (pp. 61-63)

28. Marx, *Capital*, Vol. I, Ch. IV, p. 147.

29. *Ibid.*, p. 155.

30. *Ibid.*, p. 147.

31. *Ibid.*, Ch. VI, p. 167.

32. If workers work only long enough to produce their means of subsistence and the commodities necessary to replace the means of production used up, then the only *final* (net) outputs of the system are the means of subsistence. As such the total time put in by workers is the time directly required to produce the means of subsistence, plus the time directly required to replace the means of production used up in producing these means of

subsistence. But the latter time is also the time *indirectly* required to produce the means of subsistence: hence the total time they work is the sum of the direct and indirect labor-time necessary to produce the means of subsistence—which of course is by definition the (labor) Value of these commodities, and hence the (labor) Value of the labor-power which is reproduced through their consumption.

Similarly, any surplus labor-time they work over and above this necessary labor-time is the labor Value of the surplus-product, surplus-Value.

33. See Meek's discussion of this (false) issue in [12], pp. 215-225.

34. Marx, *Capital*, Vol. III, Ch. IX, p. 157.

35. The *product* of each concrete labor-time has a definite quantity of Value—abstract or general labor-time—which is measured by the average quantity of labor-time required for the production of the average product of this type. As such, the actual quantity of labor time put in by a given worker, such as the hand-loom weaver of Footnote 13, counts only as the quantity of average value-added in the production of the average commodity.

36. Sraffa's initial point of reference is a set of prices which obtain when the rate of profit is zero. As is well known, in the simplest case relative prices are then proportional to relative Values. The subsequent movements of relative prices at alternate positive rates of profit which he then analyzes may be therefore viewed as the analysis of relative price-Value deviations at alternative levels of the rate of surplus-Value.

37. A. Emmanuel [3] provides a modern example of a neo-Smithian theory of price, in which the "labor theory" of price is valid when there is only one class of recipients of the net product (laborers), and the theory of prices of production is valid when there are two classes of recipients: capitalists and workers (see Emmanuel, *op. cit.*, Ch. 1, and Appendix V). This rejection of "labor" as a determinant of price has its roots in the confusion and difficulty surrounding the "transformation problem."

38. See Marx, *Capital*, Vol. I, Ch. 2, Section 2b, pp. 53-54.

39. Sweezy [21], Ch. V.

40. In addition to the transformation discussion in Volume III of *Capital*, see: *Theories of Surplus Value*, Part III, Ch. XX, p. 82 and pp. 167-168.

41. It has been proved in various places that, under given conditions of production, a rise in the rate of surplus-Value will increase the *money* rate of profit. Since it will also have the same effect on the *Value* rate of profit, it follows that the two move together (see, for instance, Medio [11], pp. 339-340; or Morishima [14], Ch. 6).

42. See Marx, *Capital*, Vol. I, Ch. 3; or *Contribution to the Critique of Political Economy*, Chapter 2.

43. Marx, *Capital*, Vol. III, Part III, Ch. XLVIII, p. 813.

44. *Ibid.*, p. 830.

45. *Ibid.*, p. 830. Emphasis added.

46. *Ibid.*, p. 830.

47. See Althusser's discussion of this in [1], Ch. 2-4.

Capitalist Development, Surplus Value, and Reproduction
An Empirical Examination of Puerto Rico
EDWARD N. WOLFF
Associate Professor of Economics at New York University

I. INTRODUCTION

Few opportunities exist to study the movement of basic parameters in Marxian analysis over a period of major economic and social changes as that provided by Puerto Rico. Between 1948 and 1963 real per capita income and labor productivity more than doubled, and investment rose as a share of gross national product from 12.5 to 20.0 percent. The industrial share in gross output expanded by 50 percent, and that of agriculture shrank by a similar percentage. The breakup of the agricultural sector led to a shift of population from rural to urban areas (and to emigration to the U.S. mainland). The net result was a transformation of the Puerto Rican economy from a primarily rural and agrarian one to a modern industrial and urban state.

The availability of input-output data for both the pre-industrial and post-industrial period allows us to test some basic hypotheses in Marxian economics. The first is that the rate of surplus value remains constant over time. Marx himself, as far as I am aware, offers no prediction on its movement. In chapter 13, Volume III of *Capital*, on "the law of the tendency of the rate of profit to fall," Marx assumes a constant rate of surplus value and an increasing organic composition of capital in his arithmetic examples (p. 211).[1] However, in the following chapter, Marx mentions a falling rate of surplus value, owing to an increase in relative surplus from increased labor productivity, as a "counteracting influence" to the tendency of the rate of profit to decline (vol. III, pp. 232-35). As Marx argues, the movement of the rate of surplus value over time depends on the change in the real wage—that is, the mass of wage goods consumed by workers— and the change in the labor value of the wage goods. In the case of Puerto Rico, we can determine the change in the rate of surplus value and algebraically decompose it into a real wage effect and a technology effect.

The second hypothesis is that the value rate of profit is equal to the average market rate of profit. In the transformation of labor values to prices of production Marx maintains that the sum of values equals the sum of prices, and total surplus value equals total profits (vol. III, p. 138). Though the inconsistency between these two propositions has been commented on many times,[2]

I would like to express appreciation to Richard Weisskoff for his advice and support, and to Harry Magdoff for his interesting and helpful comments. This article, revised May 1976, was previously unpublished.

a question arises as to what are the relative magnitudes of these two sets of variables. The ratio of total surplus value to total labor values can be expressed as a function of the value rate of profit, and the ratio of total profits to total prices of production can itself be expressed as a function of the price of production rate of profit.[3] Because prices of production cannot be computed from the available data (no information is available on sectoral capital stock), we shall compare, instead, the value rate of profit with the average rate of profit in market prices.[4]

The third hypothesis is that the organic composition of capital rises over time. Marx argues that the organic composition tends to increase over time because new technology, on average, embodies a higher ratio of constant capital to labor in physical terms (that is, a higher technical composition). This is the crucial presumption of the law of the tendency of the rate of profit to fall. However, Marx does argue that increased labor productivity will provide a counteracting effect on a rising organic composition because the labor required to produce constant capital and thus the labor value of constant capital will tend to decrease (vol. III, p. 236). The net effect of a rising technical composition and a depreciation in the labor embodied in the means of production will determine the movement of the organic composition.

The fourth hypothesis is that the share of Dept. I's purchases from itself (that is, the purchase of means of production) increases relative to the total value of the gross output. Though Marx provides extensive discussions of reproduction schemes in volume II of *Capital* (pp. 392-523) and in part II of *Theories of Surplus-Value*,[5] they are confined mainly to the conceptual structure of the scheme and to arithmetic examples. As far as I am aware, Marx makes no predictions of the relative magnitudes of the components of the schemes. The fourth hypothesis is suggested in an article by K. N. Raj. He remarks on "the peculiar ability of the machine-tools branch within the capital goods section to initiate and sustain a circular production process of its own and of thus 'breaking out of the determinism' laid upon the sector by the existing structural relations."[6] In fact with technological advance and increased linkages among the producing sectors, we might suspect that producing sectors will sell an increasingly larger percentage of their output to other sectors and an increasingly smaller percentage for consumer demand and other final uses. The flows within Dept. I will thus increase relative to the total product flows within the economy, as Dept. I grows increasingly internalized and self-sustaining. This should show up as an increasing share of Dept. I's purchases from itself relative to total circulation.

II. ALGEBRAIC FORMULATION

Input-output tables are constructed in terms of product flows at market prices. To examine the hypotheses proposed in the previous section, we must first convert the input-output table in market prices to one in labor values. Such a transformation was worked out by Morishima and Seton in 1961.[7] However the algebra can be presented more simply, as follows:

(i)   Let A be a 27 order matrix of interindustry coefficients in market prices.[8]

(ii)   Let a_0 be a 27 order row vector showing the number of workers employed per dollar of output in each sector.[9]

(iii) Let m be a 27 order column vector showing the consumption of each sector in market prices per worker.[10]

(iv)   Let p be a 27 order row vector showing the total labor required per dollar of output of each sector.

Therefore:

(1) $p = a_0 [I - A]^{-1}$

because this expression is precisely the direct plus indirect labor time required for each dollar of output.[11] Moreover, pm is the amount of labor embodied in the consumption of the average worker. If we define ϵ, the rate of surplus value, as the ratio of surplus (uncompensated) labor time to necessary (compensated) labor time, then

(2) $\epsilon = \dfrac{1}{pm} - 1$

because pm is the ratio of compensated labor time to total labor time.[12]

III. EMPIRICAL RESULTS[13]

A. The Rate of Surplus Value

The rate of surplus value remained relatively stable between 1948 and 1963, changing by only 4.1 percent (see Table 1).[14] The magnitude was close to 1.0, which is the figure Marx uses in most of his arithmetic examples (vol. I, p. 155, for example). The only other computations of the rate of surplus value I am aware of indicate similar magnitudes. Okishio calculated a rate of surplus value of 0.93 for the 1951 Japanese economy, though this referred only to manufacturing industries; Kýn, Sekerka, and Hejl computed one of 1.35 for the 1962 Czechoslovakian economy, though it is unclear how profit was handled in the country's socialist accounting framework; and preliminary calculations by the author yield an estimate of 0.83 for the 1963 United States economy.[15]

Table 1 / The Rate of Surplus Value (ϵ)

1948	.9729
1963	.9328

The change in the rate of surplus value can, alternatively, be seen in the change of the value of labor power. Recalling that pm, the labor embodied in the consumption goods of the average worker, is by definition equivalent to the value of labor power and equals $1/(1 + \epsilon)$, we find that it remained almost constant at 0.507 in 1948 and 0.517 in 1963. Thus the annual cost of reproducing the average worker required approximately one half a man-year of labor in the two periods.

The presence of two offsetting tendencies resulted in a stable rate of surplus value. The first was a rise in the real wage. Consumption per worker increased from \$867 in 1948 to \$2,107 in 1963, in constant 1963 prices, an increase of 143 percent.[16] The second was a fall in the labor value of the means of subsistence, which was partly a consequence of the decline in the labor value of the constant capital used to produce the wage goods. Labor values declined in each of the twenty-three sectors producing in both years (see Table 2).[17] Because labor value is the direct plus indirect labor required per unit of output, a decline in labor value can be interpreted as an increase in labor productivity, where labor productivity is understood not in the traditional sense, as the ratio of a sector's output to the (direct) labor employed in the sector, but as the ratio of a sector's output to its total labor requirement.[18] The increase in labor

Table 2 / Labor Value* and Productivity Increase by Sector

		1	2	3
		1948 Labor Values (p_{48})	1963 Labor Values (p_{63})	Productivity Increase [Col (1)/Col (2)]
1	Agriculture Nec	0.3415	0.1248	2.7367
2	Sugar Cane	1.0983	0.3154	3.4831
3	Sugar Milling	0.8693	0.2946	2.9507
4	Processed Foods	0.5291	0.1923	2.7518
5	Textiles	0.8252	0.3267	2.5253
6	Leather	**	0.3198	**
7	Furniture	0.6136	0.2928	2.0960
8	Paper Products	1.1169	0.3569	3.1299
9	Printing	0.9581	0.3219	2.9771
10	Chemical	0.4943	0.1961	2.5208
11	Nonmetal	0.6465	0.2768	2.3359
12	Petroleum & Coal	**	0.2522	**
13	Metal Industries	0.6781	0.2535	2.6752
14	Mining	**	0.2939	**
15	Other Manufacturing	0.7316	0.2868	2.5510
16	Construction	0.7500	0.3156	2.3764
17	Hotels & Restaurants	0.5127	0.2418	2.1204
18	Electricity	0.6117	0.2522	2.4254
19	Water & Sanitation	0.8702	0.2627	3.3135
20	Communication	0.9664	0.2814	3.4341
21	Trade	0.6833	0.2282	1.9940
22	Business Services	0.5865	0.2950	1.9881
23	Personal Services	0.5322	0.2767	1.9231
24	Real Estate	0.2867	0.1527	1.8779
25	Transport	0.7897	0.2637	2.9940
26	Government Services	0.9776	0.3844	2.5432
27	Depreciation	0.7162	0.2957	2.4219
28	Totals	0.7110	0.2650	2.6831

Labor value is defined as the direct plus indirect labor requirements in man-years per \$1,000 of sectoral output, in 1963 prices.

**Sectors 6, 12, and 14 did not exist in 1948.

productivity ranged from a low of 1.88 in real estate (24) to a high of 3.48 in sugar cane (2). Other large increases occurred in paper products (8), water and sanitation (19), and communications (20). The ratio of total output to the total labor required for its production increased by 168 percent. The increase in labor productivity closely offset the 143 percent growth in worker consumption, resulting in a stable rate of surplus value.

Another way of viewing this process is to consider the effect of increased labor productivity on the rate of surplus value if worker consumption had remained at the 1948 level. Marx calls the process of increasing the rate of surplus value by decreasing the labor value of the wage goods the production of "relative surplus value" (vol. I, pp. 508–18). To measure this, we substituted m^{48} for m^{63} in equation (2):

$$(3) \qquad \epsilon^* = \frac{1}{p^{63} m^{48}} - 1$$

where superscripts indicate respective years.[19] The resulting rate of surplus value, ϵ^*, was 3.8974, 318 percent above the actual 1963 level. Thus the increased consumption of labor absorbed the relative surplus value generated by increased labor productivity.[20]

B. The Market and the Value Rate of Profit

The value rate of profit was computed as the ratio of total surplus value to total constant plus variable capital in labor value terms ($S/(C + V)$), and the market rate of profit as the ratio of total surplus in price terms (taxes plus property income) to the sum of material inputs and wages in market price terms (see Table 3). The value rate of profit was 36 percent greater than the market rate of profit in 1948, and 16 percent greater in 1963. To determine the source of this discrepancy, we

Table 3 / The Rate of Profit ($S/(C + V)$)

	Market Rate	Value Rate
1948	.1904	.2596
1963	.2534	.3022

normalized labor values so that the sum of values ($C + V + S$) equaled the sum of market prices and compared the components in value and price terms (see Table 4).

Table 4 / Percentage Difference of Components in Value and Price Terms*

	1948	1963
Constant Capital	−6.7	−1.9
Variable Capital	−17.1	−7.4
Total Surplus	23.1	14.8

*Percentage difference is defined as 100 times the ratio of labor value less market price to market price.

Constant capital was relatively close in price and value terms, variable capital much less in value than in price terms, and total surplus much greater in value than in price terms. To understand the reason for the large difference between variable capital in price terms and in value terms, we analyzed the composition of worker consumption (m). Of the chief consumption items, most had a smaller labor value than market price (that is, p_i was less than 1). Moreover, of the chief items in surplus final demand (capitalist consumption plus investment plus government expenditure plus exports less imports), most had a relatively higher labor value than market price. The value of labor power thus appeared higher in market price terms than in labor value terms, and the variable capital advanced was correspondingly lower in value than in price terms. Conversely, surplus final demand was relatively greater in terms of its labor value than in terms of market prices, and surplus value greater than the surplus in market price terms.

C. The Organic Composition

The organic composition of capital (σ, which equals C/V) declined by 24 percent between 1948 and 1963 (see Table 5).[21] As discussed in section I of this paper, Marx argues that the technical composition of capital (the ratio of produced inputs to labor in physical units) tends to rise over time, while the labor value of produced inputs tends to fall. The net effect of these two counteracting tendencies determines whether the organic composition rises or falls. As Marx predicts, the technical composition did rise with capitalist development in Puerto Rico.[22] In fact, it more than doubled. However the depreciation in the labor value of constant capital more than offset the rise in technical composition.

Table 5 / The Organic and Technical Composition of Capital

	Organic Composition (σ)	Technical Composition
1948	2.75	1.95
1963	2.09	4.15

The stable rate of surplus value and the falling organic composition of capital account for the fall in the value rate of profit (see Table 4). The value rate of profit, r, can be decomposed as follows:

$$(4) \qquad r = \frac{S}{C + V} = \frac{S/V}{(C/V) + 1} = \frac{\epsilon}{1 + \sigma}$$

A decrease in the organic composition therefore results in a rise in the value rate of profit. As discussed above, the basis of Marx's law of the tendency of the rate of profit to fall is the tendency of the organic composition to increase over time with capitalist development.

D. Reproduction Schemes

The 1948 and 1963 input-output tables were aggregated into three-department reproduction schemes. Though we tried to follow Marx's description in volume

II of *Capital* as closely as possible, some adjustments were necessary. First, input-output tables show the distribution of the total output of each sector between intermediate and final demand. Because most sectors sell their output to both producers and final users, the sectors could not be directly split into Depts. I, II, and III. Instead if a sector supplied x percent of its output to Dept. I (intermediate producers), y percent to Dept. II (labor consumption), and the remainder, z percent, to Dept. III (surplus final demand components), the constant and variable capital and surplus value in that sector were divided in those proportions among the three departments. Second, Dept. III was divided into its constituent components—capitalist consumption, investment, government consumption, and exports—to allow greater detail. Third, because imports comprised a large part of Puerto Rico's inputs, constant capital was divided into a domestic and imported component. The 1948 and 1963 reproduction schemes, in thousands of man-years, are shown in Table 6.

Table 6 / Reproduction Tables for Puerto Rico*

		Constant Capital		Variable Surplus		
		Domestic	Imported	Capital	Value	Total
A. 1948						
I.	Constant Capital	313.5	213.7	122.0	118.7	768.0
II.	Labor Consumption	104.8	112.2	31.7	30.8	279.5
III.a	Capitalist Consumption	93.8	100.4	28.3	27.6	250.1
III.b	Investment	15.5	20.0	4.7	4.5	44.7
III.c	Government	25.3	0	22.3	21.7	69.3
III.d	Exports	215.0	0.4	70.5	68.6	354.5
	Imports	0	−446.7	0	0	−446.7
	Total	768.0	0	279.5	271.9	1,319.3
B. 1963						
I.	Constant Capital	257.1	203.4	106.9	99.7	667.1
II.	Labor Consumption	103.3	135.2	42.0	39.2	319.7
III.a	Capitalist Consumption	42.1	55.1	17.1	16.0	130.3
III.b	Investment	45.5	23.6	20.9	19.5	109.4
III.c	Government	28.0	0	47.8	44.6	120.5
III.d	Exports	191.1	19.2	84.9	79.2	374.5
	Imports	0	−436.4	0	0	−436.4
	Total	667.1	0	319.7	298.2	1,285.1

*All figures are in thousands of man-years.

In contrast to input-output tables, the rows show the inputs, and the columns the distribution of the output. Each row shows the constant capital, both domestically produced and imported, purchased, the variable capital advanced, and the surplus value generated in that department. The sum of variable capital and surplus value in each row is the newly added labor time in the department. The first two columns show the distribution of the domestic and imported constant capital among the departments, and the third and fourth the distribution of the labor force.

The hypothesis we wish to test is that Dept. I's purchases from itself increased relatively to total output. There are three ways to measure the circulation within Dept. I. The first is the value of domestically produced constant capital purchased in Dept. I because this represents the flow of value within Puerto Rican industries. The second is the value of domestic plus imported constant capital used in Dept. I because this measures the interdependence of Puerto Rico's producing sectors with those in Puerto Rico and the rest of the world (primarily the United States). The third is the total constant capital used in Dept. I and in investment because investment is primarily constant capital purchased by the producing sectors. Moreover there are two ways of measuring the share of each of these magnitudes with respect to total circulation. The first is the value of the total constant capital used in the economy, which represents the total flow of material goods required for the economy's reproduction. The second is the gross domestic output, which measures the total domestic circulation within the economy. Each of the six shares is shown in Table 7 for 1948 and 1963. The share of Dept. I's purchases from itself fell according to five of the measures and rose according to only one. The percentage change between 1948 and 1963 was less than 16 percent in every case. Thus, by all the measures, the relative magnitude of constant capital used to produce constant capital remained relatively stable between 1948 and 1963.

Table 7 / Measures of the Relative Share of the Circulation within Dept. I

	Total Constant Capital		Gross Domestic Output	
	1948	1963	1948	1963
Flows within Dept. I				
(a) Domestically Produced Constant Capital	.258	.233	.237	.200
(b) Domestic plus Imported Constant Capital	.434	.417	.400	.358
(c) Domestic plus Imported Constant Capital, including the Investment Sector	.463	.480	.426	.412

IV. SUMMARY

Rapid capitalist development in Puerto Rico has provided an opportunity to measure the movement of key Marxian economic variables over a period of significant historical change. Four results are of particular import. First, the rate of surplus value remained virtually stationary over the 1948–63 period. The stability was found to be due to a rise in the level of worker consumption and a corresponding increase in labor productivity. Second, the organic composition of capital declined substantially, even though the technical composition more than doubled. The reason for this was that the decrease in the labor value of the components of constant capital more than offset the rise in the technical composition. Third, the value rate of profit rose considerably. This resulted from a stationary rate of surplus value and a fall in the organic composition.

Fourth, the circulation of constant capital within Dept. I changed very little as a share of the total circulation within the Puerto Rican economy. Moreover, the percentage composition of the components of the reproduction scheme remained remarkably stable over the 1948–63 period.

Three provisos are in order. First, no distinction between productive and unproductive labor has been drawn. Such a division will affect the estimate of the mass of surplus value and consequently its rate. Second, only a rough adjustment was made for different skill and occupational composition by sector. A correct handling would require a systematic procedure to "reduce" skilled to unskilled labor and to net out the surplus component of professional and managerial wages. Such corrections will affect the estimate of the rate of surplus value. Third, circulating capital instead of the sum of fixed and circulating capital was used to estimate the organic composition and the rate of profit, biasing downward the estimate of the former and upward the estimate of the latter. Data limitations prevented corrections for these problems in our study of Puerto Rico. Current work on the United States economy, for which most of the necessary data are available, will enable us to assess the effect of each of these adjustments on the rate of surplus value, the rate of profit, and the organic composition.

NOTES

1. All page references in parentheses refer to: Karl Marx, *Capital* (New York: International Publishers, 1967).

2. For example, see Paul Sweezy, *The Theory of Capitalist Development* (New York: Modern Reader Paperbacks, 1968).

3. Let C represent total constant capital, V total variable capital, and S total surplus value. Total labor values equal $C + V + S$. Thus, $S/(C + V + S)$ equals $1/(1 + 1/r)$, where $r = S/(C + V)$, the value rate of profit. The same argument holds for the price of production rate of profit.

4. Marx, in fact, argues that the deviation of market prices from prices of production does not affect the mass of surplus value but only its distribution among competing capitals (vol. III, chap. 10). It is unclear how the inequality between total profits and total surplus value would affect this argument.

5. Karl Marx, *Theories of Surplus-Value* (Moscow: Progress Publishers, 1968), pt. II, pp. 470–92.

6. K. N. Raj, "Role of the 'Machine Tool Sector' in Economic Growth," in C. H. Feinstein, ed., *Socialism, Capitalism and Economic Growth: Essays Presented to Maurice Dobb* (Cambridge University Press, 1967).

7. M. Morishima and F. Seton, "Aggregation in Leontief Matrices and the Labour Theory of Value," *Econometrica* 29 (April 1961).

8. The original input-output tables had twenty-six industrial sectors. They were augmented by adding a row of depreciation coefficients and a column of fixed capital replacement coefficients because depreciation is considered part of constant capital in Marxian theory but part of value added in standard input-output accounting. The fixed-capital replacement column was estimated from the investment column of final demand.

9. "Labor coefficients," indicating the man-years per dollar of output in each sector, are unavailable for Puerto Rico. To estimate the labor coefficients, we used the wages generated per dollar of output in each sector. In a way, "wage coefficients" are preferable to labor coefficients because wage rates are roughly proportional to skill level, whereas labor coefficients do not differentiate between skilled and unskilled labor. Wage coefficients can therefore be considered a very rough index for "reducing" various kinds of skilled labor to unskilled labor.

10. The vector m was estimated from the household consumption column in final demand. Some error is introduced because household consumption includes both worker and capitalist consumption. Moreover, we implicitly assume that the value of labor power is equivalent to the labor embodied in the average consumption of labor.

11. Though imports are not explicitly mentioned, they are valued as follows: Competitive imports are valued according to the labor value of domestic substitutes. Noncompetitive imports are valued according to the labor value of the average export mix.

12. In Marx's symbols,

$$pm = \frac{v}{v + s} = \frac{1}{1 + (s/v)} = \frac{1}{1 + \epsilon}$$

Two additional assumptions should be mentioned in this derivation. First, to compute m, we assume that workers do not save. Second, we assume that the rate of surplus value is the same for each occupation and for each sector.

Morishima and Seton's derivation is as follows:

(a) $pA + (pm)a_0(1 + \epsilon) = p$

This imposes the condition that the rate of surplus value is the same in each sector because pm is the value of labor power. Solving for p, we obtain:

(b) $p[ma_0(I - A)^{-1}] = \lambda p$

where $\lambda = 1/(1 + \epsilon)$. The largest eigenvalue λ and its corresponding eigenvector yield the rate of surplus value and the total labor required for each dollar of sectoral output.

To see that (b) is equivalent to equation (2), note that pm is equal to λ. Therefore:

(c) $\lambda a_0(I - A)^{-1} = \lambda p$

(d) $p = a_0(I - A)^{-1}$

and

(e) $\frac{1}{1 + \epsilon} = a_0(I - A)^{-1}m$

13. For a description of the data, see R. Weisskoff, with R. Levy, L. Nisonoff, and E. Wolff, "A Multi-Sector Simulation Model of Employment, Growth and Income Distribution in Puerto Rico: A Re-evaluation of 'Successful' Development Strategy," U.S. Department of Labor Research Reports (July 1971), technical appendices.

14. For greater detail on the transformation of market prices to labor values, see Edward Wolff, "The Rate of Surplus Value in Puerto Rico," *Journal of Political Economy* 83 (October 1975).

15. Nubuo Okishio, "Measurement of the Rate of Surplus Value," *The Economic Review* (Hitotsubashi University Institute of Economic Research) 10 (October 1959); and O. Kýn, B. Sekerka, and L. Hejl, "A Model for the Planning of Prices," in Feinstein, ed., *Socialism, Capitalism and Economic Growth*.

16. Price indices were computed for each of the twenty-six sectors and supplied by Richard Weisskoff.

17. The labor value of a commodity is the total labor embodied in one (physical) unit of output. Because sectors in an input-output table produce a mix of commodities, we approximate the change in physical output in a sector by the increase in dollar output in constant (1963) prices.

18. See Michio Morishima, *Marx's Economics* (Cambridge University Press, 1973), chap. 1.

19. m^{48} was first recomputed in 1963 prices.

20. Theoretically a change in labor's average consumption mix will also affect the rate of surplus value. However, the composition of worker consumption was very similar in 1948 and 1963.

21. The theoretically correct concept of organic composition is the ratio of the stock of capital plus the value of produced inputs and depreciation in one turnover period to the variable capital advanced in one turnover period (vol. II, chap. 8). Because capital stock and turnover data are unavailable, we estimated the organic composition by the ratio of produced inputs plus depreciation per annum to the variable capital advanced per annum.

22. The technical composition was estimated as the ratio of the total cost of inputs in thousands of 1963 dollars to the total number of man-years.

Rosa Luxemburg and the Economics of Militarism

K. J. TARBUCK

Graduate Research Student at the University of Sussex, England

I. LUXEMBURG'S MODEL

In the last chapter of her book, *The Accumulation of Capital,* Rosa Luxemburg dealt with what she called "Militarism as a Province of Accumulation." She argued that militarism has three functions in capitalist society: (1) foreign conquest, particularly in the era of primitive accumulation; (2) internal security and repression; and (3) "From the purely economic point of view, it is a pre-eminent means for the realization of surplus value, it is in itself a province of accumulation."[1] It is this latter aspect that she concentrated upon in the rest of the chapter.

In typical style, Luxemburg brushes aside arguments that armaments are, from the standpoint of total social capital, a deduction from total surplus value by insisting that taxation for armaments falls almost wholly upon the working class. Furthermore, she argues that this will not affect total surplus value because no surplus value is realized by selling commodities to the workers. She says:

> Surplus value is never realized by producing means of subsistence for the workers—however necessary this may be. . . .[2]

Here she confuses the production of surplus value and its realization. Surplus value is not realized by producing *anything,* it is realized in the act of exchange, by the sale of commodities. Even more fundamentally mistaken is her conception that surplus value is something separate and apart from the commodities consumed by the workers. It is one of the contradictions of capitalism that from the point of view of capitalism as exploiter the less wages paid the greater the profit, but from the point of view of capitalism as seller of commodities the greater the wages paid the greater the market. This contradiction is an integral part of the totality of capitalism.

Luxemburg starts her examination of arms production using Marx's scheme of expanded reproduction, in volume II of *Capital,* as the basis for her analysis. This is set out so:

Dept. I $5000c + 1000v + 1000s = 7000$
Dept. II $1430c + 285v + 285s = 2000$
Total $6430c + 1285v + 1285s = 9000$

Ken Tarbuck has written extensively on Rosa Luxemburg. This article was prepared especially for this book.

She then proceeds by suggesting that one hundred units of value should be deducted from the combined total of $Iv + IIv$. This, she says, is done by indirect taxation. This tax will fall wholly upon the working class and does not fall upon surplus value. Therefore the net effect is to increase relative surplus value.

The one hundred units of value are used to create "an appropriate branch of production," that is, a third department of social production, the arms industry. This she lays out so:

$$71.5c + 14.25v + 14.25s = 100 \text{ weapons of war}$$

So far the matter is dealt with clearly. However, Luxemburg then rather confuses the issue by stating:

> Now, if the means of subsistence for the workers are cut by 100 units, the corresponding contraction of both departments will give us the following equations:
>
> I $4949c + 989.75v + 989.75s = 6928.5$
> II $1358.5c + 270.75v + 270.75s = 1900$
>
> and for the social product as a whole:
>
> $6307.5c + 1260.5v + 1260.5s = 8828.5$[3]

Commenting upon this she says:

> This looks like a general decrease in both the total volume of production and in the production of surplus value—but only if we contemplate just the abstract quantities of value in the composition of the total product; it does not hold good for the material composition thereof. Looking closer, we find that nothing but the upkeep of labour is in effect decreased.[4]

Now, the first thing that strikes one about the above is that the equation she gives has reduced the total social product by more than one hundred units. It would seem that she reasoned as follows. The one hundred units reduced the workers' demand for the products of Dept. II; that is:

$$\begin{array}{l} 1430c + 285v + 285s \\ -(\quad 71.5c + 14.5v + 14.5s) \\ \hline = 1358.5c + 270.5v + 270.5s \end{array}$$

Because this will reduce the demand for constant capital by $71.5c$, this will be deducted from Dept. I in the following manner:

$$\begin{array}{l} 5000c + 1000v + 1000s \\ -(\quad 51c + 10.25v + 10.25s) \\ \hline = 4949c + 989.75v + 989.75s \end{array}$$

By this method Luxemburg reaches her first, and provisional, expression for total social product:

$$6307.5c + 1260.5v + 1260.5s$$

However, there is something rather odd about this equation. Luxemburg starts with the premise that a reduction of total variable capital will lead to a reduction in the demand for consumption goods produced in Dept. II. From this she infers that this would lead to a reduction in Dept. II's demand upon Dept. I for constant capital (means of production). But she is, in fact, confusing what has been *produced* with what is *demanded.*

If we look at the circuit of capital this can be elucidated. Marx gives the circuit of money capital as $M - C \begin{Bmatrix} L \\ Mp \end{Bmatrix} \ldots . P \ldots . C' - M'$.[5] If we examine one aspect of the circuit we shall see Luxemburg's mistake. Let us look at $M - C$. First the capitalist advances M to buy labor power, so we have $M - C^L$. Looked at from the *worker's* point of view, what we have is this:

worker
C (labor power)

capitalist 1 $M \longrightarrow (C^L - M)$

C (means of consumption)

Similarly, when capitalist 1 buys means of production:

C (means of production and labor power for capitalist 2)

capitalist 1 $M \longrightarrow (C_{Mp} - M)$ (M' for capitalist 2)

C' (commodity capital, with increment value, of capitalist 2)

Looking at the diagrams above, we can see that for the workers the sale of their labor power, which is the precondition for capitalist 1 to engage in production, is a means to acquire money to buy *existing* means of consumption. The same applies in the case of the sale and purchase of means of production, they pre-exist on the market before they are bought by capitalist 1 from capitalist 2.

For capitalist 1 the circuit would still be, $M - C \ldots P \ldots C'$. Any tax imposed upon the workers will not affect the *material* production of the given production period, although it may affect the metamorphoses of $C' - M'$.

If one assumes a given quantity of commodities being *produced,* then a diversion of part of their *value* will not affect demand until the next production period. Luxemburg makes the mistake of confusing the commodity labor power with the commodities that form the fund for the means of consumption.

Looking at the schemes of reproduction, they represent an *ex post* picture of what *has* happened. Therefore there could not be a reduction in the demand for constant capital in the manner in which Luxemburg depicts it. A diversion of a part of the workers' *revenue* would not affect the application of the labor power that the capitalist had bought. Given a constant organic composition of capital, this labor power would set in motion the same quantity of means of production.

Only if one assumes a reduction in the quantity of *labor power* would there be a reduction in the demand for means of production in a given period. If this were the case, and assuming a constant technology, then a reduction of 100 units of labor power would mean a reduction of 500 in constant capital, not, as Luxemburg assumes, merely 71.5.

However, what is interesting is Luxemburg's attempt to introduce a multiplier effect into her argument. Unfortunately she did not allow for time lags in its effects, nor did she attempt to develop the point further.

(It is useful to remark here that although Luxemburg says that the arms industry is a field for accumulation, she consistently fails to include its product in the new total social product.)

Reverting back now to Luxemburg's first equation for the total social product, she draws back at this point and tells us:

If the total cost of maintaining the workers employed in the society came to 1285 units in the first instance, the present decrease of the total social product by 171.5—the difference of $(9000 - 8828.5)$—comes off the maintenance charges, and there is a consequent change in the composition of the social product:

$$6430c + 1113.5v + 1285s = 8828.5 \text{ total social product.}[6]$$

Here Luxemburg has deducted the whole of her 171.5 from the total variable capital, that is, $1285v - 171.5 = 1113.5$.

But then rather unsure of herself, she gives an alternative equation that includes a reduction of the total constant capital. She says:

. . . in case there are any doubts about constant capital being unaffected— we may further allow for the event. . . . The equation for the total social product would be:

$$6307.5c + 1236v + 1285s = 8828.5[7]$$

Again, Luxemburg has not carried through her own thinking correctly; the above equation gives an incorrect ratio of c to v. She has deducted 122.5 from total constant capital, that is, $6430 - 122.5 = 6307.5$; and from the total variable capital we have $1285 - 49 = 1236$. Her ratio of v to c, that is, $49 : 122.5$ gives v as 40 percent of c. To keep the same proportions—where $v = 20$ percent of c— the 171.5 should have been divided in the following manner: $142.92c + 28.58v$. If this is deducted from the original total social capital, we have:

$$6287.08c + 1256.42v + 1285s = 8828.5 \text{ total social product}$$

What we have seen so far is that Luxemburg was rather confused and unsure in her approach to the problems of arms expenditure in relation to the schemes of reproduction. Her slapdash methods had led her into making elementary mistakes in the handling of the schemes.

However, we are still faced with the fundamental question: was Luxemburg correct in her assumption that arms production was, and is, a field for the accumulation of capital? Unfortunately she made no attempt to demonstrate

her thesis other than by giving an equation for the total social product. Without a model which can be taken from cycle to cycle it is somewhat difficult to demonstrate what she asserts, and relate it to actual situations. So it will be necessary to construct such a model, using Luxemburg's own premises in the initial construction.

II. LUXEMBURG'S MODEL—AN APPLICATION

Now to the schemes of reproduction. Luxemburg uses the figures from the first cycle of Marx's second illustration of expanded reproduction to be found in *Capital*, volume II. I shall use a modified form of this scheme to ensure ease of understanding.

I start with:

$$
\begin{array}{ll}
\text{Dept. I} & 5000c + 1000v + 1000s = 7000 \\
\text{Dept. II} & \underline{1461c +\ 292v +\ \ 292s = 2045} \\
& 6461c + 1292v + 1292s = 9045 \text{ total social product}
\end{array}
$$

In the above scheme the capitalists in both departments accumulate 50 percent of s and consume unproductively the other 50 percent. Therefore we have a balanced scheme of reproduction, in equilibrium from the first cycle onwards. Luxemburg's assumption would be that although the workers are paid 1292 total variable capital (that is, the 1292 becomes revenue in the hands of the workers) because of taxation this is reduced to 1192 in real terms. This is a reduction of 7.74 percent, that is, $77.5v1$ and $22.5v2$ (allowing for rounding), and gives us the following:

$$
\begin{array}{llllll}
\text{Dept. I} & 5000c & +\ 922.5v & +\ 1000s & = 6922.5 \\
\text{Dept. II} & 1461c & +\ 269.5v & +\ 292s & = 2022.5 \\
\text{Dept. III} & \underline{\ \ 71.5c} & \underline{+\ 14.25v} & \underline{+\ \ 14.25s} & \underline{=\ \ 100} \\
& 6532.5c & + 1206.25v & + 1306.25s & = 9045 \text{ total social product}
\end{array}
$$

After Luxemburg, I have used the one hundred units deducted from $v1$ and $v2$ to create a third department of production for arms production. These one hundred units have been divided in the same proportions as the original scheme, again as Luxemburg does.

Let us now examine how the process of accumulation will proceed. I begin by showing the allocation of the surplus value in each department; sk = surplus value consumed unproductively by the capitalists, sc = surplus value accumulated in constant capital, and sv = surplus value accumulated as additional labor power, that is, wages for extra workers. I assume that 50 percent of the surplus value is accumulated in all departments. This will give us:

$$
\begin{array}{llllll}
\text{Dept. I} & 5000c & +\ 922.5v & +\ 500sk & +\ 417sc & +\ 83sv \\
\text{Dept. II} & 1461c & +\ 269.5v & +\ 146sk & +\ 122sc & +\ 24sv \\
\text{Dept. III} & 71.5c & +\ 14.5v & +\ 7.125sk & +\ 5.945sc & +\ 1.18sv
\end{array}
$$

Let us now see if supply and demand are in equilibrium:

Means of Production

Supply	Demand	
Production Period 1	Production Period 2	
5000c	5000	c1
1000v	417	sc1
1000s	1461	c2
7000 Units of constant capital	122	sc2
	71.5	c3
	5.945	sc3
	7077.445	

77.445 Excess Demand

Means of Consumption

1461c	922.5	v1
292v	83	sv1
292s	500	sk1
2045 Units of means	269.5	v2
of consumption	24	sv2
	146	sk2
	14.25	v3
	1.18	sv3
	7.125	sk3
	1967.555	

77.445 Excess Supply

Means of Destruction

71.5c	100 From State
14.25v	
14.25s	
100	

It can be seen that using Luxemburg's own assumptions—diverting the one hundred units to arms production—far from providing a field for further accumulation, has pushed the economy into a crisis. This is because her assumptions violated the basic postulates of the schemes of reproduction. Marx consistently maintains that workers are paid the full value of their labor power; there is no sleight of hand by way of cheating on the part of the capitalists. (I am referring to the theoretical aspects here, not the actuality of capitalist relations with workers.) Yet, the capitalists are able to extract surplus value from the workers.

The schemes of reproduction are built on this assumption because they are not designed to deal with the particular aspect of the exploitation of labor—that being dealt with elsewhere by Marx—but rather to illuminate the circulation of the total social capital, in relation to the two main departments of production.

The schemes of reproduction do not take into account the division of surplus value into industrial profit, commercial profit, rent, interest, and so on. Moreover, they are built using value relations, not market price calculations. This being the case it is incorrect to introduce taxation into the scheme in mid-stream, as Luxemburg does, because taxation as applied belongs to the realm of prices. Taxation belongs to the sphere of *money* prices, and today this does not mean commodity money but state paper money. Luxemburg introduces a mechanism that belongs to the sphere of *nominal* wages and attempts to fasten it on, in mid-stream, to a scheme that deals with *real wages*.

What results from Luxemburg's method is a loss of proportionality, on which the scheme is based. It is irrelevant to a *value* scheme that the workers receive X pounds or dollars, with or without taxes being deducted; the unit of account here is not money, but value. Therefore a value scheme would indicate immediately that there was a different amount of value going to variable capital if it had changed from a previous cycle. It is a matter of indifference that the state appropriates the one hundred units of value, or how it does it, in a *value* scheme. The exact mechanism is of no concern at this level of abstraction. What matters is the result. And this result is an increase in relative surplus value, at the direct expense of the workers because they are assumed to produce as much value as they did previously, but receive less. It is, of course, *not* a matter of indifference to the workers that their living standards would have declined. But that is a separate problem from that pertaining to a formal value model. It is not possible in such a model to demonstrate the actual class struggle that ensues when the capitalist class attempts to force down the living standards of the working class. It is only possible to show the *result* of such a struggle. Like all models the schemes of reproduction have to be built with severe restrictions, which, while not necessarily divorced from reality, do not present the whole picture of society, only a partial one.

Whilst appearing to approach the question of arms production from the standpoint of total social capital, Luxemburg, in reality, examined it from the *individual* capitalist's point of view. From the latter point of view, arms production is certainly profitable for the arms producers. However from the macro level of total social capital, arms production *is* unproductive of surplus value. It was this confusion between surplus value and profit, at the micro level, and a confusion between value and price calculations, that led Luxemburg astray.

If one wishes to use Marx's schemes of reproduction, then one must adhere to the assumptions implicit in them. One cannot make an *arbitrary* switch from value to market price calculation in mid-stream without incorporating the results into the process in a conscious manner. Luxemburg was *not* conscious of what she had done in this respect. If one also adds the condition that only the state buys arms, then this will impose further restrictions upon any model one constructs. This further delimiting is perfectly acceptable because on the scale envisioned only the state does buy arms.

III. PRODUCTIVE AND REPRODUCTIVE CAPITAL CONSIDERED

Given the parameters of the schemes of reproduction, one must assume that all the state income is derived from revenue; that is, the state does not engage in capitalist production. Moreover because we are dealing—by definition—with a closed economy, there cannot be any sale of arms to external buyers.

We must ask, therefore, how does the value embodied in armaments reenter the productive cycle? In Marx's two-department scheme of expanded reproduction each of the departments contributes toward the total social process of production and reproduction, that is, accumulation. This is true even though part of the total social product is unproductively consumed. With the introduction of a special department for the production of armaments we have to ask what contribution does it make to this process? Do its products reenter the productive cycle as means of production? Do they reenter the productive cycle as productive consumption, or as means of consumption? Patently not, in none of the cases under consideration. In this respect arms production is akin to the capitalists' own unproductive consumption, but on a collective basis.

The "labor power" expended upon arms production is exchanged for the revenue of the state, and this as such is *not capital*. Combined with the non-reproductive nature of armaments, this makes the labor expended unproductive, even though it may be necessary for the capitalist class as a whole. Without an increase in the rate of exploitation in Depts. I and II, arms production will actually lead to a slower rate of growth and a decline in the average rate of profit. This is because the revenue expended upon arms acts as fictitious capital.

If we compute the average rate of profit, after Marx, as $s/(c + v)$ in the productive sectors of the economy, then with the introduction of an arms-producing sector (which I designate as u) we have $(s - u)/(c + v + u)$. This is the case where u is deducted from s in each cycle and added to $c + v$ for the purpose of computing the average rate of profit. For example, if we take $20c + 10v + 10s$, $s/(c + v) = 10/30 = 33.33$ percent; if one deducts 2 from s and adds it to $c + v$, we have $8/32 = 25$ percent. The rate of profit can only be the same if $u = 0$.

Luxemburg's creation of a special arms production department can only be carried through on her terms, that is, of increasing the rate of exploitation; if one is, at the same time, prepared to drop at least one of the previous assumptions, that of the same rate of accumulation in Depts. I and II in the first cycle of the changeover. Up to now it was assumed that Dept. II would accumulate one half of the surplus value generated in that department, and the capitalists would consume the other half unproductively, as in Dept. I.

Let us examine what will happen if we follow this method. Luxemburg suggested that new taxes are levied on the workers, thereby depressing the real wage and increasing the rate of exploitation and the rate of surplus value; that is, that there would be an increase in the relative surplus value. As we have seen, she used Marx's second illustration of expanded reproduction as the basis for her exposition. I shall use the modified scheme set out earlier and demonstrate what I consider to be a correct exposition of the question.

First, I shall show expanded reproduction in equilibrium without arms production, and this I call scheme (A). From this we shall be able to compare the results when arms production is introduced; the arms production scheme I call scheme (B).

We start with scheme (A):

$$
\begin{array}{lll}
\text{Dept. I} & 5000c + 1000v + 1000s = 7000 \\
\text{Dept. II} & \underline{1461c + 292v + 292s = 2045} \\
& 6461c + 1292v + 1292s = 9045
\end{array}
$$

s/v = 100 percent, variable capital is 20 percent of constant capital, and $s/(c + v)$ = 16.66 percent. 50 percent of the surplus value is accumulated, and the other 50 percent is consumed unproductively in both departments.

Allocating s for accumulation and consumption we have:

$$
\begin{array}{lll}
\text{Dept. I} & 5000c + 1000v + 500sk + 417sc + 83sv = 7000 \\
\text{Dept. II} & \underline{1461c + 292v + 146sk + 122sc + 24sv = 2045} \\
& 6461c + 1292v + 646sk + 539sc + 107sv = 9045
\end{array}
$$

From the above we can state that $c1 + sc1 + c2 + sc2 = 7000$, and $c1 + v1 + s1 = 7000$; therefore the sum of c demanded is equal to the product of Dept. I. And, $v1 + sv1 + sk1 + v2 + sv2 + sk2 = 2045$, and $c2 + v2 + s2 = 2045$; therefore the sum of v, sv, and sk is equal to the product of Dept. II. For the scheme to be in equilibrium the exchanges between the two departments must also balance.

Therefore, $c2 + sc2 = 1583$, and $v1 + sv1 + sk1 = 1583$. Because $c2 + sc2$ are in the material form of means of consumption and $v1 + sv1 + sk1$ are in the material form of means of production, these quantities must be exchanged for expanded reproduction to take place. From this we can say that $c2 + sc2 = v1 + sv1 + sk1$ is the fundamental equation for expanded reproduction with a two-department scheme of reproduction.

Now let us look at Luxemburg's proposals and see how they affect this scheme. She suggests that the total variable capital should be reduced by one hundred units. Whilst maintaining the same amount of newly produced value, $v + s$, we can divide it differently. This is so we can indicate an increase in the relative surplus value immediately. This is deducted from $v1$ and $v2$ in the same proportions as in the previous example and added to $s1$ and $s2$. We then have scheme (B):

$$
\begin{array}{lll}
\text{Dept. I} & 5000c + 922.5v + 1077.5s = 7000 \\
\text{Dept. II} & \underline{1461c + 269.5v + 314.5s = 2045} \\
& 6461c + 1192v + 1392s = 9045
\end{array}
$$

A glance at the above scheme will show that three proportions have changed; v/c = 18.45 percent, s/v = 116.77 percent, and $s/(c + v)$ = 18.18 percent. Luxemburg at this point would have deducted the one hundred units from Depts. I and II, creating a third department. This would have taken the form of $71.5c + 14.5v + 14.5s$.

Apart from all the problems noted earlier, to create such a new department in this manner would have the odd result of an arms industry with a lower organic composition of capital than that in the other two departments. Moreover because this is assumed to be the *first* cycle with a diversion of resources to arms production, surplus value would not be created at this point. The allocation for arms production must be at least of the same organic composition of capital as in the other two departments and will have to be deducted from the respective departments proportionately. Therefore I will divide the one hundred units allocated for arms production in the following manner: $84.44c + 15.56v$. Thus we can lay out the first cycle for accumulation su; designating the portion of surplus value going to arms production u:

$$
\begin{array}{lll}
\text{Dept. I} & 5000c + 922.5v + 538.75sk + 383.61sc + 70.7sv & + 84.44su \\
\text{Dept. II} & 1461c + 269.5v + 214.95sk + 70.95sc + 13.04sv & + 15.56su
\end{array}
$$

We can now see how supply and demand will be in equilibrium.

Dept. I—Means of Production

Supply Production Period 1 Output (PP1)		Demand Production Period 2 Input (PP2)	
5000	$c1$	5000	$c1$
922.5	$v1$	383.61	$sc1$
1077.5	$s1$	1461	$c2$
7000.0		70.95	$sc2$
		84.44	$uc3$
		7000.00	

Dept. II—Means of Consumption

1461	$c2$	922.5	$v1$
269.5	$v2$	70.7	$sv1$
314.5	$s2$	538.75	$sk1$
2045.0		269.5	$v2$
		13.04	$sv2$
		214.95	$sk2$
		15.56	$uv3$
		2045.00	

It will be noted that the $84.44su1$ and the $15.56su2$ of Production Period 1 represent a demand for c and v from Dept. III arising in PP2. Thus at the end of the cycle we have the same total social product—9045—as in scheme (A). However if one compares the increase in productive and reproductive capital, one can see the difference between the two schemes. Scheme (A) started with a total social capital of 7753, and during the course of the cycle 646 new capital was added to this ($sc1 + sv1 + sc2 + sv2$), giving a new total social productive capital

of 8399. With scheme (B) we started with a total social capital of 7653, and only 538.3 reproductive capital was added during the cycle, giving a new total social reproductive capital of 8191.3. Thus from the point of view of the total social capitalist the increase has been less with arms production than it was without it. Not only was less accumulated in absolute terms but also as a percentage; 8.33 percent was added in scheme (A), and 7.03 percent in scheme (B).

Of course from the point of view of the individual capitalist the portion of surplus value "invested" in Dept. III is also capital. Up to now I have ignored the question of the production of surplus value in Dept. III. Let us follow scheme (B) from Production Period 2 to Production Period 3, *using Luxemburg's thesis that surplus value is created in Dept. III.*

PP2 Input

Dept. I $5383.61c + 993.2v$
Dept. II $1531.95c + 282.5v$
Dept. III $84.44c + 15.56v$

I assume an average rate of surplus value of 116.77 percent, that is, the same as in PP1, and this gives us:

Dept. I $5383.61c + 993.2v + 1159.75s$
Dept. II $1531.95c + 282.5v + 329.92s$
Dept. III $84.44c + 15.56v + 18.17s$

I again assume that one hundred units from Depts. I and II are allocated for arms production, and allocate the surplus value in all departments for accumulation:

Dept. I $579.87sk + 418.35sc + 77.09sv + 84.44su = 1159.75s$
Dept. II $174.38sk + 118.21sc + 21.77sv + 15.56su = 329.92s$
Dept. III $9.09sk + 7.68sc + 1.4sv = 18.17s$

We are now in a position to test Luxemburg's thesis that armament production is a field for accumulation.

Dept. I—Means of Production

Supply—Output of PP2	Demand—Including Input of PP3
5383.61 $c1$	5383.61 $c1$
993.2 $v1$	418.35 $sc1$
1159.75 $s1$	1531.95 $c2$
7536.56	118.21 $sc2$
	84.44 $uc3$
	7.68 $sc3$
	7544.24

Excess Demand of 7.68

Dept. II—Means of Consumption

Supply—Output of PP2	Demand—Including Input of PP3
1531.95 $c2$	993.2 $v1$
282.54 $v2$	77.09 $sv1$
329.92 $s2$	579.87 $sk1$
2144.41	282.54 $v2$
	21.77 $sv2$
	174.38 $sk2$
	15.56 $uv3$
	1.4 $sv3$
	9.09 $sk3$
	2154.90

Excess Demand of 10.49

It can be readily seen that the excess demand in Depts. I and II are a total of 18.17—equal to the "surplus value" supposedly generated in Dept. III. If this "surplus value" is deducted, it will be seen that supply and demand will balance in the two main departments of production. However this leaves unresolved the question of surplus value in Dept. III because it is obvious that the capitalists in that department do not "work" for nothing. So it is to that question we must now turn.

IV. THE ARMS PRODUCERS DO NOT LIVE BY STEEL ALONE

It can be seen that from the standpoint of the total social capital Dept. III is unproductive of surplus value and its products are nonreproductive. However because the capitalists who engage in such production obviously do so to make a profit, such a value scheme as set above should indicate that portion of surplus value accruing to them to be consumed for their own unproductive consumption.

The simplest method is to take the sum of $sk1 + sk2$ and divide this among the capitalists of the three departments according to the "capital" therein. It should be emphasized that because this is a value scheme this is all that is required. This method is adopted because it has the merit of simplicity and also separates out the disproportionate burdens falling upon the working class. This can be seen in the following manner. If we assume that in Depts. I and II the same number of workers are employed after the increase in the rate of surplus value as before, then the same workers receive 1275.74 total variable capital, in the form of wages, instead of 1382.705, a decline on the order of 8 percent. The capitalists of Depts. I and II will receive a total of 744.95, for unproductive consumption, instead of 754.25, a reduction of 1.23 percent.

In total, the sum of $c3 + v3 + sk3 = 109.3$, and this is equal to 7.337 percent of the total surplus value. To have deducted the whole sum in this way would have masked the above disparities.

I set out below a reproduction scheme indicating a special department for

arms production, with all the necessary adjustments made as stated above. I start from the second cycle of scheme (B):

PP2 Output

Dept. I $5383.61c + 993.2v + 1159.75s$
Dept. II $1531.95c + 282.54v + 329.92s$
Dept. III $84.44c + 15.56v$

Allocation of accumulation and consumption:

Dept. I $5383.61c + 993.2v + 579sk + 418.35sc + 77.09sv + 84.44su$
Dept. II $1531.95c + 282.54v + 165.95sk + 118.21sc + 21.77sv + 15.56su$
Dept. III $84.44c + 15.56v + 9.3sk$

We are now in a position to see how supply and demand will equilibrate.

Dept. I—Means of Production

Supply—Output PP2	Demand—Including Input for PP3
5383.61 $c1$	5383.61 $c1$
993.2 $v1$	418.35 $sc1$
1159.75 $s1$	1531.95 $c2$
7536.56	118.21 $sc2$
	84.44 $uc3$
	7536.56

Dept. II—Means of Consumption

1531.95 $c2$	993.2 $v1$
282.54 $v2$	77.09 $sv1$
329.92 $s2$	579.0 $sk1$
2141.41	282.54 $v2$
	21.77 $sv2$
	165.95 $sk2$
	15.56 $uv3$
	9.3 $usk3$
	2141.41

Dept. III—Means of Destruction

84.44 $uc3$	109.3 State
15.56 $uv3$	
9.3 $usk3$	
109.3	

It can be seen that from a decision to create a third department for arms production there has been an actual transfer of 109.3 as the "price" for obtaining the arms. This result is not so peculiar as it may at first sight appear. Insofar as

the state buys arms it deals in physical quantities, but to obtain these in the commodity *form* of sale and purchase it must command *value* of 109.3.

At this point it will be instructive to compare scheme (A) with scheme (B), taking both to the end of PP2:

(A)		**(B)**
7753	Total social capital at the beginning of PP1	7653
9045	Total social product of PP1	9045
8399	Total social capital at the end of PP1	8191.26
8399	Total social capital at the start of PP2	8191.26
9798	Total social product of PP2	9680.93
9098	Total social capital at the end of PP2	8826.68

Not only has scheme (A) grown more than scheme (B) in absolute terms but also in percentage terms; that is, 17.34 as against 15.33 percent. We can see that far from arms production being a field for accumulation, or even merely a reshuffle of the total social product, it will in fact lead to a smaller total social product and smaller total social capital.

However, if armaments are sold outside of the closed economy, then it is possible that they will gather an increment of surplus value. But then we are faced with exogenous accumulation for the particular economy, and for the world economy it will still be a deduction from total surplus value. As such the gain of one particular capitalist economy would merely be at the expense of another, a transfer of surplus value, not the creation of it.

Luxemburg tells us that the arms industry is a field for accumulation, for the production and realization of surplus value. But she laid out the one hundred units that she deducted from variable capital as:

$$71.5c + 14.25v + 14.25s = 100 \text{ weapons of war}$$

Thus we have not the creation of surplus value, but a *transfer* of value. Luxemburg shows, with her own presentation, that the supposed extra surplus value accruing to the capitalist class has not been *produced* by the arms industry, but is merely a portion of the existing value transferred from both $v1$ and $v2$. It is also noteworthy that Luxemburg does not include the product of the arms industry when she gives her modified equations for the total social product.

The one situation in which arms production could be considered to have a stimulating effect upon a capitalist economy is where there are idle resources. State expenditure in a period of economic slump can give the economy an upwards impulse. Arms production has the "merit" from the capitalists' point of view that it does not compete with normal commodity circulation. However, such expenditure is a call upon existing or future surplus value. Only insofar as military expenditure is able to call upon idle resources will it have no inflationary effects. With a situation of near or full capacity working in an economy, arms production will tend to have inflationary consequences.

It would be beyond the scope of this essay to make more than this mention of such a situation. What it does indicate is that although Luxemburg was wrong

in her main assumption—that arms production was a field for accumulation—it did highlight the possibilities inherent in state expenditure for the manipulation of capitalist economies. The full flowering of such activities did not emerge until after the second World War.

V. THE ANTI-REVISIONIST PURPOSE OF LUXEMBURG'S THESIS

From what I have said up to now, it would be wrong to assume that Luxemburg had any conception other than that armaments were a drain upon socially useful resources. She had a very lively appreciation of the true nature of militarism, and this dated from her earliest days within the German Social Democratic movement. In 1899 she polemicised against Max Schippel, who had suggested that arms production could provide some relief from overproduction within capitalist society. It is clear from what Luxemburg wrote that she either misunderstood what Schippel was saying or that she pushed his ideas to their "logical" conclusion, a method of disputation that still finds favor in some quarters.

Luxemburg led off by saying that "Schippel thinks current militarism is economically indispensable because it 'relieves' society from economic pressures. . . . When he speaks of 'relief' he is plainly thinking of *capital*. And to that extent he is correct: for capital, militarism is one of the most important forms of investment; from the point of view of capital, militarism is certainly a *relief*. And the fact [is] that Schippel speaks here as a true representative of the interests of capital."[8]

We can see that fourteen years later, when she came to write *Accumulation*, Luxemburg had not changed her fundamental position on this question. However, against Schippel she continued:

> Now, it is indeed clear that if the same money, which the government gets its hands on through taxes and uses to maintain the military, were to remain in the hands of the people, it would stimulate an increased demand for foodstuffs, or if a greater proportion were used by the state for cultural ends, it would at the same time create a corresponding demand for socially productive labour. It is of course clear that because of this fact, militarism is in no way a "relief" for society as a whole. The question appears differently only from the point of view of capitalist profits, from the entrepreneur's point of view.[9]

The thread of continuity runs through this essay of Luxemburg's to her later writings. She continually looked at the question of profitability from the standpoint of the *individual* capitalist, not from that of the total social capitalist. This explains her confusion and uncertainty when trying to grapple with the problem on the abstract level of the reproduction schemes. She explicitly equates capitalist profits with "the entrepreneur's point of view." Certainly she understood the social evils of militarism, and that the wealth squandered on it could have been used to greater advantage in a rationally ordered society. But she failed to see that militarism is a *necessity* and a permanent item of cost for the capitalist *class*. When discussing militarism and arms production one cannot abstract them from the insane "logic" of a class society.

Schippel, who had been castigated in no uncertain manner, attempted to explain his position in a letter to the *Leipziger Volkszeitung*:

> In the *Neue Zeit*, I merely explained that the enormous unproductive expenditures—whether those of the private sector for crazy luxuries and sheer foolishness, or those of the state for the military, sinecures, and all kind of junk—cool the fever of the crisis by which a society which "overproduces" would be continually shaken if the unproductive waste did not occupy an ever broader space alongside accumulation for productive purposes. Obviously I did not therefore in the least approve of wasteful and unproductive expenditures, and even less did I *demand them in the interests of the working class*. I only tried to point to *objective* consequences of these expenditures "for modern society" which are *different* from those consequences which are generally emphasised.[10]

Luxemburg curtly dismissed Schippel's explanation, yet the difference between them on this particular point is very narrow. Both obviously regard armaments as wasteful, both see them as profitable for certain sections of the capitalist class. Luxemburg's objection is really centered on Schippel's suggestion that such arms expenditure could be used countercyclically; yet there is nothing in Luxemburg's own basic theory on arms production that would run counter to this. Indeed, a whole school of thought in the modern Marxist movement has taken up and elaborated this very point of Schippel's, while at the same time swearing fealty to Luxemburg.

Perhaps the most significant difference between the two points of view is that Luxemburg sees arms production as a field for the realization of surplus value and the accumulation of capital, while Schippel sees the problem as one of the disposal of excess surplus value. Modern readers will no doubt see the affinity between Schippel's line of thought on the need for waste expenditure to "occupy an ever broader space alongside accumulation" and Baran and Sweezy's concept of the rising economic surplus under monopoly capitalism.[11] In this respect Luxemburg was on surer ground from an orthodox Marxist point of view, because she locates the problem within the sphere of production rather than in the sphere of circulation, as do Schippel and the later theorists.

However, Luxemburg did point to other aspects of arms production that had, and still do have, considerable influence upon the development of capitalism:

> . . . the most important advantage of military contracts over state expenditure for cultural purposes (schools, roads etc.), is the endless technical innovations and the ceaseless growth of expenditures, so that militarism provides an inexhaustible, indeed ever increasing source of capitalist profit and erects capital as social power which the worker comes against. . . . Militarism, which for society as a whole is a completely absurd squandering of huge productive forces, which for the working class signifies a reduction of its economic standard of living . . . creates for the *capitalist classes* an irreplaceable, and economically the most advantageous kind of investment.[12]

The really prescient point in the above is Luxemburg's foresight into the technological and scientific consequences of a significant sector of an economy

being devoted to arms production. The full impact of such activity came to fruition after the second World War, with manifest and palpable consequences for the whole of the world capitalist economy.

The domination of Keynesian theories of state intervention into the economy for countercyclical purposes helped to give economic "rationality" and "respectability" to the high levels of military expenditures in the capitalist economies. The arms race between East and West—to use a conventional euphemism—saw an accelerated tempo of scientific research and technological innovation, very often first in arms production and then rapidly spilling over into the rest of the economy. In this respect, Luxemburg was fully vindicated.[13]

Nevertheless, right at the heart of Luxemburg's approach to arms production lay a flaw that was contradictory and misleading. She was never able to resolve, in her own mind, this problem in a satisfactory manner because there was the inability to distinguish between the individual capitalist and the collective capitalist. Had she made this distinction, she would have had to acknowledge that the profitability of the singular was at the expense of the plural.

All of the above must be set in the context in which Luxemburg was working; this was the debate with the revisionists in the German Social Democratic Party (SPD), headed by Bernstein. No doubt the particular bite in her polemic with Schippel was due to the critical importance that Luxemburg, quite correctly, placed upon the controversy. Luxemburg was concerned that the SPD should not lose sight of its ultimate goals in an attempt to obtain short-term advantages:

> The essential characteristic of opportunist politics is that step by step it always leads to sacrificing the final goal of the movement, the interests of the working-class liberation, to its more immediate, and in fact imagined, interests.[14]

So far as Schippel, and the other revisionists, had a *political* aim, Luxemburg homed in on it with great precision.

> ... insofar as he [Schippel] supposes that every economic advantage for the investors is necessarily an advantage for the working class, he also takes as his starting point the basic position of the *harmony of interests between labour and capital*.[15]

This was the key to her assault upon Schippel. Her revolutionary politics carried her through to correct political conclusions *despite* some of the flaws in the analysis of the economic questions.

Luxemburg linked Schippel's arguments about the economic effects of arms production with his advocacy of a revision of the SPD's program on militia. The SPD advocated the abolition of the standing army and its replacement by a universal militia under democratic control. Schippel argued that the militia should grow out of the existing standing army, that is, an evolutionary projection rather than one that initiated a fundamental rupture of the existing *class* structures. It was because of this that Luxemburg saw the *whole* of Schippel's "practical politics":

> Schippel's defence of militarism is an obvious elaboration of the entire revisionist tendency in our Party, and at the same time an important step in its development. . . . In one case *bourgeois tactics* were merely suggested in place of Social Democratic tactics, now the *bourgeois programme* boldly takes the place of the Social Democratic programme.[16]

The results of such policies as Schippel, Bernstein, and so on advocated were seen in August 1914, when the SPD collapsed into the arms of imperialist militarism. It was not militarism that had faded away through the adoption of evolutionary politics, but rather the revolutionary socialist soul of the SPD. Luxemburg sat in jail, in 1914, for her opposition to militarism and the war, whilst the SPD accepted "the harmony of interests between labor and capital." The historical judgement, in this respect, is clearly with her.

NOTES

1. Rosa Luxemburg, *The Accumulation of Capital* (London: Routledge and Kegan Paul, 1951), p. 454.
2. Ibid., p. 461.
3. Ibid., p. 462.
4. Ibid.
5. M = money capital, C = commodity capital, L = labor power, Mp = means of production, P = productive capital (production process), C' = commodity capital with an increment of value, and M' = money capital with an increment of value. In value terms $C' = C + c$, $M' = M + m$, and $C' > C$, $M' > M$.
6. Luxemburg, *Accumulation of Capital*, p. 462.
7. Ibid., p. 463.
8. Rosa Luxemburg, "Militia and Militarism," in *Selected Political Writings of Rosa Luxemburg*, ed. Dick Howard (New York: 1971), p. 137.
9. Ibid., p. 141.
10. Schippel, reprinted in Luxemburg, "Militia and Militarism," p. 151.
11. See P. Baran and P. Sweezy, *Monopoly Capital* (New York: Monthly Review Press, 1966).
12. Luxemburg, "Militia and Militarism," p. 140.
13. For an early post second World War attempt to use Luxemburg's ideas on arms and accumulation see Fritz Sternberg, *The Coming Crisis* (London: 1947).
14. Luxemburg, "Militia and Militarism," p. 140.
15. Ibid., p. 142.
16. Ibid., p. 145.

PART III

The System
of Capitalism:
A Permanent State
of Emergency

10

Marxist Theory, Class Struggle, and the Crisis of Capitalism

PETER F. BELL

Associate Professor of Economics at State University of New York, at Purchase

Capital is not a thing, but rather a definite social production relation, belonging to a definite historical formation of society, which is manifested in a thing and lends this thing a specific social character. Capital is not the sum of the material and produced means of production. Capital is rather the means of production transformed into capital, which in themselves are no more capital than gold or silver in itself is money. It is the means of production monopolized by a certain section of society, confronting living labour-power as products and working conditions rendered independent of this very labour power, which are personified through this antithesis in capital.—Karl Marx, *Capital,* vol. III (New York: International Publishers, 1967), pp. 814–15.

World capitalism is in the midst of a profound crisis. There are high rates of unemployment, inflation, declining living standards, and widespread political instability. Bourgeois economic theory is in disarray. Faced with the bankruptcy of neoclassical economics and the failure of Keynesian policies, there has been a marked revival of interest in Marxian theories. Indeed capital and its theorists are looking increasingly to radicals and Marxists for explanations.[1]

There are, however, profound disagreements within the Marxist movement regarding the nature of the current crisis of capitalism. These are not mere academic squabbles but form part of a larger political struggle as to the theory and practice of Marxism.[2] Clarification of these issues is essential if Marxian theory is to be used as a weapon by the working class and not as a tool by capital to solve its problems.

The differences originate in the most basic issues; it is the purpose of this essay to clarify these issues. The methodological character of Marx's work may seem to involve remote philosophical issues, yet it serves as a basis for profound political disagreement. Within the broad spectrum of tendencies within the Marxist movement, broadly defined, we find the following groups: (1) those

An earlier version of this paper was presented at the Meetings of Union for Radical Political Economics, Dallas, Texas, December 28, 1975. I would like to thank Harry Cleaver for continuous discussion and assistance in clarifying the issues in this paper, and Ellen Grasso for the typing and production.

with radical and anarchistic tendencies who see capitalism as immoral, anarchic, conspiratorial, or alienating;[3] (2) the old sectarian groups on the Left who share a common basis in "dialectical materialism" and who engage in a debate over Marxology concerning which "laws of capitalist production" can be used as a guide to "praxis";[4] (3) Hegelian Marxists, stimulated by the Frankfurt School, who are attracted to the completeness of the Hegelian system and seek to locate Marx within Hegel's project by completing a *theory* of bourgeois society in which Marx becomes part of the realization of the Idea;[5] and (4) Marxist economists who read *Capital* in the light of bourgeois economic theory, as a set of technical problems to be unravelled with the aid of modern mathematical tools, to complete a better *theory* of the capitalist economy.[6]

The debate regarding Marx's crisis theory grows out of this broader disagreement.[7] Three opposed economic views of the crisis have gained some measure of support in recent years:[8] (1) neo-Ricardian, which focuses on distributional aspects of the class struggle; (2) underconsumptionist, which centers on the realization crisis; and (3) falling rate of profit/organic composition of capital theorists, who see these relationships as a necessary expression of the law of value. Although each of these views embodies important political differences, this paper will attempt to identify the important theoretical inadequacies of each position so far as their respective grasps over Marx's method and the theory of capital accumulation are concerned. These differences are often posed as a problem of selecting *one* of the many elements contained in Marx's discussion of crises and attempting to validate it as the correct theory through careful citation of the texts and/or empirical data.[9] This has introduced a stasis into the discussion that is itself antithetical to Marx's method. Such an approach is also akin to bourgeois theory which proposes "models" of partial aspects of reality to serve as monocausal explanations for the whole around which complexity can be fitted. Much of the current debate is misplaced in that it denies the dialectical nature of reality, replacing it with cause-and-effect relationships. It will be argued, to the contrary, that capitalist reality must be seen as unity of many complex determinations that derive from the nature of capital.

It is necessary to first distinguish the character of capitalist production *in general* from the particular *forms* in which crises develop because there are many forms consistent with the process of accumulation. It will be argued that there is but a single theory of crises *in general*, and that Marx's theory is neither incomplete nor contradictory. It must be grasped by seeing how he develops an understanding of the character of capitalist production as a whole, seen as the unity of both production and circulation.

Crises will be seen as specific determinations of the process of accumulation in general, appearing in different forms at different stages in the development of capitalism, and emanating from the central dialectic of capital, the relationship between capital and labor. A concrete analysis of the current crisis will be discussed by applying this understanding to the specific conditions of contemporary capitalism.

These conclusions differ from the widely accepted approaches in terms of Marxian theory, particular readings of *Capital,* and the analysis of crises. A critique of existing theories must therefore set forth a methodological basis at the outset. The first section does this with a brief discussion of epistemology, of

the manner in which class relations form the basis of the logic of capitalism, and
of the process of accumulation in particular. It will be shown later that this
suggests a relationship between theory and praxis that brings a political immediacy to the discussion of crises.

I. MARXIAN METHODOLOGY AND
THE ANALYSIS OF CAPITALISM

A. Epistemology

For Marx, Hegel's dissolution of the old philosophical problem of epistemology
had important political implications.[10] He argues that *Capital* is not based on
arbitrary mental categories, but is thought reproducing the reality of which it is
a part. The manner in which the theory is generated captures the actual forms in
which things appear. Responding to a critic with regard to his notion of "value"
at the beginning of *Capital,* volume I, he states:

> At the outset I do not start from "concepts" and hence do not start from
> the "concept of value," and therefore do not have to "divide" the latter
> in any way. What I start from is the simplest social form in which the
> labour product is represented in contemporary society, and this is the
> *commodity.* I analyse this, and indeed, first in the *form in which it appears.*
> Here I find that on the one hand it is in its natural form a thing of use,
> alias a *use-value,* on the other hand *a bearer of exchange value. . . .* it is
> not I who divide "value" into use-value and exchange-value as opposition
> into which the abstraction "value" divides itself, but the concrete *social
> form* of the labour product. . . .[11]

Discussing the concept of abstract labor he argues analogously:

> This abstraction labour is *not merely the mental product* of a concrete
> totality of labours. Indifference towards specific labours corresponds to a
> form of society in which individuals can with ease transfer from one
> labour to another. . . . Not only the *category,* labour, but labour in *reality*
> has here become the means of creating wealth in general. . . . [In the
> United States] the abstraction of the category "labour," "labour as such,"
> labour pure and simple, becomes true *in practice.*[12]

These passages suggest clearly the breakdown of the traditional theory/
reality dualism and give an immediacy to the analysis in *Capital.* The concept of
abstract labor contains the real process of capital's impact on the working class,
its social power in turning labor into a homogeneous mass, "indifferent to its
particular specificity, but capable of all specificities."[13] With the dissolution of
the old dualistic distinctions, the theory-practice dichotomy of the sectarian
left (Marx provides the economic theory, Lenin the political practice) is called
into question. Thus the political implications of this epistemological approach
are profound and must be drawn out in terms of our understanding of crises.

A second essential difference lies in the manner in which Marx's method
is distinct from that of the political economists and from bourgeois conceptions
of science in general. Theory must be developed dialectically.

> The method of arising from the abstract to the concrete is the only way
> in which thought appropriates the concrete, reproduces it as the concrete
> in the mind.[14]

This movement, which Marx terms the "scientifically correct method," is
not a movement from the world of thought to the real world (for the reasons
discussed above); it is rather a movement from a reality with few determinations
to one that is a "rich totality of many determinations and relations . . . unity of
the diverse." Theory reproduces reality by building from the simplest relations
to a complex and unified whole. It is important to see that *Capital* is a development of the simplest relations, that of capital and wage labor, to the complex
forms in which this is expressed in the system as a whole.

B. Class Relations and *Capital*

Marx stated that the "guiding principle" of his studies was that the social relations of production constituted the real foundation of society and conditioned
its development in general.[15] In *Capital* the relation between capital and labor
constitutes the essential and most abstract relation of capitalist society and is
therefore the foundation of the entire analysis. The three volumes of *Capital*
reveal successively more determinate levels of understanding of how the relations between capital and labor determine the character of exchange, production,
circulation, and their unity in terms of the process as a whole.

The starting point of the analysis is dictated by the manner in which the
results of inquiry must be presented.[16] The discussion of the sphere of exchange
reveals that the social relations of capitalist society are *value* relations (because
socially necessary labor time serves as the basis of commodity exchange). For
labor to serve as the substance and magnitude of value, it must take on a particular form. Labor-value is the basis of exchange only because abstract labor is
the historically determined form of labor under capital; the social relations of
exchange are determined by the social relations of production. Value analysis
reveals the basis of class power: for labor to form the basis of capitalist wealth,
capital must have the ability to impose the commodity form on the working
class, to reproduce labor as abstract labor.[17] The logic of capitalism is an amplification of these class relations that center on the ability of capital to appropriate value from the owners of labor-power:

> The secret of the self-expansion of capital resolves itself into having the
> disposal of a definite quantity of other people's unpaid labour.[18]

The concept of capital that is developed in *Capital* consists in this relation:

> In order to become capital, it itself presupposes labour as not-capital as
> against capital; hence it presupposes the establishment at another point of
> the contradiction it presupposes to overcome . . . capital, too cannot con-
> front capital, if capital does not confront labour, since capital is only
> capital as not-labour; in this contradictory relation. Thus the concept and
> relation of capital itself would be destroyed.[19]

The movement from the abstract to the concrete is thus a process of seeing the manner in which the capital-labor relationship determines the nature of capitalist production, from the nature of commodity exchange and production in *Capital*, volume I, to the movement of the whole in volume III.

From the perspective of seeing *Capital* as successively determinate forms of class struggle, volume I reveals how the various forms that this struggle takes in the sphere of direct production center on the terms on which surplus value can be extracted. The self-expansion of capital depends on its strength vis-à-vis the working class as measured by the rate of exploitation. Absolute and relative forms of surplus value are concrete strategies employed by capital to enlarge surplus value and include lengthening of the working day, the intensity, the organization, and the productivity of work. The latter includes mechanization or changes in the organic composition of capital as responses to working-class resistance.[20]

Class struggle provides the logic and the dynamic of capitalist production, which proceeds in terms of offensives and counteroffensives by both capital and the working class, which Marx documents at length for his own day. The dialectic of struggle is the self-expansion of capital and constitutes the basis of accumulation and, as we shall see below, of crises as well. The outcome of this struggle must be seen in historically specific conditions. There is no single predictable outcome. In volume I accumulation is not merely seen as the growing size of means of production, a physical notion, as many commentators have implied,[21] but is the continuous extension of the class relation. Reproduction is reproduction of the working class: "The maintenance and reproduction of the working-class is and must ever be, a necessary condition to the reproduction of capital."[22] This involves the sphere of workers' consumption and the production of labor-power as a means to the enlargement of capital. The individual consumption of the laborer is "the production and reproduction of that means of production so indispensable to the capitalist: the laborer himself."[23] The *rate* of accumulation depends on the outcome of the class struggle and the dividing and recomposition of the working class as a whole, as between the waged and unwaged segments, through the reserve army of the unemployed. (These ideas are discussed later, in section IV.)

From the discussion in volume I it is clear that the "laws of motion" are inseparable from historically concrete stages of development of the capital-labor relationship. Crises are not the movements of "things," but the breakdown of the smooth reproduction of the class relationship. Crises are not the expression of abstract theoretical categories, but the real statement of the actual cycles of struggle between capital and the working class.

Although this point is often grasped in volume I, there is a tendency in the Marxist literature to argue that class struggle is confined to the direct process of production and does not underlie the rest of the analysis. This is based on a misunderstanding of the method outlined above, and it will be argued here that volumes II and III are more determinate levels of the capital-labor relationship. Some elements can be briefly stated here.

In volume II the relation of capital to labor underlies the circuit of money capital:

The capital relation during the process of production arises only because it is inherent in the act of circulation, in the different fundamental economic conditions in which buyer and seller confront each other, in their class relation.[24]

Through the analysis of circulation, capital is seen "not only as class relations," but as "a movement, a circuit-describing process" in which "capitalist production exists and can endure only so long as capital-value is made to create surplus-value. . . ."[25]

Marx returns to the question of the reproduction of social capital to emphasize again that the circulation of commodities (and thus the reproduction of labor-power) is an essential part of the process of reproduction and lies outside of the circuit of individual capital. As in volume I the reproduction of total social capital is seen not merely as the sum of capitals, but as the reproduction of social relations.[26] As part of this discussion, the proportional growth of means of production and consumption is discussed in terms of Departments. Although not explicitly analyzed by Marx, the size of Department II reflects the strength of the working class in raising the value of labor-power and hence enlarging the production of subsistence goods.

There is a tendency to ignore the process of circulation or to see it in terms of movements of *things* (money, means of production, or commodities), whereas for Marx it is an extension of the character of capital as self-expanding value; it is a circular movement or circuit, based on class relations.[27]

As the process of production and circulation are analyzed for the first time together in volume III, the manner in which class struggle underlies the movements of total social capital is harder to discern. Yet Marx insists on these connections when establishing the analysis as a more concrete but inseparable stage in the analysis of volume I:

Surplus-value and the rate of surplus-value are, relatively, the invisible and unknown essence that wants investigating, while rate of profit and therefore the appearance of surplus-value in the form of profit are revealed on the surface of phenomenon.[28]

He also insists on these connections when discussing the complex manner in which the unity of production and circulation reveal themselves concretely:

The actual process of production and the process of circulation intertwine and intermingle continually, and thereby adulterate their typical distinctive features. . . . Capital passes through the circuit of its metamorphoses. Finally, stepping beyond its inner organic life, so to say, it enters into relations with outer life, into relations in which it is not capital and labour which confront one another, but capital and capital in one case, and individuals, again simply as buyers as sellers, in the other. *The original form in which capital and wage-labour confront one another* is disguised through the intervention of relationships seemingly independent of it.[29]

The original manner in which class struggle determines these "seemingly independent" relationships is "disguised" in the relations between capitals and

between individuals. In the realm of appearance, surplus value *appears* as an excess of selling price, and profit as excess selling price over value. In reality, in surplus value "the relation between capital and labour is laid bare" and profit is "a converted form of surplus-value." Appearances suggest looking at costs, profit, prices of production, and so on, but the underlying relations are not seen through the consciousness of the agents of production, and the object of science is to uncover these relations.[30] Another important tendency in Marxist literature, reflected in the discussion of crises, is to detach the movement of social capital from its underlying basis in the social relations. The accumulation process becomes reified in terms of costs, technical relations, and competition, and the analytical focus becomes the individual firm and its relations to other firms and its own products.

Through the work of neo-Keynesians such as Kalecki, Steindl, Baran, and Sweezy accumulation is divorced from class relations.[31] It is argued that relations between capitals (that is, competition) express the unity of production and circulation. The reading of *Capital* suggested above argues that the movements of social capital are more determinate expressions of the abstract analysis, showing how class struggle appears at the level of the whole, on the surface of society.

II. ACCUMULATION AND CRISES

It is not the intention to set out Marx's analysis of accumulation, but four points must be stressed in order to distinguish the position of this paper from existing interpretations of crises. (1) The analysis of accumulation and crises in *Capital* is of capital *in general*,[32] indicating that it is an understanding that remains abstract. In particular the role of competition is not developed, so that relations between capitals and the role of markets are not part of the central determinations of crises.[33] Indicating the place of competition in his theoretical schema Marx states: "Competition executes the inner laws of capital . . . it does not invent them. It realizes them."[34] Thus competition is included in the discussion of the mechanisms of crises, particularly through its effects on the concentration and centralization of capital.[35] Therefore, interpretations of accumulation that are based on interfirm rivalry and market structures as the central focus are working from a different theoretical framework.[36]

(2) Although the "general conditions of crises . . . must be explicable from the general conditions of capitalist production," there is no general *form* of crises. The form must also be distinguished from the cause of crises: "If one is to ask what its cause is, one wants to know why *its abstract form*, the form of its possibility, turns from possibility into *actuality*."[37] Thus Marx's analysis provides a set of basic determinations for crises but not a predictive model nor a single formula for the manner in which crises present themselves.

(3) Although crises may appear in both the sphere of production and of circulation and may be expressed as a lack of markets, financial breakdown, falling rate of profit, and so on, Marx is at pains to establish the *unity* of the two spheres and their inseparability from the standpoint of the movement of social capital. It was argued above (see section I.B.) that the capital-labor relationship is the determinant of both production and circulation, and not merely of the former. The central feature of most existing interpretations of crises is that they

focus on one or the other of these spheres and ignore their unity. There are several important sections in *Capital*, volume III, on the falling rate of profit tendency that underline both the complexity of interaction of the two spheres, and the impossibility of any monocausal theory of crisis. These passages include some key sections that require close examination. This unity is to be understood dialectically, as the contradiction between the two spheres (which crises bring out clearly):

The contradiction between production and realization—of which capital, by its concept, is the unity—has to be grasped more intrinsically, than merely as the indifferent, seemingly reciprocal independent appearance of the individual moments of the process, or rather of the totality of the processes.[38]

A precise statement of the link between production and circulation appears in chapter 15, "Exposition of the Internal Contradictions of the Law," and must be quoted at length:

But this production of surplus-value completes but the first act of the capitalist process of production—the direct production process. Capital has absorbed so and so much unpaid labor. With the development of the process, which expresses itself in a drop in the rate of profit, the mass of surplus-value thus produced swells to immense dimensions. Now comes the second act of the process. . . . The entire mass of commodities must be sold. . . . The conditions of direct exploitation, and those of realizing it, are not identical. They diverge not only in place and time, but also logically. The first are only limited by the productive power of society, the latter by the proportional relation of the various branches of production and the consumer power of society. But this last named is not determined either by the absolute consumer power, but by the consumer power based on antagonistic conditions of distribution, which reduce the consumption of the bulk of society to a minimum varying within more or less narrow limits. It is furthermore restricted by the tendency to produce surplus-value on an expanded scale. . . . The market must, therefore, be continually extended, so that its interrelations and the conditions regulating them assume more and more the form of a natural law working independently of the producer, and become ever more uncontrollable. This internal contradiction seeks to resolve itself through expansion of the outlying field of production. But the more productiveness develops, the more it finds itself at variance with the narrow basis on which the conditions of consumption rest. It is no contradiction at all on this self-contradictory basis that there should be an excess of capital simultaneously with a growing surplus of population. For while a combination of these two would, indeed, increase the mass of produced surplus-value, it would at the same time intensify the contradiction between the conditions under which surplus-value is produced and those under which it is realised.[39]

The production of surplus value is the "first act"; realization is the second. Although the conditions of the latter are logically distinct from the former, they are in turn limited by the proportional relation of branches of production and the consumer power of society. This latter is in turn limited by income

distribution and by capital's need for a constantly expanding market. A falling rate of profit is consistent with a rise in the mass of profits; hence, the narrow basis of consumption is a contradiction to the increased productivity of labor and mass of surplus value that must be realized.

Although Marx is definitely not an underconsumptionist (he frequently attacks the view that markets alone could be a barrier to expansion),[40] the sphere of circulation is linked to that of production through proportionality, income distribution, and markets. Distribution relations, although linked to the overall process, serve as a constraint on accumulation but do not determine the rate (contrary to the neo-Ricardian views discussed in the next section).

(4) An important element in the falling rate of profit tendency is the changing organic composition of capital. Marx locates this as capital's attempt to increase relative surplus value through productivity increases:

> Like every other increase in the productiveness of labour, machinery is intended to cheapen commodities and, by shortening the working-day in which the labourer works for himself, to lengthen the other portion he gives without an equivalent to the capitalist. In short, it is a means for producing surplus-value.[41]

The substitution of constant for variable capital is determined by the terms on which capital can exploit the working class. It is not an autonomous law that the organic composition must change, but it is a strategy in the class struggle and reflects conditions of profitability.[42]

The falling rate of profit tendency is the center of Marx's accumulation theory, expressing the contradictory character of value production and realization. An important function of crises is to restore the conditions under which accumulation can occur.

The possibility of crises exists at many points where struggle may rupture the process of production or circulation,[43] where the value of labor-power is pushed up faster than increases in productivity, through the breakdowns in the circuits of capital in any of the points at which money capital is transformed into commodity capital (through strikes, refusal to work, the demand for wages by the unwaged segments of the working class, failure of the educational system to produce labor-power as a commodity, and so on).

It has been argued in the first two sections that the inner mechanism of accumulation is the capital-labor relationship, and that the dynamic movement of the whole is provided by the logic of this relationship. Class struggle is internal to the concept of capital, thus the barriers to expansion are posed by the form that this antagonism takes in the real world. Crises are the expression of the specific working-out of this class relation and assume a historically specific form conditioned by the character of the class relation and also by the particular features of capitalist development, including many elements that lie outside of the analysis of capital in general: competition, credit, finance, and so forth.

Crises cannot be understood as the movement of formal, purely theoretical relations, but take their life from the concrete social conditions of struggle in capitalist society. The perspective that this suggests as an interpretation of the current crisis will be outlined briefly in the final section.

III. CRITIQUE OF EXISTING INTERPRETATIONS OF CRISIS

The discussion of Marxist theory up to this point has attempted to provide a methodological basis for a critique of existing interpretations of Marx's crisis theory. This task will be undertaken through an examination of the three dominant views of the crisis: (1) underconsumptionist; (2) falling rate of profit/rising organic composition of capital theorists; and (3) neo-Ricardian. Because a detailed discussion of the arguments in the recent literature have been presented elsewhere,[44] this critique will deal selectively with the issues involved.

It should be noted that these three main views are interwoven with the pattern of capitalist development in the last thirty years, particularly with the crises of the 1960s and 1970s.[45] They represent concrete developments in the class struggle. For example, Baran and Sweezy's *Monopoly Capital*,[46] disillusioned with the prospects of revolution by the American working class, reflected a certain mood on the Left in the 1960s that was associated with a looking towards the Third World. The second tendency, led by Mattick,[47] attempted to revive Marxist theory by reasserting in traditional terms Marx's theory of value and accumulation. The third group, the neo-Ricardians, reflected a growing recognition of working-class power and the problems that this created for capitalist accumulation in the late 1960s and early 1970s.

A. Underconsumptionist Theories

Although the analysis of underconsumptionism has roots in (among others) Hobson, Bauer, and Luxemburg,[48] the modern formulations derive essentially from two interwoven theoretical traditions: the neo-Keynesian, represented by Robinson, Steindl, and Kalecki;[49] and the neo-Marxist, represented by Sweezy and much of contemporary U.S. Marxism. The difference between them turns centrally upon the manner in which underconsumption is analyzed, particularly whether it is seen to arise from income distribution or from excess capacity.[50] Joan Robinson has argued the former, Steindl and Sweezy the latter. The modern formulation of underconsumption as presented by Sweezy in his *Theory of Capitalist Development* is neo-Keynesian. It is presented in terms of a mathematical example in which, by the behavioral assumptions chosen, it necessarily follows that the means of production will grow at a rate that constantly outstrips the growth of means of consumption. The core of the argument hinges on the investment decisions of capitalists and their attempts to improve productivity, under the assumption of profit maximization.[51] The problematic of the proof is Keynesian; it ignores Marxian categories, most critically the concepts of the rate of surplus value and organic composition of capital that would have linked the analysis of underconsumption to the sphere of production. As it stands there is no link, and the central tendency of capitalist accumulation is discussed solely within the sphere of circulation.

In the later work, *Monopoly Capital*, underconsumption is treated additionally through a synthesis of the above with the work of Steindl and Kalecki who develop their analyses of accumulation on the effect of noncompetitive market conditions on profit margins and the mobility of capital. Baran and Sweezy

argue that market conditions are the decisive influence on the contemporary form of capitalist accumulation. The individual, representative firm is taken as the analytic unit to develop a theory of accumulation based on cost patterns and pricing behavior of monopolistic corporations. From this "model" it is observed that the mass of profits tends to rise over time for the economy as a whole, providing a new "law of political economy," that of "rising economic surplus," which replaces the Marxian falling rate of profit tendency.[52]

Although it has since been argued[53] that the notion of "surplus" is consistent with surplus value, it is in fact a category of distribution.[54] It offers a critique of the composition of output but it does not explain from where the surplus derives. The latter depends on the neoclassical theory of imperfect competition: on the cost and revenue behavior of individual firms. The contradictions of accumulation thus emerge not from an analysis of the social relations but from changes in market forms which, Baran and Sweezy argue, are substantial enough to warrant a new conceptual framework and new theoretical laws. The contradictions are expressed in terms of the manner in which society uses its surplus (its "irrationality"), that is, between the material base ("economic structure") and the ideological superstructure.[55] This links the analysis with the prevailing critique of the Frankfurt School, and with Marcuse in particular. Thus *Monopoly Capital* includes extended discussion of the "quality of life" under advanced capitalism, ignoring class struggle and the material contradictions of accumulation.

The eschewal of Marxian analysis (and value theory in particular) forces attention to the realm of ideology, away from the revolutionary implications of class struggle to the relations between firms, and to the Third World for the prospects of revolution.[56]

Methodologically the theory of accumulation is constructed from the micro analysis of the representative firm, through a process of aggregation, to the economy as a whole. Rising surplus focuses attention upon the neo-Keynesian problem of insufficient aggregate demand. Most importantly, as in Sweezy's earlier formulation, the essential link between the spheres of production and realization are again severed. Underconsumption triumphs and the worldwide expansion of capital is ensured except for possible resistance from the reserve army at home or abroad (such as liberation movements in the Third World).

To recall the earlier argument, for Marx, markets could not determine the conditions of accumulation, and competition was not the main determinant of the movement of capitalism in general. Also monopoly was analyzed in terms of the movement towards concentration and centralization of capital which accompanies accumulation and all attempts to increase surplus value.

Nevertheless, this view of Marxian theory has provided a consistent thread to U.S. Marxism and, as the conventional wisdom of the Left, has been widely used as a basis for analyzing imperialism, the role of the state, and crises.[57]

Other approaches to underconsumptionism, apart from this central one, include theorists who are close to Luxemburg's argument concerning the need for external markets, or who argue for a "permanent arms economy" to overcome the insufficiency of internally generated demand. The problems of these approaches have been examined elsewhere.[58]

B. Falling Rate of Profit/Organic Composition of Capital Theorists

In a fundamental sense the reassertion of the Marxian theory of value and accumulation represents a rejection of underconsumptionism and a revival of the Old Left. Mattick,[59] Mandel,[60] and others from a variety of political tendencies have led the movement to focus again upon class struggle through the traditional Marxian categories. Nevertheless the position that they and their followers (Yaffe, Cogoy, and so on[61]) have formulated remains trapped in the rigidity of the Marxism of the Second International. The Mattick School has argued for the strict mathematical necessity for the organic composition of capital to rise over time, thus making the falling rate of profit inevitable in the long run regardless of the rate of surplus value. This perspective has been subject to criticism on both empirical and theoretical grounds, so the critique here will restrict itself to methodological issues in the light of the discussion of Marxian theory above.

First, in arguing that the falling rate of profit emanates from the law of value there is a tendency to reify both these concepts and to substitute rigid, formal relations for the dialectic of real social processes. Marxian theory becomes rigidified, and a monocausal explanation is substituted for a complex set of determinations that express the fundamental social relations of capitalist society.

One critic sees an additional element: "[Yaffe's] theory falls into a type of Hegelian Marxism with laws of capitalism unfolding relentlessly in the realm of theory and the concept of capital taking the role of the Idea."[62] Second, the analysis of accumulation is one-sided, ignoring the sphere of circulation entirely and focusing solely on movements that emanate from the sphere of production, most importantly those affecting the organic composition of capital. For example, citing Marx's critique of Malthus, Yaffe denies *any* possible role to markets or the problem of realization in determining the rate of accumulation.[63]

Although not denying the most fundamental theoretical premise of these theorists that the falling rate of profit is, as Marx said, "the most important law of political economy," it in no way follows that it can be understood as a single, pervasive law that asserts itself for reasons internal to it as a *concept*. It depends rather on the concrete manner in which class struggle affects the path of accumulation through three elements: surplus value, productivity (and hence, by extension, the organic composition of capital), and also (as argued in section II above) the conditions that determine realization.

It is important to note briefly that the Mattick-Yaffe argument is critically linked to an attack on the state as part of the unproductive sector and as the primary contradiction of advanced capitalism.[64] The productive/unproductive distinction has generated a heated debate among Marxologists;[65] a debate that, from the perspective of social capital underlying this paper, is largely irrelevant.[66] The political conclusion that the Yaffe position supports is that the working class is more exploited because, with a rising organic composition of capital, fewer productive workers produce the surplus value and more are supported from revenue. Class struggle is not seen as a cause of crises, it is rather the changing organic composition of capital that lies behind these contradictory movements—the swelling of the unproductive sector and the falling tendency of

the rate of profit.[67] The removal of the theory from the class relations of accumulation is again evident in this rigid formulation of theoretical "laws."

The other main emphasis in the literature concerning the falling rate of profit are attempts to test its empirical validity. The pioneering work of Mage and Gillman[68] has been followed in recent years by that of Hodgson, Mandel, Perlo, and others.[69] For the most part these empirical studies do not support a rising organic composition of capital and a falling rate of profit in any consistent manner. The methodological problems with these studies are numerous, most particularly with the manner in which they conceptualize the relationship between the empirical data and Marx's categories.[70] The extreme positions would have Marx's categories (1) untranslatable into empirical terms, such as Mattick; or (2) synonymous with empirical data, such as Mandel. These problems have not been adequately resolved, although (as will be argued in the next section) there are strong indications to believe that the rate of profit has fallen since the mid-1960s.

Typical of the methodology in this debate is Hodgson's attempt[71] to dispose of the falling rate of profit in Marxian theory by developing a "testable model," subjecting it to empirical examination, and concluding on the basis of this test that the theory itself is invalidated!

C. Neo-Ricardian Theories[72]

The revival of the analysis of the older generation of Marxists of the falling rate of profit, particularly in the formulations of Yaffe, are especially unconvincing in a period when throughout the capitalist world class struggle has moved into the center of the political arena. In both England and the United States, empirical studies began to show clearly a relationship between rising wages and a "profits squeeze." Glyn and Sutcliffe[73] in England, and Body and Crotty[74] in the United States focused on the problem of distributive shares. The latter, in addition, integrate this into an analysis of state macroeconomic policy that is seen to regulate the business cycle in the interests of capital in attempts to offset wage pressure.

These analyses are an important advance in that they deal with actual social processes and place class struggle at the center of the explanation of the crises of capitalism. Nevertheless, there remain significant methodological problems with this work. The central issue hinges upon the role of distribution in the process of accumulation.

First, to recall the remarks above (section II), Marx's analysis of accumulation is an analysis of class struggle, which is centered upon, but by no means restricted to, the sphere of production. This struggle is about absolute and relative forms of surplus value, as alternative strategies used by capital to exploit workers. It is critically about productivity in relationship to the value of labor-power. Increased productivity permits the value of labor-power to be lowered behind the backs of workers, by lowering the value contained in necessary costs of reproducing the proletariat.[75] Changes in the organic composition of capital may also lead to the displacement of workers. The overall impact of the struggle must be analyzed therefore in value terms, in its effect on the rate of surplus value and rate of profit. Marx warns of the danger of representing this process in terms of distributive categories:

The habit of representing surplus-value and value of labour-power as fractions of value created—a habit which originated in the capitalist mode of production itself . . . conceals the very transaction that characterises capital namely the exchange of variable capital for living labour-power and the consequent exclusion of the labourer from the product.[76]

Marx argues in many places that distribution (and thus the share of wages) is determined by the process of production and circulation. He specifically argues this in discussing accumulation in *Capital,* volume I, in the very passages that these writers have used to support a distributive shares argument.[77] He argues: (1) although both an excess and a diminution of means of production make the available supply of labor power seem alternately scarce and excessive, thus determining the rate of accumulation, this is only an appearance; and (2) the relationship between the expansion/contraction of capital and wages are in fact adjustments of the ratio of unpaid to paid labor that is appropriated from the working class as a whole (including the reserve army):

The correlation between accumulation of capital and the rate of wages is nothing else than the correlation between the unpaid labour transformed into capital and the additional paid labour necessary for setting in motion this capital . . . it is . . . at bottom, only the relation between the unpaid and the paid labour of the same labouring population.[78]

The point is that accumulation is to be understood here not as a business cycle determined by distributive shares and a profits squeeze, but in terms of the manner in which the working class as a whole is reproduced and the relative proportions of waged to unwaged workers within the class. Fluctuations in wages are the outward expression of the differential exploitation of different segments of the working class, as capital divides the class through the reserve army, and imposes control through attacking wages and by destroying class unity through segmentation. This movement, which appears to capital as a business cycle, is merely a condition for further accumulation leaving "intact the entire foundations of the capitalistic system," and also "securing its reproduction on a progressive scale."[79] Marx explicitly denies that wages determine the rate of accumulation: "The rate of accumulation is the independent, not the dependent, variable; the rate of wages, the dependent, not the independent, variable."[80]

Accumulation is seen throughout *Capital* in terms of the class relation of capital to labor and its effects on the condition of the working class:

Pauperism forms a condition . . . of the capitalist development of wealth. It enters into the *faux frais* of capitalist production; but capital knows how to throw these, for the most part, from its own shoulders on to those of the working-class and the lower middle class.[81]

The barriers to capitalist accumulation hinge, as we have seen, on both production and circulation, but they revolve critically around the contradictory manner in which the process of value expansion must occur: through control over the working-class to ensure the production of surplus value, through

changes in productivity, and the changes in value that are brought about through alterations in the organic composition of capital. Class struggle limits the expansion of value through the growing productivity of social labor.

Thus although class struggle certainly occurs around the distribution of national product, in the sphere of circulation, it must first be analyzed in terms of value relations in the sphere of production: "specific distribution relations are . . . merely the expression of specific historical production relations."[82]

D. Summary of Critiques of Existing Theories

In the light of the understanding of Marxian theory presented in this paper, the main points of criticism may be briefly summarized:

1. A Tendency to Monocausal Explanation

Social reality is reduced to a theoretical construct or "law" that drives capitalism toward crises. This reductionism equates Marxism with developing an explanatory model of selective relationships around which reality can be fitted. These laws or models are often verified by use of statistical data, and crises appear as confirmation of the monocausal explanation of accumulation contained in the model. This positivistic methodology reduces reality to a single determination, denying the dialectical movement from the abstract to the concrete.[83]

2. Reification of Marxian Theory

Because of the duality between theory and reality that these theories maintain, accumulation and crises are not always seen as expressions of social relations. Crises appear to emanate from "things" and to have a technical rather than a social character. For Yaffe, capital and accumulation appear to have a life and a movement outside of the class relations that they express.[84] Thus crises are governed by laws of things, which are either purely technical (for economists), or purely theoretical (for Hegelians). In either case, the theory remains a set of *mental* abstractions. For Marx, on the other hand, capitalist production was the outcome of a complex set of determinations that derive from the nature of capital seen as a class relation. The categories of analysis describe how these determinations actually occur, through struggle.

The fetishizing of capitalism that occurs through the categories of bourgeois society, against which Marx warns in the first chapter of *Capital*,[85] would serve as a critique of much of contemporary political economy. It is the "peculiar social character of labor" that masks the relations between people from view, turning them into relations between things.

3. Marxology and the Stasis of Theory

The removal of Marxist theory from real social processes, which undoubtedly reflects the distance of the Left from the working class, has its reflection in endless debates regarding a "correct" reading of Marx's texts. Although this paper has attempted to support a particular understanding of Marx's method, with textual support, it is fruitless to argue over interpretations of particular passages that support or refute, for example, the problem of underconsumption.

Marxism is not the application of a formula to the movements of capitalism, and textual debate serves to rigidify the theory in such a manner that it becomes static and ahistorical. What is required is that the method and the understanding of crises in general be applied to concrete historical conditions. The forms of class struggle, the institutional context in which accumulation occurs, and thus the barriers to expansion have altered the conditions under which capitalist reproduction takes place. The crises of the period since 1945 must be seen in terms of the concrete forms that the capital-labor relationship takes, in particular the strategies at the disposal of capital (for example, Keynesian theory) and the power of the working class. The institutions, including the state, that shape the process of production and circulation all require specific analysis as more concrete determinations of the social relations.

It should be noted that the capital-labor relationship is not a "formula" but a statement of the particular character of the material relations that form the basis of capitalist society. It is the insistence on seeing how these material relations generate the "laws of motion" of capitalism that separates Marx's project from all idealistic thought.

4. The Separation of Production and Circulation

A formal critique of the crisis theories revealed a one-sidedness in locating the barriers to accumulation in *either* the sphere of circulation (underconsumptionists and neo-Ricardians) *or* in the sphere of production (the falling rate of profit/organic composition of capital theorists), considered separately. Of the attempts to combine the two spheres into a single framework, that of Mandel is remarkable for its eclecticism. Although it discusses the falling rate of profit, it places its primary emphasis on a variation of the underconsumptionist thesis.[86]

Marx is at pains to establish that capitalism as a whole involves the unity of both production and circulation and that their intertwined movements are both expressions of the underlying capital-labor relationship. Overlooking this has the consequence of leading to partial theories that ignore either the importance of markets or the importance of class struggle in production.

5. Market Structures and the "Theory of the Firm"

Stimulated by the work of Left Keynesians such as Robinson, Kalecki, and Steindl, Marxist theory of accumulation has become transformed into a theory of firms and market structures. This analysis has obvious appeal to theorists who ignore value theory and class struggle and who build their theories upon movements within the sphere of circulation. It is argued by these theorists that the relationship between firms provides the necessary link between production and circulation by providing prices and profit margins, and thus giving Marx's system a theoretical determinacy. Linked with this is the view that competition is the central mechanism in determining the movement of total social capital. These views have been both implicitly and explicitly rejected in the discussion above. Although this requires a more extended critique,[87] suffice it to reiterate here that this theoretical work seems part of a different project. It reifies economic categories and is powerless to analyze the class forces that constitute the basis of accumulation.

6. *The Politics of Crisis Theory*

Without entering into the sectarian debates that are associated with the theoretical disagreements outlined above, it is important not to see these differences in an idealistic manner, as struggles solely about theory. The issues involved touch on the most basic meaning of Marxism and different conceptions of the relation of theory and praxis in particular. For this reason they are not resolvable through appeals to scientific correctness, but involve struggle within the Left itself.

Some of the striking features of the debate are (1) the denial of politics in the attempts to complete "theories" *of* capitalism, rather than theories *against* capitalism; that is, to ignore the revolutionary implications of Marxian analysis. (This is particularly evident in the work of economists.) (2) Ignoring the impact of working-class struggle on capital's ability to accumulate (the neo-Ricardians being a clear exception). Crises are viewed from the perspective of capital, not as a matter of class sympathy but because capital itself is not viewed as a class relation, whose movements express class struggle. Marxists unwittingly find themselves working to solve capital's problems in unravelling the technical limitations of accumulation. This may indeed explain some of the renewed interest in Marxist theory in recent years. (3) The separation of the economic from the political, which relegates class struggle to the sphere of the state, to conflict over distribution shares, and so on.

IV. CLASS STRUGGLE AND THE CURRENT CRISIS

This final section will not attempt to provide a comprehensive account of the current crisis, but rather set out the key elements upon which such an examination must rest. Although recognizing that a more concrete analysis would require seeing the role of class struggle in determining such phenomena as competition, credit, inflation, fictitious capital, and so on, the perspective of this paper is that this struggle provides a determination of the whole. It is the character and strength of class struggle as it affects the progress of accumulation that determines the movement of the whole. Its form must be examined in the context of "social capital" (the particular historical stage of capitalist accumulation), in the impact of this struggle on the rate of surplus value, and finally in terms of the mechanisms of the current crisis.

A. Surplus Value, Productivity, and the Value of Labor-Power

It has been argued that the "inner organic life" of capital is the antagonistic relation between capital and wage labor. Accumulation is the continuous extension of the class relationship. The impact of class struggle on the process of accumulation can be seen through the rate of surplus value, which is an index of the varying strength of capital in relation to labor, in terms of capital's ability to impose the commodity form on the working class and to extract unpaid labor.

The actual rate of surplus value involves two key elements: the value of labor-power and the productivity of labor. The actual rate is a concrete historical question centering on a power struggle between the classes:

The maximum of profit is, therefore, limited by the physical maximum of the working day. It is evident that between the two limits of the maximum rate of profit an immense scale of variations is possible. The fixation of its actual degree is only settled by the continuous struggle between capital and labour, the capitalist constantly tending to reduce wages to their physical minimum, and to extend the working day to its physical maximum, while the working man constantly presses in the opposite direction. The matter resolves itself into a question of the respective powers of the combatants.[88]

This is not to imply that wages are determined solely in the sphere of direct production. Real wages depend on struggles around distribution and also upon price manipulations at the level of the state (through inflation, wage-price freezes, and so forth) and upon capital flows in response to differential profitability. The important point here is that as the working class struggles to win new standards of living and to work less, it pushes up the value of labor power and attempts to have these newer standards accepted as elements of a "traditional way of life."[89] Capital, in its turn, seeks to prevent the rise in the value of labor power, by increasing absolute surplus value or by changes in productivity that increase relative surplus value and reduce the value of labor power. Crises occur when capital's plans to enlarge surplus value are inadequate in the face of working-class resistance and where they lead to contradictory tendencies, such as the diminution of the living labor employed in production. Both a lowering of the rate of surplus value and the rising organic composition of capital are determinations of class struggle and lead to a fall in the rate of profit.

To understand this concretely we must therefore explore the forms of struggle that have emerged recently and the organizational characteristics of capitalist society in this period.

B. Social Capital

Stages of capitalist development are to be understood in terms of the degree of integration of society into the overall process of capitalist reproduction. This view differs from attempts to periodize this development in terms of market characteristics (competitive/monopoly),[90] the growth or "decay" of forces of production (technical characteristics),[91] changes in the sphere of circulation (such as rising surplus or a growing unproductive sector),[92] or changes in the ideological sphere (the repressive aspects of the state).[93] Rather this view focuses upon the degree to which capital, through its organizational forms, has been generalized to cover all of society: "The social character of production has been extended to such a point that the entire society functions as a moment of production."[94] At a particular stage in historical development, this process transforms society into a "social factory." This implies that all aspects of social life become dominated by capital and become moments in its reproduction.[95] Consequently all labor is working directly or indirectly, in household or in factory, to maintain or reproduce elements of constant or variable capital, and hence to expand capital, as a class relation.

This implies also that these class relations have been transformed in the era of, as Tronti calls it, "social capital":

Social capital is not merely just the total capital of society; it is not the simple sum of individual capitals. It is the whole process of socialization of capitalist production; it is capital that becomes uncovered at a certain point of its development as *social power*.[96]

More specifically, as Marx saw, the class struggle takes the form of a relationship between collective capital and collective labor:

> In each particular sphere of production the individual capitalist, as well as the capitalists as a whole, take part in the exploitation of the total working class by the *totality of capital* and in the degree of that exploitation, not only out of general class sympathy, but also for direct economic reasons . . . the average rate of profit depends on the intensity of the exploitation of the *sum total of labour by the sum total of capital* . . .[97]

Thus the productivity of labor becomes the concern of collective capital, and its development is revealed in the diminution of living labor, the growth of the working class. These two processes lead to intensification of accumulation and concentration of capital.[98] It is here that the basis of "monopoly capitalism" must be located, as an organizational form of capital to structure society, to control the working class and to organize and plan movements of capital on a global basis.[99] In addition the state serves as a major medium for the integration of society into capital's organization and rationale.

A further aspect of the changing class relation is the absorption of the working class into capital, and the integration of the class struggle within capitalist planning: "the tension between capital and labor becomes a 'legal institution of society' [i.e., unions], and all the institutions which *guarantee* an orderly bourgeois development of particular labor claims can be legally recognized in their full autonomy." As Tronti has also argued,[100] this stage was a response to the class struggles in the United States in the period between the two World Wars, and most specifically in the period 1933–47. As a result of intense struggle the working class secured enormous gains in establishing their legitimacy through collective bargaining and gains in income.

The rate of surplus value was sustained through a rapid accumulation of capital accompanied by managed recessions during the 1950s and 1960s. A series of "deals" between capital and labor, which reached their highest point in the "productivity deal" of the Kennedy era, were used alongside Keynesian economic policies to sustain high rates of profit.[101] The 1960s was characterized by a concern for relative surplus value. Capitalist strategy focused upon "human capital" and the sociology of work became a major area of concern.

By the late 1960s the levels of both industrial unrest (strikes, absenteeism) and social unrest (riots in the cities and schools) made it clear that these programs had failed. Productivity fell dramatically from the early 1960s, and there was a fall in the rate of profit.[102] In addition capital was faced with demands from the traditionally unwaged segments (such as those of welfare). Seen through the perspective of social capital, capital's initiative during the current crisis is to dismantle working-class organization, reduce its power, cut back the social service sector under the guise of fiscal austerity, and to reestab-

lish control over a working class that throughout the capitalist world has broken the link between wages and productivity, upon which an adequate rate of accumulation hinges.

C. Mechanisms of the Current Capitalist Offensive

Periods of crisis, such as the 1974–75 recession, are crises for the working class in terms of unemployment and falling standards of living, but for capital they are strategies to resolve the crisis of profitable accumulation. These strategies focus on the rate of surplus value and direct and indirect attacks on the working class.

The international reduction of social expenditures and attempts to dismantle the "welfare state" of the post-1945 period[103] are attacks on the value of labor power, which function by reducing those elements (such as education or health care) that have not succeeded in contributing directly to labor productivity and by shifting more of the cost of reproduction of labor power onto the working class itself. In New York City, which serves as a model of this strategy, deals are being attempted to restructure education and social services under the threat of fiscal bankruptcy.[104] In Britain the Labor Party returned to power to effect this program.[105]

Capital is also attempting to reduce the value of labor power through inflationary attacks on wages, and by recomposing the reserve army of the unemployed it has hoped to alleviate the pressure of union demands and effect changes in attitudes towards work.[106] The constant threat of immigrant labor and run-away shops are efforts to stir concern for job security and create a new willingness to work harder for less money. Ideological mechanisms serve to further divide the class through hostility based on race, ethnic difference, and gender. On the function of this Marx remarked (discussing the antagonism of British workers to Irish immigrant labor):

> This antagonism is kept artificially alive and intensified by the press, pulpit, comic papers, in short, by all the means at the disposal of the ruling classes. This antagonism is the secret of the impotence of the English working-class, despite its organization. It is the secret by which the capitalist class maintains its power. And the latter is quite aware of this.[107]

While this offensive continues, the limits on capital's ability to overcome the difficulties that have been building since the late 1960s depend not on "laws" but on the continuation of working-class resistance.

The power to disrupt capitalist accumulation that the working class has demonstrated forms the root of the current crisis. Our understanding of Marxist theory, by breaking down the separation between theory and practice, leads to a grasp of the actual forces at work in capitalist society and to the possibility of intervention in the process of reproduction. In this way Marxism can be developed as an instrument of class struggle. The perspective suggested in this paper is an essential step in this direction.

NOTES

1. This can be seen most obviously in the attention given in the bourgeois press to radicals of all kinds (e.g., articles in *Business Week*, and *New York Times Magazine*, April 27, 1975), but also in the pages of the highly conservative *American Economic Review* whose December 1975 issue carried a critique of the Report of the Council of Economic Advisors.

2. This is developed in the Preface to Harry Cleaver, "Reading *Capital* Politically: An Essay on Chapter One" (Manuscript, New School for Social Research, 1976). In the body of this work capital is grasped as the struggle between the capitalist and working classes over the imposition of work through the commodity form. The determinations of the commodity form are understood politically as the fundamental determinations of the class struggle. The "political reading" involves a two-class perspective that insists that each concept reflects the perspective of one or the other of the classes, or must be understood differently from each perspective. For an example of this two-class reading, see note 17 below.

3. The critique that emerged from the New Left is strikingly similar to that put forward by the Old (revisionist) Left, particularly of the Communist Party, who attack bankers and the ruling class for the problems of capitalism on the grounds of their personal greed. To this moral critique, the New Left has added the dimension of "alienation." Both of these ignore the logical character of capitalism, and Marx's specific critique.

4. Engels' "dialectical materialism," based on a profound misreading of Marx, has been popularized by Stalin and Mao and remains the basic orthodoxy of the Marxist Left in the United States. Inherent in this "science" is a sharp dualism between theory and practice, politics and economics, and theory and the real world. For a critique see below (esp. section II.A.). For an extended critique see L. Colletti, *From Rousseau to Lenin* (New York: Monthly Review Press, 1972); Colletti, *Marxism and Hegel* (London: New Left Books, 1973); S. Hook, *From Hegel to Marx* (Ann Arbor: University of Michigan Press, 1971); and S. Avineri, *Social and Political Thought of Karl Marx* (Cambridge: Cambridge University Press, 1969).

5. In the United States, *Telos* magazine represents an important element of this tendency. For a brief background to the Hegel revival see articles by Poster and Heckman in *Telos*, no. 16 (Summer 1973). On the influence of the Frankfurt School on Marxism see G. Lichteim, *From Marx to Hegel* (New York: Seabury Press, 1974); R. Jacoby, "Towards a Critique of Automatic Marxism: The Politics of Philosophy from Lukacs to the Frankfurt School," *Telos*, no. 10 (Winter 1971); for an example of this position see R. Winfield, "The Logic of Marxist *Capital*," *Telos*, no. 27 (Spring 1976). A useful introductory critique is Goran Therborn, "Frankfurt Marxism: A Critique," *New Left Review*, no. 63 (September–October 1970).

6. The tradition of reading *Capital* as "economic theory" was made popular by Paul Sweezy, *Theory of Capitalist Development* (New York: Monthly Review Press, 1942). A more recent mathematical treatment is that of Morishima, *Marx's Economics* (Cambridge: Cambridge University Press, 1973). In general the building of economic theory from *Capital*, removed of the critical elements of Marx's method, puts the theory at the disposal of capital. This helps to explain also the attention paid to Sraffa and the post-Keynesian theorists in recent years.

7. It is also, in many respects, a revival of earlier debates in the socialist movement that are discussed, for example, in Sweezy, *Theory of Capitalist Development*, chap. 11; and R. Jacoby, "Politics of the Crisis Theory," *Telos*, no. 23 (Spring 1975).

8. For a more extended discussion of the range of current positions see Eric Olin Wright, "Alternative Perspectives in the Marxist Theory of Accumulation and Crises," *The Insurgent Sociologist*, Fall 1975.

9. See, for example, G. Hodgson, "The Falling Rate of Profit," *New Left Review*, no. 84 (March–April 1974); David Yaffe, "The Marxian Theory of Crisis, Capital and the State," *Economy and Society* 2 (1973).

10. On this point see W. T. Stace, *The Philosophy of Hegel* (New York: Dover, 1955), esp. pt. I; and Colletti, *Marxism and Hegel*. The specific way in which Marx distinguishes himself from Hegel is a central point of disagreement in the current Marxist "revival." (See note 5 above.)

11. Marx, "Marginal Notes on Adolph Wagner's 'Lehrbuch der politischen Okonomie,' " *Theoretical Practice*, no. 5 (Spring 1971), pp. 50–51.

12. Marx, *Grundrisse: Introduction to a Critique of Political Economy* (New York: Vintage Books, 1973), pp. 104–105. Emphasis added.

13. Ibid., p. 296. This is discussed in Cleaver, "Reading *Capital* Politically."

14. Ibid., pp. 100–101.

15. Marx, "Preface" to *A Contribution to the Critique of Political Economy*, in L. Colletti, ed., *Marx's Early Writings* (New York: Vintage Books, 1975), p. 425.

16. Marx distinguishes the mode of inquiry from that of presentation. The beginning of *Capital* presupposes the conclusions as a result of prior inquiry; thus although reality appears as the *result* of theoretical inquiry, it is in fact the inquiry's point of departure. This is to emphasize that the early part of the analysis of value and exchange in *Capital*, vol. I, presupposes for its understanding the entire three volumes. See Marx, "Afterword" to *Capital*, vol. I, 2nd German ed. (New York: International, 1967), p.19; and Marx, *Grundrisse*, p. 101. Mandel has a helpful discussion of this and other issues in *Late Capitalism* (New Left Books, 1975), chap. 1, although his methodological position of a "mediated unity between theory and history" (p. 20) differs in some important respects from that taken in this paper.

17. Cleaver, "Reading *Capital* Politically." The analysis of abstract labor in Cleaver's piece is a good example of reading *Capital* politically through a two-class perspective. Abstract labor designates both the struggle of capital to control the working class (maintain its ability to allocate and exploit labor—homogeneity through heterogeneity) and the working class struggle to overcome capital's divisions in order to achieve the unity necessary to defeat capital.

18. Marx, *Grundrisse*, p. 534.

19. Ibid., p. 288.

20. The concept of the organic composition of capital is central to the debate concerning crises. The position developed in this paper suggests that this relationship is critically determined by the rate of exploitation and must be understood in terms of it rather than as an autonomous outcome of exogenous changes in the "forces of production," or technical change in the sense of bourgeois economics. This is developed further below. The concept is discussed in *Capital*, vol. I, chaps. 8, 25, and in vol. III, chaps. 5, 14.

21. See, for example, Sweezy, *Theory of Capitalist Development*, chaps. 9, 10, where accumulation is seen as the accumulation of means of production; that is, as a *thing* rather than a class relation.

22. Marx, *Capital*, vol. I, p. 572; vol. III, p. 219.

23. Marx, *Capital*, vol. I, p. 572.

24. Marx, *Capital*, vol. II, p. 30. We are discussing here the circuit of industrial capital that begins $M—P$ $(MP + LP)$. . . .

25. Ibid., p. 105.

26. Ibid., pp. 351–54. For an insightful exegesis of this section see M. Tronti, "Social Capital," *Telos*, no. 17 (Fall 1973). Tronti is one of the few to have grasped some of the meaning of Marx's notion of social capital.

27. A very helpful discussion of the importance of the sphere of circulation is Ben Fine, "The Circulation of Capital, Ideology and Crises," *Bulletin of the Conference of Socialist Economics*, No. 12, October 1975.

28. *Capital*, vol. III, p. 43.

29. Ibid., p. 44, emphasis added.

30. "All science would be superfluous if the outward appearance and the essence of things directly coincided." *Capital*, vol. III, p. 817. See also N. Geras, "Essence and Appearance: Aspects of Fetishism in Marx's *Capital*," *New Left Review*, no. 65 (January-February 1971). Further discussion of this relationship would require an analysis of Hegel's *Logic*, which is not attempted here.

31. For references to these works, and their influence on crisis theories, see section III.A. The important problem with their work is that accumulation is seen in terms of competition between capitals and not, as Marx insists, in terms of class struggle. Their work, it is argued below, converges with the neoclassical theory of the firm (and thus of markets), and with the neo-Keynesian view of accumulation.

32. For a discussion of this point see Marx, *Theories of Surplus-Value*, pt. II, pp. 492–93.

33. This is clear from the plans of *Capital* that Marx drafted and from reminders in the text itself. See Marx's letter to Engels of April 2, 1858, cited in Martin Nicholaus, "Foreword," in Marx, *Grundrisse*, p. 55.

34. Ibid., p. 752.
35. See the discussion in *Capital*, vol. I, chaps. 15, 25, and in vol. III, chap. 15.
36. See note 31 above.
37. Marx, *Theories of Surplus-Value*, pt. II, p. 515.
38. Marx, *Grundrisse*, p. 415.
39. Marx, *Capital*, vol. III, pp. 244–45.
40. Marx nevertheless stresses the importance of consumer power and exchange as limits to the expansion of capital and as a possible source of crises in *Grundrisse*, esp. pp. 418–23. See also Marx, *Theories of Surplus-Value*, pt. II, p. 493.
41. *Capital*, vol. I, p. 371.
42. See note 20 above.
43. See the suggestive discussion in M. Tronti, "Social Capital," and in Tronti, "Workers and Capital," *Telos*, no. 14 (Winter 1972). See also the analysis in *Zerowork*, no. 1 (December 1975). This is discussed in section IV. below.
44. Wright, "Alternative Perspectives in the Marxist Theory."
45. The historical context of these theoretical developments is discussed in Bell and Cleaver, eds., "Marxist Theories of Accumulation and Crises" (in preparation).
46. Paul Baran and Paul Sweezy, *Monopoly Capital: An Essay on the American Economic and Social Order* (New York: Monthly Review Press, 1966).
47. Paul Mattick, *Marx and Keynes* (Boston: Porter Sargent, 1969). See also Ernest Mandel, *Marxist Economic Theory*, 2 vols. (New York: Monthly Review Press, 1968).
48. J. Hobson, *Imperialism* (Ann Arbor: University of Michigan Press, 1965); Rosa Luxemburg, *Accumulation of Capital* (New York: Monthly Review Press, 1968); Otto Bauer, *Zwischen zwei Weltkrigen* (Bratislava: Eugen Prager Verlag, 1936).
49. Joan Robinson, *An Essay on Marxian Economics* (London, 1942); J. Steindl, *Maturity and Stagnation in American Capitalism* (Oxford: Blackwell, 1952); and M. Kalecki, *Theory of Economic Dynamics* (London, 1954).
50. Mario Cogoy, "Les Theories Neo-Marxistes, Marx et l'Accumulation du Capital," *Les Temps Modernes*, September-October 1972.
51. Sweezy, *Theory of Capitalist Development*, esp. pp. 180–89. The critical assumptions of the analysis are set out on p. 181.
52. Baran and Sweezy, *Monopoly Capital*, pp. 10, 72.
53. Paul Sweezy, "Monopoly Capital and the Theory of Value," *Monthly Review*, January 1974.
54. Mario Cogoy, "The Fall in the Rate of Profit and the Theory of Accumulation," *Bulletin of the Conference of Socialist Economists*, No. 7, Winter 1973.
55. Baran and Sweezy, *Monopoly Capital*, p. 8. See their discussion in chaps. 10 and 11.
56. Ibid., pp. 9, 363–67.
57. Among recent contributions that confirm the widespread acceptance of the Baran and Sweezy position are: James O'Connor, *Fiscal Crisis of the State* (New York, 1973); Harry Braverman, *Labor and Monopoly Capital* (New York: Monthly Review Press, 1974); S. Amin, "Toward a Structural Crisis of World Capitalism," *Socialist Revolution*, no. 23 (April 1975); and Douglas Dowd, "Accumulation and Crisis in U.S. Capitalism," *Socialist Revolution*, no. 24 (June 1975).
58. For critiques see Yaffe, "Marxian Theory of Crisis"; David Purdy, "The Theory of the Permanent Arms Economy: A Critique and an Alternative," *Bulletin of the Conference of Socialist Economists*, no. 5 (Spring 1973).
59. Mattick, *Marx and Keynes*, also, "Marxism and Monopoly Capital," *Progressive Labor*, nos. 7, 8 (1969).
60. E. Mandel, "The Labor Theory of Value and Monopoly Capitalism," *International Socialist Review* 28, no. 4, July-August 1967; "Surplus Capital and Realization of Surplus Value," *International Socialist Review* 28, no. 1, January-February 1967. See also the critique of Baran and Sweezy from the "Old Left" in *Science and Society* 30, no. 4 (Fall 1966), where reviews by Dobb, Gillman, Lumer, and others appear.
61. Yaffe, "The Marxian Theory of Crisis"; Cogoy, "The Fall in the Rate of Profit." The discussion has been continued and extended by Yaffe and others in *Revolutionary Communist*, nos. 1, 3, 4.
62. Ben Fine and Laurence Harris, "The British Economy Since March 1974," *Bulletin of the Conference of Socialist Economists*, no. 12 (October 1975), pp. 10–11.

63. Yaffe, "Marxian Theory of Crisis," pp. 38–43.
64. Ibid., pp. 11–14. See also *Revolutionary Communist*, nos. 3, 4, pp. 16–17.
65. Contributions to the voluminous literature can be found in articles by Gough, Seacombe, Gardiner, Coulson, and others, *New Left Review*, nos. 76, 83, 89; in articles by Harrison, Bullock, Fine, Gough, and exchanges between them in *Conference of Socialist Economists*, nos. 6, 7, 9, 10, 11. See also, C. Colliet-Hélène, "Remarques sur les statuts du travail productif dans la théorie marxiste," *Critiques de l'Economie Politiques*, no. 10 (January-March 1973).
66. See section IV below and the discussion of social capital.
67. See Yaffe, "Marxian Theory of Crisis," and *Revolutionary Communist*, Nos. 3 and 4.
68. S. H. Mage, "The Law of the Falling Tendency of the Rate of Profit" (Ph.D. Thesis, Columbia University, 1963); J. M. Gillman, *The Falling Rate of Profit* (London: Dobson, 1957).
69. Hodgson, "The Falling Rate of Profit"; Victor Perlo, *The Unstable Economy* (New York: International Publishers, 1973), chaps. 3, 5; Mandel, *Marxist Economy Theory*; Mandel, *Late Capitalism* (London: New Left Books, 1975), esp. chap. 5.
70. See, for example, the discussion in Geoff Hodgson, "Marxian Epistemology and the Transformation Problem," *Economy and Society* 3, no. 4 (November 1974).
71. Hodgson, "The Falling Rate of Profit."
72. The term *neo-Ricardian* is used to stress the importance placed upon distributive shares. It is not intended to suggest that the writers discussed tend also to the neo-Ricardian view of value theory as formulated by Sraffa, and recently embraced by Dobb, Meek, and Eatwell. See Maurice Dobb, *Theories of Value and Distribution Since Adam Smith* (Cambridge: Cambridge University Press, 1973); Ronald Meek, *Studies in the Labor Theory of Value*, 2nd ed. (London: Lawrence and Weishart, 1973), esp. Introduction; J. Eatwell, "Controversies in the Theory of Surplus Value, Old and New," *Science and Society* 38, no. 3 (Fall 1974).
73. A. Glyn and R. Sutcliffe, *British Capital, Workers and the Profits Squeeze* (London: Penguin, 1972).
74. R. Body and J. Crotty, "Class Conflict and Macro-Policy: The Political Business Cycle," *Review of Radical and Political Economics* 7, no. 1 (1975), also their "Class Conflict, Keynesian Policies and the Business Cycle," *Monthly Review*, October 1974; Alan Nasser, "The Twilight of Capitalism: Contours of an Emerging Decline," *The Insurgent Sociologist* 6, no. 11 (Winter 1976).
75. David Yaffe, "The Crisis of Profitability: A Critique of Glyn-Sutcliffe Thesis," *New Left Review*, no. 80 (July-August 1973).
76. *Capital*, vol. I, p. 533, cited in Yaffe, ibid., p. 49.
77. *Capital*, vol. I, chap. 25, esp. pp. 612–21.
78. Ibid., p. 620.
79. Ibid., p. 620.
80. Ibid., p. 620.
81. Ibid., p. 644.
82. *Capital*, vol. III, p. 882. See also *Theories of Surplus-Value*, pt. II, p. 493, where Marx makes the following observation concerning consumer power and distribution: "[the] way in which they [consumers] spend their revenue [from profits and wages], and the very size of the revenue gives rise to very considerable modifications in the economy and particularly in the circulation and reproduction process of capital."
83. Amin, "Toward a Structural Crisis of World Capitalism."
84. Although Colletti grasps this point well in his discussion of abstract labor, he nevertheless fails to see the manner in which it is determined by capital in the sphere of production and limits himself to a notion of value derived in exchange. This leads him in a false direction to alienation and fetishism, rather than class relationships. See *From Rousseau to Lenin*, pp. 82–92.
85. *Capital*, vol. I, chap. 1, sec. 4.
86. Mandel, *Late Capitalism*, chap. 14. The theoretical basis for this was presented in his *Marxist Economic Theory*, vol. I, chap. 11, esp. pp. 349–61.
87. A fuller discussion would elaborate on the movement of capital between branches of production as a way of understanding vol. III, pt. II, rather than competition as normally understood.
88. Marx, *Wages, Price, and Profit*, cited in Mandel, *Late Capitalism*, p. 150. Mandel focuses on the rate of surplus value, but this relationship tends to get lost among "technical"

variables to which it is never fully related. Accumulation is seen as an "interplay of six variables." See *Late Capitalism*, p. 39.

89. Although Marx refers to the "physical minimum" in the passage cited, he refers also to the "historical and social elements" which establish this level. (See also *Capital*, vol. I, p. 171.) The capitalist countries are unusual in that the value of labor power has been pushed above the biological minimum.

90. Discussed in Wright, "Alternative Perspectives in the Marxist Theory," pp. 30-35.

91. This is the position broadly taken by Trotskyite groups and is evident in Mandel's work.

92. Baran and Sweezy, *Monopoly Capital*; Yaffe, "Marxian Theory of Crisis."

93. See Wright, "Alternative Perspectives in the Marxist Theory"; O'Connor, *Fiscal Crisis of the State*. This view is most developed in Marcuse and the Frankfurt School.

94. Tronti, "Social Capital," p. 105.

95. See Mariarosa Dalla Costa and Selma James, *The Power of Women and the Subversion of the Community* (London: Falling Wall Press, 1972), and the Wages for Housework literature.

96. Tronti, "Social Capital," p. 105.

97. *Capital*, vol. III, pp. 196-97, emphasis added.

98. Tronti, "Social Capital," pp. 106-7.

99. Bell and Cleaver, "Marxian Theory of Accumulation and Monopoly Capitalism" (paper delivered to meetings of Union for Radical Political Economics, San Francisco, December 28, 1975).

100. Mario Tronti, "Workers and Capital," esp. pp. 37-54.

101. For a discussion of the phases of struggle in the 1950s and 1960s see Paolo Carpignano, "U.S. Class Composition in the Sixties," *Zerowork*, no. 1 (December 1975).

102. For data see William Nordhaus, "The Falling Share of Profits," *Brookings Papers*, no. 1 (1974); William Wycko, "The Work Shortage: Class Struggle and Capital Reproduction," *Review of Radical Political Economics* 7, no. 2 (Summer 1975); and David Gordon, "Recession Is Capitalism as Usual," *New York Times Magazine*, April 27, 1975.

103. Ian Gough, "State Expenditure in Advanced Capitalism," *New Left Review*, no. 92 (July-August 1975).

104. For a study of the New York City crisis, see article by Philip Matero in *Zerowork* no. 2 (forthcoming).

105. For background which shows how the Conservative Party were unable to control the working-class in Britain see Anthony Barnett, "Class Struggle and the Heath Government," *New Left Review*, No. 77 (Jan/Feb. 1973).

106. This is clear from articles in the business press; see, for example, "Workers unrest: Not dead but playing possum," *Business Week*, May 10, 1976, pp. 133-134. "Grinding Out More: How the Current Gain in Productivity Looks From a Factory's Floor," *Wall Street Journal*, Dec. 8, 1975.

107. Letter from Marx to Engels, April 9, 1870, in *Selected Correspondence* (Moscow: Progress Publishers, 1965), p. 222. Cited in Cleaver, *Reading Capital Politically*.

11

Alternative Perspectives in Marxist Theory of Accumulation and Crisis

ERIK OLIN WRIGHT

Assistant Professor of Sociology at the University of Wisconsin

INTRODUCTION

Everyone agrees that the world economy in the 1970s is in the midst of a serious economic crisis. The inadequacies of the standard neoclassical and Keynesian economic paradigms for understanding the current crisis—let alone for providing solutions—is becoming more and more apparent. The major alternative paradigm is Marxist political economy, and it is hardly surprising that the Marxist theory of economic crisis has begun to attract considerably more attention in recent years.

The difficulty is that there is not one Marxist theory of economic crisis, but several competing theories. Although all Marxist perspectives on economic crisis tend to see crisis as growing out of the contradictions inherent in the process of capital accumulation, there is very little general consensus on which contradictions are most central to understanding crisis, or even on how the contradictions in accumulation should be conceptualized in the first place.

This paper will attempt to lay bare the logical structure of each of the general Marxist perspectives on economic crisis and to provide a preliminary synthesis. I will argue that there is no intrinsic incompatibility in these diverse conceptions of the contradictions in accumulation if they are viewed as part of a historical process. Specifically, I will make the following argument:

1. At different stages of capitalist development the accumulation process faces different dominant constraints or impediments. These impediments are not exogenous factors that interfere with the accumulation process but are generated by the accumulation process itself.
2. In order for capitalist production to continue, these constraints must be overcome. In a fundamental sense capitalists do not have the choice of passively accepting the impediments to accumulation. As individuals, capitalists must attempt to overcome these impediments in order to survive in a competitive world; as a class, capitalists must strive to remove the impediments to accumulation in order to contain the class struggle.

Many of the core ideas in this paper have grown out of the numerous intense discussions on the capitalist system that I have had as a member of the San Francisco Bay Area Kapitalistate Collective. I would also like to thank especially David Gold, Jens Christiansen, Clarence Lo, and Michael Reich for helpful criticisms. An earlier version of this paper appeared in The Insurgent Sociologist *(Fall 1975).*

3. The systemic solutions to the dominant impediments at a given stage of capitalist development generate the new impediments that constrain the accumulation process in the subsequent stage. It is in this sense that the impediments to accumulation can be considered *contradictions* in accumulation rather than merely obstacles to accumulation. They are contradictions because the "solutions" to a particular impediment become themselves impediments to accumulation.

4. The worldwide capitalist economic crisis of the 1970s can be (tentatively) understood as part of a transition from one pattern of constraints on accumulation, characterized by Keynesian solutions, to a new set of emergent constraints, which were in part caused by those very Keynesian strategies in earlier crises and which are no longer amenable to Keynesian solutions.

The paper will be divided into three sections. Part I will briefly discuss the meaning of accumulation and the reasons why accumulation is such an integral part of capitalist society. Much of this discussion will involve a somewhat painstaking exposition of the basic concepts of Marxist political economy. Such a discussion of basic concepts is necessary both to make the conceptual apparatus of the argument accessible to readers relatively unfamiliar with the Marxist categories, and because many of the actual debates over the theory of accumulation are rooted in differing conceptualizations of the basic categories. I hope that by making my particular formulations of these concepts quite clear it will be easier for the weaknesses of the more substantive parts of the paper to be criticized. In part II of the paper this conceptual apparatus will be used to examine the underlying logic of several potential constraints on the accumulation process. Finally, in part III, these potential constraints on accumulation will be systematically related to the general stages of capitalist development. The paper will conclude with a more speculative discussion of likely developments in the immediate future.

I. THE MEANING OF ACCUMULATION

At some stage early in every Marxist textbook of political economy it is stressed that "capital" is not a *thing*, but a *social relation*, and an antagonistic social relation at that. But frequently, after this proclamation is made, the accumulation of capital is substantively treated as the accumulation of things, of the machinery, buildings, raw materials, and so forth that are usually grouped under the rubric "constant capital." This is fundamentally incorrect from a Marxist point of view: capital accumulation must be understood as *the reproduction of capitalist social relations on an ever-expanding scale through the conversion of surplus value into new constant and variable capital.* Before explaining this statement, it will be helpful to very briefly define two of its constituent elements.

1. *Capitalist social relations.* As a first approximation, all class societies, whether capitalist or not, can be understood as consisting of two broad categories of people: direct producers, the men and women who produce the goods and services that allow the society to continue; and nonproducers, those who live off the production of others. Corresponding to this distinction between

classes is an analytic distinction between two categories of labor of the direct producers: "necessary labor" and "surplus labor." *Necessary labor* constitutes the expenditure of human activity for the production of the means of livelihood of the direct producers. *Surplus labor* represents the human activity that produces a surplus beyond the requirements of simply reproducing the direct producers themselves, a surplus that is appropriated by the nonproducing classes.

These categories of direct producers and nonproducers, necessary and surplus labor, pertain to all class societies. What fundamentally distinguishes one kind of class society from another are the types of social relations between the direct producers and nonproducers, and the social mechanisms by which surplus labor is extracted from the direct producers. The characteristic social relations in a capitalist society involve on the one hand propertyless workers who own neither the means of production nor the products of production and are thus forced to sell their labor power—their capacity to produce goods and services—in order to survive, and on the other hand capitalists who own the means of production and purchase labor power on the labor market for the purpose of setting those means of production in motion. The essential social mechanism by which surplus labor is extracted from the direct producers is through the creation of *surplus value* in the process of production.

2. *Surplus value.* Much of the Marxist analysis of capitalism revolves around the concept of surplus value, and thus it is important to make this concept as clear as possible. In order to do this it is first necessary to define briefly a number of other concepts:

a. *Commodity:* A commodity is something that is produced for exchange rather than simply for its direct use. Whereas in all societies the objects of production must in some sense be useful (or have "use value"), it is only in a capitalist society that production in general is primarily organized around exchange.

b. *Labor power:* Labor power is a special kind of commodity—human productive capacity sold on a labor market for use in the production of other commodities.

c. *Value:* If one wants to analyze the division of the total social product among the various classes of society, it is obviously necessary to have units for measuring different quantities of products. In principle a wide variety of metrics could be adopted: one could weigh the total social product and state that so many tons went to the working class, so many tons went to the capitalist class, and so on. One could measure the price of the commodities that make up the social product. Or, one could measure the total hours of average human labor that directly and indirectly went to produce the social product. All these represent some kind of quantitative "value" of the social product.

The premise of the labor theory of value is that *if one is interested in understanding the relationship of class forces to social production, then a measure of value based on hours of human labor embodied in commodities is the most useful.* There are two basic justifications for this claim: First, if one is interested in social relations, in understanding social dynamics, then intuitively a measure of value that directly taps social activity—labor time in production—is attractive. Second, it can be shown that the embodied labor times in commodities bear a systematic relationship to the ratios at which commodities

exchange (see Desai, 1974: 41–76; Koshimura, 1975: 64–94).[1] This does not mean that other theories of value cannot also predict exchange ratios. Piero Sraffa (1960) has shown, for example, that relative prices can be predicted from a value theory based on a "standard commodity" rather than embodied labor times. The point is that only the labor theory of value provides a link between the *quantitative* ratios at which commodities exchange and the *qualitative* social relations that underlie the production process.

Because of the relationship of embodied labor time to the ratios at which commodities exchange, labor time is generally referred to as the *exchange* value of a commodity (to distinguish it from the *use* value of the commodity). More precisely, the *exchange value of a commodity* is defined as the average number of hours of labor of average skill and intensity used directly and indirectly in the production of the commodity, or more succinctly, the socially necessary labor time used to produce the commodity. (For a discussion of the problems involved in this definition, see Mage, 1963; Marx, 1906; Rowthorn, 1974; Sweezy, 1942).

We can now return to the question of how surplus labor is appropriated in capitalist relations of production. The most convenient way to approach this process is to examine the capitalist system at the level of abstraction that Marxists refer to as "capital in general."[2] At this level of abstraction, the capitalist system is analyzed as if capital were a single, homogeneous entity. Under this assumption, it is easy to show that all commodities, including the commodity labor power, will exchange in direct proportion to the socially necessary labor time used in their production. (For a simple explanation of this point, see Sweezy, 1942, chap. 4, especially pp. 69–71.)

Like every other commodity in capitalist society, labor power is produced for exchange on the market, and, like every other commodity, the exchange value of labor power is itself determined by the socially necessary labor time for its production (and reproduction). Labor power, however, is in one crucial respect qualitatively different from all other commodities: it not only has an exchange value but also has the capacity to create new values greater than its own exchange value. This follows from the very definition of exchange value discussed above. Let us suppose that, given the average level of productivity in the economy, it takes a worker four hours to produce the equivalent of his/her daily livelihood (that is, it takes four hours to produce/reproduce the labor power of the worker), but that the capitalist hires the worker for a total of eight hours. In this case the exchange value of labor power would be four "socially necessary labor time hours," but the labor would be used by the capitalist for eight hours worth of production, thus producing eight hours of new value. The difference between the total value produced by the worker and the value of the worker's labor power is called "surplus value."

The only commodity that can produce *surplus* value is labor power. Machines can certainly create value in the sense that they can transfer the exchange value that they contain to new commodities. But machines cannot create surplus value, new value in excess of the exchange value of the machine itself.

The total value of the commodities produced during a production period can be represented by the traditional Marxist formula $c + v + s = P$, where:

P = the total value produced (gross product).

c = the value of the constant capital (machines, buildings, raw materials) used up in production.

v = the value of the labor power used up in production, or variable capital. (It is called variable capital because it produces a variable amount of new value—surplus value—in the production process.)

s = the value of the surplus product produced by the workers.

$v + s$ = the total amount of living labor time used in production (or the value of the net product, i.e., the gross product minus depreciation, raw materials, etc.).

This expression, $c + v + s = P$, reflects the essential mechanism by which surplus labor is extracted in capitalist society: surplus labor is extracted from the working class within the process of production itself through the appropriation of surplus value by the capitalist class.

We are now in a position to explain our definition of capital accumulation as the reproduction of capitalist social relations on an ever-expanding scale through the conversion of surplus value into new constant and variable capital. To understand what is meant by "reproduction on an ever-expanding scale," it is first necessary to understand what reproduction on a static scale (or simple reproduction) means. The traditional Marxist conception of simple reproduction is as follows: Imagine an economy with two sectors, one of which produces the means of production, the other of which produces consumption goods. Within each sector, the total value of the commodities produced can be expressed by the value equation $c + v + s = P$:

sector 1 (production goods): $c_1 + v_1 + s_1 = P_1$
sector 2 (consumption goods): $c_2 + v_2 + s_2 = P_2$

Each of the terms in these equations can be considered simultaneously a supply of and a demand for certain commodities, expressed in value terms: P_1 represents the value of the total supply of production goods; P_2 the value of the total supply of consumption goods; v_1 constitutes that part of the total supply of production goods which must be exchanged for consumption goods in order to reproduce the labor power used in the production of production goods; c_1 represents that part of the total supply of production goods which must be used to replace the means of production used up in the production of production goods; and so on. The equilibrium condition for simple reproduction is that year after year, the magnitude of each of the terms in these equations remains unchanged. That is, the total amount of constant capital used up in production in both sectors is equal to the total supply of constant capital produced in sector 1, and the total consumption by capitalists and workers is equal to the total production of the consumption goods sector. For this to be true, the entire surplus value (s_1 and s_2) must be consumed by the capitalist class.

Expanded reproduction constitutes the situation in which at least part of the surplus value is used to augment the level of constant and variable capital in production. Part of the supply of production goods represented by s_1 is used to increase the level of constant capital, c_1 and c_2, and part of the supply of con-

sumption goods represented by s_2 is used to increase the level of variable capital, v_1 and v_2. Expanded reproduction thus consists of the accumulation of both constant capital and variable capital, and the *rate* of accumulation can be expressed as $\frac{\Delta c + \Delta v}{c + v}$. It is because accumulation involves an expansion both of the means of production controlled by capitalists and of the size of the working class that it constitutes "the reproduction of capitalist social relations on an ever-expanding scale."

Let us examine a bit more closely exactly what it means to say that constant and variable capital are "accumulated." In Marxist terms, the accumulation of constant capital is not the accumulation of machines and the like in any physical sense but the accumulation of the means of production *in value terms*. The accumulation of constant capital can thus be interpreted as the accumulation of labor time performed in the past (often called "dead labor") and embodied in the means of production.

When we turn to the accumulation of variable capital the problem becomes even more complex. Variable capital represents the costs of reproducing the labor force. The total amount of variable capital is a function of at least three critical processes:

1. The total amount of living labor involved in production, that is, $v + s$ (where "amount" must not be interpreted as the number of workers or total worker hours, but rather as the total number of labor hours of average skill level and average labor intensity).
2. The level of the standard of living won by the working class through class struggle.
3. The exchange value of the consumption goods that constitute this standard of living (that is, the level of productivity in consumption goods sector).

If the rate of exploitation (s/v) remains constant and if the rate of productivity does not decrease, then any increase in v must imply an accumulation of variable capital (that is, an expansion of the labor power brought into the production process). But what happens if workers manage to win substantial wage increases through class struggle (without any corresponding increases in the level of productivity of the wage goods sector) and thus tend to push up the level of v per worker at the expense of surplus value? Should this be called a situation of "accumulation of variable capital"?

The usual way out of this ambiguity is through the theory of the "reserve army of the unemployed." The argument is made that, when the working class manages to win sizable wage increases, capitalists respond by introducing new technologies that substitute machines for labor. This has the effect of increasing the pool of unemployed workers—the reserve army—and, accordingly, increasing the competition among workers for jobs. This in turn tends to push the wage rate back to its "true" value. Thus, while it is acknowledged that in the short run the "price" of labor power may exceed its value, it is held that in the long run there is a definite dynamic at work that tends to keep wages in line with the value of labor power. Thus, it is argued, it is reasonable to interpret any long-term aggregate increases in variable capital as accumulation, as part of the self-expansion of capital.

This does not seem to me to be an adequate solution to the ambiguities in the notion of the accumulation of variable capital, especially for periods in which there is a strong labor movement. The problem is that the very notion of the "value" of labor power is itself ambiguous. Whenever the value of constant capital increases, it can be said that the amount of past labor power embodied in means of production has expanded; but an increase in variable capital can mean either that the total amount of living labor in production has expanded, or that the costs of reproducing the same amount of living labor have increased (through successful class struggles over wages). Marx recognized this issue when he stated in volume I of *Capital* that "In contradistinction therefore to the case of other commodities, there enters into the determination of the value of labor power a historical and moral element" (Marx, 1906: 190), and furthermore that:

> The fixation of the value of labor power . . . is only settled by the continuous struggle between capital and labor, the capitalist constantly tending to reduce wages to their physical minimum and to extend the working day to its physical maximum, while the working man constantly presses in the opposite direction.
>
> The matter resolves itself into a question of the relative powers of the combatants. (Marx, 1962: 443)

As a result of this variability in the value of labor power itself, the ratio $\frac{\Delta c + \Delta v}{c + v}$ is an ambiguous expression for the real rate of accumulation. This ratio could be positive simply because workers are winning wage gains without there being any real expansion of capital.

What we would like is some way of representing accumulation that excludes the situation where variable capital increases because labor costs are rising even without an expansion of production taking place. One way of doing this is to shift the analysis from the rate of accumulation per se to the aggregate rate of profit expressed in value terms, that is, $s/(c + v)$.[3] This ratio constitutes the maximum potential rate of accumulation for the society as a whole, given whatever increases or decreases in real wages and in the value of labor power that may have occurred because of class struggle. To the extent that variable capital increases at the expense of surplus value (that is, s/v declines), the rate of profit will be reduced; to the extent that real accumulation is taking place, the increases in variable capital will generate corresponding increases in surplus value, and thus the rate of profit will not decrease. The rate of profit thus has an unambiguous relationship to the possible rate of accumulation: When the rate of profit is high, possible accumulation is high; when the rate of profit is low, possible accumulation is low.[4] Throughout this paper, therefore, we will use the rate of profit as the key expression for the analysis of accumulation.

One final issue needs at least brief discussion before we turn to the analysis of the contradictions and impediments in the accumulation process. Why is accumulation so important for the survival of capitalism? Is a stagnant, no-growth, nonaccumulating capitalism a viable possibility? The example of the British economy in the past twenty-five years certainly indicates the possibility of there being a capitalist system in which little accumulation takes place. Marxists have generally tended to discount the possibility of a return to an

economy of simple reproduction under the conditions of advanced capitalism. Paul Mattick, for example, has written:

> . . . a non-accumulating capitalism is only a temporary possibility; it is a capitalism in crisis. For capitalist production is conceivable only in terms of accumulation. (1969: 60)

As will become clear in the rest of this paper, I do not feel that a non-accumulating capitalism is an impossibility or that it necessarily leads to economic and social breakdown. But I do feel that a nonaccumulating capitalism is a precarious capitalism, and that a variety of repressive social mechanisms have to be created or expanded in order to cope with such a situation. This precariousness can be understood at the level of both "capital in general" and "many capitals" (see footnote 2). At the level of capital in general, of the capitalist system understood as the essential confrontation of capital and labor, accumulation plays a vital role in containing and channeling the class struggle. Accumulation underpins much of the ideological legitimation of the inequalities of capitalist society. The ever-expanding pie enables the standard of living of the working class to increase slowly without threatening relations of production. At the same time it helps to legitimate the vastly higher standard of living of the capitalist class. A prolonged period of nonaccumulation (let alone disaccumulation) would seriously undermine such legitimations and would lead to a considerable intensification of class conflict.

At the level of many capitals, nonaccumulation would considerably intensify competition on both a national and an international scale. In a period of general economic growth, the expansion of individual capitals occurs partially because each capitalist tries to increase his share of the market at the expense of other capitalists and partially because the total size of the market is increasing. In a period of nonaccumulation, the latter of these disappears, and all individual expansion takes the form of a zero-sum game. Marx describes such a situation elegantly:

> So long as everything goes well, competition effects a practical brother-hood of the capitalist class as we have seen in the case of the average rate of profit, so that each shares in the common loot in proportion to the magnitude of his share of investment. But as soon as it is no longer a question of sharing profits but of sharing losses, everyone tries to reduce his own share to a minimum and load as much as possible upon the shoulders of some other competitor . . . competition then transforms itself into a fight of hostile brothers. The antagonism of the interests of the individual capitalists and those of the capitalist class as a whole then makes itself felt as previously the identity of these interests impressed itself practically as competition. (Marx, 1967: 253)

Such an intensification of class conflict and capitalist competition does not, however, necessarily imply the end of capitalism. Contradictions can increase, and social systems can muddle through, especially if new institutional arrangements are created in the attempt to contain those contradictions. The point of an analysis of contradictions in and impediments to the accumulation process is not to prove the inevitability of the collapse of capitalism, but to understand the kinds of adaptations and institutional reorderings that are likely to be attempted in the efforts to counteract those contradictions. Such an understanding is crucial to the development of a viable socialist politics.

II. IMPEDIMENTS AND CONTRADICTIONS IN THE ACCUMULATION PROCESS

Contemporary Marxist literature on contradictions in the accumulation process generally focuses on one of four critical impediments to accumulation: (1) the rising organic composition of capital (Cogoy, 1973; Mage, 1963; Mattick, 1969; Yaffe, 1973a); (2) the problem of realizing surplus value, and in particular problems of underconsumption in capitalist society (Baran and Sweezy, 1966; Gillman, 1965; Sweezy, 1942); (3) a low or falling rate of exploitation resulting from rises in wages (Body and Crotty, 1975; Glyn and Sutcliffe, 1972); and (4) the contradictory role of the state in accumulation (Cogoy, 1972; O'Connor, 1973; Offe, 1973, 1974; Yaffe, 1973a). Most of our discussion of these four impediments to accumulation will be based on the value categories discussed in part I. It is important to stress that such a value analysis does not exhaust the Marxist work on economic crisis. A complete understanding of crisis would also involve an analysis of monetary instability, credit imbalances, and other problems strictly in the sphere of circulation. These issues will not be discussed in the present paper because, although such problems are important, there is a theoretical priority to analyzing the impediments to accumulation in terms of contradictions in the sphere of production. It is on these contradictions that my analysis will be focused. (For a collection of papers on economic crisis that is not restricted to value analysis, see Mermelstein, 1975.)

A. The Organic Composition of Capital and the Falling Rate of Profit

As discussed in part I, it is a fundamental premise of Marxist political economy that only living labor can produce surplus value, and thus profits. The rate of profit, however, is based not merely on labor costs of the capitalist (v) but on all capital costs ($c + v$). Therefore, the reasoning goes, if it should happen in the course of capitalist development that the value of the dead labor used in production should grow much more rapidly than the living labor, there will be a tendency, all other things being equal, for the rate of profit to decline. This constitutes the basic logic for studying the relationship between changes in the productive forces of capitalist society—the technology broadly conceived—and the rate of profit. The "organic composition of capital" is a ratio that is designed to reflect the salient aspects of technology that impinge on the rate of profit. The most useful simple expression for this is the ratio of dead labor (constant capital) to living labor in production.[5]

$$Q = \frac{c}{v + s}$$

One other expression, the rate of exploitation (also called the rate of surplus value), will be important in the discussion of the falling rate of profit.

The *rate of exploitation* is defined as the ratio of the unpaid to the paid portions of the working day (see the discussion of surplus value above), or, alternatively, the ratio of surplus value to variable capital:

$$e = \frac{s}{v}$$

One note of caution before we proceed further. It is very important not to interpret the rate of surplus value, s/v, as an expression simply reflecting the state of class struggle, and the organic composition of capital as an expression simply reflecting the nature of the technology. Both ratios are affected by both class struggle and technology, although in different ways. The average level of productivity in the society, especially in the wage goods sector, has a direct bearing on the rate of surplus value; and the class struggle has a direct bearing on the length of the working day and the intensity of work, and thus on the denominator of the organic composition of capital. Although we will interpret the organic composition of capital as *reflecting* technical relations, this does not imply that it is a purely technical coefficient.

Using the expression

$$Q = \frac{c}{v + s}$$

for the organic composition of capital, and

$$e = \frac{s}{v}$$

for the rate of exploitation, we can write the rate of profit as

$$(1) \qquad r = \frac{s}{c + v} = \frac{s/(v + s)}{\dfrac{c}{v + s} + \dfrac{v}{v + s}} = \frac{e/(1 + e)}{Q + [1/(1 + e)]} = \frac{e}{Q(1 + e) + 1}$$

This function is graphed in Figure 1 (for convenience in this graph, the reciprocal of the rate of exploitation is used).

Equation (1) and Figure 1 will help us to explain the theory of the falling tendency of the rate of profit. There are six propositions in the argument:

1. There are forces intrinsic to the process of capital accumulation that tend to raise the level of the organic composition of capital.
2. As the organic composition of capital rises, there is a tendency for the rate of profit to fall *unless* the rate of exploitation increases sufficiently to counterbalance the rise in the organic composition of capital (or unless some other counteracting force intervenes).
3. In the long run, rises in the rate of exploitation cannot completely counteract the rising organic composition of capital, and thus there will be a definite tendency for the rate of profit to decline.
4. When the decline in the rate of profit becomes sufficiently serious and can no longer be compensated for by the existing rate of exploitation, an economic crisis occurs: the least profitable capitals disappear as businesses go bankrupt; and capitalists increasingly withhold investments because there

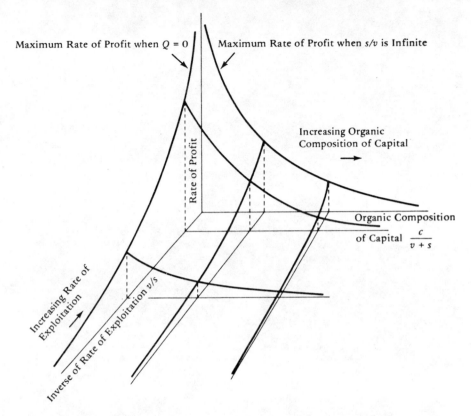

Note: In this figure, intersections of vertical planes parallel to the exploitation/rate of profit plane with the profit surface represent the rate of profit as a function of exploitation for fixed levels of the organic composition of capital. Intersections of vertical planes parallel to the organic composition/rate of profit plane represent the rate of profit as a function of the organic composition of capital for fixed rates of exploitation. And the intersection of a horizontal plane with the profit surface represents the locus of points with a common rate of profit.

Figure 1. The Rate of Profit as a Function of $\dfrac{c}{v + s}$ and $\dfrac{v}{s}$.

are no profitable outlets. Aggregate demand, which is fundamentally derived from the rate of accumulation, therefore declines with the result that the crisis takes on the *appearance* of a crisis of overproduction of commodities. Whereas underconsumptionists (see below, subsection B) argue that crisis is caused by an overproduction of surplus value, the theory of the falling rate of profit argues the exact opposite.

> Because *not enough* [surplus value] has been produced, capital cannot expand at a rate which would allow for the full realization of *what has been* produced. The relative scarcity of surplus-labor in the production process appears as an absolute abundance of commodities in circulation. (Mattick, 1969: 79)

5. These conditions of crisis, however, serve the function of restoring conditions favorable for subsequent profitable accumulation. Several mechanisms accomplish this: (a) unproductive capital is eliminated from the market, thus leaving the remaining capital at a higher level of productivity; (b) in addition, when individual capitals go bankrupt they are forced to sell their existing constant capital at prices below real exchange values. This devaluation of capital means that in the aggregate the numerator in the organic composition of capital declines, thus raising the rate of profit; (c) finally, workers are thrown out of work, the reserve army of the unemployed swells, and capitalists can push the wage below its value, thus increasing the rate of exploitation. Once these processes have advanced sufficiently to restore an acceptable rate of profit, accumulation resumes and the crisis ends.

6. Although the crisis tendency of capitalist society takes the form of periodic business cycles, there is also an overarching tendency for cycles to become progressively more severe. Each successive crisis occurs at a higher level of accumulation and thus a higher level of the organic composition of capital. The problems of restoring conditions for renewed profitable accumulation thus tend to become more difficult in each successive crisis (Mattick, 1969: 69).

With slight variations, these six propositions are all held by proponents of the theory of the falling tendency of the rate of profit. The first three constitute the heart of the theory, for if it can be demonstrated that there is a tendency for the rate of profit to fall, the particular conception of how this in turn produces economic crisis and how economic crisis itself restores conditions of renewed accumulation follows fairly naturally. We will therefore concentrate our attention on the first three propositions.

The second and third of these can be dealt with purely formally in terms of equation (1). It is immediately obvious from equation (1) that for any fixed value of the rate of exploitation, the rate of profit becomes simply a function of the inverse of the organic composition of capital. Thus, if Q rises and e remains constant, the rate of profit will necessarily fall. The second proposition in the argument therefore follows immediately from the definitions of r, Q, and e.

The validity of the third proposition is less obvious. Although it is clear that if the organic composition were to rise to infinity, even an infinite rate of exploitation could not counteract the fall in the rate of profit, this limiting case is not very helpful for understanding the movements of the rate of profit in the real world. What we would like to know is the extent to which a rise in the organic composition of capital will constrain the accumulation process at *any* arbitrary level of Q, and not just in the limiting case where Q is infinite. One way of examining this problem is to ask if the extent to which the rate of exploitation can function as a counteracting force is itself affected by rises in the organic composition of capital. It is easy to show using elementary calculus[6] that, as the organic composition of capital rises, the rate of profit becomes progressively less sensitive to changes in the rate of exploitation. Thus not only does a high organic composition of capital produce a lower possible profit, but it also makes changes in the rate of exploitation less useful as a strategy for bolstering the rate of profit. Furthermore, the higher the rate of exploitation

already is, the less sensitive will be the rate of profit to subsequent changes in the rate of exploitation. Thus *if* in fact there is a secular rise in the organic composition of capital, then, even if the rate of exploitation also rises, it becomes progressively less and less likely that it will be able to counteract completely the rising organic composition of capital. It is therefore quite reasonable to regard rises in the organic composition of capital as a significant impediment to the accumulation process and equally reasonable to assume that, if it does tend to rise, complementary rises in the rate of exploitation will not be able to counteract the fall in the rate of profit in the long run.

The first proposition in the argument is the most problematic. Neither the empirical demonstrations of a general tendency for the organic composition of capital to rise over time, nor the theoretical arguments marshaled in its support, have been particularly convincing. It is unquestionably true that in *physical* terms the amount of machines, raw materials, buildings, and so forth per worker has vastly increased with capitalist development. But the organic composition of capital is a *value* concept, and it is far from obvious that the value of constant capital per worker has risen or has a tendency to rise, especially in the later stages of capitalist development.

For the value of constant capital per worker to rise, there must be a net excess of *labor-saving* technological innovations (innovations that substitute machinery for labor power) over constant *capital-saving* innovations (innovations that substitute cheap machines—machines that require relatively little socially necessary labor time to produce—for expensive machines). When Marx wrote *Capital*, this was a fairly plausible assumption to make. Although Marx did recognize the possibility that increasing productivity in the capital goods sector of the economy might result in a "cheapening of the elements of constant capital" (Marx, 1967: 236), he regarded this as at most a transient countertendency to a generally rising organic composition of capital. In Marx's view, progressive introduction of labor-saving technologies was an intrinsic part of the accumulation process.

Two arguments have been made for why labor-saving innovations should on balance outweigh constant-capital-saving innovations. The first ties labor-saving innovations to the business cycle: as capital expands, the reserve army of the unemployed becomes depleted, and labor markets become tight. The result is that wage costs tend to rise. Capitalists will therefore look for technological innovations that replace workers by machines, both to reduce their individual wage bills and to discipline the labor force (see Yaffe, 1973a: 198).

The second argument places more stress on class struggle in general than on the cyclical expansion and contraction of the labor market. There is one fundamental difference between machines and workers: machines do not resist capitalist domination. Capitalists seek to replace workers with machines, not simply because of the technological advantages that may result from the innovation, but because workers organize to resist exploitation. The intensity of that resistance may vary with the tightness of the labor market, but it is class struggle rather than the labor market as such that is the crucial pressure for labor-saving innovations.

If the only pressures for technological innovation experienced by capitalists came from tight labor markets and class struggle, then indeed these two

arguments would support the view that labor-saving innovations should generally outweigh constant-capital-saving innovations. However real capitalists are under constant pressure to innovate because of competition with other capitalists, and in the competitive struggle, it does not matter whether costs are cut by savings on labor or constant capital. In fact, several plausible arguments can be made that suggest that in advanced capitalist economies there should be some tendency for a relative increase to occur in the selective pressures for capital-saving over labor-saving technological innovations. In earlier periods of capitalist development, when mechanization was first occurring, the introduction of machines necessarily implied the substitution of machines for workers. Once an industry is fully mechanized, however, all innovations tend to take the form of machines replacing machines. Even if such machines do in fact still replace workers, there is no reason why they should not also be cheaper machines. In the competitive struggle among the producers of machines, after all, there will be attempts to expand markets by producing less expensive machines (that is, machines that take less total labor to produce) as well as more productive machines (that is, machines that produce more output per total labor input).

Furthermore, it might also be expected that as constant capital increases as a proportion of total costs (that is, as the *value composition of capital, c/v,* rises), individual capitalists will tend to be more concerned about saving on constant capital. A capitalist in a high technology industry in which vast amounts of constant capital are used per worker is likely to be less concerned about cutting labor costs than about cutting costs of machinery, energy, raw materials, and so on. A plausible model for the rate of increase in the organic composition of capital could postulate that, all other things being equal, the *net* rate of labor-saving innovations over capital-saving innovations is inversely related to *c/v* (or directly related to the proportion of labor costs in production). Thus as the organic composition of capital rose, it would tend to rise at a slower and slower rate, perhaps even asymptotically approaching some high, relatively stable level.

Finally, even if it should happen that in highly mechanized industries the organic composition of capital continues to rise, the aggregate social level of the organic composition might remain constant if there were a relatively faster rate of growth in unmechanized sectors of the economy. The enormous growth of "service sector" employment, which is typically highly labor-intensive, could counterbalance the continuing growth in capital intensity in the industrial sector.[7] The tendency for the competitive labor-intensive sector of the economy to grow in a symbiotic relation with the monopoly sector would also tend to counter to some degree the rise in the *aggregate* organic composition (see O'Connor, 1973, chap. 2). All these pieces of suggestive reasoning indicate that, although a thorough model predicting the relative proportions of labor-saving and capital-saving innovations has yet to be worked out, there is no a priori reason to assume a general preponderance of labor-saving innovations in a developed capitalist economy.

The empirical evidence is at best indecisive on the question of whether or not the organic composition of capital has risen, done nothing, or even fallen. Because national income accounts are not figured in terms of embodied labor times, and because data on capital invested includes many entries that Marxists

would not even consider capital, it is of course highly problematic to gather reliable data on the organic composition. Even as strong a proponent of the rising organic composition thesis as Cogoy has to admit that the meager data that support his views are as equivocal as the data that oppose them (Cogoy, 1973: 63).

If the theoretical basis is weak for assuming there is a tendency for the organic composition to rise, and if the empirical evidence is nonexistent, why bother with the theory at all? There are several reasons. First, although there is considerable dispute about the relevance of the theory of the rising organic composition of capital to late twentieth century capitalism, there is general agreement among Marxists that it was a significant characteristic of nineteenth century capitalism. As we will see in section III of this paper, the theory of the rising organic composition of capital is essential for a historical understanding of the development of capitalist accumulation.

Second, even if it is true that there is no consistent long-term tendency for the organic composition of capital to rise, the organic composition still acts as a real constraint on the accumulation process. The results we discussed above indicate that when an economy is in a situation of relatively high organic composition of capital, the rate of profit becomes less sensitive to increases in the rate of exploitation. This means that if the rate of profit were to decline because of some factor other than the organic composition of capital (for example, the growth of unproductive expenditures), the system would be more rigid because of the high organic composition. No one has argued that the organic composition of capital has fallen to any great extent in the past several decades, and thus one can deny that it still acts as an impediment to accumulation, even though it may not be the great dynamic source of crisis that its defenders claim.

Finally, even if a secular rise in the organic composition of capital is not the general cause of capitalist crisis, a destruction of values and a corresponding temporary fall in the organic composition of capital may be a crucial part of the solution to crises. The movement of the organic composition of capital over the past century could be hypothesized to look something like Figure 2.[8] Sometime during the first quarter of the twentieth century, according to this hypothesis,

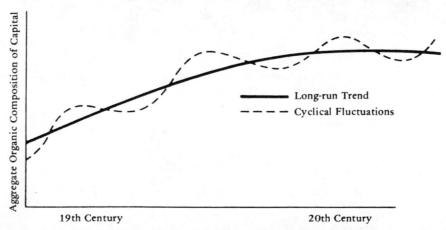

Figure 2. Hypothesized Trend in the Organic Composition of Capital.

a relatively stable, fairly high level of organic composition of capital was reached. Since that time the organic composition of capital has dropped considerably during periods of crisis and then risen back to this stable level during periods of prosperity as post-crisis un-devaluated constant capital replaced the cheap, devaluated capital acquired during the crisis. A fall in the organic composition of capital can be a solution to crisis without a rise in the organic composition being the fundamental cause of crisis. Under these assumptions, if it should happen that institutional changes in the economy—in particular, growth of government subsidies of inefficient monopolistic firms—should block the fall in capital values during a crisis, then it would be expected that a serious "crisis of crisis management" might occur. This issue will be more fully discussed in section III below.

B. Underconsumptionist Theories of Economic Crisis

Marx very explicitly states in the *Grundrisse* that the inherent tendency for the rate of profit to fall is

> . . . the most important law of modern political economy and the most essential one for understanding the most complicated relationships. It is the most important law from an historical standpoint. (Quoted in Yaffe, 1973b. 200)

But he also makes a number of statements that some Marxists have taken to indicate that Marx supported an underconsumptionist view of crisis. "The last cause of all real crisis," Marx writes in *Capital,* volume III,

> always remains the poverty and restricted consumption of the masses as compared to the tendency of capitalist production to develop the productive forces in such a way, that only the absolute power of consumption of the entire society would be their limit. (Marx, 1967)

As often happens in debates among Marxists, the dispute between the two positions has frequently taken the form of competing exegeses of passages from *Capital.* On that score it seems to me that the proponents of the falling rate of profit probably have the upper hand. While Marx did see the underconsumption of the masses as a chronic state in capitalist society, it only became a factor in crisis given the dynamics of accumulation and the problem of the rising organic composition of capital. Engels states this position very clearly:

> The underconsumption of the masses, the restriction of the consumption of the masses to what is necessary for their maintenance and reproduction, is not a new phenomenon. It has existed as long as there have been exploiting and exploited classes. . . . The underconsumption of the masses is a necessary condition of all forms of society based on exploitation, consequently also of the capitalist form; but it is the capitalist form of production which first gives rise to crises. The underconsumption of the masses is therefore also a prerequisite condition for crises, and plays in them a role which has long been recognized. But it tells us just as little why crises exist today as why they did not exist before. (Quoted in Yaffe, 1973a: 216)

A correct exegesis of Marx, however, doth not a correct interpretation of the world make. The cogency of underconsumptionist views must be assessed on the strength of their logical status, not on their formal agreement or disagreement with Marx's own work.

One of the initial problems in assessing the underconsumptionist logic is that most writings from the underconsumptionist perspective fail to lay out the assumptions and structure of the argument in as coherent a way as the falling-rate-of-profit theorists. The following account of underconsumptionist theory is thus not taken directly from any one defender of the perspective. It is rather my own construction of what I feel a coherent Marxist underconsumptionist theory would be.

A Marxist theory of underconsumption contains four basic propositions:

1. There is a general tendency in capitalist society for the absolute level of surplus value to rise. In addition, with increases in productivity, there is a tendency for the rate of surplus value to increase as well.
2. There is an intrinsic contradiction in capitalist society between the conditions of production of surplus value and the conditions of the realization of surplus value. For realization *not* to be a problem, the growth in aggregate demand must occur at the same rate as the growth in surplus value. This is always problematic in capitalist society because individual capitalists always try to minimize their wage bills and thus restrict the development of effective demand on the part of workers. The result is that there will be a tendency for the growth of demand to lag behind the growth of surplus value unless new sources of aggregate demand can be created (for example, through increases in government spending, in foreign markets, in consumer credit, in the rate of accumulation itself). In the absence of such new sources of demand, part of the surplus value will remain unrealized.
3. The inability of the capitalist to realize the full value of the produced surplus value is experienced by capitalists as a fall in the actual rate of profit. This leads to a reduction of investment, bankruptcies, unemployment, and so on. Such crisis conditions are resolved when some exogenous source of new demand—such as the state—steps in and restores conditions of profitable realization of surplus.
4. Although underconsumptionist tendencies are present at all stages of capitalist development, they become especially acute, and become the source of serious economic crisis, only in the monopoly stage of capitalism. Monopoly power greatly augments the tendency for surplus value to rise, and thus the tendency for underconsumption to occur.

There is relatively little disagreement over the first of these propositions. With some exceptions most Marxists feel that with increasing productivity, the value of wage goods tends to fall and that thus, although the standard of living of workers might even rise in real terms, the value of labor power will also tend to decline. This results in an increase in the rate of surplus value and, with expanded reproduction of capital, an increase in the mass of surplus value as well. Although the underconsumptionists and the falling-rate-of-profit theorists disagree vehemently on the relationship of monopoly to a rising rate of surplus value, they agree on the general proposition that it tends to rise.

On the second proposition there is no such agreement. The falling-rate-of-profit theorists insist that realization problems are a consequence rather than a cause of the fall in the rate of profit. Cogoy makes perhaps the most categorical statement of this view when he argues (in a somewhat cryptic way):

> Since total demand under capitalism represents accumulation (the demand for subsistence goods represents accumulation, that is accumulation of variable capital), the organic composition determines which part of the total demand consists of demand for subsistence and which for means of production. Thus a falling-off of demand must stem from capital, and capital discontinues its demand only when the rate of profit falls. Thus logically, we can only deduce the over-production of commodities from the fall in the rate of profit and not vice versa. (1973: 64)

If all aggregate demand is derived from accumulation, and if capitalists are constantly striving to maximize the rate of accumulation, then clearly the only reason there can ever be an effective demand inadequate for absorbing all of the produced surplus value would be if something happened to the rate of accumulation. This is precisely what the theory of the rising organic composition of capital attempts to provide.

The problem with Cogoy's reasoning, and that of similar critics of underconsumption theories, is that aggregate demand in capitalist society is not simply derived from accumulation. Especially under monopoly conditions, a sizable part of total demand does not come directly from accumulation but from such nonaccumulating sources as capitalist personal consumption, much of state expenses, and so on. From the point of view of the rising-organic-composition theorists, this would change nothing fundamental about the problem. Because the rising organic composition of capital creates a problem of inadequate surplus value, such "unproductive expenses"[9] (often called luxury expenses or waste expenditures) would merely exacerbate the problem whose root cause lay in the production process. But things become quite otherwise if we drop the assumption of a rising organic composition of capital.

To analyze the underconsumption problem it is useful to introduce a distinction between potential profits and actual profits. Potential profits are those that would occur in the absence of any realization problems. In terms of our previous discussion, potential profits constitute the surface on Figure 1 and the value expression in equation (1). Actual profits will always be less than or equal to such potential profits. The underconsumption argument is an analysis of why there are *tendencies* for a portion of the surplus to remain unrealized, and thus for actual profits to fall short of potential profits.

If the organic composition of capital is more or less constant and the rate of exploitation is rising, there will necessarily occur a rise in the rate of potential profits in value terms. The question then becomes, what are the equilibrium conditions such that all of this increasing surplus will be realized? That is, what total demand must be forthcoming so that the entire surplus product in value terms will be sold? From the basic value equation we have the total supply of commodities:

$$\text{Supply} = c + v + s$$

and the total demand for commodities:

$$\text{Demand} = c + v + \Delta c + \Delta v + U = c + v + I + U$$

where Δc and Δv are the demand for additional constant and variable capital or new investment, I (that is, the demand for accumulation), and U is the demand for unproductive expenditures. The equilibrium condition is therefore:

$$c + v + s = c + v + \Delta c + \Delta v + U$$

or simply:

(3) $$s = \Delta c + \Delta v + U = I + U$$

Dividing each side of this equation by total capital, $c + v$, we have:

(4) $$\frac{s}{c + v} = \frac{I}{c + v} + \frac{U}{c + v}$$

In this equation, the left-hand side is simply the potential profit rate, r; $I/(c + v)$ is the rate of investment, I' (or the rate of accumulation, ignoring the problems discussed earlier about the meaning of v in such an expression); and $U/(c + v)$ can be considered the rate of unproductive utilization of resources, U'.

Differentiating both sides of the equation with respect to time, we get:

(5) $$\frac{dr}{dt} = \frac{dI'}{dt} + \frac{dU'}{dt}$$

What can we say about the relative magnitudes of these various terms? We know that dr/dt must be positive. Can we say anything general about the relationship between the other two terms? With the assumptions we have made so far, we cannot. But if we are willing to assume that accumulation occurs at a constant rate, then we know that dI'/dt must equal zero. Under this assumption we then know that the requirement for equilibrium is that the rate of unproductive spending must grow at the same rate as the potential rate of profit.

The assumption that accumulation occurs at a constant rather than an ever-increasing rate may seem somewhat questionable. In fact, of course, this assumption can be relaxed somewhat, and it will still be necessary for the rate of unproductive spending to increase in order for the equilibrium condition to be met (that is, in order for all of the surplus value produced to be realized). The crucial point is that, unless it is assumed that the *rate* of accumulation increases exactly as fast as increases in the rate of potential profits, then a growth in the rate of unproductive expenditures must occur if the equilibrium conditions are to be met.

The tendency toward underconsumption in capitalist society stems fundamentally from the fact that there are no automatic mechanisms that guarantee that the rate of unproductive demand will grow sufficiently fast to fill the gap between the rate of accumulation and the rate of potential profit. The demand for unproductive, wasteful consumption does not grow spontaneously in the same way that demand directly derived from accumulation grows automatically

with economic growth. Waste is a social invention, and the maintenance of high levels of wasteful consumption requires conscious planning and intervention. The growth on a massive scale of consumer credit, built-in obsolescence of many consumer durables, the wide range of state interventions in the economy of the Keynesian variety, and so forth, all represent conscious strategies to increase the rate of unproductive demand and thus avoid realization/underconsumption crises.[10] As we will see in section III, these solutions themselves create new problems that the capitalist economy is only beginning to face.

While underconsumptionist tendencies are present at all stages of capitalist development, they have remained largely latent until the monopoly stage. So long as the organic composition of capital did have a tendency to rise, much of the rising surplus was in fact automatically absorbed by the accelerating rate of investment (of accumulation). With the emergence of monopoly capital, however, the situation decisively changes. To begin with, there appears to be a tendency for the organic composition of capital to be relatively stable in the monopoly stage of capitalism, or at least to rise at a much slower rate. Several mechanisms might explain this. The typical productivity bargains worked out between big unions and monopoly capital may have reduced the selective pressures for labor-saving innovations. Or, because monopolies tend to emerge in industries with already high levels of organic composition of capital (that is, high barriers to entry), it may be that the rate of increase in the organic composition capital, in the period of monopoly capital, would tend to be lower (assuming, as we did above, that the rate of labor-saving innovations is proportional to the inverse of the value composition of capital). Whatever the explanation, this relatively stable organic composition of capital, which seems characteristic of developed monopoly capital, will tend to aggravate the problem of rising surplus.

Monopoly capital has a second, and probably more important, impact on the tendency toward underconsumption. In a fundamental way, monopoly power transforms the relationship between values and prices. This is an extremely controversial issue and the cause of one of the most heated disputes between the organic composition theorists and the underconsumptionists. The falling-rate-of-profit theorists insist that the structure of market relations can in principle have no fundamental impact on value relations. All that monopoly power can hope to change is the distribution of surplus value from less monopolistic to more monopolistic capitals. It cannot have any effect on the analysis of "capital in general."

Sweezy has challenged this view head on. He argues that monopoly power results in a redistribution of value not only from competitive to monopoly capital, but also from wages to surplus value:

> Monopoly does not change the total *amount* of value produced—except indirectly to the extent that it affects the total volume of employment—but it does bring about a *redistribution* of value. Marx indicates that this can take two forms: first, a transfer of surplus value from competitive to monopolistic capitals; and second, a transfer of value from wages to surplus value. (Sweezy, 1974: 41)[11]

This means that during the stage of monopoly capital surplus labor is extracted from the working class through (at least) two mechanisms rather than merely

one: in addition to the extraction of surplus value in the labor process through the wage contract, surplus value is appropriated in the sphere of circulation through the manipulation of monopoly prices. Why don't workers then organize and force monopoly capital to pay wages equal to the "true" value of labor power? The answer, of course, is that the working class *in the monopoly sector* attempts to do precisely this, and by and large wages in the monopoly sector have tended to rise almost at the same rate as productivity. But workers outside of the monopoly sector of the economy have not been able to raise their wages in a comparable manner. The result is that monopoly sector capitalists in effect extract surplus value from competitive sector workers (and transfer surplus value from competitive sector capitalists) through the mechanism of monopoly pricing. The upshot of all this is that the aggregate rate of surplus value under conditions of monopoly capital rises more rapidly than productivity, and thus the general problem of underconsumption becomes even more acute.

Two general social processes have evolved that at least partially counteract this tendency toward underconsumption in monopoly capitalist society. The first has already been mentioned: the invention and growth of Keynesian policies designed to stimulate aggregate demand through the expansion of unproductive spending, primarily by the state. Such spending has the secondary consequence of bolstering the confidence of investors in the stability of the economy, and thus fosters a higher rate of accumulation. Thus, in equation (5), the growth of dU'/dt becomes a stimulus for the growth of dI'/dt and, consequently, for a further reduction in underconsumption pressures.

Second, the growth of collective bargaining may have the effect of reducing the rate of increase in the rate of surplus value itself. In the equilibrium condition in equation (5) this would mean a reduction in dr/dt and thus a reduced pressure towards underconsumption. Especially in monopoly sector industries, where wages since the war have been fairly closely tied to productivity increases, the gradual rise in the wage has undoubtedly lessened to some extent underconsumption tendencies. The continued growth of monopoly power, however, has at least partially neutralized this counteracting process, because much of the productivity wage increases have in turn been passed on to the working class as a whole in the form of monopoly pricing. As we argued above, this has the effect of further increasing the rate of surplus value for capital as a whole.

The most serious weakness in the underconsumptionist position is that it lacks any theory of the determinants of the actual rate of accumulation. The falling-rate-of-profit theorists have a specific theory of the determinants of the rate of accumulation. In equating the rate of profit with the rate of accumulation, they see a combination of the organic composition of capital and the rate of exploitation as the basic determinant of the actual rate of accumulation. Because they view the organic composition of capital as rising and thus constantly pushing down the rate of profit, the assumption that the rate of profit and the rate of accumulation are equivalent does no damage to their general argument. If anything, the impact of the rising organic composition of capital would be even greater if not all profits were accumulated.

In the underconsumption argument, however, the rate of profit and the rate of accumulation cannot be equated. If they were, there would not be a tendency for underconsumption (that is, there would be no need for the rate of

unproductive spending to increase). Much underconsumptionist writing has, at least implicitly, opted for Keynes' solution to this problem by focusing on the subjective anticipations of profit on the part of capitalists as the key determinant of the rate of accumulation. From a Marxist point of view, this is an inadequate solution. I have not yet seen an elaborated theory of investment and the rate of accumulation by a Marxist underconsumptionist theorist, and thus for the time being the theory remains incomplete.

C. Theories of the Profit Squeeze

Both underconsumptionists and organic-composition-of-capital theorists maintain that with capitalist development there tends to be a rising rate of surplus value. Where they differ is in their view of the relationship between this rising rate of surplus value and the movements of the rate of profit. The organic-composition theorists insist that changes in technology within the production process itself tend to negate rises in the rate of surplus value and thus produce a fall in profits; underconsumptionists argue that the forces for a rising surplus tend to be stronger than any counterforces, especially under conditions of monopoly capital.

The proponents of the profit squeeze view of crisis agree with the organic-composition theorists that the rate of profit tends to fall, but they do not agree that this has anything to do with changes in technology, and they disagree with both the organic-composition theorists' and the underconsumptionists' belief that there is any tendency for the rate of surplus value to rise.

The essential argument of the profit squeeze is very simple: the relative share of the national income going to workers and to capitalists is almost entirely a consequence of their relative strengths in the class struggle. To the extent that the working class develops a strong enough labor movement to win wage increases in excess of productivity increases, there will be a tendency for the rate of exploitation to decline and thus for the rate of profits to fall (to be "squeezed" by rising wage bills). Such a decline in profits results in a corresponding decline in investments and thus in even slower increases in productivity. The end result is economic crisis. Conditions for profitable accumulation are restored when, as a result of the economic crisis, the reserve army of the unemployed increases to the point where the bargaining power of the working class is weakened. This enables the capitalist class to increase its share of the national income and thus escape the squeeze on profits, at least temporarily.

This position has been argued by Raford Body and James Crotty (1975) for the case of the United States, and by Andrew Glyn and Bob Sutcliffe for Great Britain (1971, 1972). Body and Crotty have largely used the profit squeeze argument to explain the relationship of macroeconomic policy to the business cycle. They write:

> Throughout the post-World War II, post-Keynesian period, the profit share of income, indeed the absolute level of profits, has fallen in the latter half of every expansion. Correspondingly, wages and wage share have risen. We view the erosion of profits as the result of successful class struggle waged by labor against capital—struggle that is confined and ultimately reversed by the relaxation of demand and the rise in unemployment engineered by the capitalists and acquiesced in and abetted by the state. (1975: 1)

Cyclical crises are thus portrayed primarily as devices for disciplining the working class.

Glyn and Sutcliffe have extended this argument into an analysis of the general stagnation of the British economy in the 1960s. They argue that because of the vulnerability of British capital to international competition and because of the organizational strength of the British labor movement, British capital has not been able to use economic crisis as a mechanism for disciplining the working class. The result is that the profit squeeze has continued during the crisis itself.

The theory of the profit squeeze has the considerable merit of bringing class struggle into the very heart of a theory of accumulation and crisis. But in avoiding the mechanistic determinism that so frequently characterizes Marxists who support the rising organic composition of capital thesis, Glyn and Sutcliffe and Body and Crotty have made their own theories almost totally indeterminate. In particular, they have broken almost entirely the link between the productive forces and the relations of production (or between technology broadly conceived and class struggle) that is central to the Marxist understanding of social development. The level of productivity (the level of development of the productive forces) plays almost no role in either Glyn and Sutcliffe's or Body and Crotty's analysis of the relative shares of capital and labor, and thus no role in their view of the rate of exploitation. Although it is certainly crucial to regard class struggle as having an important impact on real wages, that impact must be seen as occurring within structural limits shaped by the level of technology and productivity.

To be fair to Body and Crotty in particular, they do not set their work out as a general theory of crisis, but as an explanation of the business cycle. However, even a theory of cycles needs to be related to an understanding of dynamics at the level of production. The same class struggles over wages will have very different consequences depending upon whether the accumulation process is dominated by the dynamics described in the rising organic composition of capital/falling rate of profit view of crisis or in the underconsumption view. If underconsumption is the essential problem facing the capitalist class, then wage increases can themselves become one of the ways in which the rising surplus is absorbed. If, on the other hand, a rising organic composition of capital is the underlying basis for crisis, then struggles over wages will tend to heighten crisis tendencies. Rising wage bills will encourage capitalists to increase the rate of labor-saving innovations, which results in a further rise of the organic composition of capital and thus greater tendencies for the rate of profit to fall.

Both Glyn and Sutcliffe and Body and Crotty largely ignore such links between the dynamics of accumulation and class struggles over wages. The result is that profit squeeze views of crisis become almost entirely circulation-based theories. Social relations of production may be important to defining the protagonists in class struggle—workers and capitalists—but contradictions within production itself cease to be the focus of the understanding of crisis. Again, this is not to deny the importance of struggles over wages as a factor contributing to economic crisis. The important point is that the class struggle must be analyzed dialectically in the context of the material relations present in the production process, rather than treated as a kind of *deus ex machina* that determines the development of the system.

D. State Expenditures and Accumulation

Marxist theories of accumulation and crisis have generally conceptualized state activity as unproductive in a double sense: first, state *revenues* (principally taxes) are seen as coming out of the existing pool of surplus value, and thus increases in state spending necessarily imply less surplus value for accumulation. Second, state *spending* itself is seen as unproductive because under normal conditions the state does not engage in direct investment in the production of commodities. In the underconsumptionist model of crisis this unproductive quality of state expenditures constitutes the central mechanism by which crisis is averted or at least minimized; in rising-organic-composition models, the expansion of such unproductive expenditures is seen as a critical factor that exacerbates the inherent crisis tendencies in the system. In both theories, however, state activity is seen as largely unproductive and as absorbing an increasing share of the surplus value produced in the economy.

This traditional conception can be criticized both in terms of its view of the *sources* of state revenue and of its view of the *impact* of state spending.

The view that all taxes constitute a tax on the *existing* pool of surplus value is based on a mechanistic and static interpretation of the meaning of the value of labor power. Because it is obviously the case that taxation reduces the real wages of workers, the view that all taxes come from surplus value implicitly assumes that prior to taxation the wages were above the "true" value of labor power. Taxation then merely appropriates that part of the surplus value which had previously been in the disguised form of an inflated money wage. The implicit logic is that if taxation did not occur, wages would be reduced to the present after-tax level anyway. In other words if the state did not tax this surplus value, it would be available to the capitalist for accumulation. These assumptions are at best dubious, if real wages and taxation are seen as at least partially the outcome of class struggle. Because of the enormous weight of the state's power of legitimation, it is reasonable to assume that many workers are willing to accept a level of taxation on their money incomes greater than a corresponding wage cut that might occur in the absence of such taxes. Taxation can thus be seen as, in part, a weapon in the class struggle by which the state appropriates a certain amount of surplus value that is *unavailable* to private capitalists. From a total social point of view, therefore, taxation, like monopoly pricing, has the capacity to increase the aggregate rate of surplus value. Taxation, of course, cannot itself create *value*, but taxation can increase the part of total value that is appropriated as *surplus value*. Tax exploitation did not die with the feudal mode of production just because wage exploitation became the dominant way that surplus is extracted from workers in capitalist society. This is not to say that there are no limits on the extent to which taxes can have this effect, and certainly not that all or even most taxation in fact expands surplus value, but merely that the assumption that all taxation constitutes a drain on the existing pool of surplus value is incorrect.

Quite apart from the problem of the relationship of taxation to existing surplus value, there is the question of the impact of taxation on the subsequent production of surplus value. It is certainly true that, with very few exceptions, state production itself is not production for the market and the state does not

accumulate capital out of any realized profits from its own production. Most state expenditures therefore do not *directly* produce surplus value. But as O'Connor (1973) has thoroughly argued, this does not keep the state from playing an important role in *indirectly* expanding surplus value and accumulation. Many state expenditures have the effect of reducing the reproduction costs of labor power by socializing many expenses that would otherwise have to be paid for by individual capitalists (medical care, training and education, social security, and so on). Furthermore a great deal of state spending on research and development, transportation infrastructures, communications, and so on has the effect of increasing the level of productivity of capital as a whole and thus contributing to accumulation. Even in terms of classical Keynesian demand-maintenance state interventions, such state spending may have the side effect of increasing capacity utilization and thus increasing productivity. Again, this is not to say that such indirectly productive expenditures are necessarily the dominant mode of state activity, but rather that it is incorrect to see the state's role in the accumulation process as being simply a drag on accumulation.

Given that to some extent taxation, as a mechanism of exploitation, can expand surplus value and that to some extent state spending can expand accumulation, the crucial thing to analyze becomes not merely the forces that produce a general expansion of state activity but also the extent to which those forces selectively expand the unproductive or indirectly productive activities of the state, and the extent to which either surplus-expanding or surplus-absorbing taxation tends to grow more rapidly.

Little can be said about the latter issue. The current growth of the so-called taxpayers' revolt might indicate that the growth of surplus-expanding taxation has reached some sort of limit. Certainly the general battering that the legitimacy of the state has taken in the last several years would tend to reduce the state's capacity to use taxes to extract extra surplus value from the working class. At any rate, for the rest of this discussion we will assume that there has not been any major trend one way or the other in the balance between surplus-expanding and surplus-absorbing taxation.

More can be said about the relationship between unproductive state expenditures and indirectly productive state expenditures. Given the under-consumptionist tendencies inherent in monopoly capital, it is obviously necessary for unproductive expenditures to grow more rapidly than productive expenditures. The growth of classical Keynesian make-work and waste programs, most notably in military spending, reflects this requirement. There are several critical contradictions contained within this role of the state, however, that disrupt the smooth adjustment of unproductive state spending to the needs of monopoly capital.

1. *Contradiction of Legitimation and Accumulation*

The state does not serve the function merely of facilitating accumulation through demand maintenance; the state also serves a vital legitimation function in capitalist society that helps to stabilize and reproduce the class structure as a whole. The legitimation function directs much state activity toward co-opting potential sources of popular discontent by attempting to transform political demands into

economic demands (see Anderson, Friedland, and Wright, 1976). The expansion of Keynesian programs beginning in the 1930s created a perfect political climate for dramatically expanding such legitimating state expenditures. For a long time it appeared that the state could kill two functional birds with one economic-policy stone.

The difficulty, however, is that once a demand on the state to provide some social service or to meet some social need is granted and becomes institutionalized, it becomes viewed as a right. There is a certain logic to legitimation that implies that the political apparatus gets progressively diminishing returns in added legitimation for a given program over time. Once a program becomes seen as a right, the continuation of that program adds little to the legitimacy of the state, whereas a cutback in the program would constitute a source of delegitimation. There is thus not only a tendency for programs once established to continue, but also a constant pressure for programs to expand, regardless of the requirements of the accumulation process. The hypothesis can therefore be advanced that once Keynesian demand maintenance programs become bound up with the legitimation functions of the state, there is a tendency for unproductive spending to rise more rapidly than the systemic requirements for realization of surplus value might dictate.

2. Military Keynesianism and Productivity

The particular institutional form that much Keynesian spending takes—specifically the system of state contracting known as the military-industrial complex—tends not only to absorb surplus but also to put a considerable damper on the subsequent development of productivity (except for occasional technological "spin-offs" from military research and development). Corporations that are major suppliers of military hardware are guaranteed a given profit rate by the state (especially in cost-plus contracts) and are thus under relatively little pressure to introduce inexpensive, efficient innovations into their production processes. Because for most military production there are only one or two potential suppliers, and because the criterion for awarding contracts generally has little to do with the efficiency of the corporation, military Keynesianism tends generally to reduce the average level of productivity in the economy. Furthermore, there is no necessary reason for the imperatives of military spending generated by imperialism to coincide with the imperatives generated by underconsumptionist tendencies. The Vietnam War is an example of a period where these two imperatives were quite contradictory (see Lo, 1975).

3. The Weakening of Mechanisms of Crisis Management

The usual scenario for crisis and recovery is for the least-productive capitals to be wiped out, capital to be devalued, and conditions for profitable accumulation to be restored. The growth of monopoly capital, and especially of the dominant role of the state in regulating the economy, tends to weaken seriously this restorative mechanism. This is most obvious in the case of corporations that become locked into production for the state. In part because of the personal ties between the corporate elite and the state apparatus (especially in the mili-

tary-industrial nexus), and in part because of the social dislocation that would result from the bankruptcy of a major monopoly corporation, the state finds it very difficult to abandon a corporation, even if that corporation's productivity declines. (Witness the enormous subsidies given to that inefficient and unproductive corporation, Lockheed.) But the state is also forced to underwrite the low productivity of many other sectors of the economy, simply in order to avoid major disruptions of the economy (the railroads are a good example).

The upshot of these contradictions in the role of the state is that Keynesian policies tend to become progressively more and more out of proportion to the requirements of accumulation. Although those policies originally emerged as a response to the problem of excessive surplus (as portrayed by the underconsumptionist model), the end result is that they begin to act as a drain on the surplus value necessary for accumulation. That is, in spite of the necessity for waste in the era of monopoly capitalism, there is a tendency for the level of waste (that is, unproductive spending) to expand more rapidly than the capacity of the system to produce waste (that is, the rate of increase in productivity). Because the crisis-solving mechanisms are partially blocked, the result is chronic inflation combined with relatively high levels of unemployment, or what has come to be called "stagflation."

The obvious solution to these dilemmas is, of course, for the state to shift the balance of its activities from unproductive to indirectly productive spending. Indirectly productive expenditures have certainly been steadily growing over the past several decades, although generally at a slower rate than unproductive expenditures. The state is increasingly involved not merely in what Offe (1974) calls "allocative" policies (policies that basically redistribute resources already produced or that mobilize the production of resources strictly for Keynesian purposes), but in "productive" policies as well (policies that directly impinge on the production process and that contribute to the productivity of the economy). As the productive forces in advanced capitalism have developed highly sophisticated technologies, increasingly interdependent productive processes, increasing needs for highly specialized technical labor, and so on, it has become more and more difficult for individual capitals to provide all the requirements for their own expanded reproduction, and they have turned to the state for various forms of socialized investments. It might well be thought, therefore, that the solution to the contradictions of Keynesian policies can be found in a dramatic expansion of these emergent forms of indirectly productive socialized investments. The problem is that the fundamentally Keynesian politics of the contemporary capitalist state—a politics rooted in pluralist interest-group demands, special interest subsidies, military production, and so on—acts as a serious constraint on the potential growth of these newer productivity-enhancing forms of state intervention. This is the heart of the "fiscal crisis of the state": The constant pressures from the growth of unproductive spending, which are exceedingly difficult to curtail (for the reasons spelled out above), make it highly problematic for the state to finance the new forms of state policy that would help reverse the problem of declining productivity itself. Until such time as new political forces can be mobilized successfully to generate what O'Connor (1973) has aptly called a new "social industrial complex," it is difficult to see how this impasse can be overcome.

III. THE HISTORICAL DEVELOPMENT OF CAPITALISM AND THE IMPEDIMENTS TO ACCUMULATION

If these various interpretations are treated as total explanations of crisis tendencies in capitalism, then indeed they are quite incompatible: one cannot, for example, argue that the basic cause of crisis is excessive surplus value (underconsumption thesis) and, simultaneously, inadequate surplus value (rising organic composition of capital thesis); one cannot posit that the reason for crises is a declining rate of exploitation caused by successful class struggle (profit squeeze) and, at the same time, that there is a general tendency for the rate of exploitation to rise (underconsumption and rising organic composition perspectives). Either we must reject outright all these views of crisis but one, or we must adopt a methodological stance which enables us to integrate them within a larger framework.

One strategy for reconciling these various perspectives is to analyze them in terms of the history of capitalist development. Instead of regarding any one crisis mechanism as the pan-historical cause of all economic crises in capitalist society, capitalist development should be viewed as continually transforming the nature of capitalist crisis. The basic logic of this historical transformation of crisis mechanism was set out in the introduction to this paper: At each stage of capitalist development there is a characteristic pattern of impediments to the accumulation process. Through a combination of class strategies by the capitalist state and individual strategies by individual capitalists attempting to maximize their profits, these impediments are overcome and the accumulation process continues in new forms. The solutions to the dominant impediments at each level of capitalist development, however, contain within themselves new contradictions that gradually emerge in the subsequent stages. This dialectic of the accumulation process is summarized in Figure 3.[12]

The chart is, of course, highly oversimplified. The structural "solutions" to a particular impediment to accumulation do not generally eliminate the problem altogether, but merely help it recede into the background. Every period of capitalist development contains, if only in a residual form, the contradictions characteristic of earlier periods. The purpose of the chart is not to present a rigid "stage theory" of capitalism, but rather to capture the overarching problems and movements of the capitalist system.[13]

There is one serious limitation to the chart and the analysis that accompanies it: They contain almost no discussion of imperialism or the world capitalist system. The changing relationships between the most advanced capitalist societies and the more backward areas have been intimately bound up with the dynamics and contradictions of capital accumulation. Indeed, there is a major strand of Marxist thought that sees imperialism as the structural solution par excellence to a variety of impediments to capital accumulation. The account that follows must therefore be read as only a partial story of the dialectic of structural contradiction and structural reorganization in the course of capitalist development.[14]

With these limitations in mind, let us briefly examine each of the stages in the chart.

Stage of Capitalist Development	Central Constraints on Accumulation	Structural Solutions to Constraints
1. Early period of primitive accumulation: transition from simple commodity production to expanded reproduction.	Limits on the *mass* of surplus value due to the restricted size of the working class; limits on the unpaid portion of the working day caused by the lack of close supervision of the labor process (low rate of "absolute surplus value").	Various institutional changes designed to expand the size of the proletariat (immigration, enclosures, etc.); creation of factories by the capitalist class to increase the control of the work process and the length of the workday.
2. Transition from primitive accumulation to manufacture.	Relatively low *rate* of surplus value because of the low level of productivity of the technology and the accompanying (relatively) high value of labor power; continuation of general shortage of labor.	Technical innovations, especially in the production of consumer goods, which result in the cheapening of labor power; especially important are labor-saving innovations that increase the reserve army of the unemployed.
3. Transition from manufacture to machinofacture.	Tendency for the organic composition of capital to rise with an accompanying tendency for the rate of profit to fall; early forms of the labor movement demanding a shorter workday.	Business cycles that devaluate capital and lead to an increasing concentration of capital; continuing pressure for labor-saving innovations to expand the reserve army and undermine the labor movement.
4. Rise of monopoly capital.	Tendency for the surplus to rise more rapidly than consumption demand, with a resulting tendency toward underconsumption/realization crises; growth of a more militant labor movement with socialist and communist currents.	Keynesian forms of state intervention designed to expand aggregate demand, especially military spending; creation of complex promotion structures, job hierarchies, etc.; general acceptance of collective bargaining.
5. Advanced monopoly capital.	Ever-increasing reproductive costs of the system as a whole stemming from the contradictions of the accumulation and legitimation functions of the state, resulting in stagnation with chronic inflation. These tendencies are considerably exacerbated by the continued growth of monopoly capital and the internationalization of capital.	Extension of state intervention from simple Keynesian manipulations of effective demand to active involvement in the production process itself: state policies geared directly to increasing productivity ("post-industrial" state policies).
6. State-directed monopoly capitalism.	Ever-deepening politicization of the accumulation process itself: heightened contradiction between the socialization of production and the continuing private appropriation and control of the surplus product. Commodity production itself requires an increasingly noncommodified sphere of production (i.e., nonmarket production organized by the state).	The emergence of a full-fledged, repressive "state capitalism." —?—

Figure 3. Historical Pattern of Constraints on Accumulation and Emergent Structural Solutions.

A. Stage 1: Transition from Simple Commodity Production to Expanded Reproduction

The two crucial constraints on the accumulation process in the early period of primitive accumulation were, on the one hand, the existence of institutional forms of production that made close supervision and control of the work force difficult, and, on the other, the relatively small size of the proletariat and thus the limited amount of exploitable labor. The lack of supervision of workers under conditions of cottage industry meant that the capitalist had little control over exactly how much the worker worked per day; it was also often exceedingly easy for the worker to embezzle considerable amounts of raw materials from the capitalist (see Marglin, 1974, for an excellent discussion of these issues). The result was that the rate of exploitation tended to be low because the effective unpaid portion of the workday was low. In combination with the restricted size of the proletariat, this meant that the mass of surplus value available for accumulation tended to be quite low.

As Stephen Marglin has argued, the creation of the factory in the Industrial Revolution provided the structural solution to the first of these constraints. Workers were brought together under a single roof and closely supervised in their work. They were forced to work as many hours as the capitalist dictated, and thus the amount of surplus labor increased considerably. The creation of factories, however, only heightened the problem of the shortage of free exploitable labor. A variety of state policies, such as open immigration, rural depopulation, closing of the poor houses, and so on contributed to the solution of the labor shortage.

B. Stage 2: Transition from Primitive Accumulation to Manufacture

The continual expansion of the proletariat and of the factory system characterizes the transition from primitive accumulation to the period of manufacture. In the early period of this transition the major way of increasing the rate of exploitation was through the expansion of "absolute surplus value" (that is, increases in surplus value resulting from the expansion of the working day and the intensity of work). Very quickly, the working day was increased virtually to its biological maximum. In spite of this, however, the actual rate of exploitation remained relatively low because of the generally low productivity of technology and the accompanying high value of labor power. Even when the standard of living of the worker was pushed down to bare subsistence, it still took a relatively high proportion of the working day for the worker to reproduce the value of his/her labor power.

The solution to the problem of the relatively low rate of surplus value came through the proliferation of technical innovations, which drastically cheapened the goods consumed by wage labor and thus lowered the value of labor power. Because many of these innovations were labor saving, they also had the effect of expanding the reserve army of the unemployed, thus further alleviating the general problem of the shortage of labor that characterized the period.

C. Stage 3: Transition from Manufacture to Machinofacture

The progressive introduction of machines into the production process defines the transition from simple manufacture to machinofacture. The earlier tendencies—expansion of factories, expansion of the proletariat, and so on—continue, but there is added a constant stream of new innovations. In addition, in this period the first effective forms of proletarian class organizations emerge. Demands are made both for a shortening of the working day and for raises in real wages. The increasing intensity of class struggle creates considerable additional pressure on capital to introduce labor-saving innovations. The result is that in the period of transition from manufacture to machinofacture there is a very rapidly growing organic composition of capital. Thus in spite of an increasing rate of surplus value, there was a definite tendency for the rate of profit to fall.

The solution to this impediment to accumulation was contained within the impediment itself. The classic pattern of business cycles, devaluations of capital, elimination of unproductive capitals, and increasing concentration and centralization of capital provided the social mechanisms for periodically restructuring capital in ways that restored conditions favorable to accumulation.[15]

D. Stage 4: Rise of Monopoly Capital

As the organic composition of capital continued to rise in the nineteenth century and into the twentieth century, two things occurred: capital tended to become ever more concentrated and centralized, and the rate of increase in the organic composition of capital tended to slow down. By some time in the first quarter of this century, it appears, the organic composition of capital more or less stabilized. The rate of exploitation, however, continued to rise, both because of general increases in productivity (both capital saving and labor saving) and because of monopoly power itself. The result was that a strong tendency toward realization and underconsumption problems emerged.

Simultaneously with these developments, the labor movement began to gather considerable strength, especially in the monopolized sectors of the economy. While demands tended to center on issues of wages and immediate working conditions, the growth of socialist and communist forces within the labor movement made the potential for a more genuinely revolutionary labor movement seem likely.

The great social invention of state-sponsored waste, academically legitimated as Keynesianism, constituted the major solution to the impediment of underconsumption. The discovery of collective bargaining and the creation of complex systems of job hierarchies and promotion structures (see Braverman, 1974, and Stone, 1974) helped to contain the labor movement in bounds compatible with such Keynesian solutions.

E. Stage 5: Advanced Monopoly Capital

The Keynesian solutions to underconsumption tended at least initially to dovetail with the political requirements for legitimation. But the initial harmony was shattered as the growth of unproductive state expenditures tended to expand

faster than the surplus-absorbing requirements of the system. The continuing growth of monopoly on both a national and international scale has further contributed to the deterioration of the trade-off between inflation and unemployment. The internationalization of capital in particular has confounded the situation by undermining the capacity of national governments in the advanced capitalist countries to regulate effectively their own national economies.

The emergent solution to these problems of the ever-expanding reproductive costs of monopoly capitalism relative to the growth in productivity is to move from simple Keynesian interventions in the economy to active state involvement in the production process itself. This is the juncture at which American monopoly capital finds itself in the mid-1970s. Qualitatively new forms of state intervention are called for, but the state apparatus seems prepared only to try once more the old Keynesian solutions. After these final attempts flounder, as they almost surely will, it is reasonable to expect that some tentative steps toward these new forms of state intervention and control of the economy will be taken.

It is dangerous to make predictions about history that has not yet happened and especially dangerous to make predictions about the new forms of contradiction that are likely to emerge in the future. Nevertheless, some things seem fairly safe to say. As monopoly capitalism moves toward qualitatively new forms of state involvement in production, toward State Directed Monopoly Capital,[16] there will be an ever-deepening politicization of the accumulation process itself. It will become increasingly difficult to apply a "neutral" market process as rationality to production; political criteria will become more and more central to production itself. Although it is almost certain that in the United States few major corporations would be formally nationalized, a greater and greater proportion of production will be de facto organized by the state. This does not mean, of course, that commodity production (production for exchange) would disappear, but rather that an increasingly important part of production would be organized outside of the market, and not directly subjected profit-maximizing criteria. Stated more abstractly, in order to perpetuate commodity production, the state will have to organize a continually growing noncommodified sphere of production (see Offe, 1974).

All of this would occur within the continuing context of capitalist social relations and a capitalist state that serves the function of reproducing the class structure of capitalist society. The expanded noncommodified sphere of production would be strictly constrained by the requirements of reproducing commodity production itself. The new forms of impediments to accumulation would therefore center on the heightened contradiction between the progressive socialization (and politicization) of the process of production and the continuing private appropriation (through commodity production) of the surplus product.

As the state assumes an ever-greater role in the actual organization of production, the ideological legitimations of the "free enterprise system" will tend to become more and more tenuous. As a result, it is likely that the socialist alternative will move more into the center of American working-class politics. Class struggles around the state and around production (which increasingly become the same struggles) will thus tend to become more ideological, more politicized, and ultimately more threatening to the capitalist system. Under such circum-

stances, it is quite possible to imagine the development of a full-fledged state capitalism in the United States (although dressed in the symbols of private capitalism) that would attempt to contain the glaring contradictions between legitimation and accumulation by means of considerable repression and centralized planning. This is, of course, a highly speculative image of the future. The important point for socialist struggles in the present is to try to understand the changing nature of contradictions within the accumulation process and to adopt political strategies that exploit those contradictions in ways that help to build a socialist movement.

REFERENCES

Amin, Samir. "Toward a Structural Crisis of World Capitalism." *Socialist Revolution,* no. 23 (1975).

Anderson, Gösta; Friedland, Roger; and Wright, Erik Olin. "Modes of Class Struggle and the Capitalist State." *Kapitalistate,* no. 4 (1976).

Baran, Paul, and Sweezy, Paul. *Monopoly Capital.* New York: Monthly Review, 1966.

Body, Raford, and Crotty, James. "Class Conflict and Macro-Policy: The Political Business Cycle." *Review of Radical Political Economics,* 7, no. 1 (1975).

Braverman, Harry. *Labor and Monopoly Capital.* New York: Monthly Review, 1974.

Cogoy, Mario. "Les Theories Neo-Marxistes, Marx et l'Accumulation du Capital." *Les Temps Modernes,* September-October 1972, pp. 396–427.

——"The Fall in the Rate of Profit and the Theory of Accumulation." *BCSE,* Winter 1973, pp. 52–67.

Desai, Meghnad. *Marxian Economic Theory.* London: Gray-Mills Publishing, 1974.

Gillman, J. *Prosperity in Crisis.* New York: Marzani and Munsell, 1965.

Glyn, Andrew, and Sutcliffe, Bob. "The Critical Condition of British Capital." *New Left Review,* no. 66 (1971).

——*British Capitalism, Workers and the Profit Squeeze.* London: Penguin Books, 1972.

Gold, David; Lo, Clarence; and Wright, Erik Olin. "Some Recent Developments in Marxist Theories of the State." *Monthly Review,* (1975).

Hodgson, G. "The Falling Rate of Profit." *New Left Review,* no. 84 (1974).

Koshimura, Shinzaburo. *Theory of Capital Reproduction and Accumulation.* Edited by Jesse Schwartz. Kitchner, Ontario: DPG Publishing Co., 1975.

Laibman, David. "The Organic Composition of Capital: A Fresh Look at Marxian Accumulation Theory." Unpublished ms., 1974.

Levine, David. *Accumulation and Technical Change in Marxian Economics.* Unpublished Ph.D. dissertation, Yale University, 1973.

Lo, Clarence. "The Functions of U.S. Military Spending." *Kapitalistate,* no. 3 (1975).

Mage, S. H. *The Law of the Falling Tendency of the Rate of Profit.* Unpublished Ph.D. dissertation, Columbia University, 1963.

Marglin, Stephen A. "What Do Bosses Do?" *Review of Radical Political Economics,* 6, no. 2 (1974).

Martinelli, Alberto. "Nation States and Multinational Corporations." *Kapitalistate,* no. 1 (1973).

Marx, K. *Capital,* vol. I (Charles H. Kerr & Company edition). New York: The Modern Library, 1906.

——*Wages, Price and Profit,* in *Selected Works,* vol. I. Moscow: Foreign Languages Publishing House, 1962.

——*Capital,* vol. III. New York: New World Paperbacks, 1967.

Mattick, Paul. *Marx and Keynes.* Boston: Porter Sargent, 1969.

Mermelstein, David. *The Economics Crisis Reader.* New York: Random House, 1975.

O'Connor, James. *The Fiscal Crisis of the State.* New York: St. Martin's Press, 1973.

Offe, Claus. "The Structural Problem of the State." Unpublished ms., 1973.

——"The Theory of the State and the Problem of Policy Formation." Unpublished ms., 1974.

Poulantzas, Nicos. *Political Power and Social Classes.* London: NLB, 1973.

Rowthorn, Bob. "Skilled Labor in the Marxist System." *BCSE,* September 1974, pp. 25–45.

Sraffa, Piero. *The Production of Commodities by Means of Commodities.* Cambridge: Cambridge University Press, 1960.

Stone, Katherine. "The Origins of Job Structures in the Steel Industry." *Review of Radical Political Economics,* 6, no. 2 (1974).

Sweezy, Paul. *The Theory of Capitalist Development.* New York: Monthly Review Press, 1942.

——"Some Problems in the Theory of Capital Accumulation." *Monthly Review,* 26, no. 1 (1974).

Yaffe, David. "The Marxian Theory of Crisis, Capital and the State." *Economy and Society,* 2 (1973a), pp. 186–232.

——"The Crisis of Profitability, A Critique of the Glyn-Sutcliffe Thesis." *New Left Review,* no. 80 (1973b), pp. 45–62.

NOTES

1. The relationship of values (embodied labor times) of commodities to actual exchange ratios among commodities (relative prices) involves two transformations: (1) the transformation of the value of the inputs into the prices of the inputs, or what is usually called the "prices of production"; and (2) the transformation of the prices of production into the concrete market prices of commodities. The first of these is the object of the debates over what is called the "transformation problem." A variety of solutions to the transformation problem have been proposed. In the present context it is not necessary to choose between them; all solutions involve a systematic relationship between embodied labor times and prices of production. The second transformation, of prices of production into market prices, lies outside of value theory proper. There are a myriad of factors other than embodied labor times—relative scarcities, monopoly power, government price fixing, and so on—that enter into the determination of concrete relative prices. The point is that embodied labor represents the characteristics *of the commodity itself* (as opposed to contingent forces external to the commodity, such as market forces) that influence prices. To the extent that one is interested in the actual market exchange rates between two individual commodities, value theory will be helpful mainly as an indicator of the strength of these external factors. On the other hand, if one is concerned with the relative magnitudes of large aggregates of commodities and the development of the capitalist system as a whole, then value theory becomes much more powerful because one can assume that many of the external, contingent factors cancel each other out.

2. The distinction in the analysis of capitalism between "capital in general" and "many capitals" must not be confused with the common distinction in economics between macroeconomics and microeconomics. The micro versus macro distinction refers to the *unit of analysis* under examination: the behavior of individual firms and consumers in the former case, of the economic system as a whole in the latter. In contrast, the distinction between capital in general and many capitals refers to the *level of abstraction* of the analysis. In the analysis of "capital in general," the capitalist system has been stripped to its barest, simplest essence: the confrontation of capital and labor. The analysis of "many capitals" does not shift the unit of analysis from system to individual, but rather adds complexity to the analysis of the system as such through the discussion of market structures, competition, diverse technologies, and so on. To say that the analysis of many capitals is at a lower level of abstraction than the analysis of capital in general does not imply that these added complexities are unimportant or that they cannot change the dynamics of the capitalist system in fundamental ways. The method of beginning with the simplest, most abstract conceptualization of capitalism and then moving to the more concrete does not mean that the propositions derived at the most abstract level are unaffected by forces that are analyzed at more concrete levels. But this method does mean that the more concrete complexities introduced in the analysis of many capitals acquire their theoretical specificity in terms of their relationship to the analysis of capital in general.

3. Technically, the ratio $s/(c + v)$ is the rate of profit only when it is assumed that the turnover time for capital stock is one production period. Because the rate of profit is usually measured on total investment (not merely on raw materials and depreciation and wages, that is, $c + v$), a more complex expression including the capital stock and turnover rates is necessary if longer turnover times are to be included in the analysis. Because I have

seen no evidence to indicate that the added complexity of including capital stock in the analysis changes any of the basic relationships, I will use the simpler model throughout this paper, assuming one-period turnovers of constant capital. (See Hodgson, 1974, on the time dating of capital.) It should also be noted that throughout this paper I will make no distinction between profit, interest, and rent as components of surplus value. The expression "profit" will be used to designate the total surplus value.

4. The reason for saying "possible" accumulation is that surplus value is used for capitalist consumption (among other things) as well as for expanded reproduction. To the extent that the capitalist class has some discretion over the proportion of surplus value reinvested as new capital, it is not necessarily true that an increase in the rate of profit will immediately produce an increase in actual accumulation, and vice versa.

5. This expression is not the traditional way that Marxists have defined the organic composition of capital. The usual practice has been to regard the ratio c/v as the organic composition of capital. This has been the usage by economists such as Sweezy, Dobb, Mattick, and Gillman. This expression constitutes the ratio of dead to living capital and is generally treated by these writers as reflecting in value terms what in bourgeois economics is called the capital-intensity of the technology.

In a number of recent works (Cogoy, 1973; Laibman, 1974; Mage, 1963) it has been argued that the ratio c/v is not an adequate measure of capital intensity because, as we argued in the discussion of the problem of the accumulation of variable capital, the level of v depends in part upon the rate of exploitation and not merely on the relative amounts of constant capital and human labor in production. The ratio of dead labor to living labor in production, $c/(v + s)$, has therefore been substituted for the ratio of constant capital to variable capital. While Marx himself is somewhat ambiguous in his own usage of the various expressions, it is possible to interpret a number of important passages in *Capital* as indicating that his notion of the organic composition of capital is best represented by this ratio. (See especially Marx's discussion at the beginning of section 1 of chapter 25 in volume I of *Capital,* "The General Law of Capitalist Accumulation." For a discussion of this section of *Capital,* see Cogoy, 1973: 56–57.) In practical terms it is not terribly important which ratio is used. None of the important results that we will derive below are substantially different if c/v is used instead of $c/(v + s)$. Nevertheless because the ratio of dead to living labor in production is a closer reflection of the technical relations of production, we will adopt it throughout this discussion.

6. Using the definition of the rate of profit in equation (1), take partial derivatives with respect to the rate of exploitation:

$$(1) \qquad r = \frac{e}{Q(e + 1) + 1}$$

$$(2) \qquad \frac{\partial r}{\partial e} = \frac{[Q(e + 1) + 1] - Qe}{[Q(e + 1) + 1]^2} = \frac{Q + 1}{[Q(e + 1) + 1]^2}$$

Because Q appears in the denominator at a higher power than in the numerator, equation (2) indicates that as the organic composition of capital rises, a given change in the rate of exploitation will produce a smaller change in the rate of profit.

7. For the moment I am ignoring the thorny question of the distinction between productive and unproductive labor and how these categories relate to the organic composition of capital. Clearly, if the service sector is categorically considered unproductive labor, then it would not in any sense offset the rising organic composition in the industrial, productive sector of the economy. The point here is that the social aggregate organic composition may be the result of a complex pattern of relative changes in the size of high-capital-intensity and low-capital-intensity sectors, rather than being merely the result of the growth of the organic composition in already high-capital-intensity sectors of the economy.

8. A pattern very similar to this has been hypothesized by David Levine (1973). Its implications will be more fully discussed when we place the theory of crisis in a more historical context in section III of this paper.

9. It must be stressed that the expression "unproductive" is being used in a non-normative sense. An expenditure is unproductive in capitalist society if it does not contribute directly or indirectly to the production of value and surplus value. Some of these expendi-

tures might in fact be "productive" in terms of meeting human needs, but they are not productive in terms of the functioning of a capitalist economy.

10. Any concrete commodity can, of course, represent both accumulation and waste. The distinction being made is an analytical one, not one between different categories of concrete commodities.

11. The passage from Marx to which Sweezy refers is extremely interesting: "If a commodity with a monopoly price should enter into the consumption of the laborer, it would increase the wages and thereby reduce the surplus value if the laborer would receive the value of his labor power the same as before. But such a commodity might also depress wages below the value of labor power, of course only to the extent that wages would be higher than the physical minimum of subsistence. In this case the monopoly price would be paid by a deduction from real wages (that is, from the quantity of use values received by the laborer for the same quantity of labor) and from the profit of other capitalists" (quoted in Sweezy, 1974: 41).

This is certainly a clear statement that monopoly can redistribute value from variable capital to surplus value and thus increase the rate of exploitation. While in Marx's own time the occurrence of monopoly may have been sufficiently rare to make this process of relatively little significance, such is hardly the case at the present time.

12. This chart draws heavily from a number of sources. The first three stages come fairly directly from Marx's discussion of primitive accumulation in part VIII of volume I of *Capital*; the shift from stage 3 to stage 4 is quite similar to the analysis by David Levine (1973), especially part III of his analysis, "The Theory of the Growth of the Capitalist Economy"; the analysis of stage 5 is based largely on the work of James O'Connor (1973); and the analysis of the emergent problems of stage 6 has grown out of the analysis of Offe (1974).

13. The chart may give the impression that the particular path of capitalist development, and the particular pattern of contradictions that emerges at each stage in the process, are rigidly determined. This raises some extremely important questions about the underlying logic of the concept of "contradiction." In what exact sense are the contradictions schematically laid out in the chart "inevitable"? Do the solutions to impediments to accumulation in one period necessarily lead to future impediments? While it is obvious that each of the "solutions" outlined in the chart have certain inherent limits, it is less obvious that the social forces in capitalist society necessarily push the system toward the limits, and thus transform a structural solution into a contradiction. Why, in other words, does each adaptive strategy of the capitalist system tend to exhaust itself in time?

The simple answer is that none of these adaptive strategies can eliminate the inherent class antagonisms of capitalism. Class antagonisms make a simple, homeostatic reproduction of the system impossible. The more complex answer is that the forms that class struggle takes are themselves molded by the dominant adaptive strategies of the system. The working class is not merely a passive force, even in its most integrated and contained periods. It adapts its strategies to the "structural solutions" that emerge in the course of capitalist development. In their most class-conscious form, these working-class strategies are explicitly focused on exploiting the structural solutions and pushing them to their limits.

A similar argument can be made about the effects of struggle among capitalists (competition): as solutions to the impediments of accumulation emerge, individual capitalists adopt new forms of competition, new strategies for maximizing their individual accumulation. Because there is no overall planning in capitalist society to coordinate these individual strategies, there is an inherent tendency for these strategies gradually to push toward the limits of the existing structure within which accumulation takes place. There is thus a dialectic between the structural solutions to earlier constraints on accumulation and the forms of class struggle and competition that develop in response to those structural solutions.

14. For an interesting discussion of the development of capitalism as a world system, which partially fills the gap in the present analysis, see Amin, 1975. The series of stages of development in Amin's analysis corresponds fairly closely to that outlined in Figure 3. Amin presents four periods of general expansion of the capitalist system (1815–40; 1850–70; 1890–1914; 1948–67), and four periods of structural crisis during which what Amin

calls a restructuring of the mode of accumulation occurs (1840–50; 1870–90; 1914–48; 1967–present). The four expansionary periods correspond roughly to stages 2 through 5 in Figure 3, and the periods of structural crisis, to the transitions from one stage to another.

15. In addition to these structural solutions, many Marxists have argued that classical nineteenth-century European colonialism provided a (temporary) structural solution to the problem of the falling rate of profit. By bringing technologically backward, labor-intensive economies into the world capitalist system, colonialism in effect lowered the organic composition of capital on a world scale. Furthermore, colonialism involved the transfer of vast amounts of surplus value from the Third World to the developed capitalist countries. This further reduced the tendency for the rate of profit to fall. For a discussion of this perspective on imperialism, see Mattick (1969, chap. 19).

16. This expression should not be confused with the theory of "State Monopoly Capital" (commonly referred to as StaMoCap theory), in which the state is seen as manipulated by the dominant financial interest groups of monopoly capital. The implicit theory of the state underlying the present discussion is much closer to O'Connor's (1973) and Offe's (1973, 1974) than to StaMoCap theory. See Gold, Lo, and Wright (1975) and Anderson, Friedland, and Wright (1976) for general discussions of the theory of the state.

A Contribution to the Criticism of Keynes and Keynesianism

Western Criticism Turns Against Keynesianism: An Attempt at a "Nonwestern" Critique

PETER ERDOS

Professor of Economics at the Hungarian Academy of Sciences

The capitalist economy has proven itself much less manageable during the last three decades than post-World War II Western economists predicted. This situation opened the door to malicious criticism of Keynesianism. It may seem odd that this kind of criticism is most vociferous not in the Marxian economic literature of socialist countries but in the West. An example of this criticism is the aggressiveness of the Chicago School of monetarists and the rapid spread of its doctrines. I think, nevertheless, that there is nothing very surprising in this phenomenon.

Marxist economists have been taken aback by the long postwar prosperity in the West, interrupted only by fairly mild recessions. This prosperity had been regarded as a vindication of Keynesian economic policy. Marxists never believed in the possibility of a more or less steady growth of capitalism. Later, when it seemed that facts had not proven them right, Marxist economists looked for the causes of such a surprising change in the transformation of capitalism into state monopoly capitalism rather than in Keynesian economic policy. They were not very illuminating when they analyzed how and by what chain of causations this transformation could have led to such unexpected prosperity.

In any case, these Marxist economists generally relied upon the following abstract argumentation. In the twentieth century the prevalence of monopolies had paralyzed the functioning of the "invisible hand." But, there appeared to exist a kind of analogy between the planned economies of the socialist countries and those elements of planning that the capitalist state introduced into the economy of Western countries. According to this line of thought, a factor that could regulate a capitalist economy with some efficiency might be found in a recent element of capitalism, that is, the pronounced economic role of the state, rather than in the use of any specific Keynesian recipes. Yet all Marxists firmly contended that under capitalism only certain elements of economic planning are possible; that such partial planning necessarily tends to aggravate the contradic-

This article was especially written for this book by Professor Erdos, who has devoted many years of study to the Keynesian system.

tions of capitalism while often engendering new forms of their manifestation. Capitalism is, in the long run, incompatible with economic growth undisturbed by major crises.

Thus Marxist economists did not try to find the roots of the evils of capitalism in the deficiencies of this or that variant of economic policy—because chance deficiencies could surely be corrected. Instead, they found those roots in the very existence of capitalism; in its insolvable contradictions. Yet for a long time they were too rigid in their convictions. Prominent Marxist economists predicted more than once the imminent outbreak of a deep crisis during the decades following the war, and they were mistaken each time. Today, therefore, in the face of a deep crisis most of them watch events with much reservation, and are cautious enough not to prophesy catastrophy. Indeed it is yet a far cry from such a state of things.

Conversely, a Western non-Marxist economist may be convinced that capitalism—whatever he may dub it—is the only economic system capable of ensuring high efficiency. In his opinion capitalism is, as if by definition, a system that could be made to work without great disturbances. And then when deep disturbances appear he is, of course, highly indignant. For him to blame them on faulty economic policy and on the theoretic school in whose name this policy had been pursued is the most natural thing in the world. An Eastern economist finds this situation much more comic because the theoretic foundations from which Western critics attack Keynesian ideas represent a definite regression as compared to those correct insights the works of Keynes succeeded in propagating.

In my opinion Keynes' scientific achievements marked a point of culmination in the history of non-Marxist economic thought. But this climax was highly relative. The present crisis of Keynesian economic policy indicates that the *General Theory* is far from being a really general theory of employment, interest, and money. Of course in this article I do not intend to criticize the whole theoretic work of Keynes, nor will I discuss every aspect of the *General Theory* or each practical feature of the economic policies thought to be Keynesian. What I will do is point out some insufficiencies in the Keynesian theoretic system that are currently most conspicuous in their consequences. My main contention will be that Keynes, while he turned against some neoclassical theses characteristic of the Marshallian-Pigouvian school, remained very much a captive of this school. I will try to demonstrate with some examples that the crucial insufficiencies of his system originate from this. I will try to show that, by his not having accepted the classical heritage, he blocked the way to a deep understanding of capitalist economy.

KEYNES' NEGLECT OF ESSENTIAL DIFFERENCES BETWEEN WAGES AND PROFITS: SOME ASPECTS OF THESE DIFFERENCES

It is common knowledge that Keynes was not very interested in questions of distribution. This was, of course, by no means a consequence of the fact that those enjoying a high income are not deeply motivated to meditate on the causes of poverty. It did not follow simply from Keynes' bourgeois *Weltanschauung*,

nor was it caused only by the fact that he lived a century after the fathers of classical bourgeois economics, who were especially interested in the problems of distribution. An excellent counterexample is given by the lifework of J. B. Clark. With Keynes, however, the roots went much deeper. Not only did he disregard the intricacies of distribution, but he regarded capitalism more as a society of free producers of commodities than as a class society. With him, incomes meant simply the compensations of useful services, and, when he looked upon them from this point of view, it seemed to be of little importance whether those incomes took the form of wages or profits. Such blindness would be unimaginable in the case of a Smith or a Ricardo.

What an economist striving to understand the capitalist economy must understand is that wages and profits are two essentially different forms of income that play utterly different roles within capitalism. The chief motive force of the capitalist economy and its growth is profit. It was not only Marx who understood this; it was understood just as well by Ricardo and even by Malthus.

Let us recall some theses on wages and profit that are necessary if one is to understand the working of a capitalist economy.

We begin by examining a two-sector economy, similar to the economy depicted by Marx in his schemas for reproduction of the social capital. This is a closed economy, whose dramatis personae are only industrial capitalists and workers, where workers' saving is zero. Marx analyzed in his schemas two departments: Department I, producing means of production, and Department II, producing consumer goods. The two departments are:

$$c_1 + v_1 + s_1 = \text{I}$$
$$c_2 + v_2 + s_2 = \text{II}$$

where c = constant capital, v = variable capital, and s = surplus value. The sum of the products, the value of which is I + II, is the social product.

In our discussions, we will deal mostly with GNP instead of the social product. In the economy we analyze, GNP is less than the social product because it does not contain intermediate products, such as raw materials. Thus the labor value of GNP equals the Marxian "new value" $v + s$ plus the value of the investment goods serving replacement (amortization).

Thus our two-sector economy, producing GNP, contains sector I, the investment goods sector, and sector II, the consumption goods sector. Here we have to assume that intermediate products are being produced in that sector where they will be utilized, in order to avoid double and multiple counting.

In formulating our definitions we have to clearly distinguish between quantities interpreted in real terms and those interpreted in money terms.

In our economy,

GNP in real terms = investment goods + consumption goods

In the case of the equilibrium, when supply equals demand,

GNP in real terms = capitalists' real investment + capitalists' real consumption + workers' real consumption

Further:

capitalists' real consumption + workers' real consumption = the whole product of sector II

capitalists' real investment + capitalists' real consumption = real gross profits (including investment goods serving replacement)

capitalists' real net investment + capitalists' real consumption = real net profits

GNP in money terms = gross money profits + money wages

real wages = all products of sector II − capitalists' consumption.

In such a two-sector economy when GNP and productivity are given, wages are an inverse function of gross investment; higher gross investment indicates lower real wages and a lower rate of wages. Gross investment is the independent variable. This relationship may be slightly modified by changes in capitalists' consumption. Such changes in capitalists' consumption tend to be minor because capitalists' consumption measured in real terms is pretty inelastic. Moreover if capitalists' consumption does increase, then capitalists' consumption acts as an independent variable in the sense that this increase implies a decrease of real wages.[1]

The decrease in real wages is brought about by the price increase of consumption goods, which resulted from the increase of capitalists' consumption. With GNP and productivity given, Kaldor's thesis is valid: wages, not aggregate profits, are the residual quantity. But even when such minor modifications occur, capitalists' consumption is the independent variable. Increasing capitalists' consumption implies, *ceteris paribus*, decreasing real wages. With GNP given, Kaldor's thesis is valid: not aggregate profits but wages are the residual quantity.

And finally, a simple truism that, when formulated in slightly different terms, is generally not accepted by the majority of people: wages are not profits. Entrepreneurs know that when workers spend more from their wages to buy goods or services offered by these same entrepreneurs, their profits will be higher. It is easy to conclude from this that higher wages bring higher profits. Thus it seems to be evident that by maintaining effective demand on an appropriate level all difficulties can be solved. But, neglecting taxes and foreign trade, NNP equals the sum of wages and net profits; net profits equal the sum of capitalists' net investments and capitalists' consumption. Given net real profits (that is, given capitalists' net investment and capitalists' consumption), suppose that NNP increases due to an increment in consumer goods produced. This increment in consumer goods could only be promoted by the increment of wages earned by the workers who produced this extra output. Thus this increment in consumer goods could only be sold at lower prices; hence the profit margin, which is defined as the difference between price and cost of production of the unit product, declines (cost of production of the unit product is assumed not to decrease).

I think that the illusionary belief in the possibility of a capitalist economy being efficiently controlled by virtually the sole means of monetary and fiscal

policy has been nourished by the lack of a full understanding of the very simple truths just mentioned. And, I think, this holds true also for Keynes.

THE NEGLECT OF THE IMPORTANCE OF PROFIT

I will begin to demonstrate the shortcomings in Keynes' methodology with his formula for the purchasing power of money, or, more exactly, for the price level of consumer goods. Here I can show how the same problem has been tackled by Marxists in Hungary. It is not without interest that Keynes' formula may be found only in his *Treatise on Money*, and that the *General Theory* not only wholly neglected this problem but it even rejected the solution of the *Treatise*. But what Keynes found to be not quite correct in his previous analysis has nothing to do with what I wish to expound.

Keynes, when obtaining his formula, began with the relation

$$E - S = P \cdot R$$

where E is the total money income of the community in a unit of time; S is the amount of saving; P the price level of consumption goods; and R the volume of these goods (and services) flowing on to the market and purchased by consumers. Thus,

$$(1) \qquad P = \frac{E - S}{R}$$

In the Hungarian textbooks we find the formula,

$$W = P \cdot (R - R_k)$$

and from this,

$$(2) \qquad P = \frac{W}{R - R_k}$$

Here W is the sum of wages paid in a unit of time, R_k is the volume of the personal consumption by capitalists, and P and R have the same meaning as in (1).

Formula (1) is seemingly more exact. In this saving is deducted from income and, indeed, workers also may save; formula (2) is based on the supposition that savings by workers equal zero. But this is a question of very little importance because formula (2) may be easily generalized without altering anything of consequence. In this more generalized form,

$$P = \frac{W - S_w}{R - R_k - L}$$

where S_w represents the possible net savings by workers, and L stands for the possible increment in the inventories of consumer goods.

The difference between the two formulae that really matters is as follows: Formula (1) brings the whole money income spent for consumer goods in comparison with the full volume of consumer goods; formula (2) relates money

wages to that amount of consumer goods which will be consumed by workers. Keynes did not distinguish between money spent on consumer goods by workers from money spent for such goods by capitalists. But these two kinds of spending are quite different both in their character and in their impact on prices—and not only on prices.

One aphoristic description of this difference is pretty well-known: "Capitalists get what they spend, workers spend what they earn." The second half of the sentence refers to the fact, verifiable also statistically, that in the not very long run the net savings of the working class are negligibly small (therefore, we neglect S_w in formula (2)). More important than this is what is meant by the first half of the sentence. As Keynes has pointed out already in his parable of the Widow's Cruse, an increase in the consumption of capitalists does not diminish their profits disposable for investments; instead, it raises money profits. In fact it increases their real profits, too, this being the sum of their real investment and consumption. And as to the money profits, an increase in capitalists' consumption increases by its own amount the receipts and money profits of the producers and sellers of consumer goods, causing also the prices of these goods to increase. That the volume of capitalists' consumption is inelastic to changes in prices is partly due to this same reason. Putting this somewhat pointedly and aphoristically: Workers as consumers influence prices by the sum of their *money* wages, while capitalists as consumers do so by the *volume* of their consumption.

As may be seen from formula (2), the price level is a linear function of the sum of wages. True, it is also a function of the sum of money spent by capitalists for consumer goods, and this is the relation to which formula (1) refers. Yet the sum of money spent by capitalists on consumer goods is itself a function of the price level of consumer goods due to its inelasticity in real terms. Moreover, the numerator $E - S$ in formula (1) is not independent of P, which it intends to explain. Thus formula (1) does not explain price level.[2] The formation of price level is much more relevantly explained by formula (2) operating with the *volume* of capitalists' consumption, instead of the *sum of money* spent by them on buying consumer goods. We may see from formula (2) that there does not exist even mathematically a symmetry between capitalists' and workers' consumption. Workers as consumers influence P with the sum of their wages according to a linear function, but capitalists as consumers influence P by the volume of their consumption in the way of a hyperbolic relationship.

Finally Keynes' Fundamental Equations, neglecting the vital difference between consumption of workers and capitalists, divert attention from the fact, that the amount of consumer goods consumed by capitalists goes entirely into real profits, while profits in money terms increase even further. Consumption by workers constitutes no part of profit. When production of consumer goods and the part taken from them by capitalists are given, then increasing money wages in order to increase purchases of consumer goods raises prices, and, by doing so, increases profits in money terms while leaving real profits unchanged. If the volume of the production of consumer goods increases and this increment does not go entirely into the consumption of capitalists, then real wages of the working class rise while prices (and profits in money terms) decrease.

A CRITICISM OF KEYNES' FRAGMENTARY THEORIES OF PROFIT

It would, of course, be absurd to interpret what I have written about the undifferentiated treatment of different kinds of income as if Keynes had utterly neglected to deal with profits or wages as specific categories of income. What I intended to say was that he often treated them indiscriminately. Actually, we may say even more than this: He had no consistent theory of profit.

According to one of his Fundamental Equations, the price level of output as a whole is

$$\pi = \frac{E}{O} + \frac{Q}{O}$$

where, besides notations already known to us, O is the volume of total output and Q is aggregate profits. The "income of the community," as already mentioned, has a peculiar meaning in the *Treatise*. As Keynes put it later in the *General Theory*, "The peculiarity in my former definition related to that part of aggregate incomes, which accrues to the entrepreneurs, since I took neither the profit . . . actually realized from their current operations, nor the profit which they expected when they decided to undertake their current operations, but, in some sense (not, as I now think, sufficiently defined if we allow for the possibility of changes in the scale of output), a normal or equilibrium profit; with the result that on this definition saving exceeded investment by the amount of the excess of normal profits over the actual profit."[3] Let us reword the end of this sentence! When actual profit exceeds normal profit, then investment exceeds saving; $I - S$ is a positive quantity. The aggregate profits in the above formula are just this positive difference between actual and normal profit; $Q = I - S$. Thus Q is a kind of surplus profit, or, as Keynes put it, a windfall profit. More exactly, it consists, in his opinion, of two parts: (1) the profit accruing to the entrepreneurs producing consumer goods, $Q_1 = I' - S$ where I' is the cost of production of the investment goods; and (2) the profits, originating from producing new investment goods, $Q_2 = I - I'$, where I is the price of those investment goods, so that $Q = Q_1 + Q_2 = I' - S + I - I' = I - S$. But when Keynes allegedly came to speak about the problem of the price level of new investment goods,[4] he committed a sudden slanting of definitions: instead of defining "investing" as "the act of the entrepreneur when he makes an addition to the capital of the community," he defined it as a "purchase of securities by members of the public" (see *Treatise*, note p. 141). So the problem of the price of investment goods became that of the price of securities—a trick that, for that matter, he repeated also in the *General Theory* and that made his analysis senseless. (Compare the price level of common stocks in 1974 with that of investment goods or with company profits!)

Nor do we find in the *General Theory* any coherent theory of profit. Perhaps we are not mistaken when saying that in Keynes' mind there coexisted some elements of two competing theories of profit, one allegedly prevailing in the short run, the other true in the long run.

As to the first of these, he seems to have followed more or less the reasoning of the theory of marginal productivity, and in this setting wages and profits occupy two polar positions.

Doubtlessly, it must be regarded as one of Keynes' major merits that he repudiated the doctrine of neoclassical economics that "the utility of the wage when a given volume of labour is employed is equal to the marginal disutility of that amount of employment." Doubtlessly, he was deeply wrong when he stubbornly championed the doctrine complementary to the aforementioned that "the wage is equal to the marginal product of labour." Many economists have from various aspects demonstrated the incorrectness of this thesis, and so I will simply state its fallaciousness. But it was this very theory that led Keynes, when considering the short-run changes in profits, to write that "in a given state of organization, equipment and technique, the real wage earned by a unit of labour has a unique [inverse] correlation with the volume of employment. Thus, *if* employment increases, then, in the short period, the reward per unit of labour in terms of wage-goods must, in general, decline and *profits increase*. This is only the adverse of the familiar proposition that industry is normally working subject to decreasing returns in the short period."[5]

Indeed, if the marginal postulates of neoclassical analysis were correct, then, with given technology, the level of real wages and of profits are uniquely determined by the amount of employment. If those postulates were correct, and if the production functions (if there existed such continuous and differentiable functions at all) were not homogenously linear, then there could exist a positive profit for the enterprise and also an aggregate positive profit of an exactly determined amount. (Although, as I have tried to demonstrate elsewhere, this would not be reconcilable with market equilibrium.)

Keynes, however, did not pursue this line of thought. First of all, the theory of marginal productivity is based (or was, at least, originally based) on the concept of the productivity of capital. But Keynes, and this too should go to his credit, rejected this: "It is much preferable to speak of capital having a yield over the course of its life in excess of its original cost, than, as being *productive*. . . . I sympathize . . . with the pre-classical doctrine that everything is *produced by labour*, aided by what . . . is now called technique, by natural resources . . . and by the results of past labour, embodied in assets . . ."—a conclusion that would have evoked most fierce rebukes from J. B. Clark. But the crucial point is this: "If capital becomes less scarce, the excess yield [that is, the profit] will diminish, without its having become less productive—at least in the physical sense" (p. 213).[6] And so, instead of a theory of (physical) marginal productivity, Keynes arrived at a different theory of profit: a theory of scarcity: ". . . the only reason why an asset offers a prospect of yielding during its life-services having an aggregate value greater than its initial supply price is, because it is *scarce*, and it is kept scarce, because of the competition of the rate of interest on money" (p. 213).

The second half of this sentence refers to Keynes' thesis that in equilibrium "the marginal efficiency of capital in general is equal to the market rate of interest" (p. 136). Now, the marginal efficiency of capital is, in the *General Theory*, the notion that usurps the place of profit (or the rate of profit) and differs from it mainly by being an *expected* yield instead of profit actually accrued. All we know about its size is that it is bounded from below by the rate of interest. As to the causes of the existence of profits we do not know anything except the hazy concept of scarcity. As to the indeterminateness of the actual

size, of *expected* profits, the best witness is Keynes himself. He devoted all of chapter 12 of the *General Theory* to this theme. The haziness of the very concept of scarcity may be perhaps best judged by those thoughts that Keynes followed when speculating about a "not so far future." In his opinion, under some circumstances, a "properly run community equipped with modern technical resources, of which the population is not increasing rapidly, ought to bring down the marginal efficiency of capital in equilibrium approximately to zero within a single generation" (p. 220). This "would mean the euthanasia of the rentier" (p. 376). Moreover, Keynes even advocated "this order of events," being, in his opinion, "the most sensible way of gradually getting rid of many of the objectionable features of capitalism," while preserving it (p. 221). Alvin H. Hansen mildly mocked such sentences of Keynes by declaring in his *Guide to Keynes* that, "The rentier euthanasia discussion is a kind of free-wheeling detour by Keynes in his less responsible moments."[7] But the matter is much more serious than this. The fact that Keynes considered, if even only for moments, a capitalist society with zero profits including interest in a state of equilibrium as a viable formation highlights how little he understood the central role of profits as *the* driving force of a capitalist economy. In my view profits are by definition sufficiently high even in the richest conceivable community as long as investment goods are being produced in a sufficient quantity having a sufficient labor value.

KEYNES' PRINCIPLE OF EFFECTIVE DEMAND USURPS PART PLAYED IN REALITY BY PROFIT PRINCIPLE

Someone could retort that the concept of marginal efficiency of capital is one of the cornerstones in Keynes' system and that this fact by itself proves that Keynes did not neglect the role of profits. Surely he did not completely neglect profits, but he missed their full importance. The central concept in his system, and even in those of his followers, is that of the effective demand.

Keynes justly regarded effective *demand* (D) as made up of two parts: "D_1, the amount which the community is expected to spend on consumption and D_2, the amount which it is expected to devote to new investment" (p. 29). More exactly, "the value of D at the point of the aggregate demand function where it is intercepted by the aggregate supply function [is] the effective demand" (p. 25).

Now Keynes is thought to have found the key to the basic problem of capitalism of his time, that is, the problem of underemployment. Keynes stated that "when employment increases, D_1 will increase, but not by so much as D," and, therefore "the greater the volume of employment, the greater will be the gap between the aggregate supply price (Z) of the corresponding output and the sum (D_1) which the entrepreneurs can expect to get back out of the expenditure of consumers. Hence, if there is no change in the propensity to consume, employment cannot increase unless, at the same time, D_2 is increasing so as to fill the increasing gap between Z and D_1." And so, contrary to the "classical assumptions," "the economic system may find itself in stable equilibrium with N (the volume of employment) at a level below full employment . . ."

(pp. 29–30). This sentence was conditional: "may find itself." But then it became stronger: "moreover, the richer the community, the wider will have to be the gap between its actual and its potential production" because, in contrast with a poor community that will be prone to consume by far the greater part of its output and where "a very modest measure of investment will be sufficient to provide full employment," a potentially "wealthy community will have to discover much ampler opportunities for investment." Thus if in the latter "the inducement to invest is weak, then . . . the working of the principle of effective demand will compel it to reduce its actual output until it becomes sufficiently poor" (p. 3).

Let us forget that Keynes' explanations of underemployment are not convincing because an increasing gap between Z and D, so long as it did not increase also proportionally (which it did not), need not cause any difficulties and that the future aspect of a weak inducement to invest is not well formed by him. We will speak about a more important deficiency in his thoughts.

When stressing the role of D (effective demand) in relation to full employment Keynes seemed to think that it would not matter whether D_1 or D_2 increased so long as their sum would be equal to aggregate supply. He seemed to think that so far as this could be ensured, prolonged growth would be warranted (at least up to the point of full employment). Keynes failed to realize that demand for consumption goods paid by wages, that is, consumption by workers, does not add to profits. (As to this, however, see also the following section of this article!)

Consumption by capitalists constitutes a part of their profits, but not the part that really matters. Capitalists as such are not consuming machines. They are servants of their capital. Capital demands growth, and, therefore, it demands accumulation of capital, that is, investment. Profits are a source of investment, but also investing is a source of profits. At the moment when they have been produced all goods are properties of the class of capitalists. One part of these goods, the wage goods, will be given to workers in exchange for printed slips of paper, serving as currency, which have been given them for their labor power. This does not happen to the investment goods serving net investment. They remain the property of the class of capitalists, constituting a part of the class' real income, of its real profits, while the price of these goods that capitalists get when they sell them to other capitalists (who, on their part, pay for them out of their money profits) constitutes a part of their money profits. An increased volume of investment goods produced is, by the same token, increased real profit and ensures increased money profit for the class. (As already told, prices will also thus increase.) This is true for the class as a whole, but not necessarily true for an individual capitalist: He cannot invest more than he can pay for. Therefore nobody will normally want to invest when general investment activity is low because in such times profits and profit expectations are low. Conversely, high investment activity stimulates, as a rule, investment, increasing thereby profits. Effective demand also becomes greater. But demand for investment goods is not just another means to enforce prosperity and full employment. The production of excess consumer goods to be consumed by workers does not satisfy the kind of demand that would automatically enhance capitalist prosperity. Malthus, so much admired by Keynes, had long ago formulated this quite

crudely: "... no power of consumption on the part of the labouring classes can ever, according to common motives which influence mankind, alone furnish an encouragement to the employment of capital ... nobody will ever employ capital merely for the sake of the demand occasioned by those who work for him."[8] Or was Malthus wrong?

INCREASED DEMAND MAY EVOKE INSTEAD OF A MULTIPLIER EFFECT A RISE IN PRICES

Was Malthus' formulation too categorical? I have tried to formulate, more cautiously, the idea that increasing demand for consumer goods does not automatically enhance prosperity. Everybody is acquainted with the concept of the multiplier and with Keynes' thesis according to which "when there is an increment of aggregate investment, income will increase by an amount which is k times the increment of investment," where

$$k = \frac{\Delta Y_w}{\Delta I_w} = \frac{1}{1 - \frac{\Delta C_w}{\Delta Y_w}}$$

This investment multiplier, k, is very nearly akin to the employment multiplier, k', meaning "the ratio of the increment of total employment which is associated with a given increment of primary employment in the investment industries" (p. 115). So much akin, that Keynes thought it convenient to deal only with the simplified case where $k = k'$ (p. 116). And, of course, Hansen was right when he remarked in a footnote to chapter 4 of his *Guide to Keynes* that the initial outlay evoking a multiplier effect represented in Keynes' multiplier theory by an increment of investment is not necessarily an outlay spent on capital goods. The result would be the same if the initial outlay would be a transfer payment to consumers or an increase in the wages brought home in consequence of tax reductions or something similar. To evoke the multiplier effect, only the demand for consumer goods need increase.

Is this really so under "normal" circumstances? When speaking about demand for consumer goods increased by wages I have argued previously that this demand is, in itself, no source of aggregate profits. When capitalists try to win a greater part of this demand for themselves by increasing the supply of consumer goods, this results in decreasing prices and decreasing profit margins. Yet if it is demand in terms of money that starts growing, this by itself increases prices. Increasing prices, even when they are not accompanied by any greater investment activity, are often taken by capitalists as a signal to increase their production. In such cases profits increase in money terms, while real profits remain unchanged. All this would be true even if the increase in demand may remain unchanged. All this would be true even if the increase in demand in terms of money were only a consequence of a rise in the rate of wages, which also causes the costs of production to rise. A final possibility exists. The forced production of consumer goods may lead—mediated by the accelerator effect—to an increase of investment activity and, by this, to that of real profits. So, in summary, increased demand for consumption goods normally stimulates the production of consumer goods. The remaining question is how effectively it will do so because prices will rise, too.

Whether an increase of consumers' demand will be followed mainly by

increased production or by a rise of prices depends, before all, on the overall economic situation. In the depth of the Depression of the thirties entrepreneurs were happy if they could sell anything, even at very low prices, and thus an increasing demand could have worked as a very efficient stimulus to production. Under less severe circumstances it will tend to manifest itself mostly in enhancing prices, but in circumstances of chronic inflation rising money demand becomes a most unreliable incentive to growth of production. Finally, as experience shows, indirect methods of slowing down investment activity are apt to choke growth, while the use of indirect incentives for investment are of very dubious effect.

STRUCTURAL CHANGES THAT LESSENED THE DANGER OF SECULAR STAGNATION AND MITIGATED THE CRISIS-PRONENESS OF CAPITALISM

But, seemingly, the methods of Keynesian economic policy did work quite well during a period of three decades! The last very severe crisis occured in the thirties. The capitalist world has experienced since World War II a period of exceptionally fast growth and prosperity, disturbed only by lesser recessions. (Great Britain, with her eternal stop-and-go periods, was quite a special case.) How did this come about?

It is, of course, impossible here to analyze all the chief causes of such a trend. Nonetheless, I wish to mention several of them.

I am not going to deny that the application of Keynesian tools have helped. They did not solve and could not have solved the innate contradictions of capitalist economy, but, under the given conditions, they could and did significantly contribute to palliating the symptoms of ailing capitalism and even to making it seemingly healthy. But, directly and chiefly, they could help because, aided by Keynesian analysis, a whole set of fatal blunders has been avoided, which during the 1930s enormously contributed to the severity of the crisis. The prototype of such blunders was the forced deflating of budgetary expenditures during a great slump. What I have tried to show in this article is that Keynesian analysis did not dig deep enough, although it clarified some causal and previously unknown relationships between economic factors.

The chief immediate cause of an unsatisfactory rate of growth or even of recessions is to be found not in a lack of general effective demand but in a lack of demand for investment goods. During and after World War II, however, a kind of second Industrial Revolution emerged. New interrelations came into being between several factors. The technical potentialities, mostly originating from military engineering and applicable also to civil industries, were utilized by the highly developed, rich economies of the leading capitalist countries. The prosperity elicited by large-scale investment activity, the continuing advances in technology, and the rapid obsolescence of assets caused by the advances created a situation in which the chief headache of capitalist entrepreneurs was not so much the problem of finding investment opportunities in a rich country as the opposite of this, mainly a kind of *embarras de richesses*. It is almost superfluous to add to this that all this has been reinforced by such trifles as the Korean or the Vietnam wars. Under such circumstances it was not by chance that the idea that richness itself, by "lessening the scarcity of capital," would lead to secular stagnation, slowly became obsolete.

All this could not, of course, prevent recessions or even lesser crises from occurring in several countries with different frequency. But since the Great Depression and at a greatly accelerated pace since World War II, structural changes took place in the economies of the leading capitalist countries that very much lessened the proneness of these economies to crises. This point deserves a more detailed explanation.

In the course of more than a century, from the first quarter of the nineteenth century up to the 1930s, crises of the classical type had shaken the capitalist economy approximately every tenth year. Each one differed from the others. Nevertheless they had enough common characteristics so that we may regard them as being of the same "classical" type, and their course may be simulated by a relatively simple economic model. One of their essential characteristics was the decline in the level of aggregate production. Moreover the causes that triggered the initial slackening initiated a whole series of cumulative reactions. These cumulative reactions turned the slackening into a backfall and the backfall into a steep crash.

To put it differently, the structure of the economy is such that there exist between some of its elements and some other ones certain positive feedback relations. Also here we have to draw a distinction between the production of consumer goods and that of investment goods. That slowing down of demand which triggers a chain reaction ending in a crash cannot be limited to the demand for consumer goods. Between the production of consumer goods and the price level, and together with the latter, the profit margin, there exists a negative, instead of positive, feedback relation. This we can see from formula (2) of the price level of consumer goods. We may break down the sum of wages W in the numerator of the formula

$$P = \frac{W}{R - R_k}$$

into W_1 and W_2, where $W_1 = n_1 w$ is the money wages in sector I, and $W_2 = n_2 w$ the money wages in sector II (n_1 and n_2 are the respective number of workers; w is the uniform rate of money wages). We write: $\frac{W_2}{W_1} = \frac{n_2}{n_1} = \lambda$, and the product volume of sector II, $R = \beta n_2 W$ (with β nearly constant). Thus,

$$(2) \qquad P = \frac{W_1(1 + \lambda)}{\beta \lambda W_1 - R_k} = \frac{1}{\beta} + \frac{W_1 + (R_k/\beta)}{\beta \lambda W_1 - R_k} \ldots$$

Because R_k, the volume of capitalists' real consumption, is pretty inelastic against changes in prices, we see from (2) that between λ and P there exists an inverse relation. If the production of consumer goods and, together with it, λ decreases, the price level P will rise. Here a *negative* feedback effect works. A slackening of the production of consumer goods increases the price level of these goods, and the profit margin will be higher, too. The secondary processes work against the primary process, that is, against the slowing down in the production of consumer goods.

A downswing in the production of investment goods brings utterly different results. Here a positive feedback process works. When investing activity

decreases, λ becomes greater, the price level of consumer goods will thus decrease too, or, if it was not allowed to decrease, then unsold stocks must pile up. Under such circumstances, further investing would be more or less senseless, and now investment activity may catastrophically fall back. The initial change evokes further and reinforced changes in the same direction and so on.

Also an initial downswing of production of consumer goods may, of course, trigger the working of a positive feedback mechanism, when potential investors think that this downward trend will last and they, therefore, abstain from further investing. This may be the case, for example, when a previous investment wave had already produced some excess capacities so that they are not fully utilized. In this way the decrease in the production of consumer goods leads indirectly, mediated by the consequent fall in the investment activity, to a general recession. The final outcome will be different depending on whether the negative feedback effect of the decreasing production of consumer goods or the positive feedback effect of the decreasing investment activity will prove to be the stronger factor. How much an economy is, owing to its structure, prone to crises, will therefore depend mainly on the intensity of the feedback relation between changes in investment activity and this activity itself.

We may obtain a very simple, although by no means exact, indicator of the change in this intensity that occurred between two periods if, for each period, we measure the percentage fall in the price level of consumer goods and in aggregate profits, which would have been caused by a decrease (of comparable magnitude) in the production of investment goods if the production of consumer goods remained unaltered.

A SIMULATION MODEL ASSESSING THE IMPACT OF THE STRUCTURAL CHANGES THAT OCCURRED

In an article written in 1969 Peter Erdos and Ferenc Molnár published a simulation model of the U.S. economy for the years 1929 and 1957 (1957 immediately preceded one of the deepest after-war crises in the United States).

It appeared that if in 1929 net investments fell back to zero, this would have caused a 13.2 percent fall in the price sum of consumption goods and a 29.2 percent fall in the incomes of those not living on wages or salaries. The same would have caused in 1957 a 6 percent fall in the price of consumer goods and a 10.8 percent fall in the money incomes of nonworkers. In calculating this, the effects of unemployment benefits and the decrease of indirect taxes paid by workers have been neglected. If we take these two factors into account, in accordance with the rules effective for 1957, the fall in the price of consumer goods would appear to be less than a tenth of 1 percent, while the percentile decrease in aggregate incomes of those not living on wages or salaries would have amounted to but 4 percent. Furthermore, after allowing for the actual increase in government purchases and the increase in government wages, which occurred in 1958, the price level of consumer goods would have been even higher, by 3 percent, than it was in 1957. This result exaggerates what happened in reality, but between those two years the price level did indeed rise somewhat, although production of consumer goods had risen, too. All this shows that the intensity of the feedback relation had much decreased since 1929.

In one of the foregoing paragraphs it has been explained that the lessening of the crisis-proneness of the capitalist economies was mainly a consequence of some structural changes they underwent. In the model depicting the behavior of the U.S. economy these changes manifested themselves in the very diminished proportion of workers producing investment goods or consumer goods as compared to overall employment. Thus, when analyzing this situation, we must abandon our model of "pure" capitalism.

The numerator W in formula (2) should contain the wages of all workers and not only of those employed in the production of investment and consumer goods. In accordance with this, ΣW is greater than the sum $W_1 + W_2$ of wages earned in these industries. That is ΣW is greater than the sum of the wages of productive workers in the Marxist sense of the word *productive*. Thus in reality $\Sigma W = W_1 + W_2 + W_3$, where W_3 is the wages of all unproductive workers. And, again, for λ we have to write $\dfrac{W_2}{W_1 + W_3}$ instead of only $\dfrac{W_2}{W_1}$. The denominator of formula (2) should contain the volume of the totality of wage goods, that is, the sum of all goods and services of the kind usually bought also by workers, diminished by that part of these that will be bought not by them but by persons not living on wages or salaries. Also those goods and services that are gratuitous (as, for example, free primary education) have to be disregarded in the denominator.

In more recent decades W_3 has been much increased. In the United States some 60 percent of the working population is employed in the service industries, and many of those belonging to the remaining 40 percent producing material goods are employed in industries whose products are neither wage goods nor investment goods for the use of enterprises. (To these belong, for example, all war materials and implements.) Since W_3 has become greater in proportion to W_1, a change in W_1, that is, an increase or decrease in the production of those investment goods, will much less modify the size of λ than if W_3 had become smaller or even negligible. This is the decisive force, stemming from structural changes, behind the diminished crisis-proneness of capitalism. In addition, the extension of the institutions of social security and taxation may be classified as a major structural change. It is well known that they act as built-in stabilizers against business fluctuations.

STRUCTURAL CHANGES AND GOVERNMENT EXPENDITURE ENGENDER A PERMANENT INFLATIONARY TENDENCY

The diminution of the crisis-proneness is, however, only one side of the consequences of those structural changes. The other side had been more or less hidden for a long time; it began to grow to full and fatal proportions only during the last few years. The greater part of Keynesian economists considered, and under the given circumstances not without reason, slow, controlled inflation as a more or less favorable phenomenon that was one of the vital incentives of growth. This mild inflation was more and more regarded to have been caused, and deliberately caused, by Keynesian economic policy. We may see also in this proposition a grain of truth, although by no means the whole truth. This

half-truth nursed the hope that inflation, at least when handled with proper circumspection, would remain controllable indefinitely; though economists always had the uneasy feeling that between price stability and the policy of full employment there existed an innate conflict.

A slow rise of prices probably stimulates to a degree economic growth because of the money illusion of entrepreneurs. Yet, more importantly, the inverse of this statement is definitely true. A decrease in aggregate demand that would lead to a fall of prices if production were not diminished certainly evokes a regression. For decades there has not been a considerable fall in prices on a general scale. But, as we may see from formula (2), prices would immediately fall when the rate of money wages decreased. This is what happened in most countries during the Great Depression. Today such a general fall in the money rate of wages does not occur. It would not be tolerated by organized labor, which, so far as it goes about money wages (and not about real wages), has become a Great Power. Their intransigency in this matter prevents capitalists, striving to diminish costs, from throttling the economy with their own hands. Of course it does not follow that prices had to remain stable if the rate of money wages did not increase. Even less would this follow if the rate of wages increased proportionally to increasing productivity. In this latter case, owing to the structural changes we have spoken about, a slow inflation is bound to occur.

One characteristic of these structural changes, namely the fact that an ever-increasing part of private enterprise does not produce wage goods or investment goods but is engaged in the service industries instead (wholesale and retail trade, together with the advertising industry, financial institutions, and *hoc genus omne*),[9] is surely not a result of Keynesian economic policy. It is an upshot of the inner tendencies of capitalism. However, wages are flowing into the economy out of these service industries, and all these wages are a part of W_3.

An increasing proportion of W_3, while moderating the changes of λ accompanying the changes in the rate of investments, increases principally the numerator of formula (2), as compared to its denominator. The price level of consumer goods will tend to rise when W_3 grows faster than W while the rate of money wages remains constant. This would be different only if an increase of productivity in the industries producing wage goods neutralized this change. In today's reality, however, the rate of money wages tends to grow at least proportionally to productivity, and this settles the matter: The growth of the portion of service industries tends to raise prices and engenders an inflationary tendency.

The other principal characteristic of the structural changes is the unprecedented swelling of government expenditure. The government's share in GNP was rather less than 10 percent at the beginning of the thirties; now it lies at about 50 percent. The chief sources of budget income are taxes together with the incomes of the social security funds. The receipts of government obtained from its purchases of goods and services are much less. It follows from this that the budget's contribution to R in the denominator of formula (2) is negligible. But government spends its incomes partly in the form of wages paid and partly for the purchase of goods and services whose production, directly or mediated by the previous stages of production, requires further wages. The transfer payments directed to workers or their families have, of course, the same effects as wages. Thus these wages form a part, actually the greater part, of W_3. The

growth of the incomes and payments of government arouse the same kind of inflationary tendencies as do the factors mentioned in the foregoing paragraph.

We can hardly tell how great a part deliberate Keynesian economic policy has played in the growth of government expenditure. It does seem to be true that the triumph of Keynesian ideas created a favorable atmosphere for that process. It is no less certain that a very considerable part of those expenditures simply could not have been avoided. To them belong most of the social and educational expenditures; social equilibrium made their rise inevitable. And to them belong the construction of roads and bridges and, generally, the government participation in the buildup of infrastructure. Nor was the immense increase of military expenditure simply a consequence of Keynesian economic policy. All this also rendered a vast growth of administration a necessity, while the well-known "Parkinson's Law" also played its part. But I will not go into further details. Government expenditure has vastly grown, engendering an inflationary tendency.

A SHORT EXCURSION INTO THE ECONOMICS OF UNPRODUCTIVE COSTS AND TAXATION

Two common misconceptions need clarification. Let us look at the first of them. For Marxian economists it is an elementary doctrine that the costs of trade and finances have to be paid out of surplus value (surplus value being the sum of profits net of interest, interest, rent, business taxes, and unproductive costs of business including W_3). Some of them, for example Gillman, extended this proposition to the wages and salaries of the major part of nonmanual workers in industry. All this is partly a question of definition and, so far, quite correct. However, departing from this, many Marxist economists, together with Gillman, arrived at an unadmissible conclusion. They think that because these costs have to be paid from the surplus value, their existence is equivalent to a reduction of, that is, a subtraction from, profits. In their opinion, it follows from this that there exists a tendency for the rate of profit to fall. This seems to be even more so with respect to taxes, and especially to profit taxes. Marxists know that taxes are a part of surplus value, and thus they think that profit taxes diminish that part of surplus value (profits) disposable for capitalists. In this matter, especially as regards the cost of circulation, they seem to be backed up by Marx's opinion. They are also backed up by Ricardo, according to whom, with the sole exception of taxes on rents, all taxes, and thus also taxes on wages, are in last analysis profit taxes. Furthermore, this idea is backed up by the voice of capitalists and of reformist labor leaders as well. They all contend that a heavy taxation imposed on capitalists would diminish after-tax profits and, by doing so, hamper investment.

Marxists, of course, listen more to Marx than to capitalists or reformists. What most of them forget is "only" that Marx's conclusions, and also those of Ricardo, could apply but to economies with gold currencies (or with any other kind of commodity money, if such existed). Their analyses have been based on the theory of Marx and Ricardo that price is governed by the labor value of the commodities and of gold (or the existing money commodity), and therefore, if money wages were to rise, prices would remain unchanged while profits would diminish.

Regardless of whether Marx and Ricardo were fully right or not, today's currency is a kind of paper money, and when money wages increase, price level will, *ceteris paribus*, increase, too. But before proving instead of only stating the fallaciousness of the foregoing ideas, I want to mention a second misconception. Many economists, Marxists as well as non-Marxists, seem to think that government expenditure has an inflationary tendency only when the budget is not balanced. However this is not the case.

Does there exist an absolute upper limit for possible taxes on profits? If there were such a limit, obviously it ought to lie at a point where taxes would take away the whole of profits—if such a state of things were possible. But this state can never be reached and not only because capitalists would not allow it. This has to be evident if we take a look at any balance of a national economy. Let us consider a set of such balances as devised by Kalecki.

The first of them depicts an economy where taxes and government expenditure may be neglected.

I

Gross profits	Gross investment
Wages and salaries	Capitalists' consumption
	Workers' consumption
GNP	GNP

Here, gross profits of capitalists or income of capitalists includes depreciation and undistributed profits, dividends, and withdrawals from unincorporated business, rents, and interests. It follows when workers' savings also can be neglected that

Gross profits = Gross investments + capitalists' consumption
Net profits = Net investments + capitalists' consumption

For a closed economy where taxes are not negligible but workers' savings are still zero, we may write:

II

Gross profits net of (direct) taxes	Gross investments
Wages and salaries net of (direct) taxes	Government expenditure on goods and services
Taxes (direct and indirect)	Capitalists' consumption
	Workers' consumption
GNP	GNP

Here gross investment does not include government's investments.

If we allow for foreign trade and reckon on a budget deficit but still disregard workers' savings, we have:

III

Gross profits net of taxes Wages, salaries, and transfers net of taxes	Gross investment Export surplus Budget deficit Capitalists' consumption Workers' consumption
GNP minus taxes plus transfers	GNP minus taxes plus transfers

Government expenditure on goods and services − (taxes − transfers) = Budget deficit.

From III follows, when taking account also of possible workers' savings,

IV

$$\text{Gross profits net of taxes} = \begin{cases} \text{Gross investment} \\ + \text{ Export surplus} \\ + \text{ Budget deficit} \\ - \text{ Workers' savings} \\ + \text{ Capitalists' consumption} \end{cases}$$

All these relations are self-explanatory; the balances contain simple identities. They indicate that after-tax profits, which, in a closed society where there is no budget deficit (or surplus) and where workers spend just what they earn, are equal to the sum of gross investment and capitalists' consumption, can be increased by an export surplus, by a budget deficit, and by workers' dissavings.

Gross profits net profit taxes do not depend on wages and salaries, nor on profit taxes. Nor do profits net of depreciation and taxes depend on them. Gross profits net taxes depend in *real* terms only on gross investment and on capitalists' consumption, while export surplus, budget deficit, or workers' dissavings may increase profits (whether gross or net) only in terms of money. (And even as for real profits only the part incorporated in investment is well apt to stimulate further growth.)

Profit taxes can never confiscate profits. So long as capitalists invest and consume, their real after-tax profit will be equal to the amount of their investment and consumption. Conversely, so long as they invest and consume, they will be able to pay for it out of their money income after tax. In terms of money their profits before tax will be equal to the money costs of their investments and consumption plus export surpluses, budget deficit, and workers' dissavings, all this increased by the amount of direct taxes they had to pay.

It is only a formal truth that profits net of taxes are equal to gross profits diminished by taxes. The deeper truth is the opposite of this. Gross profits (in money terms) are equal to profits net of taxes, increased by direct taxes upon profits. In a positive fashion we may formulate the essential difference between these two sentences by saying that profit taxes are paid out of surplus value but they are not liabilities upon surplus value; they do not diminish surplus value disposable to capitalists.

I will try to explain this, for the sake of Marxists, in a Marxian terminology.

Surplus value is, by definition, that part of national income that does not accrue directly (in the form of wages) to productive workers having produced this national income. The sum of money spent on profit taxes represents, therefore, a part of aggregate surplus value to be measured by the value of those goods and services that this sum of money can buy. (Strictly speaking, the value of services in general is not a Marxian concept, but the reader will understand what I mean by it.)

This, however, does not imply that this part of surplus value had been from the very outset produced in some mysterious way as such, that is, as surplus value. What really occurs is that a part of value produced *becomes* a part of surplus value by the very fact that a sum of money had been paid into the budget as tax on profit, and afterwards most of it will buy goods and services to the benefit of people other than those producing national income. To this I will add that the case with the unproductive costs of circulation is exactly the same. Unproductive workers are paid out of surplus value. This is a part of value that becomes surplus value not as if it had been *produced* as such but because it will accrue to unproductive workers. Its existence, therefore, does not involve any deduction from profits. It *increases* surplus value. This increment of surplus value will, however, for capitalists constitute *costs* instead of profits. The real wages of productive workers tend by their existence to diminish.

Everything I have expounded in the last few paragraphs contradicts the most elementary everyday experiences of entrepreneurs. Well, it seems to contradict common sense. Everybody knows perfectly well that the higher he is taxed, the less of his income will remain at his disposal. Every capitalist knows that the part of his pre-tax profits that is taken away from him cannot be invested by himself. Yet, he will be able to invest the money he manages to keep untaxed. I will not contend that a new or higher tax cannot frustrate the intentions of many entrepreneurs to invest, or, conversely, that loosening the tax grip cannot initiate an opposite process. What I have said in the previous paragraphs is not valid for the individual entrepreneur, and it is not necessarily true in the short run. It refers to the macroeconomy, to the class of capitalists in its entirety, and it holds true in the long run. Experience shows that in reality the volume of taxes did grow, beginning at hardly 10 percent of GNP, to 50 percent and even more of it, without having the least endangered aggregate profits net of taxes. Regarding the system of taxation from this point of view, there does not seem to exist any absolute upper limit to the part of GNP that could be taken away by the government in the form of taxes.

FAILING KEYNESIAN ANTI-CYCLIC TOOLS ENHANCE PITFALLS OF CAPITALISM

The usual Keynesian tools of anti-cyclic economic policy fall short of "a comprehensive socialization of investment," which was vaguely advocated by Keynes. Thus, capitalism slides into a world of inflation and stagnation. But this is only one side of the whole story. Increasing profit taxes, when spent by the government, while increasing pre-tax profits (in money terms), also raises

prices. Pre-tax money profits are the difference between the realized price and the costs of production. So long as these costs do not decrease and taxes rise, prices must rise. But with rising prices, costs of production, far from decreasing, rise, too. And it is not only profit taxes that raise prices. So do all indirect taxes, and not only because capitalists will try to charge the public with these expenses. No. Indirect taxes tend to increase demand also almost by their own amount. Workers spend their wages for wage goods; a part of their wages goes, by way of indirect taxes, into the state budget; from here it reaches directly or indirectly the workers producing goods or services for the government, and, in their hands, it constitutes once again demand for wage goods. The same is true for most government transfers. So prices must rise. The only kind of taxes not raising prices directly are the direct taxes on wages. They do not, by themselves, increase prices, because they diminish the disposable money wages of those affected. This is true so long, and only so long, as workers do not successfully react to an increase in their taxes by demanding higher wages. Thus we have arrived at the notorious problem of spiraling prices and wages.

Prices do not rise simply because wages rise. They rise because the proportion of workers whose wages belong to the class W_3 is increasing. W_3 is increasing mainly because of the steady growth of budget expenditures. Direct taxes do not, by themselves, augment the costs of production; they do not cause a "cost-push" variety of inflation; mediated by government expenditures they enhance demand. Nor could indirect taxes raise prices if government expenditures met by the influx of these taxes did not increase demand, except when production was to be cut. If, conversely, enhanced demand were followed by an increase of production (of consumer goods) according to the oversimplified theory of the multiplier, prices should not rise. Nor would such a state of affairs necessarily involve any sinking in *real* profits. Prices rise with rising demand because of the prevalence of oligopolistic supply, as entrepreneurs do not allow a fall in their profit margins; they rise because of what Marxists call monopoly and monopoly capitalism. In addition, prices rise because, in an inflationary situation, workers try to preserve the purchasing power of their money wages by demanding and enforcing higher wage rates. Thus prices rise *also* because of the phenomenon of the price-wage spiral. (And, of course, their rise may be caused by many other factors, which here I cannot, and need not, enumerate.)

For a long period inflation was, in the leading capitalist countries, a slow and controlled process. This was a period of prosperity disturbed only by minor setbacks. In these countries workers have long enough listened to preachings about the unequivocal advantages of capitalist prosperity and its benefits to workers and have learned to keep quiet, be patient, and believe in "social partnership." As a just price for their patriotic behavior, they took for granted their rights first to nearly full employment and, second, to growing real wages at a rate no less than the increase in productivity.[10] But this latter cannot be realized if in a situation of inflation, however controlled, the rate of money wages does not rise faster than productivity. And, when the rate of money wages rises, it must rise even in industries where productivity is stagnating. Thus, there works a built-in mechanism forcing inflation to accelerate, to run wild, and to threaten the whole economy with explosion.

The situation is somewhat analogous to ignition. Ignition does not occur below a critical temperature. However, once the critical temperature is reached,

a chain reaction follows. There seems also to exist a critical speed in the process of inflation. Inflation in the leading capitalist countries seems to have reached this critical point.[11]

Until recently it had not been too difficult to enforce a slowdown in growth by reducing effective demand through the usual weapons of Keynesian monetary and fiscal policy. Yet recently inflation has not been stopped by these weapons. Unemployment increased instead. Massive unemployment is not a situation that can be tolerated for a long period. It is not aggregate demand but production that ought to be increased in such a situation. The private investment activity ought to be somehow enhanced, for this is the method of increasing private profits, thus setting off the working of the propelling force of the capitalist economy. Nor would, so long as capitalism prevails, Keynes' "somewhat comprehensive socialisation of investment" suffice if this was to mean increased government investment. Investment goods accumulated by government are no additions to the real profits of capitalists. Nonetheless, for want of something better, capitalist governments will surely return to the "classical" tools of monetary and fiscal policy, enhancing effective demand, thereby producing even higher and more steady inflation.

The multiplier effect, working rather well in a slump when prices are falling or at least stagnating, does not work effectively enough during inflation. Not a lack of effective demand but insufficient private investment and, therefore, a low rate of profit is the central problem that ought to be tackled when growth is low. But this, when inflation has reached a critical point, is not manageable with traditional Keynesian (and even less with monetarist) methods.

EPILOGUE

My aim was not to prescribe better medicines, or to denigrate lock, stock, and barrel Keynesian economic policy, which has served in saving capitalism quite successfully for a long time. My aim was to show that Keynes or the Keynesians, hampered by their neoclassical inheritance, did not fully grasp the very essence of their economy. Only by not fully grasping the essence of their economy could they think that they had invented the way to eternal capitalist viability, while what they advocated was good only for symptomatic treatment. Capitalism is a class society and, as such, full of deep inner contradictions. Temporarily these contradictions may remain more or less hidden; any major change in economic structure may modify or thoroughly alter the forms in which these contradictions break through, but sooner or later they inevitably come to the surface, jeopardizing the very existence of capitalism.

NOTES AND REFERENCES

1. When the ratio of investment increases faster than GNP but also GNP increases, the behavior of capitalists' consumption makes the necessary conditions for the decrease of the rate of real wages more complicated. Let us suppose that at the beginning of a period n_2 workers in section II produce a volume βn_2 of consumer goods, according to their given productivity, while n_1 workers in section I produce a volume αn_1 of investment goods. The ratio n_2/n_1 is λ. Capitalists' real consumption is now R_k, so that $\omega R_k = \beta \cdot n_2$. We will suppose that investment increases by a rate p, the production of consumer goods by the rate r, so that $p > r$.

We ask how great the growth rate μ of capitalist consumption has to be for the real rate of wages not to fall.

The rate of real wages at the beginning of the period is

$$\frac{\beta n_2 - R_k}{n_1 + n_2} = \frac{\omega R_k - R_k}{n_1 + n_2}$$

We will have

$$\frac{\omega R_k - R_k}{n_1 + \lambda n_1} \geqslant \frac{r\omega R_k - \mu R_k}{p n_1 + r\lambda n_1}$$

and from this

$$\mu \geqslant r - \frac{(\omega - 1)(p - r)}{1 + \lambda}$$

If $r = 1$,

$$\mu \geqslant 1 - \frac{(\omega - 1)(p - 1)}{1 + \lambda}$$

That is, for the rate of real wages to decrease, capitalists' consumption need not grow at the same rate as GNP, and it may even grow less than the production of consumers goods. This difference between μ and r may be higher with a small ratio of capitalist consumption (a high value of ω), a small ratio n_2/n_1, and slowly growing production of consumer goods (r is small). If r is one or near to one, the real rate of wages may decrease also when R_k, too, decreases.

2. This remains true also when we take into account the fact that Keynes' interpretation of E was, in his *Treatise on Money*, a very peculiar one. If, namely, we understand by E something different from what we usually mean by this term then also S (saving out of the given income) is different from what one usually understands by the term *saving*.

3. Keynes, J. M., *General Theory of Employment, Interest and Money* (New York: Harcourt, Brace and Co. 1930), p. 66.

4. Keynes, J. M., *Treatise on Money* (New York: Harcourt, Brace and Co., 1930).

5. *General Theory*, p. 17, emphasis added.

6. All page numbers standing alone in parentheses throughout the rest of this reading refer to Keynes' *General Theory*.

7. Hansen, Alvin, *Guide to Keynes* (New York: McGraw-Hill, 1953), Chapter 8.

8. T. R. Malthus, *Principles of Political Economy Considered with a View to Their Practical Application* (London, 1820), p. 471.

9. Some statistics on employment in the tertiary sector in percentage of whole employment:

	1960	1970
Britain	53	60
France	39	47
GFR	36.5	41
Italy	30	36
Japan	41	46.5
Sweden	44.5	53.5
Switzerland	40	44
USA	57.5	62.5

10. An illusionary aim, if what is meant by "productivity" is productivity in the nonservice industries.

11. The fact that in spite of its impact on inflationary pressure collective-wage contracts often and understandably discount the expected rate of inflation may be deemed to be characteristic of such a state of things.

13

Equations of Chain Bankruptcy
From Sectoral to General Crisis

SHINZABURO KOSHIMURA
Professor of Economics at Wako University, Tokyo.

PROBLEMS

The economic crises are the momentary and forcible solutions of various contradictions that lie in the capitalist production and are widened with its development. They are strong eruptions that restore disturbed equilibrium for a while. To analyze the phenomena of crises, therefore, it is necessary to recognize the state of stable growth of the capitalist production, because it is the starting point of contradictions that lead to crises, and, at the same time, the terminal point to which they tranquilize various disturbances.

But such a stable growth can exist only in a vision and does not actually present itself in a capitalist society.

On the stage of industrial capitalism that stands on the principle of free competition and anarchy of social production, the law of uneven development is an absolute law that rules all industries or their sectors. Every capitalist can determine of his own free will the organic composition of his capital and the rates of depreciation and replacement of fixed capital. He can also decide the rate of surplus value and propensity to accumulate.

If every commodity is sold at its value, there arise differing rates of profit due to differences in the organic compositions of capitals invested in the various sectors.

Now, where free competition prevails, capitals will move from those sectors with lower rates to those with higher rates. Through such continual movement, that is, through the redistribution of capital to the various sectors, a relation between demand and supply comes into being that permits the rates of profit in various sectors to be equalized. Consequently the value of every commodity can be transformed into a price of production—that is, the cost price that the capitalist spends for its production plus a markup at the average rate of profit.

Once the price of production is formed, both stability and equilibrium will be realized at the same time. However, such a state of stable equilibrium is only a temporary aspect because all conditions of capital reproduction and accumulation inevitably change with the passage of time. If those conditions undergo changes, the actually invested capitals in each sector will deviate from those suitable for the formation of production price so that overflowing or deficient capitals are necessarily formed. Therefore the process of capital reproduction cannot run smoothly.

A theory of the propagation of crises especially written for this book.

Disequilibrium of this type might be avoided to some extent by the formation of market prices that deviate from production prices. The formation of market prices, however, naturally gives rise to different actual rates of profit in various sectors of production. As a result the instability of capital investment may come up to the surface of capitalist economy. Thus the difference of actual rates of profit gives again an impetus to and quickening of capital movement among sectors. However, any given sector would be unable to shift its capital to another if it employs a large quantity of fixed equipment that cannot be adapted to the use of other sectors. Accordingly the contradictions may gradually accumulate, and as soon as the amount of overflowing capital invested in any given sector reaches a point at which it reduces the rate of profit to naught, the sector will be struck by a panic or crisis.

When the capitalists in this sector utterly lose their profit by overproduction caused by overflowing capital they cannot obtain the maintenance of life, let alone accumulate their capitals.

Stoppage of the capital accumulation is the first effect of the sectoral crisis, which in turn calls forth some repercussions in all the other sectors. It reduces the demand for machinery, raw material, and consumption goods for laborers. As a result, the profits in sectors which are producing such commodities may decrease in proportion to the reduction of demand. The curtailment of profits in these sectors may suppress the demand for consumption goods for capitalists and cut down the profit of the sector which is producing these articles of trade.

If the first effect in one sector is so large as to reduce the profit of another sector to zero or less than zero, the flames of sectoral crisis may leap to the other sector concerned.

Moreover, the second effect of sectoral crisis may occur at the same time as the first. If the actual profit in one sector is reduced to zero, its capital no longer functions as capital, so that a part, or all of its productive functions may be paralyzed. Closure of factories, reduction of operation, and curtailment of wages or dismissal come about, and consequently there simultaneously arises suspension of machine operations, cancellation of materials orders, and unemployment. The second effect calls forth far greater repercussions upon other sectors than does the first. It provokes, together with the first, chain bankruptcy everywhere. Thus the sectoral crisis sometimes extends to general crises that threaten the capitalist system with death or war.

DEFINITIONS

In order to clarify the above propositions, let us look at some numerical models. First we will look at the classification of sectors and the definitions of *capital* and *income*.

Karl Marx classified the total annual product of a society into two major categories—means of production and articles of consumption. In accordance with their use values he has also classified all the industries of a society into two Departments: Dept. I, which produces means of production; and Dept. II, which produces articles of consumption. Means of production consist of machinery and raw materials, and articles of consumption consist, in a capitalist society, of those items produced for laborers and those for capitalists.

For the purpose of analyzing the process of capital reproduction more minutely, we can divide all industries into four Subdepartments or Sectors.

1. Sector 1, which produces machinery. It includes the subsectors that manufacture workhouses, plants, equipment, apparatus, machines, tools, and other elements of fixed capital.
2. Sector 2, which produces raw material. It embraces the subsectors that not only extract proper raw material from nature but also make auxiliary stuffs, semifinished products, and other elements of floating capital.
3. Sector 3, which produces articles of consumption for laborers. It comprehends the subsectors that produce necessities such as food, clothing, furniture, and so on, ordinarily purchased with the wages of labor.
4. Sector 4, which produces articles of consumption for capitalists. It comprises the subsectors that produce both necessities and luxuries purchased with a part of the profit capitalists secure.

According to the definition set forth by Marx, every productive capital consists of two constituent parts:

1. Constant capital, C. This is equal to the value of the means of production; that is, machinery and raw material. As these means are consumed in the process of production, their value is transferred to the newly produced product, but they do not produce additional value. That is why Marx calls this constant capital.
2. Variable capital, V. This constituent of capital is equal to the labor power employed; in other words, it is equal to the sum of the wages paid for labor power. Its function, labor, not merely reproduces its value, but produces an excess, namely surplus value M (for the German word *Mehrwert*). In view of this unique value-creating property, Marx calls this portion of capital variable capital.

Accordingly the value (or its monetary expression, simple price) of the capital K invested in the ith sector can be expressed by the formula:

$$C_i + V_i = K_i \qquad (i = 1, 2, 3, 4)$$

Now these component parts of productive capital have different modes of turnover. Some of the machinery, the instruments of labor, that is, a part of constant capital, never leave the sphere of production once they have entered it. Through wear and tear, a part of their value passes on to the product, while the rest remains fixed in the instruments. They are not renewed so long as they continue to exist. It is their durable character that leads conventional economists to call them "fixed capital." The remaining elements of productive capital consist partly of those elements of constant capital that exist as raw material and partly of variable capital invested in labor power. They are entirely consumed in the creation of the product, so that they transfer their value entirely to the product. These elements are continually renewed in kind. They confront the fixed capital as circulating or fluent capital by reason of their comparatively rapid turnover.

For the purpose of analyzing economic crises the role played by fixed capital cannot be neglected. So we must divide constant capital C into fixed capital, F, and circulating constant capital (raw material), R. Thus we have

$$
\begin{array}{llll}
\text{Sector 1:} & F_1 + R_1 + V_2 = K_1 \\
\text{Sector 2:} & F_2 + R_2 + V_2 = K_2 \\
\text{Sector 3:} & F_3 + R_3 + V_3 = K_3 \\
\underline{\text{Sector 4:}} & \underline{F_4 + R_4 + V_4 = K_4} \\
\text{Total} & F \ + R \ \ + V \ = K
\end{array}
$$

WARRANTED COURSE

When aggregate social capital K and its constituent parts F, R, and V are given and other conditions of capital reproduction—that is, the organic composition of the capital of each sector, rate of surplus value, rates of depreciation and replacement of fixed capital, and growth rate of every constituent part of capital—are settled, there exists an adequate allocation of social capital to each sector that ensures, though temporarily, both stability and equilibrium. Every capitalist can acquire the average profit and accumulate his capital smoothly under such adequate allocation of capital.

We call this situation the *warranted course* of accumulation, and, in order to distinguish this course from the actual and sometimes risky course, we add bars above the symbol letters:

$$\bar{F}_i + \bar{R}_i + \bar{V}_i = \bar{K}_i$$

Let us take a numerical example:

Capital Composition
(billion dollars)

	$\bar{F}_i$		$\bar{R}_i$		$\bar{V}_i$		$\bar{K}_i$
1:	1,735 +		386 +		193 =		2,313*
2:	2,710 +		339 +		339 =		3,388
3:	1,751 +		250 +		250 =		2,251
4:	1,280 +		512 +		256 =		2,048
Total:	7,476 +		1,486*+		1,038 =		10,000

When total capital and its constituent parts are given and certain conditions of reproduction are settled, the above sample allocation of capital is quite adequate for smooth proceeding. The reason will be explained later in the text.

We see in the above model the organic composition of capital is assumed to be

$$
\begin{aligned}
\bar{F}_1 : \bar{R}_1 : \bar{V}_1 &= 9 : 2 : 1 = 1,735 : 386 : 193 \\
\bar{F}_2 : \bar{R}_2 : \bar{V}_2 &= 8 : 1 : 1 = 2,710 : 339 : 339 \\
\bar{F}_3 : \bar{R}_3 : \bar{V}_3 &= 7 : 1 : 1 = 1,751 : 250 : 250 \\
\bar{F}_4 : \bar{R}_4 : \bar{V}_4 &= 5 : 2 : 1 = 1,280 : 512 : 256
\end{aligned}
$$

Total variance due to rounding off of numbers.

---

and the adequate allocation of capital is

$$\bar{K}_1 : \bar{K}_2 : \bar{K}_3 : \bar{K}_4 = 2,313 : 3,388 : 2,251 : 2,048$$

Here the smallest numbers show some errors because fractions of 0.5 and over were reckoned as a unit and the rest was cut away. These errors should be admitted in the succeeding calculations.

For brevity we shall express total capital by F, R, V, K instead of $\sum_{i=1}^{4} \bar{F}_i$, $\sum_{i=1}^{4} \bar{R}_i$, $\sum_{i=1}^{4} \bar{V}_i$, $\sum_{i=1}^{4} \bar{K}_i$, and so forth.

The value of annual product $\bar{X}_i$ consists of the depreciation of fixed capital $\bar{D}_i$; worn-out raw materials, $\bar{R}_i$; variable capital, $\bar{V}_i$; and surplus value $\bar{M}_i$:

$$\bar{D}_i + \bar{R}_i + \bar{V}_i + \bar{M}_i = \bar{X}_i$$

When we assume that the average useful life of fixed capital is ten years—that is, the rate of its depreciation is 0.10 per annum—that raw materials and variable capital turn over once a year, and that the rate of surplus value $\mu = \bar{M}_i/\bar{V}_i$ is 192.74 percent, then the value composition in the warranted course is estimated as follows:

Value Composition

	$\bar{D}_i$		$\bar{R}_i$		$\bar{V}_i$		$\bar{M}_i$		$\bar{X}_i$
1:	173 +		386 +		193 +		372 =		1,123*
2:	271 +		339 +		339 +		653 =		1,602
3:	175 +		250 +		250 +		482 =		1,157
4:	128 +		512 +		256 +		493 =		1,390*
Total:	748*+		1,486*+		1,038 +		2,000 =		5,272

Total surplus value M equals 2,000, and aggregate social capital K equals 10,000, as shown before, so the average rate of profit π is

$$\pi = \frac{M}{K} = \frac{2,000}{10,000} = 20\%$$

This schema expresses the value of commodities directly made in the process of production. In a capitalist society every commodity cannot always be sold at its value. Sometimes it is sold at its price of production, and sometimes at its market price. The relation between demand and supply continually regulates the actual price in the market.

The supply is determined by the value of each product. But the demand for it is regulated by the replacement and accumulation of capital.

When we consider the process of capital accumulation, it is important to distinguish the replacement of fixed capital, $\bar{H}_i$, from its depreciation, $\bar{D}_i$. The whole fixed capital $\bar{F}_i$ existing in a sector is the cumulative amount of capital increased year by year. Therefore of all fixed capitals, the only one that should be renewed or replaced at the end of the year is the wholly defunct machinery

Total variance due to rounding off of numbers.

that was invested ten years before. So the amount of $\bar{H}_i$ is smaller than the total depreciation $\bar{D}_i$, which is estimated at $\bar{F}_i$ divided by 10.

Because the circulating capitals $\bar{R}_i$ and $\bar{V}_i$ are assumed to be used up yearly, the annual replacement of fixed and circulating capitals amounts to

$$\bar{H}_i + \bar{R}_i + \bar{V}_i$$

If we denote the increment of fixed capital, circulating constant capital, and variable capital by $\Delta \bar{F}_i$, $\Delta \bar{R}_i$, and $\Delta \bar{V}_i$, respectively, then the total demand for the replacement and accumulation of capital is

$$\bar{H}_i + \Delta \bar{F}_i + \bar{R}_i + \Delta \bar{R}_i + \bar{V}_i + \Delta \bar{V}_i$$

The total of these elements may be expressed as before by

$$H + \Delta F + R + \Delta R + V + \Delta V$$

of which $H + \Delta F$ determines the demand for machinery, the output of Sector 1; $R + \Delta R$ is the demand for raw material, the output of Sector 2; and $V + \Delta V$ the demand for articles of consumption for laborers, the output of Sector 3.

The capitalists of three sectors can sell or are obliged to sell their products at prices corresponding to these demands.

If we designate the price of each sector by $\bar{Y}_i$, then

$$\bar{Y}_1 = H + \Delta F$$
$$\bar{Y}_2 = R + \Delta R$$
$$\bar{Y}_3 = V + \Delta V$$

and when we assume total value equals total price, namely

$$X = Y = \bar{Y}_1 + \bar{Y}_2 + \bar{Y}_3 + \bar{Y}_4$$

the price of the output of Sector 4, that is, articles of consumption for capitalists, can be estimated by

$$\bar{Y}_4 = X - (\bar{Y}_1 + \bar{Y}_2 + \bar{Y}_3)$$

The profit of each sector $\bar{P}_i$ is the difference between $\bar{Y}_i$ and the cost price; that is, $\bar{D}_i + \bar{R}_i + \bar{V}_i$. Then we have

$$\bar{P}_i = \bar{Y}_i - (\bar{D}_i + \bar{R}_i + \bar{V}_i)$$

or

$$\bar{D}_i + \bar{R}_i + \bar{V}_i + \bar{P}_i = \bar{Y}_i$$

Here the total profit, P, equals the total surplus value in a society; that is:

$$P = M$$

When an individual rate of profit $\bar{P}_i/\bar{K}_i$ coincides with the average rate of profit M/K, the profit acquired in each sector is called average profit, and cost price plus average profit forms the price of production.

The average profit, and consequently the production price, can be realized only under the adequate allocation of capital. The warranted course permits such realization.

As the adequately allocated capital in each sector in our example is $\bar{K}_1 = 2,313$; $\bar{K}_2 = 3,388$; $\bar{K}_3 = 2,251$; and $\bar{K}_4 = 2,048$, and the average rate of profit π is 20 percent, the average profit is reckoned as

$$\bar{P}_1 = \pi \bar{K}_1 = 463$$
$$\bar{P}_2 = \pi \bar{K}_2 = 678$$
$$\bar{P}_3 = \pi \bar{K}_3 = 450$$
$$\underline{\bar{P}_4 = \pi \bar{K}_4 = 410}$$
$$P = \pi K = 2,000$$

Thus we obtain the schema of production price:

Composition of Production Price

	Cost Price			Average Profit	Production Price
	$\bar{D}_i$	$\bar{R}_i$	$\bar{V}_i$	$\bar{P}_i$	$\bar{Y}_i$
1:	173 +	386 +	193 +	463	= 1,214*
2:	271 +	339 +	339 +	678	= 1,626
3:	175 +	250 +	250 +	450	= 1,125
4:	128 +	512 +	256 +	410	= 1,306*
Total:	748* +	1,486* +	1,038 +	2,000	= 5,272

Each sector's capital realizes average profit, so the stability condition of capital movement is, although temporarily, satisfied.

Equilibrium of demand and supply among four sectors can be attained under the assumption that the rate of replacement of fixed capital $\bar{H}_i/\bar{F}_i$ in each sector is 5.2 percent, 6.3 percent, 4.5 percent, and 6.1 percent. Then the amount of its renewal is

$$\bar{H}_1 = 5.2\% \times \bar{F}_1 = 5.2\% \times 1,735 = 90$$
$$\bar{H}_2 = 6.3\% \times \bar{F}_2 = 6.3\% \times 2,710 = 171$$
$$\bar{H}_3 = 4.5\% \times \bar{F}_3 = 4.5\% \times 1,751 = 79$$
$$\bar{H}_4 = 6.1\% \times \bar{F}_4 = 6.1\% \times 1,280 = 78$$

Next we assume the rate of growth $\Delta \bar{F}_i/\bar{F}_i$, $\Delta \bar{R}_i/\bar{R}_i$, and $\Delta \bar{V}_i/\bar{V}_i$ as follows:

$$\frac{\Delta \bar{F}_1}{\bar{F}_1} = 12\%, \quad \frac{\Delta \bar{R}_1}{\bar{R}_1} = 11\%, \quad \frac{\Delta \bar{V}_1}{\bar{V}_1} = 10\%$$

$$\frac{\Delta \bar{F}_2}{\bar{F}_2} = 11\%, \quad \frac{\Delta \bar{R}_2}{\bar{R}_2} = 10\%, \quad \frac{\Delta \bar{V}_2}{\bar{V}_2} = 9\%$$

*Total variance due to rounding off of numbers.

$$\frac{\Delta \bar{F}_3}{\bar{F}_3} = 10\%, \quad \frac{\Delta \bar{R}_3}{\bar{R}_3} = 9\%, \quad \frac{\Delta \bar{V}_3}{\bar{V}_3} = 8\%$$

$$\frac{\Delta \bar{F}_4}{\bar{F}_4} = 9\%, \quad \frac{\Delta \bar{R}_4}{\bar{R}_4} = 8\%, \quad \frac{\Delta \bar{V}_4}{\bar{V}_4} = 7\%$$

Then the increments of capital elements can be calculated. For example, the increment of $\bar{F}_1$ is

$$\Delta \bar{F}_1 = 12\% \times \bar{F}_1 = 12\% \times 1,735 = 208$$

In the same way all increments are:

$$\Delta \bar{F}_1 = 208, \quad \Delta \bar{R}_1 = 42, \quad \Delta \bar{V}_1 = 19$$
$$\Delta \bar{F}_2 = 298, \quad \Delta \bar{R}_2 = 34, \quad \Delta \bar{V}_2 = 31$$
$$\Delta \bar{F}_3 = 175, \quad \Delta \bar{R}_3 = 23, \quad \Delta \bar{V}_3 = 20$$
$$\Delta \bar{F}_4 = 115, \quad \Delta \bar{R}_4 = 41, \quad \Delta \bar{V}_4 = 18$$

The structure of reproduction in terms of production price rearranged for the purpose of accumulation under the law of uneven development takes the form of

$$\bar{H}_i + \Delta \bar{F}_i + \bar{R}_i + \Delta \bar{R}_i + \bar{V}_i + \Delta \bar{V}_i + \bar{P}_i + \Delta \bar{P}_i = \bar{Y}_i$$

The last term on the left-hand side, $\Delta \bar{P}_i$, is the decrement of average profit from which net increment of capital should be supplemented. How can we find out the amount of $\Delta \bar{P}_i$?

The schema of production price is, as stated before, written by

$$\bar{D}_i + \bar{R}_i + \bar{V}_i + \bar{P}_i = \bar{Y}_i$$

From these two equalities we obtain

$$\Delta \bar{P}_i = -(\Delta \bar{F}_i + \Delta \bar{R}_i + \Delta \bar{V}_i) + \bar{D}_i - \bar{H}_i$$
$$= -[\Delta \bar{F}_i - (\bar{D}_i - \bar{H}_i) + \Delta \bar{R}_i + \Delta \bar{V}_i]$$

Here $(\bar{D}_i - \bar{H}_i)$ is the difference between depreciation and replacement of fixed capital, so $\Delta \bar{F}_i - (\bar{D}_i - \bar{H}_i)$ is the net increment of fixed capital.

Thus the decrement of average profit for the accumulation is reckoned as follows:

$$\Delta \bar{P}_1 = -[208 - (173 - 90) + 42 + 19] = -186$$
$$\Delta \bar{P}_2 = -[298 - (271 - 171) + 34 + 31] = -263$$
$$\Delta \bar{P}_3 = -[175 - (175 - 79) + 23 + 20] = -122$$
$$\Delta \bar{P}_4 = -[115 - (128 - 78) + 41 + 18] = -124$$

By dint of these figures we obtain the remainder of average profit that should be expended in the purchase of capitalists' consumable goods; that is:

$$\bar{P}_1 + \Delta \bar{P}_1 = 463 - 186 = 276$$
$$\bar{P}_2 + \Delta \bar{P}_2 = 678 - 263 = 415$$
$$\bar{P}_3 + \Delta \bar{P}_3 = 450 - 122 = 329$$
$$\bar{P}_4 + \Delta \bar{P}_4 = 410 - 124 = 285$$

At last we have the output of each sector rearranged for the purpose of accumulation.

	$\bar{H}_i + \Delta \bar{F}_i$	$\bar{R}_i + \Delta \bar{R}_i$	$\bar{V}_i + \Delta \bar{V}_i$	$\bar{P}_i + \Delta \bar{P}_i$	$\bar{Y}_i$
1:	(90 + 208) +	(386 + 42) +	(193 + 19) +	(463 − 186) =	1,214
2:	(171 + 298) +	(339 + 34) +	(339 + 31) +	(678 − 263) =	1,626
3:	(79 + 175) +	(250 + 23) +	(250 + 20) +	(450 − 122) =	1,125
4:	(78 + 115) +	(512 + 41) +	(256 + 18) +	(410 − 124) =	1,306

This schema satisfies the equilibrium condition of capital accumulation, namely:

Equilibrium

	$\bar{H}_i + \Delta \bar{F}_i$		$\bar{R}_i + \Delta \bar{R}_i$		$\bar{V}_i + \Delta \bar{V}_i$		$\bar{P}_i + \Delta \bar{P}_i$		$\bar{Y}_i$
1:	296	+	428	+	212	+	276	=	1,214
2:	469	+	373	+	369	+	415	=	1,626
3:	254	+	273	+	270	+	329	=	1,125
4:	194	+	553	+	274	+	285	=	1,306
Total:	1,214	+	1,626	+	1,125	+	1,306	=	5,262

In this table the summation of each row expresses the supply (output) of each sector, and the summation of each column the demand (input) for the output of each sector. Every supply coincides with corresponding demand for it. Therefore, the equilibrium condition of production and consumption among sectors is satisfied. Commodities are exchanged in terms of production price.

Through the process of circulation, fixed capital, raw material, and variable capital of each sector are extended with given rates. If we denote these elements invested in the next year by F_i', R_i', and V_i', the amount will become:

$$F_1' = (1 + 0.12) \times 1,735, \quad R_1' = (1 + 0.11) \times 386, \quad V_1' = (1 + 0.10) \times 193$$
$$F_2' = (1 + 0.11) \times 2,710, \quad R_2' = (1 + 0.10) \times 339, \quad V_2' = (1 + 0.09) \times 339$$
$$F_3' = (1 + 0.10) \times 1,751, \quad R_3' = (1 + 0.09) \times 250, \quad V_3' = (1 + 0.08) \times 250$$
$$F_4' = (1 + 0.09) \times 1,280, \quad R_4' = (1 + 0.08) \times 512, \quad V_4' = (1 + 0.07) \times 256$$

The result is:

Capital Composition

	F_i	R_i	V_i	K_i
1:	1,943 +	428 +	212 =	2,583
2:	3,008 +	373 +	369 =	3,750
3:	1,926 +	273 +	270 =	2,468*
4:	1,395 +	553 +	274 =	2,222
Total:	8,272 +	1,626*+	1,125 =	11,024

However the allocation of capital cannot always run on the warranted course. The conditions of accumulation in the next year necessitate the reallocation of capital for its smooth extension. If capitalists fail to reallocate their capitals adequately, contradictions between supply and demand gradually reveal themselves and lead to the explosion of economic crisis.

CRITICAL COURSE

If the social capital and its constituents are inadequately allocated among various sectors, each capital cannot acquire average profit. Moreover if too much capital were employed in a certain sector, the profit of this sector might vanish under certain conditions.

We name this situation the unwarranted or *critical course* of accumulation.

For example, we will adopt the following schema, wherein all symbol letters have the same meaning as before but have no bars over them because they are now expressed in terms of actual value or price.

Capital Composition

	F_i	R_i	V_i	K_i
1:	2,110 +	469 +	234 =	2,813*
2:	1,378 +	172 +	172 =	1,722
3:	2,917 +	417 +	417 =	3,750
4:	1,072 +	429 +	214 =	1,715
Total:	7,476 +	1,486*+	1,038 =	10,000

Here total capital and its elements are the very same as before, and the capital composition still holds the same proportions, which are:

$$F_1 : R_1 : V_1 = 9 : 2 : 1 = 2,110 : 469 : 234$$
$$F_2 : R_2 : V_2 = 8 : 1 : 1 = 1,378 : 172 : 172$$
$$F_3 : R_3 : V_3 = 7 : 1 : 1 = 2,917 : 417 : 417$$
$$F_4 : R_4 : V_4 = 5 : 2 : 1 = 1,072 : 429 : 214$$

*Total variance due to rounding off of numbers.

Yet the social capital is inadequately allocated:

$$K_1 : K_2 : K_3 : K_4 = 2,813 : 1,722 : 3,750 : 1,715$$

The excess and deficiency of actual capital to adequate capital can be calculated by

$$
\begin{aligned}
K_1 - \bar{K}_1 &= 2,813 - 2,313 = 500 \\
K_2 - \bar{K}_2 &= 1,722 - 3,388 = -1,666 \\
K_3 - \bar{K}_3 &= 3,750 - 2,251 = 1,499 \\
K_4 - \bar{K}_4 &= 1,715 - 2,048 = -333 \\
\hline
\text{Total } K - \bar{K} &= 10,000 - 10,000 = 0
\end{aligned}
$$

From this table we can see Sectors 1 and 3 have overflowing capitals of 500 and 1,499, and Sectors 2 and 4 have underflowing capitals of -1,666 and -333. Too much capital is employed in Sector 2, which, as you will see, is enough to make the profit of this sector zero.

The value composition that leads to the critical state is displayed in the following schema under the supposition of the same rate of surplus value, 192.74 percent.

Value Composition

	D_i	R_i	V_i	M_i	X_i
1:	211 +	469 +	234 +	452 =	1,366
2:	138 +	172 +	172 +	332 =	814
3:	292 +	417 +	417 +	803 =	1,928
4:	107 +	429 +	214 +	413 =	1,164
Total:	748 +	1,486 +	1,038 +	2,000 =	5,272

If the rate of replacement of fixed capital H_i/F_i is the same as before, the amount of its renewal is estimated by

$$
\begin{aligned}
H_1 &= 5.2\% \times F_1 = 5.2\% \times 2,110 = 110 \\
H_2 &= 6.3\% \times F_2 = 6.3\% \times 1,378 = 87 \\
H_3 &= 4.5\% \times F_3 = 4.5\% \times 2,917 = 131 \\
H_4 &= 6.1\% \times F_4 = 6.1\% \times 1,072 = 65
\end{aligned}
$$

If the rate of growth $\Delta F_i/F_i$, $\Delta R_i/R_i$, and $\Delta V_i/V_i$ are all the same as before, the increments of capital constituents are

$$
\begin{aligned}
\Delta F_1 &= 12\% \times 2,110, & \Delta R_1 &= 11\% \times 469, & \Delta V_1 &= 10\% \times 234 \\
\Delta F_2 &= 11\% \times 1,378, & \Delta R_2 &= 10\% \times 172, & \Delta V_2 &= 9\% \times 172 \\
\Delta F_3 &= 10\% \times 2,917, & \Delta R_3 &= 9\% \times 417, & \Delta V_3 &= 8\% \times 417 \\
\Delta F_4 &= 9\% \times 1,072, & \Delta R_4 &= 8\% \times 429, & \Delta V_4 &= 7\% \times 214
\end{aligned}
$$

Namely:

$$\Delta F_1 = 253, \quad \Delta R_1 = 52, \quad \Delta V_1 = 23$$
$$\Delta F_2 = 152, \quad \Delta R_2 = 17, \quad \Delta V_2 = 16$$
$$\Delta F_3 = 292, \quad \Delta R_3 = 38, \quad \Delta V_3 = 33$$
$$\Delta F_4 = 96, \quad \Delta R_4 = 34, \quad \Delta V_4 = 15$$

From these figures we can determine the demand for output of each sector, that is, the total $H + \Delta F$ for machinery, $R + \Delta R$ for raw material, and $V + \Delta V$ for consumable goods for laborers.

	$H_i + \Delta F_i$	$R_i + \Delta R_i$	$V_i + \Delta V_i$
1:	363	520	258
2:	238	189	188
3:	423	454	450
4:	162	463	229
Total:	1,186	1,627	1,125

The total amount 1,186 is the demand for machinery; therefore, it regulates Y_1, the market price of output of Sector 1. Likewise 1,626 regulates Y_2, the market price of Sector 2; and 1,125 regulates Y_3, that of Sector 3.

Then how is Y_4, the market price of the output of Sector 4, determined? It is settled by the demand for articles of consumption of all sectors' capitalists, which in turn is decided by the difference between total demand and demands for outputs of the other three sectors.

Total demand is given by total value of product X, which is equal to total amount of market price Y. And demands for outputs of the first three sectors are $H + \Delta F$, $R + \Delta R$, and $V + \Delta V$. Therefore,

$$Y_4 = X - (H + \Delta F + R + \Delta R + V + \Delta V)$$
$$= 5,272 - (1,186 + 1,627 + 1,125)$$
$$= 1,334$$

Next, how can we estimate the actual profit of each sector? It is the margin between market price and cost price.

Thus in the present critical juncture of things, the structure of market price can be represented by the following schema:

Composition of Market Price

	Cost Price			Actual Profit	Market Price
	D_i	R_i	V_i	P_i	Y_i
1:	211 +	469 +	234 +	272 =	1,186
2:	138 +	172 +	172 +	1,145 =	1,627
3:	292 +	417 +	417 +	0 =	1,125
4:	107 +	429 +	214 +	583 =	1,334
Total:	748 +	1,486 +	1,038 +	2,000 =	5,272

Examining this schema, we find out the actual profit of Sector 3 comes to zero. If capital can realize no profit, its function goes numb, and crisis occurs.

Why does this sector lose its profit? It goes without saying that too much capital is invested there. The overflowing capital amounts, as we have already estimated, to 1,499. This gives rise to an overproduction. This amount is calculated by the difference between the value and market price of the product, namely:

$$X_3 - Y_3 = 1,928 - 1,125 = 803$$

The amount just equals surplus value of Sector 3, which is now nullified.

When the actual profit of any one sector comes to nothing, the capital invested there is said to be in the state of oversaturation. Such an overflowing capital marks the ignition point of sectoral crisis.

Even in such critical moments, the balance of demand and supply is kept formally.

Equilibrium

	$H_i + \Delta F_i$	$R_i + \Delta R_i$	$V_i + \Delta V_i$	$P_i + \Delta P_i$	Y_i
1:	363 +	520 +	258 +	45	= 1,186
2:	238 +	189 +	188 +	1,011	= 1,627
3:	423 +	454 +	450 −	202	= 1,125
4:	162 +	463 +	229 +	479	= 1,334
Total:	1,186 +	1,627 +	1,125 +	1,334	= 5,272

Each summation of row (supply) coincides with that of column (demand). Such an equilibrium, however, is superficial and false because capitalists' individual consumption in Sector 3 comes to have negative value. They are in danger of starvation. The situation is little better than the death sentence. They will be struck with a panic.

FROM SECTORAL TO GENERAL CRISIS

The first effect of crisis in Sector 3 is that capital accumulation of this sector cannot go smoothly because of the disappearance of its actual profit. Consequently all or a part of increments of its capital will be cut down.

In short, at the very moment of outburst of crisis, the direction of Sector 3's capital movement is switched over from a line of reproduction on an extending scale towards that of simple reproduction.

If the drastic cut is made in the increments at the rate of 93.14 percent, ΔF_3, ΔR_3, and ΔV_3 will be reduced from 292, 38, and 33 to 20, 3, and 2. The amount of abatement is 272, 35, and 31, respectively. Accordingly $H_3 + \Delta F_3 = 423$, $R_3 + \Delta R_3 = 454$, and $V_3 + \Delta V_3 = 450$ will become 151, 419, and 419, respectively.

The demand table shown above should therefore be altered.

	$\Delta H_i + \Delta F_i$	$R_i + \Delta R_i$	$V_i + \Delta V_i$
1:	363	520	258
2:	238	189	188
3:	151	419	419
4:	162	463	229
Total:	914	1,592	1,094

Now these total demands regulate the new market prices Y_1, Y_2, and Y_3. Therefore the structure of market price takes the form of

	Cost Price			Actual Profit	Market Price
	D_i	R_i	V_i	P_i	Y_i
1:	211 +	469 +	234 +	0 =	914
2:	138 +	172 +	172 +	1,110 =	1,592
3:	292 +	417 +	417 −	31 =	1,094
4:	107 +	429 +	214 +	583 =	1,334
Total:	748 +	1,486 +	1,038 +	1,662 =	4,934

Here we see that the actual profit of Sector 3 has negative value, and that of Sector 1 comes to nil. The flames of crisis leap now from Sector 3 to Sector 1. There occurs chain bankruptcy.

The second effect of crisis in Sector 3 on the same sector is the total or partial stoppage of the function of its original capital. Successive closing of factories, reduction of operations, and bankruptcy occur. Accordingly the operation of machines is suspended partially or entirely, orders for raw material are put off, and large numbers of laborers get dismissed from their jobs.

As a result of the first effect, the movement of this sector diverts its route from reproduction on an extending scale to simple reproduction. The second effect causes it to fall down from a line of simple reproduction to that of reproduction on a reducing scale.

Sometimes the first and the second effects occur successively, and sometimes simultaneously.

From our numerical example, it is clear that if 60.49 percent of its original capital is paralyzed at this juncture, the diminution of demands will lead to the reduction of actual profits of Sectors 1, 2, and 3, thus making the profit of Sector 4 zero.

In this case H_3, R_3, and V_3 will be reduced from 131, 417, and 417 to 52, 165, and 165. The amount of reduction is 79, 252, and 252, respectively.

The total demand $H + \Delta F$ becomes $914 - 79 = 835$. $R + \Delta R$ becomes $1,592 - 252 = 1,340$; and $V + \Delta V$ becomes $1,094 - 252 = 842$. These values regulate the market prices Y_1, Y_2, and Y_3 again. Thus we have:

	Cost Price			Actual Profit	Market Price
	D_i	R_i	V_i	P_i	Y_i
1:	· 211 +	469 +	234 −	79 =	835
2:	138 +	172 +	172 +	858 =	1,340
3:	292 +	417 +	417 −	283 =	842
4:	107 +	429 +	214 +	0 =	750
Total:	748 +	1,486 +	1,038 +	495 =	3,767

The actual profits of Sectors 1 and 3 have negative values, and that of Sector 4 comes to cipher. The fire of panic spreads to this sector.

The panic will also give rise to the first and second effects in these sectors. If the reduction of accumulation and of operation of capital is so large as to extinguish the profit of Sector 2, sectoral crisis spreads to all industries.

But if such effects are weakened by some reasons while spreading, crisis will be confined to one or two sectors. All industries, however, are closely related with each other through the network of reproduction, so it is inevitable that a crisis occurring in one sector reduces the demands for outputs of other sectors, and thus causes some repercussions in all economic circles.

EQUATIONS OF CHAIN BANKRUPTCY

The adequate capital invested in the four sectors can be denoted by

$$\bar{F}_i + \bar{R}_i + \bar{V}_i = \bar{K}_i \qquad (i = 1, 2, 3, 4)$$

and if we express the rate of organic composition by

$$\alpha_{1i} = \frac{\bar{F}_i}{\bar{K}_i}, \qquad \alpha_{2i} = \frac{\bar{R}_i}{\bar{K}_i}, \qquad \alpha_{3i} = \frac{\bar{V}_i}{\bar{K}_i}$$

The above equalities can be rewritten by

$$\alpha_{1i}\bar{K}_i + \alpha_{2i}\bar{K}_i + \alpha_{3i}\bar{K}_i = \bar{K}_i$$

Therefore

$$\alpha_{1i} + \alpha_{2i} + \alpha_{3i} = 1$$

Suppose that $\bar{F}_i$ rotates in T years, and $\bar{R}_i$ and $\bar{V}_i$ once a year; then the annual cost price $\bar{C}_i$ is expressed by

$$\bar{D}_i + \bar{R}_i + \bar{V}_i = \bar{C}_i$$

If we denote the average rate of depreciation of fixed capital by $\varphi = 1/T$, then the amount of depreciation is

$$\bar{D}_i = \varphi\bar{F}_i = \varphi\alpha_{1i}\bar{K}_i$$

If we define the rate of cost price as

$$\xi_i = \frac{\bar{C}_i}{\bar{K}_i}$$

then

$$\varphi\alpha_{1i} + \alpha_{2i} + \alpha_{3i} = \xi_i$$

The annual product of each sector is expressed in value terms by

$$\bar{D}_i + \bar{R}_i + \bar{V}_i + \bar{M}_i = \bar{X}_i$$

The rate of surplus value is designated by

$$\mu = \frac{\bar{M}_i}{\bar{V}_i}$$

Then we have

$$[\varphi\alpha_{1i} + \alpha_{2i} + (1 + \mu)\alpha_{3i}]\,\bar{K}_i = \bar{X}_i$$

The average rate of profit is the ratio of total surplus value to total capital; that is,

$$\pi = \frac{M}{K}$$

and the amount of average profit obtained in each sector is

$$\bar{P}_i = \pi\bar{K}_i$$

The price of production $\bar{Y}_i$ is

$$\bar{D}_i + \bar{R}_i + \bar{V}_i + \bar{P}_i = \bar{Y}_i$$

If we express the rate of production price by

$$\bar{\psi}_i = \frac{\bar{Y}_i}{\bar{K}_i}$$

we obtain

$$\varphi\alpha_{1i} + \alpha_{2i} + \alpha_{3i} + \pi = \xi_i + \pi = \bar{\psi}_i$$

The product of each sector rearranged for the purpose of accumulation is

$$\bar{H}_i + \Delta\bar{F}_i + \bar{R}_i + \Delta\bar{R}_i + \bar{V}_i + \Delta\bar{V}_i + \bar{P}_i + \Delta\bar{P}_i = \bar{Y}_i$$

The rate of replacement of fixed capital is expressed by

$$\iota_i = \frac{\bar{H}_i}{\bar{F}_i}$$

the growth rates of capital by

$$\delta_{1i} = \frac{\Delta\bar{F}_i}{\bar{F}_i}, \qquad \delta_{2i} = \frac{\Delta\bar{R}_i}{\bar{R}_i}, \qquad \delta_{3i} = \frac{\Delta\bar{V}_i}{\bar{V}_i}$$

and the rate of accumulation by

$$\bar{X}_i = \frac{-\Delta\bar{P}_i}{\bar{P}_i} = \frac{\bar{H}_i + \Delta\bar{F}_i - \bar{D}_i + \Delta\bar{R}_i + \Delta\bar{V}_i}{\bar{P}_i}$$

$$= \frac{(\iota_i + \delta_{1i} - \varphi)\alpha_{1i} + \delta_{2i}\alpha_{2i} + \delta_{3i}\alpha_{3i}}{\pi}$$

The above equalities are denoted by

$$(\iota_i + \delta_{1i})\alpha_{1i}\bar{K}_i + (1 + \delta_{2i})\alpha_{2i}\bar{K}_i + (1 + \delta_{3i})\alpha_{3i}\bar{K}_i + (1 - \bar{X}_i)\pi\bar{K}_i = \bar{\psi}_i\bar{K}_i$$

For simplicity's sake, we take the following notation:

$$\bar{\beta}_{1i} = (\iota_i + \delta_{1i})\alpha_{1i}, \qquad \bar{\beta}_{2i} = (1 + \delta_{2i})\alpha_{2i}$$
$$\bar{\beta}_{3i} = (1 + \delta_{3i})\alpha_{3i}, \qquad \bar{\beta}_{4i} = (1 - \bar{X}_i)\pi$$

Eliminating $\bar{K}_i$ from both sides, we have

$$\bar{\beta}_{1i} + \bar{\beta}_{2i} + \bar{\beta}_{3i} + \bar{\beta}_{4i} = \bar{\psi}_i$$

For the smooth accumulation of capital, demand and supply should be balanced. Therefore:

$$\Sigma(\bar{H}_i + \Delta\bar{F}_i) = \bar{Y}_1, \qquad \Sigma(\bar{R}_i + \Delta\bar{R}_i) = \bar{Y}_2$$
$$\Sigma(\bar{V}_i + \Delta\bar{V}_i) = \bar{Y}_3, \qquad \Sigma(\bar{P}_i + \Delta\bar{P}_i) = \bar{Y}_4$$

or

$$\bar{\beta}_{11}\bar{K}_1 + \bar{\beta}_{12}\bar{K}_2 + \bar{\beta}_{13}\bar{K}_3 + \bar{\beta}_{14}\bar{K}_4 = \bar{\psi}_1\bar{K}_1$$
$$\bar{\beta}_{21}\bar{K}_1 + \bar{\beta}_{22}\bar{K}_2 + \bar{\beta}_{23}\bar{K}_3 + \bar{\beta}_{24}\bar{K}_4 = \bar{\psi}_2\bar{K}_2$$
$$\bar{\beta}_{31}\bar{K}_1 + \bar{\beta}_{32}\bar{K}_2 + \bar{\beta}_{33}\bar{K}_3 + \bar{\beta}_{34}\bar{K}_4 = \bar{\psi}_3\bar{K}_3$$
$$\bar{\beta}_{41}\bar{K}_1 + \bar{\beta}_{42}\bar{K}_2 + \bar{\beta}_{43}\bar{K}_3 + \bar{\beta}_{44}\bar{K}_4 = \bar{\psi}_4\bar{K}_4$$

From these we have the following equations that satisfy the equilibrium condition:

$$(\bar{\psi}_1 - \bar{\beta}_{11})\bar{K}_1 - \bar{\beta}_{12}\bar{K}_2 - \bar{\beta}_{13}\bar{K}_3 - \bar{\beta}_{14}\bar{K}_4 = 0$$
$$-\bar{\beta}_{21}\bar{K}_1 + (\bar{\psi}_2 - \bar{\beta}_{22})\bar{K}_2 - \bar{\beta}_{23}\bar{K}_3 - \bar{\beta}_{24}\bar{K}_4 = 0$$
$$-\bar{\beta}_{31}\bar{K}_1 - \bar{\beta}_{32}\bar{K}_2 + (\bar{\psi}_3 - \bar{\beta}_{33})\bar{K}_3 - \bar{\beta}_{34}\bar{K}_4 = 0$$
$$-\bar{\beta}_{41}\bar{K}_1 - \bar{\beta}_{42}\bar{K}_2 - \bar{\beta}_{43}\bar{K}_3 + (\bar{\psi}_4 - \bar{\beta}_{44})\bar{K}_4 = 0$$

They are four homogeneous linear equations with four unknowns, $\bar{K}_i$. There are, however, only three independent equations because any one equation

vanishes when we add to it all other equations on both sides respectively according to the formula $\Sigma_j \bar{\beta}_{ji} = \bar{\psi}_i$. Therefore, the mutual relation among the four K_i's can be derived from any three equations; that is,

$$\frac{\bar{K}_1}{\Delta_{i1}} = \frac{\bar{K}_2}{\Delta_{i2}} = \frac{\bar{K}_3}{\Delta_{i3}} = \frac{\bar{K}_4}{\Delta_{i4}}$$

where Δ_{ij} is the cofactor of the (i, j) element in the determinant

$$\bar{\Delta} = \begin{vmatrix} \bar{\psi}_1 - \bar{\beta}_{11} & -\bar{\beta}_{12} & -\bar{\beta}_{13} & -\bar{\beta}_{14} \\ -\bar{\beta}_{21} & \bar{\psi}_2 - \bar{\beta}_{22} & -\bar{\beta}_{23} & -\bar{\beta}_{24} \\ -\bar{\beta}_{31} & -\bar{\beta}_{32} & \bar{\psi}_3 - \bar{\beta}_{33} & -\bar{\beta}_{34} \\ -\bar{\beta}_{41} & -\bar{\beta}_{42} & -\bar{\beta}_{43} & \bar{\psi}_4 - \bar{\beta}_{44} \end{vmatrix}$$

This determinant has a peculiar character in that the cofactors of its every column are all equal:

$$\Delta_{1j} = \Delta_{2j} = \Delta_{3j} = \Delta_{4j} \qquad (j = 1, 2, 3, 4)$$

Therefore, the above relation can be rewritten more elegantly as

$$\frac{\bar{K}_1}{\Delta_{11}} = \frac{\bar{K}_2}{\Delta_{22}} = \frac{\bar{K}_3}{\Delta_{33}} = \frac{\bar{K}_4}{\Delta_{44}}$$

where $\bar{\Delta}_{ii}$ is the principal minor of order 3 in $\bar{\Delta}$.

The aggregate social capital K is the summation of $\bar{K}_i$; that is,

$$\bar{K}_1 + \bar{K}_2 + \bar{K}_3 + \bar{K}_4 = K$$

Therefore, the adequate capital $\bar{K}_i$ is calculated by the formula

$$\bar{K}_i = \frac{\bar{\Delta}_{ii}}{\bar{\Delta}_{11} + \bar{\Delta}_{22} + \bar{\Delta}_{33} + \bar{\Delta}_{44}} K$$

When K is given, $\bar{K}_i$ can be determined by this formula. We call this coefficient, which determines the adequate allocation of social capital and permits $\bar{K}_i$ to run on warranted course, the *adequate allocator* and express it by

$$\bar{\kappa}_i = \frac{\bar{\Delta}_{ii}}{\Sigma \bar{\Delta}_{ii}}$$

Thus we can denote the system of adequate capital by the matrix form:

$$[\bar{K}] = \begin{bmatrix} \bar{F}_1 & \bar{R}_1 & \bar{V}_1 \\ \bar{F}_2 & \bar{R}_2 & \bar{V}_2 \\ \bar{F}_3 & \bar{R}_3 & \bar{V}_3 \\ \bar{F}_4 & \bar{R}_4 & \bar{V}_4 \end{bmatrix} = \begin{bmatrix} \alpha_{11}\bar{K}_1 & \alpha_{21}\bar{K}_1 & \alpha_{31}\bar{K}_1 \\ \alpha_{12}\bar{K}_2 & \alpha_{22}\bar{K}_2 & \alpha_{32}\bar{K}_2 \\ \alpha_{13}\bar{K}_3 & \alpha_{23}\bar{K}_3 & \alpha_{33}\bar{K}_3 \\ \alpha_{14}\bar{K}_4 & \alpha_{24}\bar{K}_4 & \alpha_{34}\bar{K}_4 \end{bmatrix}$$

$$= \begin{bmatrix} \bar{K}_1 & 0 & 0 & 0 \\ 0 & \bar{K}_2 & 0 & 0 \\ 0 & 0 & \bar{K}_3 & 0 \\ 0 & 0 & 0 & \bar{K}_4 \end{bmatrix} \begin{bmatrix} \alpha_{11} & \alpha_{21} & \alpha_{31} \\ \alpha_{12} & \alpha_{22} & \alpha_{32} \\ \alpha_{13} & \alpha_{23} & \alpha_{33} \\ \alpha_{14} & \alpha_{24} & \alpha_{34} \end{bmatrix}$$

$$= \begin{bmatrix} \bar{\kappa}_1 & 0 & 0 & 0 \\ 0 & \bar{\kappa}_2 & 0 & 0 \\ 0 & 0 & \bar{\kappa}_3 & 0 \\ 0 & 0 & 0 & \bar{\kappa}_4 \end{bmatrix} \begin{bmatrix} \alpha_{11} & \alpha_{21} & \alpha_{31} \\ \alpha_{12} & \alpha_{22} & \alpha_{32} \\ \alpha_{13} & \alpha_{23} & \alpha_{33} \\ \alpha_{14} & \alpha_{24} & \alpha_{34} \end{bmatrix} K$$

Our numerical example supposes:

$$K = 10,000$$

$$\begin{bmatrix} \alpha_{11} & \alpha_{21} & \alpha_{31} \\ \alpha_{12} & \alpha_{22} & \alpha_{32} \\ \alpha_{13} & \alpha_{23} & \alpha_{33} \\ \alpha_{14} & \alpha_{24} & \alpha_{34} \end{bmatrix} = \begin{bmatrix} \frac{9}{12} & \frac{2}{12} & \frac{1}{12} \\ \frac{8}{10} & \frac{1}{10} & \frac{1}{10} \\ \frac{7}{9} & \frac{1}{9} & \frac{1}{9} \\ \frac{5}{8} & \frac{2}{8} & \frac{1}{8} \end{bmatrix} = \begin{bmatrix} 0.750 & 0.167 & 0.083 \\ 0.800 & 0.100 & 0.100 \\ 0.778 & 0.111 & 0.111 \\ 0.625 & 0.250 & 0.125 \end{bmatrix}$$

$$\varphi = 0.1$$

$$\xi_1 = 0.1 \times 0.750 + 0.167 + 0.083 = 0.325$$
$$\xi_2 = 0.1 \times 0.800 + 0.100 + 0.100 = 0.280$$
$$\xi_3 = 0.1 \times 0.778 + 0.111 + 0.111 = 0.300$$
$$\xi_4 = 0.1 \times 0.625 + 0.250 + 0.125 = 0.438$$

$$\pi = 0.200$$

$$\bar{\psi}_1 = 0.325 + 0.200 = 0.525$$
$$\bar{\psi}_2 = 0.280 + 0.200 = 0.480$$
$$\bar{\psi}_3 = 0.300 + 0.200 = 0.500$$
$$\bar{\psi}_4 = 0.438 + 0.200 = 0.638$$

$$[\iota_1 \quad \iota_2 \quad \iota_3 \quad \iota_4] = [0.052 \quad 0.063 \quad 0.045 \quad 0.061]$$

$$\begin{bmatrix} \delta_{11} & \delta_{21} & \delta_{31} \\ \delta_{12} & \delta_{22} & \delta_{32} \\ \delta_{13} & \delta_{23} & \delta_{33} \\ \delta_{14} & \delta_{24} & \delta_{34} \end{bmatrix} = \begin{bmatrix} 0.12 & 0.11 & 0.10 \\ 0.11 & 0.10 & 0.09 \\ 0.10 & 0.09 & 0.08 \\ 0.09 & 0.08 & 0.07 \end{bmatrix}$$

$$\overline{X}_1 = \frac{(0.052 + 0.12 - 0.1) \times 0.750 + 0.11 \times 0.167 + 0.10 \times 0.083}{0.2} = 0.403$$

$$\overline{X}_2 = \frac{(0.063 + 0.11 - 0.1) \times 0.800 + 0.10 \times 0.100 + 0.09 \times 0.100}{0.2} = 0.387$$

$$\overline{X}_3 = \frac{(0.045 + 0.10 - 0.1) \times 0.778 + 0.09 \times 0.111 + 0.08 \times 0.111}{0.2} = 0.054$$

$$\overline{X}_4 = \frac{(0.061 + 0.09 - 0.1) \times 0.625 + 0.08 \times 0.250 + 0.07 \times 0.125}{0.2} = 0.303$$

$$\overline{\Delta} = \begin{vmatrix} 0.396 & -0.138 & -0.113 & -0.094 \\ -0.185 & 0.370 & -0.121 & -0.270 \\ -0.092 & -0.109 & 0.380 & -0.134 \\ -0.119 & -0.123 & -0.146 & 0.498 \end{vmatrix} = 0$$

$$\overline{\Delta}_{11} = 0.03737$$
$$\overline{\Delta}_{22} = 0.05473$$
$$\overline{\Delta}_{33} = 0.03636$$
$$\overline{\Delta}_{44} = 0.03308$$
$$\Sigma \overline{\Delta}_{ii} = 0.16153$$

$$\overline{\kappa}_1 = \frac{0.03737}{0.16153} = 0.2313$$

$$\overline{\kappa}_2 = \frac{0.05473}{0.16153} = 0.3388$$

$$\overline{\kappa}_3 = \frac{0.03636}{0.16153} = 0.2251$$

$$\overline{\kappa}_4 = \frac{0.03308}{0.16153} = 0.2048$$

$$\mu = \frac{\overline{M}_i}{\overline{V}_i} = \frac{M}{V} = \frac{P}{V} = \frac{P}{\overline{V}_1 + \overline{V}_2 + \overline{V}_3 + \overline{V}_4}$$

$$= \frac{\pi(\overline{K}_1 + \overline{K}_2 + \overline{K}_3 + \overline{K}_4)}{\alpha_{31}\overline{K}_1 + \alpha_{32}\overline{K}_2 + \alpha_{33}\overline{K}_3 + \alpha_{34}\overline{K}_4}$$

$$= \frac{\pi(\Delta_{11} + \Delta_{22} + \Delta_{33} + \Delta_{44})}{\alpha_{31}\Delta_{11} + \alpha_{32}\Delta_{22} + \alpha_{33}\Delta_{33} + \alpha_{34}\Delta_{44}}$$

$$= 1.9274$$

Thus we have the system of adequate capital:

$$[\overline{K}] = \begin{bmatrix} 0.2313 & 0 & 0 & 0 \\ 0 & 0.3388 & 0 & 0 \\ 0 & 0 & 0.2251 & 0 \\ 0 & 0 & 0 & 0.2048 \end{bmatrix} \begin{bmatrix} 0.750 & 0.167 & 0.083 \\ 0.800 & 0.100 & 0.100 \\ 0.778 & 0.111 & 0.111 \\ 0.625 & 0.250 & 0.125 \end{bmatrix} \times 10,000$$

$$= \begin{bmatrix} 1,735 & 386 & 193 \\ 2,710 & 339 & 339 \\ 1,751 & 250 & 250 \\ 1,280 & 512 & 256 \end{bmatrix}$$

This is nothing but the capital composition that can run on warranted course (see p. 258).

The system of reproduction in terms of market price can be expressed by the same signs without bars, namely, F_i, R_i, V_i, K_i, D_i, M_i, P_i, X_i, Y_i, H_i, ΔF_i, ΔR_i, ΔV_i, ΔP_i.

But here P_i expresses actual profit and Y_i market price. Therefore,

$$\rho_i = \frac{P_i}{K_i}$$

is the rate of actual profit and

$$\psi_i = \frac{Y_i}{K_i}$$

is the rate of market price.

When total amount F, R, V, K, D, M, P, X, Y, and H are equal in both systems, the capital composition in terms of market price can be denoted by the similar form:

$$[K] = \begin{bmatrix} K_1 & 0 & 0 & 0 \\ 0 & K_2 & 0 & 0 \\ 0 & 0 & K_3 & 0 \\ 0 & 0 & 0 & K_4 \end{bmatrix} \begin{bmatrix} \alpha_{11} & \alpha_{21} & \alpha_{31} \\ \alpha_{12} & \alpha_{22} & \alpha_{32} \\ \alpha_{13} & \alpha_{23} & \alpha_{33} \\ \alpha_{14} & \alpha_{24} & \alpha_{34} \end{bmatrix}$$

$$= \begin{bmatrix} \kappa_1 & 0 & 0 & 0 \\ 0 & \kappa_2 & 0 & 0 \\ 0 & 0 & \kappa_3 & 0 \\ 0 & 0 & 0 & \kappa_4 \end{bmatrix} \begin{bmatrix} \alpha_{11} & \alpha_{21} & \alpha_{31} \\ \alpha_{12} & \alpha_{22} & \alpha_{32} \\ \alpha_{13} & \alpha_{23} & \alpha_{33} \\ \alpha_{14} & \alpha_{24} & \alpha_{34} \end{bmatrix} K$$

Here κ_i is the *actual allocator*, which is defined by

$$\kappa_i = \frac{\Delta_{ii}}{\Sigma \Delta_{ii}}$$

Δ_{ii} is the principal minor of

$$\Delta = \begin{vmatrix} \psi_1 - \beta_{11} & -\beta_{12} & -\beta_{13} & -\beta_{14} \\ -\beta_{21} & \psi_2 - \beta_{22} & -\beta_{23} & -\beta_{24} \\ -\beta_{31} & -\beta_{32} & \psi_3 - \beta_{33} & -\beta_{34} \\ -\beta_{41} & -\beta_{42} & -\beta_{43} & \psi_4 - \beta_{44} \end{vmatrix} = 0$$

where β_{ij} is the same as $\bar{\beta}_{ij}$, except

$$\beta_{4i} = (1 - \chi_i)\rho_i$$

In order to obtain the equations of economic crisis, we must ascertain the rate of overflowing capital.

From the following supposition

$$\Sigma \bar{F}_i = \Sigma F_i$$
$$\Sigma \bar{R}_i = \Sigma R_i$$
$$\Sigma \bar{V}_i = \Sigma V_i$$

we have

$$\Sigma(F_i - \bar{F}_i) = 0$$
$$\Sigma(R_i - \bar{R}_i) = 0$$
$$\Sigma(V_i - \bar{V}_i) = 0$$

This can be rewritten as

$$\Sigma \alpha_{1i}(K_i - \bar{K}_i) = 0$$
$$\Sigma \alpha_{2i}(K_i - \bar{K}_i) = 0$$
$$\Sigma \alpha_{3i}(K_i - \bar{K}_i) = 0$$

We define the rate of overflowing (or underflowing) capital as

$$\epsilon_i = \frac{K_i - \bar{K}_i}{\bar{K}_i} = \frac{K_i}{\bar{K}_i} - 1$$

then we obtain

$$\alpha_{11}\epsilon_1\bar{K}_1 + \alpha_{12}\epsilon_2\bar{K}_2 + \alpha_{13}\epsilon_3\bar{K}_3 + \alpha_{14}\epsilon_4\bar{K}_4 = 0$$
$$\alpha_{21}\epsilon_1\bar{K}_1 + \alpha_{22}\epsilon_2\bar{K}_2 + \alpha_{23}\epsilon_3\bar{K}_3 + \alpha_{24}\epsilon_4\bar{K}_4 = 0$$
$$\alpha_{31}\epsilon_1\bar{K}_1 + \alpha_{32}\epsilon_2\bar{K}_2 + \alpha_{33}\epsilon_3\bar{K}_3 + \alpha_{34}\epsilon_4\bar{K}_4 = 0$$
$$\epsilon_1\bar{K}_1 + \epsilon_2\bar{K}_2 + \epsilon_3\bar{K}_3 + \epsilon_4\bar{K}_4 = 0$$

Thus the relation among overflowing capitals is determined by

$$\frac{\epsilon_1 \bar{K}_1}{A_{11}} = \frac{\epsilon_2 \bar{K}_2}{A_{22}} = \frac{\epsilon_3 \bar{K}_3}{A_{33}} = \frac{\epsilon_4 \bar{K}_4}{A_{44}}$$

where A_{ii} is the principal minor of

$$A = \begin{vmatrix} \alpha_{11} & \alpha_{12} & \alpha_{13} & \alpha_{14} \\ \alpha_{21} & \alpha_{22} & \alpha_{23} & \alpha_{24} \\ \alpha_{31} & \alpha_{32} & \alpha_{33} & \alpha_{34} \\ 1 & 1 & 1 & 1 \end{vmatrix} = 0$$

when $A_{ii} \neq 0$.

The above relation can be rewritten by

$$\frac{\epsilon_1 \bar{\Delta}_{11}}{A_{11}} = \frac{\epsilon_2 \bar{\Delta}_{22}}{A_{22}} = \frac{\epsilon_3 \bar{\Delta}_{33}}{A_{33}} = \frac{\epsilon_4 \bar{\Delta}_{44}}{A_{44}}$$

For the purpose of searching for the rate of overflowing capital that gives rise to a sectoral crisis, we must examine the actual rate of profit.

$$\begin{aligned} \rho_i &= \frac{P_i}{K_i} = \frac{Y_i - C_i}{K_i} = \frac{\bar{Y}_i - C_i + Y_i - \bar{Y}_i}{K_i} \\ &= \frac{\bar{C}_i + \bar{P}_i - C_i + Y_i - \bar{Y}_i}{K_i} = \frac{\bar{P}_i - (C_i - \bar{C}_i) + Y_i - \bar{Y}_i}{K_i} \\ &= \frac{\dfrac{\bar{P}_i}{\bar{K}_i} - \dfrac{C_i - \bar{C}_i}{\bar{K}_i} + \dfrac{Y_i - \bar{Y}_i}{\bar{K}_i}}{\dfrac{K_i}{\bar{K}_i}} \end{aligned}$$

Substituting

$$\frac{K_i}{\bar{K}_i} = 1 + \epsilon_i, \quad \frac{\bar{P}_i}{\bar{K}_i} = \pi, \quad \frac{C_i - \bar{C}_i}{\bar{K}_i} = \frac{\xi_i(1 + \epsilon_i)\bar{K}_i - \xi_i \bar{K}_i}{\bar{K}_i} = \xi_i \epsilon_i$$

and

$$\frac{Y_i - \bar{Y}_i}{\bar{K}_i} = \sigma_i \epsilon_i$$

where

$$\sigma_i = \frac{Y_i - \bar{Y}_i}{\epsilon_i \bar{K}_i} = \frac{Y_i - \bar{Y}_i}{K_i - \bar{K}_i}$$

we obtain

$$\rho_i = \frac{\pi - (\xi_i - \sigma_i)\epsilon_i}{1 + \epsilon_i}$$

The economic meaning of σ_i is as follows. When actual capital deviates from adequate capital, σ_i acts as a coefficient indicating in what ratio market price deviates from production price corresponding to the above alienation. In short, it is the ratio of overprice to overcapital. When overcapital has positive value, overprice comes to have negative value, and vice versa. Therefore, we call it *antinomy coefficient*.

It can be calculated by

$$\sigma_i = \frac{\sum_j \bar{\beta}_{ij} A_{jj}}{A_{ii}}$$

and it has zero or negative value; that is,

$$\sigma_i \leqslant 0$$

The second term of the numerator indicates the rate of surplus profit.

$$-(\xi_i - \sigma_i)\epsilon_i = \frac{(Y_i - C_i) - (\bar{Y}_i - \bar{C}_i)}{\bar{K}_i} = \frac{P_i - \bar{P}_i}{\bar{K}_i}$$

It is evident that the rate of surplus profit has the opposite sign of the rate of overflowing capital because $(\xi_i - \sigma_i)$ is positive. Namely, when the rate of overflowing capital is positive, the rate of surplus profit is negative, and vice versa.

Therefore, the formula

$$\rho_i = \frac{\pi - (\xi_i - \sigma_i)\epsilon_i}{1 + \epsilon_i}$$

tells us that as the rate of overflowing capital increases the actual rate of profit will *ceteris paribus* decrease.

Then, at what point during the fall of the actual rate of profit does crisis burst out? Many time points have been regarded as the ignition point of crisis by many authors. These are: (1) the point at which the actual rate of profit of an industry begins to go down from its highest level; (2) the point at which it goes down and is about to cross the level of average rate of profit; (3) the point when it falls below the average growth rate of capital; (4) the point when it begins to encroach upon the individual consumption of capitalists; (5) the point at which it comes to be equal to a rising general rate of interest; (6) the point at which it reaches zero; and (7) the point at which it starts having a negative value and eats up the net worth of industrial capital.

Time points (1) through (5) are probably too early to provoke crisis, and (7) too late. Therefore, (6) is the most probable ignition point of crisis.

If the actual rate of profit reaches zero, we obtain the equation of the ignition point of crisis in Sector i.

$$\pi - (\xi_i - \sigma_i)\epsilon_i = 0$$

From this formula we can get a theorem:

When the overinvestment coefficient of Sector i increases and comes to

$$\epsilon_i = \frac{\pi}{\xi_i - \sigma_i}$$

the actual rate of profit reaches the vanishing point, and crisis flares up in this sector.

The capital invested in it comes to the state of oversaturation. The coefficient indicates the signal of igniting sectoral crisis.

In our numerical example, Sector 3 is supposed to be in such a state; that is,

$$\epsilon_3 = \frac{\pi}{\xi_3 - \sigma_3}$$

Once ϵ_3 is given, the rate of overflowing (or underflowing) capital can be estimated from their mutual relation:

$$\epsilon_1 = \frac{\bar{\Delta}_{33} A_{11}}{\bar{\Delta}_{11} A_{33}} \epsilon_3, \qquad \epsilon_2 = \frac{\bar{\Delta}_{33} A_{22}}{\bar{\Delta}_{22} A_{33}} \epsilon_3, \qquad \epsilon_4 = \frac{\bar{\Delta}_{33} A_{44}}{\bar{\Delta}_{44} A_{33}} \epsilon_3$$

From our supposition we get

$$\pi = 0.2, \qquad \xi_3 = 0.3, \quad \text{and} \quad \sigma_3 = -0.000278$$

Therefore

$$\epsilon_3 = 0.6660$$

and

$$[\bar{\Delta}_{11} \quad \bar{\Delta}_{22} \quad \bar{\Delta}_{33} \quad \bar{\Delta}_{44}] = [0.03737 \quad 0.05473 \quad 0.03636 \quad 0.03308]$$

$$[A_{11} \quad A_{22} \quad A_{33} \quad A_{44}] = [-0.013889 \quad 0.004630 \quad -0.004167 \quad 0.000926]$$

Therefore

$$\epsilon_1 = 0.2160, \qquad \epsilon_2 = -0.4916, \qquad \epsilon_4 = -0.1626$$

Putting these values into

$$\rho_3 = \frac{\pi - (\xi_3 - \sigma_3)\epsilon_3}{1 + \epsilon_3}$$

the actual rates of profit in the four sectors can be obtained as

$$[\rho_1 \quad \rho_2 \quad \rho_3 \quad \rho_4] = [0.0966 \quad 0.6647 \quad 0 \quad 0.3402]$$

From the equation

$$\epsilon_i = \frac{\kappa_i}{\bar{\kappa}_i} - 1$$

we have

$$\kappa_i = (1 + \epsilon_i)\bar{\kappa}_i$$

Therefore the actual allocator of capital that runs on critical course can be calculated by

$$\kappa_1 = (1 + 0.2160) \times 0.231 = 0.2813$$
$$\kappa_2 = (1 - 0.4916) \times 0.339 = 0.1722$$
$$\kappa_3 = (1 + 0.6660) \times 0.225 = 0.3750$$
$$\kappa_4 = (1 - 0.1626) \times 0.205 = 0.1715$$

Putting these allocators into the system $[K]$, we have the capital composition that will lead to ignite crisis in Sector 3.

$$[K] = \begin{bmatrix} 0.2813 & 0 & 0 & 0 \\ 0 & 0.1722 & 0 & 0 \\ 0 & 0 & 0.3750 & 0 \\ 0 & 0 & 0 & 0.1715 \end{bmatrix} \begin{bmatrix} 0.750 & 0.167 & 0.083 \\ 0.800 & 0.100 & 0.100 \\ 0.778 & 0.111 & 0.111 \\ 0.625 & 0.250 & 0.125 \end{bmatrix} \times 10,000$$

$$= \begin{bmatrix} 2,110 & 469 & 234 \\ 1,378 & 172 & 172 \\ 2,917 & 417 & 417 \\ 1,072 & 429 & 214 \end{bmatrix}$$

(see p. 264.)

Or a short cut to the same result is:

$$[1 + \epsilon_1 \quad 1 + \epsilon_2 \quad 1 + \epsilon_3 \quad 1 + \epsilon_4] = [1.2160 \quad 0.5084 \quad 1.6660 \quad 0.8374]$$

$$\begin{bmatrix} F_1 & R_1 & V_1 \\ F_2 & R_2 & V_2 \\ F_3 & R_3 & V_3 \\ F_4 & R_4 & V_4 \end{bmatrix} = \begin{bmatrix} 1 + \epsilon_1 & 0 & 0 & 0 \\ 0 & 1 + \epsilon_2 & 0 & 0 \\ 0 & 0 & 1 + \epsilon_3 & 0 \\ 0 & 0 & 0 & 1 + \epsilon_4 \end{bmatrix} \begin{bmatrix} \bar{F}_1 & \bar{R}_1 & \bar{V}_1 \\ \bar{F}_2 & \bar{R}_2 & \bar{V}_2 \\ \bar{F}_3 & \bar{R}_3 & \bar{V}_3 \\ \bar{F}_4 & \bar{R}_4 & \bar{V}_4 \end{bmatrix}$$

$$= \begin{bmatrix} 1.2160 & 0 & 0 & 0 \\ 0 & 0.5084 & 0 & 0 \\ 0 & 0 & 1.6660 & 0 \\ 0 & 0 & 0 & 0.8374 \end{bmatrix} \begin{bmatrix} 1,735 & 386 & 193 \\ 2,710 & 339 & 339 \\ 1,751 & 250 & 250 \\ 1,280 & 512 & 256 \end{bmatrix}$$

$$= \begin{bmatrix} 2,110 & 469 & 234 \\ 1,378 & 172 & 172 \\ 2,917 & 417 & 417 \\ 1,072 & 429 & 214 \end{bmatrix}$$

Now we shall examine the equations of chain bankruptcy. The first effect of crisis occurring in Sector 3 is the curtailment of capital accumulation; that is, the suspension of ΔF_3, ΔR_3, and ΔV_3. Therefore they reduce the demand for outputs of Sectors 1, 2, and 3 by their amounts.

The second effect is the paralysis of capital operation in Sector 3. Let us express the paralyzed parts of capital by $\hat{F}_3$, $\hat{R}_3$, and $\hat{V}_3$, and their rates by $\hat{\delta}_3$.

$$\hat{\delta}_3 = \frac{\hat{F}_3}{F_3} = \frac{\hat{R}_3}{R_3} = \frac{\hat{V}_3}{V_3}$$

First we search for the condition of spreading flames of crisis from Sector 3 to Sector 1.

If the fixed capital F_3 goes numb with the rate of $\hat{\delta}_3$, the benumbed amount of fixed capital comes to $\hat{\delta}_3 F_3$. If a part of fixed capital goes numb, demand for the output of Sector 1 is compressed. But it is not the total benumbed amount of fixed capital, but the paralyzed part of its replacement, that affects the demand for Sector 1's output. We denote the replacement of benumbed fixed capital by $\hat{H}_3$. Its amount is denoted by

$$\hat{H}_3 = \iota_3 \hat{F}_3 = \iota_3 \hat{\delta}_3 F_3 = \iota_3 \hat{\delta}_3 \alpha_{13} K_3$$

So the reduction of demand for Sector 1's output is the total amount of $\Delta F_3 + \hat{H}_3$, and if this amount is large enough to nullify actual profit P_1, fire of Sector 3's crisis spreads to Sector 1.

Thus the condition of chain bankruptcy is

$$P_1 - (\Delta F_3 + \hat{H}_3) = 0$$

or

$$P_1 = \Delta F_3 + \hat{H}_3$$

This is rewritten as

$$\rho_1 K_1 = \delta_{13} \alpha_{13} K_3 + \iota_3 \hat{\delta}_3 \alpha_{13} K_3 = (\delta_{13} + \iota_3 \hat{\delta}_3) \alpha_{13} K_3$$

From this formula we obtain the paralysis coefficient necessary for spreading crisis from Sector 3 to Sector 1.

$$\hat{\delta}_3 = \frac{1}{\iota_3} \left(\frac{\rho_1 K_1}{\alpha_{13} K_3} - \delta_{13} \right) = \frac{1}{\iota_3} \left(\frac{\rho_1 (1 + \epsilon_1) \bar{K}_1}{\alpha_{13} (1 + \epsilon_3) \bar{K}_3} - \delta_{13} \right)$$

$$= \frac{1}{\iota_3} \left(\frac{\rho_1 (1 + \epsilon_1) \bar{\Delta}_{11}}{\alpha_{13} (1 + \epsilon_3) \bar{\Delta}_{33}} - \delta_{13} \right)$$

Putting in the necessary values, we get

$$\hat{\delta}_3 = \frac{1}{0.045} \left(\frac{0.0966 \times 1.216 \times 0.03737}{0.778 \times 1.666 \times 0.03636} - 0.1 \right)$$

$$= -0.15204$$

In this case the paralysis coefficient comes to have negative value so it means that crisis spreads to Sector 1 by curtailment of accumulation of Sector 3's fixed capital before its original capital goes numb.

At what percent is accumulation cut down? The answer is

$$\frac{\Delta F_1 + \hat{H}}{\Delta F_1} = \frac{\delta_{13} + \iota_3 \hat{\delta}_3}{\delta_{13}} = \frac{0.1 + 0.0451 \times (-0.15204)}{0.1} = 0.9314$$

Curtailment at 93.14 percent is necessary to provoke crisis in Sector 1 (cf. p. 267).

Next, the condition for the spread of crisis from Sector 3 to Sector 4 is that the actual profit P_4 is nullified by an indirect influence of the paralysis $\hat{H}_3 + \hat{R}_3 + \hat{V}_3$. Therefore

$$P_4 - (\hat{H}_3 + \hat{R}_3 + \hat{V}_3) = 0$$

is the necessary condition.

Rewriting it in the following form

$$\rho_4 K_4 = \hat{\delta}_3(\iota_3 \alpha_{13} + \alpha_{23} + \alpha_{33})K_3$$

we have

$$\hat{\delta}_3 = \frac{\rho_4 K_4}{(\iota_3 \alpha_{13} + \alpha_{23} + \alpha_{33})K_3} = \frac{\rho_4(1 + \epsilon_4)\overline{\Delta}_{44}}{(\iota_3 \alpha_{13} + \alpha_{23} + \alpha_{33})(1 + \epsilon_3)\overline{\Delta}_{33}}$$

$$= \frac{0.3402 \times 0.8374 \times 0.03308}{(0.045 \times 0.778 + 0.111 + 0.111) \times 1.666 \times 0.03636}$$

$$= 0.6049$$

That is, paralysis at 60.49 percent is enough to stir up crisis in Sector 4 (cf. p. 268).

REFERENCES

Altman, E. I. *Corporate Bankruptcy in America.* Lexington, Mass: D. C. Heath and Co., 1971.

Bouniatian, M. *Geschichte der Handelskrisen in England.* Munich: Ernst Reinhardt Verlagsbuchhandlung, 1908.

Grossmann, H. *Das Akkumulations—und Zusammenbruchsgesetz des kapitalistischen Systems.* Leipzig: C. L. Hirschfeld, 1929.

Hilferding, R. *Das Finanzkapital.* Berlin: Dietz Verlag, 1947.

Koshimura, S. *Theory of Capital Reproduction and Accumulation,* ed. J. G. Schwartz. Kitchener, Canada: DPG Publishing Co., 1975.

——. *Theory of Waves and Crises.* Tokyo: Shunju-sha, 1967.

Luxemburg, Rosa. *Die Akkumulation des Kapitals.* Berlin: Vereinigung Internationaler Verlags-Anstalten, 1922.

Marx, K. *Das Kapital,* vols. I, II, III. Moscow: Marx-Engels-Lenin-Institut, and Berlin: Dietz Verlag, 1953.

Oelssner, F. *Die Wirtschaftskrisen,* vol. I. Berlin: Dietz Verlag, 1953.

Sweezy, P. M. *The Theory of Capitalist Development.* New York: Oxford University Press, 1942.

PART IV
Post-Keynesian Theory: The Cambridge School

14

The Theoretical and Social Significance of the Cambridge Controversies in the Theory of Capital
An Evaluation*
G. C. HARCOURT
Professor of Economics at the University of Adelaide, South Australia

The editor of this volume has asked me to discuss the theoretical and social significance of the Cambridge controversies in the theory of capital. A sharp division between these two aspects logically cannot be made because, like trend and cycle, analysis and ideology, and Samuelson and Solow, they are indissolubly mixed. Nevertheless it is a convenient division for purposes of exposition, so I adopt it and deal first with the theoretical significance and then with the significance, if such there be, for society. I survey the various, very differing views of the controversies, indicating where I believe truth lies and what the ongoing implications for the theory and practice both are likely to be and should be, for the two, unfortunately, have not as yet converged into one. I proceed by outlining what I take to be the gist of the various approaches; the references at the end of the paper provide the detailed evidence from which the interested reader may check whether I have been just in my presentation. The debate is, of course, a continuing one, but I think that we have now reached a position where some broad generalizations and evaluations may be usefully made. I take it that the principal issues and results are familiar to readers. For those, however, who are either coming at them afresh or wish to refresh their memories, there are a number of convenient sources that, together, provide an exhaustive overview, from all points of view, of the whole controversy: see Blaug (1974), Dobb (1973), Hahn (1972, pp. 1-18; 1974; 1975b), Harcourt (1972, 1976), Kregel (1973), Ng (1974), Pasinetti (1974), Robinson (1974, 1975a, 1975b, 1975c, 1975d), Rowthorn (1974), Samuelson (1966, 1975), Solow (1975), Stiglitz (1974).

     The paper is in two sections. In section I the theoretical issues are examined

*I am especially indebted to Peter Kenyon for helpful discussions when the first draft of this paper was being written. I am also grateful to John Henry, Neil Laing, Harold Lydall, Eric Russell, and Bob Wallace for their comments on a draft. As usual I thank them all but implicate none. Published in the Symposium on the Cambridge-Cambridge controversies in the Revue d'Economie Politique, 1977.

and evaluated. In section II the social significance, especially the implications for policy, is speculated on.

I

1.1   The theoretical issues resolve themselves into two groups, the first of which relates to the questions actually being asked, the second, to the appropriate methodology to be used. Endless confusion has occurred in the literature because these two underlying strands have not always been made sufficiently explicit. As to the first group the principal questions being discussed, at least as seen by the post-Keynesian school (the leaders of which include Joan Robinson, Kahn, Kaldor, and, as a guiding spirit, Sraffa), are some of those with which the great classical political economists and, of course, Marx, were concerned: "the relation between accumulation and the distribution of the net product of industry between wages and profits" (Robinson, 1975e, p. 398), together with discussions of the origins of profits, their size (absolutely and as a rate) at any moment of time and over time, and the analogous aspects of wages. Solow (in his review, 1975, of Blaug, 1974, and Pasinetti, 1974) recently made clear his agreement with this evaluation. He discussed the orthodox view (the old-time religion that, according to Joan Robinson, is good enough for him) of how profits (interest) arise and what determines their size and rate in conditions of certainty, and when monopoly, short-run shortages, and risk have been ruled out by assumption. "The third component of profit is the routine return to capitalist firms under tranquil conditions in the absence of monopoly" (p. 277).[1] Also connected to these questions are those that concern the concepts of natural, as the classicals had it, or normal, as Marshall would say, prices, and the relations between distribution and the relative price system, where the latter is seen as the relative (natural) prices of broad classes of commodities. The distinguishing characteristics of the commodities are determined both by their ultimate uses and by the classes in society who principally are associated with those uses. These questions constitute a natural link between the works of Ricardo, Marx and Sraffa; they have received particular attention from Garegnani (1958, 1960, 1970a) and Eatwell (1974).

1.2   Though the debates have been designated as recurring within the context of capital theory, in fact four related strands of theory are involved: value theory (which is absolutely central), capital theory itself, growth theory, and distribution theory. Joan Robinson, who started these particular debates with her 1953 article, "The Production Function and the Theory of Capital" (1953-54), was at the time searching the literature for the orthodox theories of profits and choice of technique *at the level of the economy as a whole.* She was in the process of working out the various strands of her theory of growth, her generalization of the *General Theory,* as expressed fully in her book, *The Accumulation of Capital* (1956). (The book itself was inspired by Harrod's seminal works in this area (1939, 1948) and by leftover business from the true Keynesian revolution.)

1.3   Growing out of the preoccupations discussed above but also intimately associated with them is another set of issues that provides the link through to the second head of methodology. These relate to the post-Keynesian critique

of orthodox or mainstream neoclassical analysis, especially the theory of value, production, and distribution that loosely comes under the heading of marginal productivity theory. There have been a number of strands of this critique, emanating principally (in these contexts) from Dobb, Joan Robinson, Kaldor, Garegnani, Pasinetti and Sraffa. The critique has concerned itself, first, with the logical tenability of certain propositions thought to be associated with the traditional neoclassical approach to value and distribution, especially those theories that draw on the concepts of supply and demand as their fundamental tools. Secondly—here the link occurs—it has concerned itself with the methodological procedure of using (long-run) equilibrium comparisons in order to throw light on actual processes in capitalist economies as they evolve through actual historical time. Thus the theoretical contexts may be seen to be both classical and modern. They are classical, and especially Marxist, in that they are concerned with the "laws of motion" of capitalist economies; that is to say, the historical processes of growth, with which are associated endogenous technical changes as a result of the internal workings and possibly contradictions of the system, and of transition from one mode of production to another, the latter an aspect honored more by default than in practice or by profundity. They are modern because, with the exceptions of Harrod and some of the post-Keynesian school and, recently, Sir John Hicks (see Hicks, 1975), though orthodox economists have returned in the postwar period to a preoccupation with classical problems of accumulation, growth (both descriptive and optimal), and distribution, they have brought with them the tools and perspectives that were attained during their sojourn in the land of the margin (see Harris, 1975). There, they were preoccupied with a different set of problems, the properties—existence, uniqueness, stability—of an equilibrium state when the resources to be allocated by competitive markets are exogenous to the analysis itself. By contrast Harrod and the post-Keynesians brought with them to the renewed interest in classical and Marxist problems the Kaleckian-Keynesian solution of the realization problem, so that the advances in the theory of the short run of the 1930s could be integrated with the postwar developments.[2]

1.4   The neo-neoclassical economists, on the whole, have preferred explicitly to assume away the effective demand aspects. They have grafted the neoclassical analyses of allocation in situations of full employment onto their analyses of movements through "time" due to accumulation, in which the savings dog wags the investment tail;[3] "capital" is substituted for labor, and technical progress, whether disembodied or embodied, is usually exogenous. Initially, neoclassical growth theory was concerned principally with steady-state analysis. Very quickly, however, modifications and extensions were made as the conditions of stability were investigated outside the domain of the simple one all-purpose commodity model in which there was, in effect, perfect foresight because of the assumption of malleability of the one all-purpose commodity. The steady-state now serves merely as a reference point and as a means of flexing intellectual muscles (see Hahn, 1971; Hicks, 1975).[4] The focus of the analysis has been, to a much greater extent, on the traverse—the initial and ultimate response of the economy to a new factor, say an innovation or an autonomous change in the saving rate, the path it is likely to follow, and the possibility of it finding its way,

both technocratically and, more generally, by postulating the behavior of its economic agents, to a new equilibrium position (see Samuelson, 1975).

1.5   Bound up with the methodological issues is the further question as to which particular branch of neoclassical analysis is both relevant to the principal questions being asked and is under attack. I have argued elsewhere (see Harcourt, 1975a, 1976) that it is the neoclassical theories, which, misleadingly in my view, are dubbed "aggregative" (that is, the aggregate production function growth models and econometric studies, much of international trade and orthodox development theory, and the rate of return model at the economy level), that are both relevant and vulnerable. Those neoclassical models that are associated with (J. R.) Hicks's *Value and Capital*,[5] and the general equilibrium models of Arrow-Debreu, whatever their logical robustness (believed by Arrow and Hahn, for example, to be very great), are not designed to answer the questions at present under discussion. Rather, they are concerned with what rigorously may be said to be true of the properties of the invisible hand, another major insight and preoccupation of the classical political economists from Adam Smith on (see Arrow, 1974; Arrow and Hahn, 1971; Hahn, 1973b). The reason why it is the aggregative theories that are relevant has to do with the attempts of modern theory to tackle the classical questions, especially of the distribution of income, in the context of a class-dominated society. Perhaps it should not be necessary to stress this at the moment in an integrated capitalist world that is dominated by an inflationary crisis that is itself intimately bound up with competing class claims on national products. Admittedly, the modern scenario is much more complicated than the simple triad of landlords, capitalists, and workers of the classical stage. Nevertheless, it certainly is an indispensable element of the analysis, far more relevant than an attempt to start with isolated, utility-maximizing economic agents with their arbitrary initial distribution of resources and between whom power is diffused equally, which, on the whole, are the characteristics of the orthodox approach to these questions.

1.6   Yet the questions themselves have been rejected as uninteresting (Blaug, 1974, p. 57;[6] Vanags, 1975, p. 335) or ill-defined (Hahn, 1974, 1975b), and the consequent preoccupation with the *meaning*, much more important than the *measurement* of capital, has been rejected as irrelevant for neoclassical analysis and results (see Bliss, 1975; Stiglitz, 1974; von Weizsacker, 1971). We need only quote Steedman's view (in his review, 1975, of Blaug, 1974) to refute this point conclusively. "Their [the post-Keynesian theorists'] good reason [for emphasizing the heterogeneity of capital goods but not of labour] lies in the fact that different types of labour do not *need* to be aggregated and can receive different wages while, in long-run equilibrium theory, capital goods have to be aggregated, in value terms, since the [rate of profits] on their value is uniform" (p. i). That is to say, for those who dismiss the concept of classes as too vague and woolly to be included in rigorous economic analysis and who seek for universality of principles rather than a more modest set that is tied to time and place, in which the sort of economy that the writer has in mind is explicitly specified—its institutional framework, "rules of the game," and social relationships—the whole issue has an air of mystery and incomprehension, of being "rather silly" and

unable "to capture the interest or imagination of economists outside the circle of immediate participants in the two Cambridges" (Vanags, 1975, p. 334).

1.7   All sides of the argument are agreed that there is much wrong with the state of orthodox economic theory at the moment;[7] but here the agreement ends—or almost, for it is also almost agreed that concentration on equilibrium states, as usually or traditionally defined, is one of the root causes of the trouble. Joan Robinson has been attacking what she considers to be the characteristics of the neoclassical concept of equilibrium and equilibrium analysis since at least 1953. Especially has she attacked what she considers to be a characteristic neoclassical methodology of attempting to analyze what are essentially processes occurring in time by comparisons of long-run equilibrium states, a methodology that allows "time" to be modeled only in so far as it has the characteristics of space (see Bliss, 1974).[8]

1.8   We should note at this point an important argument by Garegnani. In his view, a belief in long-period gravitation towards natural prices has been shared by all economists up until *Value and Capital* (Hicks, 1939). It is this belief that has justified the use of comparisons as an analytical device for "studying the *permanent* effects of changes in the conditions of the economy" (Garegnani, 1976, p. 25). Furthermore, it is *not* this methodological procedure that is at fault but, rather, its use *in conjunction with the concepts of supply and demand*, the characteristic procedure of neoclassical economists, including Marshall, the original Austrians, Walras, and Wicksell. Garegnani (1958, 1960, 1970a, 1970b, 1973, 1976) has concentrated his criticisms on both the difficulties in the concepts of the supply and demand for labor and, especially, "capital," and on the need for there to be a "well-behaved" relationship between "capital" and the rate of profits in order that unique and stable equilibria may both exist *and* be attained. "It is therefore apparent that this difficulty . . . [concerns] the theory, i.e., the way in which the centres of gravitation of the system are determined, and not the static *method* of analysis based on such 'centres' . . . no similar difficulty arises for the classical economists who used the same method but did not determine the centres of gravitation as equilibria between supply and demand" (Garegnani, 1976, p. 36).[9] Be that as it may, in place of this method, Joan Robinson has called consistently for a return to a predominantly Keynesian methodology whereby actual historical time is modeled by placing an economy down in history and letting it evolve under the influence of its own past historical experiences and present expectations of the future, in which environment there is an ever-present uncertainty of the future, an uncertainty that, by its very nature, cannot be modeled by probability distributions and the like.[10]

1.9   In more formal terms, Pasinetti (1974, pp. 43-44) has described the Keynesian method as being akin to the Ricardian one; the economic theorist has a duty to name which relationships between variables exhibit a one-way direction, ". . . such an overwhelming dependence in one direction (. . . such a small dependence in the opposite direction," and which are so interrelated as properly to be treated as part of an interdependent system of simultaneous equations. "The characteristic consequence of this methodological procedure [which also includes singling out for consideration those variables that are

thought to be most important] is the emergence in Keynes, as in Ricardo, of a system of equations of the 'causal type' or . . . of the 'decomposable type,' as opposed to a completely interdependent system of simultaneous equations" (p. 44). Joan Robinson (1975e, pp. 397–98) comments at this point: "Since the word 'causal' always raises philosophical blood pressure [for a good example, see Hahn, 1974, pp. 36–37], the point may be put more concretely: the Keynesian system is designed to show the consequences, over the immediate and further future, of a change taking place as an event at a moment of time, while the equilibrium system can only compare the differences between two positions or two paths conceived as coexisting in time, or rather outside time."

1.10   Kalecki also used a similar method, in that he divided time into short periods, each with its own past and expectations of the future, and then let the process unravel as the happenings of one short period were passed on to be the historical or initial conditions of the next, the actual events now helping to form the expectations of the next period. Thus for Kalecki, at least in his later work, the trend and cycle were indissolubly mixed, not separable as in statistical techniques and much neoclassical growth theory.[11] (This approach is well exemplified in Asimakopulos and Burbidge, 1974, a post-Keynesian analysis of tax incidence at the economy level, and in Asimakopulos, 1975, an endogenous theory of investment in a Kaleckian model.)[12] Hicks, too, uses a similar methodology in *Capital and Time*, in order to trace out the immediate and ultimate consequences of a change (in technical possibilities) intruding itself into an existing equilibrium position. He uses a full-employment equilibrium path as the reference point from which to measure divergences as the story unfolds (see Hicks, 1975). It is, moreover, only the early parts of the story—what Hicks calls the Early Phase—that are likely to be of relevance to an explanation of actual events in actual time.[13]

1.11   There are, of course, parallel developments in orthodox neo-neoclassical theory, in that out-of-(long-period)-equilibrium processes and studies of transient paths are its stock in trade, as are the methods of temporary and momentary equilibria. Where the two approaches differ from one another relates especially to their modeling of economies. In one there are still, at least until very recently, isolated economic agents between whom power is diffused equally, usually price-takers *in markets that clear each instant*. In the other, we have broad distinct classes, classified by their differing functions in the economy and by their different spending, saving, and accumulating characteristics, models that, like Ricardo's, are "highly simplified but . . . not arbitrary fanciful constructions like those of Debreu."[14] Moreover, there is not the same dependence on temporary and/or momentary equilibria, in the sense of market-clearing *prices*, as the means of modeling *actual* processes.

1.12   The particular strands of the post-Keynesian approach that have been outlined above are on the whole neglected by its critics. They have tended, rather, to concentrate on the formal results, for example, those that emerged from the reswitching debates of the mid to late 1960s (see Harcourt, 1972, chap. 4; 1976). Thus Hahn in one of his many attacks on those whom he now calls "the reactionaries" (because he interprets them as a back-to-Ricardo movement) chooses to focus attention on Piero Sraffa's propositions (which are set

out in Sraffa, 1960), usually as interpreted by Sraffa's followers. Hahn argues that the post-Keynesian school is concerned with the wrong issues and uses the wrong arguments (see Hahn, 1975a, 1975b). He criticizes Sraffa's propositions for their complete lack of operational and/or empirical content (with the exception of the assumption of a uniform rate of profits, which, he says, is patently empirically false). That is to say, we have only a set of logical propositions that are of necessity true, not even in principle capable of being falsified empirically. (Presumably such an approach is all right in the theory of optimal growth but not in a prelude to a critique of economic theory.) He is willing (now) to give Sraffa and others an alpha for demonstrating that there is no *necessary* inverse relationship between the rate of profits and the value of capital;[15] he is not willing to draw the further inference that Sraffa's propositions were designed as a prelude to a critique of neoclassical-type answers via supply and demand concepts to the questions of accumulation, growth, and distribution with which the classical political economists were concerned. Hahn regards these as nonquestions for moderns. With the same breath, though, he is willing to praise modern general equilibrium theorists for having provided a rigorous (but, on the whole, negative) set of answers to another grand question that has classical origins, namely, the ability of the invisible hand in a competitive system of isolated economic agents to bring about a satisfactory disposition of economic resources (see Arrow and Hahn, 1971; Hahn, 1973b). Yet it is this sort of theory that underlies (erroneously, evidently) Milton Friedman's and Harry Johnson's apologia and propaganda for the virtues of a free market system.[16] And, just for good measure, Hahn (1975b, p. 362) regards every one of Sraffa's formal propositions as consistent with and, indeed, deducible from modern general equilibrium theory.

1.13   Hahn is very conscious of the rudimentary state of the economic theory that he champions, despite its great technical difficulty. He has, in several seminal articles, discussed the unlikelihood of a growing "capitalist" economy that contains heterogeneous capital goods (though usually no recognizable capitalists or workers) going through time in a full-employment equilibrium state. He also has been concerned with the puzzles of putting money into general equilibrium models and taking the auctioneer out, so that something akin to Keynesian involuntary unemployment may be made to appear. In passing he has ridiculed the simple neoclassical models. And he has stressed the nature of an equilibrium as a situation that, *if it were to exist*, and if the assumption of maximizing behavior were to be made—"like Marxian Economics, orthodoxy is founded on the hypothesis of the greedy, rational, self-seeking capitalist" (Hahn, 1974, p. 35)—would require as a matter of logic that certain simple relationships, sometimes akin to textbook marginal productivity relationships, would of necessity hold. But he is most insistent in stating that the proof of existence implies neither uniqueness nor local nor global stability and that it is the simple relationships that are of relevance to the issues discussed in the present theoretical debates.[17] Nor will he allow anything concerning determination or explanation to be drawn from the equilibrium relations. This is a point of view with which Joan Robinson would certainly agree because it underlies her discussions of logical and historical time and the related concepts of equilibrium and causal models respectively.[18] What Hahn is reluctant to admit—he does grant that "the

neoclassical textbook" is a fair target, hastening to add that "textbooks [and their 'vulgar theories'] are not the frontier of knowledge" (1975b, p. 363)—is that the very errors that he deplores in the post-Keynesians are more to be found in a large part of the literature that goes under the name of neoclassical economics, that is, the simple growth models, the econometric studies of the relative contributions of "deepening" and technical progress to productivity growth over time, and much of the orthodox theory of international trade and development. That there is much at stake has been witnessed to by the recent, abortive attempts to defend the neoclassical propositions that underlie these constructions *by means of analyses that consist of equilibrium comparisons* (see, for example, Gallaway and Shukla, 1974).

1.14 Solow wishes to ride two horses at once. First, he takes a pragmatic approach to the simpler stories, the neoclassical parables that underlie the econometric work[19] and that are only guides to empirical work, even if there is no rigorous theory necessarily to back them up even as possibilities. (The outcome of the reswitching and capital-reversing debates is to show that the parables do not necessarily hold, even as the outcome of long-run equilibrium comparisons, let alone as a description of actual processes; see Harcourt, 1975a, pp. 315-29.) Evidently we are to treat them as correct until refuted by empirical findings.[20] But if the world is modeled by a predisposition to find certain relationships there and if certain observations are to be viewed "as if" they were the empirical counterparts of the theoretical variables of the model, it is hard to see *how* the facts could refute them, as opposed to providing the orders of magnitude of the coefficients in the imposed relationships (see Shaikh, 1974, and Solow's reply, 1974).[21] Second, Solow is a great proponent of highbrow rigorous theory that, like Hahn and Stiglitz (1974, pp. 898-99), he argues is independent of any relationships and concepts, especially aggregate ones, against which logical objections have been established when the simpler versions of neoclassical theory are examined.

1.15 The strongest attacks in the *present* debates or, rather, those most distressing to the protagonists involved, come not from the post-Keynesians on the neo-neoclassicals, nor from the neo-neoclassicals in reply, but from the Marxist and radical economists' camp—and the attacks are on the post-Keynesians, not the neo-neoclassicals. (Of course, the post-Keynesians and the Marxists and their allies are united in the attacks on the neo-neoclassicals, though they stress somewhat different issues. It is their attitudes to each other that are under review here.)[22] Two good representatives of this aspect of the controversies are Rowthorn (1974) and Roosevelt (1975) (see also Medio, 1972).[23] Partly these attacks are misconceived because they sometimes fail to distinguish between the negative aspect of the post-Keynesian's works—the critique from within, as it were, of neo-neoclassical logic—and the positive aspect whereby the post-Keynesians try to provide an alternative approach to economic analysis, building on Marxian, Kaleckian, and Keynesian underpinnings. The main thrust of the Marxists' attack relates to the (supposed) neglect of the sphere of production in post-Keynesian analysis and the (alleged) failure also to use the concept of the mode of production, whereby the spheres of production and of distribution and exchange interrelate one with another in an organic manner.

This implies both a neglect of the characteristics of the mode of production, in this case the capitalist mode, and of an analysis of the processes whereby one mode is transformed into another. It is for this reason that the post-Keynesians have been christened neo-Ricardians by Marxists—Marx, of course, made a similar criticism of Ricardo. It is also a clue to the reason why relevance in economic analysis has been defined by some radical economists in recent years as that which adds to our understanding of the inevitable transition to socialism.

1.16 Roosevelt sees the post-Keynesians (as represented, principally, by Sraffa and Robinson and Eatwell, 1973) as falling into the same trap as J. S. Mill by holding that the laws of production are universal, technical, physical matters, but the laws of distribution reflect existing institutions and social relationships and are subject to fundamental changes as well as varying as between one society and another and being, in the main, independent of production. He criticizes at length what he takes to be a neglect of discussion of production as a set of social relationships as opposed to physical and technical ones. He objects to the undue concentration on the distribution of the surplus as opposed to discussions of how it is created, what determines its size, and the organic relationship that exists between its production and distribution through the social relationships involved, which he takes to be the principal characteristic of the capitalist mode of production. Both Rowthorn and Roosevelt are critical of the neglect of feedback relationships between the two spheres. They argue that such relationships are a characteristic of Marxian analysis but are, in their view, conspicuous by their absence in post-Keynesian analysis, especially that branch which emanates from and/or is inspired by Sraffa's work.

1.17 In contrast to Rowthorn and Roosevelt, Eatwell (1974) vigorously defends the Sraffian strands, regarding them as constituting important advances in *Marxian* analysis, especially in regard to the form of the problem of the link between "values" and "prices of production," that is, the transformation problem. The latter is not seen primarily as a problem concerned with relative prices, of the link between commodities exchanging at their Marxian or labor values and commodities exchanging at their prices of production. Rather, it is seen as the link between surplus value, a social phenomenon that is a function of the social relations in the capitalist mode of production, and profits, as seen on the surface in the sphere of distribution and exchange, as a component of the prices of production. That is to say, it is concerned primarily with the origin of profits in the essence of the capitalist mode of production, instead of with the deviations of the prices of production from Marxian values, a secondary consideration.[24] This link Sraffa provides with his standard system and standard commodity (see Sraffa, 1960, chaps. 4-6). With these constructions, Sraffa is able to demonstrate by his wage rate/rate of profits relation that, although the wage, rate of profits, and relative prices of the standard and actual systems are identical (see Sraffa, 1960, p. 23), yet in the standard system the wage/rate of profits relation and the wage/surplus value relation exist, as it were, *prior to and independently of the relative prices*, that is, the prices of production.[25] "Sraffa's standard commodity therefore possesses all the characteristics which Marx sought in the "average commodity" which was to be the key to his solution of the transformation problem" (Eatwell, 1974, p. 302).[26]

1.18   Though Eatwell criticizes Medio (1972) as well as Rowthorn in his defense of Sraffa, it does appear that Medio and Eatwell agree at least on general issues. Medio's criticism of Sraffa relates to details rather than to his general approach. Thus, Medio objects to Sraffa's assumption that the wage is paid out of the surplus rather than advanced and therefore part of the firms' capitals, as in the classical and Marxian tradition. Sraffa adopted his procedure, not without misgivings (see Sraffa, 1960, pp. 9-10), because it had the convenient by-product that the relationship between the wage (measured in terms of the standard commodity) and the rate of profits was a very simple straight-line one.[27] Medio feels that this simplification is bought at too high a price in that it obscures the Marxian insight, whereby the wage is measured in terms of labor time, so that the working day splits conveniently into the workman working first for himself and then for the capitalist (surplus value). Moreover, Medio argues, in the Sraffian scheme the wage is purely a distributive phenomenon, instead of being integrated into the social and technical relationships associated with the production of output and, more importantly in this context, the surplus. Marx's macroeconomic foundations of microeconomics are thus in Medio's view not sufficiently emphasized in Sraffa's formulation.[28] Sraffa is well aware of this criticism for he argues (1960, p. 10) that although his treatment of the wage formally implies that wage goods are nonbasics, yet their essentially basic characteristic will show up in the formation of relative prices and profits in other ways.

1.19   We may conclude that although the Marxists and radicals legitimately may take issue on the *details* of the post-Keynesians' analysis, their general criticism that there is a neglect of the concept of the mode of production, of social relationships, and of the importance of the sphere of production is not really well-founded. Marx was well-known for his method of concentrating on one aspect of a large interrelated problem and putting the other aspects theoretically in cold storage, while, at the same time, stressing the importance of their interrelationships and overlaps in a complete analysis. Presumably a charitable view would allow the post-Keynesians a similar dispensation.

II

2.1   We now consider the social significance of the controversies. The theoretical issues provide a convenient launching pad. A major result that has emerged is the view of both sides that time must be modeled seriously and that analysis of processes in an uncertain environment is the most pressing problem yet to be tackled, or, at least, tackled satisfactorily. Where the protagonists differ is over the "vision" of the economy that will go into the model to be used. Thus, Hahn (1975b, p. 363) tells us that there is "no Millsian complacence [in] the current mainstream theoretical literature" and that "[there] have been important developments in the modelling of information, sequence economies, uncertainty, coalitions and power. Results most damaging to neoclassical theory have recently been proved by Debreu, Sonnenschein and Mas-Collel." Nevertheless, as Hahn himself made clear in his Inaugural Lecture (1973a), he still wishes to have equilibrium, albeit in a considerably modified neoclassical sense, as a central

concept and Walrasian economic agents interacting in Walrasian markets, but now, of course, without the auctioneer and recontracting, but using money, as the principal actors.[29] Bliss, too, while properly aware of the limited advances that further concentration on steady-state analysis will bring, nonetheless wishes to take over to his studies of "capital theory in the short run," a framework similar to that of Hahn. Thus he intends to use a *temporary equilibrium* analysis "in which current markets and a restricted set of forward markets are clearing" (Bliss, 1974, p. 3). And, although Clower and Leijonhufvud (1975) are, at least implicitly, critical of these approaches, their own suggestions concerning the essential role of traders who hold stocks seem to make them also horses of a similar stable.

2.2   The use of these approaches means that no radical changes in "vision" are involved. Capitalism is still seen as advancing through "a process of 'deepening the structure of capital,' in which the savings decision of atomistic individuals," as expressed in their intertemporal choices between goods today and goods tomorrow, are the driving forces of the system. "The capitalist firm is seen merely as an intermediary between the individuals as suppliers of factors and the individuals as *rentiers* consuming their lifetime income" (Harris, 1975, p. 329). Consumption is the be-all and end-all of economic life; accumulation by contrast is an incidental feature, a means merely to an end. Growth in the labor force and technical advances are exogenous to the system. Crises and cycles are aberrations on a process of smooth development (though something supposedly akin to Keynesian involuntary unemployment may be deduced in some versions of these models; see, for example, Malinvaud and Younès, 1975). "There is no identifiable class of workers displaced from property in the means of production who must depend entirely on employment in capitalistic production . . . for their economic survival. It is therefore difficult to see what real historical phenomena . . . this system of thought is intended to explain" (Harris, 1975, p. 330).[30] As Pasinetti (1974) has pointed out, Keynes was modeling an industrial society. This is a tradition that his immediate followers and their pupils have followed. By contrast, "much of the pre-Keynesian economic thought [which is the base on which both the Bastard Keynesians and the "new" interpreters of Keynes—Clower and Leijonhufvud—have built] does not . . . refer to an industrial society, but to a more primitive . . . society, in which resources (. . . given) are being offered and at the same time represent the purchasing power of the single individuals. . . . [P]ushed to the extreme, the concepts are shaped into a 'model of pure exchange' expressed precisely by a system of simultaneous equations (supply . . . and demand functions) from which prices emerge as the solutions" (Pasinetti, 1974, p. 47). This gives rise to the "misleading impression . . . that all the problems of our time would disappear if only the [so-called Keynesian] 'rigidities' were to be eliminated . . . as if [they] were the cause and not . . . one of the . . . inherent consequences of the industrial society in which we live" (Pasinetti, 1974, p. 48).

2.3   By contrast, the positive contributions of the post-Keynesians are intended specifically to deal with the neglected elements that have their base in historical fact and industrial societies. Some members of the school are open to the criticism that they tend to analyze the trend independently of the cycle (for example,

Kaldor's stylized facts do not include the cycle though this has not always been true of his approach). Nevertheless, they have been attempting to provide the ingredients for a theory of growth that is *"a theory of the expanded reproduction of the capitalist mode of production on a world scale"* (Harris, 1975, p. 331). When their approach is integrated with Marxian analysis, so that we return to the boundaries of our subject, as "more generously drawn by the classical pioneers" (Dobb, 1973, p. 11), we will have a more suitable and richer framework for the analysis of historical developments, past and future. Lest this be mistaken for a plea for economists to be techniques Luddites, it should be said that there is no suggestion that we are to scrap modern methods of technical analysis. Rather, they are to be used at the appropriate places in this different context in order to refine and enrich the resulting analyses. (A good example of such an application is the analytical sections of Harris's paper, 1975, pp. 331-36. I also have in mind the valuable works of Braverman, 1974, and Marglin, 1971, both of which throw considerable light on the detailed conditions of work, technical advances, and saving in the sphere of production, aspects virtually neglected by the neo-neoclassicals and only lightly touched upon by the post-Keynesians.)

2.4   There are important social and policy implications of the two contrasting approaches. In a sense, it may not be too fanciful to argue that we are now at a position in time that is equivalent to, or at least has strong similarities with, that prior to the publication of the *General Theory*. Then, it will be remembered, both practical men and many economists were advocating pump-priming measures for raising the capitalist world from its slump, but the authoritative theory that would explain exactly *why* there was the sustained slump and *how* these measures could remove it still awaited to be written and accepted.[31] Two branches of orthodoxy dominate the discussion and implementation of policy in the capitalist world; one actually (the Bastard Keynesians), one, on the whole, potentially (the monetarist school). (Nixon at one stage gave the latter a slight run for its money, and recent United Kingdom (Conservative) and Australian (Labor) administrations have flirted with some aspects of the monetarist recommendations.) The Bastard Keynesians are in the process, which is probably very far along, of being discredited in many capitalist countries, because of the conjunction of high rates of inflation *and* unemployment. An extreme and old-fashioned form of orthodoxy is bidding to take its place. "Once again it is alleged that the private market economy can and will, without aid from government policy, steer itself to full employment equilibrium" (Tobin, 1975, p. 196). This is, of course, Friedman's monetarism with its stress on the need to get markets, especially labor markets, functioning efficiently and competitively, and to remove as much as possible the discretionary role of government as well as its absorption of the community's resources. (An even more extreme view is that of von Hayek, 1975, and his followers, the present von Mises revivalists, who are suspicious even of Friedman and who strangely, even incongruously, want a system of free markets, again especially labor markets, and fixed exchange rates for the capitalist world as a whole.) With this go also their attempts to show that the Keynesian revolution was but an aberration—and an abortive one at that —on the mainstream of the development of liberal economic thought from Adam

Smith on. That is to say, the focus is, once again, on the primary importance of substitution and flexibility, on the quick and correct, that is, stable, response of the economy to price market signals. These forces, in a correct environment, are seen as far more powerful than the major instabilities implied by the discrepancies between saving and investment, leakages and injections, which are the central features of the Keynesian-Kaleckian and Marxist approaches.

2.5   There are attempts to replace tendencies to deficiencies or excesses in the level of effective demand with the concept of the "natural" rate of unemployment, a concept that draws on an underlying Walrasian equilibrium in competitive markets in which the relative price system is the key method of allocation and inflation is a monetary phenomenon superimposed on the workings of the real sector. " '[E]quilibrium' often allows for any steady rate of deflation or inflation, not just zero" (Tobin, 1975, p. 196). In a parallel movement, the Keynesian concept of involuntary unemployment is also being replaced, or whittled away to insignificance, by the job search literature in which is employed the belated discovery that an atomistic competitor in an uncertain world nevertheless could have some direct responsibility for setting prices that themselves may well not be equilibrium ones.

2.6   In places there are also glimpses of and attempts to create consensus policies embodying genuine *money* income restraints and what Joan Robinson has called "a real social contract which would satisfy the reasonable demands of the workers for more control over their own work, more security against redundancy, better social services and so forth." This recognizes a point that Keynes (and Kalecki) clearly foresaw: that prolonged near full employment would imply inflation unless there were changing attitudes and methods of *money* wage bargaining. The post-Keynesian critique of the marginal productivity theory of distribution, together with Sidney Weintraub's work, are especially relevant at this point. These efforts tend to be timid and unsustained, to lack confidence because the authoritative theoretical backing, though by no means completely awaiting to be written, certainly does still await wide acceptance. It should also be said that amongst many of those who are attempting to provide it, there is much more ambivalence about (and/or outright hostility to) the desirability of either propping up or salvaging the capitalist mode of production than was the case when Keynes was writing the *General Theory*.[32] It is at this juncture that the post-Keynesian contributions, both methodologically and analytically, most relevantly fit into the current policy and social situation. The above scenario is one of the themes of Joan Robinson's Richard T. Ely Lecture, "The Second Crisis of Economic Theory" (1972). These very fundamental and practical implications are thus an important offshoot of the seemingly esoteric theoretical exchanges of the Cambridge controversies in the theory of capital.

REFERENCES

Arrow, K. J. "General Economic Equilibrium: Purpose, Analytic Techniques, Collective Choice." *American Economic Review* 64 (1974), pp. 253-72.
—— and F. H. Hahn. *General Competitive Analysis.* San Francisco: Holden-Day; Edinburgh: Oliver and Boyd, 1971.

Asimakopulos, A. "Profits and Investment: A Kaleckian Approach," in G. C. Harcourt and Austin Robinson, eds., *The Microeconomic Foundations of Macroeconomics*. London: Macmillan, 1975.

—— and J. B. Burbidge. "The Short-Period Incidence of Taxation." *Economic Journal*, 84 (1974), pp. 267-88.

Baumol, W. J. "The Transformation of Values: What Marx 'Really' Meant (An Interpretation)." *Journal of Economic Literature* 12 (1974a), pp. 51-62.

—— "Comment." *Journal of Economic Literature* 12 (1974b), pp. 74-75.

Blaug, M. *The Cambridge Revolution: Success or Failure? A Critical Analysis of Cambridge Theories of Value and Distribution*. London: Institute of Economic Affairs, 1974.

Bliss, C. J. "Capital Theory in the Short-Run." Mimeographed. Buffalo, N.Y.: State University of New York at Buffalo, 1974.

—— *Capital Theory and the Distribution of Income*. Amsterdam: North-Holland; New York: American Elsevier, 1975.

Braverman, H. *Labor and Monopoly Capital: The Degradation of Work in the Twentieth Century*. New York: Monthly Review Press, 1974.

Clower, R. "Reflections on the Keynesian Perplex." *Zeitschrift für Nationalökonomie* 35 (1975), pp. 1-24.

—— and A. Leijonhufvud. "The Coordination of Economic Activities: A Keynesian Perspective." *American Economic Review, Papers and Proceedings* 65 (1975), pp. 182-88.

Dobb, M. H. *Theories of Value and Distribution since Adam Smith: Ideology and Economic Theory*. Cambridge: Cambridge University Press, 1973.

—— "Ricardo and Adam Smith" in A. S. Skinner and T. Wilson, eds., *Essays on Adam Smith*. Oxford: Clarendon Press, 1975.

Eatwell, J. L. "Controversies in the Theory of Surplus Value: Old and New." *Science and Society* 38 (1974), pp. 281-303.

Gallaway, L., and V. Shukla. "The Neoclassical Production Function." *American Economic Review* 64 (1974), pp. 348-58.

Garegnani, P. "A Problem in the Theory of Distribution from Ricardo to Wicksell." Ph.D. dissertation, Cambridge University, 1958.

—— *Il Capitale nelle Teorie della Distribuzione*, ed. Dott A. Giuffrè. Milan: Pubblicazioni della Facoltà di Economia e Commercio dell' Università di Roma, XII, 1960.

—— "Heterogeneous Capital, the Production Function and the Theory of Distribution." *Review of Economic Studies* 37, no. 3 (1970a), pp. 407-36.

—— "A Reply." *Review of Economic Studies* 37, no. 3 (1970b), p. 439.

—— "Summary of the Final Discussion," in J. A. Mirrlees and N. H. Stern, eds., *Models of Economic Growth*. London: Macmillan, 1973.

—— "On a Change in the Notion of Equilibrium in Recent Work on Value and Distribution. A Comment on Samuelson," in M. Brown, K. Sato, and P. Zarembka, eds., *Essays in Modern Capital Theory*. Amsterdam: North-Holland, 1975, pp. 25-45.

Hahn, F. H. "Introduction," in F. H. Hahn, ed., *Readings in the Theory of Growth*. London: Macmillan, 1971.

—— *The Share of Wages in the National Income: An Enquiry into the Theory of Distribution*. London: Weidenfeld and Nicolson, 1972.

—— *On the Notion of Equilibrium in Economics: An Inaugural Lecture*. Cambridge: Cambridge University Press, 1973a.

—— "The Winter of Our Discontent." *Economica* 40 (1973b), pp. 322-30.

—— "Back to Square One." *Cambridge Review* 96 (1974), pp. 34-37.

—— "Comment." *Cambridge Review* 96 (1975a), p. 92.

—— "Revival of Political Economy: The Wrong Issues and the Wrong Argument." *Economic Record* 51 (1975b), pp. 360-64.

Harcourt, G. C. "A Two-Sector Model of the Distribution of Income and the Level of Employment in the Short Run." *Economic Record* 41 (1965), pp. 103-17.

—— *Some Cambridge Controversies in the Theory of Capital*. Cambridge: Cambridge University Press, 1972.

—— "The Cambridge Controversies: The Afterglow," in M. Parkin and A. R. Nobay, eds., *Contemporary Issues in Economics*. Manchester: Manchester University Press, 1975a, pp. 305-34.

—— "Decline and Rise: The Revival of (Classical) Political Economy." *Economic Record* 51 (1975b), pp. 339-56.

—— "The Cambridge Controversies: Old Ways and New Horizons—or Dead End?" *Oxford Economic Papers* 28 (1976), pp. 25-65.

—— and V. G. Massaro. "Mr. Sraffa's Production of Commodities." *Economic Record* 40 (1964), pp. 442-54.

Harris, D. J. "The Theory of Economic Growth: A Critique and Reformulation." *American Economic Review, Papers and Proceedings* 65 (1975), pp. 329-37.

Harrod, R. F. "An Essay in Dynamic Theory." *Economic Journal* 49 (1939), pp. 14-33.

—— *Towards a Dynamic Economics: Some Recent Developments of Economic Theory and Their Application to Policy*. London: Macmillan, 1948.

Hayek, F. A. von. *Full Employment at Any Price?* London: Institute of Economic Affairs, 1975.

Hicks, J. R. *Value and Capital: An Inquiry into Some Fundamental Principles of Economic Theory*. Oxford: Clarendon Press, 1939.

Hicks, John. *Capital and Growth*. Oxford: Clarendon Press, 1965.

—— *A Theory of Economic History*. Oxford: Clarendon Press, 1969.

—— *Capital and Time: A Neo-Austrian Theory*. Oxford: Clarendon Press, 1973.

—— "Revival of Political Economy: The Old and the New." *Economic Record* 51 (1975), pp. 365-67.

Johnson, H. G. "Keynes and British Economics," in M. Keynes, ed., *Essays on John Maynard Keynes*. Cambridge: Cambridge University Press, 1975, pp. 108-22.

Kalecki, M. "Trend and Business Cycles Reconsidered." *Economic Journal* 78 (1968), pp. 263-76.

Kregel, J. A. *The Reconstruction of Political Economy: An Introduction to Post-Keynesian Economics*. London: Macmillan, 1973.

Malinvaud, E. "Discussion of Koopmans' Paper," in G. C. Harcourt and Austin Robinson, eds., *The Microeconomic Foundations of Macroeconomics*. London: Macmillan, 1975.

—— and Y. Younès. "Some New Concepts for the Microeconomic Foundations of Macroeconomics," in G. C. Harcourt and Austin Robinson, eds., *The Microeconomic Foundations of Macroeconomics*. London: Macmillan, 1975.

Marglin, S. A. "What Do Bosses Do? The Origins and Functions of Hierarchy in Capitalist Production." Mimeographed. Cambridge, Mass., 1971.

Meade, J. E. "The Keynesian Revolution," in M. Keynes, ed., *Essays on John Maynard Keynes*. Cambridge: Cambridge University Press, 1975, pp. 82-88.

Medio, A. "Profits and Surplus-Value: Appearance and Reality in Capitalist Production," in E. K. Hunt and J. G. Schwartz, eds., *A Critique of Economic Theory: Selected Readings*. London: Penguin Books Ltd., 1972.

Meek, R. L. *Economics and Ideology and Other Essays: Studies in the Development of Economic Thought*. London: Chapman and Hall, 1967.

Ng, Y. K. "The Neoclassical and the Neo-Marxist-Keynesian Theories of Income Distribution: A Non-Cambridge Contribution to the Cambridge Controversy in Capital Theory." *Australian Economic Papers* 13 (1974), pp. 124-32.

Pasinetti, L. L. "Rate of Profit and Income Distribution in Relation to the Rate of Economic Growth." *Review of Economic Studies* 29 (1962), pp. 267-79.

—— *Growth and Income Distribution: Essays in Economic Theory*. Cambridge: Cambridge University Press, 1974.

Rivlin, A. M. "Income Distribution—Can Economists Help?" (Richard T. Ely Lecture, 1975.) *American Economic Review, Papers and Proceedings* 65 (1975), pp. 1-15.

Robinson, Joan. "The Production Function and the Theory of Capital." *Review of Economic Studies* 21 (1953-54), pp. 81-106.

—— *The Accumulation of Capital*. London: Macmillan, 1956.

—— *Essays in the Theory of Economic Growth*. London: Macmillan, 1962.

—— "The Second Crisis of Economic Theory." (Richard T. Ely Lecture, 1972.) *American Economic Review, Papers and Proceedings* 62 (1972), pp. 1-10.

—— *History versus Equilibrium*. London: Thames Polytechnic, 1974.

—— "The Unimportance of Reswitching." *Quarterly Journal of Economics* 89 (1975a), pp. 32-39.

—— "Reswitching: Reply." *Quarterly Journal of Economics* 89 (1975b), pp. 53-55.

—— "Introduction 1974: Reflections and Reminiscences," in *Collected Economic Papers*, vol. II, 2nd ed. Oxford: Basil Blackwell, 1975c, iii-xii.

—— "Introduction 1974: Comments and Explanations," in *Collected Economic Papers*, vol. III, 2nd ed. Oxford: Basil Blackwell, 1975d, iii-xiv.

—— "Review of L. L. Pasinetti, *Growth and Income Distribution: Essays in Economic Theory*, 1974." *Economic Journal* 85 (1975e), pp. 397-99.

—— "Letter to Editor." *Cambridge Review* 96 (1975f), pp. 91-92.

—— and J. L. Eatwell. *An Introduction to Modern Economics.* London: McGraw-Hill, 1973.

Roncaglia, A. "Labour-Power, Subsistence Wage and the Rate of Wages." *Australian Economic Papers* 13 (1974), pp. 133-43.

Roosevelt, F. "Cambridge Economics as Commodity Fetishism," in E. J. Nell, ed., *Growth, Profits and Property: Essays in the Revival of Political Economy.* Cambridge: Cambridge University Press, 1975.

Rowthorn, R. E. "Neo-Classicism, Neo-Ricardianism and Marxism." *New Left Review*, no. 86 (1974), pp. 63-87.

Samuelson, P. A. "A Summing Up." *Quarterly Journal of Economics* 80 (1966), pp. 568-83.

—— "Insight and Detour in the Theory of Exploitation: A Reply to Baumol." *Journal of Economic Literature* 12 (1974a), pp. 62-70.

—— "Rejoinder: Merlin Unclothed, a Final Word." *Journal of Economic Literature* 12 (1974b), pp. 75-77.

—— "Steady-State and Transient Relations: A Reply on Reswitching." *Quarterly Journal of Economics* 89 (1975), pp. 40-47.

Shaikh, A. "Laws of Production and Laws of Algebra: The Humbug Production Function." *Review of Economics and Statistics* 56 (1974), pp. 115-20.

Solow, R. M. "'Laws of Production and Laws of Algebra: The Humbug Production Function': A Comment." *Review of Economics and Statistics* 56 (1974), p. 121.

—— "Cambridge and the Real World." *Times Literary Supplement*, March 14, 1975, pp. 277-78.

Sraffa, P. *Production of Commodities by Means of Commodities: Prelude to a Critique of Economic Theory.* Cambridge: Cambridge University Press, 1960.

Steedman, I. "Critique of the Critic." *Times Higher Educational Supplement*, January 31, 1975, p. i.

Stiglitz, J. E. "The Cambridge-Cambridge Controversy in the Theory of Capital: A View from New Haven: A Review Article." *Journal of Political Economy* 82 (1974), pp. 893-903.

Tobin, J. "Keynesian Models of Recession and Depression." *American Economic Review, Papers and Proceedings* 65 (1975), pp. 195-202.

Vanags, A. H. "Discussion," in M. Parkin and A. R. Nobay, eds., *Contemporary Issues in Economics.* Manchester, England: Manchester University Press, 1975, pp. 334-36.

Weizsäcker, C. C. von. "Ende einer Wachstumstheorie? Zu Hajo Rieses Missverständnissen über die "neoklassiche" Theorie." *Kyklos* 24 (1971), pp. 97-101.

NOTES

1. Solow (1975, p. 277) argues that the real dispute concerns size rather than origin, but I think that this is wishful thinking. For Solow finds his clues to size in the modern versions of Fisherian theory, "the preferences of investors and savers, . . . the alternative forms of wealth available to them," while the post-Keynesian theory has its roots in the Marxian concepts of exploitation and surplus value allied with the Keynesian-Kaleckian solutions of the realization problem, that is, "mainly [in] the investment decisions of profit-seeking firms, not . . . the intentions to save of thrifty households" (Robinson, 1975e, p. 397).

2. ". . . Keynes' theory of effective demand, which has remained so impervious to reconciliation with marginal economic theory, raises almost no problem when directly inserted into the earlier discussions of the Classical economists. Similarly, . . . the post-Keynesian theories of economic growth and income distribution, which have required so many artificial assumptions in the efforts to reconcile them with marginal productivity theory, encounter almost no difficulty when directly grafted on to Classical economic dynamics" (Pasinetti, 1974, p. ix).

3. "Keynes's intellectual revolution was to shift economists from thinking normally in terms of a model of reality in which a dog called *savings* wagged his tail labelled *investment* to thinking in terms of a model in which a dog called *investment* wagged his tail labelled *savings*" (Meade, 1975, p. 82).

4. Similarly, in the initial stages, post-Keynesian theory was preoccupied with Golden Age analysis, as a preliminary flexing of muscles prior to tackling the much harder problems of actual growth processes.

5. Hicks has recently reminded us, as a result of my denseness, that the "non-neoclassic" John Hicks of *A Theory of Economic History* and *Capital and Time* is J. R.'s uncle, and that he is not all *that* well pleased with his nephew (see Hicks, 1975, p. 365).

6. "The great mystery of the modern theory of distribution is, actually, why anyone regards the share of wages and profits in total income as an interesting problem. It has after all little practical relevance." To this view, happily *and* relevantly, may be contrasted Alice Rivlin's recent "political prediction" (in her Richard T. Ely lecture, 1975) "that income shares . . . are going to become a major focus of policy debate in the next few years" (p. 1).

7. ". . . the present orthodoxy is in serious need of revision and perhaps of revolution . . . the theory of dis-equilibrium is in considerable disarray as is the theory of intertemporal allocation in the face of uncertainty" (Hahn, 1974, p. 37).

8. A similar conclusion, albeit in a rather different and more limited context, recently has been stated by Clower (1975, p. 12). Referring to the finest modern flowering of neo-classical analysis, namely, general equilibrium (or neo-Walrasian) theory, Clower says: "[T]he existing body of Neo-Walrasian analysis rests upon assumptions that preclude its use for explicit analysis of either disequilibrium trading processes or monetary exchanges. . . . [It] is closed to extensions in certain crucial directions including . . . those . . . that would permit explicit formal analysis of Keynesian short-run adjustment processes . . . precisely the kind of processes about which economists must be able to speak with scientific authority if their science is to be anything more than a body of idle speculation and a breeding ground for charlatans and quacks."

9. It is, of course, natural for Marxists to defend the traditional equilibrium concept, for most of volume I of *Das Kapital* uses this methodology, yet refute the use of supply and demand concepts as the surface phenomena of vulgar economy (see Rowthorn, 1974). I am indebted to John Henry for this point.

10. "The Keynesian method is to describe a set of relationships (intended to correspond to what are believed to be the relevant features of the economic system) and to trace the effects in the immediate and further future of a change taking place as an event at a moment of time" (Robinson, 1975f, p. 92).

11. "In fact, the long-run trend is but a slowly changing component of a chain of short-period situations; it has no independent entity" (Kalecki, 1968, p. 263).

12. See also Harcourt (1965) for an early example.

13. "'Convergence to equilibrium' has been shown to be dubious . . . also unimportant. Even at the best, it will take a long time; and in most applications before that time has elapsed, something else . . . will surely have occurred" (Hicks, 1975, p. 366).

14. Robinson (1975f, p. 92). Hahn thinks Marx would have been scornful of the post-Keynesians—those whom Hahn calls "reactionaries"—because they define classes by the orders of magnitude of their saving propensities. "The reactionaries take differences in the propensity to save as their characterisation of class—how Marx would have scoffed!" (Hahn, 1975a, p. 92). That may be. Certainly his present-day followers are rather scornful, though not for this reason (see below, paragraphs 1.15 – 1.19). But how much more scornful Marx would have been of Hahn's own peculiarly sophisticated brand of Vulgar Economy.

15. "The neo-Ricardians, by means of the neoclassical theory of the choice of technique, have established that capital aggregation is theoretically unsound. Fine. Let us give them an alpha for this" (Hahn, 1975b, p. 363). This is a resolution of a major area in favor of the critics, a resolution that surprised at least one commentator. "Economists have looked for this simple relationship, one of the main propositions of neoclassical economics, for a century; but now it is generally recognized that the property did not always hold. . . . Cambridge U.K. had been right on this point" (Malinvaud, 1975, pp. 40-41). Malinvaud adds, wrongly in my view, that he does not think the consequences are "very profound."

16. It is at this point that Garegnani's (nearly) unique stance is significant. For, as we saw in paragraph 1.8 above, he wishes both to defend a well-established methodology *and* to deduce the disquieting conclusion that when it is allied with the neoclassical emphasis on supply and demand, insuperable logical difficulties associated principally with the treatment of "capital" prevent the approach from providing a viable theory of accumulation and distribution. "Thus, after following in the footsteps of traditional theory and attempting an analysis of distribution in terms of 'demand' and 'supply,' we are forced to the conclusion that a change, however small, in the 'supply' or 'demand' conditions of labour or capital (saving) may result in drastic changes of r and w ... would even force us to admit that r may fall to zero or rise to its maximum ... without bringing to equality the quantities supplied and demanded of the two factors.... [No] such instability [has] ever [been] observed.... [In] order to explain distribution, [we] must rely on forces other than 'supply' and 'demand'" (Garegnani, 1970a, p. 426). The response of those more favorably disposed towards traditional neoclassical theory (and its modern offshoots) has been either to evade the conclusions (Friedman, Johnson) or to change the questions or the methodology, or both. Garegnani's lesson from the Cambridge controversies is thus a head-on confrontation, a full frontal attack, *even in terms of the long-run comparisons.*

17. "The abstract equilibrium tells us what value the unknowns must have if there is to be equilibrium; it does not tell us anything of any economic process which establishes such values" (Hahn, 1974, p. 36, n. 4).

18. "There is much to be learned from *a priori* comparisons of equilibrium positions, but they must be kept in their logical place ... cannot be applied to actual situations .... In a model depicting equilibrium positions there is no causation. It consists of a closed circle of simultaneous equations .... At any moment in logical time, the past is determined just as much as the future. In an historical model, causal relations have to be specified. Today is a break in time between an unknown future and an irrevocable past .... Movement can only be forward" (Robinson, 1962, pp. 25-26).

19. For a list of the parables, see Harcourt (1975a, p. 316).

20. "The mainstream replies that this is only a crude simplification made for the purpose of applying the theory to real numbers, and so is to be judged pragmatically and not by the standards of rigorous analysis" (Solow, 1975, p. 277).

22. "It merely shows how one goes about interpreting given time series if one starts by *assuming* that they were generated from a production function and that the competitive marginal-product relations apply" (Solow, 1974, p. 121).

22. The use of Keynes's name makes Marxists and radicals suspicious, for they (rightly) see Keynes as wishing to preserve the capitalist system by ridding it of its short-run effective demand deficiencies. They also suspect that something of this attitude—here they are on less firm ground—has affected the post-Keynesian approach to the analysis of the longer-run developments of capitalist economies.

23. Roosevelt (1975, n. 2) acknowledges the important influence of Medio and Rowthorn's work on his own.

24. The exchanges between Samuelson (1974a, 1974b) and Baumol (1974a, 1974b) on the transformation problem also center on these basic distinctions.

25. This, incidentally, gives a rigorous meaning to the classical view that "distribution precedes value" (Harcourt, 1975b, p. 34), which Hahn (1975b, p. 361) finds not merely mistaken but also incomprehensible. Sraffa thus bridges satisfactorily both Ricardian with Marxian thought *and* these together with modern thought. As with Ricardo of old, his editor gives "the primary emphasis of his theory" to the proposition "that a rise in wages would reduce profits equivalently [but] he [is] by no means blind to its differential effect on prices" (Dobb, 1975, p. 329).

26. Meek (1967, pp. 175-78) made a similar point many years ago in his classic review of Sraffa's book (originally published simultaneously in the June 1961 and Spring 1961 issues of the *Scottish Journal of Political Economy* and *Science and Society*, respectively). It was, however, obscured by his exposition, in which he treated the transformation problem as being directed more towards an explanation of the deviations of the "prices of production" from "values." Harcourt and Massaro (1964, pp. 453-54), in arguing that Sraffa had rehabilitated the labor theory of value, also pitched it in these terms rather than in the more correct terms, from the point of view of an interpretation of Marx, of the fundamental explanation of the origin of profits, themselves a surface phenomenon.

27. See Roncaglia (1974) on Sraffa's analysis when the wage is advanced.

28. "The theory of *value* performs [an] important function within the Marxian analysis of capitalism. It links Marx's 'macroeconomic model,' which shows the mechanism of the system setting some basic relationships between a limited number of variables, with his 'microeconomic model' of interindustry competitive relationships" (Medio, 1972, p. 330).

29. "[A]n economy is in equilibrium when it generates messages which do not cause agents to change the theories which they hold or the policies which they pursue" (Hahn, 1973, p. 28).

30. Harris's paper has influenced greatly the views I have taken in the present section.

31. With hindsight, Harry Johnson (1975) is now arguing that the *General Theory* is yet another example of unnecessary English originality. He feels, moreover, that its effects are pernicious, for it drew on the unique United Kingdom experience, a special case that was nevertheless easily explainable in orthodox terms, as the basis for an unnecessary and incorrect general theory of how capitalism works.

32. In commenting on a draft of this paper, Harold Lydall described the political attitude of the Cambridge post-Keynesians as "a sort of 'bastard' Marxism [which will get] short shift from 'true' Marxists [though its proponents serve] a useful purpose as intellectual fellow travellers, whose main function is to undermine faith in capitalism and any other kind of market economy."

15

Some Comments on the Cambridge Paradigm
An Introduction to Modern Economics

W. ROBERT NEEDHAM

Professor of Economics at University of Waterloo, Ontario, Canada

I

The publication of *An Introduction to Modern Economics* by Joan Robinson and John Eatwell (1973) should represent a significant step in modernizing the teaching of economics. This is so because the book attempts a shift in the direction of realism and away from mathematical esoterica and irrelevance, on the one hand, and what may conveniently be referred to as "trendy trivia," on the other. The former has long been a characteristic of neoclassical economics in terms of research on the so-called frontiers and to a certain extent teaching; the latter is an outgrowth of the past two decades, during which it has been in some circles fashionable and superficially radical to adopt somewhat off-the-track writing and teaching interests in response to student awareness that orthodox economics is more concerned with a particular system of thinking than with the real world. In addition, *An Introduction to Modern Economics* (hereafter, *IME*) may be seen as an attempt to present in a more complete fashion than hitherto available the vantage point from which a clear vision of the world, in general, and the operation of capitalist economies, in particular, may be obtained.[1] This vision is neither neoclassical, mathematically esoteric, nor irrelevant, and it is certainly not trendy radicalism, though radical it is. It is a vision that has come to be known as "Cambridge Economics,"[2] although Nell's (1972) description of it as the Cambridge "paradigm" is more meaningful in stressing that it is a vantage point from which the continuous motion of modern economies may be descriptively analyzed and understood. Specifically, *IME* presents the teachers and students of economics with a "positive" and all-encompassing radical alternative to orthodox economics,[3] a system within which to present and analyze the relevance and adequacy of economic doctrine itself, the operation of capitalist economies, and indeed the relevance of the former as a base from which the latter may be understood. It is likely that the book will generate a great interest in practical or applied problems at all levels of research, and in large part it will now be possible to do this in closer cooperation with other social science disci-

I would like to thank my good friend Jesse Schwartz for the invitation to write this paper for this book and indeed for the suggestions he made with respect to a previous draft. Colleagues Soichi Shinohara and Andreas Andrikopoulos read and commented on the first draft; and although it cannot be claimed that they have been fully convinced, they are certainly more appreciative of what it is that Cambridge is attempting to do.

plines. The book should do much to change the image of economics to one relevant to an understanding of the problems of mankind.

For the teacher of economics, the Cambridge and neoclassical literature (the writings of Joan Robinson not excluded) suggests that this book has been long overdue. It is true that her writings over many years are consistent in revealing a continuous attempt to hammer out an accurate description and appropriate framework for studying the operation of capitalist economies, and indeed much of her previously published work finds its place in *IME*. It seems fairly accurate, however, to say that in the last twenty years or so her main involvement has been in fighting battles (and emerging victorious) with the leading neoclassicals[4] —primarily with those of the MIT-Harvard complex, though Robert Solow (1975) would apparently like to have the losses shared more equitably—than with presenting simply and systematically the Cambridge view. Although others have taken up parts of this work (see Kregel and Nell, for example) the publication of this book hopefully signals the end of the battles at the upper end and the beginning of an attempt at grass-roots articulation and discussion. It is this that is most important in the modernizing of economics teaching, and it is most important in that the next decade or two will see significant continuations of the impressive challenges that have been thrown out to the economics establishment in the universities and in governments around the world in the last two decades.

North American economists have not given Joan Robinson's work the attention that it deserves. This seems primarily to be due to two reasons. First, they are trained in a tradition at both the graduate and undergraduate levels that may appropriately be described as in the Samuelson-McConnell-Lipsey tradition. In Canada this takes a form consistent with the country's role as a branch-plant operation of the United States. Thus branch-plant economics departments may adopt texts "adapted to the Canadian context" in co-authored editions of the major orthodox texts—thus Samuelson-Scott and Lipsey-Stiener-Sparks. Academic programs invariably require that one of these main textbooks or some reasonable facsimile be adopted in the first-year course. Upper-year undergraduate courses represent further amplification of "set" chapter topics from these encyclicals. It is rare to find a continuous and meaningful attempt to deal with the history of economic doctrine in any other way than that which is consistent with received neoclassical dogma.[5] Masters and Ph.D. programs involve more of the same with allowance being made for specialization or niche selection. Only accidentally do students obtain a firm understanding of modern economies and their operation, though they become indoctrinated in the ways of a profession dealing with worlds and small aspects of worlds that have never and will never exist. University education does little to train students to think critically of their world and how to change it. Indeed orthodox university economics is often a most reactionary institution in terms of its unwillingness to accept alternative points of view. Support for the first point is numerous and comes in different forms (Galbraith, 1974; Myrdal, 1974; Robinson, 1965; Ward, 1972). On a related tack one might note particularly Wiles' article dealing with cost inflation and the state of economic theory: ". . . of all the recognized authorities: central bankers, ministers of finance and professors of macro-economics. They have no strictly economic cure to offer except high unemployment, which they rightly

think is immoral—and in any case is a political cure after all. . . . Some even, threatened with the loss of their whole intellectual capital attribute everything to international monetary events!" (1973, p. 391). An explanation of the loss of intellectual capital may be sought in a succinct and most damning phrase of Hollis and Nell: "Neo-classicism . . . is an unsound economic theory, presupposing an unsound political theory, underwritten by an unsound theory of knowledge" (1975, p. 266). On the second point one might simply like to refer to the *New York Times* article, "Harvard Economics Teaching Criticized" (Golden, 1975) and to the associated topic in the *Harvard Gazette*, "Leontief, Nobel Economist, Will Join NYU Faculty" (1975).

The second reason for the neglect of Robinson's work, necessarily related to the first, one can derive from the work itself. No doubt most neoclassical teachers who have found their students engrossed in one or another of her writings have learned of the great difficulty experienced by the student in coming to grips with it. Even for teachers, though, if it is fashionable to list her books and articles on reading lists, it is not so fashionable to have read them or certainly not to have seriously come to grips with them in order to, through integration, amend and update particular courses in which they are unquestionably of social relevance. The indoctrination process for priest and novice alike does not allow one to dwell long on heretical points of view, however different, challenging, downright disturbing, and somehow amazingly refreshing they may be. In fact for success in the profession one is best advised to forget about social relevance and follow religiously a "follow thy leader or be damned" commandment. Thus emulation of one's leaders (sometimes self-styled) is the high road to success in the profession.

The Robinson-Eatwell textbook will be found to give students and teachers a firm foundation in modern economics, how it is that modern economies operate, and a firm foundation upon which to assess the Cambridge neoclassical literature of the past two decades or so. It, and the Cambridge paradigm that it encompasses, provides a sound guide to the main issues in the development of economic doctrine and an objective, impartial evaluative framework for current schools of thinking. Through its provision of a real alternative to the conventional wisdom of neoclassical texts, much of the neoclassical doctrine is reduced to special cases, some of it is rejected, and a few common-sense points are brought forward and integrated as useful tools or ideas in the Cambridge view of the world.

The following section of this paper deals with an overview of the Cambridge paradigm; an overview that compresses essential notions, singled out in *IME* book I and developed in some detail in book II, into a simple circular-flow diagram. The third section of this paper surveys in more detail some of the interesting points of analysis found in book II. No attempt is made here to examine book III. Though large sections of *IME* are devoted to revealing criticisms of neoclassical economics, to the extent that these are dealt with it is to show how the ideas of Robinson and Eatwell differ from the conventional. That they close their chapter on the neoclassical era with, "It is time to go back to the beginning and start again" (p. 56), reflects the problems of neoclassical economics, problems of logic, and problems of applicability. The new start is the Cambridge alternative; this article provides an introductory survey of some aspects of that alternative and hopefully will assist grass-roots articulation and understanding.

II

IME is divided into three books, dealing with economic thought or doctrine, economic analysis, and modern economic problems. The presentation of material overall departs sharply from the encyclopedic style of orthodox textbooks; rather it presents from even its introductory pages a terse yet essentially complete argument that integrates micro and macro topics in such an effective manner that distinctions traditionally drawn to allow classification of topics under these headings seem to reduce questions emphasized by neoclassical economists and economics to the second order of smalls.

Book I has three chapters, titled "Before Adam Smith," "Classical Political Economy," and "The Neoclassical Era." They contain, along with succinct statements of economic issues couched in terms of the evolution of economic doctrine that alone could form the base for an entire course, difficult analytical points that are only appreciated after book II has been fully absorbed, and for this reason the details of book I are ignored here. Although not explicitly illustrated, there is a central unifying theme running throughout *IME* that is easily captured in a circular-flow diagram conceptualizing the economic system in terms of economic production and social class relations in production. Orthodox economists are no doubt unfamiliar with this alternative to the Samuelson vision,[6] and it is useful to present the essentials of it in order to emphasize that the study of economics can *begin with a simple description of the world as it is*. It is worth particular emphasis that this is a very real point of distinction between *IME* and orthodox texts; in fact, a distinction that makes the text, first time around, more difficult for the orthodox teacher than for the more practical student! The former are accustomed to presentation of material in discrete packages of tools and concepts outside the context of reasonable social reality (in a style consistent with the programmed instruction noted above)—specifically in terms of a priori behavioral rules, initial conditions, and hypothetical observations at a logical instant of time as opposed to a framework that can absorb observations of fact obtainable from whatever evolving economy in order to dissect and explore its characteristics at a slice through time. This emphasis is paramount in *IME*; it is then specifically post-Keynesian in terms, recognizing "economic life as a process going on through time, in which the future is not known in advance" (p. 56).

As an overview of *IME* and its description of the operation of capitalist economies, the central notions of neoclassical economics, of factor rewards being in proportion to productive contributions, of rational economic man—of individual utility maximization by consumers and of profit maximization by producers—are dispensed with. Rather households are replaced by a hierarchical depiction of society in terms of income type, and firms are replaced by a blueprint that traces the actual productive interdependencies that exist amongst industries within the economy. Rewards are simply referred to as incomes received by particular classes without regard to productive contributions at all. Consumption is rooted in the class distribution of income; different classes have different consumption-to-income ratios, but none of Keynes' misbegotten

psychological law in this! Specifically this is a radical departure from orthodox texts and means that utility theory, along with the associated conceptual baggage and ideology serving notions of optimum or equilibrium supply and demand in a stationary state, disappears. The world is characterized by inherent conflict between sellers and buyers and among competitive and concentrated industries. This view carries throughout *IME*'s analysis of closed and open economies.

Production, income distribution, and consumption are viewed from the descriptive detail provided by an input-output table; but even more, legitimate Keynesian price formation falls out as a markup over prime costs or money wages, and peofit generation, accumulation, and investment are linked in a realistic frame. It is no wonder that Professor Samuelson recognizes this as the "Age of Leontief and Sraffa"![7]

In Diagram 1 industry is conceptually caught up in the lower right hand corner in the box of rows and columns of an input-output table. In this S_1, S_2, and S_3 are producing sectors or industries; y_i, $i = 1, 2, 3$, represents disposition of a proportion of sectoral output to final demands, $C_i + I_i$; the X_{oj}, $j = 1, 2, 3$, represents the total revenue of the jth industry; $\Sigma P_i f_{ij}$, $i = 1, 2, 3$, represents total commodity input costs of the jth industry; W_{oj} and π_{oj} are the wage bill and the amount of surplus, respectively, of the jth sector.

The other sections of the diagram spell out in interesting social detail the relations of income recipients in the distribution of output. Thus while the input-output table specifies the technical relations in production, the pyramid in the lower left corner specifies in terms of the class structure of society the social relations in production as an elaboration of the input-output distribution of the net-product among the claimants to it, as given by W_{oj} and π_{oj}. The social system and industry are connected *directly* only by two flows, that of work by workers and the associated return flow of wage income. There is no implication that this income stream is ever in proportion to the productive contribution of workers; it is taken to be determined by historical and institutional considerations that may vary from one industry to another. The pyramid represents an explicit attempt to dig beneath apparent accounting categories in order to extract the distribution of product, to highlight that the source of wealth and value is work, and that the surplus over the wage bill is the key to conflicting social relations in production, to institutional conflict, to inflation, to stagnation, and much else.

In an accounting sense work in combination with capital equipment and produced commodity inputs generate a total value of output for each industry. A price-formation mechanism, including produced commodity inputs, is implied for intermediate input; purchases are caught up in the scheme of structural interdependencies dictated by output levels. The proportion of total industry output that is final goods flows from industry to final goods disposition centers from which industry obtains a flow of income from the sale of output. This income, in this diagram, is the usual closed economy, with no government net product and takes two immediate forms—a wage payment to workers, and a net surplus (net of capital consumption allowances) over the return to work—and in the input-output table sits passively at the bottom. This sedate and pacific nature changes when it is realized that surplus is at the expense of workers'

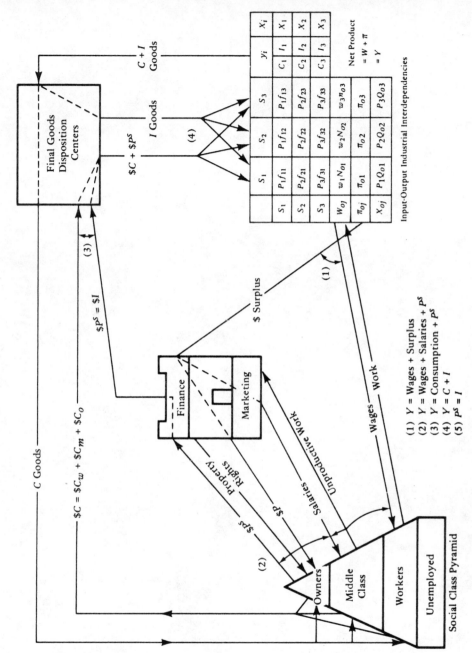

Diagram 1. Cambridge Circular Flow.

(1) Y = Wages + Surplus
(2) Y = Wages + Salaries + P^s
(3) Y = Consumption + P^s
(4) Y = $C + I$
(5) P^s = I

wages, a tax, and, laying this exploitation concept aside, that it is subject to control and distribution internally by industry without direct reference to the needs of the social system (shades of Galbraith). This control is given prominence in the diagram in the financial citadel in which the division of surplus is made. The division is between salaries of middle-class workers and owners. Salaries are viewed as an income return in payment for "unproductive" labor, a distinction that recognizes only that some workers are engaged directly in production and others in support or tertiary activities, such as marketing and operations finance. This distinction serves as a particularly useful tool as it raises, in the first instance, the question whether salaries are earned, and, ultimately, whether any income return can be so characterized.

Profits are paid to the owners of the means of production, and one might note again the importance of the above distinction in the conflict that may appear between decisions to enlarge nonproductive staff and to funnel profits to additions to plant and equipment and in turn that this may be inconsistent with the aims of labor. Profits in this scheme are paid to owners because they have an institutional or legal claim to a share of total output. In the simplest Cambridge model, developed in *IME*, only owners save,[8] and this is illustrated in the diagram. Profits received are consumed, P^e, or saved, P^s. Consumed profits are funneled back to industry in the form of an accumulation of ownership or property rights in the means of production. Savings accumulate in the financial sector and are used by industry for investment expenditures.

The simple flow of output and income is thus complete, and the national income accounting identities shown at the bottom of the diagram, though different from Marxian analysis, are analogous to those that emerge from traditional circular-flow diagrams; their interpretation and implications, however, are radically different.

Contrasting and comparing the two circular flows, the Cambridge and the usual neoclassical, emphasizes their divergent starting points—the description of fact, on the one hand, via the above scheme, and on the other, the highly imaginative and notional figure of neoclassic economic man and assumptions which tend to be the direct opposite of fact.

III

The formal points of analysis that support the conceptual ideas of the Cambridge circular flow correspond to reasonable descriptions of phases in the technical and societal development of Western capitalism.[9] In this context emphasis is given to the evolution of the techniques of production and the social division of the net product amongst the claimants to it. The story is an old one to economic historians in illustrating the accumulation of power in the hands of property owners and ultimately property managers and provides the historical and intellectual link to modern post-Keynesian theories of distribution in which the wage share is viewed as a residual.

The particular economy evolves from the most simple, nonmarket, agrarian organization in which property is vested in the individual producing and consuming unit to an economy of modern, complex, industrial characteristics. In the former, with no technical change, techniques of production are simple, and corn is both an output and an input. With land free and abundant and equally fertile,

plots are taken up in an amount optimal in size for the amount of work to be provided so that output per person is everywhere a maximum. Growth of population brings land scarcity and falling average and marginal product as a state of diminishing returns sets in. Although maximum average output is optimal under one set of conditions, an alternative extreme level can be established by assuming a Malthusian adjustment mechanism affecting population levels. This is hardly noted in *IME*; the emphasis is upon maximum output per person under given techniques, and movements from this conceptual point, as social relations in production change.

In stage 2, under a landlord-peasant social class system, the optimum position contrasts with the two possible extremes of stage 1. In comparison with maximum output per person, a landlord system pushes the intensity of cultivation towards maximum output per acre; for the other extreme, population contraction is suggested in order to allow a return to the landlord. It is rare to find a discussion of this sort in traditional texts even though the analysis corresponds to the facts of the early economic history of northwest Europe and to the central problem of underdeveloped economies today. *IME* specifically emphasizes the fundamental problem of obtaining a surplus in agriculture production over the needs of the population and the use that is made of that surplus; and generally, to the point that social relations in production dictate population levels, here through the intensity of cultivation, it stresses the pressure of legal rights, from mere ownership of the land to a share in output independent of productive contribution. Orthodox texts, it appears, slough off the conflict questions that surround the social division of surplus product; these are surely the main questions.

Capitalist farmers, introduced in the third slice through historical time, allow somewhat more freedom for neoclassical "neatly calculated less or more" and in an appropriate framework. Property-less workers are hired to work the land, which is rented by a capitalist farmer; land differs in quality, and there is a current margin of cultivation. The historically given wage rate and the capital accumulated in the wage fund determine the intensity of cultivation. With given techniques the employed labor force implies the average and marginal products of labor. If it is assumed that output is to be maximized, then labor forces should be allocated over the land in order to equalize the marginal product (MP_L) to be derived from each. The contrast with orthodox treatments is clear in defining the demand for labor not as the marginal product curve but as the capital accumulated in the wage fund from past surpluses and in the subsequent division of the surplus over the wage bill between rent and profit. Various contractual relationships may be specified; if, for example, it is assumed that the wage fund is adequate enough to allow equating MP_L and the wage per person, w_O, so that the maximum surplus is possible, the rental contract can in fact determine the maximum net profit position to be a different intensity of cultivation than that which maximizes surplus. Not to belabor the obvious, social relations in production influence the production of output apart from assumed behavioral rules of orthodoxy. The framework set up by *IME* explicitly recognizes institutional contractual relations.

In examining the question of surplus division as Ricardian rent theory, though, the departure from orthodox texts is even more marked. In traditional

texts capitalist farmers are not treated, and the wage fund is everywhere sufficient to allow $MP_L = w_o$, and there is a rising supply curve of labor at that wage; the surplus over the wage bill is therefore rent and is a return to the landlord as a result of the productivity of that which he owns, or so students are led to believe. In *IME* with capitalist farmers and landlords the wage per person and profit per person are payments from the marginal product of labor, and rent takes up the difference between the average product on the type of land considered and the marginal product on the marginal piece of land. Demonstration of this involves the assumptions that land is taken up in optimal amount for the work that is to be applied to it, so that on marginal land marginal and average products of labor are identical; and that marginal land is so abundant that in the limit no rent is chargeable on it. The argument is contained in Diagram 2. Plots of land differ only in average fertility; the intensity of cultivation has been controlled so that

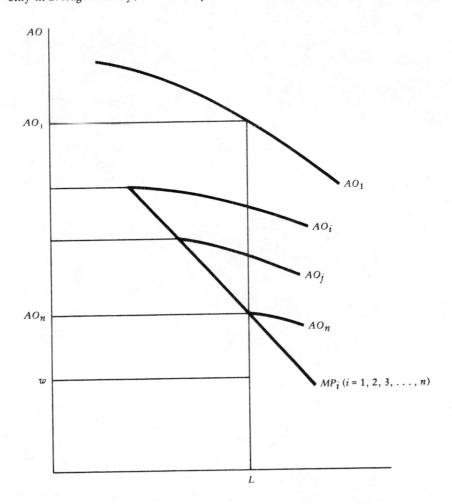

Diagram 2.

on each plot of land an equality of marginal products has been obtained at a specific intensity of cultivation. The intensive margin has been controlled, but on no plot of land is the marginal product of labor equal to the wage. Given the wage funds, at w_o per person, L units of labor are applied to each plot of land. On type n land, rent is zero; net output is $AO_n \cdot L$; profits, $AO_n \cdot L - w_o L$; and profits per person, $AO_n - w_o$. But because the marginal product and average product are everywhere equal on marginal land, both the wage per person and profit per person are returns paid from the marginal product of labor. The return to capital is a surplus over the wage bill determined not by the marginal productivity of capital but simply because land is scarce! Because of competition for the use of better land, this profit prevails on each type of land of higher fertility; surplus per person on better land is $(AO_i - w_o; i = 1, 2, 3, \ldots n)$; and of this, rent is $(AO_i - w_o) - (AO_n - w_o)$ or $(AO_i - AO_n)$ or $(AO_i - MP_n)$. Thus, in this rough way, rent is the gap between the marginal product curve on the least fertile land and the average product curve on the more fertile land considered. Profits appear as a residual component of surplus due to land scarcity; the return to the landlord is a return from the property he owns that varies not because *it* becomes more or less productive as the intensity of cultivation changes but because as the margin of cultivation expands, with population growth and the accumulation of capital, this squeezes profits per person against constant wages per person and increasing rents per person.

Another difference between *IME* and orthodox texts is that the latter attempt to expand and twist the marginal notions of Ricardo with respect to land to cover all factors so that the return to each factor contributing to production is equal to its marginal product. In fact the orthodox argument must be contrived in terms of continuous variability of each factor equivalent to variation in land/labor ratios as accomplished above. In a world with known techniques involving fixed capital equipment, multiple commodity inputs, and labor, such variation is impossible. Thus it is more realistic to start, as in *IME*, with known stocks of property, specify the level of utilization, which will have to be at given rates or prices in terms of inputs, and then analyze the resulting distribution of the net product. In Ricardo's setting, land, labor, and capital returns are scarcity returns, productive contributions of the specific property income classes are not of essential concern; that land, labor, and capital combine to jointly produce physical product is a trivial fact. The real point that emerges from *IME* is a distinction between income from work and from property ownership as institutional or contractual relationships. Ownership could obviously be altered without changing total product; the division of total product could be altered by respecifying contractual agreements. This emphasizes, in contrast to orthodox texts, that the only justification for a given distribution is prevailing legal conventions; conventions in the main protective of the interests of property. In the orthodox story the importance of property rights as legal claims is absent, though ownership is implied by property use and exchange. Indeed, in a neoclassical corn model, the power of the two classes must be in balance for nonexploitation to occur. Thus the argument requires an assumption of perfect inter- and intra-group competition; an assumption that is both counterfactual and deceiving. The tack that is suggested by *IME* requires none of this, and on balance the neoclassical view is inapplicable and fortunately unnecessary;

marginal productivity concepts as rewards can be dispensed with, unless, of course, one takes an ideological position on the matter or holds religiously a belief in the rightness of market pronouncements in the face of known inequalities in the exercise of economic power in every sphere.

In expanding the analysis to cover a two-sector economy, the Ricardian analysis can be expanded. As pointed out by Kaldor (1955-56) and *IME* (p. 188), Ricardo's argument amounts to a macro model of distribution in agriculture and in industry. Assuming a closed economy, no produced commodity inputs, and with corn as only a wage good; then from Diagram 2, if AO_i is *now* interpreted as the average product curve in all agricultural production, if MP_L is extended to the corresponding marginal curve, and $L_N = L_A$ is total labor employed in agriculture, then the wage bill in agriculture is $W_A = w_o \cdot L_A$; the national wage bill is $W_N = AO_i \cdot L_A$ and the wage bill in industry is $W_m = W_N - W_A = (AO_i - w_o) \cdot L_A$. In input-output format the Ricardian argument can be summarized in Table 1.

Table 1

	Agriculture	Industry
Agriculture	$x_{11} = $ seed	$x_{12} = 0$
Industry	$x_{21} = 0$	$x_{22} = ?$
Wages	$w_o \cdot L_A = W_A$	$(AO_i - w_o) \cdot L_A$
Profits	$(MP_L - w_o) \cdot L_A$	P_m
Rents	$(AO_i - MP_L) \cdot L_A$	R_m
Net Product	$AO_i \cdot L_A$	$AP_m \cdot L_m$
Gross Product	$AO_i \cdot L_A + x_{11}$	$AP_m \cdot L_m + x_{22}$
		$L_m = \dfrac{AO_i L_A - w_o L_A}{w_o}$

In this form the Ricardian analysis provides an intellectual link to the two-sector model developed in *IME*, in which a more Marxian approach is taken in the elimination of diminishing returns. This forces rent into the background as simply a component of profits-surplus and allows a *rentier* return to be controlled as a distributive share by capitalists.

The two-sector model is designed to illustrate problems of effective demand; the central feature of this is a detailed examination of the sectoral consequences of capitalists' decisions to invest in the face of uncertainty and a multiplier-accelerator model. The basic model also leads to a discussion of some aspects of technological change in terms of repercussions on employment, of rising real wages in mitigating the tendency for technological unemployment, and the inherent instability of capitalist economies.

In contrast to orthodox authors, Robinson and Eatwell are pointedly reluctant to specify the basic model in equation form or indeed to use graphical illustration. This is to remove any suggestion of stable behavioral relationships and equilibrium in a time flow of production in which capacity utilization is quickly alterable. The emphasis in *IME* is upon singling out aspects of an economy evolving through time, throwing out facts that provide in *themselves* (as opposed to a priori behavioral relationships) a descriptive understanding of the operation of capitalist economies. As the economy evolves, tossing up new facts, our understanding of it changes accordingly. With these acknowledgments to the intent of *IME*, as a start at what may be called "disequilibrium" analysis, the essential relationships are set out below and summarized in Diagram 3.

Basic IME Two-Sector Model: National Accounts

1) $Y = C + I$
2) $Y = W + P$
3) $W/Y = k$ 3a) $P/Y = (1 - k)$
4) $P^e/P = e$ 4a) $P^e = e(1 - k)Y$
5) $P^S/P = 1 - e$ 5a) $P^S = (1 - e)(1 - k)Y$
           5b) $P^S/Y = (1 - e)(1 - k) = s$

6) $C = W + P^e$
     $= kY + e(1 - k)Y$
     $= [k + e(1 - k)]Y$
7) $I = I_a$ 7a) $P^S_C = $ Bills
8) $Y = [1/1 - k + e(1 - k)] \cdot I_a$ 8a) $Y = (1/s) \cdot I_a$

In terms of techniques, output per person in both the corn, C, and machine, I, sectors is unity—in Diagram 3b this corresponds to $Y/E = 1$; labor and capital combine uniquely so that the employment of a machine requires the employment of one person; machines last forever, and once installed in a particular use they cannot be switched to the alternative sector nor are they alterable in form. The output of machines is valued in terms of corn and can be referred to as corn units worth of machines. The social relations in production involve as data a wage share k, in output, that, because of the techniques assumed, is equal to the wage rate; the corresponding rate and share of profit is $(1 - k)$. The Marxian "rate of exploitation" is built explicitly into this model; because k and $(1 - k)$ are known, the rate of exploitation can be expressed as $(1 - k)/k$ and, as an operative relationship of the model, represents a markup on prime costs of production, establishing the value division of output between wages and profits. Specifically the value division can be represented as:

$$C = W_c + [(1 - k)/k] \cdot W_c$$
$$C = W_c + (P_c/W_c) \cdot W_c$$
$$C = W_c + P_c$$

where W_c represents the wage bill in corn, P_c, profits in corn; and C, the total of corn output produced. The markup $(1 - k)/k$ defines a level of profits consistent

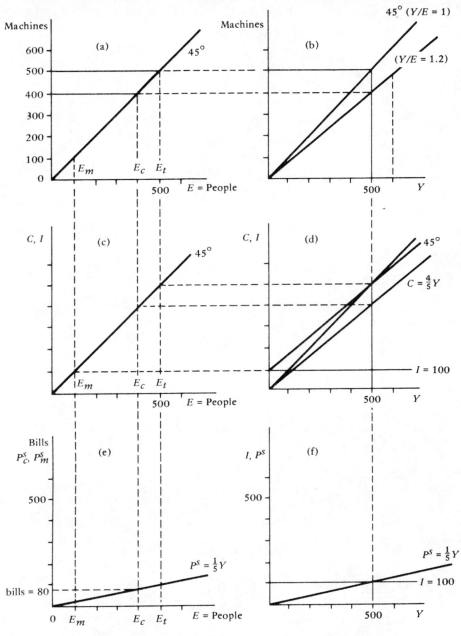

DATA: $k = 0.6$; $e = 0.5$; $I_a = 100$; P_c^S = Bills = profits saved in the corn sector.

Diagram 3.

with the observed shares in output. It is assumed that workers consume all of their wages in corn, while from profits a distributive share, in corn, provides for maintenance of the *rentier* class; P^e/P is the share of profits observed to be allowed *rentiers*, and P^S/P represents the proportion of savings from corn profits. The share of profits saved in total output is $(P^S/P)(P/Y) = s$. The comments made earlier that pertain to corn apply in context to shares in machine sector output.

In amalgamating the technical aspects with the social relations of production, the focus of power in this model is in the capitalists' decisions to invest and specifically to generate, as is appropriate in their terms, contractions and expansions in output and employment consistent with the necessity to obtain a fund of savings or finance capital to allow accomplishment of investment goals. Thus from whatever historical processes have determined k and e, the share of profits saved in total output is s. Given an investment decision requiring finance, $P^S = I$, then the output and employment level required is $Y = (1/s) \cdot I_a$. Alterable social relations in production and the animal spirits of capitalists unambiguously determine output and employment. This is the first main implication of the model to be stressed; as Keynesian analysis, "the key to the level of employment (and the utilization of the stock of machines) lies in the orders for new machines to be produced for the corn sector, which in turn, stimulate the production of machine sector machines. The determining factor is the decisions that govern the volume of investment" (*IME*, p. 107); thus in

$$\Delta I_a \rightarrow (1/s) \cdot \Delta I_a = \Delta Y$$

$(1/s)$ is an unqualified output and employment multiplier in contrast to the expenditure multiplier of orthodox texts. As Robinsonian analysis, the model demonstrates that the level of investment driving the system generates savings: "investment is causing savings to be made" (*IME*, p. 107).

$$\Delta I_a \rightarrow \Delta Y \rightarrow \Delta P^S = \Delta I_a$$

The rate of accumulation depends on the decisions of firms and not on the savings of households. This stresses the most obvious difference between *IME* and orthodox models: that consumption demand and workers' willingness to work have no independent influence in this model. In orthodox models it is households that consume and save and firms that produce and invest; this has the effect of unrealistically equalizing power through the apparent independence of savings and investment decisions and of leaving undistinguished income from property and work and the ultimate concentration of power that this allows. *IME* moves in the opposite direction and in consequence is of more relevance to understanding the operation of capitalist economies; households of workers and *rentiers* have no power, not even with respect to consumption demand. Capitalist decisions decide I and e and system instability.

As Kaleckian analysis, with consumption, savings, and investment rooted in the distribution of income, the analysis demonstrates that "workers spend what they get, and capitalists get what they spend" (*IME*, p. 109). Although in terms of profits this amounts to saying no more than that what capitalists get

is the sum of their expenditures on machines and their outpayments to *rentiers*, it more importantly focuses upon analyzing the consequences of alteration of *e*; this examination is analogous to orthodox paradox of thrift discussions of traditional texts, but *IME* places the onus of responsibility for instability in capitalist economies with capitalists rather than with autonomous household decisions to save. If the share of profits going to *rentiers* rises, output and employment rise because capitalists must now produce more to generate the level of savings required to finance investment.

At the root of the orthodox model are marginal productivity notions in explanation of individual income returns and the operation of supply and demand in competitive markets. Utility maximization assumptions lie behind consumer decisions to purchase and save. On the side of technique orthodoxy and *IME* are similarly at odds in that the former involves substitutability of factors and indeed a capital stock that can be altered in form to allow employment at marginal product wages and to guarantee full-employment equilibrium for those willing to work. In contrast techniques are fixed and unchanging in *IME*'s basic model, and the question of effective demand is addressed as a matter in which employment of any degree is dependent upon the decisions of capitalists with respect to the utilization of existing machines.

The two sectors of *IME*'s model are tied together by technical relations in corn, by the biological requirements of workers in terms of regular payment of wages, and by the distributive requirements of the economy in terms of a share of profits for *rentiers*. Taken together it is imperative that a form of credit be available to machine sector capitalists in order to allow these payments; also, because corn is perishable, corn sector capitalists link into this credit line as a means of holding wealth accumulating as P_C^S. In *IME* credit takes the form of real bills expressed in terms of corn. This, too, contrasts with orthodox texts: *IME* starts with the fundamental question of credit and the need for a form of money directly within the technical and social relations of production; in orthodox texts this link between savings, investment, and production as continuous flows through time is left, at best, to inference.

What might be called the micro theory of *IME* is mainly contained in the chapter titled, "Commodities and Prices," but the ideas are tied consistently to the aggregative model already presented. *IME* attempts a marked replacement of conventional micro market demand and supply, cast in terms of timeless Walrasian general equilibrium, with a more relevant post-Keynesian framework. The world of commodity relations and relative prices is characterized by inherent conflict between buyers and sellers within and among competitive and concentrated industries. The discussion relates to the ideas expressed by Myrdal (1957), Kaldor (1970), and others, which generally emphasize the cumulative disadvantages under which market forces place primary producing economies relative to economies producing industrial commodities. Although tools of supply and demand, of price and income elasticities, are central, when cast in a world of uncertainty and changing expectations they contrast with the usual treatment.

Briefly, the agents of *IME* are spatially separated producers and consumers and a dealer who accumulates and disposes of stocks. Immediately, then, there is a contrast with traditional texts in a more real-world concept of market and in explicitly recognizing that even in highly competitive markets some degree of

control over price may be present as a result of spatial separation. In competitive markets conditions of demand represent possible dealer sales levels; given conditions of supply, possible levels of dealer purchase from suppliers. Differences between these two levels are not taken to imply equilibrating adjustments in terms of prices and outputs; rather they simply illustrate what must be happening in terms of dealer stocks—either building up or running down. Alterations in supply and demand conditions result in price and inventory adjustments. To emphasize, though, the neoclassical notion of equilibrium prices and quantities disappears in this story; evolution may result only in a temporary "balance" in the sense that dealer stocks turn over at one level, but this is regarded as a rare happening as market conditions are constantly changing. *IME* forces explicit attention to production over time based on historical, partial information, which changes as the economy moves through time. Regarding equilibrating processes of excess demand and supply situations as inadmissible is a sharp departure from conventional texts; they implicitly eliminate history and explicitly argue as if events take place at a logical instant of time. The equilibrium argument ignores the possibility, relevant in all real world situations, that the events described may themselves alter the position towards which the phenomena under investigation are moving. *IME* succeeds in replacing conventional argument with a framework that allows description of real-world events, and it removes the equilibrium framework as a base necessary for micro-analysis.

In the treatment of concentrated industries, too, *IME* offers an alternative to conventional texts; the chief ideas involved are the Kaleckian "degree of monopoly" and the concepts of markups or gross margins. These ideas are illustrated in what may be referred to as a Chamberlain context of the survival and growth decisions of oligopolistic firms. Again marginalism, maximization, and equilibrium processes appear as special cases or rare happenings tossed up in this broader framework. In *IME* the argument runs in terms of normal conditions of excess capacity in given conditions of demand, a normal level of output for which associated prime costs may be estimated. To unit prime costs, a markup or gross margin is added to establish price. The size of the markup is related to the degree of monopoly in final product markets and to the costs of investment per unit of capacity in producing industries. Briefly, then, in the absence of full information on cost curves and revenue relationships—ingredients that are present by implication or by assumption in the orthodox story—a price is set to cover costs and to provide a return considered appropriate in the context of a particular industry; the adjustment process to unrealized expectations with respect to sales volume results not in variation in price but in stocks or inventories with ultimate consequences on output levels and employment. The link to the basic more aggregative model and variations in the degree of capacity utilization as the fundamental determinant of instability in capitalist economies is clear. The model also builds in an explicit explanation for the continuous impetus given in capitalist economies to the creation of monopolies. Specifically, with significant uncertainty about the future, and faced with a situation in which profits per unit vary with the level of plant utilization, the built-in inducements with respect to product differentiation, mergers, acquisitions, and the like, contrasts with the more usual treatment of orthodox texts, in which these topics are discussed as "aberrant appendages" to the main argument and to the overriding

concern with perfectly competitive industries, which conform to the assumptions the orthodox authors found necessary to make in order to be consistent with a predetermined argument.

The micro cost relationships dealt with in the above discussion move *IME* a further step towards dealing explicitly with produced commodity inputs. This relates directly to the format presented as an input-output table in Diagram 1. In fact the analysis stems from the total systems framework developed by Piero Sraffa (1960), within which theories of the rate of profit and of distribution may be fitted. A similar development of this fundamental contribution to the understanding of the mechanism of price formation and valuation and associated distributional questions is not to be found in conventional texts. Consequently it is dealt with here in somewhat more detail than other topics.

The specific new focus of attention is upon introducing the technological linkages that exist as facts between industries in terms of production and the use of produced commodity inputs, the pricing of commodity inputs and outputs, and the distribution of net output of the economy among the claimants to it. The introduction of produced commodity inputs is illustrated using a simple example, but it is worth emphasizing that the conclusions that are derived in the simple model are correct in form, and lack only the detail, of more complicated systems. The economy considered moves through time producing given and unchanging levels of output in each of three industries using prescribed and unvarying stocks of commodity inputs in conjunction with labor. Fixed stocks of capital are ignored, at least in this model, and no growth or net investment is allowed. The stocks of commodity inputs are used up during each production period but reappear at the end of each; as well, industry produces a net product, in real terms, of bread, which is available for distribution to workers as wages and to capitalists as profits. This net product is entirely consumed during the ensuing production period.

In ex-post terms the fundamental ideas involved for each commodity producing sector are expressed in terms of money costs and revenues and their components:

$$TR_{oj} = TC_{oj} + \pi_{oj}$$

in which:

$$TR_{oj} = P_j Q_{oj}$$
$$TC_{oj} = w_{oj} N_{oj} + \Sigma P_i f_{ij} \qquad i = 1 \ldots n$$
$$\pi_{oj} = TR_{oj} - TC_{oj}$$

TR_{oj}, TC_{oj}, and π_{oj} represent the total revenues, costs, and profits, respectively, of the jth industry; Q_{oj}, N_{oj}, and f_{ij}, $i = 1 \ldots n$, represent the physical quantities of output, labor, and produced commodity inputs used in the jth industry; and w_{oj} and P_i represent the wage rate per person in the jth industry and the commodity price of ith industry output, some part of which is used in the production of jth industry output.

The critical feature is the nature of profits; *IME*, without philosophical examination of the explanations of the existence of profits as a surplus over the

wage bill, expresses profits as a factual return on the value of investment in produced commodity inputs; thus:

$$r_{oj}\% = \frac{TR_{oj} - TC_{oj}}{\Sigma P_i f_{ij}} \cdot 100$$

Defining $N_{oj}/Q_{oj} = a_{oj}$ and $f_{ij}/Q_{oj} = a_{ij}$ as representing labor and commodity input requirements per unit of output used in the given state of technique, then

$$P_j = w_{oj} a_{oj} + \Sigma P_i a_{ij} + \Sigma P_i a_{ij}(r_{oj})$$

or $$P_j = w_{oj} a_{oj} + \Sigma P_i a_{ij}(1 + r)$$

As a system this last equation embodies, if it is assumed that the wage and the rate of profit rate is constant in all industries, n equations in $n + 2$ unknowns. Table 2 presents hypothetical data for the three-industry or commodity sector economy. I is iron, S is steel, and B is bread. Bread is a consumption good only, and iron and steel are produced commodity inputs. If it is assumed, for example, that the wage rate is a fixed amount, say $10.00 per person to be consistent with the numbers in the text, and prices are to be computed for successive rates of profit, say 0, 25, 50, and 100 percent, several interesting points emerge. First, with respect to the post-Keynesian theory of distribution with given techniques and a wage rate, however prescribed, the rate of profit assumed "values" the outputs and inputs used and produces a net product. If K represents the value of the stock of capital, Y, the value of net product, and π the level of profits, which in an accounting sense appears as a residual, it is now clear that the share of profits in net output is unambiguously

$$\pi/Y = (K/Y)(\pi/K)$$

Specifically, the capital/output ratio and the assumed rate of profit determine the share of profits in net output; but the value of the stock of capital depends on the rate of profit and is now shown to be intimately related to the net product distribution between wages and profits. From this point of view the wage share may be viewed as a residual:

$$1 - (\pi/Y) = W/Y$$

The second and related point that emerges from this analysis is a reemphasis of the power of property and the control over the valuation of the means of production in a systems sense. This complements earlier analysis of effective demand and the discussion of relative price determination in the more micro-oriented examination of commodities and prices. The specific link is with the rate of profit in a form analogous to a markup on prime costs of production and stresses the control of prices to maintain the share of profits in net output. And in turn this emphasizes the relevance of the format as a framework within which to examine inflationary processes and their primary causes in cost changes of labor and commodity inputs.

Third, and related, it raises, in the necessity of assuming a specific wage

Table 2. A Simple Scheme of Commodity Reproduction and Valuation

1 Physical units: Tons of output

	I	S	B	Q
I		4		4
S	1		3	4
B				100
People	12	32	10	
Q	4	4	100	

	I	S	B	Q
I	f_{11}	f_{12}	f_{13}	Q_1
S	f_{21}	f_{22}	f_{23}	Q_2
B	f_{31}	f_{32}	f_{33}	Q_3
People	N_{O1}	N_{O2}	N_{O3}	
Q	Q_{O1}	Q_{O2}	Q_{O3}	

2 Technology: Input Requirements per Unit of Output

	I	S	B
I		1.0	
S	.25		.03
B			
People	3.0	8.0	10
Q/Q	1.0	1.0	1.0

	I	S	B
I	a_{11}	a_{12}	a_{13}
S	a_{21}	a_{22}	a_{23}
B	a_{31}	a_{32}	a_{33}
People	a_{O1}	a_{O2}	a_{O3}
Q/Q	1.0	1.0	1.0

3 Unit Costs Formulation of Prices

	I	S	B
I		$1P_1$	
S	$.25P_2$		$.03P_2$
B			
Wages	$3w$	$8w$	$.1w$
Profits	$.25P_2r$	$1P_1r$	$.03P_2r$
Price	P_1	P_2	P_3

	I	S	B
I	$a_{11}P_1$	$a_{12}P_1$	$a_{13}P_1$
S	$a_{21}P_2$	$a_{22}P_2$	$a_{23}P_2$
B	$a_{31}P_3$	$a_{32}P_3$	$a_{33}P_3$
Wages	$a_{O1}w$	$a_{O2}w$	$a_{O3}w$
Profits	$r(\Sigma a_{i1}P_i)$	$r(\Sigma a_{i2}P_i)$	$r(\Sigma a_{i3}P_i)$
Price	P_1	P_2	P_3

4 Total Formulation of Prices

	I	S	B
I		$4P_1$	
S	$1P_2$		$3P_2$
B			
Wages	$12w$	$32w$	$10w$
Profits	$1P_2r$	$4P_1r$	$3P_2r$
Price	$4P_1$	$4P_2$	$100P_3$

	I	S	B
I	$f_{11}P_1$	$f_{12}P_1$	$f_{13}P_1$
S	$f_{21}P_2$	$f_{22}P_2$	$f_{23}P_2$
B	$f_{31}P_3$	$f_{32}P_3$	$f_{33}P_3$
Wages	$N_{O1}w$	$N_{O2}w$	$N_{O3}w$
Profits	$r(f_{i1}P_i)$	$r(f_{i2}P_i)$	$r(f_{i3}P_i)$
Price	$Q_{O1}P_1$	$Q_{O2}P_2$	$Q_{O3}P_3$

rate and rate of profit, the question of the basic indeterminacy of capitalist economies and the associated instability with the implicit policy implication of direct controls on prices and wages and ultimately the direction of output and employment by means other than the animal spirits of capitalists.

Finally, the analysis provides a framework for criticizing orthodox theory. In this regard the analysis implies no substitution between inputs in production; the emphasis in *IME* is upon specific levels of output in a given state of technology. In this context there is simply no way by which the output produced can be attributed partly to produced commodity inputs and partly to labor inputs.

So, in contrast to orthodoxy, the concept of marginal productivity has no meaning. This is illustrated most dramatically in the rising shares of net output that are claimed by capital as the rate of profit is arbitrarily increased, with no associated changes taking place in the physical quantities of capital used or of output produced. In neoclassical jargon, each of these returns would be attributed to an objective measure of each factor's marginal contribution in production; capital and labor, so the ideological justification goes, receive what each has independently earned; there is an implicit moral justification for the status quo! It should now be clear that the neoclassical view should be regarded as nonsense—to quote a well-known "Keynesian" in this context, ". . . nonsense is nonsense no matter how prestigiously pronounced [from Cambridge, Mass.] so why take it seriously. . . ."[10]

Other topics of book II of *IME* extend the basic ideas to include a discussion of technological change, of government, of fiscal and monetary policy, of a more detailed analysis of finance than covered in the "bills" concept of the basic model, and of international trade and exchange rates. Detailed examination of these topics cannot be made here. Briefly, though, the examination of *IME* contrasts with the usual equilibrium theory. There is an open and honest attempt to analyze the roots of secular inflation; it is endemic, found ". . . in the mechanism of private enterprise market economy" (*IME*, p. 214). Just as there is no full-employment equilibrium, there is no equilibrium price level. The fundamental determinant of prices is money costs and particularly the level of money wages. In an open-economy context the analysis departs sharply from the equilibrium assumptions of the orthodox story; *IME* faces directly the problem of international competition, of persistent deficits and surpluses; there is no suggestion that the system adjusts in ways appropriate for each country. There is little play for effective monetary policy in *IME*: The money supply, realistically, is a response to the needs of trade; variations in interest rates, although subject to manipulation, provide little in the way of leverage on effective demand; supply prices individually and in the aggregate can be shifted independently of demand conditions; and in an open-economy context monetary instruments are even weaker.

CONCLUDING COMMENTS

The writer was asked to produce a survey of the ideas presented in *IME* in comparison with the treatment given in orthodox texts. In attempting to fulfill this charge, only a brief illustration of the main components of the Cambridge paradigm has been given. Much of the complexity of the argument, the variety and richness of detail and the many extensions of the main core of the analysis, have necessarily been omitted; the critique of neoclassical economics developed in the text has been touched upon. In fact it can be suggested that the power of Cambridge economics as a view of the operation of modern economies leads at an increasing rate to minor attention being given to the neoclassical model in teaching introductory economics; the teacher will be led inevitably to dispense with it as a framework for analysis, and it is proper then to consider its relegation to aspects of courses in doctrinal history.

IME has been used by the writer as the text in the introductory course at

the University of Waterloo for the past two years. Student reactions to the difficulty of the text are probably somewhat more pronounced than those registered with orthodox texts. But this diminishes as more experience is gained by the teacher in "rounding the corners"; this is done with appropriate supplements, specifically a greater use of numerical examples than provided in the text, graphical illustration, and algebraic formulation. Thus the difficulty is with the terse style in which the book is written; but this seems to be a "teaching device" purposely employed by the authors to force understanding by making it necessary to figure it out first hand.

There is no doubt that students realize there is a marked difference between classes using *IME* and those using a facsimile of the Samuelson text. The difference in approach, the direct confrontation of questions that link production and social class, makes *IME* more relevant in comparison to orthodoxy. The approach to analysis via the facts, reasonable simplifications, and a presentation of the meaning of existing facts within the mechanism of the operation of capitalist economies appears to be the key. Further, reaction seems to suggest that *IME* is more appropriate than orthodox texts in preparing students for dealing with practical research questions, and indeed specifically for employment. Most students taking introductory economics do not carry the subject matter any further. With this in mind *IME* is undoubtedly of greater relevance to them, in spite of its greater difficulty. Graduate teaching assistants attached to classes using *IME* who have dealt directly with students report on the enthusiasm and understanding of basic economic relationships that are learned. Indeed it has been suggested that the orthodox-trained graduate student would benefit greatly by sitting in on the undergraduate courses using this text.

There are, however, teaching devices that must be employed to make *IME* a more useable book than it is. These include using the circular-flow diagram outlined in this paper and a greater use of algebraic, graphic, and numerical illustration. Also, there is now a wealth of supplemental literature that links directly to the view of *IME*. In light of all this it is likely, assuming that economists become familiar with this alternative paradigm and that teachers want to fulfill part of their function as teachers by presenting alternative points of view, that in the next few years we will witness a differentiation of the Cambridge, England, text as equally successful but more relevant than the Cambridge, Massachusetts, text.

As a last word, it should be clear that the Cambridge *approach* to the study of economics cannot be wrong! In the writer's view it is free of doctrine and consequently provides a framework within which proponents of particular schools of thought will find it possible to compare and improve upon their respective intellectual positions. At the same time, as an approach and a viewpoint it does not pretend to offer complete explanation; the authors offer it as a new start, and they have presented the teacher of economics with a framework that will profoundly affect the discipline, the reader's view of the world, and the solutions the reader seeks to modern problems.

Cambridge economics is based upon a sound conception of the social and political system and the inherent conflicts existing within and between nations, its prime methodology being the observation of the facts of capitalist economies in terms of objective national income account measures and their manipulation

in well-defined terms, and upon the production linkages and social relations in production as given by the wage and profit components of value added national income. It is this that makes Cambridge economics sound in theory and in application and a common reference base with which intellectuals of different ideological persuasions may put their ideas to the test.

REFERENCES

Galbraith, J. K. *Economics and the Public Purpose.* London: Andre Deutsch Ltd., 1974.

Golden, S. "Harvard Economics Teaching Criticized." *New York Times,* February 1, 1975, p. 1.

Gurley, J. G. "Some Comments on the Principles Course." *The American Economic Review: Papers and Proceedings* 65 (1975), pp. 431-33.

Harcourt, G. C. *Some Cambridge Controversies in the Theory of Capital.* Cambridge: Cambridge University Press, 1972.

Harcourt, G. C., and Laing, N. F. *Capital and Growth: Selected Readings.* Harmondsworth, England: Penguin Books, 1971.

Hunt, E. K., and Schwartz, J. G. *A Critique of Economic Theory.* Harmondsworth, England: Penguin Books, 1972.

Kaldor, N. "Alternative Theories of Distribution." *Review of Economic Studies* 23 (1955-56), pp. 83-100.

—— "The Case for Regional Policies." *The Scottish Journal of Political Economy* 17 (1970), pp. 337-47.

Kregel, J. A. *Rate of Profit, Distribution and Growth: Two Views.* London: The Macmillan Press, 1971.

—— *The Reconstruction of Political Economy.* London: The Macmillan Press, 1973.

"Leontief, Nobel Economist, Will Join NYU Faculty." *Harvard Gazette,* January 31, 1975.

Levine, A. L. "This Age of Leontief . . . and Who? An Interpretation." *Journal of Economic Literature* 12 (1974), pp. 872-81.

Marglin, S. A. "Review: Economic Heresies: Some Old Fashioned Questions in Economic Theory." *The Economic Journal* 83 (1973), pp. 535-38.

Myrdal, G. *Economic Theory and Under-Developed Regions.* London: Duckworth, 1957.

—— *Against the Stream: Critical Essays on Economics.* London: The Macmillan Press, 1974.

Nell, E. J. "Property and the Means of Production: A Primer on the Cambridge Controversy." *The Review of Radical Political Economics* 4 (1972), pp. 1-27.

Nell, E. J., and Hollis, M. *Rational Economic Man: A Philosophical Critique of Neo-Classical Economics.* Cambridge: Cambridge University Press, 1975.

Pasinetti, L. "Rate of Profit and Income Distribution in Relation to the Rate of Economic Growth." *Review of Economic Studies* 29 (1962), pp. 267-79.

Robinson, J. "Teaching Economics," in *Collected Economic Papers,* vol. III, Oxford: Basil Blackwell, 1965.

—— *Economic Heresies: Some Old Fashioned Questions in Economic Theory.* New York: Basic Books, 1971.

Robinson, J., and Eatwell, J. *An Introduction to Modern Economics.* McGraw-Hill Book Co. (U.K.) Ltd., 1973.

Rymes, T. K. *On Concepts of Capital and Technical Change.* Cambridge: Cambridge University Press, 1971.

Samuelson, P. A. "Understanding the Marxian Notation of Exploitation: A Summary of the So-called Transformation Problem Between Marxian Values and Competitive Prices." *Journal of Economic Literature* 9 (1971), pp. 399-431.

Solow, R. "Cambridge and the Real World." *The Times Literary Supplement* (London), March 14, 1975.

Sraffa, P. *Production of Commodities by Means of Commodities: Prelude to a Critique of Economic Theory.* Cambridge: Cambridge University Press, 1960.

Ward, B. *What's Wrong With Economics?* London: The Macmillan Press, 1972.

Wiles, P. "Cost Inflation and the State of Economic Theory." *The Economic Journal* 83 (1973), pp. 377-98.

NOTES

1. But reference may be made to other expositors of the Cambridge view, such as Hunt and Schwartz (1972), Kregel (1971, 1973), Nell (1972), and recently Hollis and Nell (1975).

2. In his book Rymes (1971) is quite explicit in describing a new economics emerging at Cambridge.

3. S. A. Marglin's review (1973) of Robinson (1971) ends with, "my generation of heretics owes her a debt of gratitude, not only for keeping the critical spirit alive but also for keeping the vision of an alternative before us."

4. Much of the literature is contained in Harcourt (1972) and Harcourt and Laing (1971).

5. See, for example, Gurley (1975) in support of this point.

6. Diagram 1 presented here is a modified version of the circular flow presented by Professor Nell in several publications (for example, see Nell, 1972, and Nell and Hollis, 1975); the modifications made here represent explicit treatment of the swirl of interindustry relations in the input-output table in order to link more directly with the Sraffa system discussed later in this paper.

7. Quoted in Levine (1974) from Samuelson (1971).

8. Kaldor (1955-56), Pasinetti (1962), and Kregel (1971, chap. 10) may be referred to for some analysis of the introduction of savings by workers into Cambridge models.

9. Book II contains eleven chapters. The core ideas of the Cambridge paradigm, dealt with in this paper, are found in chapters 1, 2, 3, 5, and 6; these are titled, respectively, "Land and Labour," "Men and Machines," "Effective Demand," "Commodities and Prices," and "Rates of Profit." Space does not permit examination of extension of the basic ideas to the more general topics contained in other chapters.

10. From H. G. Johnson, "Cambridge in the 1950's," *Encounter* 42 (1974), p. 38.

16

The Fall of Bastard Keynesianism and the Rise of Legitimate Keynesianism

JOHN H. HOTSON

Professor of Economics at University of Waterloo, Ontario, Canada.

INTRODUCTION

> No man can serve two masters. He is bound to hate one and love the other, or support one and despise the other.[1]

> The stone which the builders rejected has become the head of the corner.[2]

I hope to demonstrate that American textbook "neoclassical synthetic" Keynesianism is an illegitimate attempt to serve both Walras and Keynes—to hold with Walras that the economy is self-regulating and can "settle down" *only* at full employment, *and* to hold with Keynes that it can "settle down" anywhere. Further I hope to show that in attempting to serve two masters the originator of the "neoclassical synthesis" argument has clearly supported Walras over Keynes, while real-world economics must reject Walras' model of timeless equilibrium and instead take as its starting point Keynes' *General Theory*—the "stone which the builders rejected." I focus particularly upon the contrast between the "Bastard Keynesian" theory of inflation and Keynes' own theory of the price level. Finally, I sketch a "more general" theory of inflation on a Keynesian base.

THE CONCEPTION, BIRTH, AND DEATH OF BASTARD KEYNESIANISM

It is, perhaps, the fate of all profound insights to be debased and vulgarized as they are popularized sufficiently to become policy. This was especially the fate of Keynes, whose epoch-making *The General Theory of Employment, Interest, and Money* quickly attained the status of a classic—a book that everybody thinks they know about and that nobody reads. So far has the process of vulgarization gone that Joan Robinson dismisses the entire American "Keynesian" school—from the simplest version offered the college freshman in Nobel Laureate Paul A. Samuelson's textbook through the most sophisticated mathematical or econometric versions—with the spleed-did term *Bastard Keynesianism*.[3]

What are the hallmarks—the bar sinister—of Bastard Keynesianism that distinguish it from the legitimate article? I see them as including the following:

An earlier version of this paper was given at the Second Annual Convention of the Eastern Economics Association, April 16, 1976.

(1) At the level of "pure" theory, a willingness to concede that Say's Law, or Walras' Law, is "really" correct, or would be if it were not for "frictions," such as sticky wages and interest rates, from "money illusion" or other "irrationalities." This is to make the general theory merely a "special case" of the classical theory—thereby neatly exchanging the doughnut and the hole. Keynes' is a theory of life in the real world of irreversible calendar time, not one of timeless equilibrium. (2) At the level of policy, Bastard Keynesianism has been perverted into a technique for *causing* unemployment by "deflating" "excess" demand. Whether the argument for so doing is that of the "Phillips curve" or the "natural rate" of unemployment, it is a bitter irony, and a bastardization of Keynes, that we have exchanged the classical business cycle for a "policy cycle" of administered semiboom and semidepression.[4] (3) Particularly in the United States, "Keynesian" policy has been perverted into "military Keynesianism"—the maintenance of high levels of income and employment by armaments spending, CIA subversion, and "brushfire" wars. This development was, perhaps, inevitable given U.S. foreign policy imperatives. However, the Bastard Keynesian model—with its sole regard for the short-run effects of policy upon demand, its neglect of the short- and long-run supply effects of various government policies, and its lack of concern with what output is for—was particularly vulnerable to this corruption. (4) An ignoring, forgetting, or jettisoning of Keynes' more disturbing and "radical" ideas, such as "true uncertainty"; his concern with the top-heavy income distribution in a capitalistic society as the root cause of social injustice, inadequate demand, and maldistribution of resources; his call for "euthanasia of the *rentier*" via low interest rates and for partial socialization of investment. (5) Ignoring Keynes' entire analysis of aggregate supply and his wage cost theory of the price level in order to preach either an "excess demand" theory of inflation (early Samuelsonians), "Phillips curve" trade-off (later Samuelsonians), or a refurbished quantity theory (Friedmanians). These analyses restore the "classical dichotomy" between the "real" and "monetary" aspects of the economy, and between "micro" and "macro" analysis, whose elimination was one of Keynes' chief purposes.[5] It is on this last aspect of Keynes and "bad," "45°," "$IS = LM$" or "Bastard" Keynesianism that I wish especially to focus. For Keynes rejected the classical dichotomy with stinging words regarding the opposite "side of the moon" and "waking and dreaming lives,"[6] and set forth a theory of the price level that was in "close contact with the theory of value."[7] But why did economists adopt, in large part, Keynes' theory of aggregate demand, income, and employment, but neglect and even forget his theory of aggregate supply, distribution, money, and the price level and his focus upon uncertain expectations?

Space will not permit an attempt at a full answer to this question, but the following points seem most relevant.[8] Bastard Keynesianism has been useful in popularizing the basic lesson that major depressions such as that of the 1930s will not recur if proper demand-creating fiscal and monetary policy moves are made. Once the profession was converted to this new aggregate demand analysis, a great problem of salesmanship remained. The public had to be educated to the "heretical" idea that in a depressed economy easy money and deficit finance were conservative, prudent, responsible, and wise public policies, rather than the work of the great red devil. How much harder it would have been if his disciples

conceded that the expansionary medicine would be somewhat inflationary (as Keynes did).[9] Because conservatives were bound to hammer endlessly on the theme that deficit finance would cause runaway inflation, a flat denial—"this isn't going to hurt a bit"—was a better bedside manner to adopt than a completely truthful approach—"why do the *Readers Digests* work for it?"

Second, the profession was able to convince itself quite early that the law of diminishing returns, so central to Keynes' macro analysis as to neoclassical micro analysis, was of no practical importance at the macro level.[10] Further, Keynes' analysis, whether short run or long run, pointed directly to labor and, by implication, the labor union, as the chief "culprit" in secular inflation,[11] a conclusion many of his disciples wished to avoid to maintain their "liberal" *bona fides*.

But more is involved here than mere necessary simplification and the "white lies" of salesmanship. Although Hicks, Hansen, Samuelson, Patinkin, and others were quick to make *pieces* of Keynes' analysis their own, at a deeper level his vision was wholly alien and repugnant to them. The mutation from the economics of Keynes through the Keynesian counterrevolution to Bastard Keynesianism is the result of economists' attempts to behave as "normal scientists" and stuff Keynes back into the neoclassical paradigm.

It is central to Keynes' argument that there is no Say's Law to guarantee that either the short- or the long-run equilibrium of the economy be at full employment because investment decisions depend upon the state of long-run profit expectations relative to the rate of interest, which itself largely also depends upon long-run expectations. But upon what do these expectations depend? As Shackle puts it, to find Keynes' answer stated with

> . . . full uncompromising explicitness, we have to look in a part of the canon which few economists seem able to endure the sight of it. . . . It appeared in the *Quarterly Journal of Economics* for February 1937, and it declares unequivocally that expectations do not rest on anything solid, determinable, demonstrable. "We simply do not know."[12]

Keynes envisioned the economy as an underdetermined system. The human condition is not one in which "complete information" of the past or present, still less the future, can ever be obtained. Instead lack of knowledge totally dominates human affairs. There are not as many "equations" as there are "unknowns." Long-run expectation is a "wild card," exogenously given and subject to violent shifts as new information and rumor is dealt us by history's unfolding, to feed our hopes and fears. The rate of change of money wages also depends largely on expectations and, therefore, does not depend in any solid, determinable, demonstrable way on short-run market phenomena or a simple lag structure from the past, thus frustrating all attempts to find an invariant Phillips curve. The rate of interest does *not* tend to a "natural" rate that will equate saving and investment at full employment. This view is wholly alien to economic scholars "trained to treat economics as a geometry in the old sense, a complete and self-sufficient axiom-system for generating as many propositions as required."[13]

Thus Bastard Keynesian, monetarist, Walrasian general equilibrium

analysis, and *all determined* models that we can create are alien to Keynes' own vision of our situation.

> All are concerned with a model of economic society, an economic world, where knowledge of circumstance is (miraculously, impossibly, unexplainedly) *sufficient*. Keynes in many places exploited a superlative mastery of language to repudiate such a model, such an invented world, as totally alien to our real predicament. We are not omniscient, assured masters of known circumstance via reason, but the prisoners of time.[14]

But Keynes' is not a counsel of despair. The very fact that the economic system is underdetermined is what gives economic policies; monetary, fiscal, incomes, foreign trade, and international agreements—scope to move us toward desired outcomes that the market system is incapable of achieving by the interplay of blind forces and individual decisions.

In kicking their Say's Law props out from under them, Keynes invited his fellow economists to join him in facing and mastering the real world with its "horrid void of indeterminacy and irrationality."[15] Instead most economists sought to regain their mental equilibrium by a retreat into determinate systems. Say's Law is dead? Long live Say's Law! Not that anyone cared to reassert Say's Law boldly—that way lies rejection as a "classical" fuddydud.

What to do? It was Samuelson who found the answer: Substitute Walras' Law for Say's Law and go on as if nothing (essential) has happened. Thus Samuelson's "neoclassical synthesis" was born as a dash of Keynes in the Walras soup. R_x: whenever Walras' Law—that in equilibrium the sum of the excess demands and supplies is zero—seems not be yielding full employment (thus whenever the assumed law is not a law), add a dash of Keynesian monetary and fiscal policy until the "law" is "validated." For Samuelson does maintain he can "serve two masters." "On Monday, Wednesday and Friday, I can be a Say's Law man and a Keynesian on Tuesday, Thursday and Saturday."[16]

Despite Samuelson's many panegyrics on Keynes, and his great success in putting across his "caricature" of Keynes' system,[17] it is clear that the "master" he favors is Walras. A few quotations will indicate his relative evaluation of the two. In the following he comes, like Marc Antony, to bury Keynes, not to praise him:

> *The General Theory* is a badly written book, poorly organized. . . . It is not well suited for classroom use. It is arrogant, bad tempered, polemical. . . . It abounds in mares' nests or confusions. . . . In it the Keynesian system stands out indistinctly, as if the author were hardly aware of its existence or cognizant of its properties. . . . When finally mastered, its analysis is found to be obvious and at the same time new. In short it is a work of genius.[18]

The following quotation is from Samuelson's Presidential Address to the American Economic Association in 1961:

> . . . in 1935, Schumpeter rather shocked me by saying in a lecture that of the four greatest economists in the world three were French. . . . Of course,

> one was Léon Walras, whom Schumpeter had no hesitation in calling the greatest economist of all time, by virtue of his first formulation of general equilibrium. . . . the comparison that Lagrange made of Newton is worth repeating in this connection: Assuredly Newton was the greatest man of science, but also the luckiest. For there is but one system of the world and Newton was the one who found it. Similarly, there is but one grand concept of general equilibrium and it was Walras who had the insight (and luck) to find it.[19]

Schumpeter's remaining three greatest economists were Cournot, Quesnay, and Marshall. Samuelson makes it clear that he agrees with the first two choices, but rates Adam Smith somewhat more highly than Marshall.[20] And what attention does this leading "Keynesian" give Keynes in this address entitled "Economists and the History of Ideas"? Well, the motto—"For there are, in the present times, two opinions: not, as in former ages the true and the false; but the outside and the inside"—is from Keynes, and one is given to understand that, like Walras, he is more important than his father. Other than that, Keynes is mentioned merely as one who was wrong in thinking that "Ricardo's mind was the greatest that ever addressed itself to economics," and wrong in thinking that "practical men . . . are usually the slaves of some defunct economist." (Because "the Prince often gets to hear what he wants to hear.") Keynes was also, we are told, "known for one famous quotation, the casual remark: 'In the long run we are all dead'"[21] and presumably even Samuelson is prepared to concede he was right about that! He also quotes Keynes approvingly for having once dismissed Marx as "turbid" nonsense.

I remember, as a rather bastardized graduate student (I see now), reading Samuelson's presidential address and wondering whether a man who could dismiss Karl Marx as "from the viewpoint of pure economic theory . . . a minor post Ricardian"[22] was always right.

Now after the experience of watching the collapse of Bastard Keynesianism, I reread this speech as an abstract of all that is wrong with establishment economics of the first "Keynesian" generation in its decline. It is all there—the "normal science" pride in the manipulation of mathematical abstractions,[23] while ignoring the anomalies with which the neoclassical paradigm cannot cope and ignoring indeed the central contradiction of that paradigm—the putting down as an "outside opinion" the view that epoch-making economists such as Smith, Marx, and Keynes were the great economists on the showing that Smith was a mere "synthesizer" (Schumpeter's term), Marx "wrong" in "his facade of economics" but of some importance for some of his other ideas, while Keynes is at the highest level of "pure theory" a "theoretical charlatan who hid his trivial manipulation in fogs of words on irrelevant topics."[24]

If, as I would maintain, Bastard Keynesianism has collapsed, what, or who, has brought about its downfall? Certainly there have been increasing, and increasingly important, anomalies or noncorrespondence between fact and theory. But as Samuelson wrote long ago:

> Theorists can always resist facts; for facts are hard to establish and are always changing anyway. . . . Inevitably, at the earliest opportunity, the

mind slips back into the old grooves of thought, since analysis is utterly impossible without a frame of reference, a way of thinking about things, or, in short, a theory.[25]

So long as establishment Keynesians were content with their neoclassical synthesis, it was vain for empiricists to push anomalous facts at them and for Weintraub,[26] and, following him, Davidson, Wells, and myself to point out to them that their "Keynesianism" was neither Keynes nor in accord with plain facts. They knew better than Keynes—better than to read that "incomprehensible" book again, and facts were irrelevant! It remained for Joan Robinson and R. W. Clower, independently, to refute the Bastard Keynesian theory *before* the recent stagflation convinced even its practitioners that it was hopelessly inadequate. I would date the collapse of the Bastard Keynesian theory from about 1966. In that year Cambridge, Massachusetts, conceded defeat to Cambridge, England, in the "reswitching" debate,[27] and Clower's "The Keynesian Counter-Revolution" began to sink into the professional consciousness.[28]

The reswitching debate demonstrated that the neoclassical capital and profit theory—the aggregate production function with "well-behaved" marginal productivities—was untenable as an explanation of income distribution and growth. This realization undermined economists' confidence in the neoclassical paradigm and, I believe, made them more receptive of the points raised by Clower. Clower's contribution consisted of reinterpreting the *General Theory* as a refutation of Walras' Law as well as Say's Law. Clower demonstrates that once we drop the assumption that Walras' "auctioneer" (who costlessly and instantly transmits the information necessary to coordinate all markets) exists, Walras' Law goes out, and what he might have called "Keynes' Law" or "Clower's Law" takes its place. Walras' Law asserts that in equilibrium the sum of excess demands in all markets is zero; that is, if there is an excess supply of labor (involuntary unemployment) in the labor market, there is an excess demand for goods in the product market and the "auctioneer" will go to work finding and transmitting the new vector of wages and prices at which both markets will clear. However because no such miraculous auctioneer exists, unemployed workers' "notional demand" for goods (how much they would buy at current prices if they could sell all the labor they wished to) is not "effective demand," as they are income constrained to offer to buy less than their "notional" demand. It is to effective demand that the market system responds, and Walras' Law must therefore "be replaced by the more general condition, *the sum of all market excess demands, valued at prevailing market prices, is at most equal to zero.*"[29] Thus full employment is just a special case, and the classical theory is just a special case of Keynes' *General Theory*. Because this is merely common sense, as Clower shows, and it is all there in Keynes, at least tacitly as the basis of the Keynesian "consumption function," as Clower shows, what is all the fuss about? Is the trip necessary? Yes, it is necessary; theorists are immune to common sense. Given that neoclassical Keynesians are enamored with Walras, it is necessary to show that his equilibrium law wholly depends on the very special assumption of perfect knowledge—that "miraculous, impossible, unexplained" denial of the human condition. Clower concludes:

I shall be the last one to suggest that abstract theory is useless; that simply is not so. At the same time, I am convinced that much of what now passes for useful theory is not only worthless economics (and mathematics), but also a positive hindrance to fruitful theoretical and empirical research. Most importantly, however, I am impressed by the worth of Keynesian economics as a guide to practical action, which is in such sharp contrast to the situation of general price theory. As physicists should and would have rejected Einstein's theory of relativity, had it not included Newtonian mechanics as a special case, so we would do well to think twice before accepting as "useful" or "general" doctrines which are incapable of accommodating Keynesian economics.[30]

In addition to Clower's central point regarding nontransmission of notional signals, and Shackle's point regarding the impossibility of transcending the human condition, it has also been adequately demonstrated that Walras' equations describe essentially a barter world and all attempts to add a *numérare* money are artificial.[31] All goods and services are equally exchangeable—everything is liquid, so nothing is money. Again, this is not the real world, and such abstractions are not helpful, as Keynes said so clearly and as Davidson has so helpfully elaborated.[32] Finally, as Joan Robinson has shown repeatedly, Walras' model cannot be made into a useful starting point for studying the real world because it is a model of pure exchange of already existing stocks and the real world is a world of production in historical time.

Anyone who tries to introduce a flow of production with Walras immediately falls into contradictions. Either the whole of future time is collapsed into today or else every individual has correct foresight about what all others will do; while they have correct foresight about what he will do, so that the argument runs into the problem of free will and predestination. This could not be of any use to Keynes. The very essence of his problem was uncertainty.[33]

What these attacks taken together do is to prove, even to the Bastard Keynesians, that the neoclassical synthesis is hopelessly foolish and self-contradictory. If they want to progress in understanding and dealing with the real world, they must go back to the good book, *General Theory*, and this time understand it as they struggle to develop a workable paradigm. What a pity that forty years have been wasted!

To turn again to the Walras-Newton analogy used by Samuelson: As Clower mentioned, Newton's "world" is only a "special case" of Einstein's "world." However, Newton's world does happen to be the world we live in—that is, relativity makes no practical difference to an astronaut who wants to predict the motions of the planets in order to get to Mars. By exact analogy, Walras' theory of general equilibrium at full employment is only a special case of Keynes' general theory. However Walras' "world" is *not* the world we live in. It matters very much to practical affairs that notional demand is not effective demand, and that information is *never* sufficient—so that neither Say's nor Walras' laws are valid.

Furthermore, what would we think of a physicist who first gained fame and fortune explaining what Einstein "really meant," then led a retreat to Newton because he found relativity scientifically and politically disturbing and because he found uncertainty impossible to treat mathematically?

Commenting upon this strange mental aberration, Martin Shubik writes the following:

> General equilibrium economics is undoubtedly a splendid intellectual achievement. But it is not by any means on the level of Newtonian mechanics. In a world with large complicated corporations, selling thousands of goods and services (and often selling whole systems), the way we stick to our simple models (which at best cover one simple limiting case) is ludicrous. I am reminded of the story of the drunk who had lost his keys at night and spent his time searching for them under a streetlamp fifty yards from where he had lost them because that was the only place where he could see anything.[34]

Let us leave this drunken search and turn to the task of freeing Keynes' "lost" theory of the price level from the "Keynesian" incubus.

KEYNES' THEORY OF THE PRICE LEVEL VERSUS THE BASTARD KEYNESIAN THEORY

The difficulty economists have in distilling Keynes' price level theory does not come from any inherent difficulty of this theory. Keynes merely applied micro price theory to the economy as a whole with important *caveats* concerning wages. Rather the source of the difficulty is threefold. First, economists thought they already had an adequate price level theory in the quantity theory of money, and are in the habit of treating money wages as "just another price" that adjusts to clear markets.

Second, Keynes' theory has been neglected because of inconsistencies in his exposition. In chapter 4 he proposed to have nothing to do with so "vague and non-quantitative" concepts as "the price level" and "real output," and instead proposed to "make use of only two fundamental units of quantity, namely quantities of money value and quantities of employment."[35] However, Keynes later abandoned his self-imposed restriction and devoted book V to the subject of "Money—Wages and Prices."

Third, economists are unfamiliar with Keynes' price level theory because Paul Samuelson placed himself between the *GT* and a whole generation of "Keynesians," explaining that the book was a disjointed collection of "random notes" and advising the "young and innocent" to ignore book I "especially the difficult chapter 3" and book V, at least on the first reading—and clearly few ever went back for a second reading.[36]

Yet it is precisely in chapter 3 that Keynes first sketches his model of aggregate supply, aggregate demand, and price level, which he developed further in chapter 5, on expectations, and in book V. Keynes might have saved himself the trouble of writing these chapters, so completely have economists followed Samuelson's advice.

Keynes summarized his "contraquantity" or "micro based" theory of the price level as follows:

> In a single industry its particular price-level depends partly on the rate of remuneration of the factors of production which enter into its marginal cost, and partly on the scale of output. There is no reason to modify this conclusion when we pass to industry as a whole. The general price-level depends partly on the rate of remuneration of the factors of production which enter into marginal cost and partly on the scale of output as a whole, i.e. (taking equipment and technique as given) on the volume of employment"[37]

Keynes briefly considered what later became the Bastard Keynesian and monetarist models only to reject them as not the real world. He wrote:

> . . . let us . . . assume (1) that all unemployed resources are homogeneous and interchangeable . . . and (2) that the factors of production entering into marginal cost are content with the same money-wage so long as there is a surplus of them unemployed. . . . It follows that an increase in the quantity of money will have no effect whatever on prices, so long as there is any unemployment, and that employment will increase in exact proportion to any increase in effective demand brought about by the increase in the quantity of money; whilst as soon as full employment is reached, it will thenceforward be the wage-unit and prices which will increase in exact proportion to the increase in effective demand. Thus if there is perfectly elastic supply so long as there is unemployment, and perfectly inelastic supply so soon as full employment is reached, and if effective demand changes in the same proportion as the quantity of money, the Quantity Theory of Money can be enunciated as follows: "So long as there is unemployment, *employment* will change in the same proportion as the quantity of money; and when there is full employment, *prices* will change in the same proportion as the quantity of money."[38]

However, he continued:

> Having, however, satisfied tradition by introducing a sufficient number of simplifying assumptions to enable us to enunciate a Quantity Theory of Money, let us now consider the possible complications which will in fact influence events:
> (1) Effective demand will not change in exact proportion to the quantity of money.
> (2) Since resources are not homogeneous, there will be diminishing, and not constant, returns as employment gradually increases.
> (3) Since resources are not interchangeable, some commodities will reach a condition of inelastic supply whilst there are still unemployed resources available for the production of other commodities.
> (4) The wage-unit will tend to rise, before full employment has been reached.
> (5) The remunerations of the factors entering into marginal cost will not all change in the same proportion.[39]

Let us bring together Keynes' cost level considerations from chapter 21, his aggregate supply and demand analysis from chapter 3, and his expectations analysis from chapter 5 into a geometric representation of his theory of income, employment, and prices. The result of this exercise is Figure 1. In Figure 1 the supply side of Keynes' analysis is fully articulated rather than constrained to a 45° line wholly stripped of price level content and representing only the truism that real income ≡ real output.

Keynes defines the aggregate supply function, $Z = \phi(N)$, as the proceeds, the expectation of which would just make it worthwhile to hire varying numbers of employees—thus, *necessary* proceeds. He defines the aggregate demand function, $D = f(N)$, as the "proceeds which entrepreneurs expect to receive from the employment of N men,"[40] and concludes:

Now if for a given value of N the expected proceeds are greater than the aggregate supply price, i.e., if D is greater than Z, there will be an incentive to entrepreneurs to increase employment beyond N and, if necessary, to raise costs by competing with one another for the factors of production, up to the value of N for which Z has become equal to D. Thus the volume of employment is given by the point of intersection between the aggregate demand function and the aggregate supply function; for it is at this point that the entrepreneurs' expectations of profits will be maximized.[41]

Thus in Figure 1 the volume of employment offered is initially Na, based on expected proceeds of that employment ZDa. There being no godlike auctioneer to clear all markets, (1) there is no particular reason for ZDa to be the full-employment output of the economy, or for the money wage (wa) implicit at Na to result in the real wage (when wa is divided through by Pa) that would "give" full employment in a full-information system; (2) there is no particular reason for entrepreneurs to be correct in their expectation that ZDa is indeed the profit-maximizing output.

Suppose that they have been unduly pessimistic, so that when Na is employed in the expectation of proceeds of ZDa, somewhat higher proceeds of ZDb are realized. To the extent that prices are market determined, rather than supply cost determined, ZDb exceeds ZDa because of a price rise. If prices are set and maintained by producers, for an interval inventories are run down.[42] Doubtless both outcomes will be present to some extent.

By drawing in a Dr, or *realized* demand function, through ZDb and roughly parallel to D in Figure 1, we economists can see that the "equilibrium" proceeds, employment, and price level are respectively ZDe, Ne, and Pe, and we conclude, too facilely, that the economy will quickly "home in" on these values. Entrepreneurs, however, are not looking at our Figure 1, but at their sales figures, order books, and general business news. From these they learn that some divergence exists between expected and realized proceeds such that they wish they had produced and sold more goods in the most recent past. This divergence *may* cause them to adjust their short-run expectations and realizations smoothly to ZDe in the next period, or they may approach it through several periods in the familiar "stair-step" or multiplier style—expecting and producing ZDb and then

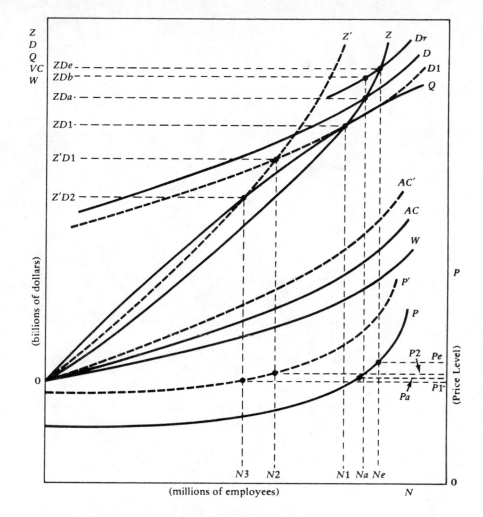

Z = Aggregate supply or *necessary* proceeds
D = Aggregate demand or *expected* proceeds
Dr = Aggregate realized demand or *realized* proceeds
Q = Real output function
VC = Variable cost function
W = Total wage function
P = Price level function
N = Employment
$D1, Z', AC', P'$ = Relevant functions after "anti-inflationary"
                    aggregate demand (and supply) restriction

Figure 1. Keynes' Model of Income, Employment, and Prices and the Bastard Keynesian "Anti-inflation" Policy.

realizing some $ZDc > ZDb < ZDe$, but eventually attaining ZDe. However, the realization of ZDb in one time period may lead to very different results: if, say, businessmen expect that "what goes up must come down," they may cut their output in the next period. Or, if "expectations are a tinder" the one-period divergence between short-run expectations and realizations may lead to an upward revision of long-run expectations—on which investment decisions depend—leading expected demand in the next period to exceed Dr and setting off a boom like that in an accelerator-multiplier model. Keynes analyzed the matter as follows:

> . . . the behaviour of each individual firm in deciding its daily output will be determined by its *short-run* expectations—expectations as to the cost of output on various possible scales and expectations as to the sale-proceeds of this output . . . . The *actually realized* results of the production and sale of output will only be relevant to employment insofar as they cause a modification of subsequent expectations.[43]

> . . . the process of revision of short-term expectation is a gradual and continuous one carried on largely in the light of realized results; so that expected and realized results run into and overlap one another in their influence. For although output and employment are determined by the producer's short-term expectations and not by past results, the most recent results usually play a predominant part in determining what these expectations are.[44]

Next let us turn to the remaining relationships of Figure 1, starting with the aggregate supply function, Z. It should be stressed that Z represents an ex ante expectation, as do all the functional relations of Figure 1 except realized demand. Thus Keynes defined the aggregate supply price of a given amount of employment as "the expectation of proceeds which will just make it worth the while of the entrepreneurs to give that employment."[45] Just as demand-side divergences between expectations and realizations will occur, so also will supply-side divergences. Thus if prices are market determined, some $Pb > Pa$ will be realized at employment level Na, and some of the more volatile elements in variable costs—such as short-term interest rates and raw material prices—may rise in an unanticipated manner. Further, these realizations will affect anticipations of the next period in complex ways, shifting the VC, P, Z, and W functions over time.

The position and shape of the total wage function, W, represent entrepreneurs' anticipations of the responsiveness of the average wage ($w = W/N$) to employment, given the anticipated price level function. The longer the time horizon we are considering and the larger the change in employment and output level that businessmen are anticipating, the greater the likelihood of divergence between the anticipated and realized level of wage costs.

It would seem that the only solidly based anticipation is that of the real output function, and it probably has a different shape than the "diminishing returns" shape Keynes gave it! (see note 10). Still, the world's work must go on, and it does; businessmen basing their decisions on imperfect anticipations of the future and adjusting imperfectly to ever-changing realizations, occasionally

brushing against a transitory "equilibrium," or even, as in 1953 or perhaps in 1969, touching "full employment." As Keynes observed,

> . . . it is an outstanding characteristic of the economic system in which we live that, whilst it is subject to severe fluctuations in respect of output and employment, it is not violently unstable. . . . Fluctuations may start briskly but seem to wear themselves out before they have proceeded to great extremes, and an intermediate situation which is neither desperate nor satisfactory is our normal lot.[46]

Thanks to Keynes and the experience of the Great Depression, rather than Walras' auctioneer, the economy does run at close to full employment because governments the world over have made it their business to see to it that it does. Thus the employment level and the rate of growth of output have long been *political*, rather than merely economic, matters. The benefits of thirty-five years of near full employment in the industrialized world have been immense, but there has been a persistent and now accelerating inconvenience—inflation.

Keynes was uneasily aware that a government guarantee of continuous near full employment would remove the restraints on cost-push inflation, which to him was almost solely wage-push inflation. Thus he saw that the rate of change of money incomes had also, via the "Keynesian revolution," become *political* matters, as he wrote to Benjamin Graham on New Year's Day, 1943:

> The task of keeping efficiency-wages reasonably stable (I am sure they will creep up steadily in spite of our best efforts) is a political rather than an economic problem.[47]

Unfortunately, instead of setting about the difficult task of designing the activist incomes policies that activist fiscal and monetary policies require, his Bastard Keynesian disciples, whether fiscalist, monetarist, or eclectic, clung to the illusion that if only they could banish "excess" demand they could end inflation. Particularly in North America employment, output, and growth were traded off for price stability and yet "flation" was not achieved. Thus for eighteen years, from 1948 to 1966, the money supply (M_1) of the United States was kept growing at a slower pace than real output so that the M_1/Q ratio fell, and even today the ratio is virtually the same as in 1948. However the price level is now one and a half *times* its 1948 level.[48]

Not only were the disciples wrong in their belief that fiscal and monetary restraints were sufficient to control inflation without complementary incomes policies, they also failed to understand that their "anti" inflationary policy moves could have inflationary effects. In terms of Figure 1, they really believed it was possible to drive the economy from ZDa, Na, Pa to $ZD1$, $N1$, $P1$ (where $Z = Q$ and therefore the price level is the same as in the previous period) by reducing demand to $D1$ by *raising* interest rates and *raising* taxes. Yet even a modicum of additional analysis, even a modicum of micro analysis, would show that such demand reduction would also be accompanied by a supply reduction, so that: (1) the price level impact of the move is indeterminate without knowledge of the degree of shift and shape of the D and Z functions; and (2) the employment and output effects of the move will prove "unexpectedly severe."

But no such insight is possible to Bastard Keynesians so long as they are blinded by 45° models with a nonoperative supply curve, $IS = LM$ models with no supply curve, or quantity theory prejudgments.

I, and others, have written extensively concerning this point elsewhere[49] and will therefore spare the reader the repetition of all of it here. Suffice to say that interest on business debts and many taxes—such as the prices of imported goods —enter into the variable cost function, thus $VC = V(w, i, t, pm)$, and thus interest and tax changes cause a parametric shift in VC. If we adhere to marginal cost pricing, as did Keynes, the price level function will be given by $P' = MC' = \Delta VC'/\Delta Q$, where ΔQ is the marginal product of the variable factors. The new aggregate supply function is given by $Z' = P'Q$. Thus, as seen in Figure 1, the anti-inflationary reduction of demand to $D1$, by tax or interest hikes, causes an upward shift in the variable cost function to VC', of the price level function to P', and in the aggregate supply function to Z'. The result of this misguided policy is stagflation; as the money GNP falls to $Z'D1$ and unemployment becomes "unexpectedly" severe, employment falling to $N2$ rather than the $N1$ "target"; the price level rises to $P2$, rather than falling to $P1$. Achievement of the price level "target," $P1$, would necessitate still greater unemployment at $N3$.

Under the markup pricing formulae actually used by businessmen, the link between cost hikes from taxation and interest hikes is equally direct. Furthermore, even hikes of direct taxes, such as the personal income tax, will lead to higher prices if they result in higher wage settlements "to pay the higher taxes." It is all there in Keynes, at least implicitly in his discussion of the "cost-unit," a "weighted average of the rewards of the factors of production entering into marginal prime-cost,"[50] but so little is he read that these matters are just now forcing themselves into the professional consciousness. Thus, in his Presidential Address to the American Economic Association in December 1974, Walter W. Heller belatedly recognized the cost effects of tax hikes, but not, interestingly enough, interest hikes:

> Further work is needed to measure the cost-push effects of anti-inflationary tax increases that offset part of their demand damping effect. In recession, the cost-easing and demand-push effects work in happy harmony. They work at cross purposes in tax increases (though not in expenditure cuts) to curb inflation. The question of how large the offsetting cost-push effects, or aggregate supply effects, may be, is unresolved. In a high inflation economy, this is a serious gap in our fiscal policy knowledge.[51]

As Blinder and Solow put it:

> The basic remark is so obvious that it is almost embarrassing that it does not appear in textbook expositions of the analytics of fiscal policy.[52] It is simply this: most taxes are . . . incorporated into business costs, and therefore . . . passed on to the consumer in higher prices. Therefore, if the contractionary fiscal medicine administrated to cure inflation takes the form of higher taxes it may well have the desired deflationary impact on aggregate demand, but also an unintended cost-push inflationary impact on aggregate supply. The net result is, in many cases, unclear on purely theoretical grounds. . . . tight money as a cure for inflation runs into

analogous objections. Restrictive monetary policies generally imply high interest rates and interest payments are a significant component to costs of many firms.[53]

What is takes to embarrass one, or "almost embarrass" one, is a matter of personal constitution. For close to a decade now I have been almost continuously blushing to be part of a profession that could advocate, as good macroeconomic policy, suppressing aggregate demand by tax and interest hikes, when we know, in the microeconomic part of our minds, that these moves boost prices by reducing supply. Now after tens of millions of man-years of unemployment and perhaps $600 billion of GNP have been sacrificed to appease the inflationary gods, the priests discover they have been feeding the idols the wrong meat! Almost embarrassing!

That we still have plenty of unfinished work is indicated by Aaron Gordon when he says:

> . . . "the forecasters fell flat on their faces when predicting price changes because they didn't have any way of estimating sectoral supply scarcity" and adds that we have not "even started to develop a theory of aggregate supply."[54]

The discussion illustrated in Figure 1 is set in a short-run comparative statics framework, while inflation has been a long-run, dynamic phenomenon. In our discussion of "anti" inflationary tax hikes the assumption was that the extra tax money would not be spent. However, the usual reason for raising taxes is to spend them, and the rise in the government sector as a percentage of GNP is a worldwide phenomenon.[55] Likewise the average rate of interest has increased mightily from Keynes' day, and interest income, which shrank greatly as a percentage of GNP in the Depression and World War II, is back to 1920s levels—a far cry from the "euthanasia of the *rentier*" he advocated. No follower of Keynes can object to the word "expectation," but instead of depending on the slogan "inflationary expectations" to explain away the failures of monetarism and fiscalism, should not economists consider fully the implications of these potent forces—tax and interest push?

As yet too little has been done by the profession. The Economic Council of Canada has focused needed attention here,[56] and the Canadian Federal Government has promised to mend its ways and slow down its growth as part of the present "attack on inflation." The most insightful analysis of this problem is William Krehm's.[57] My new book, *Stagflation and the Bastard Keynesians*, devotes two chapters to attempting to quantify the inflationary impact of the rising government sector. Beyond this there is as yet rather little to report.[58]

Still there is progress. For Bastard Keynesianism has collapsed and, increasingly I believe, will be seen to have died. However the fall of Bastard Keynesianism and its replacement by the legitimate variety, although a gain, is by no means sufficient to end our present time of troubles. Like Lear's Britain, the capitalist world has far worse sorrows than those involving Gloucester's bastard son Edmund and legitimate Edgar.

Messenger: Edmund is dead, my lord.

Albany: That's but a trifle here.
You lords and noble friends, know our intent.
What comfort to this great decay may come,
Shall be applied . . . .
[To Kent and Edgar] Friends of my soul, you twain,
Rule in this realm, and the gored state sustain.

Kent: I have a journey, sir, shortly shall I go.
My master calls me; I must not say no.

Edgar: The weight of this sad time we must obey,
Speak what we feel, not what we ought to say.
The oldest hath borne most; we that are young,
Shall never see so much, nor live so long.

(Exeunt with a dead march.)[59]

NOTES

1. Matt. 6:24.
2. Ps. 118:22-23; also Matt. 21:42.
3. Joan Robinson, *Economic Heresies: Some Old Fashioned Questions in Economic Theory* (New York: Basic Books, 1971), pp. 88, 95. See also Joan Robinson, "What Has Become of the Keynesian Revolution?" *Challenge*, January-February 1974, pp. 6-11.
4. In his prescient 1943 article, "Political Aspects of Full Employment," *Political Quarterly* 14 (1943), pp. 322-31, M. Kalecki foresaw just such a perversion as governments respond to *rentier* and business pressure to *prevent* continuous full employment. Kalecki failed to foresee, however, that it would be recurring balance of payments problems that would be central to the phases of the "stop-go" policy cycle, particularly in Britain.
5. Because Milton Friedman's "monetarists" combine all these shortcomings of Bastard Keynesianism with peculiarly simplistic analysis and policy notions, I do not regard them as constituting a separate "school" but merely as the "right wing" of illegitimate Keynesianism. Friedman once wrote, ". . . in one sense we are all Keynesians now; in another, no one is a Keynesian any longer." (M. Friedman, *Dollars and Deficits*, Englewood Cliffs, N.J.: Prentice-Hall, 1968, p. 15.) I would hold that he might better have written, ". . . we are all Bastard Keynesians now, and thus none of us are Keynesians any longer." For Friedman's own reassertion of Say's Law (without actually using the term) see "A Theoretical Framework for Monetary Analysis," *Journal of Political Economy*, March-April 1970, pp. 193-238, esp. pp. 206-7. Indeed, Friedman's entire monetarist chain of causation amounts to the assertion of Say's Law for money—the supply of money is the demand for money, though with a lag.
6. John Maynard Keynes, *The General Theory of Employment, Interest, and Money* (New York: Harcourt, 1936), p. 292, hereafter *GT*.
7. *GT*, p. 293.
8. For some exploration of these matters of Keynesian exegesis, see: Sidney Weintraub, "Keynes and the Monetarists," *Canadian Journal of Economics* 4 (February 1971), pp. 37-49; Warren S. Gramm, "Natural Selection in Economic Thought: Ideology, Power, and the Keynesian Counterrevolution," *Journal of Economic Issues* 7 (March 1973), pp. 1-27; Ron Stanfield, "Kuhnian Scientific Revolutions and the Keynesian Revolution," *Journal of Economic Issues* 8 (March 1974), pp. 97-110; Richard X. Chase, "Keynes and U.S. Keynesianism: A Lack of Historical Perspective and the Decline of the New Economics," *Journal of Economic Issues* 9 (September 1975), pp. 441-70. A look to the future is provided by Alfred S. Eichner and J. A. Kregel, "An Essay on Post-Keynesian Theory: A New Paradigm in Economics," *Journal of Economic Literature* 13 (December 1975), pp. 1293-1314.
9. "An increase in effective demand will, generally speaking, spend itself partly in increasing the quantity of employment and partly in raising the level of prices. Thus instead

of constant prices in conditions of unemployment, and of prices rising in proportion to the quantity of money in conditions of full employment, we have in fact a condition of prices rising gradually as employment increases" (*GT*, p. 296).
10. For a review of this controversy and the evidence, see Ronald G. Bodkin, "Real Wages and Cyclical Variations in Employment: A Reexamination of the Evidence," *Canadian Journal of Economics* 2 (August 1969), pp. 353-72.
11. *GT*, pp. 307, 309, 340n.
12. G. L. S. Shackle, "Keynes and Today's Establishment in Economic Theory: A View," *Journal of Economic Literature* 11 (June 1973), p. 516.
13. Shackle, "Keynes and Today's Establishment," p. 517.
14. Ibid., p. 519.
15. Ibid., p. 517.
16. Paul A. Samuelson, remarks at Conference on Keynes, Cambridge, and the *General Theory*, University of Western Ontario, October 10, 1975.
17. See Paul A. Samuelson, "A Brief Survey of Post-Keynesian Developments," in Robert Lekachman, ed., *Keynes' General Theory: Reports of Three Decades* (New York: St. Martin, 1964), p. 338.
18. Paul A. Samuelson, "Lord Keynes and the General Theory," *Econometrica*, July 1946, pp. 318-19.
19. P. A. Samuelson, "Economists and the History of Ideas," *American Economic Review* 52 (March 1962), p. 3.
20. Ibid., p. 9.
21. Ibid., p. 17.
22. Ibid., p. 12. But despair not, spirit of Marx, for lately, finding that like Keynes you can be mathematized, Samuelson has rehabilitated you, and declares (*Economics*, 9th ed.) "It is a scandal that, until recently, even majors in economics were taught nothing of Karl Marx except that he was an unsound fellow." You may yet be canonized in Cambridge, Mass. However, for a truly innovative view of economics, rejecting both capitalism and Marxism, see Eugen Loebl, *Humanomics* (New York: Random, 1976). Loebl, former Czech minister and director of the State Bank, got the "leisure" to rethink in Stalin's jails. He is now professor of economics at Vassar.
23. "My own scholarship has covered . . . questions like welfare economics and factor-price equalization; turnpike theorems and osculating envelopes; nonsubstitutability relations in Minkowski-Ricardo-Leontief-Metzler matrices of Mosak-Hicks type; or balanced-budget multipliers under conditions of balanced uncertainty in locally impacted topological spaces and molar equivalences" (Ibid., p. 1).
24. The words are Leijonhufvud's as expressing not his own opinion but that of "high brow" theorists such as Samuelson after the Hicks-Patinkin exchange of 1957-59. Axel Leijonhufvud, *Keynes and the Classics* (London: Institute of Economic Affairs, 1969), p. 19.
25. Samuelson, "Lord Keynes," p. 318.
26. Sidney Weintraub, "Classical 45° Keynesianism: A Plea for Its Abandonment," in *Classical Keynesianism, Monetary Theory and the Price Level* (Philadelphia: Chilton, 1965), pp. 1-25.
27. The debate demonstrated that a technique that minimized the cost of production with a high rate of profit, and that did not minimize costs for intermediate range, might also minimize costs with a low rate of profit. Samuelson and Levhari set off the debate by denying that reswitching (first suggested by Joan Robinson, "The Production Function and the Theory of Capital," *Review of Economic Studies* 21, no. 55 (1953-54), pp. 81-106; and D. C. Champernowne, "Comment," *Review of Economic Studies* 21, no. 55 (1953-54), pp. 112-35) can occur. P. A. Samuelson, "A New Theorem on Non-Substitution," in H. Hegeland, ed., *Money, Growth, and Methodology and Other Essays in Honor of John Akerman* (Lund: CWK Gleerup, 1961); and D. Levhari, "A Non-Substitution Theorem and Switching of Techniques," *Quarterly Journal of Economics*, February 1965, pp. 98-105. The November 1966 issue of the *Quarterly Journal of Economics* is largely given over to a symposium on reswitching that concludes with Levhari and Samuelson's retraction, "The Non-Switching Theorem is False," pp. 518-19, and Samuelson's "A Summing Up," pp. 568-83, which shows that reswitching is plausible, and possibly important. See also G. C. Harcourt, "Some Cambridge Controversies in the Theory of Capital," *Journal of Economic Literature* 7

(June 1969), pp. 369-405; Joan Robinson, "Capital Theory Up to Date," *Canadian Journal of Economics* 3 (May 1970), pp. 309-17.

28. Robert W. Clower, "The Keynesian Counter-Revolution: A Theoretical Appraisal," in *The Theory of Interest Rates,* F. H. Hahn and F. Brechling, eds. (London: Macmillan, 1965), pp. 103-25. Clower's paper was presented to a Conference on the Theory of Interest and Money at the Abbey of Royanmont, France, in 1962, but not published until 1965.

29. Clower, "Keynesian Counter-Revolution," p. 120.

30. Ibid., pp. 124-25. See also Axel Leijonhufvud, *Keynes and the Classics,* for further elucidation of Clower's central point. See further, H. I. Grossman, "Was Keynes a Keynesian? A Review Article," *Journal of Economic Literature* 10 (March 1972), pp. 26-30, for the view that Clower is too generous in attributing his own ideas to Keynes.

31. ". . . the Walrasian economy . . . is essentially one of barter," F. Hahn, "Some Adjustment Problems," *Econometrica* 38 (1970), p. 5.

32. Paul Davidson, *Money and the Real World,* chap. 6. New York: Wiley, 1972.

33. Joan Robinson, "The Second Crisis of Economic Theory," *American Economic Review, Papers and Proceedings,* May 1972, pp. 1-10.

34. Martin Shubik, "A Curmudgeon's Guide to Microeconomics," *Journal of Economic Literature* 8 (June 1970), p. 415.

35. *GT,* p. 41.

36. "Like Joyce's *Finnegan's Wake,* the *General Theory* is much in need of a companion volume providing a 'skeleton key' and guide to its contents: warning the young and innocent away from Book I (especially the difficult Chapter 3) and on to Books III, IV, and VI" (Samuelson, "Lord Keynes," p. 319).

37. *GT,* p. 294.

38. *GT,* pp. 295-96.

39. *GT,* p. 296.

40. *GT,* p. 25.

41. Ibid.

42. For a clear statement of Keynes' short-run model of employment, proceeds and output, see Paul Wells, "Keynes' Dynamic Disequilibrium Theory of Employment," *Quarterly Review of Economics and Business,* January 1974, pp. 89-92. Axel Leijonhufvud once believed the essential difference between Marshall and Keynes involved alternative assumptions concerning the relative speeds of adjustment of prices and quantities [*On Keynesian Economics and the Economics of Keynes* (New York: Oxford, 1966), pp. 24-54]. However, he later changed his mind. (See his "Keynes' Employment Function: Comment," *History of Political Economy,* Summer 1974, pp. 164-70.)

43. *GT,* p. 47.

44. *GT,* pp. 50-51.

45. *GT,* p. 24.

46. *GT,* pp. 249-50.

47. As quoted by Lord Kahn, "On Re-Reading Keynes," Keynes Lecture in Economics, *Proceedings of the British Academy* 60 (1974); Oxford University Press, 1975, p. 387.

48. If we assign 1947 magnitudes the value of 100, the M_1/Q ratio fell to 71 in 1966, was 86 in 1972, 97 in 1974, and 103 in 1975, while the price level rose from 100 in 1947 to 152 in 1966, 195 in 1972, 234 in 1974, and 254 in 1975. If we broaden the definition of money to M_2, the results are as follows: M_2/Q in 1947 = 100, 1966 = 105, 1972 = 136, 1974 = 158, 1975 = 175.

The disasters of the last two years can be seen in the following figures: between 1973 and 1975 the real output of the U.S. economy fell from $1,233 billion to $1,186 billion, or 3.8 percent, while the price index (GNP deflator) rose from 105.9 to 126.4, or 19.4 percent. M_1 rose 9.2 percent, and M_2 rose 16.7 percent over the two-year period. (All figures calculated from *Economic Report of the President,* January 1976.)

These sad facts can doubtless be rationalized by such considerations as that the continuation of inflation raised the opportunity costs of holding money and therefore shrank the demand for money even more rapidly than "tight money" was shrinking its relative supply, but the point of the operation was to stop inflation, and the operation failed while inflicting very major costs in lost output and employment.

49. See J. H. Hotson, "Neo-Orthodox Keynesianism and the 45° Heresy," *Nebraska Journal of Economics and Business* 6 (Autumn 1967), pp. 34-49. See also C. Brennan and D. A. L. Auld, "The Tax Cut as an Anti-Inflationary Measure," *Economic Record,* (December 1968), pp. 520-25; R. Harrod, "Reassessment of Keynes' Views on Money," *Journal of Political Economy* 78 (July-August 1970), pp. 63-76; J. H. Hotson, "Adverse Effects of Interest and Tax Hikes as Strengthening the Case for Incomes Policies,"* *Canadian Journal of Economics* 4 (May 1971), pp. 164-81; Robert Eisner, "What Went Wrong?" *Journal of Political Economy* 79 (May-June 1971), pp. 629-41; J. H. Hotson and H. Habibagahi, "Comparative Static Analysis of Harrod's Dichotomy," *Kyklos* 25 (1972), pp. 154-66; H. Habibagahi and J. H. Hotson, "Harrod's Dichotomy and the Price Level," **Economic and Business Bulletin.* *Reprinted in my *Stagflation and the Bastard Keynesians* (Waterloo: at the University Press, 1976).

50. *GT,* p. 302. He continued, "The cost-unit, . . . can thus be regarded as the essential standard of value; and the price-level, given the state of technique and equipment, will depend partly on the cost-unit and partly on the scale of output, increasing, where output increases, *more* than in proportion to any increase in the cost-unit, in accordance with the principle of diminishing returns in the short period."

51. Walter W. Heller, "What's Right With Economics?" *American Economic Review* 65 (March 1975), pp. 1-26.

52. It is beginning to: see Nancy S. Barrett, *The Theory of Macroeconomic Policy* (Englewood Cliffs, N.J.: Prentice-Hall, 1972), pp. 275-76 for a brief development of this point: John Lindauer, *Macroeconomics,* 2nd ed. (New York: Wiley, 1971), pp. 378-82; G. Brunhild and R. H. Burton, *Macroeconomic Theory* (Englewood Cliffs, N.J.: Prentice-Hall, 1974), pp. 439-40.

53. Alan S. Blinder and Robert M. Solow, "Analytical Foundations of Fiscal Policy," *The Economics of Public Policy* (Washington, D.C.: The Brookings Institute, 1974), pp. 98-101.

54. As quoted by Heller, "What's Right with Economics?" p. 15.

55. To cite only the U.S. and Canadian experience: U.S. government expenditures and transfers as a percentage of GNP: 1929, 10.0%; 1947, 18.3%; 1961, 28.6%; 1974, 33.0% (source: *Economic Report of the President,* February 1975, tables C-1, C-67); Canada: 1929, 15.8%; 1947, 24.3%; 1961, 32.6%; 1974, 39.3%.

56. See Economic Council of Canada, *Ninth Annual Review: The Years Ahead* (Ottawa, 1972), p. 101.

57. William Krehm, *Price in a Mixed Economy: Our Record of Disaster* (Toronto: Thornwood, 1975). Many of Krehm's coinages, such as "social lien," "social revalorization," "aggregate shift function," "core value," and "structural quotient" are, I think, useful and destined to enter our vocabulary.

58. However, see David Warsh and Lawrence Minard, "Memo to President Carter: Inflation is Now Too Serious a Matter to Leave to the Economists," *Forbes,* November 15, 1976, pp. 121-41. Warsh and Minard's insights on "Clark Gable Economics" are worth more than many "learned" books on inflation.

59. William Shakespeare, *King Lear,* V: iii.

Production of Commodities by Means of Commodities

A Review

PETER NEWMAN

Professor of Political Economy, The Johns Hopkins University

Piero Sraffa's *Production of Commodities by Means of Commodities* is remarkable on many counts. It is handsomely produced and extraordinarily terse, accomplishing a great deal in a tiny space. It is essentially and explicitly mathematical, yet gives few adequate proofs and no mathematical references (apart from the eminent mathematicians whose help is acknowledged in the preface). It is clearly tangential at several points to much modern work on general equilibrium models, but no guide is given to the similarities or differences. And, as perhaps befits a work that is partly concerned with capital theory, it has taken a very long time to come to fruition. Sraffa tells us in his preface that the "central propositions had taken shape in the late 1920's." It is an absorbing game to speculate how much more progress economics theory would have made if those propositions had been published then, before many of todays' leading theorists were born. For, with all its oddities, the book is obviously the work of an artist, working in the medium of economic theory.

It is my experience that some economists have concluded that the book gives just another Leontief-type model, subjectively original but nothing more; while others have hailed it as a great advance.[1] Part of this divergence of views is no doubt due to differences in the approaches of various schools of thought, but part must also be due to the book's extreme difficulty. Compressed and mathematically incomplete as it is, the main trouble lies not there, but in wrenching oneself out of the more usual Walrasian approach to general equilibrium, and in substituting a Ricardian viewpoint. An added potential source of difficulty stems from Sraffa's elegant but formal method of presentation. Quite detailed propositions are derived from a model that apparently has almost no assumptions about reality at all, a methodological procedure that is uncommon in modern economic theory (though not necessarily the worse for that).

Because of these difficulties, and because previous review articles have dealt ably with other aspects of Sraffa's contribution, it has seemed to me that the most useful function that this critique can serve is to *translate* his work into

A critique of Piero Sraffa, Production of Commodities by Means of Commodities (Cambridge, at the University Press, 1960). *[This article, which is almost unknown and inaccessible, is an important review of Sraffa's book. It was published in* Schweizerische Zeitschrift fur Volkswirtschaft und Statistik *98 (1962), pp. 58–75.—Ed.]*
   I am grateful to Hugh Rose for several illuminating conversations on the nature of Mr. Sraffa's system.

the more widely used Walrasian dialect of mathematical economics, and to give proofs of his main results which are acceptable to the speakers of that dialect. Translated into this more common *argot*, his system may become less opaque, although perhaps—as in good poetry—there are subtleties which defy translation; at least it seems worth trying. Because of space limitations, I shall be almost entirely concerned with Part I of the book. Once this first half has been mastered, then the rest of the book—which contains some brilliant pieces of analysis—is relatively easy territory, and may be left to the reader to explore.

I

The system discussed in chapter 1 (which consists of two and a half pages) is considerably different from the usual static inter-industry model, which superficially it resembles. It is obtained from the following assumptions:

Assumption 1. The economy is producing sufficient of each commodity to maintain itself, or is in what Sraffa calls a *self-replacing state*. This means that we are *given* total quantities of each product, and discuss the conditions under which these quantities will persist. No question of unemployment of any factor can arise, because that would imply schedules for factor supplies, which do not exist in the model.

Assumption 2. We are given certain *numbers* which tell us how much of each commodity is required to produce a *given* quantity of any one commodity (this quantity being given by Assumption 1). The collection of such numbers for any given commodity simply constitutes a *recipe*, as in a cookery-book, and no question of variation in either input proportions or *scale* of output is raised. Hence all we have for any product is one point of its production function; in particular, this is *not* the fixed coefficient model of Walras-Cassel-Leontief type which it appears to resemble.

Assumption 3. There is no surplus in the production of any commodity, i.e. all the output of each product is used to produce other products (including itself), and none goes for final consumption. To make this palatable, we must assume that workers are produced like any other commodity, requiring definite inputs of wheat and wine, etc. in order to produce the *given* amount of labor time postulated by Assumption 1.

As in all such models, we have to make some assumptions about the organization of the market. Sraffa assumes, in effect, that the market is cleared once each production period ("after the harvest")—which therefore is implicitly assumed to be the same for each commodity, a very important proviso. After the exchange takes place, all economizing activity ceases until the next "market day." The only activity pursued between whiles is production, and that goes by the simple recipes of Assumption 2, leaving no room for choice, regarding either input substitution *or* scale.

The model may now be formalized, in a notation differing from—and more convenient than—that used by Sraffa. Assumption 1 says that for each product *j* there is a *fixed* quantity A_j, so that we may take A_j as the *unit* of measurement

of the jth good; we put $A_j = 1$ for each j (and shall assume that there are n commodities). Assumption 2 then permits us to write $a_{i1}, a_{i2}, \ldots, a_{in}$ as the *proportion* of the output of the 1st, 2nd, . . . , nth good respectively, used in the production of good i. Assumption 3 tells us that $a_{1j} + a_{2j} + \ldots + a_{nj} = 1$, for each j.

The question we ask of this system (which we denote by $S1$) is: What set (if any) of exchange values relating the various products would enable production to persist indefinitely at the levels prescribed by Assumption 1? Each industry brings one unit of its product to market "after the harvest" and by means of exchange tries to secure just those amounts of each of its inputs required to produce "next year" one unit of product. Can a set of consistent exchange-ratios be found? Notice that $S1$ cannot really be asked any *other* question, since there is no guide to tell us what might happen to *anything* if the levels of production of each commodity were different from 1 (cf. the first paragraph of Sraffa's preface, p. v).

We may rephrase the question as follows: Does there exist a vector of positive exchange ratios $p_1, p_2, \ldots, p_n$—one for each commodity—such that the value of the quantities of the products used in producing each of the unit levels is equal to the value of the (unit) output of each commodity? Symbolically, is there a positive vector $\mathbf{p}^*$ which is a solution of the matrix equation:

(1) $\mathbf{Ap} = \mathbf{p}$

where $\mathbf{A}$ is the matrix of the proportions a_{ij}, and $\mathbf{p}$ is the vector of exchange ratios? Since $\Sigma_i a_{ij} = 1$ for each j, and $a_{ij} \geqslant 0$ for each element of $\mathbf{A}$, this model is formally identical with the linear exchange model introduced by Remak, and analyzed in great detail by Gale.[2]

Briefly stated, the answer is that there will always exist a solution vector $\mathbf{p}^*$ which will have *no* negative elements and at least one positive element (Gale employs the useful term "semipositive"). This solution will be unique except for a scale factor, which in this model is equivalent to requiring that one of the goods be selected as *numéraire*. In order to go beyond this statement, and assert the existence of a completely positive vector of exchange ratios, we have to make a more detailed investigation.

Suppose that there were only three industries, and that the output of one of them—number 3—was not used by either of the others. The relevant matrix equation would then be

(2) $\begin{bmatrix} a_{11} & a_{12} & 0 \\ a_{21} & a_{22} & 0 \\ a_{31} & a_{32} & a_{33} \end{bmatrix} \begin{bmatrix} p_1 \\ p_2 \\ p_3 \end{bmatrix} = \begin{bmatrix} p_1 \\ p_2 \\ p_3 \end{bmatrix}$

By putting the bottom row to the top, and then the right-hand column to the left, we can rewrite (2), as

(2a) $\begin{bmatrix} a_{33} & a_{31} & a_{32} \\ 0 & a_{11} & a_{12} \\ 0 & a_{21} & a_{22} \end{bmatrix} \begin{bmatrix} p_3 \\ p_1 \\ p_2 \end{bmatrix} = \begin{bmatrix} p_3 \\ p_1 \\ p_2 \end{bmatrix}$

Because of Assumption 3, $a_{33} = 1$, and in view of (2a) we must therefore have $p_3 + a_{31}p_1 + a_{32}p_2 = p_3$. Now a_{31} and a_{32} are both positive, by hypothesis, so that $p_1 = p_2 = 0$, in which case p_3 can assume *any* value. Since, presumably, if an industry in this system $S1$ produces a free good, it goes out of existence, the requirement that the system be in a self-replacing state *implies* positive prices, and hence that the phenomenon discussed here cannot happen. This means in turn that *each* commodity must be used directly or indirectly in the production of every commodity. It is then a theorem (e.g., Gale, op. cit., p. 226), that there exists a positive price vector, unique save for specification of *numéraire*.[3]

II

It is possible to move from the system $S1$ in a number of different directions. One such direction would be to assume that the proportions $a_{i1}, a_{i2}, \ldots, a_{in}$ remain invariant with changes in the scale of output, for any commodity i. This would lead directly to the Walras-Cassel-Leontief fixed-coefficient model already mentioned. If then alternative ways of producing any given commodity were introduced, we would be in one region of the world of Koopmans' activity analysis; a further step would take us to the von Neumann model of an expanding economy.[4]

Sraffa's direction is quite different, and is related (though not by descent) to his interpretation of an important passage in Ricardo's thought.[5] If the economy is split into two sectors, agriculture ("corn") and manufacture ("iron"), then corn necessarily enters into iron production (through its role as wage good) and also into its own production; but iron does not enter into corn production. If the economy is capable of generating a surplus, then Ricardo seems to have maintained that it necessarily follows that the rate of profit is determined solely by the physical conditions of corn production, and that the exchange-value of corn is independent of the conditions of iron production.

If we consider a more complicated model, with more than two sectors, then can we continue to make the same kind of statement? This is a natural extension of Ricardian ideas in one direction, while a further generalization would be the abandonment of wage determination through the Malthusian population mechanism. Finally, to take in another strand of the Ricardian fabric, it would be desirable to generalize the idea of a commodity which is a "standard of value," i.e. a commodity whose cost of production (and therefore price) is invariant through time, and hence which can serve as an unvarying yardstick against which to measure price changes in other commodities. A rise in the price of a good Y relative to this "fixed" commodity, X, would then be unambiguously due to a rise in Y's price, and not perhaps due also to a fall in X's price (or to a rise in X's price less steep than that in Y's price).

In order to concentrate on these problems, Sraffa makes a drastic series of simplifications in his next model, which I shall call $S2$. He retains the essentials of model $S1$, modifying only Assumption 3 in order to permit the production of each commodity to be such that there might be a *surplus* over and above the inter-industry demands for it as input. Once this is done, and once we abandon the Malthusian wage doctrine (at least in its strict form), it becomes necessary to abandon the idea of labor being produced, like any other commodity, by

recipe. This could, of course, be taken care of by a theory accounting for the distribution of the national income between wages and profits.[6]

But this would not fit in with Sraffa's main object, which is to see what happens to prices and the *rate* of profit when the allocation between wages and profits is varied. To use a simile, it is as if we varied the proportion ω of income going to wages [with a corresponding proportion $(1 - \omega)$ going to profits] by varying the resistance in a simple electrical circuit. We could then imagine observing on suitable meters the varying price of each commodity, together with the varying rate of profit.

It is important to bear in mind always that, as Joan Robinson says (op. cit., p. 54), Sraffa's $S2$ is only "half of an equilibrium system." What we are given are the production recipes of $S1$, together with the fixed quantitites of outputs. We also have *Assumption 4*, that the rate of profit (defined below) should be the same in each industry. Sraffa gives no justification for this, but it is obviously the equilibrium condition (in a world of certainty) for a dynamic process in which each capitalist tries to maximize his profits.

What $S2$ does *not* grant is the possibility of making any variation in either output scale or input proportions. Capitalists receive surplus, but do not invest it in the further expansion of outputs; nor, apparently, do they consume it, at least in the sense that there exist no demand equations for either capitalists or workers. Since we are mainly concerned with prices, there seem to be three possible alternative assumptions by which this procedure might be rationalized:

(i)   Constant returns to scale exist in each industry, which implies abandoning the fixity of the given outputs. Sraffa says in his preface that this is a harmless provisional assumption for the reader to make, but that in fact "no such assumption is made"; we shall return to this point later.

(ii) Following Mrs. Robinson's suggestion (op. cit., p. 54), no variation in the division between wages and profits can alter the commodity composition of output. This is an extremely restrictive assumption to swallow.

(iii) Some central mechanism exists for allocating the *commodity* composition of profits and wages, subject to the restraints of $S2$. This is necessary, since this commodity composition is not otherwise determined by the system, except in the two-industry case, as in Sraffa's example on p. 7. But since there is then no possibility of trade among consumer goods, this third assumption seems to rule out any rationale for equal money profit rates (and wage rates) in each industry.

Suppose that a vegetarian capitalist were allotted his profits in the form of meat; if he cannot trade, it is small consolation to be told that the money value of this meat, in proportion to the money value of the means of production he employs, is the same as that of everyone else's allocation (in proportion to the value of the means of production that *they* command).

All this is only to stress that half of an equilibrium system is just that, and not a small complete system. One wonders a little whether the striking results that Sraffa obtains would survive substantially intact in a more complete model, which would need to include a distribution theory, demand equations and some degree of factor substitution, and which would abandon the assumption of a uniform "harvest period" for each commodity.[7] But it is certainly of importance to investigate the bare logic of $S2$ and its variants, even though the discussion of variations of prices with changes in income distribution (all the while keeping to the same point of the n-dimensional output space), reminds one at times of the medieval scholastic debates concerning angels dancing on the point of a pin.

III

Let us keep to the notation of I, and replace Assumption 3 by 3a, i.e., that $\Sigma_i a_{ij} \leqslant 1$ for each j, with $\Sigma_i a_{ij} < 1$ for at least one j. We assume that each good is used in the production of every other good, either directly or indirectly. Define the rate of profit r_i in the ith industry by

$$(3\mathrm{i}) \qquad r_i = \frac{p_i - \Sigma_j a_{ij} p_j}{\Sigma_j a_{ij} p_j}$$

By Assumption 4, r_i is independent of i, and all rates of profit are equal to the uniform rate of profit r, which may be written

$$(3\mathrm{ii}) \qquad r = \frac{\Sigma_i p_i - \Sigma_i \Sigma_j a_{ij} p_j}{\Sigma_i \Sigma_j a_{ij} p_j} = \frac{\Sigma_i p_i - V}{V}$$

The first term on the righthand side of (3ii) is simply the value of total product, and the other term V is the total value of the means of production. By Assumption 4, this latter quantity is raised in each industry by the expansion factor $(1 + r)$ and the matrix equation for $S2$ becomes

$$(4) \qquad (1 + r)\mathbf{A}\mathbf{p} = \mathbf{p}$$

Setting $c = \dfrac{1}{(1 + r)}$, (4) becomes

$$(4\mathrm{i}) \qquad \mathbf{A}\mathbf{p} = c\mathbf{p}$$

Assuming for the moment that labor is a product like any other, we may ask if there is a solution to (4i) giving a positive price vector and a positive rate of profit. The answer is yes, and here we call on a remarkable theorem, due essentially to Perron,[8] and much used recently in mathematical economics. Since $\mathbf{A}$ is a matrix which is non-negative and indecomposable (a term defined below), there will by this theorem exist a real, positive root c^* of $\mathbf{A}$, which is no less in absolute value than any other root of $\mathbf{A}$, and which is unique (i.e. all other real positive roots are smaller). Moreover, with c^* is associated an eigenvector $\mathbf{p}^*$, each of whose components is non-zero and of the same sign. Since $\mathbf{p}^*$ is unique only up to a scale factor, we may always normalize it so that $\mathbf{p}^*$ is a positive vector. Hence there exists $\mathbf{p}^* > 0$ such that

$$(4\mathrm{ii}) \qquad \mathbf{A}\mathbf{p}^* = c^*\mathbf{p}^*$$

Sraffa chooses to normalize p^* by the condition that the money value of the net national income be unity (p. 12), which may be written

(5) $s'p^* = 1$

where s is the n-dimensional column vector of the physical surpluses s_j in each industry, and s' denotes the row vector which is the transpose of s (i.e. $s_j \doteq 1 - \Sigma_i a_{ij}$, so that $s_j \geqslant 0$ and s' is a semipositive vector).

As yet, however, we have only proved that the root c^* is positive; what we need to prove is that the equilibrium rate of profit r^* is positive. Since, $c^* = \dfrac{1}{(1 + r^*)}$, the requirement that r^* be positive (and finite) implies that c^* must be less than 1 and greater than zero. Fortunately this further result is also a corollary of the Perron theorem. Let M be the largest of the numbers $\Sigma_i a_{ij}$ (i.e. the largest column sum), and let m be the smallest such column sum. Then provided that m is actually less than M, we can assert that

(6) $m < c^* < M$

Since none of the column sums of **A** is greater than 1, and at least one is less (by Assumption 3a), while all column sums are positive, it follows that c^* must be between 0 and 1; if all column sums are equal, then $m = M = c^*$. Hence r^* is positive in any event. This proof also demonstrates the reasonable proposition that the equilibrium rate of profit must lie between the greatest and the smallest industry rate of surplus (measured as ratios of physically measurable quantities) in the system. Clearly r^* and p^* depend only on the "recipe" matrix **A**.

In proving those results we have assumed that: (a) each commodity is used as input, either directly or indirectly, in the manufacture of all other commodities (e.g., iron used in steel, steel used in ships, ships used in freight service, freight service used in wheat, wheat used in bread, and so on, where the chain would run through all commodities); and (b) that labor consumes fixed levels of inputs, irrespective of the rate of profit. Let us now relax these assumptions, beginning with (a). Sraffa calls those commodities which do not enter into the production of any other commodity, "non-basic commodities" (he later generalizes this definition considerably). Suppose that we have a two-sector model (think of Ricardo's "corn" and "iron"), and let the first commodity—"iron"—not enter into corn production, so that iron is "non-basic." This means that $a_{21} = 0$, and the equations corresponding to (4) will then be

(7)
$$(1 + r)a_{11}p_1 + (1 + r)a_{12}p_2 = p_1$$
$$(1 + r)a_{22}p_2 = p_2$$
$$(1 - a_{11})p_1 + (1 - a_{12} - a_{22})p_2 = 1$$

Since the unknowns are p_1, p_2 and r, it might be thought that the system (7) is sufficient to ensure the existence of a solution. But remember that the solution must contain *positive* prices and a *positive* uniform rate of profit. Let us take a particular numerical example of (7), as follows:

(7a)
$$(1 + r)0.8p_1 + (1 + r)0.3p_2 = p_1 \quad \text{(i)}$$
$$(1 + r)0.2p_2 = p_2 \quad \text{(ii)}$$
$$0.2p_1 + 0.5p_2 = 1 \quad \text{(iii)}$$

Now if $p_2 \neq 0$, we can conclude from (ii) that $(1 + r) = \dfrac{1}{a_{22}} = 5$. Substituting this into (i), we obtain $p_2 = -2p_1$, which from (iii) yields $p_1 = -\frac{5}{4}$, $p_2 = \frac{5}{2}$, and $r = 4$. Hence if $p_2 \neq 0$, the solution contains a negative price. If $p_2 = 0$, then $p_1 = 5$ and $r = \frac{1}{4}$. In either case we have a contradiction of Sraffa's combined requirements that the system be in a self-replacing state and that profit rates be uniform. If the value of p_2 is negative, then even though it uses only itself in its own production, the fact that $a_{22} < 1$ means that production of corn results in negative profit. If $p_2 = 0$, then its production cannot add to profit. Since there are positive profit opportunities in "iron," corn is not produced at all. But then iron production must cease also—since it requires corn—and the system is not self-replacing in any part.

It is possible to find necessary and sufficient conditions that a matrix containing "non-basics" will always yield prices which are all positive,[9] but these conditions appear to have little economic significance; in the present very simple example, they specialize to $a_{11} < a_{22}$, the economic rationale for which seems obscure. Therefore either we must abandon one of Sraffa's Assumptions 1-4, or we must assume that "non-basics" do not exist, if we are not to confine ourselves to a rather odd and restricted class of situations. I shall choose the course of abandoning "non-basics," since Assumptions 1-4 are the crux of Sraffa's system. This choice is reinforced by the consideration that the question of whether a good is "non-basic" is partly a matter of the degree of aggregation in the system. Thus suppose that initially we have a three-sector system as follows:

$$\begin{matrix} a_{11} & a_{12} & a_{13} \\ 0 & a_{22} & a_{23} \\ 0 & a_{32} & a_{33} \end{matrix}$$

in which the first good is non-basic. If we now aggregate the first and second sectors to one, we will obtain a new matrix

$$\begin{matrix} b_{11} & b_{12} \\ b_{21} & b_{22} \end{matrix}$$

in which there is no non-basic commodity.

This result, that non-basics will often not imply a positive price vector, means that the rather heavy emphasis placed on such commodities by Sraffa (he exemplifies them by luxury goods), seems misplaced. We may welcome the result, since it greatly simplifies the following analysis.

IV

The relaxation of the second provisional assumption, that there are fixed inputs into labor, poses such important problems that it occupies the rest of Part I.

Sraffa argues that when there is surplus in the system, it is only reasonable to expect that labor will share in it. He wistfully lingers over the possibility of dividing the wage into an "inter-industry" and a "surplus" part, but rejects it in order to conform to common usage. Such a division would seem reasonable if there were two non-competing groups of laborers—say slaves and freemen—but is (as Mrs. Robinson remarks, p. 54) very artificial otherwise. The model $S2$ was a genuine slave economy, since capitalists made profit at the usual rate on the production of labor, but in the new model, $S3$, there is no slave production. The total quantity of labor available is given (at 1 unit), and persists through time unchanged and unresponsive to prices or wages. However, we are still given quantities (this time $m = (n - 1)$ in number) which tell us the proportion of labor (l_i) used in the production of the unit level of the ith good; the vector of the l_i will be denoted by $\mathbf{L}$.

The new system involves an m-dimensional technology matrix $\mathbf{B}$, and corresponding price and "surplus" vectors, π and σ respectively. Let us denote the amount of the national income going to wages by W, and the *proportion* going to wages by ω. It is assumed implicitly that the wage rate is the same in each industry, although similar criticisms can be levelled at that as were done at the assumption of equal profit rates in section II. With these assumptions, and following the normalization rule (5), the system $S3$ may be written

$$(8) \quad \begin{aligned} (1 + r)\mathbf{B}\pi + W\mathbf{L} &= \pi & \text{(i)} \\ W &= \omega\sigma'\pi & \text{(ii)} \\ \sigma'\pi &= 1 & \text{(iii)} \end{aligned}$$

I shall postpone until the next section a consideration of whether there always exists a positive solution for r and π, given any pre-assigned value of ω (between 0 and 1), and shall simply assume provisionally that such a solution exists.

Since there is a fixed amount of labor, a reduction in ω corresponds to a fall in the wage rate. Industries that use a *relatively* small amount of labor will be worse off than those using a large amount, although complications arise since the means of production used by an industry of low labor-intensity may themselves have high labor-intensity. In any event, relative prices will almost certainly have to change if the system is to continue unperturbed, with a uniform rate of profit.[10]

Suppose, however, that there were an industry which employed labor and other means of production in such proportion that with a change in ω, the balance between wages and profits were maintained at the original level. This would imply that such a relationship held for *each* of the industries supplying the first industry's means of production; and so on back to the whole set of industries which directly or indirectly supply the first. Obviously the existence of such an industry would be very unlikely, but perhaps it could be *constructed*, as a "composite commodity," from the others.

Observe that the price of such an industry's product would never rise or fall with changes in ω, since there would never at any time be a change in the wage-profit proportion (for the full reasoning, see Sraffa's chapter 3). It could therefore serve as a standard commodity, in terms of which all other prices

could be measured. Sraffa then tackles the problem of whether such a commodity could always be constructed. I shall not follow his rather unconvincing proof of this (pp. 26-27), since an easier and much more illuminating route is available.

Sraffa starts his analysis by posing an apparently different question. Can we, by taking appropriate positive "fractions" of existing industries, construct a system such that the proportionate excess of output of each commodity, over the amount used as means of production in the system, is the same for each industry? Remembering that each output is 1 unit, this may be expressed by asking if there is a positive vector of numbers $(\lambda_1, \lambda_2, \ldots, \lambda_m)$ such that

$$(9) \quad \frac{\lambda_1}{\Sigma_i \lambda_i b_{i1}} = \frac{\lambda_2}{\Sigma_i \lambda_i b_{i2}} = \cdots = \frac{\lambda_m}{\Sigma_i \lambda_i b_{im}} = \frac{1}{v}$$

say, where all summation signs, here and in the sequel, are over the $(n - 1)$ integers $1, 2, \ldots, m$.

We may write (9) as

$$(9a) \quad \Sigma_i \lambda_i b_{ij} = v\lambda_j \qquad (j = 1, 2, \ldots, m)$$

or, in matrix form, where λ' is the row vector $(\lambda_1, \lambda_2, \ldots, \lambda_m)$

$$(9b) \quad \lambda'\mathbf{B} = v\lambda'$$

Taking the transpose of (9b), we get

$$(10) \quad \mathbf{B}'\lambda = v\lambda$$

which is of exactly the same form as (4i). $\mathbf{B}'$ is a non-negative indecomposable matrix, and its roots are the *same* as those of $\mathbf{B}$. Hence the dominant root v^* of $\mathbf{B}'$, which gives a positive equilibrium vector λ'^*, is the *same* as the maximal root of $\mathbf{B}$, which is $c^* = \dfrac{1}{(1 + r^*)}$.[11]

From a mathematical point of view, λ'^* is the *row* eigenvector corresponding to the maximal root c^* of $\mathbf{B}$, just as π^* (the price vector when all surplus goes to capital) is the *column* eigenvector corresponding to c^*. It follows that λ'^* is unique up to a normalizing factor, which Sraffa obtains by the relation

$$(11) \quad \lambda'^*\mathbf{L} = 1$$

This means that we take the *standard system* to be that which uses all the available labor supply of the *actual* system. Such a system produces the *standard national income*, and the "standard" ratio R of this income to the "standard" means of production is given, for *any* price vector π, by

$$(12) \quad R = \frac{\Sigma_j \pi_j (\lambda_j - \Sigma_i \lambda_i b_{ij})}{\Sigma_j \pi_j \Sigma_i \lambda_i b_{ij}}$$

which, from (9a), assumes the form for equilibrium situations

$$(12a) \qquad R = \frac{(1 - v^*)\Sigma_j \pi_j \lambda_j}{v^* \Sigma_j \pi_j \lambda_j}$$

Remembering that $v^* = c^* = \dfrac{1}{(1 + r^*)}$, and since each π_j and λ_j is positive, (12a) reduces to

$$(13) \qquad R = \frac{1 - c^*}{c^*} = r^*$$

Hence the standard ratio is (i) equal to the rate of profits of the actual system when none of the surplus goes to labor[12] (a rate which Sraffa calls the Maximum Rate), and (ii) is independent of prices, depending only on **B**, the technology matrix. It follows that this standard commodity has the desired properties laid down earlier.

We may pause here to enquire whether (following Sraffa) we have not implicitly smuggled an assumption of constant returns to scale into the analysis here. For we have multiplied, in each industry, each of the inputs by the fraction λ_i, and have assumed that output will now be λ_i. One could argue in defense, at least up to equation (12), that this trick has merely been a computing device to enable us to find the appropriate vector $\boldsymbol{\lambda}'^*$, given **B**, and that no changes in output actually occur. This is a little harder to maintain with equation (12), for then we actually consider what the "standard" level of production would be. But do we? We are still dealing only with a *Hilfskonstruktion*, the Standard System, and are not committed to the assertion that if we *actually* changed input levels by a fraction λ_i, we would *observe* output to be changed by the same fraction λ_i. The important point to take hold of is that at no time in part I do any output levels actually change, so that the question of whether constant returns to scale do or do not prevail can have no meaning.

Thus reassured, let us consider further properties of the standard system. Suppose that a fraction Θ of the standard national income goes to wages. This is equivalent to multiplying the numerator of (12) by $(1 - \Theta)$, which leads to the conclusion that the rate of profit r in the standard system will be

$$(14) \qquad r = R(1 - \Theta)$$

One achievement of part I is to show that such a linear relation between r and Θ is *not* confined to the standard system, but holds in the actual system, provided that wages are paid in "standard commodity" i.e. in a fixed "basket of goods," with weights $(\lambda_1, \lambda_2, \ldots, \lambda_m)$. Sraffa's proof of this in the book (p. 22) is mostly assertion, but it is fairly easy to demonstrate. The rate of profit r_a in the actual system is the amount of the national income remaining after paying away to wages the monetary equivalent of a fraction Θ of the standard national product, divided by the value of the actual means of production. Thus

$$(15) \qquad r_a = \frac{\Sigma_j \pi_j (1 - \Sigma_i b_{ij}) - \Theta(\Sigma_j \pi_j (\lambda_j - \Sigma_i \lambda_i b_{ij}))}{\Sigma_j \Sigma_i b_{ij} \pi_j}$$

Since by Assumption 4, r_a is the rate of profit in each industry, we have also [analogously to (3i)],

$$(16) \qquad r_a = \frac{\pi_i - \Sigma_j b_{ij} \pi_j - l_i \Theta(\Sigma_j \pi_j (\lambda_j - \Sigma_i \lambda_i b_{ij}))}{\Sigma_j b_{ij} \pi_j} \qquad (i = 1, 2, \ldots, m)$$

The last term in the numerator of (16) is the proportion of the total wage bill accruing to the ith industry; the same term does not appear in the denominator because Sraffa assumes (p. 10) that wages are *not* advanced from capital, but paid *ex post* as a share of the national product.

From (16), and the fact that $\lambda_i > 0$ for each i,

$$(17) \qquad r_a = \frac{\lambda_i \pi_i - \lambda_i(\Sigma_j b_{ij} \pi_j) - \lambda_i l_i \Theta(\Sigma_j \pi_j(\lambda_j - \Sigma_i \lambda_i b_{ij}))}{\lambda_i \Sigma_j b_{ij} \pi_j} \qquad (i = 1, 2, \ldots, m)$$

Summing over all i,

$$(18) \qquad r_a = \frac{\Sigma_i \lambda_i \pi_i - \Sigma_j \pi_j(\Sigma_i \lambda_i b_{ij}) - \Theta \Sigma_i \lambda_i l_i(\Sigma_j \pi_j(\lambda_j - \Sigma_i \lambda_i b_{ij}))}{\Sigma_j \pi_j(\Sigma_i \lambda_i b_{ij})}$$

From (9a) and (11), and because $v^* = c^*$,

$$(19) \qquad r_a = \frac{\Sigma_i \lambda_i \pi_i - c^* \Sigma_j \pi_j \lambda_j - \Theta(\Sigma_j \pi_j \lambda_j - c^* \Sigma_j \lambda_j \pi_j)}{c^* \Sigma_j \pi_j \lambda_j}$$

Since in this equilibrium situation each π_i and λ_i is positive, (19) reduces to

$$r_a = \frac{(1 - c^*)(1 - \Theta)}{c^*}$$

or

$$(20) \qquad r_a = R(1 - \Theta)$$

Notice that Θ is the fraction of the *standard* national income that goes to wages, and not the fraction ω of the actual national income. Sraffa adopts a new normalization rule for π, using

$$(21) \qquad \Sigma_j \pi_j(\lambda_j - \Sigma_i \lambda_i b_{ij}) = 1$$

which from (9a) can be written

$$(22) \qquad (1 - c^*)\Sigma_j \pi_j \lambda_j = 1$$

or in matrix form, from (13)

$$(23) \qquad \boldsymbol{\lambda}' \pi = \frac{R + 1}{R}$$

V

Our remaining task, left over from the early part of section IV, is to prove that the system $S3$, given by

$$(8) \quad \begin{array}{ll} (1+r)\mathbf{B}\pi + W\mathbf{L} = \pi & \text{(i)} \\ W = \omega\sigma'\pi & \text{(ii)} \\ \sigma'\pi = 1 & \text{(iii)} \end{array}$$

always has a positive solution for the price vector π, whatever the value of the wage-share parameter ω. As Sraffa remarks however (p. 33), once we cease to regard wages as physiologically given, it becomes less natural to suppose that it is ω which should be independently varied. To quote him: "The rate of profits, as a ratio, has a significance which is independent of any prices, and can well be 'given' before the prices are fixed. It is accordingly susceptible of being determined from outside the system of production."

Therefore we shall investigate the positivity of prices, profits and wages as the *rate* of profits r is varied.[13] A valid proof is not easy to find, but can be constructed with the help of material contained in a remarkable book by the mathematician Jacob Schwartz,[14] which appeared at a late stage in the preparation of this article. We begin by observing that since σ' is semipositive, (8iii) implies that a price vector which is at least semipositive must exist. Since this seems to prejudge the issue, let us reduce $S3$ to (8i) and (8ii) only; we can add (8iii) at such time as we have proved that π is positive.

It will prove convenient to rewrite (8i) in a new form, by writing $P_i = \dfrac{\pi_i}{W}$ for each i, and so obtaining

$$(24) \quad \mathbf{L} = [\mathbf{I} - (1+r)\mathbf{B}]\,\mathbf{P}$$

where $\mathbf{I}$ is the m-dimensional diagonal unit matrix, and $\mathbf{P}$ is the column vector of the P_i. Now in view of (8ii), we can only write (24) if ω is non-zero and the scalar $\sigma'\pi$ is non-zero, for otherwise W will be zero. If ω is zero, then (8i) reduces to an m-dimensional version of (4), for which we know there exist positive solutions for r and π.

If $\sigma'\pi$ is zero, however, the problem is more delicate. It follows from (3ii) that r must then be zero unless V is zero, in which case r assumes the indeterminate form $\frac{0}{0}$. Assuming temporarily that this is not the case, the conditions $r = 0$ and $W = 0$ imply that (8i) reduces to

$$(25) \quad \mathbf{0} = (\mathbf{I} - \mathbf{B})\pi$$

where $\mathbf{0}$ is a column vector of zeros. Since $(\mathbf{I} - \mathbf{B})^{-1}$ exists (actually consisting entirely of positive elements),[15] it follows that π, which is equal to $(\mathbf{I} - \mathbf{B})^{-1}\mathbf{0}$, is also a vector of zeros. If, instead, V in (3ii) is also zero, we fall back on the fact, due to Assumption 4, that r must also satisfy each of the $(m-1)$ equations (3i). Since $\sigma'\pi$ and W are both zero, those equations can clearly only be satisfied if each price is zero.

Hence $\sigma'\pi$ only vanishes for the trivial null solution $\pi = 0$; it follows that we are always entitled to write equation (24). We may now pose the problem

of this section by asking if there exist positive (i.e. every element > 0) inverses of the one-parameter family of matrices $(\mathbf{I} - (1+r)\mathbf{B})$, for a sufficiently large interval of values of the parameter r.

If so, then the equation

$$(26) \quad \mathbf{P} = (\mathbf{I} - (1+r)\mathbf{B})^{-1}\mathbf{L}$$

assures us that $\mathbf{P}$ will be a positive vector. Since (8ii) may be written

$$(27) \quad 1 = \omega\sigma'\mathbf{P}$$

it follows, by multiplying both sides of (27) by $W (\neq 0)$, that the positivity of $\mathbf{P}$ implies that W and π are both positive, and hence total profits also.[16]

An affirmative answer to our question can be derived straightforwardly from a series of results in Jacob Schwartz's lectures 2 and 3 (op. cit.), provided that we set *his* matrix π equal to his Φ, and identify both with our $\mathbf{B}$. Let us denote the maximum, or dominant, latent root of $(1+r)\mathbf{B}$ by the symbol dom $(1+r)\mathbf{B}$. Since $\mathbf{B}$ is a positive matrix, $(1+r)\mathbf{B}$ will be positive for $r > -1$, and hence dom $(1+r)\mathbf{B} > 0$ for $r > -1$.

From Schwartz's lemma 3.3, it follows that an inverse will always exist if r is such that dom $(1+r)\mathbf{B} < 1$. Suppose that r_{max} is the least upper bound of those r's for which this is true i.e. dom $(1+r)\mathbf{B} < 1$ for $r < r_{max}$. By theorems 2.2 and 2.3 of his lecture 2, it follows that dom $(1+r)\mathbf{B}$ is a strictly increasing and *continuous* function of r; hence we can equivalently define r_{max} as the unique solution of the equation

$$(28) \quad \text{dom } (1+r_{max})\mathbf{B} = 1$$

An alternative way of expressing this is to say [remembering equations (4) to (4ii)] that r_{max} is the unique number for which there exists a positive solution vector $\mathbf{P}_{max}$ of the system

$$(29) \quad (1+r_{max})\mathbf{B}\mathbf{P} = 1\mathbf{P}$$

which may be written

$$(30) \quad \mathbf{B}\mathbf{P} = \frac{1}{(1+r_{max})}\mathbf{P}$$

But (30) is just another way of writing the solution to (8i) when ω, and hence W, $= 0$. Therefore r_{max} is simply our old friend the Maximum Rate of Profit R, which obtains when the wage-share ω is zero. Moreover we know that since dom $\mathbf{B} < 1$, $r_{max} > 0$, so that the open interval $(-1, r_{max})$ is not empty. It follows that for $-1 < r < r_{max}$ we have dom $(1+r)\mathbf{B} < 1$, which in turn implies that $(\mathbf{I} - (1+r)\mathbf{B})^{-1}$ exists for all such r. Since $(1+r)\mathbf{B}$ is a positive matrix for this range of values of r, it follows from the result quoted for equation (25) that the inverses not only exist but also consist entirely of positive elements.

Hence $\mathbf{P}$ is a positive vector, which is our required main result. Utilizing Schwartz's lemma 3.6, we can assert an even stronger result. This lemma enables

us to say that if $(1 + r_1)\mathbf{B} < (1 + r_2)\mathbf{B}$, dom $(1 + r_1)\mathbf{B} < 1$ and dom $(1 + r_2)\mathbf{B} < 1$, then

$$(31) \qquad (\mathbf{I} - (1 + r_1)\mathbf{B})^{-1} < (\mathbf{I} - (1 + r_2)\mathbf{B})^{-1}$$

Now if $-1 < r_1 < r_2 < r_{max}$, (31) applies, so that we can say that the solution vector $\mathbf{P}$ is a strictly increasing function of r (Schwartz's theorem 3.7). *All prices rise in terms of wages as the rate of profits is increased towards r_{max}.*

We have spoken of the interval for r as $(-1, r_{max})$, but there is something repugnant to economic common sense in supposing that an equilibrium value of r can be less than zero. Accordingly we restrict the interval to be $(0, r_{max})$, which is not empty, by the results above. Also, utilizing $S3$ and an equation analogous to (3ii), we can write

$$(32) \qquad r = \frac{\sigma' \pi (1 - \omega)}{V}$$

When $r = 0$, then (32) means that $\omega = 1$, so that a zero profit rate implies that all income goes to labor, a reasonable result.

This completes our analysis of Sraffa's Part I;[17] all of his main results have been shown to be valid, and it is a reasonable presumption that the more extended analysis of Part II rests on secure foundations. Whether the work of the book as a whole is considered important depends partly upon the reader's view of pure economic theory. My own view would be that although particular points on which Sraffa lays stress, such as non-basics and the standard commodity, are of greater mathematical interest than economic, the book has made a serious contribution to a re-examination of our theory of general equilibrium. Such work as that of Sraffa and of Jacob Schwartz helps us realize that neo-classical Walrasian theory is not *the* general equilibrium theory, but only a *model* of general equilibrium. Other models may be much more helpful for the elucidation of important unresolved problems, especially in dynamics.

NOTES

1. For a typical reaction of the first type, see R. Quandt's review in *Journal of Political Economy* 69 (October 1961), p. 500, and for the second type of judgment, see Joan Robinson, *Oxford Economic Papers* 13 (February 1961), pp. 53-58; and R. L. Meek, *Scottish Journal of Political Economy* 8 (June 1961), pp. 119-36. An intermediate position is taken by M. W. Reder, *American Economic Review* 51 (September 1961), pp. 688-95.

2. R. Remak, "Kann die Volkswirtschaftslehre eine exakte Wissenschaft werden?" *Jahrbücher für Nationalökonomie und Statistik* 76 (1929), pp. 703-35. David Gale, *The Theory of Linear Economic Models* (New York: McGraw-Hill, 1960), chap. 8, pp. 260-71. The present model could also be treated by well-known techniques applicable to Markov (or stochastic) matrices because $\mathbf{A}$ belongs to this type. See e.g. F. R. Gantmacher, *Applications of the Theory of Matrices* (New York: Interscience, 1959), chap. 3, pp. 99-117.

Unless otherwise stated, all summation signs in this article will be over the n indices $1, 2, \ldots, n$.

3. Sraffa cites only the equality of equations and unknowns in (1) to guarantee the existence of a *positive* price vector. But it is clear that he is fully aware of these problems, both from a footnote (concerning non-viability), on p. 5, and from his assertion on p. 7 that non-basics (to be defined below) cannot appear in $S1$. This is an example of what was

meant above by saying that the book is mathematically (though not economically) incomplete. This property has misled one reviewer (Meek, op. cit., p. 119) into saying that "the mathematics used is of a very elementary character," which is akin to equating an iceberg to that part of it which shows above water.

4. Let us observe, in this connection, that in a footnote of his 1945 explication of the von Neumann model, D. G. Champernowne acknowledged the help derived from discussions with Sraffa (*Review of Economic Studies* 13, 1945-1946, p. 10). This note is, incidentally, useful in indicating the influence of the von Neumann model on the various main streams (Champernowne, Kahn, Kaldor, Joan Robinson, Sraffa) that make up current Cambridge thought on the theory of capital.

5. *The Works and Correspondence of David Ricardo*, ed. P. Sraffa, vol. I (Cambridge, 1951), pp. xxx-xxxiii. The logical structure of the Ricardian system has recently been brilliantly presented by L. L. Pasinetti, *Review of Economic Studies* 27 (1959-1960), pp. 78-98; the interested reader is recommended to study this article before attempting Sraffa's book, since it provides an excellent account of the Ricardian modes of thought immanent in Sraffa's approach.

6. Land, and hence land rent, is not introduced until part II.

7. In part II Sraffa makes considerable progress in relaxing this last assumption (whose crucial importance for Ricardo is well brought out by Pasinetti, op. cit., p. 91), by his very clever treatment of fixed capital in terms of joint products, a device due originally to Torrens, and exploited in particular by von Neumann.

8. See e.g., Gantmacher, op. cit., chap. 3, pp. 61-79. The theorem quoted is actually due to Frobenius, and represents a fairly straightforward extension of the basic result for positive matrices due to Perron. It may also be shown that no other root of $\mathbf{A}$ has a one-signed eigenvector associated with it, so that the rate of profit determined by c^* is the *only* rate which is consonant with positive prices.

Sraffa does not, at this stage, provide a proof of positivity of p^* and r^*; for his later discussion of this point, see section V below.

9. Gantmacher, op. cit., Theorem 6, p. 92. Considering now Sraffa's *generalization* of "non-basics" (which are also excluded by the considerations in the text), we may say that if there are non-basics, the matrix $\mathbf{A}$ is *decomposable*, i.e., by suitable interchanging of rows and columns, it can be put in the form

$$\begin{bmatrix} \mathbf{A}_1 & \mathbf{A}_2 \\ 0 & \mathbf{A}_3 \end{bmatrix}$$

where $\mathbf{A}_1$ and $\mathbf{A}_3$ are square matrices and 0 is a matrix of zeros. For a discussion of the economic aspects of such matrices, see e.g. Dorfman, Samuelson and Solow, *Linear Programming and Economic Analysis* (New York: McGraw-Hill, 1958), chap. 10. If a matrix is not decomposable, it is *indecomposable*, which is equivalent to containing no "non-basic" commodities.

10. There is a close similarity in method of approach here between Sraffa and Joan Robinson's "Rising Supply Price," *Economica*, 1941, reprinted both in *Readings in Price Theory*, ed. Boulding and Stigler, and in Mrs. Robinson's *Collected Economic Papers*, vol. I (Blackwell, 1951). Sraffa does not refer to this paper nor, indeed, to any literature of post-World War I vintage.

11. Sraffa asserts that if λ' is to be positive (he uses q's rather than λ's), then no non-basic can enter the system. This is not quite correct, as we have seen earlier (note 9), though the conditions *are* very stringent. However, using a result of Gantmacher, op. cit., (p. 96), we can assert that if *both* π and λ are to be positive, $\mathbf{B}$ must be indecomposable, so that there are then no non-basics.

12. In $S3$, unlike $S2$, labor does not get any reward at all when $w = 0$, since labor is not included in $\mathbf{B}$. This enhances the desirability of considering two non-competing types of labor, a device discussed above.

13. Sraffa's proof of this (pp. 27-28) is deficient, mainly because it assumes that wages and profits remain positive throughout; since these are partly the resultant of prices, the argument appears to be circular.

This is one example of the inadequacy of several of Sraffa's proofs. Since most of his theorems are essentially correct, it is an open question whether Sraffa in fact (perhaps with

the help of Besicovitch, Ramsey et al.) has more adequate proofs up his sleeve, proofs which he did not include for fear of making the book "too mathematical." Given the present temper of pure economic theory, such a fear seems misplaced; their inclusion (should they exist) would have made the book *less* difficult.

14. Jacob L. Schwartz, *Lectures on the Mathematical Method in Analytical Economics* (New York: Gordon and Breach, 1961). It is my impression that part C of Schwartz's book does, in a sense, carry forward the programme announced in Sraffa's preface, of preparing a systematic critique of neo-classical general equilibrium theory, a critique based on Sraffa-type models. The similarity in methods of approach is striking, especially in their similar conclusions regarding the relatively minor role in price formation played by individual demand functions. Since Schwartz makes no reference to Sraffa, this may be taken as supporting evidence for the considerable originality displayed in the former's work.

15. This is another consequence of the Perron theorem. See e.g. G. Debreu and I. N. Herstein, "Non-negative Square Matrices," *Econometrica* 21 (1953), Theorem III, p. 602.

16. Strictly speaking our argument only shows that W and each price must have the same sign, which could be negative. But since we have already shown that for $W = 0$, π is positive, it follows by simple continuity arguments that the common sign must in fact be positive.

17. The last chapter of Part I is a straightforward "reduction" of prices to dated quantities of labor, a process familiar from Leontief models in which labor is the only primary input. A somewhat similar analysis is to be found in section 3 of Schwartz's lecture 4.

Further results from the latter's lecture 3 would enable us to carry through a similar analysis to that in the text for the case where there are several grades of labor, instead of just one.

PART V
Toward a New Political Economy: A Dialogue between Mr. Ricardo, Mr. Sraffa, and Karl Marx

18

Ideology and Analysis

JOAN ROBINSON
Professor of Economics at Cambridge University

It is natural that a student of the social sciences should choose the school to which he attaches himself according to his ideological sympathies. But when he judges all points of logical and factual analysis by ideological standards and refuses to learn anything from the work of any school whose ideology he does not accept, he cuts himself off from making any useful contribution to the development of his subject and ends by substituting slogans for the insight that led him to form his ideological beliefs in the first place.

Some writers purport to deny that analysis and interpretation of evidence can have any validity apart from ideology. (I say purport to deny, for the fact that they deploy arguments in favor of the ideology that they support shows that they do not accept in practice that argument cannot have any validity.) This point is discussed by Dr. Barrington Moore in a book entitled *Reflections on the Causes of Human Misery and upon Certain Proposals to Eliminate Them.*

> There are many people today who apparently believe that once moral judgments enter a discussion, science necessarily flies out the window. Since, they agree, moral considerations are unavoidable, there can be no such thing as a scientific approach to human affairs. Moral judgments are inevitably arbitrary, this line of argument continues, and therefore no two people with different moral positions can possibly agree in their interpretation of social facts.
>
> That aspect of the issue may have stirred up more dust than is really necessary. If the factual evidence and the logic in a political treatise are sound, the moral starting point plays a very minor role towards the intellectual contribution that the treatise can make. One can reverse the moral premise without affecting the rest of the argument. In the case of this little book, if the general arguments are correct, presumably anyone who wished to increase human suffering would find the discussion pertinent.[1]

In what follows I offer a few examples of how confusing logic with ideology has impoverished the development of economics.

It is obvious enough that the academic schoolmen, from Böhm-Bawerk to Samuelson, cut themselves off from studying the classical problems of accumulation and distribution for fear of being contaminated by Marxism. This has reduced latter-day orthodoxy to mere triviality. There is no need to dwell upon that point. I want rather to discuss some aspects of academic economics of

This article was first published in Sozialismus, Geschichte und Wirtschaft; Aus der Festschrift für Eduard März, Europa-Verlag, Zurich, 1977.

which Marxists might have made good use if they, also, had not been nervous about ideological contamination.

1. VALUE AND PRICES

The flow of production taking place in an industrial economy is an extremely complex entity that cannot be represented in any simple measure. It is something which exists. It is *there* in reality. It is not affected by the way we choose to represent it, but various ways of representing it are connected with various alternative ways of diagnosing its behavior through time, its distribution between classes, and so forth.

In a drastically simplified schematism, it may be represented as a flow of money values corresponding to the market prices at which goods change hands or are entered in the books of business and government organizations. Or it may be represented in money values deflated by a chosen index of prices. It may be represented as a list of quantities of commodities, in tons, pints, and yards. Or it may be represented in labor value, that is as a number of man-hours of work.

When "gross national product" is represented by labor value, it consists of two parts—c, the pre-existing "constant capital" used up during, say, a year, and net labor value $(v + s)$, the labor time worked during the year. The constant capital was produced in the past by labor time working with then pre-existing constant capital and so on, *ad infinitum* backwards. It therefore cannot be reduced simply to a number of labor hours that can be added to the net value of the current year. And there is no advantage in trying to do so. The constant capital used up and replaced can be subtracted in physical units from gross physical product of the year's work. The physical net product is then represented by the man-hours of work performed during that year.

What is the relation between a calculation in money values and in labor values? Total net national product in terms of money and in terms of labor hours are two different ways of presenting the same physical facts, but when we want to discuss the division of the total between wages and surplus we cannot treat them as identical.

As a first approximation, let us suppose that money prices are such that there is a uniform rate of profit on capital throughout the economy and that workers are all alike, so that a man-hour is a simple unit in which values can be measured.

Now, in the special case where "organic composition of capital" is the same in all lines of production, money value and labor values coincide, not only for total output, but for each segment of output. In that case the rate of exploitation, s/v, is identical with the ratio of profits to wages in money terms, P/W. Moreover, the real wage regarded as what the workers get is identical with the real cost of labor that the capitalists have to pay.

When prices do not correspond to labor values, we have to work out the "prices of production" in the particular economy that we are examining. This involves valuing the stock of capital, for the value of his capital determines the profit that each capitalist receives.

Marx made this calculation in a very rough and ready way. He identified c, the means of production used up in a year, with C, the stock in existence, and v,

the annual wage bill, with V, the wage fund. And he valued both elements in capital in terms of labor values instead of at prices corresponding to the ruling rate of profit. With the assistance of Piero Sraffa, we can work out the "transformation problem" correctly, at least in principle. When the physical conditions of production and the overall share of wages in output is given there is one pattern of prices of commodities, including the elements making up the stock of means of production, and one rate of profit on capital. Or, the other way round, there is one share of wages and profits in total net income corresponding to each rate of profit on capital. Thus, when either the rate of profit or the rate of exploitation is given, the relation of labor values to prices of production is determined.

Anwar Shaikh has shown that the same result is arrived at by treating Marx's calculation as the first round in a procedure of iteration, as though the transformation took place as a historical process; prices proportional to labor values are conceived to obtain at some base date and they are then modified, step by step, until a uniform rate of profit on capital is established.[2]

Now consider the meaning of s/v and P/W. We may consider the real wage—the value of labor power—as a specific bundle of commodities (as in von Neumann's system, or like Ricardo's "corn"). The commodities the capitalists receive as net profit are a different bundle, containing inputs for investment and luxury consumption goods. When money prices of the two bundles of commodities are not proportional to their labor values, P/W does not necessarily coincide with s/v.

This is a significant difference when the real wage is, in real life, a specific bundle of goods that remains more or less constant through time. But in modern conditions, with the composition of output continuously changing and the level of consumption of industrial workers rising, there does not seem to be much point in calculating labor values. For practical purposes, P/W is both more accessible in terms of statistics and more significant in terms of the diagnosis of the behavior of the economy. However, it is still necessary to distinguish between W deflated by the prices of commodities that workers consume (that is, the real wage) and W deflated by prices in general (that is, the cost of labor to the capitalists as a whole).

There has been a great deal of unnecessary controversy and fuss over all this because the ideological aura attached to the labor theory of value has dazzled Marxists and blinded academics so that neither could find their way through the analysis.

2. EFFECTIVE DEMAND

In the three volumes of *Capital* there are a number of theories of the instability of production under capitalism—the mechanism of the absorption and re-creation of a reserve army of unemployed labor; the problem of realization of the surplus; an echo cycle, due to bunching of replacements of equipment at ten-year intervals; underconsumption ("the last cause of all real crises") due to unequal distribution of income—but in the main line of the argument, capitalists continuously invest the surplus that they extract. ("Accumulate! Accumulate! That is Moses and the prophets.") There may be in some far future an absolute over-production of capital, or there may be a falling rate of profit because organic

composition rises, as time goes by, relatively to the rate of exploitation, but before the Keynesian revolution, no one found in Marx a systematic treatment of chronic or cyclical deficiency of effective demand in a market economy.

Marxists, of course, have no sympathy with Keynes' ideology. His meliorist philosophy, his "moderately conservative" politics, and his ludicrous comments on Marx naturally raise prejudice. But this is not a valid reason for refusing to understand his analysis.

In this connection we have a striking illustration of the independence of analysis from ideology (when logic is not deliberately fudged or evidence cooked). Michal Kalecki found out independently all the main points in Keynes' analysis. He, in spite of much disillusionment, was all his life devoted to the cause of socialism, and he found the basis for his theory in the Marxian schema of expanded reproduction. His version of the general theory of employment is in some respects more coherently argued than Keynes', but Keynes is more useful in shooting down academic orthodoxy, because he understood it from within.

With the aid of Kalecki's analysis, it is possible to sort out all the various elements in Marx's theories of crises, get them into perspective, and apply them, with necessary adaptions, to the problems of capitalist, socialist, and so-called developing economies in the world today.

3. THE RATE OF PROFIT

In reality, of course, there is no such entity as *the* rate of profit. Investment by capitalist firms is guided by estimates of future profits, while the distribution of income is governed by realized profits. The two are never exactly in line with each other, for expectations never turn out to have been exactly correct. Moreover, the level of profits (either *ex ante* or *ex post*) is not uniform throughout an economy. There are systematic variations due to differences in monopolistic power, and there are chance variations in the fortunes of particular industries or particular firms:

All the same, it is useful to set up a model of an economy developing in sufficiently tranquil conditions to make outcomes fairly consonant with expectations, with sufficiently pervasive competition to make the rate of profit uniform. Moreover it is convenient to assume that organic composition is the same in all sectors, so that we do not have to bother about whether s/v has the same meaning as P/W.

Before discussing Marx's treatment of the rate of profit, we must clear up some points in his notation.

When $v + s$ and c, or $W + P$ and A, represent the flow per annum of net income (wages and net profits) plus replacement (amortization) of wear and tear of equipment and stocks consumed, then we cannot write $s/(c + v)$ as the rate of profit on capital. The stock of capital as a quantity of labor time embodied in physical means of production should be written as C and the wage fund (which is related to v, the wage bill, by the average of the periods of throughput in different industries), should be written as V. Then (assuming that labor value prices have always ruled) $s/(C + V) = P/K$ where K is the value of the stock of capital in wage units, at the ruling rate of profit.

Marx habitually assumed that $v = V$, because he had taken over the

Ricardian system based on an annual harvest. Given the wage rate, V per man employed is a stock of corn in the barn after harvest, to be used to pay out v, a week at a time, over the year until the next harvest. In industry, the period of throughput varies with technology and is neither uniform between industries nor constant through time. It is important in relation to finance—bank loans are used for working capital rather than for investment in equipment—but on the level of generality of Marx's argument it is not of any importance at all.

Clearly, the rate of exploitation must be written s/v. The extent to which an employer exploits labor does not depend upon the amount of V that he owns or borrows but on the amount of v that he pays out, relatively to the net output $(v + s)$ that he makes the workers produce.

Organic composition cannot be written as c/v or C/V. Neither of these ratios is of any interest, either technologically or economically. Technically C and c consist of two parts, fixed equipment, and materials, power, and so on used up in the process of production. The latter element together with V constitutes working capital. The distinction between working and fixed capital is of importance in some connections, but it has only a remote connection with the power of capital to exploit labor or with the determination of the rate of profit. The important relationship is $(C + V)/v$ which, on our assumptions, is the same ratio as K/W.

Now, what is the theory of the determination of the rate of profit in *Capital*?

In Volume I, the mechanism of the reserve army will keep commodity wages more or less constant, while accumulation and technical change are raising output per head. Therefore the rate of profit on capital is rising over the long run.

Rosa Luxemburg pointed out that it is impossible to predict a falling rate of profit if commodity wages are to remain constant, and that the danger for capitalism lies in the sphere of realization.

In Volume III, it seems that the rate of exploitation (s/v) is expected to be more or less constant. This implies that commodity wages will be rising. The tendency to a falling rate of profit will be due to technological changes raising K/W faster than P/W. In the counteracting causes, Marx points out that the labor value of the physical ingredients in C may fall, but he did not emphasize the point that the labor value of a constant commodity wage falls towards zero as output per man rises so that there is no necessary limit to s/v.

Whether technology tends to raise K/W through capital-using innovations is a matter of fact, not of logic. No doubt in the phase of industrialization that Marx was observing, C/v was rising. Nowadays the "stylized facts" seems to correspond to more or less neutral innovations that raise the money value of capital per man in more or less the same proportion as the money value of output per man. Then an overall rate of profit on capital, constant through time, is compatible with a constant rate of exploitation (s/v or P/W) which entails commodity wages rising in proportion to output per head.

Once he has left the anchorage of constant commodity wages, Marx does not give any systematic account of what determines the rate of exploitation, but from his general argument we can see that there are two interconnected forces at work.

The first is the relation of accumulation to the growth of the labor force. When capital is accumulating rapidly, the reserve army is absorbed into employment, and the share of wages in net income rises. Marx refused to admit that growth of population is deleterious to the interests of the workers, but his argument clearly shows that it is, and modern experience certainly confirms this.

The second element, which is not unconnected with the first, is the growth of political power of organized labor. This also is clearly seen in modern times. We find that the share of wages in value added in industry is highest in countries like Australia, Sweden, and Finland; in the capitalist countries in general it is twice or three times that in the Third World. It has been rising in Japan since the reserve army from agriculture was absorbed into industry.

It is easy to understand why the academic economists have not devoted much attention to this subject. The Marxists, absorbed in theological arguments about the relation of surplus value to profits, have also neglected to study it.

To return to formal theory, Sraffa has shown that, when we know the technical conditions of production and the overall rate of exploitation, we can find the unique set of prices that is compatible with a uniform rate of profit. This determines the wage in terms of commodities and the cost of labor to each group of capitalists. There is then no need to continue to confine the argument to the case of labor value prices. When organic composition varies between industries, prices are not simply proportional to labor values but are related to them in a systematic way.

Sraffa does not offer any theory of what determines the rate of profit. His argument begins and ends with the relation of the rate of profit to the rate of exploitation in one system of technical relationships. His purpose was to vindicate Marx by showing that the orthodox theory is quite empty, rather than to discuss how to fill the void.

A Marxian analysis of the historical evolution of the rate of exploitation provides the setting, in broad terms, for a theory of profits; some detail can be fitted into it with the aid of Kalecki.

In an industrial economy, there is, at any moment, a particular amount of productive capacity in existence. Prices of commodities are formed, not by supply and demand, but by the decisions of firms, who fix the gross margin or markup on prime cost, at levels calculated to cover total cost of production at some standard rate of utilization of plant, plus an allowance for net profit that depends mainly on the weakness or strength of competition in the various markets in which the goods are to be sold.

The amounts that will be sold, at these prices, of the total flow of output, depends on the level of effective demand. When the economy can be divided exhaustively into two classes—workers and capitalists—and when the workers are spending their wages week by week as they receive them, it follows that total gross profits going to the capitalists as a whole are equal to their expenditure on investment and on their own consumption. "The workers spend what they get, and the capitalists get what they spend."

There are many complications that have to be introduced into Kalecki's simple model to analyze a modern economy, but the basis is there.

It is possible also to work out a long-period version of the theory, in which accumulation is going on at a steady rate. This, however, is only a first step that

should not be given much weight. In reality, all the interesting and important questions lie in the gap between pure short-period and pure long-period analysis.

Analysis that is put at the service of ideology is not interesting because we know in advance what the answer is going to be. When we consider the world evolving around us, we see a great number of questions that need to be explored because the answers are not obvious at all.

NOTES

1. Moore, B., *Reflections on the Causes of Human Misery and Upon Certain Proposals to Eliminate Them* (Boston: Beacon Press, 1972), pp. 4 and 5.
2. "The So-called 'Transformation-Problem': Marx Vindicated," mimeo. New School for Social Research, April 1973. [Reading No. 7 above is a revised version.]

19

Sraffa and Price Theory
An Interpretation

ALESSANDRO RONCAGLIA
Professor of Economics at University of Perugia, Italy

I

The main objective of Sraffa's *Production of Commodities by Means of Commodities* (1960) is an analysis of prices of production, and their relationship with the distribution of income between wages and profits. Yet his analysis implies deep conceptual changes that make it completely different from traditional economic theory; thus it has a bearing on the whole corpus of economic analysis.

Up to now, however, the implications of Sraffa's analysis have not been fully appreciated. Both marginalist economists and Marxists have put forward interpretations of Sraffa's analysis that greatly reduce its scope, although from divergent viewpoints. From the "right wing," marginalist economists (for example, Quandt, 1961, and Reder, 1961) maintain that Sraffa's book simply presents a new version of an already large genus, that of linear models of price determination. Sraffa would have been the first to present a complete and rigorous linear model, had he published his results in the 1920s, when (as Sraffa, 1960, p. vi, tells us) it was conceived. Today, however, it cannot add much to what is already known. These critics thus argue that Sraffa's analysis must be considered as a special case of the general neoclassical model of economic equilibrium. From the "left wing," a number of Marxists consider Sraffa a neo-Ricardian, meaning that (1) his contribution is limited to a solution of the Ricardian problem of finding a standard of value invariant to changes in distribution; and (2) Sraffa's analysis reproduces a number of errors implicit in Ricardo's analysis, errors already criticized by Marx (see, for example, Medio, 1972, and Rowthorn, 1974; Nuti, 1974, succeeds in combining both right-wing and left-wing criticisms).

As we will see, both these interpretations are based on a number of misunderstandings, especially on the side of the marginalists, who fail to see the conceptual and methodological contribution implicit in Sraffa's analysis. In the following sections, we will evaluate Sraffa's contribution by analyzing, and

This article, previously unpublished, supposes the reader to be acquainted with Sraffa's book. The interpretation of Sraffa's analysis here adopted is presented in Roncaglia (1975, 1976). Thanks are due to P. Garegnani, J. Kregel, and L. Spaventa for helpful comments on a first draft of this paper; responsibility for all remaining errors is obviously mine.

criticizing, these opposite interpretations. We will first consider the marginalist viewpoint, which helps, by contradistinction, to place the main elements of Sraffa's analysis in their proper persepctive.

II

The starting point for the right-wing assessments of Sraffa's analysis is the introduction of the assumption of constant returns to scale into the system. This assumption is considered necessary for Sraffa's results, especially for the construction of the standard system (see, for example, Collard, 1963, Dominedò, 1962, Quandt, 1961. However, as Sraffa himself stresses on three occasions on the very first page of his book, "no such assumption is made" (p. v); and indeed those passages in the book that seem to contradict the author's denial only imply mental experiments requiring purely virtual, not actual, changes in output levels.

The superfluity of constant returns is fundamental, both for rejecting the marginalist interpretation that Sraffa's analysis of prices is based on the usual framework of supply and demand, and for understanding the main aspects of the development of Sraffa's thought.

To understand Sraffa's position concerning returns, it is necessary to go back to 1925, when Sraffa published a paper on the relations between cost and quantity produced. In this paper Sraffa shows that the "laws" of increasing and decreasing returns cannot be used to determine equilibrium prices and quantities in "partial" analysis. Originally, classical economists used these laws in different contexts. The law of diminishing returns was used in the theory of distribution in order to determine rent; the law of increasing returns, which was based on the connection between market size and division of labor, was used to explain technical progress within the context of the theory of production. Marshall, and other neoclassical economists, transposed these laws in the analysis of prices, using them jointly as the basis of a law of supply in individual markets. Analytically this law took the form of a connection between costs and quantity produced, a form that was required to produce a theory of supply prices parallel with the corresponding law of demand, based on a connection between utility and quantity demanded. The two laws could then be coordinated to obtain the quantity produced and sold at the equilibrium price in any individual market.

Sraffa does not deny the existence of a connection between the level of output of an industry and its average unit costs. He simply stresses that the variations in unit costs brought about by changes in the level of output in any industry are accompanied by variations in costs in other industries. These variations are generally of the same order of magnitude as the variations in costs in the industry under consideration, for both of them are brought about by the same basic underlying causes: the decreasing returns generated by a more intense utilization of some scarce factor of production, and the increasing returns due to general technical progress associated with the economies of production on a large scale. In other words both increasing and decreasing returns cannot be taken into account in the analysis of partial equilibria, as they are incompatible with the *ceteris paribus* assumption.

Once this point is established, there are three possible alternative methods for the analysis of prices consistent with the conceptual framework of marginalist

theory: (1) dropping both types of variable returns to scale and concentrating on constant costs [Sraffa points to this possibility, stressing however that it "constitutes only a preliminary approximation of reality" (1925, p. 328)]; (2) abandoning the assumption of perfect competition—the method adopted in Sraffa (1926), a paper that marks the beginning of a vast literature on imperfect competition; and finally (3) the analysis of general economic equilibrium. Interpreting *Production of Commodities by Means of Commodities* as an attempt in this third direction is the obvious alternative to interpreting it as a critique of marginalist theory. But to constrain Sraffa's analysis to the traditional framework, where equilibrium prices correspond to equality between supply and demand, forces one to introduce the assumption of constant returns into Sraffa's analysis in order to separate the determination of prices from the determination of levels of output. This explains why marginalist interpreters are so insistent on searching for hints of constant returns assumptions here and there in Sraffa's book, notwithstanding Sraffa's explicit and repeated denials of their existence. The rejection of the constant returns assumption, conversely, leads us to interpret Sraffa's analysis as a rejection of the conceptual framework of marginalist economic analysis.

III

The new path opened by Sraffa is different from the traditional one on many accounts, while at the same time it offers many similarities to the conceptual frameworks of classical political economy and Marxism. In this section we will sketch the main characteristics of Sraffa's analysis by comparing it with the marginalist, the classical, and the Marxian conceptual frameworks.

Let us start with value theory. As we have seen above, Sraffa rejects the traditional approach to the problem of price determination based on the concepts of supply and demand curves. Wicksteed, named by Sraffa "the purist of marginal theory" (Sraffa, 1960, p. v), had already recognized that this approach is a hybrid of irreconcilable objective (cost) and subjective (demand) elements. According to Wicksteed (1934, pp. 785, 788) when prices are determined on the basis of consumers' tastes, technology, and availability of resources, the subjective elements (consumers' tastes, represented by the demand functions) necessarily tend to dominate the theoretical scheme; the objective elements (technology and availability of resources, represented by the supply functions), ultimately have to be translated into subjective terms in order to allow comparisons between the two. Thus costs are interpreted as opportunity costs, that is, the utility that might be obtained in uses other than the one considered; and supply curves are absorbed, as an "inverted" genus, in the all-embracing category of subjective demand curves. The marginalist analytical framework necessarily corresponds to subjective value theory.

On the contrary, the subjective element represented by demand is excluded from Sraffa's analysis because prices of production are determined on the basis of "physical production costs," that is, the quantities of the various means of production (labor included) required to obtain a given quantity of product. In other words Sraffa reproposes the "objective" approach that characterizes the analysis of classical economists, such as Petty and Ricardo, and, we might add,

Marxian analysis (even if, as we will see later on, Sraffa's analysis has been condemned as non-Marxian precisely for being based on "physical" data).

The distinction between the subjective and the objective approach has been presented by some writers (for example, Arcelli, 1964) in a modified way, as a distinction between the "scarcity" and the "reproducibility" approaches, whereby prices are interpreted on the one hand as indices of scarcity relatively to final demand, and on the other hand as prices of production, representing the conditions of exchange to be satisfied to keep in motion the productive process. Although still useful for stressing yet another aspect of the basic difference between the marginalist and the Sraffian conceptual framework (scarcity of land and other nonreproducible means of production is dealt with in Sraffian as in Ricardian analysis, but it influences prices only indirectly, through technology), this distinction introduces some elements of ambiguity into the comparison. In fact, one could be led to consider only differences in the problems that the various theoreticians have posed, thereby completely overlooking what is indeed a fundamental difference in their conceptions of the world (their "visions," as Schumpeter, 1954, calls them). The eclectic attitude of considering alternative models representing the same phenomena as compatible because they tackle different problems is out of place when those models originate from completely opposite "visions," as is the case with Sraffian and marginalist analyses.

The difference in value theory between the subjective and the objective approaches corresponds to a basic difference in the vision of the working of the economic system. As Sraffa notes, the "picture of the system of production and consumption as a circular process," which he accepts on a line with classical economists and Marx, "stands in striking contrast to the view presented by modern theory, of a one-way avenue that leads from 'Factors of production' to 'Consumption goods'" (1960, p. 93).

When the concept of surplus is a central feature of the analysis, then reproduction, and not consumption, is conceived to be the end of the production process. This has a bearing on the way various problems are dealt with; in particular, the problem of income distribution is tackled in terms of division of the surplus among social classes. As Sraffa's analysis shows, within this framework the problem of distribution is distinguished from that of price determination, and the way is left open for the consideration of the influence of economic, social, and political factors on wages or profits. On the other hand, traditional theory usually considers distribution as part of the theory of prices. The prices of "factors of production" are determined, as are those of all other goods, on the basis of such data as technology, availability of resources, and consumers' tastes; in particular, the rate of profits is considered as the price of a specific "factor of production" called "capital." A logical criticism of this theoretical approach is part of the achievement of Sraffa's book. The same criticisms have been independently developed with reference to the various forms of marginalist theory by Garegnani (1960), who shows that the aggregate concept of capital is necessary for all marginalist theories wishing to determine a uniform rate of profits in the long run.

As for price theory proper, the changes in the analytical scheme of price determination imply a radical modification in the concept of price itself. In

traditional theory prices are determined on the basis of interaction between the forces of supply and demand: equilibrium prices are defined as those prices that ensure equality between supply and demand. In Sraffa's, as in the classical or Marxian analysis, "prices of production" (or "natural prices") are those prices that simply ensure a uniform rate of profits in all sectors. It is this condition that replaces the stricter condition of equality between supply and demand in all sectors.

The new concept of equilibrium prices implies a return to the classical (and Marxian) concept of "free" competition, based on freedom of entry of new firms into any sector. Discrepancies between the sectoral and the general profit rate would provoke new entries in sectors with a profit rate higher than average. New entries would increase production relative to demand, and prices would fall until the common rate of profit is restored. There is no need for the conditions that under marginalist theory are necessary for the existence of "perfect" competition; that is, the impossibility for individual firms to influence the price of their own product and their means of production, or, in more precise analytical terms, a small (infinitesimal) size of firms as compared to the size of the industry, and a high (infinite) number of firms. It is clear that the marginalist concept of perfect competition stems from the necessity of the *ceteris paribus* assumption for partial analysis (that is, for the analysis of equilibrium in an industry considered in isolation), which allows us to consider the set of relative prices as a datum from the viewpoint of each individual firm. This conception, as we have seen, has already been criticized by Sraffa (1925).

Finally, in Sraffa's analysis, demand no longer directly influences prices, and, as a consequence of this, there is no longer the simultaneous determination of prices and quantities that characterizes marginalist theory. The Marxian framework, in which the problem of the levels of output is distinguished from the so-called realization problem, is thus brought to mind. Entrepreneurs decide how much to produce, on the basis of expected sales; once the levels of output are fixed, prices of production follow from technology and the prevailing rate of profits (or of real wages). It is only at this point that we are confronted with the realization problem, which concerns the relationship between quantities produced and quantities sold, between prices of production and market (actual) prices. From a logical viewpoint levels of output are uphill of the price problem, while realization is down-dale. Sraffa does not deal with either problem, but concentrates his analysis on prices of production, distinguishing them from market prices and assuming levels of output as given. As a consequence Sraffa's analysis is compatible with the Keynesian theory of employment based on the principle of "effective demand" and with the rejection of "Say's Law."

IV

All these differences between the conceptual frameworks of marginalist and Sraffian analysis point to a basic difference in methodology. Sraffa's methodological position, implicit in *Production of Commodities*, can be deduced from his care in identifying the specific problem with which he is dealing and in distinguishing it from all other problems, so that the set of data to be taken into account in the analysis is reduced to a minimum. As Sraffa (1951) showed with

reference to the Ricardian analysis of an invariant measure of value, the confusion between different problems (invariant to what?) and the attempt at solving more than one problem at a time (invariance to changes in distribution and to changes in technology), may even render the problem insoluble. A precise understanding of the problem dealt with is also needed when we consider someone else's work: We cannot grasp Ricardo's contribution to economic analysis if we do not recognize his supposition that "to determine the laws which regulate . . . distribution, is the principal problem in Political Economy" (1951, p. 5), and that he utilized the labor theory of value to this end (as Sraffa, 1951, shows). Thus in *Production of Commodities* Sraffa distinguishes the problem of prices of production, and their relationship with changes in distribution, from all other problems: distribution, levels of output and employment, realization, technological change, accumulation, development . . . . But this is not an unrealistic *ceteris paribus* assumption; it is rather an attempt to isolate *in vacuo* certain particular relationships among specific economic variables.

Marginalist methodology, as exemplified by Robbins (1935) or Samuelson (1947) tends in the opposite direction. Samuelson expresses this at the very beginning of his book by quoting the mathematician E. H. Moore: "The existence of analogies between central features of various theories implies the existence of a general theory which underlies the particular theories and unifies them with respect to those central features" (1947, p. 3). Thus economics is defined as "the science which studies human behaviour as a relationship between ends and scarce means which have alternative uses," with the proviso that "there exists a hierarchy of ends" (Robbins, 1935, pp. 14 and 16). That is, the purpose of marginalist economists is the building of a *general* theory. The existence of a unifying analytical structure is granted by the identification of economics with one general problem, the optimal allocation of scarce resources between alternative uses. All specific problems (from international trade to the theory of the firm) are considered as only particular aspects of the general problem. Thus finding a method for solving the general problem means also being able to solve any particular problem.

Elsewhere (Roncaglia, 1975, chap. 6) I have compared the methodological position of marginalist economists to that implicit in Wittgenstein's *Tractatus Logico-Philosophicus* (1922), and the methodological position implicit in Sraffa's work to that implicit in Wittgenstein's *Philosophical Investigations* (1953). Here I simply want to stress that a finding of this examination of methodological differences is that marginalist methodological categories are no longer applicable to Sraffa's analysis. Thus the distinctions between general and partial, static and dynamic analysis, do not apply to Sraffa's analysis. In fact, these distinctions are both based on the existence of a single analytical model fully describing the working of an economic system, while particular models analyzing specific aspects of the economic process are only considered as parts of the general model and are defined according to what is missing in them and present in the general model. This classification scheme does not apply to Sraffa's analysis. An instant's reflection will show that it is neither general (it does not attempt to explain the determination of *all* economic variables) nor partial (it considers *all* economic variables necessary to solve the problem dealt with, and does not limit itself to a single industry); neither dynamic (it does not consider the evolution of an economic system in time) nor static (it considers a particular instant in the process of development of an economic system, and is not "atemporal," that is, out of historical time).

Obviously, the attempt at building a general analytical scheme is something different from the adherence to a general conceptual framework. Sraffa's analysis is an implicit rejection of the first kind of approach to economic theory; at the same time, the similarities to classical and Marxian analysis noted above point to the existence of a basically common conceptual framework in the treatment of different problems. In particular, the existence of commodities with a uniform price in Sraffa's system presupposes a reference to a mercantile economic system; more specifically, the distinction between wages and profits, and the rule of a uniform rate of profits, presupposes a reference to a capitalistic system. Therefore to understand the conceptual content of Sraffa's economic variables (as distinct from their logical relationships) we may usefully refer to an analysis of the capitalistic mode of production such as the Marxian one.

V

In the preceding sections we have seen that Sraffa's analysis points to a conceptual framework similar to that of classical and Marxian analysis. In this section we will examine the attempts to question this, basically from a Marxian point of view—that is, the attempts to prove that some essential element in Sraffa's analysis is inconsistent with some essential element in Marx's analysis. Our attention will be limited to the left-wing criticisms of Sraffa's analysis, and we will avoid dealing directly with the interpretation of Marxian thought. However, the so-called Sraffian or neo-Ricardian school may be considered nothing more than a particular interpretation of Marx's thought; so that the left-wing criticisms of Sraffa's analysis appear as criticisms of a particular interpretation of Marxism, advanced on the basis of different interpretations of the same corpus.

The different criticisms are but variations on a single theme—that Sraffian analysis can be identified with Ricardian analysis, and thus that Sraffa can be compatible with Marx only if Marx is reduced to Ricardo. In the attempt to prove this, sometimes Sraffa's contribution to economic theory is itself reduced to the solution of the Ricardian problem of the invariable standard of value (see, for example, Nuti, 1974, p. 17). In fact, if it were so, Sraffa's contribution would be insignificant. The exact solution greatly reduces the importance of the problem: the standard commodity, as presented by Sraffa, is invariant only in the very specific sense that its price in terms of its own means of production does not change when distribution changes; but its price in terms of any other commodity changes with distribution, and the standard commodity itself takes a different form when there are technological changes. The standard commodity, as is well known, also ensures the determination of the rate of profits as a ratio of purely physical quantities, but this is only true for the standard system, so that (contrary to what Eatwell, 1974, 1975, and Medio, 1972, affirm) the standard commodity cannot substitute for Marx's "average commodity," which was used for another purpose, requiring more stringent analytical properties (Roncaglia, 1975, pp. 83-86). From this viewpoint we might say that Sraffa's contribution, more than giving the solution of the Ricardian problem, consists

of specifying its limits (as Sraffa already tends to do in his introduction to Ricardo's *Works*, 1951, pp. xlvi-xlvii). From a more general viewpoint we should recognize that Sraffa's main contribution to economic theory consists of the rigorous solution of a fundamental analytical problem, the determination of prices of production; and this within a conceptual framework completely different from that of traditional economics but similar to that of classical economists and Marx.

However, although the conceptual framework is similar, the central object of Sraffa's analysis (prices of production and their relationship with distribution —Ricardo's problem) is at least partly different from the more general object of Marx's analysis. This (and Marx's failure to build a fully consistent theory of relative prices) is a sufficient reason for all the differences existing between *Production of Commodities* and *Das Kapital*. All specific criticisms of Sraffa's analysis from a left-wing point of view do consider what in fact are differences in the analyses due to the difference in the objectives, as basic inconsistencies in the conceptual framework, due to Sraffa's duplication of a number of Ricardian errors already criticized by Marx.

The first and easiest criticism is the statement that Sraffa does not use the Marxian concept of labor power in his analysis, "thus obscuring the nature of capital as a relation," that is, exploitation (Lebowitz, 1973, p. 390; see also Benetti, de Brunhoff, and Cartelier (1973); de Brunhoff, 1974, p. 480). Here "obscuring" simply means "not dealing with." We should remember that Marx criticized Ricardo for confusing labor and labor power; this confusion was due to the fact that Ricardo did not introduce the distinction into his analysis where necessary. For the specific purposes of Sraffa's analysis, as is shown elsewhere (Roncaglia, 1974; 1975, chap. 4), the concept of labor power is not required: its introduction into the analysis is possible, but this does not change the basic results.

A second, and more subtle, "left-wing" criticism is attributing to Sraffa's analysis, on the basis of its similarity with the classical conceptual framework, the classical vision of the "harmonic" working of the capitalistic system (see, for example, Bianchi, D'Antonio, and Napoleoni, 1973). As is well known, classical economists represent the capitalistic mode of production as fulfilling its positive task, accumulation. The possibility of general overproduction crises was always denied by reference to "Say's Law." Hence a representation of the capitalist system as accomplishing "a triumphant onward march" (Schumpeter, 1954, p. 618). This vision was criticized by Marx, who stressed the possibility, and indeed the necessity, of general overproduction crises. Here it is not necessary to repeat Marx's arguments; we only want to stress that there is nothing in Sraffa's analysis that allows us to attribute to him this aspect of the classical vision. In fact, as we have seen above, Sraffa includes the levels of output among the data of his analysis, and rejects the approach to the problem of price determination based on the equality of supply and demand at equilibrium prices. All this shows that adherence to Say's Law is alien to the conceptual framework of Sraffa's analysis. Instead it should lead us, as we have seen above, to consider Sraffa's analysis of prices as consistent with the Marxian formulation of the problem of realization, which is distinct and logically subsequent to the determination of levels of output, and of prices.

A third criticism is based on the fact that Sraffa builds a model of price determination not founded on labor values. Sraffa's analysis is interpreted (for example, by Benetti and Cartelier, 1976) as a model of exchange relations based on use values and concrete labor; it is thus opposed to the Marxian model of the "essence" of a capitalistic mode of production based on abstract labor, which is the necessary foundation of exchange value. Something of this kind, more or less confused, is probably in the back of the minds of all those who criticize Sraffa for leaving aside labor values. Without considering the question at length, as it would involve us in the complexities of the so-called transformation problem, we would like simply to recall two points: (1) Sraffa's model of price determination is based on "physical production costs," that is, quantities of *commodities*. We cannot speak of use values or of exchange values as something existing in a vacuum—a contraposition of use values and exchange values requires a hypostasis of both these attributes of commodities, which are the only really existing entities. (2) A distinction between Sraffa's and Marx's analyses on the basis of the absence of labor values in the former is no proof of logical errors in Sraffa's scheme of price determination. Insistence on this point may be due to the idea that Marx's analysis would fall if price determination is not grounded on labor values; but then the missing link between values and prices should rather be a basis for criticizing Marx than for criticizing Sraffa. In fact, this point of view is adopted by those "right-wing Sraffians"—Samuelson (1971) is the best-known instance—who maintain that Marx's analysis in terms of labor values should be replaced by an analysis conducted in terms of prices of production. However, this means forgetting the need for an analysis in terms of labor values to "reveal," as Marx says, the social relations among men that are concealed by the relationships between commodities established in the markets—that is, the need for a labor theory of value in the analysis of commodity fetishism and alienation (on this problem, which concerns Marx's thought more than Sraffa's, see Roncaglia, 1975, chap. 7).

Finally, Marxists criticize Sraffa for assuming as given, like the classical economists, as a datum of his problem, the existence of the capitalistic mode of production. But this is no criticism, given the limited purpose of Sraffa's analysis. It is impossible to show that Sraffa falls into the trap that constitutes the major error of the classical economists: the interpretation of economic laws concerning a specific mode of production, historically determined, as if they were natural laws. Nowhere does Sraffa suggest this pre-Marxian conception; and the Marxian priests who would require Sraffa to recite the catechism of Marxian thought before starting his own analysis sound dogmatic and absurd!

REFERENCES

Arcelli, M. "Analisi a livello soggettivo e a livello oggettivo nella determinazione di un sistema di prezzi relativi." *L'industria*, no. 3 (1964), pp. 287-318.
Benetti, C., and Cartelier, J. "Prix de production et étalon," in C. Benetti, C. Berthomieu, and J. Cartelier, *Economie classique—Economie vulgaire*. Grenoble: Maspero, 1975.
——, De Brunhoff, S., and Cartelier, J. "Eléments pour une critique marxiste de Sraffa," 1973. (Published in *Cahiers d'Economie politique*, no. 3, 1976.)
Bianchi, M., D'Antonio, M., and Napoleoni, C. "Per la ripresa di una critica dell'economia politica." *Rinascita*, no. 43 (November 2, 1973), pp. 19-20.

de Brunhoff, S. "Controversies in the Theory of Surplus Value: A Reply to John Eatwell." *Science and Society* 38, no. 4 (Winter 1974), pp. 478-82.

Collard, D. A. "The Production of Commodities." *Economic Journal* 73 (1963), pp. 144-46.

Dominedò, V. "Una teoria economica neo-ricardiana." *Giornale degli economisti* 21 (1962), pp. 710-31.

Eatwell, J. "Controversies in the Theory of Surplus Value, Old and New." *Science and Society* 38, no. 3 (1974), pp. 281-303.

—— "Mr. Sraffa's Standard Commodity and the Rate of Exploitation." *Quarterly Journal of Economics* 89, no. 4 (1975), pp. 543-55.

Garegnani, P. *Il capitale nelle teorie della distribuzione.* Milano: Giuffrè, 1960.

Lebowitz, M. A. "The Current Crisis of Economic Theory." *Science and Society* 37, no. 4 (1973), pp. 385-403.

Medio, A. "Profits and Surplus-Value: Appearance and Reality in Capitalist Production," in E. K. Hunt and J. G. Schwartz, eds., *A Critique of Economic Theory.* Harmondsworth: Penguin, 1972.

Nuti, D. M. "Introduction" to V. K. Dmitriev, *Economic Essays on Value, Competition and Utility.* Cambridge: Cambridge University Press, 1974.

Quandt, R. E. "Production of Commodities by Means of Commodities," *Journal of Political Economy* 69 (1961), p. 500.

Reder, M. W. "Production of Commodities by Means of Commodities." *American Economic Review* 51 (1961), pp. 688-95.

Ricardo, D. "Principles of Political Economy and Taxation," in *Works and Correspondence,* ed. P. Sraffa, vol. I. Cambridge: Cambridge University Press, 1951.

Robbins, L. *An Essay on the Nature and Significance of Economic Science*, 2nd ed. London: Macmillan, 1935.

Roncaglia, A. "Labour-power, Subsistence Wage and the Rate of Wages." *Australian Economic Papers* 13 (1974), pp. 133-43.

—— *Sraffa e la teoria dei prezzi.* Rome: Laterza, 1975. (English edition forthcoming, Wiley.)

—— "The Sraffian Revolution," in S. Weintraub, ed., *Trends in Modern Economics.* Philadelphia: Pennsylvania University Press, 1976.

Rowthorn, R. "Neo-Classicism, Neo-Ricardianism and Marxism." *New Left Review,* no. 86 (1974), pp. 63-87.

Samuelson, P. A. *Foundations of Economic Analysis.* Cambridge, Mass.: Harvard University Press, 1947.

—— "Understanding the Marxian Notion of Exploitation: A Summary of the So-Called Transformation Problem Between Marxian Values and Competitive Prices." *Journal of Economic Literature* 9 (1971), pp. 399-431.

Schumpeter, J. *History of Economic Analysis.* London: Allen, 1954.

Sraffa, P. "Sulle relazioni fra costo e quantità prodotta." *Annali di economia* 2 (1925), pp. 277-328.

—— "The Laws of Returns under Competitive Conditions." *Economic Journal* 36 (1926), pp. 535-50.

—— "Introduction," in Ricardo, *Works and Correspondence,* ed. P. Sraffa, vol. I. Cambridge: Cambridge University Press, 1951.

—— *Production of Commodities by Means of Commodities.* Cambridge: Cambridge University Press, 1960.

Wicksteed, P. *The Common Sense of Political Economy and Selected Papers,* ed. L. Robbins. London: Routledge and Kegan Paul, 1934.

Wittgenstein, L. *Tractatus Logico-Philosophicus.* London: Kegan and Co., 1922.

—— *Philosophische Untersuchungen,* ed. G. E. Anscombe and R. Rhees. Oxford: Blackwell, 1953.

20

Neoclassicals, Neo-Ricardians, and Marx

ALFREDO MEDIO

Visiting Lecturer in Economics at The New School for Social Research

INTRODUCTION

The aim of this paper is to discuss some recent tendencies in economic theory and to clarify some controversial issues. In particular, I shall focus on the relations between neoclassical, neo-Ricardian and Marxian theories.

In the last 10 or 20 years the orthodox, neoclassical theory of value and distribution has been subjected to a radical critique by a group of authors who have been labelled "neo-Ricardians" in view of their affinity with the classical economists, and in particular with Ricardo. The revival of interest in the classical writers, stimulated by the neo-Ricardians' work, has been accompanied by renewed discussions of the Marxian theory, which, alas, have mainly been focused on the "transformation problem."

Whereas the classical character of the neo-Ricardian theory is clear, there remains a certain ambiguity, however, as regards the relation between this theory and Marx's. Following the publication of *Production of Commodities by Means of Commodities* (1960), Sraffa and his school's work were often regarded as a rehabilitation of the Marxian point of view as well as a devastating critique of the neoclassical orthodoxy. This seems to have been the interpretation, for example, by Dobb (1970) and Meek (1967). More recently, however, doubts have been raised as regards the scope of the Sraffian criticism of the neoclassical theory. Moreover, some have wondered whether it is legitimate to treat Sraffa's and Marx's theories as coextensive, the former being a modern and rigorous version of the latter.

The two questions are important and they are by no means unrelated. The originality of Marx's theory of value and the limits of the neo-Ricardian "critique of economic theory" will therefore be the objects of the following discussion.

THE MARXIAN THEORY OF VALUE

The way in which economists are grouped into schools or currents is only meaningful when the problems are defined in relation to which the classification is

This is a slightly modified version of a paper privately circulated in Cambridge in the Winter of 1973-74, and subsequently published in Italy. A. Medio, Neoclassici, Neoricardiani e Marx, *in S. Veca, ed.,* Marxismo e critica delle teorie economiche *(Milan: Mazzotta, 1974), pp. 107-167.*

suggested. Thus, according to a popular view, the neoclassical economists are distinguished from the classicals (including Smith, Ricardo, and Marx), in that the former propound an impersonal and politically neutral theory of distribution of income. This distinction obviously possesses some interpretative validity. However, I should like to emphasize the existence of a different classification that discriminates between the Marxian and the bourgeois doctrines, the latter being characterized by an impersonal and politically neutral theory of the *mode of production*. This point deserves some comments, as its correct understanding is essential to a proper assessment of the Marxian theory of value and price.

The current opinion in this respect is that Marx started his economic investigation (in *Capital*, vol. I) with a theory of value and surplus-value—expressed in terms of quantities of labor embodied—and that he later reached a more sophisticated stage of analysis (in *Capital*, vol. III), with his theory of prices of production. This may well correspond to the order of presentation followed by Marx in *Capital*, but it does not reflect the logical succession of the different stages of his analysis. In fact, it must be pointed out that when Marx began his study of economic problems, a well-developed theory of exchange already existed—the cost of production price theory—which was based on Ricardo's work, and which had its best-known academic formulation in Mill's *Principles* (1848).[1]

The cost of production theory of price explains the exchange-values of commodities[2] as functions of the methods of production and of the distribution of income between profits and wages. In equilibrium, the price of each commodity must be equal to its cost of production (itself valued at the equilibrium prices and including wages), plus a profit calculated as a uniform proportion of the cost of production.

Marx was well aware of this theory long before writing volume I of *Capital*.[3] In particular, he knew that the exchange-values determined in this way are not proportional to the quantities of labor embodied in commodities. Marx also clearly understood that such divergency was determined by the joint effect of two factors, i.e.: (1) the different organic compositions of capital in the various sectors; (2) the uniformity of the (equilibrium) rate of profit.

The idea that the theory of value developed in volume I of *Capital* is a (bad) theory of relative prices is therefore untenable, unless one is prepared to argue that Marx deliberately formulated a set of theoretical propositions that he knew to be simply wrong. The alternative interpretation, which I suggest, is that Marx's theory of value was directed to a different problem.

The cost of production theory of price seemed to be unsatisfactory for two reasons. First of all, it contained an *apparent* element of circularity. In fact, in this theory the rate of profit is defined as the ratio

$$\frac{(\text{product}) - (\text{cost of production})}{(\text{cost of production})}$$

As product, wage-goods, and means of production are heterogeneous aggregates of commodities, the calculation of the rate of profit requires that they be made dimensionally homogeneous by valuing them at their equilibrium prices. The latter, however, cannot be calculated without knowing the rate of profit. Hence the *apparent* element of circularity.

Marx, however, had a second, more fundamental reason for dissatisfaction. In fact, the cost of production theory presupposes the existence of a (uniform) rate of profit, without supplying any explanation of the origin of the profit itself. Of course both Ricardo and Mill had pointed out that the existence of a surplus over and above the cost of production requires that the net product of society exceed the remuneration of laborers. However, this fact does not characterize the capitalist economy: it has been true of almost every kind of society for thousands of years. In pre-capitalist societies the appropriation of surplus takes place according to the "rules of the game" clearly recognizable (for example, the belonging to a caste or to an "estate"). Under competitive capitalism, on the contrary, there is no obvious mechanism through which a surplus may be produced and distributed among the different social groups. Instead formation and distribution of surplus appear to be the result of a general mechanism—the exchange of commodities—in which, at least in principle, direct coercion and tradition (as well as conscious agreement) do not play any role.

The analysis of the process of exchange convinced Marx that the origin of capitalist surplus could not be found in the sphere of circulation. The latter is seen by Marx as the *locus* of competition among capitalists, which ensures that, in equilibrium, profits are allocated in proportion to capitals. But nothing can be allocated (uniformly or otherwise) unless it is first produced, and, before talking of a uniform *rate* of profit, one would like to know how *a profit* may exist at all. According to Marx, this question can only be answered by considering the sphere of production, where working activity takes place, and which is the *locus* of the struggle between capitalists and laborers.

During the production process, commodities and labor-power temporarily leave the market and undergo a process of transformation as a result of which other commodities emerge, whose value exceeds the value of the means of production and labor-power used up. The *existence* of this surplus-value—Marx argues—does not depend on the particular set of "weights" we employ in order to confront the heterogeneous aggregates of commodities that constitute means of production, wage-goods, and product. Whatever set of exchange-ratios we may use, a positive surplus will emerge only if the labor-time generated by the labor-power engaged in the productive process exceeds the labor-time directly and indirectly necessary to reproduce that labor-power.[4]

In order for such a surplus to materialize, a social mechanism must therefore exist that forces (or somewhat "persuades") laborers to work longer and/or harder than would be necessary to produce those commodities that represent their actual standard of living.

This question did not concern classical economists very much, but it was at the heart of Marx's analysis. Marx's well-known argument runs as follows. Capitalist society is characterized by private[5] property of the means of production. This fact has two symmetrical consequences. On the one hand, private property means that property-less people, i.e. workers, have to choose between starving and selling their labor-power for a wage. On the other hand, private property means that the proprietors, capitalists, have the control of working activity, i.e. they are in a position to determine its length, its intensity, and its general conditions. A corollary of this situation is that workers are not even permitted to work, unless they can produce an "acceptable" surplus.

Under capitalism, production takes place according to "rules of the game" entirely different from those prevailing in the process of circulation. The latter is characterized by the equality between dealers, whereas the process of production is characterized by the subordination of laborers to capitalists. In the process of exchange freedom prevails; in the process of production, despotism.

From this point of view the Marxian theory is *unique*. Bourgeois theories (classical as well as neoclassical) consider the laboring process as an essentially technical element and, to the extent that they deal with property relations, the attention is focused on the distributive process. That is, proprietors are those people who have a special claim on social product (see Rowthorn, 1974). To Marx, on the contrary, the essence of capitalist property is the control of the productive process and therefore the control over laborers. Forced labor rather than low wages, alienation of labor rather than alienation of the product of labor are, according to Marx, the essence of capitalist exploitation.

From this analysis two conclusions can be drawn. From an analytical point of view, it follows that, if one accepts Marx's theory of capitalist surplus, the basic determinant of profit is surplus-value, defined as the excess of total labor-time generated in the economy over the amount of labor-time embodied in wage-goods. Accordingly the *rate* of surplus-value, i.e. the ratio

$$\frac{(\text{total labor-time}) - (\text{labor embodied in wage-goods})}{(\text{labor embodied in wage-goods})}$$

gives us the most significant measure of exploitation.

From a political point of view, it follows from the Marxian analysis that: (1) as capitalist production is based on despotism and subordination, capitalism is an essentially oppressive society, however democratic its regime may be; (2) as production relations are basic, their radical change is a necessary (although not sufficient) condition of a nonillusory political revolution.

All that said, the fact remains that the spheres of production and circulation do not exist independently of one another, but they are inextricably connected. In equilibrium, commodities are exchanged according to their prices of production, not their values, and capitalists make their calculations in terms of the rate of profit rather than in terms of the rate of surplus-value. It is therefore necessary to find a satisfactory logical relation between the world of values and the world of prices; in particular, between the rate of surplus-value and the rate of profit. This problem has become famous (or notorious) as the "transformation problem," and it did not receive a fully rigorous solution by Marx himself. The problem—which is analytically related to the question of "circularity" in the cost of production price theory—*can* be solved, however. It has indeed been rigorously dealt with by a number of authors since the beginning of the century. (A formal discussion of this point is provided in Appendix A.)

THE NEOCLASSICAL THEORIES

Following the historical developments of economic theory, I shall now consider the reactions of bourgeois economists to the Marxian analysis.

The "neoclassical revolution," which took place in the 1870s, can be

interpreted, to some extent, as a theoretical answer (and a political antidote) to Marx's doctrine. In particular, neoclassical authors attempt to reduce the theory of production (and surplus) to the theory of exchange. Production is looked at as a special case of exchange—i.e. the exchange between inputs and outputs. The determination of profits and wages is presented as a special case of price determination.

However, two strains can be distinguished within the neoclassical tradition (and sometimes within the same author's work). The first variant of the theory—which I shall henceforth label as "vulgar"—is characterized by the explicit or implicit attempt to provide a theory of profit alternative to Marx's. Vulgar economists try to identify, or to relate unambiguously, two distinct phenomena, i.e. (1) "capital" as the set of means of production technically necessary to carry out production; (2) "capital" as a fund of value, which gives its owner command over commodities and labor-power, and which is connected with a particular kind of income, profit. Thus, according to vulgar economists, certain properties of capital value can be derived from the technological properties of capital-goods. In particular they argue that the gain capitalists obtain from their ownership of means of production is determined as a function of a technical relation between output per head and capital per head. This and a set of presumably genetic preferences (chiefly time preference and disutility of labor) fix the equilibrium interest and wage-rates.

Had the vulgar claims been correct, certain important results could have been established. In particular, as J. B. Clark aptly observed, the laws that govern distribution of income could have been given the *status* of natural laws. As nobody in his or her senses should question natural laws, workers' struggles to improve their lot at the expense of profits would have been proved futile.

Unfortunately, the vulgar neoclassical theory had to face some logical difficulties, which could not be overcome. The truth of the matter is that there is no way of finding any simple relation between changes of "capital" as a fund of value and corresponding changes of "capital" as a set of physical objects (quite apart from the difficulty of unambiguously defining changes of a vectorial quantity).

There exists, however, a second strain of the neoclassical theory that is based on the concept of general equilibrium, the latter being defined as a combination of prices and input-output relations such that, when existing and not disturbed, it tends to perpetuate itself. This variant of the neoclassical theory originates in Walras's work, and it has undergone considerable developments in the last decades.[6]

In the general equilibrium theory the concepts of "capital in general" (and the related concept of "marginal productivity of capital") do not play any essential analytical role. No attempt is made to measure "capital" independently of prices. Instead each individual item of the collection of capital-goods is measured in terms of its own technical unit. The dimensions of the various items are then made homogeneous by multiplying each of them by its equilibrium price.

Therefore, the general equilibrium theory appears, in principle, free from the logical problems that have troubled the vulgar theory. On the other hand, together with the concept of "capital," such theory has had to abandon any attempt to provide a causal theory of profit.

THE NEO-RICARDIAN SCHOOL

The Neo-Ricardian and the Marxian Theories

While the neoclassical theory rapidly became predominant in academic circles (mainly in its vulgar version), a different line of thought was developed— neo-Ricardianism—which was to remain largely ignored until the publication of Piero Sraffa's book, *Production of Commodities by Means of Commodities* (1960) brought it to the forefront of economic debate.

The methodological foundations of the neo-Ricardian theory can be traced back to the work of V. K. Dmitriev and L. von Bortkiewicz, who wrote between the end of the nineteenth and the beginning of the twentieth century.[7] The main element that distinguishes the neo-Ricardian from the Marxian approach is a restrictive definition of the concept of "value," which is in fact identified with that of exchange-value or price. Accordingly, of the two problems connected with the cost of production theory (the "circularity" and the origin of profit), only the first one is regarded as relevant.

According to Bortkiewicz, the "true" objective of a theory of value is the study of the quantitative relations between the rate of profit, the wage-rate, and the relative prices of commodities (Bortkiewicz, 1906-07, p. 53). Essentially the same idea is repeated by the modern neo-Ricardians (see, for example, Garegnani, 1970, p. 427). It follows that the concepts of value and surplus-value, as analyzed by Marx in *Capital*, volume I, became superfluous, and the entire "transformation problem" turns out to be just a red herring. It also follows, however, that this approach—contrary to Marx's—does not provide any explanatory theory of capitalist profit. Böhm-Bawerk—the "bourgeois Marx"—clearly understood this aspect of Ricardian thought when, in his historical analysis of the various theories of profit, he labelled Ricardo's as "colorless."

The Neo-Ricardian Critique of the "Vulgar" Theory

I shall now turn to considering the relations between the neo-Ricardian and the neoclassical theories.

The controversy between the neo-Ricardian and the vulgar neoclassical theory has played an important role in the economic debate of the last twenty years, and in this field the neo-Ricardians have scored some good points. In particular, the following vulgar neoclassical propositions have been questioned:

1. In equilibrium, the rate of interest is equal to the "marginal product of capital."
2. In equilibrium, there exist *inverse* relations between the rate of interest, on the one hand, and the capital-labor ratio, the capital-output ratio, and output per man, on the other hand.

The "capital controversy" is mostly concerned with logical aspects of economic theory, and it is best treated by means of mathematical reasoning. A formal discussion of the problem is provided in Appendix B. Here I shall try to capture the economic essence of the debate by means of verbal arguments.

Consider first the fundamental proposition of the neoclassical theory, that is, in equilibrium, the rate of profit, or the rate of interest,[8] is equal to the

marginal product of capital. A certain ambiguity exists as regards the meaning of the phrase "is equal to." Some authors take it to indicate that, in equilibrium, the marginal product of capital *measures* the rate of interest, and consequently they deny the proposition of any causal implication.[9] However, it seems to me that the vast majority of neoclassical economists implicitly or explicitly intend to say that the marginal product of capital, together with other factors (chiefly, "time preference"), *determines* the equilibrium rate of interest.

I must hasten to add at this point that not all vulgar economists are equally vulgar. Thus, the long tradition inspired by Clark (1899) and, more recently, by the work of Cobb and Douglas (1928) (the inventors of the notorious aggregate production function), interprets "capital" as a homogeneous factor of production, having the same dimension as net product, and possessing the same theoretical *status* as land or labor.

In the simplest case in which land is neglected, the productivity of capital can be defined as the ratio:[10]

$$(I) \qquad \frac{\text{increment of net product}}{\text{increment of capital}}$$

(labor being constant).

This ratio is technically determined, and in particular it does not depend on the wage or interest rates (since only one commodity exists there are no relative prices). Moreover, it can be proved that, in this case, the four neoclassical "parables" hold true.[11]

Clearly, results whose validity is limited to a one-commodity economy are not very interesting. Therefore a second group of vulgar economists, chiefly the "Austrian school" and Wicksell, endeavored to reconcile the hard fact that means of production and output are not homogeneous quantities, with the use of aggregate theoretical concepts such as "capital" (and its marginal product) and the rate of interest on capital. However, when the fact is accepted that capital and output are collections of physically heterogeneous commodities, their ratio cannot be correctly formulated without making recourse to some criterion of valuation that makes them dimensionally comparable. In economic problems this valuation will be naturally provided by relative prices.

If net output, of a given and constant physical composition, is taken as *numéraire*, the definition of productivity of capital can be rewritten thus:

$$(II) \qquad \frac{\text{increment of net output}}{\text{increment of the value of real capital}}$$

(again, labor being kept constant).

It is evident that in this general case the productivity of capital depends on two distinct elements, which in the aggregate model were confused, i.e. (1) a technical element, namely the variations of production made possible by corresponding variations of the quantities of means of production; (2) an economic element, namely the variations of the exchange-values of these means of production (in terms of net output). The first consequence of this fact is that, in general, it will no longer be possible to establish the equality between the equilibrium rate of interest and the marginal product of capital.

To prove this, let us first consider that in equilibrium the rate of interest must be equal to the rate of return on investment, i.e. to the ratio[12]

(III) $$\frac{\text{increment of net profit}}{\begin{array}{c}\text{value of the increment of real capital}\\ (= \text{value of net investment})\end{array}}$$

The equality between the rate of interest and the productivity of capital therefore implies the equality between the ratios (II) and (III), or, since their numerators are equal, it implies the equality of the denominators.[13]

The economic significance of this point can be best understood by means of a simple example. Suppose the economic system is in a state of stationary equilibrium, which will be designated by E_0. The latter can be roughly defined as a situation in which the actual capital stock and the related actual income flow are equal to the corresponding desired quantities, and consequently net saving is zero. E_0 will also be characterized by a certain set of relative prices and by certain wage and interest rates.

Let us now consider a different stationary state, designated by E_1, in which: (1) employment is the same as in E_0; (2) net product (whose physical composition is assumed to be the same as in E_0) is marginally greater; and (3) the amounts of capital-goods are correspondingly larger. In an economy where more than one capital-good exists, the phrase "larger amounts of capital-goods" is ambiguous. To overcome this difficulty, and to focus on the main point of the argument, I shall assume that, in order to increase net output per head from $(NP)_0$ to $(NP)_1$, some means of production are increased, but none of them is decreased. Therefore, if we indicate the capital-good vectors of the stationary states E_1 and E_0 by $(K)_1$, $(K)_0$, respectively, the non-negative vector

(IV) $[(K)_1 - (K)_0]$

may be unambiguously interpreted as the net investment, in real terms, that is required to increase the permanent flow of net output per head.

In addition, if p is a price vector, the positive quantity

(IV)' $[(K)_1 - (K)_0] \cdot p$

will designate the value of net investment unambiguously.

In the new stationary state E_1 we shall in general have a different set of prices, and different wage and interest rates. Therefore the variation of the value of the capital stock that takes place when we move (notionally) from E_0 to E_1 is equal to

(V) $[(K)_1 \cdot (p)_1] - [(K)_0 \cdot (p)_0]$

i.e. by the difference between the value of *all* capital-goods employed in E_1 and the value of *all* capital-goods employed in E_0, each of them valued at the corresponding price.[14]

It is self-evident that only by a fluke will *the increment of the value* of the capital stock [as indicated by (V)] be equal to *the value of its increment*, i.e. the

value of net investment, [as indicated by (IV)'], whether the latter is calculated at the old or at the new prices. Moreover, *since the prices of capital-goods may change in either direction*, the expression (V) may well be negative, i.e. there may well be a *devaluation* of capital stock, even if net investment in real terms is positive.[15]

The basic vulgar neoclassical proposition asserting the equality between rate of interest and marginal product of capital is therefore proved incorrect. From the argument developed above—and in particular from the possibility that a positive net investment may be associated with a devaluation of the capital stock—it is perhaps intuitively clear that this result implies the fallacy of the other neoclassical "parables." A formal proof of this point is at any rate provided in Appendix B.

These results do not have just a theoretical significance, but they can be used to falsify certain important commonplaces still found in textbooks, specialized journals, and "experts'" reports. For example, it is not possible to maintain, on a purely a priori ground, that long-run unemployment depends on "too high" wages that induce the adoption of techniques with higher "capital intensity," and which therefore imply a lower level of employment for any given amount of capital invested. As a matter of fact, employment is a function of the number and kinds of capital-goods, and we have seen that there exists no definite relation between such physical magnitudes and their equilibrium values.

Nor can we argue correctly that society—by forsaking present consumption in favor of future consumption—moves from equilibria characterized by high rates of interest and low levels of output per head (owing to capital being "scarce"), towards equilibria characterized by low interest rates and high output per head (owing to capital being "abundant"). It is instead perfectly possible to conceive of two equilibria that are technically identical except that one of them has a lower value of the *same* capital stock and a higher rate of interest. In this case, clearly, distribution of income cannot be explained in terms of "relative scarcities of capital and labor."

The discovery that there are flaws in the vulgar argument is not recent. Wicksell, himself one of the most outstanding neoclassical exponents, was aware that, owing to the revaluation of the capital stock that takes place in the presence of net investment, the equilibrium rate of interest may diverge from the marginal product of capital (Wicksell, 1934, pp. 148-49). However, Wicksell failed to draw the correct conclusions from this result, and he wrongly believed that, when the equilibrium rate of interest falls, the corresponding changes of equilibrium prices always lead to an *appreciation* of the capital stock, so that the marginal product of capital is always less than the rate of interest. (In this case the other vulgar neoclassical propositions would be saved.)

Gustav Åkerman, a brilliant (but largely ignored) Swedish economist, did better than Wicksell and clearly suggested that a *devaluation* of the capital stock may well take place when the equilibrium rate of interest falls. His early analysis (1923) was neglected, however, and Wicksell, who knew Åkerman's work, misinterpreted this point entirely.

The divergence between equilibrium rate of interest and marginal product of capital was pointed out subsequently by Lange (1936) and Stigler (1941), both of whom, however, adopted the defective Wicksellian analysis.

In 1950 Lloyd Metzler, in a splendid but little-known article, presented a discussion of the problem, in which practically all the elements were provided that would prove essential in the following critique of the vulgar theory. Analogous results, although in a different context, were reached in the fifties by the general equilibrium theorists (see Malinvaud, 1953).

The academic world as a whole, however, did not pay much attention to the logical difficulties of the vulgar theory, and the false neoclassical "parables" continued to be disseminated remorselessly. Only when Joan Robinson raised the issue once again in her famous article of 1954 did the economics profession seem to realize that a problem existed indeed, and that certain bits of the traditional wisdom might have to be reconsidered. What followed is well known. Especially after the publication of Sraffa's book, a school of thought developed that was able to conduct a rigorous and comprehensive critique of the vulgar theory, drawing the logical conclusion from the "curious divergence" between rate of interest and marginal product of capital.

The theoretical and practical significance of the neo-Ricardian critique is beyond dispute. An element of perplexity remains, however. The refutation of the vulgar neoclassical propositions does not require particularly complex analytical tools. The basic propositions of such a critique were formulated as far back as at the beginning of the century, and have since been repeated by several economists. The fact that legions of highly intelligent scholars insisted (and some still insist) on defending scientifically wrong propositions; the fact that miracles of ingenuity have been performed in order to find out all sorts of theoretical objects (jelly, clay, mecano-sets, lego, leets, etc.), which, like the Christian god, have the property of being one and trine; all this may only partially be explained in terms of internal developments of economic science. The phenomenon to a considerable extent belongs to sociology (and to politics) of knowledge.

The Neo-Ricardians and the General Equilibrium Theory

Let us now turn to considering the relations between the neo-Ricardians and the general equilibrium theory. The latter had its first rigorous formulation in Walras's work and has undergone substantial developments between the two World Wars and during the last few decades. Owing to the heavily mathematical character of the theory and to its inherent difficulty and level of abstraction, the general equilibrium theory in its modern versions has largely been ignored by most vulgar neoclassical authors as well as by most of their opponents.

In simple terms, a general equilibrium theory may be defined as a theoretical model aiming to define a set of equilibrium quantities and prices as functions of:

1. The state of technology, i.e. the set of production possibilities.
2. The consumer's "preferences," concerning present as well as future goods, and including a set of functions that relate supply of labor to its "disutility."
3. The resources available in the economy.
4. The distribution of the property rights on the said resources.

Moreover, certain assumptions are made as regards the economic agents' behavior. In particular, it is assumed that consumers maximize their utility within the limits of their budget, and that producers maximize their profits within the limits of the available resources.

Equilibrium is defined as a situation such that, if the system is there *at rest*, it will remain there, i.e. there will be no economic forces tending to change it.

The best way of properly grasping the relations between the neo-Ricardian and the general equilibrium theories is perhaps to consider the analysis of the forerunners of the modern neo-Ricardian theory, Bortkiewicz and Dmitriev. It is very interesting to observe that neither of these authors thought that the Walrasian theory of general equilibrium and the Ricardian cost of production theory of prices are contradictory. In his criticism of Marx, Bortkiewicz observed that

> The mathematical method, however, achieves still more: by its means, the cost of production theory can, without any difficulty, be brought into harmony with the law of supply and demand or with the determination of prices by the subjective valuations of buyers (and, if need be, of sellers). Following the example of Walras, this is done by inserting the cost equations into a more comprehensive set of equations, in which regard is paid also to those subjective valuations.
>
> It is in this connection that the superiority of the mathematical method over the Marxian method appears particularly clearly. Marx was unable to grasp that the determination of prices by costs could perfectly well be reconciled with their determination by supply and demand. He therefore strove to explain away supply and demand as factors of value or price (1906-1907, pp. 54-55).

Dmitriev discussed the relations between Walras's and Ricardo's theory in a more comprehensive way. His conclusion was that the system of prices determined as functions of costs of production (Walras's "frais nécessaire") constitutes a special case of the system of prices that corresponds to the competitive equilibrium. In particular, Dmitriev mentioned two cases in which the two systems of prices may not coincide:

1. When returns to scale are not constant, so that the costs of production themselves depend on the composition of output and therefore on demand.
2. When potential supply is different from actual supply, and the difference is a function of the level of demand.[16]

Both Bortkiewicz and Dmitriev clearly anticipated certain propositions of the modern general equilibrium theory and, in particular, they clearly argued that the cost of production price system is only a half-system of equilibrium, since demand considerations are excluded from the analysis *by definition*. Both authors regarded the cost of production theory of prices as a special case of the general equilibrium theory, which can be analytically isolated and dealt with separately.

This point deserves some further comments, as failure to properly understand it has caused much heat (and a number of silly mistakes) in the recent controversies.

In the general equilibrium model the unknowns to be determined are

prices *and* quantities. In the neo-Ricardian model only prices and the wage-rate are determined simultaneously as functions of the methods of production and of the condition that the (given) rate of profit should be uniform in the various sectors. (Alternatively, we can fix the wage-rate exogenously, and prices and the uniform profit-rate will be determined.) Therefore, in the neo-Ricardian model (as well as in the Marxian model of prices of production), there is no theory of allocation of resources. The influence of prices on quantities and the reciprocal influence of quantities on prices are ignored. This may well be a reasonable way of proceeding for certain analytical purposes, but the implicit assumptions on which the approach is based have to be defended in terms of realism and relevance, rather than in terms of logic. Little has been done in this direction.

As concerns the influence of prices on quantities demanded ("utility functions"), there exists a classical tradition that considers the composition of output as a function of distribution of income, rather than of consumers' tastes. (Marx seems to basically share this view when formulating his concept of "social needs.") This position might have been correct in 1870, but a scanty treatment of the problem of demand is hardly satisfactory in 1970. Those who are not happy with the neoclassical theory of demand (I am not) cannot beg the question by saying that demand is irrelevant: they should instead try to formulate an alternative theory.

A similar argument can be used with regard to the neoclassical concepts of "disutility of labor" and "time preference." The rejection of these concepts (and of the theory based on them) is admissible, but the neglect of the real problems to which the concepts refer is not.

As concerns the impact of quantities produced on equilibrium prices, we can distinguish two main possibilities, within a neo-Ricardian approach:

1. Output is taken as given and, therefore, for each technique, input of labor is also given. This is the case in Sraffa's model.
2. Constant returns to scale are assumed and the supply of labor is taken to be infinitely elastic at the equilibrium wage-rate. This is the approach taken, for example, by Schwartz (1961).

Once again, either of these assumptions may be justified, but neither of them constitutes a criticism of the neoclassical general equilibrium model. They are simply analytical devices permitting one to ignore certain aspects of the problem. This is a commonly accepted scientific procedure that should not be confused, however, with the claim that the aspects in question do not exist.

These general considerations open the way to a more correct assessment of certain propositions concerning the general equilibrium theory, which have been the sources of many a misunderstanding. Thus, the statement that "demand plays no role in the determination of equilibrium prices" is either trivial or false.[17] It is trivial if it refers to Sraffa's model, in which, output being given, any influence of demand on prices is excluded by hypothesis. The proposition is obviously false when it refers to real economies in which nonconstant returns to scale, the presence of stocks, natural and artificial scarcities, monopolistic elements, etc., make demand an important causal factor in the determination of equilibrium prices.

Second, the idea that, according to the neoclassical theory in all its versions,

the rate of profit (interest) and the wage-rate are *governed* by demand and supply of "capital" and labor is not correct. The general equilibrium theory, at least in its modern versions, rejects the idea that there is any simple relation between the rate of interest (and the wage-rate) and certain pseudo-technical characteristics of the system such as the "relative scarcities of capital and labor." Instead, equilibrium interest and wage-rates are determined by the interaction of all the elements of the system. This of course makes the general equilibrium theory much less suitable for apologetic purposes. Indeed, some of the data on which the determination of the equilibrium depends, explicitly or implicitly, reveal the conflictive nature of a competitive capitalist system. For example, distribution of income crucially depends on the allocation of property rights, and there is no implication in the theory that the existing distribution of wealth is in any sense "fairer" or "better" than any other conceivable distribution. In addition, the determinants of "disutility of labor" and of "time preference"—in spite of the rather "neutral" appearance of the concepts—obviously depend on the class structure of society and on the power relations of the various social groups.

Some authors have maintained that the general equilibrium model is underdetermined as it contains fewer equations than unknowns. This view is based on a lack of understanding of the determination of the equilibrium rate of interest in the general equilibrium model, and it deserves some comments. The general equilibrium models aim to determine not only the present but also the future prices of commodities and services. (*Or, more exactly, the "today" prices for commodities and services to be delivered at various future times.*) For each commodity i, the rate of interest between the instant t and $(t + 1)$ will be equal to

$$(\text{VI}) \qquad \pi_t^i = \frac{p_t^i - p_{(t+1)}^i}{p_{(t+1)}^i} \qquad i = 1, 2, \ldots, n; t = 0, 1, 2 \ldots$$

where p_t^i designates the amount of a certain commodity j—the *numéraire*—that must be paid at the time 0 to buy one unit of the ith commodity *to be delivered at the time t* (which may or may not be equal to 0).

In general, therefore, we shall have different rates of interest for different commodities and, for any given commodity, we shall have different rates of interest for different pairs of time instants. It can be demonstrated, however (see Malivaud, 1972, pp. 260-62), that in a stationary state that is efficient, the rates of interest concerning different commodities and different periods of time are equal, provided that the prices of commodities are measured in terms of a common *numéraire*.

Of course in order to determine a stationary *equilibrium* we need some "utility functions," and in particular we need some "time preference" functions.

The relation between the quantity π defined by equation (VI) and the rate of interest that appears in the equations of the cost of production theory can be illustrated as follows. In the intertemporal model of general equilibrium, outputs and inputs concerning a given productive process can be interpreted as commodities available at two different instants t, $(t + T)$ — T being the production period. In a competitive equilibrium in which capitalists obtain the pure interest on capital, we shall have

$$p_{(t+T)} \cdot b = p_t \cdot a$$

where b and a are vectors, respectively indicating (gross) outputs and inputs, and p_t and $p_{(t+T)}$ are vectors designating *discounted* prices (i.e. prices to be paid at time t for commodities to be delivered at time t and $(t + T)$, respectively. Inputs and outputs, however, may be valued at *undiscounted prices*. The latter indicate the amounts of the commodity-*numéraire* to be paid at a certain time to obtain one unit of a certain commodity *at the same time*. By designating undiscounted prices by $\tilde{p}$, we shall have

$$\tilde{p} \cdot b = (1 + \pi)\tilde{p} \cdot a$$

where π is defined as in equation (VI) and is of course fixed as soon as the equilibrium (intertemporal) prices are known. Therefore the rate of interest is not determined directly, rather it is implicit in the intertemporal price determination.

It might be (and indeed it has been) argued that this formulation assumes the existence of forward markets for all commodities and services, which is hardly a realistic assumption. Moreover, the definition of forward market for labor-power presents special difficulty, and it may be argued that it is in contradiction with the capitalist "rules of the game." These are strong and meaningful criticisms, which should be developed further, but they have nothing to do with the false claim that the general equilibrium model is lacking one equation. This of course does not imply that a solution can always be found, or that it is unique or economically meaningful (not to mention the problem of stability).

A third point to clarify is the claim that, in the neo-Ricardian (or, indeed, in the classical) approach, distribution of income is a fundamental *datum* of the system that must be fixed before and independently of equilibrium prices. In order to assess the validity of this proposition, one must first clearly define the meaning of the phrase "distribution of income." This is sometimes taken to indicate a pair of quantities that designate the uniform rate of profit (π) and the uniform wage rate (w), measured in terms of some commodity (composite or otherwise). In this case, within the neo-Ricardian model, it is certainly possible to treat either of these quantities as a parameter, and then to determine the other simultaneously with the equilibrium prices. This of course follows from the fact that the model possesses one degree of freedom (apart from the choice of the *numéraire*). It also follows, however, that the neo-Ricardian model is compatible with a number of theories of distribution of income. For example, we might introduce into the analysis a set of functions that relates the demand for commodities and the supply of labor to relative prices and distribution of income. If returns to scale are constant, demand for commodities will not affect prices directly, but it will affect demand for labor. We might then write a supplementary equation of the type

(VII) $D(\pi) = S(\pi)$ or, alternatively, $D(w) = S(w)$

where D and S indicate demand and supply of labor as functions of distribution of income. *If the functions D and S have the required properties*, the equilibrium distribution of income will thereby be determined.[18]

Alternatively, the neo-Ricardian model may be "closed" by introducing a "Cambridge equation," in which the rate of profit is related to capitalists' pro-

pensity to save (Sp) and to the rate of growth (g). Assuming that only capitalists save, we shall have the well-known formula:

$$\pi = \frac{g}{Sp}$$

If Sp and g are given, π (and consequently w and the relative prices) will be determined, too.

Sometimes, by "distribution of income" one intends to refer to the *shares* of wages (W) and of profits (P) in the national income. In this case, however, "distribution of income" cannot be determined unless the rate of profit, or the wage-rate, is known. Otherwise, we would not even know in terms of what the distributive shares have to be measured, except in the case in which only one technique exists.[19]

The last point to discuss is the relation between the equilibrium rate of interest and the marginal product of capital. This involves a matter of definition and failure to understand it has caused a lot of futile debates. If *marginal product of capital* is defined in the same way as I have suggested earlier in this paper, there is no implication in the general equilibrium model that the equilibrium rate of interest is equal to the marginal product of capital. On the contrary, it has been clearly stated and proved (see Malinvaud, 1953) that, in general, these two quantities will be different. If, on the other hand, the marginal product of capital is calculated *taking the equilibrium prices as constants*, it can be proved that, under certain conditions regarding the input-output relations, the equality in argument will indeed hold (see Appendix B).

It must be immediately added, however, that the second definition of marginal product of capital is different from the traditional one (as, for example, appears in Wicksell's analysis and in the "Austrian" tradition), and, more important, its explanatory power is very limited. In fact, the condition that the equilibrium prices should be taken as constants in the determination of the marginal product of capital implies that the latter is defined only *at the equilibrium point*, and it is determined simultaneously with it. This is a completely different view from that of the vulgar economists, who maintained that a marginal productivity *curve* could be defined on a purely technological ground and that such a curve could be taken as one of the *determinants* of the equilibrium prices and distribution of income (or, even more ambitiously, that the property of the marginal product of capital curve could be used to derive certain considerations concerning the stability of equilibrium).

From what we have been saying, it is now easy to see why the general equilibrium theory is not touched, *on the logical ground*, by the criticisms that have been raised against the vulgar theory. In a sense this is self-evident if one considers that the concept of "capital in general," which has been the main target of such criticisms, is essentially foreign to the general equilibrium theory. The vulgar neoclassical propositions that have been proved false by the neo-Ricardian critique can similarly be (and some have been) falsified by making use of a general equilibrium theoretical apparatus.

This conclusion should not be surprising. In fact, the neo-Ricardian argument basically shows that propositions which are valid in a unidimensional system are not necessarily correct in a multidimensional one. The general

equilibrium theory, in its turn, is by definition aimed at studying the interdependence of the elements of a multidimensional system. It would indeed be strange if, as far as the limitations of aggregate models are concerned, the two approaches provided contradictory results.

We are now in a position to recapitulate the main conclusions of our analysis.

1. The Marxian theory of value and surplus-value provides a logically sound and historically relevant analysis of capitalist profit. This theory is significant and adequate with respect to the object of Marx's investigation. It is still useful today in grasping some fundamental mechanisms of the capitalist social system.
2. The vulgar neoclassical theory constitutes an attempt to provide a causal explanation of profit alternative to Marx's. This theory is relevant as to the problem investigated, but it is logically false as to the solution suggested.
3. The neo-Ricardian theory has played two important roles. First of all, it has rebuilt the cost of production theory of prices on sounder bases. In so doing it has also contributed to overcoming certain logical difficulties existing in Marx's theory of prices of production. Second, the neo-Ricardian theory has brought the critique of the vulgar neoclassical theory to the extreme conclusions, showing its logical inconsistency.

 On the other hand, the neo-Ricardian theory does not provide any causal theory of profit, and it is indeed logically compatible with a number of different possible theories of distribution of income. In a sense, it brings us to a pre-Marxian stage of economic analysis—although a more rigorous and sophisticated one.
4. The general equilibrium theory is intrinsically immune from the criticisms that have been raised against the neoclassical theory *on a logical ground*. Indeed, the main results of such criticisms are implicit in the general equilibrium model.
5. From a formal point of view, the neo-Ricardian theory may be interpreted as a special case of the general equilibrium theory. It is indeed possible to reduce the latter to the former by means of a limited number of restrictive assumptions. A full discussion of the empirical foundations of these assumptions—a problem of realism and relevance, not of coherence—is still lacking.
6. The general equilibrium theory does not provide any causal explanation of capitalist profit. Strictly speaking, concepts like "capital" or "*the rate of profit (interest)*" do not play any significant role in the model of general equilibrium.
7. The general equilibrium theory cannot deal with most socially relevant problems as it lacks the necessary theoretical tools of analysis. Methodological individualism applied to the analysis of economic agents' behavior, technologism applied to the investigation of the productive process and, in general, the vision of the economy as an optimizing device seem to be the weakest points of the theory (see Rowthorn, 1974). The concepts of class, social relations of production, and power are absent. The financial institutions of capitalism, and in particular money, do not appear in the general equilibrium scheme. Expectations, uncertainty, irrevocable mistakes (and therefore

disequilibrium conditions) are not dealt with satisfactorily or are altogether ignored. Consequently the general equilibrium does not provide the instruments to analyze processes, i.e. the dynamics of the system from one state to another (not necessarily a state of equilibrium).
8. The critique of the general equilibrium theory (by Marxists as well as by non-Marxist economists) should be directed to the coherence of the theory with the object of investigation, rather than to the internal consistency of the theory itself. This, of course, makes the task much more difficult. Indeed the deductive inference possesses a character of logical necessity that inductive inference lacks. It follows that, while the falsity of a proposition (with respect to another taken as true) can be conclusively established by means of analytical critique, no obvious criterion exists as regards the choice between two theories, both logically consistent. If we think of it, however, the freedom and creativity of scientific investigation depends precisely on this apparent weakness.

APPENDIX A

The Transformation of Values into Prices

This Appendix is a formal mathematical discussion of some points dealt with *verbatim* in the main text. As the problems in question have already been discussed extensively in the literature, I shall limit myself to the essential.

Consider an economy with n industries (designated by the subscript $i = 1, 2, \ldots, n$) each of which produces a given amount of one commodity over a certain period of time, say one year, by means of given amounts of various inputs and of homogeneous labor. The yearly gross output of each commodity is taken as its physical unit of measure. Fixed capital and nonproduced inputs like land are ignored here. The symbology adopted is the following:

c_{ij} = amount of the jth commodity ($j = 1, 2, \ldots, n$) used up to produce one unit of the ith commodity.

$C = (c_{ij})$ = input-output matrix in physical terms.

ℓ_i = amount of labor-time required to produce one unit of the ith commodity. (The amount of labor-time generated in the entire economy during one year is taken as unit of measure, i.e.

$$\sum_{i=1}^{n} \ell_i = 1.)$$

$\ell = (\ell_1, \ell_2, \ldots, \ell_n)$ = column vector of labor inputs.

$b = (b_1, b_2, \ldots, b_n)$ = row vector whose elements represent the wage-goods received by laborers, per unit of labor-time. (It is assumed that the composition of the wage-good basket is the same in all sectors.)

λ_i = amount of labor embodied in one unit of the ith commodity, i.e. "value" of one unit of the ith commodity in the sense of Marx.

$\lambda = (\lambda_1, \lambda_2, \ldots, \lambda_n)$ = column vector of "values."

$K = (k_{ij})$ = input-output matrix in which the elements are measured in terms of labor embodied. Therefore, we have

$$K = C \langle \lambda \rangle$$

where

$$\langle \lambda \rangle = \begin{bmatrix} \lambda_1, 0, \ldots, 0 \\ 0, \lambda_2, \ldots, 0 \\ \vdots \\ 0, \ldots, \quad \lambda_n \end{bmatrix}$$

$v = (v_1, v_2, \ldots, v_n)$ = row vector of wage-goods in which the elements are measured in terms of labor embodied. Therefore, we have

$$v = b \langle \lambda \rangle$$

σ = rate of surplus-value in the sense of Marx, i.e.

$$\frac{1 - \sum\limits_{j=1}^{n} v_j}{\sum\limits_{j=1}^{n} v_j}$$

$p = (p_1, p_2, \ldots, p_n)$ = column vector of the prices of commodities *per unit of labor embodied*, i.e.

$$p_i = \frac{\text{price per physical unit of the } i\text{th commodity}}{\text{"value" of one unit of } i}$$

π = uniform rate of profit.

ω_i = organic composition of capital in the ith industry in "value" terms, i.e.

$$\frac{\sum\limits_{j=1}^{n} k_{ij}}{\ell_i \sum\limits_{j=1}^{n} v_j}$$

Knowledge of the technical conditions of production permits us to calculate the "values" of commodities. Adopting matrix symbology, we have

(A.1) $C\lambda + \ell = \lambda$

from which, solving for λ, we obtain

(A.2) $\lambda = [I - C]^{-1}\ell$

where I is the identity matrix.

The system of equations (A.1) determines the n positive "values" of commodities on condition that the matrix $(I - C)$ can be inverted. Of course, we want

our system to be capable of producing some net output, and therefore we assume that

$$\sum_{j=1}^{n} (c_{ij} + \ell_i b_j) \leqslant 1$$

for all i's, and that the inequality holds at least for one commodity. Let us now assume that the "values" thus determined are used as exchange-ratios of commodities. In each industry i we shall have

(A.3) $\sum\limits_{j=1}^{n} (c_{ij} + \ell_i b_j)\lambda_j (1 + \pi_i) = \lambda_i$

from which we obtain

(A.4) $\pi_i = \dfrac{\lambda_i - \sum\limits_{j=1}^{n} (c_{ij} + \ell_i b_j)\lambda_j}{\sum\limits_{j=1}^{n} (c_{ij} + \ell_i b_j)\lambda_j}$

where of course the numerator indicates surplus-value in Marx's sense, and the denominator indicates the "value" of total capital (constant and variable) for the ith industry.

Let us now divide the numerator and the denominator of the R.H.S. of equation (A.4) by

$$\ell_i \sum_{j=1}^{n} b_j \lambda_j$$

i.e. by the "value" of the wage-goods of the ith industry. Remembering the definition of rate of surplus-value and of organic composition of capital, we obtain

(A.5) $\pi_i = \dfrac{\sigma}{\omega_i + 1}$

(The rate of surplus-value is the same in all industries, if the length of the working day and the composition of the basket of the wage-goods are the same, which we assume.)

From equation (A.4) it is evident that the rates of profit which result from the exchange of commodities at their "values" are different in the different industries, unless the organic compositions of capital are the same. If we exclude this exceptional case, and we want to obtain a uniform rate of profit, we shall have to "correct" the exchange-ratios as follows:

(A.6) $[K + \ell v] p (1 + \pi) = \langle \lambda \rangle p$

If the matrix $[K + \ell v]$ (and therefore the matrix $[C + \ell b]$, from which it is derived) is non-negative and indecomposable (i.e. if all commodities are "basic" in the sense of Sraffa), system (A.6) will determine a unique set of prices *per unit of labor embodied* all positive (in terms of a unit of measure) and a unique positive rate of profit.

It is therefore possible to correctly transform "values" into prices of production, whose column vector is

$$\langle \lambda \rangle p.$$

In *Capital*, volume III, Marx argues that the relation between the rate of surplus-value and the rate of profit is

$$(A.7) \qquad \pi = \frac{\sigma}{\omega + 1},$$

where ω is the simple average of the organic compositions of capital in the various sectors. That is

$$\omega = \frac{\displaystyle\sum_{i=1}^{n} \sum_{j=1}^{n} k_{ij}}{\displaystyle\sum_{j=1}^{n} v_j}.$$

We are now in a position to correct equation (A.7). In order to simplify notation, let us introduce a new matrix

$$A = (a_{ij}) = [C + \ell b] = [K + \ell v] \langle \lambda \rangle^{-1},$$

and a new column vector

$$\tilde{p} = \langle \lambda \rangle p.$$

Remembering equation (A.6) and making use of a well-known theorem of matrix algebra, we can write

$$(A.8) \qquad (1 + \pi) A \tilde{p} = \tilde{p}$$

$$(A.9) \qquad (1 + \pi) A' b = b$$

where A' is the transpose of A and b is a column vector such that, if we use its elements as multipliers to determine the levels of activity in the various industries, the total input will have the same physical composition of total output. By making use of the degree of freedom of system (A.9) we can postulate that

$$\sum_{i=1}^{n} b_i \ell_i = \sum_{i=1}^{n} \ell_i = 1.$$

From (A.8) – (A.9) we have then:

$$(A.10) \qquad \pi = \frac{b'[I - A]\tilde{p}}{b'A\tilde{p}}$$

where b' is a row vector having the same elements as the column vector b.

But from (A.9) we know that the vectors $[b'(I - A)]$ and $[b'A]$ only differ by a scale factor. Therefore the ratio on the R.H.S. of (A.10) is independent of the particular price vector which is used. We can therefore write

$$(A.11) \qquad \pi = \frac{b'[I - A]\lambda}{b'A\lambda}.$$

A moment's reflection will suggest that the numerator of (A.11) is in fact equal to the total surplus-value of the *original* system. The denominator of (A.11) can be decomposed thus:

$$b'A\lambda = b'C\lambda + b'\ell b\lambda = b'Ku + vu$$

(where u is the column vector $[1, 1, \ldots, 1]$).

Upon dividing throughout by (vu) (i.e. by the "value" of the wage-goods) and by putting $\omega^* = [b'Ku/vu]$, we finally have

$$(A.12) \qquad \pi = \frac{\sigma}{\omega^* + 1},$$

which is the correct formula relating the rate of surplus-value to the rate of profit.

The term ω^* may be interpreted as a particular weighted average of the organic compositions in the different sectors. However, only those sectors that produce "basic" commodities in the sense of Sraffa will have non-zero weights. This means that the technical conditions of production in nonbasic sectors do not influence the uniform rate of profit *directly*.[21]

From the formula (A.10) the Sraffian equation for the rate of profit can be easily obtained. For this purpose we shall reinterpret the matrix A, excluding from it the wage-goods. The wage will now be calculated as a share of the net product of the system and will be indicated by w.

We shall therefore have

$$(A.13) \qquad \pi = \frac{b'[I - A]\tilde{p}}{b'A\tilde{p}} (1 - w)$$

Indicating by π_{max} the rate of profit which obtains when $w = 0$, we can write

$$(A.14) \qquad \pi = \pi_{max}(1 - w),$$

which is indeed Sraffa's equation for the rate of profit.[22]

APPENDIX B

Analytical Critique of the "Vulgar" Neoclassical Propositions

In this appendix, I shall provide a formal mathematical discussion of some problems dealt with in the main text. In particular, it will be proved rigorously that the neoclassical "parables" do not have general validity. This result is not new. A clear and comprehensive survey of the literature on this point can be found in Harcourt (1972).

The originality of this appendix, if any, consists in the use of an analytical apparatus different from the neo-Ricardian one, and based on the general equilibrium model. I have chosen this form of presentation in order to substantiate my earlier claim that the results of the neo-Ricardian critique are by no means incompatible with the general equilibrium theory, indeed they are implicit in such a theory.[23]

Consider a simple model in which (net) outputs are designated by y, inputs by a, prices by p, all these magnitudes being vectors.[24] The total labor input is designated by ℓ (labor being assumed homogeneous), the uniform wage-rate by w, the uniform interest rate by π, all these magnitudes being scalars.

In general, we shall have

(B.1) $p \cdot y = \pi(p \cdot a) + \widetilde{w}\ell$

where $\widetilde{w} = (1 + \pi)w$.

Consider now two stationary equilibria, E_0 and E_1, respectively, characterized by the quantities

$$(y_0, a_0, \ell_0; p_0, w_0, \pi_0)(y_1, a_1, \ell_1; p_1, w_1, \pi_1).$$

The condition that in each of these equilibria profits be maximized implies that at E_0, we have

(B.2) $p_0 \cdot \Delta y - \pi_0(p_0 \cdot \Delta a) - \widetilde{w}_0 \Delta\ell \leqslant 0,$

and at E_1, we have

(B.3) $p_1 \cdot \Delta y - \pi_1(p_1 \cdot \Delta a) - \widetilde{w}_1 \Delta\ell \geqslant 0,$

where Δ is an operator such that

$$\Delta y, \Delta a, \Delta\ell = (y_1 - y_0), (a_1 - a_0), (\ell_1 - \ell_0).$$

The meaning of the inequalities (B.2), (B.3) should be obvious: in equilibrium, for any given set of prices, interest and wage-rates (to determine which we also need certain demand functions that are not considered here), no input-output configuration should be more profitable than the actual one.

If we now subtract (B.2) from (B.3), and if we assume that employment is kept constant, i.e. $\Delta\ell = 0$, we shall have

(B.4) $\Delta p \cdot \Delta y - \Delta(\pi p) \cdot \Delta a \geqslant 0.$

The inequality (B.4) can be used to verify the validity of the neoclassical "parables."

Let us first consider an aggregate model in which the vectors that appear in (B.4) have only one element, and are therefore reduced to scalars. In such a model, the relative price p will be by definition equal to 1, and therefore $\Delta p = 0$. In this case expression (B.4) can be simplified thus:

(B.5) $\Delta\pi\Delta a \leqslant 0,$

where Δa can be unambiguously interpreted as a variation of capital per head. It follows that, when $\Delta\pi$, $\Delta a \neq 0$, they must have opposite signs, i.e. equilibrium capital intensity and equilibrium interest rate are always inversely related. In addition, in the aggregate model we are considering, equation (B.2) can be re-written thus (being $\Delta\ell = 0$),

(B.2)' $\Delta y - \pi_0 \Delta a \leqslant 0$

from which it follows

(B.6) $\dfrac{\Delta y}{\Delta a} - \pi_0 \begin{cases} \leqslant 0, \text{ for } \Delta a > 0 \\ \geqslant 0, \text{ for } \Delta a < 0. \end{cases}$

Taking the limit of expression (B.6) we shall have

(B.7) $\lim\limits_{\Delta a \to 0} \dfrac{\Delta y}{\Delta a} \equiv \left(\dfrac{dy}{da}\right)_0 = \pi_0$

which shows that the equilibrium interest rate is equal to the marginal productivity of capital, the latter being defined in terms of purely technical considerations.

By making use of the simplifying assumptions discussed above, we can rewrite (B.3), as follows:

(B.3)' $\Delta y - \pi_1 \Delta a \geqslant 0$

from which, by dividing by Δa, we obtain

(B.8) $\dfrac{\Delta y}{\Delta a} - \pi_1 \begin{cases} \geqslant 0, \text{ for } \Delta a > 0 \\ \leqslant 0, \text{ for } \Delta a < 0. \end{cases}$

If π_0, $\pi_1 > 0$, i.e. if the rate of interest has to be positive, it must be $(\Delta y/\Delta a) > 0$. Consequently, by multiplying (B.5) by $(\Delta y/\Delta a)$, we obtain

(B.9) $\Delta\pi\Delta y \leqslant 0$

i.e. when $\Delta\pi$, $\Delta y \neq 0$, they must have opposite signs. This proves the neoclassical "parable" that equilibrium output per head and equilibrium interest rate are always inversely related.

Let us now assume that the production function

$$y = f(a, \ell)$$

is homogeneous of first degree, i.e. $f(ta, t\ell) = ty$. In economic terms this implies constant returns to scale (i.e. an increment of the capital stock *with constant labor* leads to a less than proportional movement of net output). It follows that

$$(B.10)^{25} \qquad \Delta\pi\Delta\left(\frac{y}{a}\right) \geq 0$$

or, in economic terms, equilibrium interest rate and equilibrium capital-output ratio are inversely related.

All this stated, I must hasten to add that the results illustrated by (B.5), (B.7), (B.9), and (B.10) all depend on the assumption that only one commodity exists in the system, and therefore $p = 1$ and $\Delta p = 0$. The results are of little interest, unless one can prove that they also hold in the more general case, in which the presence of a multiplicity of commodities is admitted.

In order to analyze this problem, however, we have to abandon the simple inequality (B.5). The conditions of equilibrium have now to be stated according to the "complete" inequality (B.4), i.e.

$$\Delta p \cdot \Delta y - \Delta(\pi p) \cdot \Delta a \geq 0.$$

This formula does have general validity, but, unfortunately, it does not permit us to draw any simple conclusion with regard to the relations between Δp, $\Delta\pi$, Δa, and Δy. It is instead possible to show that the cases in which the neoclassical "parables" do *not* hold are, in principle, no less numerous or less "normal" than the opposite cases. Such "parables," therefore, cannot claim the *status* of scientific laws—no more than the propositions stating the contrary.

To clarify this point let us consider a simple case in which two commodities exist, y and a, only commodity a is used as input and its *net* output is zero. Let ℓ be the input of (homogeneous) labor, assumed constant; let p be the price of a in terms of y, and finally let π be the uniform rate of interest. In this case the inequality (B.4) will take the following form:

$$(B.11) \qquad \Delta(\pi p) \cdot \Delta a \leq 0.$$

Inequality (B.11) can also be written

$$(B.12) \qquad [\pi_0 \Delta p + p_1 \Delta\pi] \cdot \Delta a \leq 0$$

or, equivalently,

$$[\pi_1 \Delta p + p_0 \Delta\pi] \cdot \Delta a \leq 0.$$

The expression (B.12) can now be used to study the relation between capital intensity and interest rate. Suppose that in the equilibrium E_1 the amount of capital per head is greater than in E_0, i.e. $\Delta a > 0$. The necessary (but not sufficient) condition for (B.13) to hold, in this case, is that at least one of the two quantities Δp, $\Delta\pi$ should be negative. If $\Delta a > 0$ and, by hypothesis, $\Delta p < 0$, the (necessary, but not sufficient) condition for $\Delta\pi > 0$ is

$$(B.13) \qquad |\Delta p| > \left|\frac{p_1}{\pi_0}\Delta\pi\right|$$

or, in terms of continuous analysis,

$$(B.14) \qquad \left|\frac{dp}{p}\right| > \left|\frac{d\pi}{\pi}\right|.$$

That is to say, in order for $\Delta\pi\Delta a > 0$ when $\Delta p\Delta a < 0$ the proportional change in p should be greater, in absolute value, than the proportional change in π. A more rigorous approach should measure capital per head in terms of the *value* of the capital stock, i.e. in terms of (pa). Consider now that $\Delta(pa)$ can be written thus:

$$(B.15) \qquad [p_0\Delta a + a_1\Delta p]$$

or, equivalently,

$$[p_1\Delta a + a_0\Delta p].$$

If the hypotheses that $\Delta a > 0$ and $\Delta p < 0$ are maintained, it will be $\Delta(pa) > 0$ if

$$(B.16) \qquad |\Delta p| < \left|\frac{p_0}{a_1}\Delta a\right|$$

or in terms of continuous analysis,

$$(B.17) \qquad \left|\frac{dp}{p}\right| < \left|\frac{da}{a}\right|.$$

By combining the inequalities (B.14) and (B.17), we obtain the conditions for which $\Delta(pa) > 0$ and $\Delta\pi > 0$, i.e. the conditions for changes in capital-value per head to be associated with changes of the interest rate in the *same* direction, namely

$$(B.18) \qquad \left|\frac{da}{a}\right| > \left|\frac{dp}{p}\right| > \left|\frac{d\pi}{\pi}\right|.$$

Thus, for example, if the proportional change of a when we (notionally) move from E_0 to E_1 is, say, +10%, and the corresponding changes of p and π are, say, −5% and +2%, respectively, the value of capital per head will *increase* by 5% "in spite" of the increase of the interest rate, and contrary to the neoclassical teaching. The questions whether Δp has the same sign as Δa or not,[26]

and whether the conditions *sub* (B.14) and (B.18) may hold, cannot be answered a priori. It all depends on the specifications of the model, and in particular on the form of the input-output relations.

Let us now consider the relation between output per head and interest rate. For this purpose, let us multiply both sides of (B.11) by $(\Delta y/\Delta a)$, which is greater than zero if $\pi > 0$. We shall have

(B.19) $\Delta(\pi p) \cdot \Delta y \leqslant 0$

which can be conveniently rewritten thus:

(B.20) $[\pi_0 \Delta p + p_1 \Delta \pi] \cdot \Delta y \leqslant 0$

or, alternatively,

$[\pi_1 \Delta p + p_0 \Delta \pi] \cdot \Delta y \leqslant 0.$

When $\Delta y > 0$, and $\Delta p, \Delta \pi \neq 0$, i.e. when net output per head increases, and the price and the rate of interest change accordingly, it must be

(B.21) $[\pi_0 \Delta p + p_1 \Delta \pi] < 0.$

Suppose now that $\Delta p < 0$, and

(B.22) $|\Delta p| > \left| \dfrac{p_1}{\pi_0} \Delta \pi \right|$

or, in terms of continuous analysis, $dp < 0$, and

(B.23) $\left| \dfrac{dp}{p} \right| > \left| \dfrac{d\pi}{\pi} \right|.$

In this case we may have $\Delta \pi > 0$, and the relation between the equilibrium rate of interest and net output per head may be *positive*, not negative as the orthodox teaching would have it.

Similar considerations can be used to show that the relation between equilibrium capital-output ratio and interest rate may be "perverse." Consider again the case just discussed in which $\Delta y, \Delta a, \Delta \pi > 0$. If there are constant returns to scale (with respect to capital and labor), the increase in y will be proportionally less than the corresponding increase in a (labor is taken to be constant). It follows that, in the case under discussion, the relation between the capital-output ratio measured by (a/y) and the equilibrium rate of interest is *positive* (see above, p. 404). In general, the capital-output ratio is more conveniently measured by the ratio between net output per head and the corresponding *value* of capital per head, i.e. the ratio (pa/y). In terms of continuous analysis, we can write

(B.24) $d\left[\dfrac{(pa)}{y} \right] = \dfrac{-(pa)dy + yd(pa)}{y^2}.$

Therefore, the condition for $d[(pa)/y] > 0$ is:

$$yd(pa) > (pa)dy$$

or

(B.25) $\dfrac{dy}{y} < \dfrac{d(pa)}{(pa)}.$

Upon combining the expressions (B.25) and (B.18), we obtain the conditions for $d[(pa)/y] > 0$ and $d\pi > 0$, i.e.

(B.26) $\left\{ \left| \dfrac{da}{a} \right| > \left| \dfrac{dp}{p} \right| > \left| \dfrac{d\pi}{\pi} \right| \right\}$

$\left\{ \dfrac{dy}{y} < \dfrac{dp}{p} + \dfrac{da}{a} \right\}$

(where, by hypothesis, $da, dy > 0$ and $dp < 0$).

For example, if a increases by 10%, y increases by 6%, p decreases by 3%, and π increases by 2%, we shall have an increase of the capital-output ratio (in *value* terms) of 1%, and a corresponding increase (not decrease) of the rate of interest of 2%.

I should like to point out once again that there are no a priori reasons for excluding that the conditions *sub* (B.26) can obtain, or for believing that such conditions represent special cases.

We have postponed the discussion of the neoclassical proposition affirming the equality, in equilibrium, between the rate of interest and the marginal product of capital, since a problem of definition is involved.

If we accept the definition of marginal product of capital suggested by Malinvaud (see above p. 395), such an equality can be easily proved (in our simple case).

Consider the disequality (B.2). Under the assumptions of the present model, it can be simplified thus:

(B.27) $\Delta y - \pi_0 p_0 \Delta a \leqslant 0.$

Upon dividing (B.27) by $(p_0 \Delta a)$, we shall have

(B.28) $\dfrac{\Delta y}{p_0 \Delta a} - \pi_0 \begin{cases} \leqslant 0, \text{ for } \Delta a > 0 \\ \geqslant 0, \text{ for } \Delta a < 0 \end{cases}$

(p_0 being of course positive).

Let us now take the limit of expression (B.28),[27] *taking the price p_0 as a constant*. We shall have

(B.29) $\lim\limits_{\Delta a \to 0} \dfrac{\Delta y}{p_0 \Delta a} = \pi_0,$

where of course the L.H.S. of the equation is the marginal product of capital á la Malinvaud. However, if we consider the definition of marginal product of capital á la Wicksell, where prices are taken to be variables rather than constant, we shall obtain a quite different result. In terms of our simple model, we have

$$\text{m.p.c.} = \lim_{\Delta a \to 0} \frac{\Delta y}{\Delta(pa)}$$

or

$$(B.30) \quad \text{m.p.c.} = \lim_{\Delta a \to 0} \frac{\dfrac{\Delta y}{\Delta a}}{p_0 + a_1 \dfrac{\Delta p}{\Delta a}}$$

or, equivalently

$$\text{m.p.c.} = \lim_{\Delta a \to 0} \{(\Delta y/\Delta a) \div [p_1 + a(\Delta p/\Delta a)]\}.$$

By comparing the expressions (B.30) and (B.29), it may be readily seen that there does not exist any unambiguous relation between the R.H.S. of (B.30) and the equilibrium rate of interest. But this is not all. Whereas the existence of the limit of the ratio $(\Delta y/\Delta a)$ for $\Delta a \to 0$ may be guaranteed by certain assumptions economically meaningful, we cannot even be sure that the limit of $(\Delta p/\Delta a)$ is determinate. The very concept of marginal product of capital seems therefore to rest on rather shaky theoretical bases.

REFERENCES

Äkerman, G. *Realkapital und Kapitalzins.* Stockholm, 1923.
Arrow, K. J., and Hahn, F. H. *General Competitive Analysis.* Edinburgh: Oliver & Boyd, 1971.
Böhm-Bawerk, E. *Capital and Interest.* Illinois: Libertarian Press, 1959.
Bortkiewicz, L. von. "Value and Price in the Marxian System." *International Economic Papers*, no. 2 (1952).
Clark, J. B. *The Distribution of Wealth.* New York: Macmillan, 1899.
Cobb, C. W., and Douglas, P. H. "A Theory of Production." *American Economic Review* 18, supplement (1928), pp. 139-65.
Dmitriev, V. K. *Economic Essays.* Cambridge: Cambridge University Press, 1975.
Dobb, M. "The Sraffa System and Critique of the Neoclassical Theory of Distribution." *The Economist* 118 (1970), pp. 347-62.
Garegnani, P. "Heterogeneous Capital, the Production Function and the Theory of Distribution." *Review of Economic Studies* 37 (1970), pp. 407-36.
Hahn, F. H. *The Share of Wages in the National Income.* London, 1972.
—— and Matthews, R. C. O. "The Theory of Economic Growth: A Survey." *Economic Journal* 74 (1964).
Harcourt, G. C. *Some Cambridge Controversies on the Theory of Capital.* Cambridge: Cambridge University Press, 1972.
Koopmans, T. C. *Three Essays on the State of Economic Science.* New York: McGraw-Hill, 1957.
Lange, O. "The Place of Interest in the Theory of Production." *Review of Economic Studies* 3 (1936), pp. 159-62.
Malinvaud, E. "Capital Accumulation and Efficient Allocation of Resources." *Econometrica* 21 (1953).
—— *Lectures on Microeconomic Theory.* Amsterdam and London: North Holland, 1972.

Marx, K. *Capital*, vol. I. Moscow: Foreign Languages Publishing House, 1961.
—— *Capital*, vol. III. Moscow: Foreign Languages Publishing House, 1968.
Medio, A. "Profits and Surplus Value: Appearance and Reality in Capitalist Production," in E. K. Hunt and J. G. Schwartz, eds., *A Critique of Economic Theory.* Harmondsworth: Penguin Books, 1972.
Meek, R. L. *Economics and Ideology and Other Essays.* London: Chapman & Hall, 1967.
Metzler, L. A. "The Rate of Interest and the Marginal Product of Capital." *Journal of Political Economy*, 1950, pp. 289-306.
Mill, J. S. *Principles of Political Economy.* London: Longmans, Green & Co., 1909.
Morishima, M. *Marx's Economics.* Cambridge: Cambridge University Press, 1973.
—— and Seton, F. "Aggregation in Leontief Matrices and the Labour Theory of Value," in G. C. Harcourt, and N. S. Laing, eds., *Capital and Growth.* London, 1971.
Pasinetti, L. L. "Switches of Technique and the 'Rate of Return' in Capital Theory." *Economic Journal* 79 (1969), pp. 508-31.
Ricardo, D. *Principles of Political Economy.* Cambridge: Cambridge University Press, 1951.
Robinson, J. "The Production Function and the Theory of Capital." *Review of Economic Studies* 21 (1954), pp. 81-106.
Rowthorn, R. "Neoclassicism, Neo-Ricardianism and Marxism." *New Left Review*, no. 86 (1974).
Schwartz, J. T. *Lectures on the Mathematical Method in Analytical Economics.* Gordon & Breach, 1961.
Seton, F. "The 'Transformation Problem,'" *Review of Economic Studies* 24 (1957), pp. 146-60.
Sraffa, P. *Production of Commodities by Means of Commodities.* Cambridge: Cambridge University Press, 1960.
Stigler, G. J. *Production and Distribution Theories.* New York, 1941.
Walras, L. *Elements of Pure Economics.* London: Allen & Unwin, 1954.
Wicksell, J. G. K. (1901), *Lectures on Political Economy*, vol. I. London: Routledge & Kegan Paul, 1934-1935.
—— "A Mathematical Analysis of Dr. Äkerman's Problem." *Lectures on Political Economy,* op. cit. (1923), pp. 274-99.

NOTES

1. However, in Mill's work some elements can be found that will be later developed by marginalist authors, in particular by Marshall.

2. In what follows, by the term "commodities" I intend to refer to "freely reproducible goods." Therefore, problems connected with rent, monopoly, etc., are ignored here.

3. On this point, see Medio (1972), pp. 317-18.

4. This is a necessary but insufficient condition. For a surplus to exist it is also necessary that, in the "basic" system (in Sraffa's sense), the output of each commodity be at least equal to the amounts of the same commodity used up as inputs. Moreover, an excess of output over total inputs should exist for at least one commodity. However, whereas the input-output relation of, say, steel may be looked at as a technical fact, the generation of labor-time in excess of the labor embodied in wage-goods is primarily a social and political fact. This is why a theory of surplus value is socially more significant than a theory of surplus steel.

5. Notice that the term "private" to Marx has a meaning different from the ordinary one. Thus, a state-owned industry is "private" in Marx's sense so long as workers as a class do not control the social productive process.

6. To avoid misunderstandings, I want to make it clear that, in what follows, I shall refer to the modern versions of the general equilibrium theory. In particular, I have in mind the presentations supplied by Arrow and Hahn (1971) and Malinvaud (1972).

7. The terms "neo-Ricardian school" or "Cambridge school" sometimes refer also to the contributions of Joan Robinson, Nicholas Kaldor, Luigi Pasinetti, and others to the theory of growth. In this essay, we only consider the neo-Ricardian theory of price, in the formulation given it by Sraffa.

8. In the present discussion the expressions "rate of interest" and "rate of profit" are taken as equivalent. Neoclassical authors usually prefer the former.

9. See, for example, Hahn (1972), introduction.

10. The marginal product of capital is the limit of the ratio (I) when the denominator tends to zero.

11. See Appendix B.

12. As will become clear in a moment, this definition is not entirely free from ambiguity when more than one commodity exists. For the present discussion, however, definition (III) can be temporarily accepted.

13. More rigorously, I should say that the equality between the rate of interest and the marginal product of capital implies the equality between the limits of the ratios (II) and (III). We shall see later (see Appendix B) that the determination of these limits presents some difficulties.

14. It must be pointed out that this revaluation of the stock of capital, which occurs when a new equilibrium replaces the old one, is not just an accounting convention. On the contrary, it reflects the fundamental economic fact that in different situations economic agents value the same commodities differently.

15. But this is not all. Indeed, the existence of the limit of the ratio (I) as net investment tends to zero may be guaranteed by assumptions that have some economic plausibility. In particular, it is necessary to assume that the input-output functions are differentiable where required. But this is not the case as regards the ratio (II). When the increment of net product and the corresponding increment of the stock of capital are reduced without limit, equilibrium prices undergo changes in either direction of unspecified magnitude, and in general there is no presumption that the ratio (II) tends to a determined limit. The very concept of marginal product of capital is, therefore, vitiated by ambiguity.

16. As a matter of fact, the second case may be regarded as a special case of the first.

17. The author is not entirely innocent in this respect. See Medio (1972), p. 325. In the revised editions of this article this passage has been changed, however.

18. This approach has been considered by Schwartz (1961) within models of Walras-Leontief and of Walras-Keynes types. Schwartz's conclusions are that, given certain plausible assumptions with regard to the functions $D(\pi)$ and $S(\pi)$, it will not be possible to uniquely determine distribution of income in terms of demand and supply of labor only. In Schwartz's view, it will instead be necessary to take into account other factors, which are traditionally excluded from economic analysis (unions, political pressures and counterpressures, etc.) (1961, pp. 192-97, 227-30). Formally speaking, the Marxian model can be "closed" by taking the physical *composition* of wages as given, and by formulating an additional equation which relates the rate of profit to the rate of surplus-value. For any given technique the latter depends on the length of the working day and on the value of labor-power (in Marx's sense). Once the rate of surplus-value is fixed, the rate of profit and the equilibrium prices corresponding to each technique can also be determined. For a study of the functional relation between the rates of profit and of surplus-value, see Medio (1972); Morishima (1973, esp. chap. 6); Morishima and Seton (1961).

19. Notice that, whereas the relation between π and w is always inverse (with no joint products), the relations between π and W, or between w and P, may not be so. In other words, we may have a higher *rate* of profit corresponding to a higher wage share.

20. A rigorous proof of this statement is provided in Appendix B.

21. A more comprehensive discussion of this point especially in relation to the concept of "average commodity" in Marx, can be found in Medio (1972, pp. 330-41).

22. Sraffa (1960, p. 22). A discussion of this formula vis-à-vis the Marxian formula (A.12) can be found in Medio (1972, pp. 342-44).

23. What follows has been inspired by E. Malinvaud (1972, pp. 265-70).

24. In this model there are no fixed capital or nonreproducible inputs.

25. In fact, from the definition of Δ, we have that $\Delta(y/a) \gtreqless 0$ if

$$\frac{\Delta y}{y_0} \gtreqless \frac{\Delta a}{a_0} .$$

With constant returns to scale it will be

$$\frac{\Delta y}{y_0} \gtreqless \frac{\Delta a}{a_0} \quad \text{if} \quad \Delta a \gtreqless 0$$

(y_0 and a_0 being positive). From this and from (B.5), (B.10) follows.

26. Notice that with more than one capital good the sign of Δa is not clearly defined.

27. It is readily seen that the expression ($\Delta y/p_0 \Delta a$) is but a special case of the formula (III) above.

Cambridge Economics as Commodity Fetishism

FRANK ROOSEVELT

Assistant Professor of Economics at Vassar College

ABSTRACT: This article presents a Marxist critique of the Cambridge school, focusing particularly on the work of Piero Sraffa and Joan Robinson. Taking issue with those who see Cambridge economics as a contribution in the Marxian tradition, the author stresses the differences between the approaches of Marx and the Cantabrigians. After pointing out that the latter view history in a non-Marxian way, he goes on to argue that their economics has the effect of mystifying the basic social relations of capitalism. Finally, it is noted that Cambridge economics leads to a political strategy which aims at improving the distribution of income without altering the hierarchical structure of capitalist production.

They fail generally from limiting themselves to a guerrilla war against the effects of the system instead of simultaneously trying to change it, instead of using their organized forces as a lever for the final emancipation of the working class, that is to say, [for] the ultimate abolition of the wages system.
—Karl Marx, *Wages, Price and Profit*

INTRODUCTION

The purpose of this essay is to help students of radical political economics understand two of the main approaches available to them. On the one side, I present the basic concepts of Karl Marx and, on the other, I examine the recent work of the Cambridge school—a group of economists associated with the University of Cambridge, England (hereafter referred to as the Cantabrigians).[1] As the reader will see, my own preference is for the Marxian approach. Indeed, in the last section of the essay I argue that the approach of the Cantabrigians can be criticized in much the same way that Marx criticized the economics of his own time.

The ideas presented in this paper were developed with the help of the following members of the faculty of the New School for Social Research: David Gordon, Robert Heilbroner, Edward Nell, Anwar Shaikh, and Thomas Vietorisz. I enjoyed invaluable assistance from the late Stephen Hymer, and I have had the benefit of constant criticism and support from Philip Harvey. As earlier drafts were circulated, I received helpful comments from Frances Foster, Richard Garrett, Makoto Itoh, Jinx Roosevelt, Lillian Salzman, Jesse Schwartz, Tom Seidl, Nina Shapiro, Paul Sweezy, and members of the editorial board of the Review of Radical Political Economics. *I of course take responsibility for the remaining defects.*

The task undertaken here is important for two reasons. Since the Cambridge school originally gained its fame by attacking some of the central concepts of neoclassical economics,[2] it has attracted the attention of many radicals. In addition, several writers have treated the new economics of Cambridge as if it were a continuation of the Marxian tradition: Maurice Dobb and Ronald Meek have praised one of the founders of the Cambridge school, Piero Sraffa, for having "rehabilitated" Marx;[3] Geoffrey Harcourt has asserted that Cantabrigians such as Amit Bhaduri, Joan Robinson and Edward Nell "look to Marx's theory of exploitation" to explain the distribution of income;[4] Nell himself has used the word "neo-Marxian" as a label for the Cantabrigian approach;[5] and others have even talked about "the Sraffa-Marx model."[6] If the interpretation of these writers is correct, it would seem that radicals have a lot to learn from the Cambridge school.

The position taken in this essay is that it is fundamentally incorrect to link together the approaches of Marx and the Cantabrigians. In what follows it is argued that the two define their basic concepts in different ways, employ contrasting methods of analysis, orient themselves to different questions, paint conflicting pictures of the economy, and suggest alternative strategies for political action.

As broad as it is, this essay confronts only one part of a larger task. In its fullest development, radical political economics should be able to help us answer two kinds of questions, one *static* and the other *dynamic*:

1. How can one type of society be *differentiated* from another?
2. How does one type of society become *transformed* into another?

In this essay I consider the economics of Marx and the Cantabrigians only in relation to the first question; the whole problem of dynamic analysis is not dealt with here. Nevertheless, by pointing out how the Cantabrigians diverge from Marx in their method of differentiating societies it is possible to argue that they mystify the defining characteristics of capitalism and fail to grasp what the struggle for socialism is all about. This, in a nutshell, is the argument of the present essay.

In the first part of the essay I contrast the Marxian and Cantabrigian approaches to the *general* problem of differentiating societies. This requires taking up the question of historical periodization, for we usually demarcate and identify historical periods according to the type of society that is dominant in each one. In the second part of the essay I explain how the application of the Marxian and Cantabrigian approaches to the *specific* case of capitalism results not only in two very different views of our own society but also in diverging images of what a socialist society of the future ought to look like.

In my examination of Cantabrigian economics I refer mainly to the writings of two people, Piero Sraffa and Joan Robinson. Sraffa is the author of *Production of Commodities by Means of Commodities*,[7] the book generally treated by the Cantabrigians as the cornerstone of their theoretical edifice.[8] Robinson is the most distinguished of the Cantabrigians and is widely regarded as their leader. She was the one who heralded their attack on neoclassical economics in a 1953 article,[9] and, in the years since then, she has advocated the

Cambridge position all over the world. In the U.S., for example, she recently published an article in *Monthly Review* urging the new generation of American radical economists to train themselves in Cantabrigian economics.[10] In 1973, Robinson joined with a Cambridge colleague, John Eatwell, and published the first Cantabrigian textbook: *An Introduction to Modern Economics*.[11] Since this text explicitly presents the Cantabrigian approach, I refer to it frequently in this essay.

I. METHODS OF HISTORICAL PERIODIZATION

In parts A and B of this section I present the Marxian and the Cantabrigian approaches to the problem of periodizing history. In each approach the method of periodization is based on a particular way of looking at production in human societies; the way production is seen depends in turn on certain theoretical abstractions. Hence, in contrasting Marx and the Cantabrigians I trace the connections between their basic abstractions, their views of production, and their perspectives on history.

A. Marx's Approach

Marx's approach to the problem of historical periodization was based on his concept of a *mode of production*.[12] The earliest discussion of this concept may be found in *The German Ideology* where it is defined as "the way in which men produce their means of subsistence."[13] As straightforward as this definition is, the concept of a mode of production is not a simple one. Indeed, the only way one can grasp its full complexity is to take it apart, examine each of its components, and then see how its various parts are related to each other in the whole.

To take something apart in one's mind for the purpose of understanding it is to use the technique of *analysis*, and the intermediate results that one arrives at by using this technique are called *abstractions*. Thus the procedure employed here is essentially the one Marx referred to in the preface to the first edition of *Capital*:

> In the analysis of economic forms . . . neither microscopes nor chemical reagents are of use. The force of abstraction must replace both.[14]

In what follows, we will see what it means to rely upon "the force of abstraction."

Marx's Basic Abstractions*

Marx's concept of a mode of production may best be understood as a combination of two basic abstractions. Marx himself must have arrived at these abstractions before 1846 as they appear in *The German Ideology* in a passage explaining the materialist approach to history:

> This conception of history depends on our ability to expound the real process of production, starting out from *the material production of life itself*, and to comprehend *the form of intercourse* connected with this . . . (Italics added.)[15]

*In this section I present an exposition of the two notions that Marx often referred to as the "forces" and "relations" of production. However, for reasons which are elaborated in Balibar, *op. cit.* (pp. 233ff.), I prefer not to use these terms.

Since the context indicates that what is meant by "the form of intercourse" in this sentence is identical with what Marx would later refer to as the social form of production, we can see in this passage the two basic abstractions that make up his concept of a mode of production:

1. The material aspect of production.
2. The social form of production.

These two abstractions play a role in all of Marx's mature work for in his view the essence of any given society is the particular way that the material and social aspects of its production process are combined. But what is the nature of each of these abstractions, and how did Marx distinguish one from the other?

In *The German Ideology* Marx's basic abstractions are presented *as if* one of them refers to the *physical* aspect of production and the other to its *social* aspect. Near the beginning of this work, for example, the material aspect of production is described in the following way:

> The first premise of all human history is, of course, the existence of living human individuals. Thus the first fact to be established is the physical organization of these individuals and their consequent relation to the rest of nature.[16]

On the same page, the social form of production is introduced in this fashion:

> [A] mode of production must not be considered simply as being the production of the physical existence of individuals. Rather it is a definite form of activity of these individuals, a definite form of expressing their life . . .[17]

After reading these two passages one might get the impression that Marx arrived at his basic abstractions simply by separating the social and the physical aspects of human production. This, however, is not the case. The basis for a correct interpretation of the above passages may be found a few pages later in *The German Ideology* where the discussion of the mode of production concept is summed up as follows:

> The production of life, both of one's own in labour and of fresh life in procreation, now appears as *a double relationship*: on the one hand as a natural, on the other as a social relationship. (Italics added.)[18]

The key phrase here is "a double relationship." These words capture the essence of Marx's concept of a mode of production. Their full significance will become evident as we examine the view of production that Marx developed in his later work.

Marx's View of Production

In *Capital* Marx treated production as a process involving the interaction of four crucial elements. The three which he regarded as necessary to *all* human production were presented in the chapter on the labor-process:

The elementary factors of the labour-process are 1, the personal activity of man, i.e., work itself, 2, the subject of that work, and 3, its instruments.[19]

An additional element was introduced by Marx in his chapter on cooperation; it comes into play when production is carried on by a substantial number of people working together:

> All combined labour on a large scale requires, more or less, a directing authority, in order to secure the harmonious working of the individual activities, and to perform the general functions that have their origin in the action of its separate organs. A single violin player is his own conductor; an orchestra requires a separate one.[20]

Relating these two passages, and modifying the terminology somewhat, we may say that Marx regarded all human production on a large scale as a process involving the following four elements:

1. A coordinating agency.
2. Work itself (the activity of the direct producers).
3. The instruments of production.
4. The objects transformed in production.

The interaction of these four elements may be seen with the help of a simple diagram:

$$\begin{matrix} \text{PEOPLE} \\ \left(\right) \\ \text{PEOPLE} ===== \text{NATURE} \end{matrix}$$

In this diagram, the "people" at the top are the "coordinating agency" while those on the lower level are the "direct producers" who do the "work itself." The symbol = = = = = represents "the instruments of production" and the word "nature" stands for "the objects transformed in production." Production, then, was seen by Marx as a process in which these four elements interact.

But in what sense did Marx think of production as a process which involves "a double relationship"? And how did he apply his two basic abstractions to the four elements listed above? To answer these questions we must consult the *Grundrisse*, the notebooks written by Marx in 1857 and 1858. At one point in these notebooks Marx temporarily treats the production process of a capitalist society as if it were "only a *material relation* . . . as distinct from its *formal relation* as capital."[21] (Italics added.) Then, using the word "capital" to refer to the specific character of production in a capitalist society, he proceeds as follows:

> Regarded from this side [i.e., regarded as a material relation], the process of capital coincides with the simple process of production as such. . . . Thus the process of the production of capital does not appear as the process of the production of capital, but as the process of production in general. . . . Its formal character is completely extinguished.[22]

In the same place Marx went on to define the *labor-process* as the aspect of production that one sees when "its formal character is completely extinguished." In his view, the labor-process is nothing more than the material aspect of production which, "owing to its abstractness, its pure materiality, is common to all forms of production . . ."[23] We will shortly be drawing out the implications of these quotations with regard to Marx's method of periodizing history. At this point, however, they are cited to indicate that *his basic abstractions are merely two different ways of looking at the interaction of the various elements in the production process.* In other words, when Marx used one or the other of his dual abstractions he simply pretended that the aspect of production not under consideration at the moment had ceased to exist.

Marx's two ways of looking at production may be distinguished in the following manner: (1) When the elements in the production process are regarded from the standpoint of their material interaction, the relations among them can be described in socially neutral terms. As we have noted, Marx himself used the metaphor of an orchestra and its conductor to express the quality of these relations in such a context. Using another kind of analogy, we might think of the material relations between the coordinating agency and the other elements as a set of information flows, the role of the coordinating agency being similar, let us say, to that of the main computer in an automated process of production. In any case, the hallmark of this way of looking at the production process is that each element in it is considered solely with regard to the material function it fulfills. (2) When one looks at production from the standpoint of its social form, on the other hand, both the elements and the relations among them appear in a different light. In this case, the elements themselves are either identified with or used by specific historical classes of people, and the relations among them are seen as antagonistic. (This statement applies of course only to societies in which there are class divisions: different wording would have to be used to discuss the social form of production in a classless society.)

The point which needs to be stressed here is that Marx conceived of his basic abstractions as but one-sided views of a total reality. Thus, even when he was focusing on one or the other aspect of the production process, *he always took into account the presence of all four of its constituent elements.* Referring to the social form of production in the first chapter of *Capital*, for example, he spoke of "the social relations within the sphere of material life, between man and man, and between man and Nature . . ."[24] Similarly, when he looked at the other aspect of the production process he continued to treat it as a relationship between four different elements. It is for this reason that his concept of a mode of production may be described as involving "a double relationship."

Marx on Periodizing History

Marx's method of historical periodization was cogently summed up in a few sentences in volume II of *Capital*. Here, the word "labourers" refers to the direct producers and the term "means of production" encompasses the two elements previously referred to as "the instruments of production" and "the objects transformed in production":

Whatever the social form of production, labourers and means of production always remain factors of it. But in a state of separation from each other either of these factors can be such only potentially. For production to go on at all they must unite. The specific manner in which this union is accomplished distinguishes the different economic epochs of the structure of society from one another.[25]

In speaking here of "the specific manner in which this union is accomplished" Marx was clearly bringing to bear his concept of a mode of production. But how, exactly, do the two aspects of this concept enter into his method of periodizing history?

It is not difficult to see how Marx used the social form of production to differentiate one historical type of society from another. Consider, for example, the passage in *Capital* in which he drew a dividing line between the feudal and the capitalist epochs in history:

The starting point of the development that gave rise to the wage-labourer, as well as to the capitalist, was the servitude of the labourer. The advance consisted in *a change of form* of this servitude, in the transformation of feudal exploitation into capitalist exploitation. (Italics added.)[26]

From this we can see that Marx differentiated class-divided societies from one another on the basis of their form of exploitation. He could do this because, in his view, exploitation is the chief characteristic of the social form of production in such societies.

Marx's concept of exploitation was based on his distinction between "necessary" and "surplus" labor—the former being the amount of labor required to produce what the workers in any given society need to sustain and reproduce themselves, and the latter being the additional labor which a society's dominant class is able to induce its workers to perform.[27] Thus, it was no accident that he gave us a clear statement of his method of differentiating societies in the middle of a discussion of necessary and surplus labor:

The essential difference between the various economic forms of society, between, for instance, a society based on slave-labour, and one based on wage-labour, lies only in *the mode in which this surplus-labour is in each case extracted from the actual producer*, the labourer. (Italics added.)[28]

In Marx's view, then, exploitation is the extraction of surplus labor from those who do the work in a given society, and the particular form of this exploitation is what differentiates one type of society from another.

So much for the social form of production as a tool for periodizing history. What about the other part of Marx's concept of a mode of production, the material aspect of the production process? Does it not also have a role to play?

A passage has already been quoted from the *Grundrisse* in which Marx defined the labor-process as a material relation "common to all forms of production." This definition reappears in a more developed form in the chapter on the labor-process in *Capital*:

The labour-process . . . is the necessary condition for effecting exchange of matter between man and Nature: it is the everlasting Nature-imposed condition of human existence, and therefore is independent of every social phase of that existence, or rather, is common to every such phase. . . . As the taste of the porridge does not tell you who grew the oats, no more does this simple process tell you of itself what are the social conditions under which it is taking place, whether under the slave-owner's brutal lash, or the anxious eye of the capitalist . . .[29]

Such a passage could conceivably be interpreted to mean that Marx believed that the labor-process goes on in basically the same way throughout history. If this were in fact the case, he could hardly have referred to it in his method of historical periodization. As it happens, however, Marx did not think of the labor-process in this way.

Marx's comments on the labor-process may be understood if we recall that in his work this term refers only to the abstraction we have labelled "the material aspect of production." In the passage already quoted from the *Grundrisse* he defined this aspect of the production process as the side of it that one sees when "its formal character is completely extinguished." And, in the very same passage, he went on to issue the following qualification: "It will be seen that even within the production process itself this extinguishing of the formal character is merely a semblance."[30] We may interpret this to mean that, in Marx's view, the labor-process itself takes on new forms as societies evolve. This interpretation is confirmed by a statement Marx himself made near the end of volume III of *Capital*:

To the extent that the labour-process is solely a process between man and Nature, its simple elements remain common to all social forms of development. But each specific historical form of this process further develops its material foundations and social forms.[31]

Taking this passage as our guide, then, we may say that, for Marx, the presence of the various elements of production is a general requirement of all human societies, but the form they take and the way they are connected changes materially as well as socially from one historical epoch to the next. As a result, both the social form and the material aspect of production are taken into account in Marx's method of periodizing history.

We saw earlier that Marx's two basic abstractions may be thought of as alternate ways of looking at the "double relationship" connecting the various elements of the production process. We have now seen that both of these aspects of his concept of a mode of production are used in his method of historical periodization. All that remains to be discussed is the particular way in which Marx's basic abstractions are related *to each other* in his approach to history.

The way in which Marx thought of the relationship between his basic abstractions may be seen in a passage in *Capital* in which he stressed the importance of looking at one of the elements of production—namely, the instruments of production—when attempting to differentiate one type of society from another:

Relics of bygone instruments of labour possess the same importance for the investigation of extinct economic forms of society as do fossil bones for the determination of extinct species of animals. It is not the articles made, but how they are made, and by what instruments, that enables us to distinguish different economic epochs. Instruments of labour not only supply a standard of the degree of development to which human labour has attained, but they are also indicators of the social conditions under which that labour is carried on.[32]

Since Marx was clearly treating the instruments of production here from the standpoint of the material aspect of production, we may interpret his "fossil bones" metaphor to mean that he regarded the connection between his two basic abstractions as an *organic* one: Though the material and social aspects of production may be distinguished from each other—just as the bones of an animal may be distinguished from its flesh—the organic relationship between them allows the form of the first to serve as an "indicator" of the form of the second.

Marx's method of periodizing history may then be summed up as follows: His approach to history was based on his concept of a mode of production which, in turn, may be thought of as a combination of two basic abstractions, the social form and the material aspect of production. These abstractions are simply two ways of looking at the interaction of four key elements in the production process; and, because they are but two perspectives on the same interaction, they are organically related to each other.

B. The Cantabrigian Approach

The Cantabrigians are also interested in developing a method of periodizing history. At one point in *An Introduction to Modern Economics*, for example, Robinson and Eatwell make the following statement:

> [W]e cannot pretend to give an account of actual historical situations, but [our analysis] is intended to show the main principles underlying identifiable periods of economic evolution.[33]

In developing their method of historical periodization, however, the Cantabrigians take an approach which differs from that of Marx at every step of the way.

The Cantabrigians' Basic Abstractions

Though they do not employ Marx's concept of a mode of production, Robinson and Eatwell begin their analysis by separating all economic relationships into two basic abstractions: "technical relations" and "social relations."[34] "Technical relations" are defined as those which occur "between mankind and the physical universe."[35] Whenever Robinson and Eatwell discuss such relations they isolate them from the surrounding social framework and focus only on the quantitative relationships between the inputs and outputs of the production process. (An example of such relations would be a situation in which additional increments of labor applied to a fixed quantity of land produce smaller and smaller increases in the output from the land.) When Robinson and Eatwell discuss "social relations," on the other hand, they abstract from the interaction between people

and nature and focus exclusively on "relationships between people."[36] In contrast with Marx's view of production as "a double relationship," then, the Cantabrigians treat the productive interaction of people among themselves and with nature as if it consisted of *two separate relationships:*

Social Relations   *Technical Relations*

$$\begin{pmatrix} \text{PEOPLE} \\ \text{PEOPLE} \end{pmatrix} \qquad \text{PEOPLE} = = = = = = \text{NATURE}$$

With the help of these diagrams (which employ the same symbols that were used to represent Marx's view of production) we can see that when the Cantabrigians use one or the other of their two basic abstractions *they alternately disregard the presence in the production process of one or more of its constituent elements.* For example, when Robinson and Eatwell define "technical relations" with reference only to "mankind" and "the physical universe" they collapse two of the elements of production, the coordinating agency and work itself, into one category. This procedure has the effect of obscuring an important aspect of the production process, namely, the interaction between the people who coordinate it and those who do the work itself. Similarly, when Robinson and Eatwell define "social relations" exclusively in terms of "relationships between people" they neglect the role of the two non-human elements in the production process (i.e., the instruments of production and the objects transformed in production). As we will see, the consequence of defining "social relations" in this manner is that the Cantabrigians find themselves able to think of such relations only as occurring outside of the production process itself.

The Cantabrigian View of Production

In contrast with Marx (who employed both of his abstractions in his analysis of production), the Cantabrigians use only one of their basic abstractions to represent the production process: In their view, *production consists of those interactions between people and nature which can be portrayed as technical relations.*

The most important statement of the Cantabrigian view of production is Piero Sraffa's *Production of Commodities by Means of Commodities.* In this book production is represented by rows of mathematical symbols, each row showing the physical quantities of inputs that are required to produce a given amount of a certain type of output. Sraffa himself refers to the connections among these quantitative symbols as "relations"[37] and, as we will see, they are one example of what Robinson and Eatwell have in mind when they speak of "technical relations." Sraffa's view of production has been summed up by Nell as follows: "The basic constituents of [the] theory are industries, sectors, processes, or activities, defined in technological terms."[38] Thus people as human beings—and, more importantly, as historical social classes—are given no role in the process of production.[39]

The absence of social relations in the Cantabrigian view of production may also be observed in the Robinson and Eatwell textbook. In one of its chapters, for example, we are presented with a model of an economy consisting of only

two activities, one producing corn and the other turning out machines. In this economy the following role is assigned to technical relations:

> [T]he technical relations of our model consist of one technique for producing corn and one for producing machines. These govern the relation of work to machines and to output in each sector.[40]

Upon reading this passage, one wonders whether "technical relations" by themselves are sufficient to determine how much work gets done on each machine or how much output is produced in each sector. The authors themselves seem to be aware that something is missing since they do point out that the output per machine in each sector depends "firstly, on output per man hour of a team of men working [the] machines, and secondly, [on] the hours per day and days per year that the machines can be worked."[41] But, after noting that "the length of the working day for a team of men involves problems of great social and political significance," they immediately fall back to the following position: "These questions we leave on one side; we assume that there is a standard length [of the working day]."[42] And nowhere do they explain how the direct producers in their economy are actually induced to perform the amount of work required on each machine by the model's "technical relations."

It should be clear from what has been said that the Cantabrians define and use their most fundamental concepts in a way that separates their approach from that of Marx. But how, we may ask, do they think of the relationship *between* their two basic abstractions? Again, the answer is to be found in Robinson and Eatwell.

The main part of *An Introduction to Modern Economics* is devoted to "Analysis," and near the beginning of this part the authors make the following statement: "Here, we shall first set up a model of very simple technological specifications and consider how it operates in various social settings."[43] They then proceed to posit the existence of a particular set of technical relations and to speculate on what would happen to output and distribution if these technical relations were associated first with a society of independent families, then with feudal social relations and, finally, with capitalist social relations.[44] Since this procedure is only valid if one assumes that there are no necessary connections between particular sets of technical relations and specific kinds of social relations, we may conclude that Robinson and Eatwell think of their two basic abstractions as fundamentally *independent* of each other. Recalling that Marx thought of his abstractions as organically connected, this is yet another instance of the divergence between Marx and the Cantabrians.[45]

The crucial difference between the Marxian and the Cantabrian views of production may now be pinpointed. By having both of his abstractions encompass all of the elements of production, Marx was able to develop an *integrated* view of the interaction of human beings with each other and with their physical environment: He saw production as a dual process, and he took into account both its material and its social aspects. In contrast, the Cantabrians begin their analysis by setting up abstractions which *separate* the two aspects of our economic life. As a result, they end up thinking of production not as a social affair but, rather, as a purely technical process involving only quantitative relationships among physical phenomena.

The reader might wish at this point to raise the objection that the Cantabrians frequently do refer to social classes—and, certainly, no one familiar with their work would dispute such a statement. What needs to be pointed out, however, is that whenever they mention social classes the reference is always to phenomena *external to the process of production*. For example, many of the Cantabrians refer to classes and class conflict when they discuss the distribution of income.[46] In this case, however, classes are seen as fighting over the product *after* it has been produced, not as engaged with each other *in the process* of producing it. As Nell has summed up the matter, the Cantabrian approach is one which involves "analysis of the system of production and of the social relations *surrounding* production."[47] (Italics added.)

The Cantabrian practice of dividing the economy into a physical process of production and a social process of distribution is not without precedent in the history of economic thought. John Stuart Mill set forth a century ago the view that although, on the one hand, "the laws and conditions of the production of wealth partake of the character of physical truths," distribution is, on the other, "a matter of human institution solely."[48] To make the transition to our next section, we may note that it was precisely in reference to such a view that Marx spoke of "the ineptitude of those economists who portray production as an eternal truth while banishing history to the realm of distribution."[49]

The Cantabrians on Periodizing History

When we turn our attention to their method of periodizing history, we see a further consequence of the way the Cantabrians set up and use their basic abstractions. Since they treat production as if it consists only of "technical relations," they end up having to differentiate one type of society from another solely on the basis of what they call "social relations."

If production is treated merely as a set of technical relationships connecting various inputs and outputs, it cannot be thought of as assuming different forms in different historical epochs. For this reason the Cantabrians inevitably regard the production process as occurring in essentially the same way throughout history. (A corollary of this is that their method of representing production may be applied without modification to any historical form of society.)[50] But then, if production is viewed as going on in essentially the same way in all societies, what characteristics can we use to differentiate one type of society from another? Here is how Robinson and Eatwell deal with the problem:

> [T]echnical relations . . . exist in every kind of society. But production is not merely a technical process, it involves social relations as well, in particular, legal rules and accepted conventions concerning claims to property. . . . Social systems may be differentiated by the patterns of ownership they have adopted.[51]

Since it is stated here that "production is not merely a technical process, it involves social relations as well," one might infer that the term "social relations" refers to an aspect of the production process itself. As we can see, however, the authors immediately proceed to define this term with reference only to institutional phenomena *outside of* the actual process of production, namely, "patterns

of ownership." Thus, for the Cantabrigians, "social relations" refers to property relations, and, in contrast with Marx (who focused on the complex way in which its various elements are connected with each other in production), societies are differentiated solely on the basis of juridical phenomena.

The differences between the Marxian and the Cantabrigian methods of historical periodization may now be summarized. First, the Cantabrigians depart from Marx both in the definitions they give to their basic abstractions and also in the way they conceive of the relationship between them. Then, separating "technical relations" from "social relations"—and treating each as if it were independent of the other—the Cantabrigians use the first to represent production and the second to periodize history. Whereas Marx regarded history as a succession of modes of production, the Cantabrigians see it as a succession of different types of property relations.

II. PERSPECTIVES ON CAPITALISM

Having outlined the differences between the approaches of Marx and the Cantabrigians to the general problem of periodizing history, we may now examine the way in which they apply their various analytical tools to the specific case of capitalism. As we proceed through this examination, the political implications of the differences between the two approaches will become evident.

A. Marx's View of Capitalism

In the first part of this essay we saw that Marx distinguishes class-divided societies according to the *form of exploitation* characterizing their process of production. Exploitation, in his view, is the extraction of surplus labor from those who do the work in a given society, and the particular form of this exploitation is what differentiates one type of class society from another. Accordingly, when Marx looked at capitalism as a distinct form of society he located its distinctiveness in the fact that, in the capitalist mode of production, surplus labor is extracted from the direct producers in the form of *surplus-value*.

In applying his concept of a mode of production to the study of capitalism Marx used his two basic abstractions in the following way: Looking at the capitalist process of production from the standpoint of its material aspect, he analyzed the interaction of its constituent elements as a *labor-process*; when focusing on the social form of this process, on the other hand, he treated it as a *process of creating surplus-value*.[52] To understand Marx's view of capitalism, then, we have to investigate what it means to say that *the labor-process takes the form of a process of creating surplus-value*.

In what follows we will see how Marx analyzed each one of the elements in the capitalist production process *both* with regard to its material interaction with the other elements *and* from the standpoint of the creation of surplus-value. Moreover, we will see that the specific form taken by each of these elements is determined, in Marx's view, by the unique way in which all of them are related to each other in the capitalist mode of production.

Whenever he analyzed a society's production process, Marx always gave priority to examining the activity of the direct producers. We have already quoted him to the effect that the "essential difference" between a slave-owning

society and capitalism is that, while the former is "based on slave-labour," the latter is "based on wage-labour."[53] In presenting Marx's view of capitalism, therefore, it is appropriate to begin with his analysis of the form that "work itself" takes in the capitalist mode of production.

"Work Itself" as Commodity-Producing Labor

At the beginning of *Capital* Marx introduces us to the capitalist form of productive activity by discussing the case of "simple commodity production."[54] In the first chapter of this work he establishes the minimum conditions, or social relations, that must be present before one can say that *commodities* are being produced:

> As a general rule, articles of utility become commodities only because they are products of the labour of *private individuals* or groups of individuals *who carry on their work independently of each other*. (Italics added.)[55]

While he does not refer to capitalists or wage-laborers at this point, Marx is already talking about one of the fundamental characteristics of the capitalist form of work, namely, that it is *not organized by the community as a whole*. As he put it in another part of the same chapter, "a community, the produce of which in general takes the form of commodities [is one in which] the useful forms of labour . . . are carried on independently by individual producers, each on their own account . . ."[56]

While Marx introduces us to the capitalist form of work by stressing its independent character, he does not of course ask us to think of society as a collection of Robinson Crusoes. The independent producers he has in mind are not self-sufficient; to meet their needs, they must exchange at least a portion of their products with the other producers in the society. Thus another part of Marx's definition of commodities is that they are "produced for the purpose of being exchanged."[57]

Since commodities are generally exchanged, they necessarily possess both *use-value* and *exchange-value*. The first of these categories simply refers to the fact that a commodity must be useful in some way, otherwise no one will want to buy it. The exchange-value of a commodity, on the other hand, reflects the condition that it must be exchanged before it is consumed. Marx's conception of exchange-value is fairly complicated, but here we may think of it simply as a quantitative relationship between commodities.

For our present purposes, the use-value/exchange-value distinction is important because Marx employs it in his discussion of commodity-producing labor in the first chapter of *Capital*. After distinguishing between use-value and exchange-value in the first section of this chapter, he goes on in the second section to discuss "the two-fold character of the labour embodied in commodities."[58] Since commodities have two aspects, he argues, commodity-producing labor must also have a dual character. Just as the use-value of a commodity may be thought of as the quality of it which enables it to satisfy a particular need, so also may the work that goes into it be regarded as a particular kind of work. Marx spoke of work in this sense as *concrete labor*, and he defined it as "produc-

tive activity of a definite kind and exercised with a definite aim."[59] The other aspect of commodity-producing labor was referred to by Marx as *abstract labor*. For a clear presentation of the distinction between concrete and abstract labor, it is best to quote directly from *Capital*:

> As use-values, commodities are, above all, of different qualities; but as exchange-values they are merely different quantities . . .
> If then we leave out of consideration the use-value of commodities, they have only one common property left, that of being products of labour. But . . . [looking at] the product of labour itself. . . . If we make abstraction from its use-value, we make abstraction at the same time from its material elements and shapes that make the product a use-value; we see in it no longer a table, a house, yarn, or any other useful thing. Its existence as a material thing is put out of sight. Neither can it any longer be regarded as the product of the labour of the joiner, the mason, the spinner, or of any other kind of productive labour. Along with the useful qualities of the products themselves, we put out of sight both the useful character of the various kinds of labour embodied in them, and the concrete forms of that labour; there is nothing left but what is common to them all; all are reduced to one and the same sort of human labour, human labour in the abstract.[60]

From this passage we can see that Marx arrives at his distinction between concrete and abstract labor by employing his two fundamental abstractions: Looking at the capitalist process of production from the standpoint of its material aspect he sees a labor-process in which concrete labor produces use-values; examining the same process from the standpoint of its social form, on the other hand, he is able to deduce the notion of abstract labor from the specifically social aspect of commodities, namely, their exchange-value.

The main significance of Marx's concept of abstract labor is that it reflects the particular social relations that exist in a commodity-producing society. We have already noted that, in such a society, the concrete labors of individuals are not coordinated on a society-wide basis: Individuals make their own decisions as to the specific kind of productive activity they will perform, and they do not think of their particular skills and energies as integral parts of the total productive capacity of the society. As a result, the various work activities of these individuals are coordinated only indirectly, through the exchange of their products, and their efforts have a social character only in the sense that each individual's work amounts to a quantity of abstract labor.

Because abstract labor reflects a particular set of social relations Marx refers to it as a "social substance."[61] As such, he treats it as the substance of value.[62] "Value" itself, then, is what is created by abstract labor and, in Marx's work, it is something different from exchange-value. Whereas the latter is a quantitative relationship between commodities, "value" may be thought of as a quality possessed by a single commodity, in particular, that quality which it has as a result of the social conditions under which it was produced. Thus, for Marx, "value" refers to the very structure of a society in which individual producers relate to each other only through the exchange of their products:

> The value-form of the product of labour. . . . in bourgeois production . . . stamps that production as a particular species of social production, and thereby gives it its special historical character.[63]

As is well known, the "law of value" is for Marx the mechanism through which *both* the exchange-ratios of commodities *and* the activities of their producers are regulated.[64] In a commodity-producing society—or what is nowadays called a "market society"—individuals have to shuttle around to different productive activities (or, in some cases, to no productive activity at all) as the exchange-ratios between commodities go up and down. In Marx's view, this type of social arrangement is defective in the sense that people living under such conditions lack control over the mechanism by which their individual productive activities are coordinated. As he put it in the *Economic and Philosophic Manuscripts* of 1844, this lack of control amounts to the alienation of people from the products of their labor:

> [T]he object produced by labour, its product, now stands opposed to it as an *alien being*, as a *power independent* of the producer. The product of labour is labour which has been embodied in an object and turned into a physical thing. . . . The *alienation* of the worker in his product means not only that his labour becomes an object . . . but that it exists independently . . . and that it stands opposed to him as an autonomous power.[65]

As Marx saw it, then, commodity-producing labor is alienated labor, and the "market mechanism" that we learn about in our textbooks is nothing more than the products of our own labor set against us as an "autonomous power."

The last point that needs to be considered here in relation to commodity-producing labor is that, in Marx's view, it necessarily gives rise to certain *illusions* in the minds of those who perform it. Since the individuals in a commodity-producing society have no relationships with each other until they come to exchange their products, it appears to them as if the relationships between these products are the only ones that actually exist. Marx called this illusion *commodity fetishism* and he gave the following description of it in the first chapter of *Capital* just after he defined commodities as "products of the labour of private individuals . . . who carry on their work independently of each other":

> The sum total of the labour of all these private individuals forms the aggregate labour of society. Since the producers do not come into contact with each other until they exchange their products, the specific social character of each producer's labour does not show itself except in the act of exchange. In other words, the labour of the individual asserts itself as a part of the labour of society only by means of the relations which the act of exchange establishes directly between the products, and indirectly, through them, between the producers. To the latter, therefore, the relations connecting the labour of one individual with that of the rest appear, not as direct social relations between individuals at work, but as what they really are, material relations between persons and social relations between things.[66]

Thus, as Marx had indicated in his earlier work, *A Contribution to the Critique of Political Economy*:

> A social relation of production appears as something existing apart from individual human beings, and the distinctive relations into which they enter in the course of production in society appear as the specific properties of a thing . . .[67]

Since the notion of commodity fetishism is of central importance in our later discussion of Cambridge economics, it should be noted here that Marx himself thought of the economics of his own time as an exalted form of such fetishism. His views on this topic were aptly summed up by Engels in a review of the book from which we have just quoted:

> Political Economy begins with *commodities*, with the moment when products are exchanged. . . . The product being exchanged is a commodity. But it is a commodity merely by virtue of the *thing*, the product, being linked with a *relation* between two persons. . . . Here is at once an example of a peculiar fact which pervades the whole economy and has produced serious confusion in the minds of bourgeois economists—[In our view] economics is not concerned with things but with relations between persons, and in the final analysis between classes; these relations however are always *bound to things* and *appear as things*.[68]

In Marx's system, the doctrine of commodity fetishism is simply the logical extension of his original injunction against separating relationships between things from relationships between people. Recondite as it may seem, this doctrine is the thread that runs through the "Critique of Political Economy" contained in *Capital*:

> Political Economy has indeed analysed, however incompletely, value and its magnitude, and has discovered what lies beneath these forms. But it has never once asked the question *why labour is represented by the value of its product and labour-time by the magnitude of that value*. (Italics added.)[69]

Because bourgeois economists have a tendency to separate physical and social relationships, Marx argued, they end up confining themselves to the analysis of such superficial phenomena as the exchange-ratios between commodities. His own purpose, in contrast, was to explain the character and consequences of the social relations of capitalist production.

"Work Itself" as Wage-Labor

Thus far we have presented Marx's analysis of capitalism with reference only to the point that, in his view, it is a system in which "work itself" takes the form of commodity-producing labor; on this basis we have been able to explain, at least in a preliminary fashion, the meaning he attached to such terms as value, abstract labor, alienation, and commodity fetishism. As noted at the outset, however, Marx thought of capitalism as a system "based on wage-labour." To

penetrate to the heart of his analysis of it, therefore, we must go on to investigate why he referred specifically to wage-labor as the basis of the capitalist mode of production.

At this point it is necessary to point out that Marx made a distinction between (1) commodity production in general—or simple commodity production—and (2) commodity production in its specifically capitalist form. While he defined the former solely in terms of *horizontal* social relations (independent private producers exchanging their products), he thought of the latter as involving *vertical* as well as horizontal social relations (capitalists supervising workers in the production of commodities). Marx was well aware of the fact that simple commodity production has occurred in a variety of different societies throughout history; the point that interested him was that only with the development of capitalism does commodity production become not just a peripheral activity but the dominant form of social production: "Only when and where wage-labour is its basis does commodity production impose itself on society as a whole . . ."[70] What, then, is wage-labor?

In Marx's analysis the phenomenon of wage-labor is one of the results of the historical process that established the pre-conditions of capitalist production:

> The capitalist system pre-supposes the complete separation of the labourers from all property in the means by which they can realise their labour . . . The process, therefore, that clears the way for the capitalist system can be none other than the process which takes away from the labourer the possession of his means of production; a process that transforms, on the one hand, the social means of subsistence and of production into capital, on the other, the immediate producers into wage-labourers.[71]

As is well known, this process is described in *Capital* as the process of "primitive accumulation."[72] Under this heading Marx recites the gory details of how, on the one hand, the direct producers were forcibly separated from the land (by such measures as the Enclosures in England) and, on the other, the means of production became concentrated in the hands of capitalists. The upshot of this process, as we are concerned with it here, is that when people are deprived of direct access to "the means by which they can realise their labour" they have no other choice but to sell their productive potential to those who control these means. Wage-labor, then, is that historical category of people who must sell their capacity to work and, hence, whose very life-sustaining activity is a commodity.

In order to analyze what happens when "work itself" takes the form of wage-labor Marx made a distinction between labor and labor-power. *Labor-power*, according to his definition, is a person's capacity to work; it is the commodity which the worker *sells* to the capitalist in return for wages. *Labor*, on the other hand, is not a commodity in Marx's system; rather, it is what the worker *does* under the control of the capitalist after the latter has purchased his labor-power. In terms of the definitions introduced earlier, labor was regarded by Marx as the use-value of the commodity labor-power; like other use-values, it is consumed by the buyer of the commodity, the capitalist.

With the help of his distinction between labor and labor-power Marx was able to explain why wage-labor is the essential ingredient of capitalism. In order for capitalist production to occur, he argued, capitalists must first be able to

make contact with people who are willing to part with their productive potential: "The whole system of capitalist production is based on the fact that the workman sells his labor-power as a commodity."[73] Once labor-power has been purchased by the capitalist, Marx went on to point out, it becomes labor. Thus the essence of capitalist production, as he saw it, is that it is a process in which labor-power gets transformed into labor. (To bring about this transformation is the task which faces the capitalist in the realm of production.)

Labor is the basis of capitalist production in a sense both similar to and different from the sense in which it is the basis of simple commodity production. Just as it does in simple commodity production, labor also produces value when it is performed under the supervision of capitalists; likewise, when such labor is regarded from the standpoint of its value-creating aspect, it may be thought of as abstract labor. In Marx's system, however, the notion of abstract labor acquires a special significance in the context of capitalist production: Transcending its origins as a concept deduced from the mere fact that commodities are exchanged, it becomes a category that reflects the actual conditions of labor in a capitalist society. As Marx explained it in the "Introduction" to the *Grundrisse*:

> This abstraction of labour is . . . by no means simply the conceptual resultant of a variety of concrete types of labour. The fact that the particular kind of labour employed is immaterial is appropriate to a form of society in which individuals easily pass from one type of labour to another, the particular type of labour being accidental to them and therefore irrelevant.[74]

Clearly, the "form of society" Marx had in mind here is capitalist society, for only after masses of people have been separated from the means of production do "individuals easily pass from one type of labour to another," and only when such individuals are put in the position of having to accept whatever jobs are offered in the market does "the particular type of labour [become] accidental to them and therefore irrelevant." Under capitalist conditions, then, abstract labor refers to the historical phenomenon of wage-labor and, in this specific sense, it is regarded by Marx as the source of value.

The value created in the capitalist process of production is divided by Marx into two parts. One part of it corresponds to the value of the means of subsistence required by the workers and is actually paid to them in the form of wages. The other part of the total value produced is appropriated by the capitalists and, as we all know, is referred to by Marx as *surplus-value*.

The main significance of surplus-value in the Marxian system is that it reflects a division within the workers' labor-time itself. As we have already noted, Marx separated the total quantity of labor performed by the workers into necessary and surplus labor, the former being the amount needed to produce their own means of subsistence, and the latter being the additional labor extracted from them by the society's dominant class. The importance of surplus-value in Marx's analysis, then, is that it is the form in which surplus labor is extracted from wage-laborers and, as such, it refers to the form of exploitation characteristic of the capitalist mode of production.

The specific nature of capitalist exploitation was explained by Marx in terms of his distinction between labor and labor-power. Workers can be exploited by capitalists, he pointed out, because they are capable of performing more hours of labor than are required to produce the value of their labor-power. Thus, workers can be exploited in production even at the same time that they are paid the full value of the commodity which they sell to the capitalist. In Marx's view, it does no good to bewail the fact that the value of this commodity, like that of all other commodities, is determined by the quantity of labor time needed to reproduce it:

> It is a very cheap sort of sentimentality which declares this method of determining the value of labour-power, a method prescribed by the very nature of the case, to be a brutal method. . . .[75]

Marx's point was not that workers are gypped in the market but, rather, that they are exploited in production.

As Marx analyzes it, the capitalist form of exploitation both generates and is reinforced by a peculiar form of commodity fetishism. When workers sell their labor-power to a capitalist, the deal is made in terms of a certain amount of money for so many hours of labor. Hence, to the workers it appears as if they are being paid for each and every hour of labor that they perform. In Marx's words: "The wage-form thus extinguishes every trace of the division of the working day into necessary labour and surplus-labour . . ."[76] In another part of *Capital* Marx pointed out that, as a consequence of this mystifying effect of wages, working people have a hard time seeing the true character of the relations that connect them with capitalists: "The Roman slave was held by fetters; the wage-labourer is bound to his owner by invisible threads."[77] Just as in simple commodity production the relationships between the producers are seen by them as relations between their products, under capitalism the relationships between workers and capitalists are obscured by the fact that the former sell their labor-power to the latter as a commodity. Thus, in Marx's view, the fetishism that arises with commodity production per se becomes an element in the perpetuation of the specifically capitalist form of such production.

Finally, when "work itself" takes the form of wage-labor Marx identifies it as an advanced form of alienated labor. Since workers must give up control over their productive activity when they sell their labor-power to a capitalist, they become alienated not only from the products of their labor but from the process of production itself. Marx described this aspect of alienated labor in the *Economic and Philosophic Manuscripts* as follows:

> What constitutes the alienation of labour? First, that the work is *external* to the worker, that it is not part of his nature; and that consequently, he does not fulfil himself in his work but denies himself, has a feeling of misery rather than well-being, does not develop freely his mental and physical energies but is physically exhausted and mentally debased. The worker, therefore, feels himself at home only during his leisure time, whereas at work he feels homeless. His work is not voluntary but imposed, *forced labour*. It is not the satisfaction of a need, but only a *means* for satisfying other needs. Its alien character is clearly shown by the fact that as soon as there is no physical or other compulsion it is avoided like the plague.[78]

In Marx's view, alienation is one of the defining characteristics of capitalism for, as he pointed out, the latter is a system that requires workers to alienate themselves from their own labor. Because the wage-transaction is the vehicle through which this alienation occurs he once referred to it as "the very transaction which characterises capital."[79]

To conclude this discussion of wage-labor and to enable us to shift our attention to other elements in the capitalist process of production, let us examine a passage from *Capital* in which Marx translates his concept of alienated labor into a definition of capital itself:

> . . . the labourer, on quitting the process [of production], is what he was on entering it, a source of wealth, but devoid of all means of making that wealth his own. Since, before entering on the process, his labour has already been alienated from himself by the sale of his labour-power . . . it must, during the process, be realised in a product that does not belong to him. Since the process of production is also the process by which the capitalist consumes labour-power, the product of the labourer is incessantly converted, not only into commodities, but into capital, [that is] into value that sucks up the value-creating power, into means of subsistence that buy the person of the labourer, into means of production that command the producers. The labourer constantly produces material, objective wealth, but in the form of capital, of an alien power that dominates and exploits him . . .[80]

As is evident from this passage, Marx used the word "capital" to refer to both the means of subsistence and the means of production concentrated in the hands of the capitalist. In the next section, I focus on the means of production, looking in particular at the way Marx analyzed the specifically capitalist form of the *instruments of production* and the *objects transformed in production*.

The Means of Production as "Capital"

In the "Introduction" to the *Grundrisse* Marx noted that "All periods of production . . . have certain features in common: they have certain common categories . . . Production without them is inconceivable."[81] In the same place, however, he pointed out that "it is necessary to distinguish those definitions which apply to production in general, in order not to overlook the essential differences [between the various historical periods]."[82] To illustrate his point Marx referred to the instruments of production and argued that, although they are a necessary element in all human production, they should not be routinely identified in all times and places as "capital":

> For example, no production is possible without an instrument of production, even if this instrument is simply the hand. It is not possible without past, accumulated labour. . . . Capital is among other things also an instrument of production, and also past, materialized labour. Consequently, capital is a universal and eternal relation given by nature—that is, *provided one omits precisely those specific factors which turn the "instrument of production" or "accumulated labor" into capital.* (Italics added.)[83]

Thus, in Marx's approach, "instruments of production" is one of "those definitions which apply to production in general" but "capital" is a specific historical category. Conversely, since "capital" is—"among other things"—the form which the instruments of production take in a capitalist society, it is one of the qualities which can help us to differentiate such a society from other historical types of societies.

But what exactly did Marx have in mind when he spoke of "those specific factors which turn the 'instruments of production' or 'accumulated labour' into capital"? One might say that what he had in mind when he wrote these words was at least the whole of the first volume of *Capital*. Consider, however, one passage from this volume in which we can see Marx using his two basic abstractions to analyze the form taken by the means of production in a capitalist society:

> If we consider the process of production from the point of view of the simple labour-process, the labourer stands in relation to the means of production, not in their quality as capital, but as the mere means and material of his own intelligent productive activity. In tanning, *e.g.*, he deals with the skins as his simple object of labour. . . . But it is different as soon as we deal with the process of production from the point of view of the process of creation of surplus-value. The means of production are at once changed into means for the absorption of the labour of others. It is now no longer the labourer that employs the means of production, but the means of production that employ the labourer. Instead of being consumed by him as material elements of his productive activity, they consume him as the ferment necessary to their own life-process. . . .[84]

This of course is the kind of analysis which led Marx to refer (in the same volume) to capitalism as "a state of society in which the process of production has the mastery over man, instead of being controlled by him."[85]

It is clear, from the passage just quoted, that Marx looked at the objects transformed in production in the same way that he treated the instruments of production: Together, they constitute the means of production and, in his approach, they both assume a specific form in a capitalist society.

On the basis of his analysis of the means of production, Marx criticized other economists for failing to see that they take the form of "capital" only in the context of a specific set of social relations. In his view, the bourgeois conception of capital was an expression of commodity fetishism in the sense that it referred only to *things* and was applied indiscriminately to objects facilitating production in any form of society. In the third volume of *Capital* he attacked this way of thinking and once more brought out the connection between capital and alienated labor:

> Capital . . . is not a thing, but rather a definite social production relation, belonging to a definite historical formation of society, which is manifested in a thing and lends this thing a specific social character. Capital is not the sum of the material and produced means of production. Capital is rather the means of production transformed into capital . . . It is the

means of production monopolised by a certain section of society, confronting living labour-power as products and working conditions rendered independent of this very labour-power . . .[86]

We have now looked at three of the four elements that interact in the production process, explaining in each case how Marx treated them in the context of capitalist society. It is appropriate at this point, therefore, to focus our attention on the remaining element of production, the *coordinating agency*, and to examine the way that he analyzed it in its specifically capitalist form.

Coordination Performed by Capitalists

Marx discussed the specific form taken by the function of coordination in a capitalist society at the very point in *Capital* where he first mentioned the need for this function. Here, immediately after saying that all large scale production requires a "directing authority," he went on to make two points: (a) With the emergence of capitalism, "the work of directing, superintending, and adjusting becomes one of the functions of capital," and (b) as a result of this, "it acquires special characteristics."[87] In the next paragraph Marx explained what these "special characteristics" are, and here—once again—we can see how he used his two basic abstractions to analyze a particular element in the production process:

> The directing motive, the end and aim of capitalist production is to extract the greatest possible amount of surplus-value, and consequently to exploit labour-power to the greatest possible extent. As the number of the co-operating labourers increases, so too does their resistance to the domination of capital, and with it, the necessity for capital to overcome this resistance by counter-pressure. The control exercised by the capitalist is not only a special function, due to the nature of the social labour-process, and peculiar to that process, but it is, at the same time, a function of the exploitation of a social labour-process, and is consequently rooted in the unavoidable antagonism between the exploiter and the living and labouring raw material he exploits.[88]

Because Marx saw production as a dual process—with both a material and a social aspect—he was able to analyze the role of the capitalist as one which involves not only the responsibility of coordinating production but also the power to exploit it for his own benefit.

It is interesting to note that in the passage just quoted, as in others throughout *Capital*, Marx refers to "capital" almost as if it were human: He attributes to it an impulse to dominate workers and to overcome their resistance by "counter-pressure." This may seem strange to readers who are used to thinking of capital merely as a collection of things, but it represents a deliberate effort on Marx's part to get us to think of things as elements within social relations and people as connected with each other through things. In his work, "capital" refers to *the whole structure of things and people* against which workers must struggle in order to put an end to their exploitation.

Just as Marx rejected the notion of capital conceived of as things, so also did he warn against thinking of *capitalists* simply as individuals: "I paint the capitalist . . . in no sense *couleur de rose*. But here individuals are dealt with

only in so far as they are the personifications of economic categories, embodiments of particular class-relations and class interests."[89] Marx's usual procedure, when discussing the role of capitalists, was to refer to them as *personified capital*. He did this to indicate that they should be thought of not as individuals acting solely on the basis of their own free choices but as people caught up in, and molded by, a particular socio-economic structure. Thus capitalists are treated by Marx as a specific historical class of people whose special relationship to the means of production puts them in the position of dominating and exploiting workers.

We have now presented Marx's analysis of how all four of the elements of production interact with each other in the capitalist mode of production. It is appropriate at this point, then, to quote a brief passage from *Capital* which seems to sum up his view of capitalism:

> Within the process of production . . . capital acquired the command over labour, *i.e.*, over functioning labour-power or the labourer himself. Personified capital, the capitalist takes care that the labourer does his work regularly and with the proper degree of intensity.
>
> Capital further developed into a coercive relation which compels the working-class to do more work than the narrow round of its own life-wants prescribes. As a producer of the activity of others, as a pumper-out of surplus-labour and exploiter of labour-power, it surpasses in energy, disregard of bounds, recklessness and efficiency, all earlier systems of production based on directly compulsory labour.[90]

Thus, from Marx's standpoint, capitalism is a system in which "work itself" takes the form of labor performed under the direction of capitalists; capitalists are merely personified capital; and capital itself is defined as "a coercive social relation which compels the working-class to do more work than the narrow round of its own life-wants prescribes."

Before turning our attention to the Cambridge view of capitalism we should briefly consider two questions on which Marx's position contrasts sharply with that of the Cantabrigians: What is the relationship between production and distribution? In what way will socialism be different from capitalism?

Production and Distribution

One of the distinguishing features of Marx's approach to economics is that he always treated the distribution of the products in any given society as a mechanism integral to that society's mode of production. His views on this topic were most clearly stated in the "Introduction" to the *Grundrisse*.

> In the shallowest conception, distribution appears as the distribution of products, and hence as further removed from and quasi-independent of production. But before distribution can be the distribution of products, it is: (1) the distribution of the instruments of production, and (2), which is a further specification of the same relation, the distribution of the members of society among the different kinds of production. (Subsumption of the individuals under specific relations of production.) The distribution of products is evidently only a result of this distribution, which

is comprised within the process of production itself and determines the structure of production. To examine production while disregarding this internal distribution within it is obviously an empty abstraction; while conversely, the distribution of products follows by itself from this distribution which forms an original moment of production.[91]

The point of this passage is that, for Marx, distribution is not independent of production but, since particular class relations tend to perpetuate themselves, is actually determined by it. He believed, for example, that wages could not rise and profits fall beyond a certain point without bringing into question the very survival of the capitalist mode of production.[92] Marx also held that even the forms in which income is distributed are determined by the way in which the elements of production are connected with each other:

> The relations and modes of distribution thus appear merely as the obverse of the agents of production. An individual who participates in production in the form of wage-labour shares in the products . . . in the form of wages. The structure of distribution is completely determined by the structure of production. Distribution is itself a product of production . . . in that the specific kind of participation in production determines . . . the pattern of participation in distribution.[93]

How Socialism Would Be Different

As is well known, Marx never offered a detailed blueprint for a post-capitalist society. In the *Communist Manifesto* he asserted that "the history of all hitherto existing society is the history of class struggles,"[94] and he clearly believed that such struggles would also shape the society of the future. In spite of his general aversion to utopian thinking, however, Marx's analysis of capitalism itself contains clear indications of what he thought would be different about a socialist society.

Having analyzed capitalism as a mode of production based on wage-labor, Marx clearly expected that socialism would be based on something else. As early as 1844 in the *Economic and Philosophic Manuscripts* he argued that wages are "only a necessary consequence of the alienation of labour" and, hence, higher wages would not really change the conditions of labor:

> An enforced *increase in wages* . . . would be nothing more than a better *remuneration of slaves*, and would not restore either to the worker or to the work their human significance and worth.[95]

The point of view expressed here was not just a fancy of Marx's youth; throughout his work he consistently maintained that the point of socialism is to eliminate alienated labor. Consider, for example, the following passage from the first volume of *Capital* in which he pointed out that, even in a capitalist society, workers may at times receive an increase in wages:

> A larger part of their own surplus-product . . . comes back to them in the shape of means of payment, so that they can extend the circle of their enjoyments; can make some additions to their consumption-fund of

clothes, furniture, etc., and can lay by small reserve-funds of money. *But just as little as better clothing, food, and treatment . . . do away with the exploitation of the slave, so little do they set aside that of the wage-worker.* A rise in the price of labour . . . only means, in fact, that the length and weight of the golden chain the wage-worker has already forged for himself, allow of a relaxation of the tension of it. In the controversies on this subject the chief fact has generally been overlooked, viz., the *differentia specifica* of capitalistic production. (Italics added.)[96]

Even at the end of his life Marx took issue with those who would try to improve the distribution of income without changing the fundamental relations of production. Thus, in one of the last things he wrote, he criticized the followers of Ferdinand Lasalle for giving priority to the goal of "a fair distribution of the proceeds of labour":

> Quite apart from the analysis so far given, it was in general a mistake to make a fuss about so-called *distribution* and put the principal stress on it.
>   Any distribution whatever of the means of consumption is only a consequence of the distribution of the conditions of production themselves. The latter distribution, however, is a feature of the mode of production itself. The capitalist mode of production, for example, rests on the fact that the material conditions of production are in the hands of non-workers in the form of property in capital and land, while the masses are only owners of the personal condition of production, of labour-power. If the elements of production are so distributed, then the present-day distribution of the means of consumption results automatically. If the material conditions of production are the co-operative property of the workers themselves, then there likewise results a distribution of the means of consumption different from the present one. Vulgar socialism . . . has taken over from the bourgeois economists the consideration and treatment of distribution as independent of the mode of production and hence the presentation of socialism as turning principally on distribution. After the real relation has long been made clear, why retrogress again?[97]

As far as Marx was concerned, then, the "real relation" is that the distribution of the product is determined by the way it is produced; hence, we can achieve a "fair" distribution of products only by changing the mode of production itself. Although Marx was intentionally vague about what the new mode of production would look like, he did express himself clearly on one point. In the same essay from which we have just quoted, he described socialism with reference to the category that he had used to begin his analysis of capitalism:

> Within the co-operative society based on common ownership of the means of production, the producers do not exchange their products; just as little does the labour employed on the products appear here *as the value* of these products . . . since now, in contrast to capitalist society, individual labour no longer exists in an indirect fashion but directly as a component part of the total labour [of society].[98]

In his discussion of commodity fetishism in the first chapter of *Capital* Marx had made the following statement: "The life-process of society . . . does

not strip off its mystical veil until it is treated as production by freely associated men, and is consciously regulated by them in accordance with a settled plan."[99] Under socialism, he believed, people would not only be free from exploitation but would also be able to develop a clear view of the relations which bind them together in production.

B. Cambridge Economics as Commodity Fetishism

Up to this point, we have presented the views of Marx and the Cantabrigians as if they were just alternative approaches in economics. As we proceed to examine the Cambridge view of capitalism, however, it becomes necessary to point out that the positions taken by the Cantabrigians are similar to the ones Marx criticized a hundred years ago. We will see in fact that the Cantabrigians' practice of separating the physical from the social aspects of production leads them to present the economic relationships of capitalism in precisely the way that Marx described as "commodity fetishism." In this section, therefore, I argue not only that the Cantabrigian view of capitalism differs from that of Marx but also that it mystifies the real nature of the system in a way that can only becloud our understanding and impede our practical efforts to work towards socialism.

Production of Things by Means of Things

To establish a framework for thinking about Piero Sraffa's *Production of Commodities by Means of Commodities*, it is helpful to consider the following passage from Marx's discussion of commodity fetishism in the first chapter of *Capital*:

> A commodity is . . . a mysterious thing, simply because [1] in it the social character of men's labour appears to them as an objective character stamped upon the product of that labour; because [2] the relation of the producers to the sum total of their own labour is presented to them as a social relation, existing not between themselves, but between the products of their labour. . . . [Thus] the value-relation between the products of labour which stamps them as commodities . . . is a definite social relation between men that assumes, in their eyes, the fantastic form of a relation between things.[100]

Since Sraffa's book features the word "commodities" twice in its title, one might guess it would contain an analysis of a particular social form of human production. As we have already noted, however, Sraffa defines production solely in terms of technical relations and makes no references to social relations within the production process. Can we not say, therefore, that production, as seen by the Cantabrigians, "is a definite social relation between men that assumes, in their eyes, the fantastic form of a relation between things"?

If one accepts Marx's concept of a commodity, Sraffa's book turns out not to be about commodity production at all. Since he insists upon separating relations between things from relations between people, Sraffa merely adds to that "serious confusion in the minds of bourgeois economists" which Marx called commodity fetishism. Instead of writing about the way in which commodities are actually used to produce commodities in a capitalist society, Sraffa

has constructed an imaginary world in which things produce things (by means of magic). Had he been writing in the Marxian tradition, his book might better have carried the title *Production of Classes by Means of Classes* for, as Engels pointed out, the Marxist approach "is not concerned with things but with relations between persons, and in the final analysis between classes."[101]

Price Theory Without Value Theory

Since the Cantabrigians do not see capitalist production as something which involves specific social relations, they do not think of *value* in the way that Marx did. As we have seen, the latter founded his entire study of capitalism on an analysis of "the value-form of the product of labour."[102] The Cantabrigians, on the other hand, "never once ask the question *why labour is represented by the value of its product and labour-time by the magnitude of that value.*"[103] The most that can be said of their work is that they shed light on certain issues that were discussed in volume III of *Capital*. But, as Marx noted on the first page of that volume, to analyze such things as the effects of changes in distribution on relative prices is to deal with economic phenomena "in the form which they assume on the surface of society."[104] However ingenious the Cantabrigians are in analyzing price phenomena, they never connect such phenomena with social relations in the way that Marx did in *Capital*.[105]

The gulf between the Cantabrigian and the Marxian conceptions of value may be demonstrated by quoting a passage from Joan Robinson's introduction to her first book, *The Economics of Imperfect Competition*:

> The main theme of this book is the analysis of value. It is not easy to explain what the analysis of value is, without making it appear extremely mysterious and extremely foolish. The point may be put like this: You see two men one of whom is giving a banana to the other, and is taking a penny from him. You ask, how is it that a banana costs a penny rather than any other sum?[106]

While Robinson referred here to "the analysis of value"—what she actually had in mind was the analysis of *prices*. Indeed, in a later book she dismissed the whole notion of value as "one of the great metaphysical ideas in economics . . . [which] when you try to pin it down turns out to be just a word."[107] Her total lack of understanding of Marx's concept of value was displayed in her *Essay on Marxian Economics* wherein she stated that "under socialism the law of *value* will come into its own . . ."[108] (Italics in original.)

Sraffa's book too, it should be noted, is oriented to the traditional economists' problem of analyzing prices. Since it is not specifically a study of commodity production, one could hardly expect it to deal with "value" in the Marxian sense. Though some have praised him for having "rehabilitated" Marx,[109] Sraffa does not in fact adopt Marx's approach to the analysis of value. Not only does he neglect to ask the question "why labour is represented by the value of its product," but, taking the existence of exchange-values for granted, he asserts that in an economy without a surplus "such values spring directly from the [technical] methods of production."[110] Even after introducing a surplus, Sraffa continues to emphasize the role of a society's technical relations

in determining its pattern of relative prices, for he sees prices only as relationships between things. Since he excludes social relations altogether from his view of production, it is not feasible for him to relate price phenomena to the social relations of capitalist production.

Distribution Exogenous and Independent of Production

How do the Cantabrigians approach the question of distribution in a capitalist economy? In the Robinson and Eatwell textbook we are given the following clue:

> Sraffa's analysis of the distribution of the product of industry between wages and profits in given technical conditions provides the indispensable framework for an understanding of the problem of distribution in a private-enterprise economy.[111]

However, another Cantabrigian, Krishna Bharadwaj, has written as follows:

> Distribution in Sraffa's system is not endogenously generated through production relations. . . . No theory of distribution is offered in the book.[112]

Upon reading Sraffa himself, this statement by Bharadwaj proves to be entirely accurate. One can only conclude, then, that when Robinson and Eatwell talk about Sraffa's "indispensable framework" for understanding distribution in a capitalist economy, what they have in mind is Sraffa's practice of treating distribution as an independent variable, the determinants of which (in his view) lie "outside the system of production."[113]

If distribution is treated as an independent variable, it is possible to think of it as being determined in some way by class struggle. Thus D. M. Nuti has credited Sraffa with opening the way for the re-introduction of political considerations into economics:

> The relation between the real wage rate and the profit rate uncovered by Sraffa . . . restates the conflict between capitalists and workers in the problem of income distribution, and provides scope for the concept of class struggle in the determination of relative shares.[114]

From this insight, some have jumped to the conclusion that the Cantabrigians are in fact reviving Marx's approach to distribution. Geoffrey Harcourt, for example, has commented on the work of certain Cantabrigians as follows:

> Some writers, for example, Bhaduri, Joan Robinson, and Nell, look to Marx's theory of exploitation, brought up to date in the guise of relative bargaining strengths, to explain the distribution of the product, treated as a surplus, between profit-earners and wage-earners.[115]

Whether or not what Harcourt calls "Marx's theory of exploitation" actually resembles Marx's own theory of exploitation after the Cantabrigians have brought it "up to date" is a question we will deal with shortly. One thing which can be said immediately, however, is that it is inappropriate to link Marx's name with the Cantabrigian treatment of distribution.

The Cantabrigians generally follow Sraffa in treating distribution as an exogenously determined, independent variable. The reason Sraffa took this approach is that he wanted to construct a theory of how prices will change when distribution is altered and, in order to accomplish this task, it was convenient for him to *assume* that distribution is completely flexible and independent of production. Sraffa's followers, however, have translated this theoretical assumption into a way of thinking about distribution in the real world and, as a result, have neglected to tie distribution to the class relations of production.[116] Indeed, after reading the Cantabrigians one might form the impression that, once the means of production have been replaced, the output of the economy can be distributed in any proportions whatever between capitalists and workers without affecting the way production itself is carried on.

Marx, on the other hand, treated distribution as an endogenous variable, entirely interlocked with production. As we have seen, he believed that the distribution of the product in any given society is determined by the way in which people relate to each other in the process of producing it. In a capitalist society, for example, he argued that the product will be distributed in such a way that, after it has been distributed, capitalists and workers will again be ready and willing to perform their respective roles in the production process. He would have thought it ludicrous that someone might assume that distribution could vary in a capitalist society to the point where there were zero profits and wages absorbed all of the surplus product.

It is all well and good that certain Cantabrigians mention the class struggle when discussing distribution—but this hardly justifies placing them in the tradition of Marx. The distinguishing feature of Marx's approach was that he analyzed class conflict as a struggle rooted in the process of production. As we have noted, however, the Cantabrigians see only "technical relations" where production actually goes on. In a passage quoted above . . . [pp. 435-436], Marx criticized such a view of production as "an empty abstraction" and argued that it can only lead to "the shallowest conception" of distribution. Would he not therefore have included the Cantabrigians among those to whom he referred when (in the same passage) he spoke of "the ineptitude of those economists who portray production as an eternal truth while banishing history to the realm of distribution"?[117]

We may now see that the Cantabrigian separation of production and distribution derives from the way they originally define their fundamental abstractions. Because they insist upon isolating the physical and the human elements of production—rigidly bifurcating them into "technical" and "social" relations—they end up blinding themselves not only to the complexity of the production process itself but also to the real connection between production and distribution.

"Surplus" Rather than Surplus-Value

Perhaps the most obvious difference between the Cantabrigians and Marx is that they use the term "surplus" in place of the category of "surplus-value." This is more than a semantic difference for, as we will see, the Cantabrigian practice of

referring to the "surplus" is a reflection of the fundamental difference between their approach and that of Marx.

The Cantabrigian conception of the surplus is presented most clearly in Sraffa's book. Here, in the first sentence of the second chapter, we are simply told that "the economy produces more than the minimum necessary for replacement and there is a surplus to be distributed. . . ."[118] This comes as something of a surprise because the entire first chapter of the book is concerned with "an extremely simple society which produces just enough to maintain itself,"[119] and nowhere does Sraffa tell us how the surplus suddenly arises. Since he does not see social relations in the production process, there is of course nothing in his discussion of the surplus comparable to Marx's concept of capital as "a coercive relation which compels the working-class to do more than the narrow round of its own life-wants prescribes."[120]

When Sraffa elaborates his view of the surplus, the differences between his approach and that of Marx become clear. Consider, for example, the following passage in which Sraffa defines his concept of the surplus using the "national income" terminology of modern economics:

> The national income of a system in a self-replacing state consists of the set of commodities which are left over when from the gross national product we have removed item by item the articles which go to replace the means of production used up in all the industries.[121]

In this definition we can detect three ways in which Sraffa's idea of a surplus is different from Marx's concept of surplus-value.

In the first place, Sraffa's surplus is a physical rather than a value phenomenon. It is "the set of commodities" (read: things) which are left after removing from the total output of the economy those "articles" which are needed "item by item" to replace the ones which have been used up in production. (Sraffa's decision to define the surplus in physical terms was a consequence, once again, of his initial choice of the problem to be solved. Since the task he set for himself was to explain the effects on prices of changes in the distribution of the surplus, it was necessary for him to define the surplus in such a way that its own measurement would not be affected by changes in prices.)

The second way in which Sraffa's conception of the surplus differs from Marx's notion of surplus-value is that both its existence and its precise magnitude appear to be technologically determined. In Sraffa's system, an economy's replacement needs are fixed by the technical relations that happen to exist in each of its industries—for these indicate the quantities of inputs that are required to produce given amounts of each kind of output. Hence, once we know the characteristics of a society's technology we can tell whether or not it will have a surplus and how large this surplus will be. The following argument has thus been put forward by Nell in defense of Sraffa's concept of the surplus: "The idea is important . . . for it anchors the concept of national income firmly in the sea of technology . . ."[122]

The third distinguishing feature of Sraffa's surplus is that, unlike Marx's concept of surplus-value, it includes the part of the economy's output that is consumed by workers. As can be seen in the definition quoted above, only those

products are subtracted from the total output which are needed to replace used-up means of production. All the rest of the economy's products are included in the surplus, and workers' consumption—as well as the capitalists' share of the total output—is provided for out of this surplus. (In Marxian value terms, Sraffa's surplus includes both V and S, whereas Marx's surplus-value only includes S.)

From a Marxian point of view, Sraffa's treatment of the surplus mystifies the actual relations of capitalist production in the following ways. First, his presentation of the surplus as something physical obscures the historical significance of the fact that all the products of a capitalist economy come into being as values. After reading Sraffa, one might think that there is really no difference between the surplus product of a capitalist society and that of any other type of society.

Secondly, Sraffa's preoccupation with the technical relations of production leaves the impression that the existence and magnitude of a surplus in any given society can be explained with reference only to such relations. Since he does not mention the social relations of capitalist production—or, for that matter, *any* social relations of production—we are not led to ask how it happens that a given amount of labor is performed in his system, neither more nor less, but just the amount that is required to produce the surplus. Although Sraffa does not actually say that the surplus is a gift of nature or that it results, as Marx once put it, "from some occult quality inherent in human labour," he certainly does nothing to combat such misconceptions.[123]

The most serious shortcoming of Sraffa's treatment of the surplus is that, since it includes workers' consumption as part of the surplus, it obscures Marx's distinction between necessary and surplus labor. The reason Marx did not include workers' consumption as a part of surplus-value is that he wanted to bring out the relationship between surplus-value and the value received by workers, on the one hand, and the two parts of the workers' labor-time, on the other. As we have seen, he treated the value received by workers as the product of necessary labor, and he related surplus-value to surplus labor.

Sraffa, on the other hand, never distinguishes between necessary and surplus labor. He does make a distinction between "basic" and "non-basic" *industries*, but this has nothing to do with Marx's separation of the working day into two parts.[124] As far as Sraffa is concerned, there is no difference between the labor which produces the surplus and that which merely replaces the means of production that are used up; even if there were, such a difference would not correspond to Marx's way of dividing up the workers' labor-time. From Sraffa's point of view, then, every hour of labor seems to be just as necessary as every other hour.

Because Sraffa fails to distinguish surplus from necessary labor, on the one hand, and treats the surplus as a physical phenomenon, on the other, he leads us to believe that the surplus we produce is a surplus of *things* rather than of *labor*. To put it another way, the surplus in Sraffa's system is a relationship not between people but between two sets of products, one comprising the total output of the economy and the other consisting of what is needed to replace used up means of production. Sraffa's conception of the surplus may thus be seen as an example of commodity fetishism for, as Marx might have said, "the

relation of the producers to the sum total of their own labour is presented to them as a social relation, existing not between themselves, but between the products of their labour."[125]

The Cambridge View of "Capital"

Since the Cantabrigians think of the surplus as a relationship between things, they fail to see that its very existence reflects an actual struggle between social classes in production. (As we have pointed out, they refer to class struggle only in connection with the distribution of the surplus after it has been produced.) This same blind spot prevents them from seeing, as Marx did, that the means of production take a particular form in the context of the specific class relations that define the capitalist mode of production.

When the Cantabrigians discuss "capital" they take the position that there are actually two meanings of the word. In order to avoid confusion, they say, we should distinguish between "capital" on the one hand, and "capital goods" on the other. The difference has been explained by Nell as follows:

> "Capital" has two meanings. On the one hand, it is property in the means of production, enabling owners of equal amounts of claim in these means to receive equal returns. . . . On the other hand, "capital" also means produced means of production—that is, specific materials, tools, instruments, machines, plant, and equipment, on which, with which, and by means of which labor works. . . . *Capital goods are not the same thing as capital.*[126]

This way of dividing up the concept of capital follows more or less automatically from the Cantabrigians' basic tendency to separate physical and social phenomena. In contrast to Marx, who defined capital with reference to *both* the physical *and* the human elements of production, they treat capital as if it must be *either* a physical *or* a social phenomenon. Moreover, when the Cantabrigians divide capital into two separate categories they entirely overlook the aspect of it which was most crucial for Marx, namely, its quality as a specific social relation of production. Given the way they define capital, one can hardly imagine the Cantabrigians making the kind of statement that we have already quoted from *Capital*: "It is now no longer the labourer that employs the means of production, but the means of production that employ the labourer."[127]

The Cantabrigians' divided view of capital reflects their separation of distribution from production. Consider, for example, the statement which Nell makes immediately after saying that "capital goods are not the same thing as capital":

> "Capital" is relevant to the analysis of the division of income among the members of society, but . . . has no bearing on production. "Capital goods" are relevant to the study of production but have no bearing on the distribution of income.[128]

Here again we can see how the Cantabrigians' inability to comprehend the dual nature of production prevents them from grasping the way in which production

("capital goods") and distribution ("capital") are actually connected with each other.

The lacuna in the Cambridge conception of capital is also evident in the work of Joan Robinson. In a "postscript" to her 1953 article, for example, she criticizes the neoclassical economists for their "failure to distinguish between 'capital' in the sense of means of production with particular technical characteristics and 'capital' in the sense of a command over finance."[129] Nowhere in Robinson's work do we find anything comparable to Marx's view that "within the process of production . . . capital acquired the command over labour, *i.e.*, over functioning labour-power or the labourer himself."[130]

By some ironic twist, the way in which the Cantabrigians arrive at their non-Marxian conception of capital may be seen most clearly in an article by Amit Bhaduri, the point of which is to place Cantabrigian economics in the Marxian tradition. Calling his article "On the Significance of Recent Controversies on Capital Theory: A Marxian View,"[131] Bhaduri first takes us through a brief review of Marx's basic abstractions. Having labelled these with their standard Marxian terms, the "forces" and "relations" of production, he immediately proceeds to *identify* these with the Cantabrigian abstractions we have come to know as "technical" and "social" relations. When Bhaduri discusses the "forces of production," for example, he makes no reference to the interaction between the human elements in the production process. When he presents Marx's concept of the "relations of production," on the other hand, he first translates it into "rules of the game" and later refers to it as "a social ownership relation." Bhaduri sums up his discussion of Marx's basic abstractions by distinguishing the "forces of production" from the "relations of production" in the following way: "The former concept relates to man's relation to nature and technology while the latter corresponds to man's relation to man in a social organization of production."[132] Marx, of course, did not begin with such a separation of the "man-man" and the "man-nature" interactions; his view was that people must always relate to each other *and* to nature and technology in a social organization of production.

Bhaduri's misinterpretation of Marx's basic abstractions leads him to make a truly astonishing error in his discussion of capital. Here, he presents the Cambridge definition of capital as if it were Marx's:

> Thus, "capital" as a Marxian "category" notion is: (a) an instrument of production—a pure physical object (belonging to the Marxian notion of "forces of production"); and (b) a social ownership relation giving rise to capitalists' income (belonging to the Marxian notion of "relations of production").[133]

This is of course not the way Marx defined capital. In fact, it is precisely the kind of thinking he rejected. The following passage from volume III of *Capital* must be quoted again at this point because in it Marx seems to be speaking directly to the Cantabrigians:

> Capital . . . is not a thing, but rather a definite social production relation, belonging to a definite historical formation of society, which is manifested

in a thing and lends this thing a specific social character. Capital is not the sum of the material and produced means of production. Capital is rather the means of production transformed into capital. . . . It is the means of production monopolised by a certain section of society, confronting living labour-power as products and working conditions rendered independent of this very labour-power . . .[134]

The point that needs to be emphasized here is that there is an enormous difference between treating capital as something "confronting living labour-power" in the realm of production (Marx) and thinking of it as "a social ownership relation giving rise to capitalists' income" (Bhaduri). The first view involves treating the means of production as an integral part of the social relations of capitalist production; the second leads inevitably to treating these same means of production not as capital but as "pure physical objects." Marx had this to say about the latter way of thinking in volume II of *Capital*:

> This brings to completion the fetishism peculiar to bourgeois Political Economy, the fetishism which metamorphoses the social, economic character impressed on things in the process of social production into a natural character stemming from the material nature of those things.[135]

In Marx's view, the consequence of this form of mystification is that it prevents people from seeing that the character of production itself is socially determined and therefore susceptible to change.

"Work" Rather than Alienated Labor

At one point in their textbook Robinson and Eatwell make the following observation: "The fundamental element in production . . . is work."[136] As we have noted, however, they do not concern themselves with the conditions under which work is actually performed in the capitalist mode of production. To put it in Marxian terms, they do not treat work as alienated labor. As pointed out above . . . [p. 442], they merely assume that the amount of work specified in their technical relations will somehow be forthcoming. In this section, I argue that this kind of obliviousness to the actual character of work in capitalist production is widely shared by the Cantabrigians and that it stems from an inadequate treatment of the phenomenon of wage-labor.

One of the most surprising things about Sraffa's book, for example, is that it claims to be a study of commodity production but does not treat labor-power itself as a commodity. Although Sraffa frequently refers to the payment of wages, he never once mentions the sale of labor-power. In his system, wages are the form in which income is received by workers, but this particular form of income does not have any implications regarding the nature of the work the workers must do in order to receive it. Like Robinson and Eatwell, Sraffa simply posits various quantities of labor-time among the inputs of his production activities.

A good example of the influence Sraffa has had on other Cantabrigians is the diagram Edward Nell uses to portray a capitalist economy.[137] In this diagram Nell places "workers" on one side and "industry" on the other.

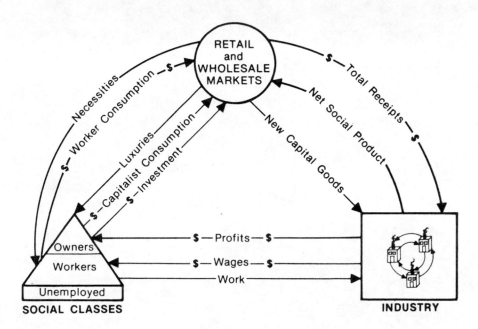

Figure 1.

Between them are two long arrows, one running from the "workers" to "industry" labelled "work," and one running from "industry" to the "workers" labelled "wages." In the diagram, however, there is no indication that the workers themselves ever enter the box where "industry" is located; and, even if we were to assume that they do, we would have no way of telling anything about their experiences there or of making a connection between these experiences and the arrows labelled "wages" and "work."

The shortcomings of Nell's diagram are also evident in the text of his article. Here, he first mocks the orthodox economists for treating distribution merely as an outcome of the process of exchanging commodities: "An exchange . . . means that *value equivalent is traded for value equivalent*. No exploitation there."[138] So far so good. Marx took the same position. In order to explain exploitation, however, Nell goes on to deny that the wage-transaction is a proper exchange of value equivalents: "the payment of wages is not an exchange . . . or at any rate, not a fair one."[139] Here, of course, Nell departs from Marx, for the latter explained how exploitation can go on even when workers are paid the value of their labor-power.

At the root of the difference between the Cantabrigian and the Marxian treatments of work is a difference regarding the nature of exploitation. For Marx, as we have seen, exploitation is the extraction of surplus labor in the process of production. For the Cantabrigians, on the other hand, exploitation has to do with the way a society's product is distributed. For example, Nell, in the same article from which we have been quoting, refers to exploitation in the following way:

. . . the work of labor . . . has produced the entire product. Is labor not therefore exploited? Does it not deserve the whole product?[140]

The implication here is that if workers could somehow receive the whole product they would no longer be exploited. While this is not actually wrong, it focuses on the symptom rather than on the disease itself. As Marx once said in reference to trade unions:

> They fail generally from limiting themselves to a guerilla war against the *effects* of the system instead of simultaneously trying to change it, instead of using their organized forces as a lever for the final emancipation of the working class, that is to say, [for] the ultimate abolition of the wages system. (Italics added.)[141]

In Marx's view, it does no good just to raise ethical questions about the distribution of the product; capitalist exploitation will be with us as long as production itself continues to be based on wage-labor.

The Cantabrigians' tendency to focus exclusively on the distribution of the product may be seen as just another manifestation of their pervasive commodity fetishism. Instead of pointing to the need to eliminate wage-labor, it limits our attention to such things as increasing the bargaining power of workers. As we will see, this leads to emphasis on shifting the distribution of income in favor of workers rather than changing the mode of production itself.

Capitalists as Workers

Since the Cantabrigians fail to bring out the fact that work is performed in the capitalist mode of production under oppressive social conditions, it is not surprising that they also mystify the role that capitalists play in the production process. In this section I will argue that the Cantabrigians portray the functioning capitalist as if he were just a particular kind of worker and thus lead us to believe that the realm of production is a place of harmony rather than conflict.

Robinson and Eatwell describe their model of "a pure capitalist economy" as follows:

> Production is controlled by *firms* which own machines, employ labour, and make profits. Consumption takes place in *households*, which receive income from the firms. There are two kinds of households, those of workers who receive wages, and those of *rentiers*, who have a claim on a share of profits.[142]

At first glance, this seems to be a realistic view of capitalism, for it at least implies that workers participate in production. On second glance, however, one begins to wonder exactly *who* are these "firms" which control production, own machines, employ labor, and make profits. The answer given by Robinson and Eatwell is closely related to their view of *rentiers* as a specific group of "households."

"The *rentiers* are identified with the households of the capitalists," say Robinson and Eatwell.[143] Reading this statement, we might imagine that "the

capitalists" are the people who exploit workers in the process of production, and the rentiers, those to whom surplus-value is distributed. Search as we might, however, we cannot find anywhere in the Robinson and Eatwell textbook a reference to capitalists as exploiters of workers in the process of production. What we find instead are references to people such as "*entrepreneurs*, who organize production."[144]

The more one reads the Cantabrigians the more one realizes that they completely overlook the dual nature of the capitalists' role in production. Instead of recognizing that this role involves exploitation as well as coordination, they tend to see it only in terms of coordination. It would seem, therefore, that the Cantabrigians are subject to the same criticism that Marx addressed to his contemporaries:

> . . . the political economist . . . when considering the capitalist mode of production . . . treats [1] the work of control made necessary by the co-operative character of the labour-process as identical with [2] the different work of control necessitated by the capitalist character of that process and the antagonism of interests between capitalist and labourer.[145]

What happens when these two aspects of the capitalists' role are confused is that one tends to forget that capitalists as such have anything to do with production. Thus it turns out that when Robinson and Eatwell refer to capitalists, they actually have in mind only the people outside of the production process whom they classify as "rentiers."

At one point in their text Robinson and Eatwell do refer to "entrepreneurs" as members of the capitalist class:

> With the spread of capitalism . . . the capitalist class became divided into *rentiers*, who receive income from property and *entrepreneurs*, who organize production.[146]

Being part of the capitalist class, however, does not apparently mean that these "entrepreneurs" must come into conflict with workers. In the sentence immediately following the one just quoted, Robinson and Eatwell put their entrepreneurs on the same side of the social split as workers:

> Thus, the division of the community into idle consumers and active producers becomes a division between rentiers of all kinds (including landowners), on the one hand, and managers and workers on the other.[147]

This division of society into rentiers on one side and managers and workers on the other corresponds to what Robinson and Eatwell say in another place is one of "the most important differences" between their approach and that of the neoclassical economists, namely, "the distinction between income from work and income from property."[148] Both managers and workers receive "income from work," while only rentiers receive "income from property." From this one is led to believe that managers and entrepreneurs are really just particular varieties of workers and that their role in the production process is not in any way antagonistic to that of the rest of the workers.

By obscuring the role of capitalists in the production process itself and treating them merely as people who happen to *own* the means of production, the Cantabrigians engage in what Marx regarded as the most "complete" form of commodity fetishism:

> The ossification of [the] relations [of production], their presentation as the relation of men to things having a definite social character is here likewise brought out in quite a different manner from that of the simple mystification of commodities. . . . The transubstantiation, the fetishism, is complete.[149]

In the section of *Theories of Surplus-Value* from which this quote was taken, Marx criticizes as "vulgar political economy" the very thing that we have just associated with the Cantabrigians, namely, the tendency to displace from the realm of production the most essential feature of capitalism, the capital-labor relationship, and to project it as nothing more than a juridical relationship which gives certain people the right to an income from property. Thus, in the same passage Marx seems to be commenting directly on the writings of the Cantabrigians:

> Since the *alienated character* of capital, its opposition to labour, is displayed outside the exploitation process, that is, outside the sphere where the *real action of this alienation* takes place, all the contradictory features are eliminated from this process itself. Consequently, *real* exploitation, the sphere where these contradictory features are put into practice and where they manifest themselves in reality, appears as its exact opposite. . . . The work of the exploiter is identified here with the labour which is exploited.[150]

If one had the space—and if this essay were not already too long—one could proceed directly from the above quotation to a critique of the way the Cantabrigians deal with the question of social change. (In Marx's view, a proper understanding of social transformations can only be arrived at by examining the "contradictory features" of the production process itself.)[151] Since space is limited, however, I will end with a brief look at how Robinson thinks our society *ought* to be changed.

"A Drastic Remedy"

In *Economics: An Awkward Corner*, Joan Robinson surveys the contemporary crisis of capitalism and makes certain suggestions for dealing with it.[152] In her last chapter she takes the view that what we have now is something called "managerial capitalism," the main defect of which is the existence of an anachronistic class of rentiers who receive "unearned income." To improve the distribution of income, eliminate "functionless wealth," and provide the state with more revenue for improving health and educational services, she proposes that we gradually eliminate rentiers and move toward a society in which there would be something that she calls "the nation as rentier."[153]

To institute "the nation as rentier," Robinson first suggests that a surplus

in the government's budget be used to purchase corporate shares of stock. Then, after discussing the extreme inequality in the present distribution of income and wealth, she offers "a drastic remedy":

> The concept of the nation as rentier points the way out of this situation. Concentrations of private property could be wiped out in a generation by confiscatory death duties (leaving a reasonable life interest to widows and orphans, and buttressed by equally heavy taxation on gifts). The titles to property could be handed over in the form in which it exists, to be held like any other endowment of a trust, and the income from it devoted to public purposes. This would not only check the growth of rentier income . . . but take a large bite out of it.[154]

This proposal may seem somewhat naive—especially with regard to the benevolent character of the state—but it is remarkably consistent with the overall approach of the Cantabrigians. Have we not seen that they distinguish different forms of society according to "patterns of ownership"?[155] If the present social system is repugnant, then, what could be more logical than transferring the ownership of corporate shares from individuals to the state?

The question that must be asked, however, is how much of the present system would Robinson's proposal really change? If capitalism is the kind of system in which most people have to perform alienated labor under the direction of an autocratic elite, would it not still be capitalism even if the surplus-value produced were to be appropriated by the state rather than by a group of wealthy families? If our economic system were to continue to be based on wage-labor, would it not still be capitalism? And, if the state were to assume the functions that had previously been performed by private capitalists, would it not be fair to call the resulting system "state capitalism"?

Michael Lebowitz has argued that the Cantabrigian approach to economics should be understood as an expression of the interests of the *functioning capitalist* in opposition to those of the *money capitalist*.[156] This interpretation explains, among other things, why Robinson and Eatwell seem to be in such sympathy with their "entrepreneurs" and "managers"—picturing them as hard-working, talented, but not exploitative people.[157] It also explains why the Cantabrigians criticize only the ownership of the means of production by capitalists and the distribution of income to rentiers while neglecting the actual relations which characterize the capitalist process of production. For it makes little difference to the functioning capitalist whether the means of production are owned by private individuals or whether they are owned by the state. What counts is control, and this, as Robinson tells us, the Cantabrigians fully expect to be retained by the managers:

> In spite of its drawbacks, managers generally value the freedom that this peculiar system [managerial capitalism] gives them. For the most part, they dislike the idea of being nationalized or even of being financed by a public body which would have a right to supervise them. The great financial institutions such as insurance companies, which actually own a great deal of industry, lean backwards not to interfere. In principle, there is no

reason why the state should not also enjoy ownership without control where management by private enterprise is considered preferable.[158]

The Cantabrigian dream, then, is a society in which the managers of its economic activities are free to run things as they please. This is not a very new kind of utopia; Thorstein Veblen had something similar in mind around the turn of the century. The only astonishing thing about it is that the Cantabrigians imagine that it has something to do with socialism.

Joan Robinson has long been a sympathetic observer of the transition to socialism in the People's Republic of China,[159] but her familiarity with China does not seem to have had much effect either on her understanding of socialism or on her attitude toward the struggle for it in the West:

> It is now clear that the revolutionary transition to socialism does not come in the advanced capitalist nations, but in the most backward . . . Current experience suggests that socialism is not a stage beyond capitalism but a substitute for it—a means by which the nations which did not share in the Industrial Revolution can imitate its technical achievements; a means to achieve rapid accumulation under a different set of rules of the game.[160]

The inadequacy of Robinson's view of socialism stems from her limited understanding of what is wrong with capitalism in the first place:

> If the capitalists . . . invested the whole surplus there would be no need for socialism. It is the rentier aspect of profit, as a source of wealth . . . that makes the strongest case for socialism.[161]

While both of the above statements were made by Robinson in 1955, nothing in her later work indicates that she has altered her view of socialism. Since the Cantabrigians mystify the basic social relations of capitalism, one could hardly expect them to think of socialism as a radical alternative.

In closing, it is appropriate to recall Marx's argument that, in our analysis of contemporary society, we should be careful to distinguish those aspects of it which are historically specific from those which are common to all human societies.[162] His reasoning was that if we fail to distinguish the "particular" from the "general"—if we falsely attribute universality to something which is transient—we will have a harder time bringing about the transition from capitalism to socialism: ". . . on failure to perceive this fact depends the entire wisdom of [those] modern economists who prove the eternity and harmony of existing social relations."[163]

[Author's Note: For a more scholarly and careful development of the argument presented in this essay the reader is referred to my Ph.D. dissertation: "Towards a Marxist Critique of the Cambridge School," New School for Social Research, September 1976, available from: Xerox University Microfilms, 300 N. Zeeb Road, Ann Arbor, Michigan 48106.]

NOTES

1. In *Webster's New World Dictionary of the American Language* (New York: World Publishing Co., 1960), we find the following definition: "*Cantabrigian* . . . 1. a native or inhabitant of Cambridge, England. 2. a student or graduate of the University of Cambridge." In the same place the corresponding definitions for the adjective are also given.

2. For a concise survey of the Cambridge critique of neo-classical economics, see: G. C. Harcourt, "Some Cambridge Controversies in the Theory of Capital," *Journal of Economic Literature* 7, no. 2 (June 1969), pp. 369-405. A Marxist view of the same controversy—one which has influenced my own thinking—is presented in Bob Rowthorn, "Neo-Classicism, Neo-Ricardianism and Marxism," *New Left Review*, no. 86 (July-August 1974), pp. 63-87.

3. Maurice Dobb, *Theories of Value and Distribution since Adam Smith* (Cambridge: Cambridge University Press, 1973), pp. 248-66; Ronald Meek, "Mr. Sraffa's Rehabilitation of Classical Economics," in his *Economics and Ideology and Other Essays* (London: Chapman and Hall Ltd., 1967), pp. 161-78.

4. Harcourt, *op. cit.*, p. 394.

5. Edward J. Nell, "A Note on Cambridge Controversies in Capital Theory," *Journal of Economic Literature* 8, no. 1 (March 1970), p. 43.

6. E. K. Hunt and Howard Sherman, "Value, Alienation, and Distribution," *Science and Society* 36, no. 1 (Spring 1972), p. 35.

7. Cambridge: Cambridge University Press, 1960.

8. See, for example, Joan Robinson, "The Relevance of Economic Theory," *Monthly Review* 22, no. 8 (January 1971), p. 34; see also Edward J. Nell, "The Revival of Political Economy," *Social Research* 39, no. 1 (Spring 1972), p. 39, wherein it is stated that Sraffa's book is "the basic work laying the foundation of the new [Cambridge] paradigm."

9. Joan Robinson, "The Production Function and the Theory of Capital," *Review of Economic Studies* 21, no. 2 (1953), pp. 81-106.

10. Robinson, "The Relevance of Economic Theory."

11. Joan Robinson and John Eatwell, *An Introduction to Modern Economics* (London: McGraw-Hill, 1973).

12. My presentation of Marx's concept of a mode of production in this section relies heavily on Etienne Balibar, "The Basic Concepts of Historical Materialism," in Louis Althusser and Etienne Balibar, *Reading Capital* (New York: Pantheon Books, 1970), pp. 199-308.

13. Karl Marx and Friedrich Engels, *The German Ideology* (New York: International Publishers, 1970), p. 42.

14. Karl Marx, *Capital* (New York: International Publishers, 1967), vol. I, p. 8. All references to *Capital* hereafter are to this edition.

15. Marx and Engels, *op. cit.*, p. 58.

16. Ibid., p. 42.

17. Ibid.

18. Ibid., p. 50.

19. Marx, *Capital*, vol. I, p. 178.

20. Ibid., pp. 330-31.

21. Karl Marx, *Grundrisse: Foundations of the Critique of Political Economy*, tr. by Martin Nicolaus (Harmondsworth: Penguin Books Ltd., 1973), p. 302.

22. Ibid., pp. 303-04.

23. Ibid., p. 304.

24. Marx, *Capital*, vol. I, p. 79.

25. Marx, *Capital*, vol. II, p. 34.

26. Marx, *Capital*, vol. I, p. 715.

27. For Marx's distinction between necessary and surplus labor, see *Capital*, vol. I, pp. 216-17.

28. Ibid., p. 217.

29. Ibid., pp. 183-84.

30. Marx, *Grundrisse*, p. 304.

31. Marx, *Capital*, vol. III, p. 883.

32. Marx, *Capital*, vol. I, pp. 179-80.

33. Robinson and Eatwell, *op. cit.*, p. 62.
34. Ibid., p. 63.
35. Ibid., p. 54.
36. Ibid.
37. Sraffa, *op. cit.*, p. 3.
38. Nell, "The Revival of Political Economy," *op. cit.*, p. 39.
39. See, for example, Nell's Sraffa-inspired drawing of a capitalist economy in which the realm of production is represented by a box containing factories but not people. Ibid., p. 46.
40. Robinson and Eatwell, *op. cit.*, p. 90.
41. Ibid., p. 91.
42. Ibid.
43. Ibid., p. 61.
44. Ibid., pp. 64-77.
45. This particular divergence between Marx and the Cantabrigians becomes extremely important when the problem of *dynamic analysis* is taken up: The organic relationship between Marx's basic abstractions allows him to focus on *contradictions* between the different aspects of the production process; the independence of the Cantabrigians' abstractions prevents them from engaging in the same kind of analysis.
46. See, for example, Harcourt, *op. cit.*, p. 394; and D. M. Nuti, "'Vulgar Economy' in the Theory of Income Distribution," *Science and Society* 35, no. 1 (Spring 1971), pp. 27-33.
47. Nell, "The Revival of Political Economy," *op. cit.*, p. 39.
48. John Stuart Mill, *Principles of Political Economy* (London: Routledge and Kegan Paul for the University of Toronto Press, 1965), p. 199.
49. Marx, *Grundrisse*, "Introduction," p. 97.
50. The Sraffa approach has actually been applied to the analysis of feudal society in Edward J. Nell, "Economic Relationships in the Decline of Feudalism: An Examination of Economic Interdependence and Social Change," *History and Theory* 6, no. 3 (1967), pp. 313-50.
51. Robinson and Eatwell, *op. cit.*, p. 63.
52. For a clear illustration of the way Marx used his two basic abstractions to analyse the capitalist process of production see the two sections of chapter 7 of *Capital*, volume I.
53. See note 28 above.
54. While Marx never used this term, it has been frequently employed by commentators on his work. See, for example, Paul M. Sweezy, *The Theory of Capitalist Development* (New York: Monthly Review Press, 1942), p. 23.
55. Marx, *Capital*, vol. I, pp. 72-73.
56. Ibid., p. 42.
57. Ibid., p. 73.
58. Ibid., p. 41.
59. Ibid., p. 42.
60. Ibid., pp. 37-38.
61. Ibid., p. 38.
62. Ibid., p. 537.
63. Ibid., p. 81, note 2.
64. Marx first discussed the law of value (without referring to it as such) in volume I of *Capital*, p. 75.
65. Karl Marx, *Early Writings*, tr. and ed. by T. B. Bottomore (New York: McGraw-Hill, 1964), pp. 122-23.
66. Marx, *Capital*, vol. I, p. 73. For an excellent discussion of this aspect of Marx's thinking, see: Norman Geras, "Essence and Appearance: Aspects of Fetishism in Marx's *Capital*," *New Left Review*, no. 65 (January-February 1971), pp. 69-85, reprinted in Robin Blackburn, ed., *Ideology in Social Science* (New York: Pantheon Books, 1972), pp. 284-305.
67. Karl Marx, *A Contribution to the Critique of Political Economy* (New York: International Publishers, 1970), p. 49.
68. Ibid., p. 226.
69. Marx, *Capital*, vol. I, p. 80.

70. Ibid., p. 587.
71. Ibid., p. 714.
72. Ibid., pt. VIII.
73. Ibid., p. 430.
74. Marx, *A Contribution to the Critique of Political Economy*, p. 210.
75. Marx, *Capital*, vol. I, p. 173.
76. Ibid., p. 539.
77. Ibid., p. 574.
78. Marx, *Early Writings*, pp. 124-25.
79. Marx, *Capital*, vol. I, p. 533.
80. Ibid., pp. 570-71.
81. Marx, *A Contribution to the Critique of Political Economy*, p. 190.
82. Ibid.
83. Ibid.
84. Marx, *Capital*, vol. I, p. 310.
85. Ibid., p. 81.
86. Marx, *Capital*, vol. III, pp. 814-15.
87. Marx, *Capital*, vol. I, p. 331.
88. Ibid.
89. Ibid., p. 10.
90. Ibid., pp. 309-310.
91. Marx, *Grundrisse*, p. 96.
92. Marx, *Capital*, vol. I, p. 619.
93. Marx, *Grundrisse*, p. 95.
94. Karl Marx and Friedrich Engels, *Selected Works* (New York: International Publishers, 1968), p. 35.
95. Marx, *Early Writings*, p. 132.
96. Marx, *Capital*, vol. I, p. 618.
97. Marx and Engels, *Selected Works*, "Critique of the Gotha Program," p. 325.
98. Ibid., p. 323.
99. Marx, *Capital*, vol. I, p. 80.
100. Marx, *Capital*, vol. I, p. 72.
101. See note 68 above. The point I am trying to make here was stated explicitly by Marx in *Capital*, vol. I, p. 578: "Capitalist production . . . produces not only commodities, not only surplus-value, but it also produces and reproduces the capitalist relation; on the one side the capitalist, on the other the wage-labourer."
102. See note 63 above.
103. See note 69 above.
104. Marx, *Capital*, vol. III, p. 25. In the same volume, Marx devoted a chapter to the question that Sraffa deals with, "Effects of General Wage Fluctuations on Prices of Production," but at the end of it he remarked: "This is but a very secondary question." (pp. 200-204).
105. For a lucid treatment of this point, see Alfredo Medio, "Profits and Surplus-Value: Appearance and Reality in Capitalist Production," in E. K. Hunt and Jesse G. Schwartz, *A Critique of Economic Theory* (Harmondsworth: Penguin Books, 1972), pp. 312-46.
106. Joan Robinson, *The Economics of Imperfect Competition* (London: Macmillan, 1933), p. 6.
107. Joan Robinson, *Economic Philosophy* (Chicago: Aldine, 1963), p. 26.
108. Joan Robinson, *An Essay on Marxian Economics* (London: Macmillan, 1966), p. xviii.
109. See note 3 above.
110. Sraffa, *op. cit.*, p. 3.
111. Robinson and Eatwell, *op. cit.*, p. 187.
112. Krishna Bharadwaj, "Value Through Exogenous Distribution," *Economic Weekly* (Bombay, India), 24 August 1963, pp. 1450-1454; reprinted in G. C. Harcourt and N. F. Laing, eds., *Capital and Growth* (Harmondsworth: Penguin Books, 1971), p. 184.
113. Sraffa, *op. cit.*, p. 33.

114. D. M. Nuti, "'Vulgar Economy' in the Theory of Income Distribution," p. 32.

115. Harcourt, "Some Cambridge Controversies in the Theory of Capital," pp. 394-95.

116. An exception may be cited here: The following statement was made by Edward Nell in a review article, "Two Books on the Theory of Income Distribution," *Journal of Economic Literature* 10, no. 2 (June 1972), p. 445: "Given the power structure of corporations, executives at the top largely set their own pay; from these levels down the pay structure reflects relative position in the hierarchy." This kind of consideration, however, is generally not taken into account by the Cantabrigians.

117. See note 49 above.

118. Sraffa, *op. cit.*, p. 6.

119. Ibid., p. 3.

120. See note 90 above. The contrast between Sraffa's and Marx's approaches may be highlighted here by quoting the following passage from *Capital*, vol. I, p. 515:

> In the midst of our West European society . . . the idea easily takes root that it is an inherent quality of human labour to furnish a surplus-product. But consider, for example . . . the eastern islands of the Asiatic Archipelago, where sago grows wild in the forests. "When the inhabitants have convinced themselves, by boring a hole in the tree, that the pith is ripe, the trunk is cut down and divided into several pieces, the pith is extracted, mixed with water and filtered; it is then quite fit for use as sago. One tree commonly yields 300 lbs., and occasionally 500 to 600 lbs. There, then, people go into the forests, and cut bread for themselves, just as they cut fire-wood." Suppose now such an eastern-bread-cutter requires 12 working-hours a week for the satisfaction of all his wants. Nature's direct gift to him is plenty of leisure time . . . before he spends it in surplus-labour for strangers, compulsion is necessary. If capitalist production were introduced, the honest fellow would perhaps have to work six days a week, in order to appropriate to himself the product of one working-day. The bounty of Nature does not explain why he would then have to work six days a week, or why he must furnish five days of surplus-labour. It explains only why his necessary labour-time would be limited to one day a week. But in no case would his surplus-product arise from some occult quality inherent in human labour.

121. Sraffa, *op. cit.*, p. 11.

122. Edward J. Nell, "Property and the Means of Production," *Review of Radical Political Economics* 4, no. 2 (Summer 1972), p. 9.

123. See note 120 above.

124. If the reader has difficulty accepting this point, think about it with reference to an imaginary economy which consists only of "basic" industries (in Sraffa's sense) but which is characterized by the performance of surplus as well as necessary labour (in Marx's sense).

125. See note 100 above.

126. Nell, "The Revival of Political Economy," p. 40.

127. See note 84 above. See also *Capital*, vol. I, p. 423.

128. Nell, "The Revival of Political Economy," p. 40.

129. Joan Robinson, "The Production Function and the Theory of Capital: Postscript," in G. C. Harcourt and N. F. Laing, eds., *Capital and Growth*, p. 63.

130. See note 90 above.

131. Amit Bhaduri, "On the Significance of Recent Controversies on Capital Theory: A Marxian View," *Economic Journal* 79 (September 1969), pp. 532-39.

132. Ibid., p. 533.

133. Ibid., p. 534.

134. See note 86 above.

135. Marx, *Capital*, vol. II, p. 225.

136. Robinson and Eatwell, *op. cit.*, p. 61.

137. Nell, "The Revival of Political Economy," p. 46.

138. Ibid., p. 43.

139. Ibid., p. 47.

140. Ibid.

141. Marx and Engels, *Selected Works*, "Wages, Price and Profit," p. 229. I am grateful to Bill Lazonick for bringing this passage to my attention.

142. Robinson and Eatwell, *op. cit.*, p. 92.

143. Ibid.

144. Ibid., p. 77. The single exception to the statement in the preceding sentence occurs where Robinson and Eatwell discuss Marx's approach to economics (see ibid., p. 28).

145. Marx, *Capital*, vol. I, p. 332.

146. Robinson and Eatwell, *op. cit.*, p. 77.

147. Ibid.

148. Ibid., p. 99.

149. Karl Marx, *Theories of Surplus-Value*, pt. III (Moscow: Progress Publishers, 1971), p. 494.

150. Ibid., p. 495.

151. See note 45 above.

152. Joan Robinson, *Economics: An Awkward Corner* (New York: Pantheon Books, 1967).

153. Ibid., p. 59.

154. Ibid., p. 61.

155. See note 51 above.

156. Michael A. Lebowitz, "The Current Crisis of Economic Theory," *Science and Society* 37, no. 4 (Winter 1973-1974), pp. 385-403.

157. The sympathy which Robinson and Eatwell have for managers comes through, among other places, in the discussion of "socialist states" in their textbook (bk. 3, chap. 2). Here, focusing on recent events in the U.S.S.R., they make the following statement: "The main obstacle to reforms . . . comes from the objections of the bureaucracy to giving up the power that it enjoys over industry and allocating more independence and initiative to managers, technicians, and engineers." (*Op. cit.*, p. 320.) True as this may be, whatever happened to the idea of socialism as a system of workers' control?

158. Robinson, *Economics: An Awkward Corner*, p. 59.

159. See, for example, Joan Robinson, *The Cultural Revolution in China* (Harmondsworth: Penguin Books, 1969).

160. Joan Robinson, *Collected Economic Papers*, vol. II (Oxford: Basil Blackwell, 1960), "Marx, Marshall and Keynes," p. 15.

161. Ibid., pp. 10-11.

162. See note 81 above.

163. Marx, *A Contribution to the Critique of Political Economy*, p. 190.

22

Some Comments on Marx's Theory of Value

LUCIO COLLETTI
Professor of Philosophy at the University of Rome

The inadequacy and simplification of the concept of 'economy', which, as we have seen, is an element more or less common to all the tendencies of Marxism in the Second International, helps to explain the foundation, during the same period, of an interpretation of the *labour theory of value* from which even later Marxism has been unable to free itself. This interpretation consisted in the reduction of Marx's theory of value to that of Ricardo, or even to the theory of value which developed in the course of the 'dissolution of the Ricardian School'. Its hallmark is the inability to grasp, or even to suspect, that Marx's theory of value is identical to his *theory of fetishism* and that it is precisely by virtue of this element (in which the crucial importance of the relation with Hegel is intuitively evident) that Marx's theory differs in principle from the whole of classical political economy.

'Political economy has indeed analysed, however incompletely, value and its magnitude and has discovered what lies beneath these forms. But it has never once asked the question why labour is represented by the *value* of its product and labour-time by the *magnitude of that value*.'[1]

The achievement and the limitation of classical political economy are indicated here with extraordinary clarity. First, the achievement: political economy, in spite of its incompleteness and its various inconsistencies, understood that the *value* of commodities is determined by the *labour* incorporated in them, or, in other words, that what appears as the 'value' of 'things' is in reality (here is 'the content hidden in the form') the 'human labour' necessary for their production. Second, the limitation: it never posed the problem of why that content assumes this particular form, why human labour takes on the form of *value of things*, or, in short, on the basis of what historical-social conditions the product of labour takes the form of a *commodity*. This problem could not be posed by political economy, since, Marx goes on to explain, the economists could not see that 'the value-form of the product of labour is not only the most abstract but is also the most universal form taken by the product in bourgeois production'. They wrongly held instead that the production of commodities, far from being a *historical* phenomenon, was a 'self-evident necessity imposed by nature'.[2] They believed, in other words, that there could be no production in society without this production being *production of commodities*, that in all societies the product of human labour must necessarily assume this form.[3]

The main consequence of this different approach is as follows. Classical political economy, taking the existence of the *commodity* as a 'natural' and hence non-problematical fact, restricted itself to investigating the proportions in which commodities exchange for one another, concentrating their analysis on *exchange value* rather than *value* in the strict sense: 'The analysis of the magnitude of value almost completely absorbs the attention of Smith and Ricardo,' Marx wrote.[4] For Marx, on the contrary, the essential problem, prior to that of exchange rates of commodities is to explain *why* the product of labour takes the form of the *commodity*, why 'human labour' appears as a 'value' of 'things'. Hence the decisive importance for him of his analysis of 'fetishism', 'alienation' or 'reification' (*Verdinglichung*): the process whereby, while *subjective* human or social labour is represented in the form of a quality intrinsic in *things*, these things themselves, endowed with their own *subjective, social* qualities, appear 'personified' or 'animated', as if they were independent subjects.

Marx writes:

> Where labour is in common, relations between men in their social production are not represented as 'value' of 'things'. Exchanges of products as commodities is a certain method of exchanging labour, and of the dependence of the labour of each upon the labour of the others, a certain mode of social labour or social production. In the first part of my work I have explained that it is characteristic of labour based on private exchange that the social character of the labour is 'represented' as a 'property' of the things; and inversely, that a social relation appears as a relation of one thing to another (of products, values in use, commodities).[5]

Marx explained the operation of this exchange of the subjective with the objective and vice versa—in which the fetishism of commodities consists—with his celebrated concept of *'abstract labour'* or *'average human labour'*. Abstract labour is what is equal and common to all concrete human labouring activities (carpentry, weaving, spinning, etc.) when their activities are considered apart from the real objects (or use-values) to which they are applied and in terms of which they are diversified. If one abstracts from the material to which labour is applied, one also abstracts, according to Marx, from the determination of productive activity, that is from the concrete character that differentiates the various forms of useful labour. Once this *abstraction* is made, all that remains of all the various sorts of labour is the fact that they are all *expenditures of human labour-power*. 'Tailoring and weaving, though qualitatively different productive activities, are each a productive expenditure of human brains, nerves and muscles, and in this sense are human labour.'[6] It is this equal or *abstract* human labour—labour considered as the expenditure and objectification of undifferentiated human labour-power, independently of the concrete forms of activity in which it is realized—that produces *value*. Value is 'a mere congelation of homogeneous human labour, of labour-power expended without regard to the form of its expenditure'. As products of *abstract labor*, all the products of concrete forms of labour lose their perceptible or real qualities and now represent only the fact that 'human labour-power has been expended in their production, that human labour is embodied in them; . . . as crystals of this social substance, common to them all, they are—Values.'[7]

The point to be emphasized here is that not only Marx's critics, but indeed his own disciples and followers—and not only those of the Second International but also more recent ones, to this very day—have all shown themselves incapable of understanding or realizing fully the significance of this concept. 'Abstract labour' seems at least to be a perfectly straightforward and clear notion. And yet neither Kautsky in his *Economic Doctrines of K. Marx*[8] nor Hilferding in his important reply to Böhm-Bawerk,[9] nor Luxemburg in her ample *Introduction to Political Economy*,[10] nor Lenin and *tutti quanti*, have ever really confronted this 'key' to the entire theory of value. Sweezy, who has gone further than most, writes: 'Abstract labour is abstract only in the quite straightforward sense that all special characteristics which differentiate one kind of labour from another are ignored. Abstract labour, in short, is, as Marx's usage quite clearly attests, equivalent to "labour in general"; it is what is common to all productive human activity.'[11]

The meaning of this argument is clear. 'Abstract labour' is an abstraction, in the sense that it is a mental *generalization* of the multiplicity of useful, concrete kinds of labour: it is the general, *common* element of all these kinds of labour. This generalization, moreover, as Sweezy goes on to point out, corresponds to capitalist reality, in that in this kind of society labour is shifted or diverted according to the direction of capital investments; hence a determinate portion of human labour is, in accordance with variations of demand, at one time supplied in one form, at another time in another form. This proves the secondary importance in this regime of the various specific kinds of labour, as against labour in general or in and for itself. In spite of Sweezy's plea that 'the reduction of all labour to a common denominator . . . is not an arbitrary abstraction, dictated in some way by the whim of the investigator' but 'rather, as Lukács correctly observes, an abstraction "which belongs to the essence of Capitalism",'[12] despite this, in the absence of what seems to me the decisive point, 'abstract labour' remains, in the last analysis, essentially a *mental generalization*.

The defect of this interpretation of 'abstract labour' lies not only in the fact that—if abstract labour is a mental generalization—it is not clear why what this labour is supposed to produce is something real—*value*; but also in the fact that this opens the door to the transformation of value itself into an abstract generality or *idea* as well. For, in the sense that here only useful and concrete kinds of labour are regarded as real, whereas 'abstract' labour is seen as a merely *mental* fact, so too only the products of useful kinds of labour or *use-values* are real, whereas *value*, the merely general element *common* to them, is abstract.

The interpretation that Bernstein adopted was precisely this one. 'Value' is *ein Gedankenbild*, a mere thought-construct: it is in Marx's work a formal principle which serves to bring system and order to the complexity of the analysis, but itself has no real existence. 'Insofar as we take into consideration the individual commodity', Bernstein comments, 'value loses any concrete content and becomes a mere mental construction'. Hence it is clear that 'the moment that labour-value is only valid as a mental formula (*gedankliche Formel*) or scientific hypothesis, surplus value also becomes a pure formula, a formula based on a hypothesis'.[13]

This interpretation had, of course, already been advanced before Bernstein by Werner Sombart and Conrad Schmidt, in time for Engels to confront it in his

Supplement to Volume III of *Capital*.[14] Value, according to Sombart, is 'not an empirical, but a mental, a logical fact' while for Schmidt the law of value within the capitalist mode of production is a 'pure, although theoretically necessary fiction'.

It is striking that even at this point, decisive for the genesis of 'revisionism', Engels's response is both uncertain and substantially erroneous. Even if he makes some reservations towards Sombart and Schmidt, he ends up by accepting their essential thesis (that is, the unreal nature of the law of value when commodities are produced under *capitalist conditions*), and hence falls back to the position of Smith (already criticized in its time by Marx)[15] which had relegated the action of the law of value to *precapitalist* historical conditions.

In other words, 'abstract labour' and 'value'—the point on which everything hangs—are understood simply as mental generalizations introduced by the scientist, in this case by Marx; ignoring the fact that, if this were effectively so, in introducing these generalizations Marx would have been committing a 'clumsy error' and the whole of Böhm-Bawerk's critique would indeed be correct. The central argument of Böhm-Bawerk's critique—already present in *Geschichte und Kritik der Kapitalzinstheorien* (pp. 435ff.) and restated in 1896 in *Zum Abschluss des Marxchen Systems* (a text which may have influenced Bernstein)—was that if 'value' is the generalization of 'use-values', it is then *use-value* 'in general' and not, as Marx had argued, a qualitatively distinct entity. Marx's error, according to Böhm-Bawerk, was the error of those who 'confuse abstraction from the *circumstance in general (von einem Umstande überhaupt)*, and abstraction from the *specific forms* in which this circumstance manifests itself';[16] the error of those who believe that to abstract from the *differences* between one use-value and another is to abstract from use-values *in general*; for the real value is *use-value*, the true theory of value a theory of *value-utility*. According to Böhm-Bawerk, this 'wrong idea' he attributes to Marx means that instead of seeing in 'exchange value' a relation or a mere quantitative proportion between use-values, and hence, like any relation, an unreal value outside the entities related together, Marx invoked the existence behind exchange-value of an objective being 'value', without seeing that this 'entity' was only a 'scholastic-theological' product, a hypostasis arising from his defective logic.[17]

The response that has traditionally been given to these objections by Marxists is well known. It consists, at most, in an appeal to the original conception of Ricardo who had, as can be seen from his last incomplete memoir, already before Marx distinguished between *Absolute Value and Exchangeable Value*. However, apart from Marx's remarks on the tendency of Ricardo's analysis to dwell more on 'exchange-value' than on 'value' itself, this response is further weakened by the fact that, confronted by the non-coincidence of 'values' and 'costs of production', this interpretation has continuously been forced to fall back on to Sombart-Schmidt positions or even Bernstein positions. For once it is accepted that value is not identified with the concrete exchange-values or competitive prices at which the capitalistically produced commodities are in fact sold, this interpretation retreats to a position of attributing to 'value' the significance, essentially, of an abstraction. Dobb's case is typical. After stating that 'value [is] only an abstract approximation to concrete exchange-values', that this 'has generally been held to fatal to the theory, and was the *onus of*

Böhm-Bawerk's criticism of Marx', he limits himself to concluding that 'all abstractions remain only approximations to reality . . . it is no criticism of a theory of value merely to say that this is so'.[18]

THE THEORY OF VALUE AND FETISHISM

The decisive point which, I believe, remains misunderstood in all these interpretations is, as already indicated, the concept of 'abstract labour'; i.e. (a) how this abstraction of labour is produced, and (b) what it really means.

The first part of the question is relatively straightforward. According to Marx, the products of labour take the form of *commodities* when they are produced for *exchange*. And they are produced for exchange when they are products of autonomous, *private* labours carried out independently of one another. Like Robinson Crusoe, the producer of commodities decides by himself how much and what to produce. But unlike Robinson Crusoe he lives in society and hence within a *social division of labour* in which his labour depends on that of others and vice versa. It follows that while Crusoe carried out *all* his indispensable labour *by himself* and relied only on his own labour for the satisfaction of his needs, the producer of commodities carries out only *one* determinate form of labour, the products of which are destined for others, just as the products of the other producers' different forms of labour go to him.

If this social division of labour were a conscious and planned distribution to all its members on the part of society of the various necessary types of labour and quantities to be produced, the products of individual labour would not take the form of *commodities*. For example, in a patriarchal peasant family there is a distribution of the work which the members themselves must carry out, but the products of this labour do not become commodities, nor do the members of the family nucleus buy or sell their products to each other.[19] On the other hand, in conditions of commodity production, the work of individual producers is not labour carried out at the command or on behalf of society: rather it is *private, autonomous* labour, carried out by each producer independently of the next. Hence, lacking any conscious assignment or distribution on the part of society, individual labour is not *immediately* an articulation of social labour; it acquires its character as a part or *aliquot* of aggregate labour only through the *mediation* of exchange relations or the market.

Now Marx's essential thesis is that in order to *exchange* their products, men must *equalize them*, i.e. abstract from the physical-natural or use-value aspect in which one product differs from another (corn from iron, iron from glass, etc.). In abstracting from the object or concrete material of their labour they also abstract *ipso facto* from that which serves to differentiate their labours. 'Along with the useful qualities of the products themselves, we put out of sight both the useful character of the various kinds of labour embodied in them and the concrete forms of that labour; there is nothing left but what is common to them all . . . human labour in the abstract.'[20]

Hence in abstracting from the natural, sensory *objectivity* of their products, men also and simultaneously abstract from what differentiates their various *subjective* activities. 'The Labour . . . that forms the substance of value is homogeneous labour-power, expenditure of one uniform labour-power. The

total labour-power of society which is embodied in the sum total of the values of all commodities produced by that society counts here as one homogeneous mass of human labour-power, composed though it be of innumerable individual units. Each of these units is the same as any other, so far as it has the character of the average labour-power of society and takes effect as such.'[21]

By now it should be clear that the process whereby 'abstract labour' is obtained, far from being a mere *mental* abstraction of the investigator's, is one which takes place daily in the *reality of exchange itself*. ('When we bring the products of our labour into relation with each other as values, it is not because we see in these articles the *material receptacles* of homogeneous human labour. Quite the contrary: whenever by an exchange we equate *as values* our *different products*, by that very act we also equate, as human labour, the different kinds of labour expended upon them. We are not aware of this, nevertheless we do it.')[22]

It remains to deal with the second aspect of the problem, the real significance of this abstraction. The crucial point here is again quite simple. Unlike those interpreters who think it is obvious and non-problematical that in commodity production each individual labour-power is considered as a 'human labour-power identical to all others' or as 'average social labour power', and hence have never asked themselves what this equalization of labour signifies— unlike them, I believe that this is precisely where the significance of 'abstract labour' and the entire theory of value is to be found. For while the working capacities or labour-power of the various producers are in fact different and unequal, just as are the individuals to whom they belong and who *'would not be different individuals if they were not unequal'*,[23] in the reality of the world of commodities, on the other hand, individual labour powers are equalized precisely because they are treated as abstract or *separate* from the real empirical individuals to whom they belong. In other words, precisely insofar as they are regarded as a 'force' or entity 'in itself', i.e. separated from the individuals whose powers they are. 'Abstract labour', in short, is *alienated* labour, labour separated or estranged with respect to man himself.

'The labour-time expressed in exchange value is the labour-time of an individual', Marx wrote, 'but of an individual in no way differing from the next individual and from all other individuals insofar as they perform equal labour. . . . It is the labour-time of an individual, *his* labour-time, but only as labour-time common to all; consequently it is quite immaterial whose individual labour-time it is.'[24] Hence labour is considered here precisely as a process in itself, independent of the man who carries it out. We are not concerned with the particular man who performs the labour, nor with the particular labour he accomplishes, but with the labour-power thus expended, leaving aside *which* particular individual it belongs to and to what particular labour it has been applied. In short, we are concerned here with human energy *as such*, labour-power and nothing more, outside and independently of the man who expended it, as if the *real subject* indeed were not the man but labour-power itself, nothing being left to the man but to serve as a mere function or vehicle for the manifestations of the latter.[25] Labour-power, in other words, which is a property, a determinant or an attribute of man, becomes an independent subject, by representing itself as the 'value' of 'things'. The human individuals, on the other hand, who are the

real subjects become determinations of their determination, i.e. articulations
or appendages of their common, reified labour-power, 'Labour, thus measured
by time, does not seem, indeed, to be the labour of different persons, but on
the contrary the different working individuals seem to be mere organs *of this
labour*.'[26] In short: 'men are effaced by their labour . . . the pendulum of the
clock has become as accurate a measure of the relative activity of two workers
as it is of the speed of two locomotives.' Hence 'we should not say that one
man's hour is worth another man's hour, but rather that one man during an
hour is worth just as much as another man during an hour. Time is everything,
man is nothing; he is at the most time's carcass.'[27]

An analogy may be of help here. Hegel separated human thought from
man, turning it into an 'independent subject' called 'the Idea'; for him it was no
longer the thinking individual who thinks but the Idea or Logos which thinks
itself through man. In this case, as Feuerbach pointed out, 'abstraction means
placing man's essence outside himself, the essence of thought outside the act of
thinking'. Hence 'speculative philosophy has theoretically fixed the separation
of the essential qualities of man from man himself and thus ends by turning
abstract qualities into divinities as if they were self-sufficient essences'.[28] The
effect of the world of commodities on real men has been similar. It has factually
separated or *abstracted* from man his 'subjectivity', i.e. his 'physical and mental
energies', his 'capacity' for work, and has transformed it into a separate essence.
It has fixed human energy *as such* in the 'crystal' or 'congelation' of labour
which is *value*, turning it into a distinct entity, an entity which is not only independent of man, but also dominates him.

As Marx writes:

> There is a definite social relation between men, that assumes in their eyes
> the fantastic form of a relation between things. In order, therefore, to
> find an analogy we must have resource to the mist-enveloped regions of
> the religious world. In that world the productions of the human brain
> appear as independent things endowed with life, and entering into rela-
> tion both with one another and the human race. So it is in the world of
> commodities with the products of men's hands. This I call the Fetishism
> which attaches itself to the products of labour, so soon as they are pro-
> duced as commodities, and which is therefore inseparable from the pro-
> duction of commodities.[29]

To conclude, 'abstract labour' is not only that which is 'common' to all
human productive activities, it is not only a mental generalization; rather, it is in
itself a real activity, if of a kind opposed to all concrete, useful kinds of labour.
More precisely, unlike all the others, it is an activity which does not represent
an *appropriation* of the objective, natural world so much as an *expropriation of
human subjectivity*, a separation of labour 'capacity' or 'power' conceived as
the totality of physical and intellectual attitudes, from man himself. This in
turn implies that in a society in which individual activities have a *private* character, and in which therefore the interests of individuals are divided and counterposed, or, as we say, *in competition* with one another, the moment of *social
unity* can only be realized in the form of an *abstract equalization*, ignoring the
individuals themselves; hence, in this case, as a reification of labour-power—a

labour-power which is said to be *equal* or *social*, not because it genuinely belongs to *everyone* and hence mediates between the individuals, but because it
belongs to *nobody* and is obtained by ignoring the real inequalities between the
individuals. This is precisely what Marx is expressing when he writes that abstract
labour is 'labour in which the individual characteristics of the workers are oblit-
erated'; or that, when buyer and seller exchange their products and hence *equalize* their labour in the act of exchange, both 'enter into it only insofar as their
individual labour is negated, that is to say, turned into money as *non*-individual
labour';[30] or, finally where he defines capital as an 'independent *social force*'
which, because it has acquired its own autonomous existence, has become 'the
power *of a portion of society*' over the rest—a power, therefore, maintaining and
multiplying itself *'by means of its exchange for direct, living labour power'*.[31]

I cannot stop here to show how this conception of the theory of value
constitutes the element of deepest continuity between the works of the young
Marx and those of his maturity. Even in *The German Ideology*, Marx underlines
the fact that, under modern conditions, the productive forces 'appear as a world
for themselves, quite independent of and divorced from the individuals', alongside the individuals'. As a result, on the one hand 'we have a totality of productive forces, which have, as it were, taken on a material (objective) form and
are for the individuals no longer the forces of the individuals, but of private
property and hence of the individuals only insofar as they are owners of private
property themselves'. On the other hand, 'standing over against these productive
forces we have the majority of the individuals from whom these forces have
been wrested away and who, robbed thus of all real life-content, have become
abstract individuals'.

Nor can we deal here with the fact that our own interpretation of the
theory of value which assimilates 'value' to Hegel's hypostasization processes,
also links together the *equalization* which is the precondition of 'abstract labour'
and the *purely* political equality realized in the modern representative state.
(The collective interest, according to Marx in *The German Ideology*, 'takes an
independent form as the *State*, divorced from the real interests of the individual
and community', insofar as 'just because individuals seek *only* their particular
interest which for them does not coincide with their communal interest—in fact
the general is the illusory form of communal life—the latter will be imposed on
them as an interest "alien" to them and "independent" of them, as in its turn
a particular, peculiar "general" interest.' Hence 'the social power' transformed
into the power of the state 'appears to these individuals . . . not as their own
united power, but as an alien force existing outside them, of the origin and goal
of which they are ignorant.')[32] We can, however, deal with one other point
here: this confluence of the theory of value and the theory of fetishism or alienation in Marx represents not only his main difference of principle with the classical political economists, for whom the theory of alienation is absolutely
inconceivable; it also constitutes the viewpoint from which he explained the
birth and destiny of political economy as a science. Firstly, its *birth*: the precondition for the emergence of economic reflection lay for Marx in the process
whereby social relations became obscured and objectified in the eyes of men as
a consequence of the *generalization*, with the emergence of modern bourgeois
society, of the production of commodities and the fetishism inherent in it. ('The

ancient social organisms of production are far more simple and transparent than the bourgeois organism'; even though commodity production occurs within them, it emerges as a secondary or marginal branch among kinds of production based on a natural economy—based, that is, on the immediate consumption of products rather than their sale on the market.) Secondly, its later *destiny*: the task of political economy as a science consisted for Marx essentially—if we can accept a neologism—in the de-fetishization of the world of commodities, in the progressive comprehension that what represents itself as the 'value' of 'things' is in reality not a property of these things themselves, but reified human labour. This theme, according to Marx, runs through the entire history of economic theory from mercantilism to Smith: the gradual rediscovery, beneath the mask of fetishized objectivity, of the alienated human subject. In the 'Introduction' of 1857, he wrote: 'The Monetary system, for example, still regards wealth quite objectively as a thing existing independently in the shape of money. Compared with this standpoint, it was a substantial advance when the Manufacturing Mercantile System transferred the source of wealth from the object to the subjective activity—mercantile or industrial labour—but it still considered that only this circumscribed activity itself produced money.' He continues: 'In contrast to this system, the Physiocrats assume that a specific form of labour—agriculture—creates wealth, and they see the object no longer in the guise of money, but as a product in general, as the universal result of labour. In accordance with the still circumscribed activity, the product remains a naturally developed product, an agricultural product, a product of the land *par excellence*.' Finally, a tremendous step forwards was achieved by Smith in rejecting 'all restrictions with regard to the activity that produces wealth—for him it was labour as such, neither manufacturing, nor commercial, nor agricultural labour, but all types of labour.'[33]

We have already seen how, despite its real merits, classical political economy as well as *Vulgärökonomie*, remained in the end a prisoner of fetishism,[34] because of its inability to pose the problem of why the product of labour takes the form of the commodity and hence why human labour is presented as the 'value' of 'things'. This gives us the chance to raise a crucial point, which today has been entirely forgotten. Marx considered that with the end of commodity production, the *political economy* born with it would *also come to an end*. It is in this sense that his work is a *critique* of political economy itself, rather than the work of an economist in the strict sense.[35] Hence the subtitle of *Capital*, the title of the *Contribution to the Critique* of 1859, not to mention the vast *brouillon* of 1858 which goes by the name of *Grundrisse der Kritik der politischen Ökonomie*.

'Value' is the product of human labour. 'Surplus-value', which is produced by human wage labour, is subdivided into profit and rent (besides, of course, the restitution of the wage). To *political economy*, which fails to coordinate or reduce these categories to a unity, rent appears as the product of land as such, as some *rudis indigestaque moles*; profit appears as a product of the notorious 'productivity of capital', that is of machines and raw materials as such; the wage appears as the product of labour. Physical, natural categories (land, means of production) and economic-social categories (profit, rent, etc.)—i.e. magnitudes which cannot be compared with one another—are fetishistically confused and muddled together, as Marx points out in his

famous chapter on 'The Trinity Formula'.[36] In Marx's own *critique* of political economy, on the other hand, the whole picture is decisively altered. The mysterious trinity of Capital, Land and Labour is swept away. Since 'value' is now considered as the objectification of human labour-power, the critical-scientific or anti-fetishistic discourse of *Capital* comes to coincide with the *self-consciousness of the working class* (a further proof of the unity of science and ideology). For just as wage labour, by recognizing the essence of 'value' and 'capital', sees that essence as an objectification of 'itself' (and hence reaches self-consciousness through this knowledge), the working class, by becoming conscious of itself, achieves—for profit and rent are forms derived from surplus value—the knowledge of the origin and basis of other classes and hence of society as a whole.[37]

This point serves to indicate the profound differences between Marx and his Marxist but (more or less consciously) Ricardian interpreters. They failed to grasp the organic unity between the *theory of value* and the *theory of fetishism* and therefore could not avoid confusing two totally distinct things. On the one hand, in dividing its total labour force between different employments, society must take account of the *labour-time* involved in each of these employments.[38] On the other hand, we have the specific way in which this law operates *under capitalism* where, in the absence of a conscious or planned division of social labour, the labour-time required by the various productive activities is presented as an *intrinsic quality* in the products themselves, as the 'value' of a 'thing'. This confusion between the law of labour-time (which applies to all societies) and its fetishized realization in the world of capital and of commodities, or between the *principles of planning and the law of value* (to bring the confusion up to date), is the root of modern revisionism, as is all too evident in the present economic debates in the Soviet Union. In Italy, it is the basis for the recent theoretical positions, which I cannot accept, of two theorists, Galvano della Volpe and Giulio Pietranera, to whom in other respects I am much indebted. First, in the case of della Volpe: to Sweezy's wholly correct statement that 'value and planning are as opposed to each other, and for the same reasons, as capitalism and socialism', della Volpe objects that 'between value and planning there is only a difference of *degree*, that is of *development*: there is nothing negatively "opposed" or "contrary" in the two terms'.[39] As for Pietranera, he follows Oscar Lange in referring to the 'market' and 'profit' in socialist society, not as survivals of bourgeois institutions that are inevitable in what is *par excellence a transitional* society but as 'rational criteria and indices of economic efficiency, and hence something *positive*, to be maintained in a planned socialist economy' —in other words as institutions *socialist* by their very nature.[40] This brings to mind a further, more recent error of della Volpe. The latter presents (in the most recent edition of *Rousseau e Marx*) the state under socialism—the state, mark you, i.e. the hypostasis of the 'general interest', which (as Marx says) has become independent and 'alien' from the generality of interests that compose it—not as a *survival*, but as a state which is wholly new, socialist in its inner structure. (Compare Lenin's conception of the state in *State and Revolution*: the presence in socialism of 'bourgeois right in regard to the distribution of consumption goods inevitably presupposes the existence of the *bourgeois state*, for right is nothing without an apparatus capable of *enforcing* the observance of the standards of right'. It follows that 'there remains for a time not only bourgeois right but even the bourgeois state without the bourgeoisie!')[41]

EQUIVALENCE AND SURPLUS VALUE

If we now turn to Bernstein, we can see that the first and most important consequence of his interpretation of 'value' as a mere 'mental construction' is that—since he is quite incapable of explaining value, and *a fortiori* surplus value as a result of capitalist *production*—he is obliged to transfer its point of origin from the sphere of production to the sphere of circulation and exchange, as though surplus value originated, in other words, in a violation of *commutative* justice, i.e. in a violation of the law of exchange on the basis of equivalents. He thus reinstated the old mercantilist conception of 'profit upon alienation', i.e. of the origin of profit in the difference between selling and buying prices (indeed, this is why 'consumer cooperatives' assume such importance in Bernstein's thought).

This viewpoint, which restores the schema of 'utopian socialism', and in this case Proudhon's account of exploitation as *theft* and hence of the *contradiction* between exploitation and legality, constitutes the essential core of 'revisionism'. For Marx modern *social inequality* or capitalist exploitation occurs simultaneously with the fullest development of *juridical-political equality*; here, on the contrary, juridical-political equality—and hence the modern representative State—becomes the instrument for the progressive elimination and dissolution of real inequalities, which seem arbitrarily produced rather than an organic consequence of the system as such.

The importance of this connection between equality and inequality in Marx's thought deserves emphasis here; besides its repercussions in political philosophy, which we shall examine, it also contained one of Marx's most important scientific achievements, his solution of the so-called 'paradox' of the law of value.

The law of value, according to Smith, is the law of the exchange of equivalents. It presupposes, besides the equal value of the commodities exchanged, the equality, as Marx pointed out, of the contracting parties in the act of exchange. In exchange the owners of commodities 'mutually recognize in each other the rights of *private proprietors*' establishing '*a juridical relation* which thus expresses itself in a contract, whether such contract be part of a developed legal system or not'.[42] Now the 'paradox' is that the production of commodities (production for exchange) becomes dominant for the first time only under purely capitalist conditions; yet just when the law of value should find its fullest application it seems to be contradicted by the existence of surplus value and exploitation, in other words, the emergence of an *unequal* exchange.

Smith, of course, reacted to this 'paradox' by turning away from a labour theory of value *contained*, to a theory of value based on *command* of labour, thus relegating the validity of the law of value to precapitalist conditions. Ricardo, while he showed the difference between equal exchange of commodities for commodities, and the inequality characterizing the exchange of commodities for labour-power (specifically capitalist exchange), failed to explain "how this *exception* could be in accordance with the law of value'.[43] Marx's theory explains the phenomenon of expropriation or of modern inequality precisely through the generalization of *property rights* or purely *juridical* equality.

Capitalism for Marx is the *generalization* of exchange; under capitalism all important social relations become exchange relations, starting with the productive relations themselves, which presuppose the buying and selling of labour-power. With this generalization of exchange a sphere of *juridical equality* is created, extended for the first time to all. The modern labourer is a holder of rights, a *free* person, and therefore is capable of entering into a contract, just as much as the employer of labour. 'Wage labour on a national scale, and hence also the capitalist mode of production, is not possible unless the labourer is personally free. It is based on the personal freedom of the labourer'.[44] Both the seller and buyer of labour-power are juridically equal persons because they are *private-proprietors*, owners of commodities.

However, according to Marx, what makes this relation of equality *formal* and conceals the real inequality is the fact that the property at the disposal of the worker (his own labouring *capacity*) is only property in *appearance*. In reality, it is the opposite, a state of need, so that 'if his capacity for labour remains unsold, the labourer derives no benefit from it, but rather he will feel it to be a cruel, nature-imposed necessity that this capacity has cost for its production a definite amount of the means of subsistence and that it will continue to do so for its reproduction'.[45]

In short, 'in the concept of the *free labourer*, it is already implicit', Marx writes, 'that he is a *pauper*, or virtually a pauper. According to his economic conditions he is *pure living working capacity*', which, since it is endowed with living requirements yet deprived of the means to satisfy them, is in itself not a *good* or form of *property*, but 'indigence from all points of view'.[46]

Hence the *generalization* of exchange—the typical phenomenon of modern capitalism—not only for the first time extends to all the sphere of juridical equality, making even the modern labourer into a *free person*; it achieves this liberation in a dual way, since the extension of contractual relations to production through the buying and selling of labour power means on the one hand that the laborer is free in the sense that he is 'a *free owner* of his own working capacity and of his own person' and on the other that he is free in the sense of *expropriated* from the means of production, i.e. 'deprived of *everything* necessary for the realization of his labour-power'.[47]

Now the application of equal rights or property rights to two persons, of whom only one is really a property owner, explains why this formal equality of rights is in reality the *law of the stronger*. This is Marx's point when he writes that 'the bourgeois economists have merely in view that production proceeds more smoothly with modern police than, e.g. under club law. They forget, however . . . that the law of the stronger, only in a different form, still survives even in their "constitutional State".'[48]

In conclusion: the law of value which is indeed a law of exchange of *equivalents*, as soon as it is realized and becomes *dominant*, reveals its true nature as the law of *surplus value* and capitalist appropriation.

The exchange of equivalents, the original operation with which we started, has now become turned round in such a way that there is only an *apparent* exchange. This is owing to the fact, first, that the capital which is exchanged for labour power is itself but a portion of *the product of others' labor appropriated without an equivalent*; and secondly, that this capital must not only be replaced by its producer but replaced together with an *added surplus*. . . . At first the rights of property seemed to us to be based

on a man's own labour. At least, some such assumption was necessary since only commodity owners with equal rights confronted each other, and the sole means by which a man could become possessed of the commodities of others was by alienating his own commodities; and these could be replaced by labour alone. Now, however, property turns out to be *the right* on the part of the capitalist to appropriate *the unpaid labour of others* or its product and to be the impossibility on the part of the labourer of appropriating his own product. The *separation of property from labour* has become the necessary consequence of a law that apparently originated in their identity.[49]

Hence Marx's opposition to 'utopian socialism' or 'revisionism' *ante litteram*, which, he claimed, 'especially in its French version' (Proudhon) saw socialism 'as the realization of the ideas of *bourgeois* society enunciated by the French Revolution'; as though the full realization of the 'rights of man', the principles of 1789—or, as we would now say, the republican Constitution—could dissolve the modern *social* inequalities which these legal and constitutional principles have claimed were the precondition for their own appearance, and which they have reinforced ever since. These socialists

affirm that exchange, exchange-value, etc. *originally* (in time) or in their *concept* (in their adequate form) are a system of liberty and equality for all, but have since been adulterated by money, capital, etc. . . . The answer to them is that exchange-value, or more precisely the monetary system, is in fact the system of equality and liberty, and that what seems to them to distort the subsequent development of the system is distortions immanent to that system itself, precisely the realization of the *equality* and freedom which reveal themselves as inequality and despotism. . . . To want exchange-value not to develop into capital, or the labour, which produces exchange-value, not to become wage-labour, is as pious as it is stupid. What distinguishes these gentlemen from the bourgeois apologists is, firstly, their awareness of the contradictions contained in the system; but secondly, the utopianism which prevents them from discerning the necessary distinction between the real and ideal forms of bourgeois society, and hence makes them want to undertake the vain task of trying to re-realize the ideal expression itself, while in fact this is only a reflected image of existing reality.[50]

Legal reforms cannot, therefore, grasp or transform the fundamental mechanisms of the system. This is so because, as Rosa Luxemburg acutely pointed out in the polemic against Bernstein, what distinguishes bourgeois society from preceding class societies, ancient or feudal, is the fact that class domination does not rest on 'inherited' or *unequal* rights as previously, but on real economic relations mediated by *equality* of rights.

No law obliges the proletariat to submit itself to the yoke of capitalism. Poverty, the lack of means of production, obliges the proletariat to submit itself to capital. . . . And no law in the world can give to the proletariat the means of production while it remains in the framework of bourgeois society, for no laws, but economic development, has torn the means of production from the producers. . . . Neither is the exploitation

inside the system of wage labour based on laws. The level of wages is not fixed by legislation but by economic factors. The phenomenon of capitalist exploitation does not rest on a legal disposition. . . . In short, the fundamental relation of domination of the capitalist class cannot be transformed by means of legislative reforms, on the basis of capitalist society, because these relations have not been introduced by bourgeois laws, nor have they received the form of such laws.

In our legislative system, as Rosa Luxemburg points out, not one legal formulation of the present class domination can be found. 'How then can one overcome wage slavery gradually, by legal means, when this has never been expressed in legislation?' That, she continues, is

why people who pronounce themselves in favour of the method of legislative reform *in place of* and *in contradistinction to* the conquest of political power and social revolution, do not really choose a more tranquil, calmer and slower road to the *same goal*, but a *different goal*. Instead of taking a stand for the establishment of a new society, they stand for surface modifications of the old society. If we follow the political conceptions of revisionism, we arrive at the same conclusion that is reached when we follow the economic theories. They aim not towards the realization of *socialism*, but the reform of *capitalism*, not the suppression of the system of wage labour but the 'diminution' of exploitation, that is the suppression of the *abuses* of capitalism instead of the suppression of capitalism itself.[51]

NOTES

1. Marx, *Capital*, Vol. I, p. 80.

2. Ibid., p. 81 and n.

3. This identification is already present in the first pages of *The Wealth of Nations*, where Smith identifies the 'division of labour' with 'exchange'. For this question, see Sweezy, op. cit., pp. 23-4, and Rosa Luxemburg, *Einführung in die Nationalökonomie*, in *Ausgemählte Reden und Schriften*, Vol. I, Berlin, 1951, p. 675.

4. Marx, *Theories of Surplus-Value*, Part II, London, 1969, p. 172: Ricardo 'does not even examine the form of value—the particular form which labour assumes as the substance of value. He only examines the magnitude of value'; in consequence, 'Ricardo is rather to be reproached for very often losing sight of this "real" or "absolute value" and only retaining "relative" and "comparative value".' And in Part III (Marx-Engels, *Werke*, Vol. 26.3, p. 28): 'The error Ricardo makes is that he is only concerned with the *magnitude of value* . . .' Cf. also p. 135. Schumpeter, too (*History of Economic Analysis*, New York, 1954, pp. 596-7) sees this as the most important distinction between Ricardo's theory of value and Marx's theory of value.

5. Marx, *Theories of Surplus-Value*, Part III (op. cit., p. 127).

6. Marx, *Capital*, Vol. I, p. 44.

7. Ibid., p. 38.

8. K. Kautsky, *Karl Marx's ökonomische Lehren*, Jena, 1887.

9. R. Hilferding, *Böhm-Bawerk's Marx-Kritik* (Offprint from *Marx Studien*, Vol. I), Vienna, 1904.

10. Luxemburg, *Einführung in die Nationalökonomie*, op. cit., pp. 412-731.

11. P. Sweezy, op. cit., p. 30.

12. Ibid., p. 31.

13. Op. cit., p. 22.

14. Marx, *Capital*, Vol. III, pp. 871 ff.

15. For this critique of Smith by Marx, see *Theories of Surplus-Value*, Part I, London n.d., pp. 71-2.

16. E. Böhm-Bawerk, *Zum Abschluss des Marxschen Systems* (in a volume of writings in honour of Karl Knies), Vienna, 1896; English translation by Paul Sweezy: *Karl Marx and the Close of His System*, New York, 1949, pp. 73-4. Hilferding's reply to Böhm-Bawerk, which is the best Marxist critique of the theory of marginal utility, is nonetheless deficient on this question—cf. Hilferding, op. cit., p. 127: 'We have in fact nothing more than a disregard by Marx of the specific forms in which use-value manifests itself.'

17. E. Böhm-Bawerk, op. cit., pp. 68-9. The same critique is to be found in E. Calogero, *Il metodo dell' economia e il marxismo*, Bari, 1967, pp. 37 ff.

18. M. Dobb, *Political Economy and Capitalism*, London, 1960, pp. 14-15.

19. Cf. *Capital*, Vol. I, pp. 77-8.

20. Ibid., p. 38.

21. Ibid., p. 39.

22. Ibid., p. 74.

23. Marx, 'Critique of the Gotha Programme', in Marx and Engels, *Selected Works*, op. cit., p. 324.

24. Marx, *Contribution to the Critique of Political Economy*, op. cit., p. 32.

25. Some clarifications may help the reader to follow more easily the argument presented here. Where labour is in common (the simplest example is the primitive community) *social* labour is simply the sum of individual, concrete labours: it is their totality and does not exist separately from its parts. In commodity production, where social labour appears instead in the form of *equal* or *abstract* labour, it is not only calculated apart from the individual concrete labours, but acquires a distinct and independent existence. An individual labour of, say, ten hours may as social labour be worth five. For example: 'The introduction of power-looms into England' meant that 'the hand-loom weavers, as a matter of fact, continued to require the same time as before; but for all that, the product of one hour of their labour represented after the change only half an hour's social labour and consequently fell to one-half its former value' (cf. *Capital*, Vol. I, p. 39). This *self-abstraction* of labour from the concrete labouring subject, this acquisition by it of independence from man, culminates in the form of the modern wage-labourer. The inversion whereby labour no longer appears as a manifestation of man but man as a manifestation of labour assumes here a real and palpable existence. The wage-earner is *owner* of his working capacity, his labour-power, i.e. of his physical and intellectual energies. These energies, which are in reality inseparable from the living personality, are *abstracted* (or separated) from man to such an extent that they become *commodities*, i.e. as a 'value' which has the man as its 'body' (or 'use-value'). The wage earner is merely the vehicle, the support of the commodity labour-power. The subject is this commodity, this private property; the man is the predicate. It is not that labour-power is a possession of the man's but rather that the man becomes a property or mode of being of 'private property'. 'For the man who is nothing more than a *labourer*', Marx writes, 'his human qualities exist, to the extent that he is a labourer, only insofar as they are for him *foreign* capital.' Indeed, insofar as it manages to realize itself on the market as a commodity (in purchase and sale), labour power becomes part of capital. This is the part that Marx defined as 'variable capital', as we know. The inversion to which we referred reappears here in a more precise form: as the 'value' of labour-power, which, in that as a 'value' it is itself part of capital, annexes the *use* of a working capacity, that is the labourer himself. In his labour, the man does not belong to himself, but to whoever has purchased his labour-power. His energies are no longer 'his own' but 'someone else's'. The productive capacity of his labour becomes the *'productive power of capital'*. This 'self-estrangement', or acquisition by labour of independence from man, culminates in modern industry, where it is not the labourer who 'applies the conditions of labour, but inversely, the conditions of labour which apply the labourer' (cf. also *Capital*, Vol. I, p. 422: 'In the factory we have a lifeless mechanism independent of the workman who becomes its mere living appendage.'); modern industry, which, for Marx, represents 'the essence of capitalist production or, if you will, wage labour; labour alienated from itself which confronts the wealth it creates as the wealth of a stranger, its own productivity as the productivity of its product, its own enrichment as self-impoverishment, its social power as the power of society over it' (*Theorien über den Mehrwert*, Part III, op. cit., p. 255).

26. Marx, *Contribution to the Critique of Political Economy*, op. cit., p. 30.

27. Marx, *The Poverty of Philosophy*, New York, 1969, p. 54.

28. L. Feuerbach, *Grundsätze der Philosophie der Zukunft* (Principles of the Philosophy of the Future), in *Sämtliche Werke*, ed. W. Bolin and F. Jodl, Stuttgart, 1959, Vol. II, pp. 227 and 243.

29. Marx, *Capital*, Vol. I, p. 72.

30. Marx, *Contribution to the Critique of Political Economy*, op. cit., pp. 29, 95.

31. Marx, *Wage Labour and Capital*, in *Selected Works*, op. cit., p. 82.

32. Marx and Engels, *The German Ideology*, London, 1965, pp. 82, 45-6.

33. Marx, '1857 Introduction' to *A Contribution to the Critique of Political Economy*, op. cit., p. 209.

34. *Theorien über den Mehrwert*, Part III, op. cit., p. 255. 'In proportion as political economy developed—and this development, at least in its basic principles, found its highest expression in Ricardo—it represented labour as the only element of value. . . . But to the extent that labour is conceived as the *only* source of exchange-value, . . . 'capital' is conceived by the same economists and especially Ricardo (but even more by Torrens, Malthus, Bailey, etc., after him) as the regulator of production, the source of wealth and the goal of all production. . . . In this contradiction, political economy merely expressed the essence of capitalist production, or if you like of wage labour: Labour alienated from itself, to which the wealth it creates is counterposed as the wealth of a stranger, its own productivity as the productivity of its product, its own enrichment as self-impoverishment, its social power as the power of society over it.'

35. This theme of the end of political economy was taken up by Hilferding. *Böhm-Bawerk's Criticism of Marx*, op. cit., pp. 133-4; by Luxemburg, *Einführung*, op. cit., p. 491; and finally was central to the work of the Russian economist and member of the Trotskyist opposition, E. Preobrazhensky, *The New Economics*, Oxford, 1966. An extremely interesting discussion of these problems can be found in Karl Korsch, *Karl Marx*, London, 1938.

36. Marx, *Capital*, Vol. III, chapter 48.

37. This point was developed by Lukács in *History and Class Consciousness*, op. cit.

38. Marx, *Grundrisse der Kritik der politischen Ökonomie*, Berlin, 1953, p. 98: 'In conditions of communal production the determination of time obviously remains essential. The less time it takes society to produce corn, cattle, etc., the more time it gains for other forms of production, material or spiritual. As in the case of a single individual, the universality of his development, of his pleasures, of his activity, depends upon the way he economizes his time. The economy of time, ultimately all economy is reduced to this. Society must distribute its time functionally so as to obtain a production in accordance with all its needs; so the individual must also divide his time correctly to acquire knowledge in the right proportions and to fulfil the various demands on his activity. In conditions of production in common the first economic law remains, therefore, the economy of time, the planned distribution of labour-time between the different branches of production. This law becomes even more important under these conditions. But all this is quite distinct from the measurement of exchange-values (labours or labour products) by "labour-time".'

39. G. della Volpe, *Chiave della dialettica storica*, Rome, 1964, p. 32 n.

40. G. Pietranera, *Capitalismo ed economia*, Turin, 1966, p. 236.

41. Lenin, *Selected Works*, op. cit., Vol. II, pp. 342-3.

42. Marx, *Capital*, Vol. I, p. 84.

43. Marx, *Theorien über den Mehrwert*, Part III, op. cit., p. 170.

44. Ibid., p. 424.

45. Marx, *Capital*, Vol. I, p.173.

46. Marx, *Grundrisse*, op. cit., p. 497.

47. Marx, *Capital*, Vol. I, p. 169.

48. Marx, 'Introduction' to *A Contribution to the Critique of Political Economy*, op. cit., p. 193.

49. Marx, *Capital*, Vol. I, pp. 583-4.

50. Marx, *Grundrisse*, op. cit., p. 160.

51. Rosa Luxemburg, *Social Reform or Revolution?*, op. cit., pp. 50-2.

23

There Is Nothing Simple About A Commodity

JESSE GEORGE SCHWARTZ

Assistant Professor of Economics at San Diego State University

"A commodity appears at first sight, a very trivial thing, and easily understood. Its analysis shows that it is, in reality, a very queer thing, abounding in metaphysical subtleties and theological niceties."
—Karl Marx

PART I

A. Exchange-Value Becomes Independent

Ricardo begins his *Principles* with a discussion of the peculiar form taken by the products of human labor under capitalism; he does not consider previous social forms. He starts with a commodity, the elemental social cell, the smallest unit wherein social mediations are discernible. His inquiry is exclusively concerned with a form of capitalism in which production, exchange, money, circulation, and banking have fully matured; as he says, his study is directed to "such commodities only as can be increased in quantity by the exertion of human industry and on the production of which competition operates without restraint."

Now a commodity, Ricardo tells us, possesses two qualities. "The one may be called *value in use*; the other *value in exchange*." The first refers to the size, texture, shape, structure, and so on of the commodity. These physical properties make it a useful object. The second, the power to exchange with other commodities, is purely social. Use-value is the abode of lovers of tangible facts. Here they can appeal to the certainty of perception to assure us, say, of the texture, color, or weave of a piece of cloth. This is the realm of solid fact. What indeed can vie with it in solidity? The "man of common sense" has always applauded as academic economists have sought to "measure" use-value and fill textbooks with an unceasing rumination over utility, tastes, and indifference curves.

The other category, "exchange-value," has proven somewhat less amenable. Indeed, the power of one commodity to exchange for others has long been a subject of speculation. Aristotle pondered it, as did scholars during the Middle Ages and much later William Petty and Benjamin Franklin. In previous social forms exchange occurred mainly on the periphery or boundaries of com-munities, while the production and distribution of useful objects within them was settled according to custom or decree. Only after a very gradual process, in the late Middle Ages, do we see exchange seizing hold of relations within communities. Perhaps, at first in Italian and Hanseatic maritime republics as Engels tells us,[1] labor began to be sold as a commodity replacing earlier forms of bondage, indenture, and serfdom. By the nineteenth century exchange had reached a level of universality, so that the general and abstract qualities of a commodity could be discerned in theory. This was accomplished by Karl Marx.

B. The Theory of Value

Marx's theory represents the fullest and most complete statement of the notion of value. Let us outline it and view Ricardo's work from its perspective.

Any commodity, no matter how humble, can exchange for an unlimited variety of other commodities. Potatoes in sufficient quantity can exchange for a watch, a house, or gold. Consider the expression

$$(1) \qquad A \text{ (potatoes)} = B \text{ (watches)} = C \text{ (houses)} = D \text{ (gold)}$$

where a quantity of potatoes is expressed in terms of watches, houses, and innumerable other commodities. How is it that things so different can exchange as equivalents?

Here the voice of common sense might say that it is their "price" that brings them into equality. This is simply repeating our question. True, we can express the watch, house, or gold in terms of potatoes and thus arrive at "potato prices," if you will. This is but an expression for the exchange-value of watches, houses, and gold in terms of one particular use-value, namely, potatoes. The point is that the potatoes can be compared with the watch or the house only because they are qualitatively identical, homogeneous magnitudes. The potatoes, watch, and house exist as values, as things that are equal and different from their existence as potatoes, watches, and so on. The potatoes here are full-fledged citizens of the world of commodities with the inalienable right to exchange, in sufficient quantity, with watches, houses, gold, and so forth. These mirror the value of the potatoes.

Let us try to understand something more of value.

The man of common sense looking at the exchange

1 watch = 50 pounds of potatoes

sees only the value of the watch as expressed in so many potatoes and the value of the watch is nothing apart from this. Apart from its "potato price," no meaning can be given to the "value" of the watch.[2] "Hear! Hear!" exclaims the man of common sense. If, the next day, a watch should exchange for 60 pounds of potatoes or 40 pounds of potatoes, well then, that is its value.

This is another way of saying that value denotes *nothing*.[3] If one watch equals 50 pounds of potatoes, what is the value of one watch? Fifty pounds of potatoes. Of 50 pounds of potatoes? One watch. Because one watch equals 50 pounds of potatoes and 50 pounds of potatoes equals one watch, it follows that

the value of one watch is equal to one watch, and, by the same reasoning, the value of 50 pounds of potatoes is equal to 50 pounds of potatoes.

(Very sound. You know where you're at with a theory like that.) This paralysis of the ability to abstract, this narrowing of reality to factual immediacy, reduces economics either to a cataloging of each and every of the myriad million exchanges occurring daily or to an equally empty conjecture that "everything depends on everything."

Furthermore, if we are restricted to saying that value is whatever has occurred in exchange, how then is it possible to express the price of a palace in terms of potatoes, or a milling machine in terms of a house? We can indeed do this, though the exchanges in question have never occurred. This would not be possible unless there is a substance common to both palaces and potatoes.

It is not with the mere fact of exchange that we are dealing. Watches have no intrinsic property that makes them exchange with a certain quantity of potatoes. Only because the watches and potatoes are values can the value of one be expressed in terms of the other. The watch must have a value independent of potatoes and must be equal to a third thing. "What," we may ask, "is the difference between a nail in one's boot and Pushkin?" Unless the watch and potatoes can be subsumed in a common space of commodities, we have as much chance of comparing them! Their existence as commodities is a purely social creation. Their separate existences as things is brought into unity by the social substance common to each.[4] This can only be social labor. Now considering expression (1) representing exchange in general, we see that it is a purely quantitative relation and abstracts from the specific qualities of commodities. In exchange, the particular qualities of commodities are subsumed and only the quantitative relation, the proportion in which the commodities exchange, has any importance. Now various concrete labors of farming, watchmaking, carpentry, and so on have produced the commodities. With the reduction of useful things to values, concrete labor is subsumed into universal abstract labor. The qualities of the commodities disappear when they are considered as values; the labor that has produced them also has no particular quality; it is abstract, universal social labor brought about by the universal alienation of labor.

As humanity in the West is totally immersed in commodity production, an individual understandably finds it hard to gaze with wonderment at the historical specificity of a mode of production where every commodity is something different from its own physical makeup. That a commodity is exchangeable for any other commodity, that is, so many potatoes for a palace, so much cloth for gold, this universal exchangeability demonstrates that exchange-value has become independent, separate from the mundane properties of potatoes or cloth. This universal exchangeability shows that all act as social labor and can be exchanged for other commodities in proportion to the amount of social labor they contain.

This remarkable independence of exchange-value from use-value finds its fullest expression in money. Here one commodity is set aside, and the others are measured in terms of the use-value of this one; that is, so many ounces of gold for so many potatoes or watches. We can rewrite this expression as

$$1 \text{ potato} = x \text{ gold}; \quad 1 \text{ watch} = y \text{ gold}; \quad 1 \text{ house} = z \text{ gold}$$

In this way we arrive at money prices of potatoes, watches, and houses.

Indeed, the concept of value first arose from a consideration of the properties of money. In money, commodities acquire a definite *measure* of their value in terms of the use-value of some particular commodity. Indeed, when a commodity is sold, transformed into money, we see clearly its exchange-value acquiring an independent existence. But note our path of reasoning from the nature of a commodity as a value to money to price; a progress from the essence to the phenomenological form. Consider:

Commodity	Money
Labor of private individuals transformed into abstract social labor.	Universal exchangeability; different magnitudes measured in terms of one exclusive use-value.
Individual labor represented as social labor.	Individual price related to total price.
Exchange-value becomes independent from use-value.	Price separate from use-value.

This underlines that the power of one commodity to exchange with any other (potatoes for a palace) reflects how the labor of private individuals must be a proportionate part of the labor of society. That the price of a commodity is separate from its use-value and is related to the prices of all other commodities reflects that exchange-value is independent of use-value and that commodities are but different expressions of the same substance.

Had we followed the Samuel Baileys of this world (who insist on designating as "real" that which can only be counted on ten fingers) by starting with price and not value, we would be doing violence to a world of understanding. Only by seeing the inner structure that prices hide can we speak of them meaningfully, otherwise we are limited to repeating "a price . . . is a price . . . is a price."

> Labour-time is the measure of both gold and commodities, and gold becomes the measure of value only because all commodities are measured in terms of gold; it is consequently merely an illusion created by the circulation process to suppose that money makes commodities commensurable. On the contrary, it is only the commensurability of commodities as materialized labour-time which converts gold into money.[5]

Money then is an intimation of the secret language of commodities.

C. "One Beaver Should Naturally Exchange for, or Be Worth, Two Deer"

With the rudiments of the theory of value, we can discuss Ricardo's achievement. First of all, we see that when Ricardo speaks of labor, it is not of the particular labor in potato growing, watchmaking, or house building he talks, but of abstract social labor. He contents himself with presupposing it and considers only the quantity or *magnitude* of this abstract labor contained in different commodities.

Taking this abstract labor as "the foundation of the exchangeable value of all things," without reflecting upon it was bound to encumber his doctrine.

For example, he invokes Adam Smith's "rude and early state" as justification for his theory of value. Recall Smith's famous example of a society of hunters—if it took twice as long to kill a beaver as a deer, then one beaver should "naturally" exchange for two deer. Smith's example does not answer altogether to Ricardo's purpose. In this mythical economy, trade consists of the exchange of the labor of one sort, beaver hunting, for another sort, deer hunting. Now these are specific types of labor and we are not told what has brought them into equality.

Why is the expenditure of the sort of labor in beaver hunting a measure of that in deer hunting or vice versa? There is no natural property of beaver that permits it to exchange for two deer. Exchange here would be settled by custom, or chance, or even whim. Only where specific labor has been reduced to a common standard or measure is exchange governed by general laws. This occurs only with commodity production seizing all sectors and labor itself becoming a commodity. Unfortunately Ricardo rests his theory for capitalism on such a primitive basis.

But this example does show, strikingly enough, that the rate at which commodities exchange does not determine their value, rather their value determines the rate at which they exchange. That is, *value is prior to exchange*. The labor materialized in beaver or deer hunting determines that they exchange 1:2. If we could not ascertain value except where an exchange had occurred, how could we estimate the value of a house or airplane in terms of potatoes?

D. Adam Smith Tries to Speak the Language of Commodities

Ricardo's theory of value is a further development and critique of Smith's view. Indeed, much of his chapter on "Value" is an ongoing argument with Smith. Let us consider, for a moment, some of Smith's ideas.

As we have seen, he took labor to be the source of exchange-value in his "rude and early state." Here the whole product of labor goes to the laborer. At this level of abstraction, commodities exchange for equivalents, as values. This, according to Smith, requires that part of the labor of the worker must pay his wages and another part must be due for profits. But then this bucolic social order of small artisans gives way to one in which instruments, raw materials, machinery, and land are appropriated by one class as capital, confronting a mass of humanity who live by selling their labor-power.

At first Smith maintained that here part of the labor of the worker goes to pay his wages and another part goes for profit. That is, with the separation of materialized labor (machinery, equipment, raw materials, and so forth) from living labor, the worker no longer receives the full value of what he produces. In a remarkable anticipation of Marx's theory of surplus-value, Smith sees profit and rent as coming from that portion of the product of labor remaining after wages. In other words, Smith clearly sees how the profit of the capitalist is an appropriation of the unpaid labor of others. Then he does a remarkable reversal. In one sentence he says,

As the price or exchange value of every particular commodity taken separately resolves itself into some one or other or all of these three parts

so that of all the commodities which compose the whole annual labour of every country, taken complexly, must resolve itself into the same three parts, and be parcelled out among different inhabitants of the country, either as wages of their labour, the profits of their stock or the rent of their land.

He clearly resolves here the value of either an individual commodity or the total annual product into profit, rent, and wages. But two sentences later, "Wages, profit and rent are the three original sources of all revenue as well as all exchangeable value."[6] Now he declares wages, profit, and rent to be independent elements that are added up to form exchange-value. He goes on to say that there exist average or ordinary rates of rent, of profit, and of wages, independently determined. The natural price of a commodity, he goes on to tell us, is equal to the sum of these three components when at their natural levels. Instead of having their source in value created by labor now wages, profit and rent become the source of value. This is merely a recitation of how an individual capitalist sees things—so much for wages, so much for profit, so much for rent.

It puts the question of exchange-value at one remove. Rather than the value of the commodity itself, we must consider its components and are still at a loss as to how to find them. There is also a logical error here in that it assumes that the total social product is resolvable into only wages, profit, and rent, thereby neglecting constant capital. Smith had to assume what he did, or he would have had to convince us not only of "natural" rates of wages, profits, and rent but of machinery, buildings, raw materials, and semifinished goods as well. He had to omit these elements of constant capital—"For otherwise he would have to say: The value of a commodity consists of wages, profit, rent and that part of the value of the commodity which does not consist of wages, profit, rent."[7]

There is nothing simple about a commodity.

E. Smith's Confusion of Tongues— Materialized and Living Labor

Ricardo everywhere contested Smith's second conception. He felt that not merely in Smith's "rude and early state" but even in circumstances of full-blown capitalism that Smith's first conception was true. As we have said this requires on the one hand a mass of instruments and means of production appropriated by a small number of people and a mass of humanity on the other who have only one commodity, their life energy, to sell. This they exchange for wages with which they replenish their muscles, nerves, and tissues. Viewing this as a process, we can say that only a part of the labor of the workers materialized in their product is returned to them. The rest becomes the property of another who blithely gives the worker chits or claims on each round, to a fraction of their product. Thus the labor materialized in wage-goods exchanges for a greater quantity of labor than itself.

Ricardo accepts this as the way things are under capitalism. He felt that not merely in Smith's "rude and early state," where the whole product of labor goes to the laborer, but even in circumstances of full-fledged capitalism, where only part goes to the worker and the rest goes to capitalists and landlords, that

Smith's first conception was true. Regardless of how the product is distributed—no matter how much goes to A or B—this does not affect its value. Value is created in production and unaffected regardless of whether the mass of commodities is owned by A or B or both.

Regardless of how much or little of their product is received by the workers, he held that if the quantity of labor regulated exchange when *all* was received by the workers, it should continue to do so when only a part is received by them. Now if only a part of the value of the product goes to the laborer, it follows that the materialized labor in wages commands a greater quantity of labor than it contains. But the exchange of living for materialized labor is not done on the basis of equivalents. This is not a mere exchange between commodities but between commodities acting as capital on the one hand and labor-power on the other.

Imagine a society where individual workers produce and sell their commodities. Each worker expends a quantity of labor in producing some commodity that he exchanges for an equal value of the other commodities. Therefore, each worker receives the full value of his product in the form of use-values produced by other workers. In effect, each worker exchanges his living labor for an equivalent quantity of the materialized labor of others. Here a definite quantity of materialized labor always commands an equal quantity of living labor. We are, formally speaking, indifferent as to whether we take labor commanded or materialized, "value of labor," or "quantity of labor" as our measure. When Smith finds that under capitalism a quantity of materialized labor commands a greater quantity of living labor, he should have realized that "value of labor" and "quantity of labor" are no longer identical. As Ricardo says forthrightly,

> . . . if the reward of the labourer were always in proportion to what he produced, the quantity of labour bestowed on a commodity, and the quantity of labour which that commodity would purchase, would be equal . . . but they are not equal.[8]

This peculiar exchange between capital and labor-power so impressed Smith that he no longer maintained his first conception, as we have seen. Rather he felt that value could be "added up" from "natural" rates of wages, profits, and rent. Furthermore, he drops his first conception of the determination of the value of commodities by the labor required for their production and takes as his measure the quantity of living labor that a definite quantity of commodities can command or, which is the same thing, the quantity of commodities that a definite quantity of labor can command. In other words, he takes wages to be a measure. But as Marx comments:

> The value of labour, or rather of labour-power, changes like that of any other commodity and is in no way specifically different from the value of other commodities. Here value is made the measuring rod and the basis for the explanation of value—so we have a vicious circle.[9]

Ricardo believed that Adam Smith was guilty of the rather obtuse error of taking "as two equivalent expressions the labour materialized in a commodity and that which it could command." But Smith nowhere asserts that "these were two equivalent expressions." On the contrary, he argues:

> Because in capitalist production, the wage of the worker is *no* longer equal to his product, therefore, the quantity of labour which a commodity costs and the quantity of commodities that a worker can purchase with this labour are two different things—*for this very reason* the relative quantity of labour contained in commodities ceases to determine their value, which is now determined rather by *value of labour*, by the quantity that I can purchase, or command with a given amount of commodities. Thus the value of labour (or the compensation paid for labour) becomes the measure of value.[10]

Ricardo does not understand the causes for Smith's abandoning the theory of value when dealing with capitalism. As he says:

> Adam Smith thought, that as in the early stages of society, all of the produce of labour belonged to the labourer, and after stock was accumulated, a part went to profits, that accumulation, necessarily, without any regard to the different degrees of durability of capital, or any other circumstance whatever, raised the prices or exchangeable value of commodities, and consequently that their value was no longer regulated by the quantity of labour necessary to their production. In opposition to him, I maintain that it is not because capital accumulates, that exchangeable value varies, but it is in all stages of society, owing only to 2 causes: one the more or less quantity of labour required, the other the greater or less durability of capital:—that the former is never superseded by the latter, but is only modified by it.[11]

Ricardo thinks that it was only because labor no longer obtains its entire product, that is, because a part goes to the owner of "stock," that Smith no longer held his first conception. Thus he reads into Smith his own overriding concern with distribution.

But Smith's difficulty arises from the inner essence of capitalism. As Marx points out:

> Adam Smith feels the difficulty of deducing the exchange between capital and labour from the law that determines the exchange of commodities, since the former apparently rests on quite opposite and contradictory principles. And indeed the contradiction could not be solved so long as capital was set directly against labour instead of labour-power. Adam Smith was well aware that the labour-time expended on the reproduction and maintenance of labour-power is very different from the labour, which it [i.e., labour-power] itself can perform.[12]

Therefore Smith is "startled,"[13] as Marx says, to find that the general law that commodities exchange according to the labor materialized in them ceases to apply in the exchange between capital and wage-labor, materialized, and living labor.

There is another reason why he drops the general law. We have seen when a commodity functions as capital it can command or exert power over more of the labor of others than it itself contains. When Smith adopts labor commanded as his standard he brings this into relief.

Smith's labor-commanded measure, although not scientifically correct, nonetheless reflected a poignant truth—the unequal exchange between capital and wage-labor. Indeed, "commanded" bespeaks coercion; it hints of something very different from a mere exchange of commodities among free, equal, and independent sellers and buyers of commodities, which ideologists have tried so hard to demonstrate as an eternal law of nature and reason. The essence of capital is its power to appropriate labor without exchange, without an equivalent. It is not merely that capital commands labor, it is the command over *unpaid* labor.

"Something is happening here, but you don't know what it is, do you Mr. Smith?"!

"There is nothing simple about a commodity."[14]

F. The Necessity for a Standard of Value

There is still a *hidden reason* as Marx[15] tells us for Smith's view that as soon as capital and wage-labor intervene it is the labor commanded, not materialized, in a commodity that regulates its value. It is that labor has a *permanent* relative value with respect to corn. Smith, taking corn to denote food in general, reasoned that so long as labor is sold at its "natural price," it will exchange for a certain quantity of corn, or a given quantity of corn will always exchange for the same amount of labor. The one will always command the same use-value of the other. For this reason, we can take either the corn or labor that a commodity could purchase as a measure of its value.

Suppose that the labor expended per bushel of corn falls by half. A bushel of corn would, by Smith's assumption, purchase a week's labor as before. Smith would say that the value of corn is unchanged as it commands the same amount of labor; he would also have to say that its value has fallen as it can command a lesser quantity of other commodities. How then can we find out whether the value of the corn has changed? Let us return to our discussion of exchange for a moment.

Suppose that we observe a quantity of potatoes to exchange for wrist-watches in the proportions

50 pounds of potatoes = 2 watches

Then suppose that one day we find

50 pounds of potatoes = 1 watch

We are at a loss to say whether a greater quantity of labor has been expended in making watches or a lesser quantity in making potatoes, or a greater quantity in making both though proportionately more in watches or a lesser quantity in both, though lesser still in potatoes.

Suppose we know for certain that the value of potatoes has remained unchanged, then we can say with confidence that the value of a watch has risen. We can call potatoes an *external measure* of value. It is a commodity in terms of which we can measure the values of the other commodities. We can contrast this to an *immanent measure*.

Suppose the labor materialized in the potatoes and watches doubled. We would still have

50 pounds of potatoes = 2 watches

The value of watches in terms of our external measure, potatoes, remains unchanged.

Only with an immanent measure can we ascertain that the absolute value of watches has changed, that more labor has been expended. We can also see that relative value cannot change without a change in absolute value, but the converse is not true.

As we have argued, the rate at which potatoes and watches exchange does not determine their value, but their value determines the rate at which they exchange. (If there were no immanent measure common to both, the value of potatoes could not be expressed in terms of watches before it had been exchanged against watches.)

We can thus distinguish between *external* and *immanent* measures of value. As the former must be a commodity, its value must be variable and subject to the same fluctuations as any commodity.

We have tried to show that the very nature of value necessitates that one commodity be taken as the measure of value of the rest. Such a commodity—gold, for instance—serves as money allowing the relative values of other commodities to be measured in terms of it. If the value of gold changes, it does so to an equal degree with respect to all commodities. The money price of a commodity, therefore, is a relative measure of its value.

Before watches, however, can be expressed in potatoes or gold, the watches and the rest must be represented as equivalents, as expressions of the same substance. How the potatoes have been made qualitatively equal to watches so that the measurement can occur is left unanswered by Ricardo.

An immanent measure of value, on the other hand, cannot be another commodity, another value, and consequently cannot be subject to the same variations in value as other commodities. It is the common substance that renders physical objects qualitatively equal so that they differ only quantitatively. This is labor-time, in its unique form as abstract social labor,[15a] which is found only under capitalism. It should not be thought that labor time is the answer to Ricardo's puzzle of an invariable standard in the same way as corn, gold, wages, or silver have been proposed at various times. The latter can play a role only in finding the magnitude of value, wherein they serve as a form of money, presupposing value. Labor-time, on the other hand, qualitatively transforms useful objects into values and is their substance as values.

This is not to deny the historic meaning and validity of the search for a standard of value. Ostensibly it arose from a need to compare the value of commodities in different times. It could be used, for example, to find whether

the rise in the price of corn sold in the eighteenth century was due to the circumstances of its production or to the medium in which it was measured. If we knew that the value of gold remained the same during this time, then by observing the proportions in which corn exchanges with gold we can ascertain the variations in the value of corn, knowing for certain that our measurements are not obfuscated by changes in our standard. But such a rather academic concern concealed, as Marx tells us, a profound question, that of the nature of value itself.[16] The mazy entanglements of the classicals, in their effort to define value in terms of some particular value, were inevitable stages in the inquiry. It culminated in the discovery that abstract social labor is the substance of value. "A quantity of labor has no value, is not a commodity, but is that which transforms commodities into values, it is their common substance."[17]

Scholars have assiduously rummaged the lumberyard of commodities for an "invariable standard." Scattered in the archaeological museum of bygone doctrine we find corn, gold, wages, or "silver picked up on the seashore in a day." Of late there has been an ingenious attempt by Piero Sraffa to construct, artificially, a "standard commodity" from a mass of commodities. All these can only measure with respect to themselves. If the value of corn, gold, wages, and so on changes, it does so with respect to all commodities. Hence the relative values remain unchanged. Rather than go through the cumbersome and tedious task of expressing values in silver or corn, it is just as well to simply read them from a price list—to express them in money. One external measure is as good as another. Insofar as Ricardo sought his "invariable measure" in terms of some commodity, he might just as well have chosen money. Hence Marx concludes, "The problem of finding an 'invariable measure of value' is thereby eliminated."[18]

PART II

A. Ricardo Progresses from Value to Capital

Ricardo was seeking to establish a general law of exchange with an image of individual commodity producers in mind. Now he tries to apply it to the realm of wage-labor and capital. That is, past labor materialized in machinery and raw materials is concentrated in a few hands and confronts living labor. Here we have not only an independent expression of value, as in money, but dynamic value, value in the process of expansion.

Ricardo begins by considering the relation of the value of raw materials, semifinished products, and machines to the finished product. These simply transfer their value to the product, though their use-values undergo the most varied changes. The entire value of cotton cloth is transferred to the shirt, whereas only a small part of the value of the weaving machine is also given up; the more durable an instrument, the less value it transfers to the product. The value of a commodity is simply the sum of the materialized and living labor expended on it. The formal difference between the two sorts of labor does not affect its value. Marx stops and asks at this point, "If this difference is of no significance in the determination of the value of commodities, why does it assume such decisive importance when past labour (capital) is exchanged against living labour?"[19] How it is that the exchange of past for living labor is not on

the basis of equivalents, that the one commands a greater quantity of the other? (If only Ricardo had inquired further!)

Ricardo continues his discussion of capital in section IV by classifying it as "circulating" or "fixed" according to its period of turnover. (Smith, by the way, had no need to make such a distinction because in his time, means of production of relatively long life were rare.)

B. Ricardo Bypasses Mediations to Confound Value and Price

With this, Ricardo leaps in with a uniform rate of profit. How he jumps from exchange value to profit and, what is more, a general rate of profit, is difficult to understand. Instead of presupposing a general rate of profit, he should have tried to explain it. In order to scientifically discuss these matters, it seems that at the very least we must go from value to money, to the nature of prices, and then to the creation and functioning of capital. But Ricardo, in bypassing these questions, encumbers his doctrine, and his followers imitate him, even to this day.

The question that he faces and with which he struggled all his days can be briefly put by looking at one of his examples.

Suppose that a farmer employs one hundred men at a wage of £50 per year, and a cotton manufacturer likewise employs one hundred men at £50 to construct a machine. Each employs a capital of £5000 and because, as Ricardo tells us, profits are 10 percent, the "value" of the machine and the corn at the end of the first year must be £5500. In the second year, the farmer again employs one hundred men, advances a capital of £5000, and sells his corn for £5500. The manufacturer also employs one hundred men to use the newly created machine in weaving cloth. The manufacturer, to be on a par with the farmer, must not only obtain £5500 but must receive in addition £550, the profit on the £5500. Hence the cloth must sell at £6050.[20]

Ricardo concludes, "Here then are capitalists employing precisely the same quantity of labour annually on the production of their commodities, and yet the goods they produce differ in value on account of the different quantities of fixed capital, or accumulated labour." He gives a number of examples, in essence the same, that show that in the following circumstances the value of commodities will differ from their relative prices:

1. Differing degrees of durability of fixed capital
2. Differing periods of durability of circulating capital
3. Differing proportions in which materialized and living labor are combined.
4. Differing times required to bring commodities to market.

He has proven in fact with his examples that the establishment of a general rate of profit brings into being prices that are determined and regulated by it and are quite different from the values of commodities. *Indeed, the cause of the variation of prices from values is the general rate of profit.*

But does Ricardo see things in this light? Not at all.

Just a few pages before, Ricardo tells us that there is "another cause, besides the greater or less quantity of labour necessary to produce commodities,

for the variations in their relative value—this cause is the rise or fall in the value of labour," i.e., changes in the wage rate. But he does not vary the wage in three of the four examples he gives. Yet "relative values" or prices differ from values. This he takes to be an exception or modification to his general rule, "The quantity of labour bestowed on the production of commodities regulates their relative value," and he ascribes this variation *solely* to changes in wages.

I maintain that all the elements of a correct solution to this problem have been provided by Marx. Its essence is that capitals, regardless of their compositions, regardless of the proportion of machinery and raw materials to wages, must yield the same return. This can come about only if there is a permanent deviation of prices from values, "permanent" because it occurs with the wage rate remaining the same. (We will call it the "Marx effect"; it is very different from the "Ricardo effect," the change in relative prices consequent upon a change in the wage, which we will consider later on.)[21]

Now a capital consisting of £5000 of machinery and raw materials and £5000 in labor must yield the same profit as a capital of £7500 in machinery and £2500 in labor. It is only the variable capital that sets in motion living labor productive of surplus-value. The proportion of constant to variable capital is accordingly most significant and Marx calls it the "organic composition." It is 1 : 1 in the first case and 3 : 1 in the second. He shows how surplus-value regardless of where it originates can be thought of as going into a kind of pool from which it is redistributed back to each capital in proportion to its size. The resulting prices deviate from values, but total price is equal to total value, and total profit is equal to total surplus value. Marx's solution is a wondrous description of industrial competition.

How then would Marx have solved the problem that Ricardo proposes? This is not hard to guess, as he discusses several problems of the same sort in the third volume of *Capital*.[22] Let us try to work it out:

During the first year both the manufacturer and the farmer employ only variable capital of £5000. The total value of machines and corn at the end of the year is £5500, and, as Ricardo has not considered raw materials or depreciation of the machines used in the production process, the augmentation of £500 in the value of the corn and machines is due solely to living labor. From this we can conclude that the rate of surplus value S/V is 500/5000 or 10 percent. That is, it is equal to the rate of profit that Ricardo assumed.

To help our discussion of the second year we can set up a table of much the same sort that Marx used:

	Manufacturer	Farmer
Capitals	$5500C + 5000V$	$5000V$
Surplus Value S	500	500
Rate of Profit	4.75%	10.00%
Value of Commodities $C + V + S$	5500	5500
Cost-Price $C + V$	5000	5000

The manufacturer employs the newly constructed machine of value £5500 and also outlays £5000 in wages as does the farmer. With a rate of surplus-

value of 10 percent, each produces a mass of surplus value of £500. As Ricardo assumes that the machine does not depreciate, the value of the cloth is £5500, as is the value of the corn. Marx calls "cost-price" the cost of materials and labor and, as only labor is considered, the cost-price of both the cloth and corn is £5000. The rate of profit of the manufacturer, the proportion of surplus-value to his total capital, $S/(C + V)$, is 4.75 percent, while that of the farmer is 10 percent.

Now both capitals must yield the same rate of return. This can only occur if they sell at prices different from their values. Let us construct another table to show how this can come about:

	Manufacturer	Farmer	Total
Capitals	$5500C + 5000V$	$5000V$	$5500C + 10,000V$
Surplus Value	500	500	1000
Value of Commodities	5500	5500	11,000
Cost-price of Commodities	5000	5000	10,000
Price of Commodities	5677	5323	11,000
Rate of Profit	6.45%	6.45%	
Deviation of Price from Value	+ 177	− 177	

The total mass of surplus-value is £1000, dividing this by total capital, $5500C + 10,000V$, we have an overall rate of profit $S/(C + V) = 1000/15,000 = 6.45$ percent.

Reckoning this rate on the capital of the manufacturer and farmer, respectively, and adding the resulting mass of profit to the "cost-price," we have the prices of production of the two commodities. The price of the cloth is above its value by +177 and that of the corn is below its value by the same amount. What has occurred is that the mass of surplus-value has been redistributed in order to equalize the profit rate on both capitals. The selling price of each commodity is no longer equal to its value, but total price is equal to total value, and total profit is equal to total surplus-value.

In summary, the capital of the manufacturer and the farmer set in motion the same amount of labor and produce the same amount of surplus-value. But as the total capital of the manufacturer is greater than that of the farmer, their rates of profit are originally very different. These different rates are equalized by competition into a single uniform rate. The profit accruing to each capital depends only upon its magnitude, not upon its organic composition. The price of production of each commodity is equal to its cost-price plus the profit reckoned on the total capital.

We see that the manufacturer secures not merely the £500 surplus-value that he has produced but an additional £177. The farmer on the other hand produced £500 in surplus but secures only £323 of this. We may think of the capital of the manufacturer, £10,500, and the farmer, £5000, regardless of its composition, as drawing an amount of surplus-value from the total pool of £1000 in proportion to their magnitudes.

So far as profits are concerned, the various capitalists are just so many stockholders in a stock company in which the shares of profit are uni-

formly divided per 100, so that profits differ in the case of the individual capitalists only in accordance with the amount of capital invested by each in the aggregate enterprise, i.e., according to his investment in social production as a whole, according to the number of his shares.[23]

We have sketched the steps from values to the derivation of a uniform rate of profit and prices of production. When a capitalist sells at these prices he recovers the cost-price of his commodities and a profit in proportion to his capital advanced as a part of the total social capital. We have shown how a uniform rate of profit is derived.[24] By leaping in with his uniform rate of profit Ricardo ignores a world of understanding right in front of his nose. Instead of showing that a uniform rate of profit necessitates that prices of production be different from values, he forcibly asserts their identity and talks only of changes in prices consequent upon changes in wages.

To fix this in our minds let us recall that the divergence of cost of production from value is the "Marx effect." Changes in prices of production consequent upon a change in the wage rate, the "Ricardo effect," we will next consider.

There is nothing simple about a commodity.

C. "Another cause, besides the greater or less quantity of labour necessary to produce commodities, for the variations in their relative value—this cause is the rise and fall in the value of labour."[25]

In the example cited above, Ricardo has proven, although he does not know it, that a general rate of profit implies prices will differ from values. Following this he considers the effect of a change in the wage rate.[26] Suppose that in the previous example wages rise so that the profit rate falls from 10 percent to 9 percent— "instead of adding £550 to the common price of their goods (to £5500) for the profits on their fixed capital, the manufacturers would add only 9 percent on that sum, or £495; consequently, the price would be £5995 instead of £6050. As corn would continue to sell for £5500, the manufactured goods in which more fixed capital was employed would fall relatively to corn." This is a striking result. In general a rise in wages will cause some prices to fall, namely, those of commodities with higher organic composition than average; the rest will rise. It demolishes both Smith's view that a rise in wages would cause all prices to rise as well as the flim-flam of "supply and demand."

The value of the mass of "corn" equal to £5500 does not change when wages rise. Before, £5000 went to the workers as their wages and £500 to the farmer in order to yield 10 percent on his capital. Now the farmer must lay out £5045.9 in wages, and his profit is £454.1, to yield him $454.1/5045.9 = 9\%$ on his capital. The manufacturer, like the farmer, sets in motion the same quantity of labor as before. It produces a product equal to £5500 in value. As with the farmer £5045.9 goes in wages, and £454.1 to profits. However instead of earning £500 on his machine built last year, the manufacturer earns only 9 percent or £495. Hence his selling price is £495 + £5500 = £5995. It has fallen by £55 from its previous level of £6050, whereas the price of corn remains unchanged. Note that presupposing a rate of profit of first 10 percent (and later 9 percent)

necessitates prices differing from values at each respective rate. But Ricardo considers only *changes* in prices consequent upon *changes* in the wage rate. He has not told us how the general rate of profit came into being. As Marx notes, "This illustration has nothing to do with the essential question of the *transformation of values into cost-prices.*"[27]

D. Ricardo Leaves a Legacy of Confusion

By confounding value and cost of production, Ricardo has left for his followers, old and new, a legacy of confusion. He criticized relentlessly Smith's confounding of labor materialized in a commodity and labor commanded by it but was guilty of the same with value and cost of production.

Consider this: "Mr. Malthus appears to think that it is a part of my doctrine, that the cost and value of a thing should be the same;—it is, if he means by cost, 'cost of production' including profits,"[28] and, "consequently a tax upon income, whilst money continued unaltered in value, would alter the relative *prices* and *value* of commodities."[29]

Marx refers to the first passage several times to show how Ricardo consciously identifies value with cost of production. Thanks to Piero Sraffa's profound scholarship we can see, perhaps more clearly, what he meant. Ricardo wrote detailed notes on Malthus' *Principles of Political Economy*, which appeared in 1820. Only in 1919 were these discovered, and they were not published until 1928.

> If by cost Mr. Malthus means the wages paid for labour, I do not confound cost and value, because I do not say that a commodity the labour on which cost £1000, will therefore sell for £1000: it may sell for £1100, £1200 or £1500—but I say it will sell for the same as another commodity the labour on which also cost £1000; that commodities will be valuable in proportion to the quantity of labour expended on them. If by cost Mr. Malthus means cost of production, he must include profits, as well as labour; he must mean what Adam Smith calls natural price, which is synonymous with value.
>
> A commodity is at its natural value, when it repays by its price, all the expenses that have been bestowed, from first to last to produce it and bring it to market. If then my expression conveys the same meaning as cost of production, it is nearly what I wish it to do.[30]

Ricardo is telling us that his theory of value is not that vulgar conception that wages regulate prices (presumably for some such reason as wages are a large portion of a capitalist's expenses). However he does say that the wage can serve as an *index*, an indicator of the quantity of labor expended, though only the latter determines value. (Needless to say, this index depends on there being a uniform working day and wage rate.)

But after all this, he unsays his high language by taking value to be the same as Smith's natural price. Let us remember that Adam Smith's "natural price" of a commodity is compounded from separate and independently determined rates of wages, profit, and rent. These are taken to be "natural rates" that commonly prevail; aside from this, we are not told whence they are found (see pt. I.D. above). Ricardo sees well enough through Smith's "adding up" theory

of price as an inconsistency. Adam Smith, however, succeeded in ensnaring him again with his natural price.

E. Ricardo's Theory Further Encumbered by Lack of Distinction between Surplus-Value and Profit

Ricardo constructed categories, "fixed" and "circulating" capital, according to its durability and period of turnover. This tells us something of the observable nature of capital though nothing of its role in value creation. Marx's categories reflect that process. His "constant" capital denotes the materials, semifinished products, and wear and tear of machinery that simply transfer their value to the product. His "variable" capital is that portion of capital that exchanges for living labor; it is self-expansive capital, the mother of surplus-value. Ricardo's categories are phenomenological; Marx's are etiological. Ricardo's analysis is thus narrowly limited from the onset.

Ricardo's concept of capital is related closely to his view of profit. Marx maintained that a telling inconsistency of his system was his failure to distinguish between the ratio of surplus-value and the ratio of profit. The one is the ratio of surplus-value to the variable part of capital, the other is the ratio of surplus-value to the *total* capital advanced. A capital of £500C may consist of £400C of constant and £100V of variable capital and produce a surplus-value of £100S. Then the rate of profit would be $S/(C + V) = 25\%$, and the rate of surplus-value $S/V = 100$ percent. Evidently any number of rates of profit can correspond to one particular rate of surplus-value, and to any one rate of profit there can be any number of rates of surplus-value. We see then that the rate of profit is quite different from the rate of surplus-value and may depend on many circumstances that do not affect the latter. Even though it is not reflected in his categories and he talks only of "profit," Ricardo gives views on surplus-value quite distinct from profit. The two are identical only when the capital advanced goes entirely for wages.

> In his observations on profit and wages, Ricardo . . . abstracts from the constant part of capital, which is not laid out on wages. He treats the matter as though the entire capital were laid out directly in wages. *To this extent*, therefore, he considers *surplus-value* and *not profit*, hence it is possible to speak of his theory of surplus-value.[31]

For example, throughout his *Essay on Profit* he maintains that only a fall in wages can increase profits utterly neglecting constant capital.[32]

Ricardo was an acute observer. He crystallized into language several facets of capitalism that had only just developed in his day. He introduced the category of fixed capital to underline the importance of machinery that was, at that time, just becoming prominent. Indeed he startled his contemporaries with his notorious chapter 31, "On Machinery," wherein he gives his opinion as to its effects on the working class. Why then did he omit, by and large, any consideration of constant capital in his discussion of the rate of profit?

This is well explained, in my view, by Marx:

> It is so much in the nature of the subject-matter that surplus-value can only be considered in relation to the variable capital, i.e., capital laid out directly in wages—and without an understanding of surplus-value no theory of profits is possible—that Ricardo treats the entire capital as variable capital and *abstracts* from constant capital, although he occasionally mentions it in the form of advances.[33]

It seems then that Ricardo's neglect of constant capital in determining the profit rate is no mere slip, but rather an intimation of genius. A glimpse just beyond recognition that somehow variable capital, the component of capital that exchanges with living labor, is solely productive of surplus-value, the stuff of profits.

In our example Ricardo, by neglecting the constant capital, C, would say that the rate of profit was 100 percent. Suppose he had considered it. If for some reason the value of the constant capital employed fell from £400 to £300, the rate of profit would rise from 20 percent to 25 percent, while the same quantity of labor would be employed. It would seem as if the mass of capital, too, played some essential role as regards profit. His intuition indicated, it seems, that it was labor alone. He never succeeded in working out the intermediate steps (see pt. II.B. above) from this recognition to profit, and so he omitted constant capital; he did this, it appears, instinctively. Hence his laws of profit are really of surplus-value.

Perhaps Ricardo comes closest to the notion of surplus-value when he tells us that profit depends on the "proportion of the annual labour of the country . . . devoted to the support of the labourers" and "in all countries, and all times, profit depends on the quantity of labour requisite to provide necessaries for the labourers."[34] Consider also, "Although a greater *value* is produced, a greater proportion of what *remains of that value*, after paying rent, is consumed by the producers, and it is this, and this alone, which regulates profits."[35]

After rent is deducted, then the mass of profit (read surplus-value) is equal to the excess of the value of the commodities minus the value of the labor-power. By "producers," Ricardo means the workers. This is an exact description of surplus-value as the value created by the actual producers that the capitalist appropriates. (Ricardo, though, is not correct in maintaining that after rent is deducted what remains goes entirely to workers and capitalists, as he neglects constant capital—see pt. II.A.)

He accepts as a fact, though, that the value of the product is greater than that of the wages. The nature of capital as a coercive social relation in which the laborer must perform surplus-labor is neglected. Here Adam Smith is to the point:

> The value which the workmen add to the materials, therefore, resolves itself in this case [with the advent of capitalism] into two parts, of which the one pays their wages, the other the profits of their employer upon the whole stock of materials and wages which he advanced. . . .
> In this state of things, the whole produce of labour does not always belong to the labourer. He must in most cases share it with the owner of

the stock which employs him. Neither is the quantity of labour commonly employed in acquiring or producing any commodity, the only circumstance which can regulate the quantity it ought commonly to purchase, command, or exchange for. An additional quantity, it is evident, must be due for the profits of the stock which advanced the wages and furnished the materials of that labour.[36]

This statement is perhaps the most explicit before Marx of the origin of surplus-value.

Ricardo's inability to distinguish between surplus-value and profit gets him into difficulties. Consider his well-known doctrine that a rise in the wage rate would cause a lowering of the rate of profit (and vice versa) with the overall price level remaining unchanged. It is possible in fact for the wage rate and the profit rate to move in the same direction. As he neglects constant capital, as usual, what this refers to is the wage rate and the rate of surplus-value. Suppose that the wage rate rises so that the rate of surplus-value falls, but the mass of surplus-value and hence profit may increase if more workers at the same time are being employed. Hence the wage rate and the profit rate may both rise. The same will occur if, as the wage rate rises with the same number of workers, the length of the working day is extended, the labor process is intensified, or there is a marked cheapening in the elements of constant capital.[37] His inability to explicate the causal relation of labor to surplus-value removes all this from his field of vision and we are left with a narrowly restricted theorem that does not tell much of the underlying process.[38]

Ricardo, alas, steadfastly maintained that the rate of profit could be influenced only by changes in the wage rate. But consider the following:

I must again observe, that the rate of profits would fall much more rapidly than I have estimated in my calculation: for the value of the produce being what I have stated it under the circumstances supposed, the value of the farmer's stock would be greatly increased from its necessarily consisting of many of the commodities which had risen in value. Before corn could rise from £4 to £12 his capital would probably be doubled in exchangeable value, and be worth £6000 instead of £3000. If then his profit were £180 or 6 per cent on his original capital, profits would not at that time be really at a higher rate than 3 per cent; for £6000 at 3 per cent gives £180; and on these terms only could a new farmer with £6000 money in his pocket enter into the farming business.[39]

Ricardo is dealing here with the consequences of an increase in the price of necessaries. (Note his talk of "absolute profit," still another anticipation of surplus-value.) He speaks of a further fall in the rate of profit due to a rise in the value of the capital stock. As Marx comments, "He throws overboard his identification of profit with surplus-value and [admits] that the rate of profit can be affected by a variation in the value of constant capital independently of the value of labour."[40] This is quite by way of exception however.

PART III

A. Ricardo's Paper on "Absolute Value and Exchangeable Value"

Ricardo's final vision, written in his last few weeks, is a worthy sequel to a life dedicated to truth. He bequeaths to humanity riches painstakingly gleaned. Sometimes those beings in harmony with the spirit of their age have such final prophetic visions as did the poet Shelley in his *Triumph of Life.*

The paper is, sad to say, unfinished. It is a record of intellectual struggle. Amidst the whirls and eddies of images, some beyond those in his previous writings, others vexingly the same, there are glimpses of sunlight. Needless disputation could have been avoided had this been known long before its fateful discovery in a little tin box in 1943. Marx would have clapped his hands had he read of the rudiments of ideas he was to evolve, laboriously, thirty-five years later.

Malthus' *Measure of Value* had just appeared. He had argued that the value of a given quantity of labor, or the wage rate, should be the measure of value. (A suggestion not conspicuous by its originality.) Ricardo had no trouble in showing its pitfalls as this, after all, is what Smith had said. Furthermore, Ricardo clearly sees the true nature of the conflict between capital and labor. Consider, "If all commodities were produced by labour employed only for one day there could be no such thing as profits for there would be no capital employed, beyond that of which every labourer is in possession before he commences to work."[41]

In other words, profit arises where the means of production are concentrated in a few hands and the mass of people sell their labor-power. This cannot occur in a society of self-employed artisans. This is an advance over his *Principles,* in which there is not much discussion of the social organization of capitalism.

He goes on to paint a charming vista:

One class gives its labour only to assist towards the production of the commodity and must be paid out of its value the compensation to which it is entitled, the other class makes the advances required in the shape of capital and must receive remuneration from the same source. Before a man can work for a year a stock of food and clothing and other necessaries must be provided for him. This stock is not his property but is the property of the man who sets him to work. Out of the finished commodity they are in fact both paid—for the master who sets him to work and who had advanced him his wages must have those wages returned with a profit or he would have no motive to employ him, and the labourer is compensated by the food, clothing and necessaries with which he is furnished, or which is the same thing which his wages enable him to purchase.[42]

In no other writing of Ricardo is the spirit of capitalism so lucidly portrayed.

Compare this with Marx:

What flows back to the labourer in the shape of wages is a portion of the product that is continuously reproduced by him. The capitalist, it is true, pays him in money, but this money is merely the transmitted form of the product of his labour. While he is converting a portion of the means of production into products, a portion of his former product is being turned into money. It is his labour of last week, or of last year, that pays for his labour-power this week, or this year. The illusion begotten by the intervention of money vanishes immediately, if, instead of taking a single capitalist and a single labourer, we take the class of capitalists and the class of labourers as a whole. The capitalist class is constantly giving to the labouring class order-notes, in the form of money, on a portion of the commodities produced by the latter and appropriated by the former. The labourers give these order-notes back just as constantly to the capitalist class, and in this way get their share of their own product. The transaction is veiled by the commodity-form of the product and the money-form of the commodity.[43]

Ricardo goes on to say of profits:

It greatly depends then on the proportion of the finished work which the master is obliged to give in exchange to replace the food and clothing expended on his workman what shall be his profits. It not only depends on the relative value of the finished commodity to the necessaries of the labourer, which must always be replaced, to put the master in the same condition as when he commenced his yearly business but it depends also on the state of the market for labour . . . for if labour be scarce the workman will be able to demand and obtain a greater quantity of necessaries and consequently a greater quantity of the finished commodity must be devoted to the payment of wages and of course a less quantity remains as profit for the master.[44]

Ricardo still resolves the finished product into wages and profit, neglecting the replacement of machines, equipment, and raw material; hence when he speaks of the profit rate here, it is the rate of surplus-value. He rightly sees that it is the value of the finished product to the value of the wages on which depends surplus-value (what he calls profits). Here once more he considers only commodities already produced, with *given* values determined by labor. If only Ricardo had followed Mr. Moneybags through the factory gates (as did Marx), instead of remaining outside and observing the outflows of finished products and inflows of wage-goods. For it would have been but a small step to have said that as the value of the product is created by labor and the mass of profit is equal to the remaining or "surplus" value after wages are deducted, then this "surplus" value is the unpaid labor or *surplus-labor* that the worker is forced to perform for the capitalist.

Socialists were not slow to see the connection between profit and surplus-labor. Indeed, the first jump in understanding appears to have occurred in an anonymous pamphlet, *The Source and Remedy of the National Difficulties: A Letter to Lord John Russell* (London, 1821). It appeared during Ricardo's lifetime but apparently never came to his notice.[45]

In the sentences following the passage on page 494, Ricardo returns to his old problem of the effects on "relative value" of a change in the wage rate as not only the value of the labor materialized in commodities but also the rise and fall of wages "does affect the value of commodities." If only he had distinguished between price and value! Rather he pursues the academic subject of a measure of value: "In this then consists the difficulty of the subject that the circumstances of time for which advances are made are so various that it is impossible to find any one commodity, which will be an unexceptional measure."

Against Malthus' proposal of a wages measure, Ricardo argues as he did with Smith that wage-goods are commodities like any other and so are subject to as much variability. If one supposes that a given quantity of corn will purchase the same amount of labor (the "permanent relative value of labor" notion cited earlier), even if half the quantity of labor is required to produce corn, its value in this measure will always be the same. Ricardo remarks, "But still Mr. M says it would not fall in absolute value, because it did not vary in his measure."[46] What would happen is that all things would rise with respect to corn or wages; and gold, too, the standard of money, would rise. But Ricardo goes on, "In Mr. Ricardo's measure everything to which such improvements were applied would fall in value and *price and value would be synonymous* while gold the standard of money cost the same expenditure of capital and labour to produce it."[47]

Following his thinking in the reference to absolute value, two sentences before, the improvements would cause a diminution in the "absolute" value of those commodities in which they were applied—*both* their prices and their values would fall (provided the value of gold were unchanged)—whereas with Malthus' corn or wages standard their prices would remain the same but they would have risen in value. Here at last is a recognition that price and value need not be synonymous, indeed, that they can move in different directions.

As an archaeologist succeeds in re-creating a lost civilization from broken bits of pottery, so Marx poring over Ricardo's texts had speculated, "Ricardo . . . doubtlessly realized that his prices of production deviated from the value of commodities."[48]

But shortly after, in discussing James Mill's thoughts on value, Ricardo takes up the venerable example of wine and cloth. The same quantity of labor has been bestowed on both, but the wine is brought to market years after the cloth. Rather than saying that the values of both are the same, but their prices different, he confounds value and price nicely by telling us that if the wage rate falls the "wine would alter in relative value to the cloth." Then he discusses an example of McCulloch's showing the "Marx effect"—the permanent deviation of prices from values without any change in the wage-rate—and closes the section by again considering effects of a change in the wage-rate. Here we have it—"Ricardo effect," "Marx effect," "Ricardo effect"—all confounded by identifying price and value as the same. No wonder that Ricardo is puzzled: "The subject is a very difficult one for with the same quantity of labour employed a commodity may be worth £100 or £35 of a money always produced under the same circumstances, and always requiring the same quantity of labour."[49] Then, as if by way of collecting his thoughts and affirming his doctrine, he sets out twelve basic principles. The first is:

1. All commodities having value are the result either of immediate labour, or of immediate and accumulated labour united.

The third is:

3. That part of the value of a commodity which is required to compensate the labourer for the labour he has bestowed on it is called wages, the remaining part of its value is retained by the master and is called profit. It is a remuneration for the accumulated labour which it was necessary for him to advance, in order that the commodity might be produced.[50]

Once again we see that he starts with given values of commodities. Although he sees clearly enough that labor creates a larger value than the share it receives as wages, by ignoring production he cannot relate this to necessary and surplus labor. Instead he talks legalistically of the distribution of the product: A part goes to "compensate" the laborer, another part to "remuneration" for the "master." (The part that must go to replace raw materials, semifinished goods, and wear and tear is neglected.)

But then he returns to the puzzle of a measure of value. He is in agreement with Marx that the relative value of all commodities can be found with respect to any commodity,[51] but he wishes to go further and seek an absolute measure of value.[52] Such a measure could be used "to ascertain the variations in the values of commodities for one year, for two years, or for any distant portions of time."

Here he considers for a moment using labor materialized in a commodity:

All then we have to do it is said to ascertain whether the value of a commodity be now of the same value as a commodity produced 20 years ago is to find out what quantity of labour for the same length of time was necessary to produce the commodity 20 years ago and what quantity is necessary to produce it now.

With such a measure we could find the *absolute* value of a commodity, he goes on to say. But then he gives this up by saying, "A commodity that requires the labour of 100 men for one year is not precisely double the value of a commodity that requires the labour of 100 men for 6 months."[53] Again confounding, alas, price and value!

His examples of wine and cloth led him to regard differences in time of production as the core of the difficulty. "This then seems to hold universally true that the commodity valued must be reduced to circumstances precisely similar (with respect to time of production) to those of the commodity in which the valuation is made." This leads him to choose gold or cloth as his measure, reasoning rather dubiously that most commodities are produced under the same circumstances.

In considering one of Malthus' arguments he returns to the example of wine. This he rightly sees will exchange for more labor than it cost. It will, Ricardo sees, exchange for, say, the labor of 1,000 men, although it cost that of 200 men. Therefore, "the value of the labour of 800 men will constitute the profit and the whole value of the wine is divided into fifths, one fifth of which is the value of the wages and four fifths the value of the profits." Recall our example of the cloth manufacturer and the farmer. We saw that a surplus-value of £177 accrues to the cloth manufacturer above what his laborers produce because its selling price is above its value. The same occurs with the wine. Ricardo sees, though as if looking through the wrong end of a telescope, an essential of Marx's solution to the "transformation problem."

He ends reaffirming his principle:

That the greater or less quantity of labour worked up in commodities can be the only cause of their alteration in value is completely made out as soon as we are agreed that all commodities are the produce of labour and would have no value but for the labour expended upon them. Though this is true it is still exceedingly difficult to discover or even to imagine any commodity which shall be [a] perfect general measure of value.[54]

It appears from this that the measure of value is not a secondary inquiry; rather, it is organically related to his theory of value. The examples of wine, cloth, and so forth refute it, *prima facie*, and his search for a measure was really an attempt to establish his great principle in a full generality.

B. Ricardo's Faulty Architectonics

Ricardo relying on the certainty of immediate perception regards capitalism as a mode of production eternal, reasonable, and natural. Hence he was not under any compulsion to scrutinize the nature of value and the *differentia specifica* that sets a commodity-producing society apart from the multitude of other historical social forms in which useful things are merely useful things. Had he done so, he would have caught the dim shape of the future amidst the fog of fetishism.

Rather, immersing himself at the onset in a sea of commodities, he concerns himself, understandably enough, with the magnitude of value. His surmise that this was determined by labor-time was an advance. But he posited at the onset a mass of commodities of given value, a crystallized quantity of human labor, and asked only what part goes to the worker as his wages and what is appropriated by capital. By concerning himself with the distribution of commodities already produced, he cannot inquire into the creation of value. Furthermore, the unequal exchange between capital and labor seems to contradict his general law that value is determined by labor-time. This was to lead eventually to the shipwreck of the Ricardian school. (Decades later Marx solved the problem with the distinction between labor and labor-power, rightly calling it the "fulcrum upon which Political Economy turns.")

Instead he takes the difference between the value that labor produces and what it receives as matter-of-factly as an apple falling from a tree. By not asking why the exchange between living and materialized labor should be singularly different from exchange among the immense mass of other commodities, he could not discover the source of surplus-value.

Other, apparently contradictory, phenomena present themselves. In the face of these, Ricardo instinctively maintained his law, vindicating it by a violent

abstraction. Thus he confounded values and prices. By leaping in with his general rate of profit, by accepting the rate of profit as something pre-existent, he was unable to consider how, through the competition of capitals, a general rate of profit is established and how this necessitates that values are transformed into prices of production.

His struggle with the apparently arid, academic question of an "invariable standard" is really an attempt to reconcile his premises with things that at first sight apparently contradict it.

If only Ricardo had paid less attention to a dead mass of things and more to how they came into being! Although he steadfastly maintained that only living labor was productive of value, he does not progress from this understanding to seeing profit and rent as manifestations of surplus-value created by unpaid labor.

Later on others would turn Ricardo's vision of capitalism into a reification of a stock market where capital and labor receive "dividends" or shares in the total product.[55] His followers would drop that part of his doctrine dealing with value as materialized labor and put in its place a mechano-mystical view of the value of commodities as originating in dead matter; "economic science" would come to be a ceaseless meditation on the "allocation" or "distribution" of a mass of things. Marx, on the other hand, saw in the exchange between *living* and *dead* labor a clue to the subtle anatomy of capitalism.

NOTES

1. Friedrich Engels, Supplement to *Capital,* vol. III (Moscow: Progress Publishers, 1971).

2. This is how Samuel Bailey argued against Ricardo's theory. See Marx's brilliant discussion, *Theories of Surplus-Value* (London: Lawrence and Wishart, 1972), pt. III, pp. 142-43.

3. Ibid., p. 141.

4. Ibid., p. 143.

5. Karl Marx, *A Contribution to the Critique of Political Economy* (London: Laurence & Wishart, 1971), pp. 67-68.

6. Adam Smith, *Wealth of Nations,* vol. I, ed. E. Canaan (London: Methuen, 1950), pp. 58-59.

7. Marx, *Theories of Surplus-Value,* pt. II, p. 219.

8. Ricardo, *The Works and Correspondence of David Ricardo,* ed. Piero Sraffa (Cambridge: Cambridge University Press, 1970), vol. I, p. 14.

9. Marx, *Theories of Surplus-Value,* pt. I, p. 71.

10. Ibid., pt. II, p. 396.

11. Ricardo, "Letter to James Mill, 28 December 1818," in *Works and Correspondence,* vol. VII, p. 377

12. Marx, *Theories of Surplus-Value,* pt. I, p. 73.

13. Ibid., p. 74.

14. Raya Dunayevskaya, *Marxism and Freedom* (London: Pluto Press, 1971), p. 99.

15. The author cannot but marvel at the image of a mighty intellect, traversing many valleys, snow-clad mountain tops and chilly plateaus—such is Karl Marx in his quest in *Theories of Surplus-Value.* This essay is but a pale reflection of the truth therein.

15a. This abstract social labor should not be confused with unskilled or *simple* labor. Unskilled labor is after all "a particular form of concrete labor and as such cannot be abstract labor. Even if all labor were unskilled the reduction of concrete to abstract labor would not be less of a problem." See Geoffrey Kay's outstanding discussion, *Bulletin of the Conference of Socialist Economists,* vol. V, no. 1; March 1976.

16. Ibid., pt. III, pp. 133-35.

17. Ibid., p. 135.

18. Ibid., pt. III, p. 133.

19. Ibid., pt. II, p. 399.

20. One peculiarity here is that neither the farmer nor the manufacturer expend capital on raw materials and equipment, they only purchase labor. We will see the significance of this omission later on.

21. These terms were suggested by Frank Roosevelt.

22. Marx, *Capital,* vol. III (Moscow: Progress Publishers, 1971), chap. 9.

23. Ibid., p. 158.

24. By following Marx in deriving prices of production from values, we may meet with the same objections raised so long ago by Böhm-Bawerk and L. von Bortkiewicz. Though we have "transformed" the value of the output of each Department to a price of production, we have left the inputs unchanged, thereby saying in effect that though the price of production of each item of output deviates from its value, the price of production of each input item is equal to its value. We are guilty of the same error as Marx but we maintain that our solution shows the essence of what any solution must be. Qualitatively our solution correctly shows the production and redistribution of surplus-value in accordance with the total value of the capital stock in each sector. While an approximation, Marx's solution explicates causal relations and is further along the path to totality than the "exact one proposed by L. von Bortkiewicz.

25. Ricardo, *Works and Correspondence,* vol. I, p. 30.

26. Ibid., p. 35.

27. Karl Marx, *Theories of Surplus-Value,* pt. II, pp. 191-92. The author would like to express his thanks to Professor Tsuyoshi Sakurai for his helpful comments on the above example.

28. Ricardo, *Works and Correspondence,* vol. I, p. 47.

29. Ibid., p. 208, emphasis added.

30. Ibid., vol. II, pp. 34-35.

31. Marx, *Theories of Surplus-Value,* pt. II, p. 373.

32. It was vital for British capitalism to import cheap raw materials, thereby cheapening constant capital. But Ricardo myopically maintained that foreign trade could only increase profits to the extent that cheap food was imported. Marx notices one instance where Ricardo takes a different position (ibid., p. 431).

33. Ibid., pt. II, p. 374.

34. Ricardo, *Works and Correspondence,* vol. I, pp. 49 and 126.

35. Ibid., p. 125, emphasis added.

36. Adam Smith, *Wealth of Nations* (London: Methuen, 1950), vol. I, pp. 54 and 55.

37. That Ricardo nowhere considers the consequences of an extension of the working day underlines his failure to explicate the causal relation of labor to profit.

38. With the Ricardian vogue, Ricardo's "law" has come to the fore again. We should always bear in mind how severely limited it is. Ricardo did make a singular contribution here in considering wages with respect to profits, that is, by speaking of relative wages. By focusing on the amount of wages relative to the total product, the social relation of workers to capital is underlined. The dynamics of class struggle depends more on relative shares that on absolute quantities.

39. Ricardo, *Works and Correspondence,* vol. I, p. 122.

40. Marx, *Theories of Surplus-Value,* pt. II, p. 431.

41. Ricardo, *Works and Correspondence,* vol. IV, p. 365.

42. Ibid., pp. 365-66.

43. Marx, *Capital,* vol. I, pp. 567-68.

44. Ricardo, *Works and Correspondence,* vol. IV, pp. 365-66.

45. See Friedrich Engels' discussion in *Capital,* vol. II (Moscow: Progress Publishers, 1967), pp. 12-13.

46. Ricardo, *Works and Correspondence,* vol. IV, p. 373.

47. Ibid., emphasis added. Compare this with the quote where he says, "natural price . . . is synonymous with value" (see footnote 30).

48. Marx, *Capital,* vol. III, p. 179.

49. Ricardo, *Works and Correspondence,* vol. IV, p. 378.

50. Ibid., p. 380.

51. "We are possessed then of plenty of measures of value," ibid., p. 381.
52. Ibid., p. 381.
53. Ibid., p. 382.
54. Ibid., p. 397.
55. See Karl Marx, *Grundrisse* (Harmondsworth: Penguin Books, 1973), p. 553.

Dear Reader,

Ricardo says, "For from no source do so many errors, and so much difference of opinion in that science proceed, as from the vague ideas which are attached to the word 'value.'"

I quite agree and would be delighted with your comments on this rudimentary beginning.

Jesse Schwartz
San Diego
February 1977

SUGGESTIONS FOR FURTHER READING

Dear Reader,

I've set down a few works which I've found vibrant and which lead, I believe, to deeper and more profound truths. Those wishing to follow the winding pathways of political economy might consider them.

1. Amin, Samir. *Accumulation on a World Scale.* Vols. I and II. New York: Monthly Review Press, 1974.
2. Braverman, Harry. *Labor and Monopoly Capital.* New York: Monthly Review Press, 1974.
3. Böhm-Bawerk, E. "Karl Marx and the Close of his System," R. Hilferding, "Böhm-Bawerk's criticism of Marx," and L. von Bortkievicz, "Transformation of values into prices of production in the Marxian System," all in *Karl Marx and the Close of His System.* Edited by P. M. Sweezy. London: Merlin Press, 1975.
4. Flamant, Maurice and Singer-Kérel, Jeanne. *Modern Economic Crises and Recessions.* Translated by Pat Wardroper. New York: Harper and Row, 1968.
5. Hunt, E. K. and Schwartz, J. G., eds. *Critique of Economic Theory.* Harmondsworth: Penguin Books, 1972.
6. Koshimura, Shinzaburo. *Theory of Capital Reproduction and Accumulation.* Edited by J. G. Schwartz. Kitchener, Ontario: Dumont Press, 1975.
7. Meek, Ronald. *Studies in the Labor Theory of Value.* New York: International Publishers, 1956.
8. O'Conner, James. *The Fiscal Crisis of the State.* New York: St. Martin's Press, 1973.
9. Rubin, Isaak I. *Essays on Marx's Theory of Value.* Detroit: Black & Red Press, 1973.
10. Sweezy, Paul. *The Theory of Capitalist Development.* New York: Monthly Review Press, 1942.

Contradiction pervades all human ideas and beliefs. Every system of ideas when isolated and set out as an absolute truth becomes yet another episode in the comedy of human delusions. "Marxian Economics" (12 weeks, 3 credits!) as often taught in colleges and universities shows signs of assuming the character of its adversaries and degenerating into an inflexible and scientist excursus confined to the realm of having. I've set down below a few works that I hope will be helpful to people in seeing political economy as but a chart or map of a small part of the continuous outpouring of life and consciousness.

1. Boadella, David, ed. *Energy and Character* (a journal of Bio-energetic Research). Abbotsbury, Dorset: England, 1968-present.
2. Dunayevskaya, Raya. *Philosophy and Revolution.* New York: Delacorte Press, 1973.
3. Frankel, George. *The Failure of the Sexual Revolution.* London: Kahn & Averill, New York: Humanities Press, 1974.

4. Georgakas, Dan and Surkin, Marvin. *Detroit: I Do Mind Dying.* New York: St. Martin's Press, 1975.

5. Goodman, Paul and Percival Goodman, *Communitas.* New York: Vintage Books, 1947.

6. Lefebvre, Henri. *Dialectical Materialism.* London: Jonathan Cape, 1970.

7. Lewin, Moshe. *Lenin's Last Struggle.* New York: Random House, 1968.

8. Loewenberg, Jacob. "Introduction" in *Hegel: Selections.* New York: Charles Scribner, 1957.

9. Lukacs, George. *History and Class Consciousness.* Translated by R. Livingstone. London: Merlin Press, 1971.

10. Marcuse, Herbert. *Reason and Revolution.* London: Routledge and Kegan Paul, 1955.

11. Meszaros, Istvan, *Marx's Theory of Alienation.* London: Merlin Press, 1970.

12. Orwell, George. *Homage to Catalonia.* London: Penguin Books, 1966.

13. Reich, Wilhelm. *The Mass Psychology of Fascism.* New York: Noonday Press, 1970.

14. Reich, Wilhelm. "What is Class-consciousness" in *Sex-Pol Essays, 1924-34,* ed. Lee Baxandall. New York: Vintage Books, 1972.

15. Rowbotham, Sheila. *Woman's Consciousness, Man's World.* Harmondsworth: Penguin Books, 1973.

ACKNOWLEDGMENTS

Howard, Dick, *Selected Political Writings of Rosa Luxemburg,* pp. 140, 141, and 151. Copyright © 1971 by Monthly Review Press. Reprinted by permission.

Keynes, J. M., *The General Theory of Employment, Interest, and Money.* Copyright © 1936. Reprinted by permission of Harcourt Brace Jovanovich.

——, *The General Theory of Employment, Interest and Money.* Reprinted by permission of Macmillan and Co., Ltd.

Luxemburg, Rosa, *Accumulation of Capital.* Copyright © 1951 by Routledge and Kegan Paul Ltd., pp. 461-463. Reprinted by permission.

——, *Social Reform or Revolution.* Copyright © 1973 by Pathfinder Press, pps. 50-52. Reprinted by permission.

Marx, Karl, *Capital, Vols. I and II.* Copyright © 1970 and 1972, respectively, by International Publishers. Reprinted by permission.

——, *Grundrisse: Foundations of the Critique of Political Economy,* translated by Martin Nicolaus. Copyright © 1974 by Random House, Inc. Reprinted by permission.

——, *Grundrisse,* edited by David McLellan. Copyright © 1971 by Macmillan Administration (Basingstoke) Ltd.

——, *Grundrisse,* translated by Martin Nicolaus. Copyright © 1973 by Penguin Books Ltd. Translation copyright © Martin Nicolaus, 1973. Reprinted by permission.

——, *Theories of Surplus-Value, Parts I, II and III.* Copyright © 1968, 1969 and 1972, respectively, by Lawrence and Wishart Ltd. Reprinted by permission.

Nell, Edward, *Revival of Political Economy.* Copyright © 1972 by Journal of Social Research. Reprinted by permission.

Robinson, Joan and Eatwell, John, *An Introduction to Modern Economics.* Copyright © 1973 by McGraw-Hill Book Co. (UK) Ltd. Reprinted by permission.

——, *Economics: An Awkward Corner.* Copyright © 1967 by Random House, Inc., pp. 59, 61. Reprinted by permission.

*Gray are all the theories, but
green is the Tree of Life.*

—GOETHE